Fodor's
Afford
Great Britain

"These books succeed admirably; easy to follow and use, full of cost related information, practical advice and recommendations...maps are clear and easy to use."
—Travel Books Worldwide

"Good helpmates for the cost-conscious traveler."
—Detroit Free Press

"Concentrates on life's basics...without skimping on literary luxuries."
—New York Daily News

"The Fodor's series puts a premium on showing its readers a good time."
—Philadelphia Inquirer

Portions of this book appear in *Fodor's Great Britain*
Fodor's Travel Publications, Inc.
New York • Toronto • London • Sydney • Auckland

Copyright © 1995 by Fodor's Travel Publications, Inc.

ISBN 0–679–02967–2

Fodor's Affordable Great Britain

Editor: David Low
Contributors: Robert Andrews, Robert Blake, Samantha Cook, Jules Brown, Linda Schmidt, Mary Ellen Schultz, M.T. Schwartzman, Kate Sekules, Dinah Spritzer, Gilbert Summers, Roger Thomas, Greg Ward
Creative Director: Fabrizio La Rocca
Cartographers: David Lindroth, R. R. Donnelley & Sons Co., Maryland Cartographics
Cover Design: Tigist Getachew
Cover Photograph: Charlie Waite/TSW

Design: Vignelli Associates

Special Sales

PRINTED IN THE UNITED STATES OF AMERICA
10 9 8 7 6 5 4 3 2 1

Contents

Maps

How This Guide Will Save You Money

If you're one of the rock-bottom-budget travelers who sleep on park benches to save money and would never, ever dress up for duck à l'orange at Jean-Louis, then look to another guidebook for your travel information.

But if you're among those who budget some of the finer things into their traveling life, if you would stay home before spending a night in a hostel dormitory with strangers, and if you're willing to pay a little more for crisp sheets, a firm bed, a soft pillow, and a really superb dining experience every now and again, read on. It's for you that Fodor's team of savvy, budget-conscious writers and editors have prepared this book.

We share your traveling style and your champagne tastes, and we know that saving money is all about making choices. Some of us do it by sticking to public transportation and picnic lunches. Others spend more on a hotel with amenities but don't care about fancy meals. Still others take the hostel route in order to go shopping.

In this guide, we've tried to include enough options so that all of you spend time and money in the ways you most enjoy. The hotels we suggest are good values, and there are no dives, thank you—only clean, friendly places with an acceptable level of comfort, convenience, and charm. We also recommend a range of inexpensive and moderately priced restaurants where you can eat well in pleasant surroundings. You'll read about the best budget shopping and how to make the arts-and-nightlife scene without breaking the bank. And we'll tell you how to get around inexpensively by public transportation.

As for planning what to see and do, you'll find the same lively writing and authoritative background information available in Fodor's renowned Gold Guides.

Please Write to Us

Everyone who has contributed to Affordable Great Britain has worked hard to make the text accurate. All prices and opening times are based on material supplied to us at press time, and Fodor's cannot accept responsibility for any errors that may have occurred. The passage of time always brings changes, so it's a good idea to call ahead to confirm information when it matters—particularly if you're making a detour to visit specific sights. When making reservations at a hotel or inn, be sure to mention if you have a disability or are traveling with children, if you prefer a private bath, or if you have specific dietary needs or any other concerns.

Do let us know about your trip. Did you enjoy the restaurants we recommended? Was your hotel comfortable and were the museums you visited worthwhile? Did you happen upon a treasure that we haven't included? We would love to have your feedback, positive and negative. If you have suggestions or complaints, we'll look into them and revise our entries when it's the right thing to do. So please send us a letter or postcard (we're at 201 East 50th Street, New York, New York 10022). We look forward to hearing from you. In the meantime, have a wonderful trip!

Karen Cure
Editorial Director

Fodor's Choice for Budget Travelers

Stately Homes **Blenheim Palace, The Thames Valley.** Britain's largest stately home and the birthplace of Winston Churchill, this early 18th-century Italianate mansion in Woodstock stands majestically in 2,000 acres of parkland and exquisite gardens landscaped by Capability Brown.

Buckland Abbey, The Southwest. Perfect for a day's outing from Plymouth, this 13th-century Cistercian monastery became the home of Sir Francis Drake in 1581 and is now full of fascinating memorabilia related to Drake and the Spanish Armada.

Castell Coch, Wales. A remarkable 1870s exercise in Victorian-Gothic whimsy, Castell Coch (The Red Castle), on a hill above Tongwynlais village, has furnishings, carvings, and murals that were designed to re-create one of the fantastic castles of Ludwig of Bavaria.

Castle Howard, York and the Northeast. Built over 60 years (1699–1759), this famous home (the setting for TV's *Brideshead Revisited*) is without equal in Northern England; a magnificent central hallway spanned by a handpainted ceiling leads to staterooms and galleries overflowing with precious furniture and works of fine art.

Melford Hall, East Anglia. Distinguished from the outside by its turrets and topiaries, this mid-16th-century house in Long Melford is surrounded by parkland and filled inside with porcelains and other fine antiques that came from the *Santissima Trinidad*, a ship captured on its way to Spain by one of the house's 18th-century owners.

Scone Palace, Scotland: Glasgow and Environs. An easy bus ride from Perth, this grandly embellished, castellated mansion, the home of the earl of Mansfield, has vast collections of 16th-century needlework, china, furniture, vases, and other objets d'art. Within its grounds is **Moot Hill,** the ancient coronation place of the Scottish kings.

Restaurants

Blas ar Gymru, Cardiff, Wales. At this first-rate, welcoming Welsh restaurant, waitresses in traditional costume will serve you such local fare as laverbread (made with seaweed) and bacon; lean lamb cooked in honey cider and ginger; poacher's pie, a scrumptious beef, rabbit, chicken, and game dish; and ewe's cheese marinated in mead.

Cherwell Boathouse, Oxford, The Thames Valley. Be prepared to linger at this ideal spot for a meal in a riverside setting with a changing weekly menu that may include popular entrées such as mussels in white wine and cream; loin of lamb with red wine, lime and garlic; or tagliatelle with fennel and cashew nuts.

Marco's, Norwich, East Anglia. The Georgian architecture of this building is complemented inside by paneled walls, open fires, and pictures, all of which create a warm, friendly, private atmosphere at this Italian eatery. Don't miss the *salmone al cartoccio* (salmon baked in parchment) and *gnocchi alla Marco* (potato dumplings).

The Moon, Kendal, The Lake District. A bistro ambience prevails in this small, centrally located restaurant, whose fine reputation has been earned with quality vegetarian dishes and homemade foods, sometimes prepared with Mediterranean and Asian accents.

St. John, London. This former smokehouse in the City area has soaring white walls, stone floors, and plain wooden chairs; crowds flock here for the buzz and the trendy but great food—roast bone marrow and parsley salad; smoked eel, beets, and horseradish; deviled crab—as well as for the affordable French wine list.

Hudson's Below Stairs, York, York and the Northeast. Revel in traditional English food, including fish dishes, roast beef, and Yorkshire pudding, at this atmospheric Victorian hotel restaurant a five-minute walk from the Minster.

Kalpna, Edinburgh, Scotland: Edinburgh and Environs. At this vegetarian Indian restaurant with a great buffet, Indian art adorns the walls, enhancing your enjoyment of the exotic specialties like *shahi sabzi* (spinach and nuts in cream sauce), and mushroom curry.

Admiral Benbow, Penzance, The Southwest. Once a smugglers' inn, this 15th-century gem serving good solid bar food (steak and Guinness pie, for instance) is now filled with seafaring bric-a-brac, including a brass cannon, model ships, figureheads, and ropes everywhere. Budget.

Haunch of Venison, Salisbury, The South. At this historic pub, parts of which date to 1430, the wood-panel restaurant upstairs has a fireplace that's more than 500 years old and a mummified hand holding some 18th-century playing cards. The downstairs bar, with timber walls and black-and-white tile floors, is small, noisy, and comfortable, serving simple pub fare. Budget

New Inn, Ironbridge, The Welsh Borders. Part of an open-air museum, this Victorian building is a fully functioning pub—with gas lamps, sawdust on the floor, and traditional ales served from the cask—where you can try a ploughman's lunch, a pasty from the antique-style bakery, or a pork pie from the butcher's store next door. Budget

Wagamama, London. This ultrapopular, Bloomsbury high-tech café has the best Japanese noodles in town. Ramen, in soup, topped with meat or fish, are supplemented by rice dishes and curries, plus "raw energy" dishes for the jaded. Budget

Hotels

The Britannia Inn, Ambleside, The Lake District. At this splendid family-owned inn with quaint, modern little rooms and hearty homemade food, you're close to some of the region's best walking country.

Curzon Lodge and Stable Cottages, York, York and the Northeast. Near the racecourse, this attractive, white-painted, 17th-century building is furnished with antiques, such as four-poster beds; breakfast is served in a cozy, rustic dining room.

Eagle House, Hastings, The Southeast. This well-regarded guest house with generous size rooms in a large, detached Victorian building, stands in its own attractive garden; the kitchen uses fresh produce from local farms.

Fielding, London. This friendly hotel with very comfortable, small bedrooms is adored by regulars, especially for its great location–it's tucked away in a quiet alley by the Royal Opera House in Covent Garden.

The Black Hostelry, Ely, East Anglia. You'll have lots of privacy at this very popular bed-and-breakfast with enormous rooms and old-fashioned English furnishings—it's right on the city's cathedral grounds, in one of the finest medieval domestic buildings still in use.

Caterham House, Stratford, The Heart of England. At this landmark 1830 building in the center of town and near the theater, you may spot an actor or two among the guests who enjoy the individually decorated bedrooms in early 19th-century style, featuring brass beds and antique furniture.

The Town House, Cardiff, Wales. This tall Victorian home within walking distance of Cardiff's city center has immaculate guest rooms and a choice of traditional British and American breakfasts served in a lovely dining room.

Vicarage, London. A family-run establishment for nearly 30 years, the Vicarage feels like a real home—it's beautifully decorated and quiet, overlooking a garden square near Kensington's shopping streets.

Eglinton Youth Hostel, Edinburgh, Scotland: Edinburgh and Environs. Located on a tree-lined court in Edinburgh's west end and only a 10-minute walk from downtown, this IYH affiliate has small, bargain-priced bedrooms, recently renovated dining rooms, kitchens, and a cafeteria. Budget

Neville's Cross Hotel, Durham, York and the Northeast. This small, family-run hotel, in a former 19th-century coaching inn on the western outskirts of the city, has open fires, a warm hospitable atmosphere, and very good homemade steak-and-kidney pie. Budget

University of Strathclyde, Glasgow, Scotland: Glasgow and Environs. If you want to be right in the city center, but at a low price, book one of the university's very pleasant single, double, or twin rooms, or apartments with kitchen facilities in the Campus Village, a five-minute walk from George Square. Budget

Cathedrals and Churches

Canterbury Cathedral, The Southeast. The focal point of the city of Canterbury, this cathedral is a living textbook of medieval architecture, combining Gothic and Norman styles. The church is well-known as the site of archbishop Thomas á Becket's murder in 1170, and a series of 13th-century stained glass windows illustrates Becket's miracles.

Durham Cathedral, York and the Northeast. Architectural historians from around the world come to study Durham Cathedral's impressive Norman features, such as its rib vaulting. The Chapel of Nine Altars has soaring pillars made of polished Frosterly marble.

King's College Chapel, East Anglia. One of the most beautiful buildings in England, this church in late English Gothic style has a great fan-vaulted ceiling supported by soaring side columns. The huge space is lit by ever-changing light from the vast stained-glass windows. Every Christmas Eve, a festival of carols sung by the chapel's famous choir is broadcast around the world.

Salisbury Cathedral, The South. Built in a short span of only 38 years (1220–58), the towering cathedral has a spire that is a miraculous feat of medieval engineering and an interior with remarkable lancet windows and sculpted tombs of crusaders and other medieval heroes.

Westminster Abbey, London. Britain's monarchs have been crowned at this most ancient of great churches since 1066. The present abbey, a largely 13th- and 14th-century rebuilding of an 11th-century church, has many memorials to royalty, writers, and statemen, and the famous Tomb of the Unknown Warrior; its Henry VII Chapel is an exquisite example of the rich late Gothic style.

York Minster, York and the Northeast. The city of York has the largest Gothic church in England. Contributing to its singular beauty and magnificence are its soaring columns; the ornamentation of its 14th-century nave; the great east window, one of the world's finest examples of medieval glazing; and the splendid Rose Window commemorating the marriage of Henry VII and Elizabeth of York.

Museums and Galleries

British Museum, London. In a monumental Greek edifice built in the first half of the 19th century, the vast collection of treasures here includes Egyptian, Greek, and Roman antiquities; Renaissance jewelry, pottery, coins, glass; and drawings from virtually every European school since the 15th century.

Corinium Museum, Cirencester, The Heart of England. This excellent museum has a superb collection of Roman artifacts and full-scale reconstructions of local Roman interiors, including a kitchen, dining room, and workshop.

Fitzwilliam Museum, Cambridge, East Anglia. In a classical building with an opulent interior, you'll discover an outstanding collection of art (including paintings by John Constable, Gainsborough, and the French Impressionists) and antiquities, including a notable Egyptian section, a large display of English Staffordshire and other pottery, and a fascinating room full of armor and muskets.

Jorvik Viking Centre, York, York and the Northeast. On an authentic Viking site, archaeologists have re-created a Viking street with astonishing detail. Its "time-cars" whisk visitors through the streets to experience the sights, sounds, and smells (!) of the past, while excellent displays show visitors the breadth of Viking culture and society.

Museum of the Moving Image, London. In the South Bank Arts Complex, MOMI joyfully celebrates every aspect of the moving image, from Chinese shadow plays of 2,500 BC to the latest fiber optics and satellite images; cinema and television take center stage.

National Gallery of Scotland, Edinburgh, Scotland: Edinburgh and Environs. The attractively decorated spacious rooms display a wide-ranging selection of paintings, from Renaissance times to Postimpressionism, with works by Velásquez, El Greco, Rembrandt, Turner, Degas, Monet, and van Gogh, among many others, as well as a fine collection of Scottish art.

Welsh Folk Museum, Wales. In 100 acres of parkland and gardens in St. Fagans lie farmhouses, cottages, and terraced houses that show the evolution of Welsh building styles, and an Elizabethan mansion built within the walls of a Norman castle. The museum has fine craft workshops, a saddler, cooper, blacksmith, and woodturner.

Great Britain by Road

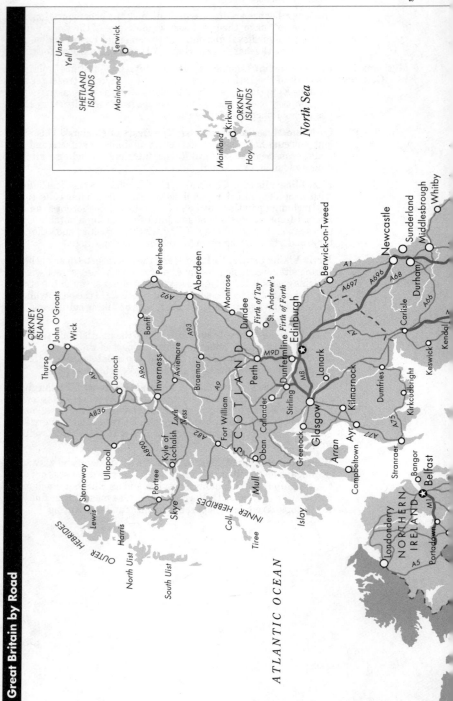

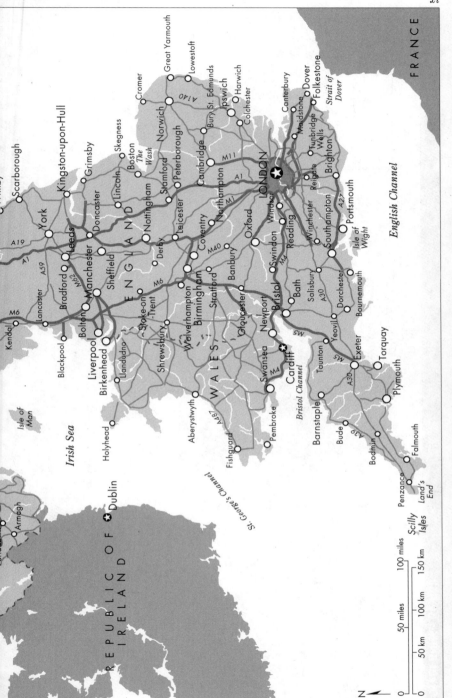

Great Britain by Rail

Great Itineraries for Budget Travelers

Writers at Home: Southwest England

Britain contains a wealth of associations with fictional and real literary figures; there are several literary walking tours of London alone that will cost you nothing if you do them without a guide. For those who like to venture out on their own and explore more than just isolated plaques commemorating who slept (or was born or died) where, the following excursion takes in some lovely settings as well as enough artistic associations to keep any literature buff happy. Some of the towns mentioned may not appear in the text because they may be more difficult to reach by public transportation. Many of these sites, however, are accessible by local bus services; local tourist offices can give you specific information.

Duration   4 days

Getting Around   **By Car.** 220 miles round-trip from London (southwest).

By Public Transportation. Trains and buses depart regularly from London to Dorchester and Bath. Local bus and train services are available once you are within the region, but plan carefully to avoid time-consuming waits.

Two days: Hardy's Wessex

The environs of Dorchester are the place to begin any exploration of Hardy country. The early years of his life were spent in **Higher Brockhampton** (2 miles west of Dorchester on A31), part of the parish of Stinsford, which appears in his writings as "Mellstock." It is best to leave at least a day to visit Sherborne, Cranborne, and Bridport, and to travel to Lullworth Cove, to get a true sense of the countryside that inspired so much of his work. All of these are within 25 miles of Dorchester.

This excursion can also include Salisbury and Stonehenge, which figure prominently in *Jude the Obscure* and *Tess of the D'Urbervilles,* respectively. They can be reached by traveling northwest for 30 miles on A31/A350/A30.

Two days: The Homes of Jane Austen

From rural delights we head for the civilized society of Jane Austen's world and novels. *Persuasion* and *Northanger Abbey* are especially associated with the city of **Bath** (105 miles west of London on A4). Jane Austen visited Bath frequently in her youth and lived here between the ages of 26 and 31 (1801–1806).

In 1809, Austen moved with her mother and sister Cassandra to **Chawton,** 50 miles south and 30 miles east of Bath on A36/A31, back through Salisbury and across Wiltshire. You will also pass through Southampton, where she lived for three years, although all records of precisely where have been lost. She lived in Chawton until 1817, and her home there is now a museum. In the last year of her life she moved to lodgings in **Winchester,** 10 miles south on A31. She lived here at 8 College Street, and is buried at Winchester Cathedral.

Further Information   *See* Chapter 4, The South; Chapter 7, The Heart of England.

The Best of Roman Britain

The Romans occupied much of Britain from the Cornish coast up into Scotland. Ruins dot the landscape, and a few of Britain's major highways (as well as many minor ones) overlie Roman roads. The following two journeys present some highlights, but you can find impressive evidence of the Roman occupation almost anywhere in the country. The first excursion covers parts of western Britain not far north of London, an area that seems to have been particularly prosperous in Roman times; the second takes us north to explore that feat of engineering, Hadrian's Wall.

Duration 4 to 5 days

Getting Around **By Car.** 150 miles round-trip from London (St. Albans and westward); 150 miles round-trip from Newcastle (Hadrian's Wall).

By Public Transportation. Although there is train and bus service to the major cities covered, as well as to the smaller sites, you may have to put up with delays. Some towns and sites may not appear in the text because they may not be so easily accessed by public transportation, but the British Tourist Association sometimes offers organized tours covering these regions.

Two to three days: St. Albans and Westward

This excursion begins in **St. Albans** (known in Roman times as Verulamium), 20 miles northwest of London on A1, and continues due west to the Roman "villas" of **North Leigh, Chedworth,** and **Gloucester** before heading back south through **Cirencester** to **Bath.** Along the way you will see some fantastic artifacts, tombs, forts, and amphitheaters, as well as the world-famous baths in, naturally, Bath. You may want to do some research in London's **British Museum,** where you will discover a wealth of archaeological finds.

One to two days: Hadrian's Wall

Following the 72-mile-long wall (built AD 122–126) from east to west, this journey offers several museum stopping points along the way, the first in **Newcastle-upon-Tyne,** then in **Corbridge, Chester, Chesterholm,** and **Carlisle.**

Further Information *See* Chapter 2, London; Chapter 4, The South; Chapter 7, The Heart of England; and Chapter 12, York and the Northeast.

Castles and Strongholds

This itinerary, concentrated in northeastern Kent, offers a quick history of castle architecture and the opportunity to visit some of the best examples Britain has to offer.

Duration 2 to 3 days

Getting Around **By Car.** 150 miles round-trip from London.

By Public Transportation. Check with British Rail and National Express or other bus companies for full information.

Heading southeast from London on A2/A257 for Sandwich brings you to **Richborough Castle,** originally a Saxon fort built in the 4th century. From here take A258 to Deal, where you will find both **Deal Castle,** dating from 1540, and **Walmer Castle,** a Renaissance fortification converted in the 18th century. Next comes **Dover Castle,** one of England's most impressive, which was still in military use as late as World War II. South down the coast is the town of Hythe and **Lympne Castle,** a 14th- to 15th-century building with a 13th-century Norman east tower. Leaving the best for last, M20 northwest will take you to **Leeds Castle,** a magnificent Norman fortress with 19th-century additions, set on two islands in a lake and surrounded by lovely landscaped park.

Chronology

2800 BC First building at Stonehenge (later building 2100–1900)

54 BC Julius Caesar's exploratory invasion of England

AD 43 Romans conquer England, led by Emperor Claudius

60 Boudicca, a native British queen, burns the first Roman London (Londinium) to the ground

122–27 Emperor Hadrian completes the Roman conquest and builds a wall across the north to keep back the Scottish Picts

145 The Antonine Wall built, north of Hadrian's, running from the Firth of Forth to the Firth of Clyde

300–350 Height of Roman colonization, administered from such towns as Verulamium (St. Albans), Colchester, Lincoln, and York

383–410 Romans begin to withdraw from Britain; waves of Germanic invaders—Jutes, Angles, and Saxons

c. 490 Possible period for the legendary King Arthur, who may have led resistance to Anglo-Saxon invaders; in 500 the Battle of Badon is fought

563 St. Columba, an Irish monk, founds monastery on the Scottish island of Iona; begins to convert Picts and Scots to Christianity

597 St. Augustine arrives in Canterbury to Christianize Britain

550–700 Seven Anglo-Saxon kingdoms emerge—Essex, Wessex, Sussex, Kent, Anglia, Mercia, and Northumbria—to become the core of English social and political organization for centuries

731 Bede completes his *Ecclesiastical History*

800s Danish Viking raids solidify into widespread colonization

871–99 Alfred the Great, king of Wessex, unifies the English against Viking invaders, who are then confined to the northeast

919–54 Short-lived Norse kingdom of York

1040 Edward the Confessor moves his court to Westminster and founds Westminster Abbey

1066 William, duke of Normandy, invades; defeats Harold at the Battle of Hastings; is crowned at Westminster on Christmas Day

1086 Domesday Book completed, a survey of all taxpayers in England, drawn up to assist administration of the new realm

1167 Oxford University founded

1170 Thomas à Becket murdered in Canterbury; his shrine becomes center for international pilgrimage

1189 Richard the Lion-Hearted embarks on the Third Crusade

1209 Cambridge University founded

1215 King John forced to sign Magna Carta at Runnymede; it promulgates basic principles of English law: no taxation except through Parliament, trial by jury, and property guarantees

1272–1307 Edward I, a great legislator; in 1282–83 he conquers Wales and reinforces his conquest with a chain of massive castles

1295 The Model Parliament sets future parliamentary pattern, with membership of knights from the shires, lower clergy, and civic representatives

1296 Edward I invades Scotland

1314 Robert the Bruce routs the English at Bannockburn

1337–1453 Edward III claims the French throne, starting the Hundred Years War. In spite of dramatic English victories—1346 at Crécy, 1356 at Poitiers, 1415 at Agincourt—the long war of attrition ends with the French driving the English out from all but Calais, which finally fell in 1558

1348–49 The Black Death (bubonic plague) reduces the population of Britain to around 2½ million; decades of social unrest follow

1381 The Peasants' Revolt is defused by the 14-year-old Richard II

1399 Henry Bolingbroke (Henry IV) deposes and imprisons his cousin Richard II; beginning of the rivalry between houses of York and Lancaster

1402–10 The Welsh, led by Owen Glendower, rebel against English rule

1455–85 The Wars of the Roses—the York/Lancaster struggle erupts in civil war

1477 William Caxton prints first book in England

1485 Henry Tudor (Henry VII) defeats Richard III at the Battle of Bosworth and founds the Tudor dynasty; he suppresses private armies, develops administrative efficiency and royal absolutism

1530s Under Henry VIII the Reformation takes hold; he dissolves the monasteries, finally demolishes medieval England and replaces it with a new society

Henry's marital history—in 1534 he divorces Catherine of Aragon after 25 years of marriage; in 1536 Anne Boleyn (mother of Elizabeth I) is executed in the Tower of London; in 1537 Jane Seymour dies giving birth to Edward VI; in 1540 Henry marries Anne of Cleves (divorced same year); in 1542 Catherine Howard is executed in the Tower; in 1542 he marries Catherine Parr, who outlives him

1554 Mary I marries Philip II of Spain; tries to restore Catholicism to England

1555 Protestant bishops Ridley and Latimer are burned in Oxford; in 1556 Archbishop Cranmer is burned

1558–1603 Reign of Elizabeth I—Protestantism re-established; Drake, Raleigh, and other freebooters establish English claims in the West Indies and North America

1568 Mary, Queen of Scots, flees to England; in 1587 she is executed

1588 Spanish Armada fails to invade England

1603 James VI of Scotland becomes James I of England

1605 Guy Fawkes and friends in Catholic plot to blow up Parliament

1611 King James Version of the Bible published

1620 Pilgrims sail from Plymouth on the *Mayflower* and settle in New England

1629 Charles I dissolves Parliament, decides to rule alone

1642–49 Civil War between the Royalists and Parliamentarians (Cavaliers and Roundheads); the Parliamentarians win

1649 Charles I executed; England is a republic

1653 Cromwell becomes Lord Protector, England's only dictatorship

1660 Charles II restored to the throne; accepts limits to royal power

1665 The Great Fire of London, accession of William III (of Orange) and his wife, Mary II, as joint monarchs; royal power limited still further

1694 Bank of England founded

1706–09 Marlborough's victories over the French under Louis XIV

1707 The Act of Union: England, Scotland, and Wales join in the United Kingdom of Great Britain

1714 The German Hanoverians succeed to the throne; George I's lack of English leads to a council of ministers, the beginning of the cabinet system of government

1700s Under the first four Georges, the Industrial Revolution develops and with it Britain's domination of world trade

1715/1745 Two Jacobite rebellions fail to restore the House of Stuart to the throne; in 1746 final defeat takes place at Culloden Moor

1756–63 Seven Years War; Britain wins colonial supremacy from the French in Canada and India

1775–83 Britain loses its American colonies

1795–1815 Britain and its allies defeat French in the Napoleonic Wars; in 1805 Nelson is killed at Trafalgar; in 1815 Battle of Waterloo is fought

---

1801 Union with Ireland

1811–20 Prince Regent rules during his father's (George III's) madness—the Regency period

1825 The Stockton to Darlington railway, the world's first passenger line with regular service, is established

1832 The Reform Bill extends the franchise, limiting the power of the great landowners

1834 Parliament outlaws slavery

1837–1901 The long reign of Victoria—Britain becomes the world's richest country and the British Empire reaches its height; railways, canals, and telegraph lines draw Britain into one vast manufacturing net

1851 The Great Exhibition, Prince Albert's brainchild, is held in the Crystal Palace, Hyde Park

1861 Prince Albert dies

1887 Victoria celebrates her Golden Jubilee; in 1901 she dies, marking the end of an era

---

1911–12 Rail, mining, and coal strikes

1914–18 World War I: Fighting against Germany, Britain loses a whole generation, with 750,000 men killed in trench warfare alone; enormous debts and inept diplomacy in the postwar years undermine Britain's position as a world power

1919 Ireland declares independence from England; bloody Black-and-Tan struggle results

1926 General Strike in sympathy with striking coal miners

1936 Edward VIII abdicates to marry American divorcée, Mrs. Wallis Simpson

1939–45 World War II—Britain faces Hitler alone until Pearl Harbor; London badly damaged during the Blitz, September '40–May '41; Britain's economy shattered by the war

1945 Labour wins a landslide victory; stays in power for six years, transforming Britain into a welfare state

1952 Queen Elizabeth accedes to the throne

1969 Serious violence breaks out in Northern Ireland

1972 National miners' strike

1973 Britain joins the European Economic Community after referendum

1975 Britain begins to pump North Sea oil

1981 Marriage of Prince Charles and Lady Diana Spencer

1982 Falklands regained

1987 Conservatives under Margaret Thatcher win a third term in office

1990 Glasgow is European Cultural Capital for the year

1990 John Major takes over as prime minister, ending Margaret Thatcher's illustrious, if controversial, career in office

1991 The Persian Gulf War

1992 Great Britain and the European countries join to form one European Community (EC), whose name is officially changed to European Union in 1993.

1994 Official opening of the Channel Tunnel by Queen Elizabeth II and President Mitterand

Kings and Queens

To help you sort out Britain's monarchs, we give here a list of those who have sat on the throne and the dates of their reigns.

	1042–66	Edward the Confessor
	1066	Harold
House of Normandy	1066–87	William I—The Conqueror
	1087–1100	William II—Rufus (murdered)
	1100–35	Henry I
	1135–54	Stephen
House of Plantagenet	1154–89	Henry II
	1189–99	Richard I—the Lion-Hearted (killed in battle)
	1199–1216	John
	1216–72	Henry III
	1272–1307	Edward I
	1307–27	Edward II (murdered)
	1327–77	Edward III
	1377–99	Richard II (deposed)
	1399–1413	Henry IV
	1413–22	Henry V
	1422–61	Henry VI (deposed)
House of York	1461–83	Edward IV
	1483	Edward V (probably murdered)
	1483–85	Richard III (killed in battle)
House of Tudor	1485–1509	Henry VII
	1509–47	Henry VIII
	1547–53	Edward VI
	1553	Jane (beheaded)
	1553–58	Mary I
	1558–1603	Elizabeth I
House of Stuart	1603–25	James I (VI of Scotland)
	1625–49	Charles I (beheaded)
Commonwealth	1653–58	Oliver Cromwell (Protector)
	1658–59	Richard Cromwell
House of Stuart (Restored)	1660–85	Charles II
	1685–88	James II (deposed and exiled)
	1689–95	William III and Mary II (joint monarchs)
	1695–1702	William III (reigned alone)
	1702–14	Anne
House of Hanover	1714–27	George I
	1727–60	George II
	1760–1820	George III
	1820–30	George IV (Regent from 1811)
	1830–37	William IV
House of Saxe-Coburg	1837–1901	Victoria
	1901–10	Edward VII
House of Windsor	1910–36	George V
	1936	Edward VIII (abdicated)
	1936–52	George VI
	1952–	Elizabeth II

1 Essential Information

Important Contacts

No single travel resource can give you every detail about every topic that might interest or concern you at the various stages of your journey—when you're planning your trip, while you're on the road, and after you get back home. The following organizations, books, and brochures will supplement the information in *Fodor's Affordable Great Britain '96*. For related information, including both basic tips on visiting Great Britain and background information on many of the topics below, study Smart Travel Tips A to Z, the section that follows Important Contacts A to Z.

Air Travel

The major gateways to Great Britain are London's Heathrow and Gatwick airports. Flying time to London is 6½ hours from New York, 7½ hours from Chicago, and 10 hours from Los Angeles.

Carriers   Carriers serving Great Britain include **American Airlines** (tel. 800/433–7300); **British Airways** (tel. 800/247–9297); **Continental Airlines** (tel. 800/231–0856); **Delta** (tel. 800/241–4141); **Northwest Airlines** (tel. 800/447–4747); **TWA** (tel. 800/892–4141); **United** (tel. 800/538–2929); and **Virgin Atlantic** (tel. 800/862–8621).

Complaints   To register complaints about charter and scheduled airlines, contact the U.S. Department of Transportation's **Office of Consumer Affairs** (400 7th St. NW, Washington, DC 20590, tel. 202/366–2220 or 800/322–7873).

Consolidators   Established consolidators selling to the public include **BET World Travel** (841 Blossom Hill Rd., Suite 212-C, San Jose, CA 95123, tel. 408/229–7880 or 800/747–1476), **Council Charter** (205 E. 42nd St., New York, NY 10017, tel. 212/661–0311 or 800/800–8222), **Euram Tours** (1522 K St. NW, Suite 430, Washington DC, 20005, tel. 800/848–6789), **TFI Tours International** (34 W. 32nd St., New York, NY 10001, tel. 212/736–1140 or 800/745–8000), **Travac Tours and Charter** (989 6th Ave., 16th Fl., New York, NY 10018, tel. 212/563–3303 or 800/872–8800; 2601 E. Jefferson, Orlando, FL 32803, tel. 407/896–0014 or 800/872–8800), and **UniTravel** (Box 12485, St. Louis, MO 63132, tel. 314/569–0900 or 800/325–2222). **FLY–ASAP** (3824 E. Indian School Rd., Phoenix, AZ 85018, tel. 800/359–2727) isn't a discounter, but gets good deals from among published fares and discount tickets from consolidators.

Publications   For general information about charter carriers, ask for the Office of Consumer Affairs' brochure **"Plane Talk: Public Charter Flights."** The Department of Transportation also publishes a 58-page booklet, **"Fly Rights"** ($1.75; Consumer Information Center, Dept. 133-B, Pueblo, CO 81009).

For other tips and hints, consult the Consumers Union's monthly **"Consumer Reports Travel Letter"** ($39 a year; Box 53629, Boulder CO 80322, tel. 800/234–1970) and the newsletter **"Travel Smart"** ($37 a year; 40 Beechdale Rd., Dobbs Ferry, NY 10522, tel. 800/327–3633); *The Official Frequent Flyer Guidebook,* by Randy Petersen ($14.99 plus $3 shipping; 4715-C Town Center Dr., Colorado Springs, CO 80916, tel. 719/597–8899 or 800/487–8893); *Airfare Secrets Exposed,* by Sharon Tyler and Matthew Wonder (Universal Information Publishing; $16.95 plus $3.75 shipping from Sandcastle Publishing, Box 3070-A, South Pasadena, CA 91031, tel. 213/255–3616 or 800/655–0053); and *202 Tips Even the Best Business Travelers May Not Know,* by Christopher McGinnis ($10 plus $3 shipping; Irwin Professional Publishing, 1333 Burr Ridge Pkwy., Burr Ridge, IL 60521, tel. 800/634–3966).

Within Great British Airways operates shuttle services between London/
Britain Heathrow and Edinburgh, Glasgow, Belfast, and Manchester. Passengers can simply turn up and get a flight (usually hourly) without
booking. There are also shuttle services from Gatwick. **British Midland** operates from Heathrow to Teesside, Belfast, Glasgow, Liverpool, and the Isle of Man. The Scottish islands are served by
Loganair from Glasgow and Edinburgh.

You can book all flights through **British Airways** (Bulova Center, 75–
20 Astoria Blvd., Jackson Heights, NY 11370, tel. 800/247–9297) or
a travel agent.

Better Business Bureau

For local contacts in the home town of a tour operator you may be
considering, consult the **Council of Better Business Bureaus** (4200
Wilson Blvd., Arlington, VA 22203, tel. 703/276–0100).

Bus Travel

Information can be obtained from **Victoria Coach Station** (Buckingham Palace Rd., London SW1W 9TP, tel. 0171/730–0202) or from
Eastern Scottish (Saint Andrew's Sq., Edinburgh, tel. 0131/558–
1616).

National Express, with its Scottish associate of the same name, is
the British equivalent of Greyhound and by far the largest British
operator. Victoria Coach Station in London is the hub of its network, which serves about 1,500 destinations. Information is available from any of the company's 2,500 agents nationwide or from
National Express offices at London's Heathrow and Gatwick airport
coach stations.

Discount Pass National Express's **Tourist Trail Pass** costs £49 for three consecutive
days of travel, £79 for five days travel out of 10 consecutive days,
£119 for eight days out of 16, and £179 for 15 days out of 30. A **Brit
Express** card qualifies you for 30% discounts on those prices and
costs £7. Both can be bought for U.S. dollars from **British Travel Associates** (Box 299, Elkton, VA 22827, tel. 703/298–2232 or 800/327–
6097).

Bicycling

Contact the **Cyclists' Touring Club** (69 Meadrow, Godalming, Surrey
GU7 3HS, tel. 01483/417217; basic membership £25 a year). Members receive free advice and information, a detailed route-planning
service for any region of Britain, a handbook of recommended bed-
and-breakfast accommodations for cyclists, and *Cycle Touring and
Campaigning* magazine.

Car Rental

Major car-rental companies represented in Great Britain include **Al-
amo** (tel. 800/327–9633, 0800/272–2000 in the U.K.); **Avis** (tel. 800/
331–1084, 800/879–2847 in Canada); **Budget** (tel. 800/527–0700,
0800/181–181 in the U.K.); **Hertz** (tel. 800/654–3001; 800/263–0600
in Canada, 0181/679–1799 in the U.K.); and **National** (sometimes
known as Europcar InterRent outside North America; tel. 800/227–
3876, 0181/950–5050 in the U.K.). Rates in London begin at $21 a
day and $126 a week for an economy car with unlimited mileage. This
does not include tax, which in Great Britain is 17.5% on car rentals.

Rental Contact **Auto Europe** (Box 7006, Portland, ME 04112, tel. 207/828–
Wholesalers 2525 or 800/223–5555); **Europe by Car** in New York City (write 1
Rockefeller Plaza, 10020; visit 14 W. 49th St.; or call 212/581–3040,
212/245–1713, or 800/223–1516) or Los Angeles (9000 Sunset Blvd.,

90069, tel. 800/252–9401 or 213/272–0424 in CA); **Foremost Euro-Car** (5658 Sepulveda Blvd., Suite 201, Van Nuys, CA 91411, tel. 818/786–1960 or 800/272–3299); or the **Kemwel Group** (106 Calvert St., Harrison, NY 10528, tel. 914/835–5555 or 800/678–0678).

Channel Tunnel

For information, contact **Le Shuttle** (tel. 01345/353535 in the U.K., 800/388–3876 in the U.S.), which transports cars, or **Eurostar** (tel. 0171/922–4486 in the U.K., 800/942–4866 in the U.S.), the high-speed train service between London (Waterloo) and Paris (Gare du Nord). Eurostar tickets are available in the United Kingdom through **InterCity Europe,** the international wing of BritRail (London, Victoria Station, tel. 0171/834–2345 or 0171/828–8092 for credit-card bookings), and in the United States through **Rail Europe** (tel. 800/942–4866) and **BritRail Travel** (1500 Broadway, New York, NY 10036, tel. 800/677–8585).

Children and Travel

If you're taking the family to Britain, get the British Tourist Authority's cost-conscious brochure "Families Welcome" before you go. For information and advice when in London, call **Kidsline** (tel. 0171/222–8070) or the tourist board's **Visitorcall** service (tel. 01839/123456 for menu; costs 49p/min, 39p off-peak). *See also* Home Exchange *under* Lodging, *below.*

Baby-sitting **Nanny Service** (9 Paddington St., London WIM 3LA, tel. 0171/935–3515) and **Universal Aunts** (19 The Chase, London SW4 ONP, tel. 0171/738–8937) are reliable sources.

Family Travel Organizations The **American Institute for Foreign Study** (AIFS, 102 Greenwich Ave., Greenwich, CT 06830, tel. 203/869–9090) offers a family-vacation program in Britain specifically designed for parents and children.

Flying Look into **"Flying with Baby"** ($5.95 plus $1 shipping; Third Street Press, Box 261250, Littleton, CO 80126, tel. 303/595–5959), cowritten by a flight attendant. **"Kids and Teens in Flight,"** free from the U.S. Department of Transportation's Office of Consumer Affairs, offers tips for children flying alone. Every two years the February issue of *Family Travel Times* (*see* Know-How, *below*) details children's services on three dozen airlines.

Games The gamemeister, Milton Bradley, has games to help keep little (and not so little) children from getting fidgety while riding in planes, trains, and automobiles. Try packing the *Travel Battleship* sea battle game ($7); *Travel Connect Four,* a vertical strategy game ($8); the *Travel Yahtzee* dice game ($6); the *Travel Trouble* dice and board game ($7); and the *Travel Guess Who* mystery game ($8).

Know-How *Family Travel Times,* published four times a year by Travel with Your Children (TWYCH, 45 W. 18th St., New York, NY 10011, tel. 212/206–0688; annual subscription $40), covers destinations, types of vacations, and modes of travel.

The *Family Travel Guides* catalogue ($1 postage; Box 6061, Albany, CA 94706; tel. 510/527–5849) lists about 200 books and articles on family travel. Also check *Take Your Baby and Go! A Guide for Traveling with Babies, Toddlers and Young Children,* by Sheri Andrews, Judy Bordeaux, and Vivian Vasquez ($5.95 plus $1.50 shipping; Bear Creek Publications, 2507 Minor Ave., Seattle, WA 98102, tel. 206/322–7604 or 800/326–6566). *Innocents Abroad: Traveling with Kids in Europe,* by Valerie Wolf Deutsch and Laura Sutherland ($15.95 hardcover, $5.95 paperback plus $2 shipping; Penguin USA, 120 Woodbine St., Bergenfield, NJ 07621, tel. 201/387–0600 or 800/253–

6476), covers child- and teen-friendly activities, food, and transportation.

Local Info Helpful local publications include *Children's London*, a free booklet from the London Visitor and Convention Bureau (Tourist Information Centre, Victoria Station Forecourt, London SW1V 1JT; personal callers only). Also consult *Kids' London*, by Elizabeth Holt and Molly Perham (St. Martin's Press, 175 5th Ave., New York, NY 10010; $5.95).

Lodging **Novotel** (tel. 800/221–4542) hotels allow up to 2 children to stay free in their parents' room. **Forte Hotels** (various London locations) in Britain have special Babycare Kits and children's menus; children under 5 stay free and ages 6–13 in parents' room enjoy reduced rates. (Keep in mind that in Britain, hotels will often allow only three people in a room.)

Tour Operators Contact **Grandtravel** (6900 Wisconsin Ave., Suite 706, Chevy Chase, MD 20815, tel. 301/986–0790 or 800/247–7651), which has tours for people traveling with grandchildren ages 7 to 17; **Families Welcome!** (21 W. Colony Pl., Suite 140, Durham, NC 27705, tel. 919/489–2555 or 800/326–0724); or **Rascals in Paradise** (650 5th St., Suite 505, San Francisco, CA 94107, tel. 415/978–9800 or 800/872–7225).

Customs

U.S. Citizens The **U.S. Customs Service** (Box 7407, Washington, DC 20044, tel. 202/927–6724) can answer questions on duty-free limits and publishes a helpful brochure, "Know Before You Go." For information on registering foreign-made articles, call 202/927–0540.

Canadians Contact **Revenue Canada** (2265 St. Laurent Blvd. S, Ottawa, Ontario, K1G 4K3, tel. 613/993–0534) for a copy of the free brochure **"I Declare/Je Déclare"** and for details on duties that exceed the standard duty-free limit.

For Travelers with Disabilities

Complaints To register complaints under the provisions of the Americans with Disabilities Act, contact the U.S. Department of Justice's **Public Access Section** (Box 66738, Washington, D.C. 20035, tel. 202/514–0301, TDD 202/514–0383, fax 202/307–1198).

Organizations
For Travelers with Hearing Impairments Contact the **American Academy of Otolaryngology** (1 Prince St., Alexandria, VA 22314, tel. 703/836–4444, fax 703/683–5100, TTY 703/519–1585), which can provide information to travelers with hearing impairments.

For Travelers with Mobility Problems Contact the **Information Center for Individuals with Disabilities** (Fort Point Pl., 27–43 Wormwood St., Boston, MA 02210, tel. 617/727–5540, 800/462–5015 in MA, TTY 617/345–9743); **Mobility International USA** (Box 10767, Eugene, OR 97440, tel. and TTY 503/343–1284, fax 503/343–6812), the U.S. branch of an international organization based in Belgium (*see below*) that has affiliates in 30 countries; **MossRehab Hospital Travel Information Service** (1200 W. Tabor Rd., Philadelphia, PA 19141, tel. 215/456–9603, TTY 215/456–9602); the **Society for the Advancement of Travel for the Handicapped** (347 5th Ave., Suite 610, New York, NY 10016, tel. 212/447–7284, fax 212/725–8253); the **Travel Industry and Disabled Exchange** (TIDE, 5435 Donna Ave., Tarzana, CA 91356, tel. 818/344–3640, fax 818/344–0078); and **Travelin' Talk** (Box 3534, Clarksville, TN 37043, tel. 615/552–6670, fax 615/552–1182).

For Travelers with Vision Impairments Contact the **American Council of the Blind** (1155 15th St. NW, Suite 720, Washington, DC 20005, tel. 202/467–5081, fax 202/467–5085) or the **American Foundation for the Blind** (15 W. 16th St., New York, NY 10011, tel. 212/620–2000, TTY 212/620–2158).

In the U.K. Contact the **Royal Association for Disability and Rehabilitation** (RA-DAR, 12 City Forum, 250 City Rd., London EC1V 8AF, tel. 0171/250–3222) or **Mobility International** (Rue de Manchester 25, B–1070 Brussels, Belgium, tel. 00–322–410–6297), an international clearinghouse of travel information for people with disabilities.

Publications Several free publications are available from the U.S. Information Center (Box 100, Pueblo, CO 81009, tel. 719/948–3334): **"New Horizons for the Air Traveler with a Disability"** (address to Dept. 355A), describing legally mandated changes; the pocket-size **"Fly Smart"** (Dept. 575B), good on flight safety; and the Airport Operators Council's worldwide **"Access Travel: Airports"** (Dept. 575A).

The 500-page *Travelin' Talk Directory* ($35; Box 3534, Clarksville, TN 37043, tel. 615/552–6670) lists people and organizations who help travelers with disabilities. For specialist travel agents worldwide, consult the *Directory of Travel Agencies for the Disabled* ($19.95 plus $2 shipping; Twin Peaks Press, Box 129, Vancouver, WA 98666, tel. 206/694–2462 or 800/637–2256) and the *Directory of Travel Agencies for the Disabled,* by Helen Hecker ($19.95 plus $3.50 handling; Disability Bookshop, Box 129, Vancouver, WA, 98666; tel. 206/694-2462).

Travel Agencies and Tour Operators The Americans with Disabilities Act requires that travel firms serve the needs of all travelers. However, some agencies and operators specialize in making group and individual arrangements for travelers with disabilities, among them **Access Adventures** (206 Chestnut Ridge Rd., Rochester, NY 14624, tel. 716/889–9096), run by a former physical-rehab counselor. In addition, many general-interest operators and agencies (*see* Tour Operators, *below*) can also arrange vacations for travelers with disabilities.

For Travelers with Hearing Impairments One agency is **International Express** (7319-B Baltimore Ave., College Park, MD 20740, tel. TDD 301/699–8836, fax 301/699–8836), which arranges group and independent trips.

For Travelers with Mobility Impairments A number of operators specialize in working with travelers with mobility impairments: **Flying Wheels Travel** (143 W. Bridge St., Box 382, Owatonna, MN 55060, tel. 507/451–5005 or 800/535–6790), a travel agency that specializes in European cruises and tours; **Hinsdale Travel Service** (201 E. Ogden Ave., Suite 100, Hinsdale, IL 60521, tel. 708/325–1335 or 800/303–5521), a travel agency that will give you access to the services of wheelchair traveler Janice Perkins; **Nautilus Tours** (5435 Donna Ave., Tarzana, CA 91356, tel. 818/344–3640 or 800/345–4654); **Wheelchair Journeys** (16979 Redmond Way, Redmond, WA 98052, tel. 206/885–2210), which can handle arrangements worldwide.

For Travelers with Developmental Disabilities Contact the nonprofit **New Directions** (5276 Hollister Ave., Suite 207, Santa Barbara, CA 93111, tel. 805/967–2841), for travelers with developmental disabilities and their families as well as the general-interest operations above.

Discount Clubs

Options include **Entertainment Travel Editions** (fee $28–$53, depending on destination; Box 1068, Trumbull, CT 06611, tel. 800/445–4137); **Great American Traveler** ($49.95 annually; Box 27965, Salt Lake City, UT 84127, tel. 800/548–2812); **Moment's Notice Discount Travel Club** ($25 annually, single or family; 163 Amsterdam Ave., Suite 137, New York, NY 10023, tel. 212/486–0500); **Privilege Card** ($74.95 annually; 3391 Peachtree Rd. NE, Suite 110, Atlanta GA 30326, tel. 404/262–0222 or 800/236-9732); **Travelers Advantage** ($49 annually, single or family; CUC Travel Service, 49 Music Sq. W, Nashville, TN 37203, tel. 800/548–1116 or 800/648–4037); and **Worldwide Discount Travel Club** ($50 annually for family, $40 single; 1674 Meridian Ave., Miami Beach, FL 33139, tel. 305/534–2082).

Driving

Auto Clubs The **Automobile Association** (Fanum House, Basingstoke, Hampshire, RQ21 2 EA, tel. 01256/20123) and the **Royal Automobile Club** (RAC House, Bartlett St., Box 10, Croydon, Surrey CR2 6XW, tel. 0181/686–2525) offer associate membership for overseas visitors and a wealth of detailed information about motoring in Britain.

Maps Good planning maps are available from the **AA** and the **RAC** (*see above*).

Electricity

Send a self-addressed, stamped envelope to the **Franzus Company** (Customer Service, Dept. B50, Murtha Industrial Park, Box 142, Beacon Falls, CT 06403, tel. 203/723–6664) for a copy of the free brochure "Foreign Electricity Is No Deep Dark Secret."

Gay and Lesbian Travel

Organizations The **International Gay Travel Association** (Box 4974, Key West, FL 33041, tel. 800/448–8550), a consortium of 800 businesses, can supply names of travel agents and tour operators.

Publications The premier international travel magazine for gays and lesbians is **Our World** ($35 for 10 issues; 1104 N. Nova Rd., Suite 251, Daytona Beach, FL 32117, tel. 904/441–5367). The 16-page monthly "Out & About" ($49 for 10 issues; tel. 212/645–6922 or 800/929–2268) covers gay-friendly resorts, hotels, cruise lines, and airlines.

Tour Operators Cruises and resort vacations are handled by **Hanns Ebensten Travel** (513 Fleming St., Key West, FL 33040, tel. 305/294–8174), one of the nation's oldest operators in the gay market, and **Toto Tours** (1326 W. Albion Suite 3W, Chicago, IL 60626, tel. 312/274–8686 or 800/565–1241), both of which offer group tours worldwide.

Travel Agencies The largest agencies serving gay travelers are **Advance Travel** (10700 Northwest Fwy., Suite 160, Houston, TX 77092, tel. 713/682–2002 or 800/695–0880); **Islanders/Kennedy Travel** (183 W. 10th St., New York, NY 10014, tel. 212/242–3222 or 800/988–1181); **Now Voyager** (4406 18th St., San Francisco, CA 94114, tel. 415/626–1169 or 800/255–6951); and **Yellowbrick Road** (1500 W. Balmoral Ave., Chicago, IL 60640, tel. 312/561–1800 or 800/642–2488). **Skylink Women's Travel** (746 Ashland Ave., Santa Monica, CA 90405, tel. 310/452–0506 or 800/225-5759) works with lesbians.

Health Issues

Medical-Assistance Companies Contact **International SOS Assistance** (Box 11568, Philadelphia, PA 19116, tel. 215/244–1500 or 800/523–8930; Box 466, Pl. Bonaventure, Montréal, Québec H5A 1C1, tel. 514/874–7674 or 800/363–0263); **Medex Assistance Corporation** (Box 10623, Baltimore, MD 21285, tel. 410/296–2530 or 800/573–2029); **Near Services** (Box 1339, Calumet City, IL 60409, tel. 708/868–6700 or 800/654–6700); and **Travel Assistance International** (1133 15th St. NW, Suite 400, Washington, DC 20005, tel. 202/331–1609 or 800/821–2828). Because these companies also sell death-and-dismemberment, trip-cancellation, and other insurance coverage, there is some overlap with the travel-insurance policies sold by the companies listed under Insurance, *below*.

Insurance

Travel insurance covering baggage, health, and trip cancellation or interruptions is available from **Access America** (Box 90315, Richmond, VA 23286, tel. 804/285–3300 or 800/284–8300); **Carefree Travel**

Insurance (Box 9366, 100 Garden City Plaza, Garden City, NY 11530, tel. 516/294–0220 or 800/323–3149); **Near Services** (Box 1339, Calumet City, IL 60409, tel. 708/868–6700 or 800/654–6700); **Tele-Trip** (Mutual of Omaha Plaza, Box 31716, Omaha, NE 68131, tel. 800/228–9792); **Travel Insured International** (Box 280568, East Hartford, CT 06128-0568, tel. 203/528–7663 or 800/243–3174); **Travel Guard International** (1145 Clark St., Stevens Point, WI 54481, tel. 715/345–0505 or 800/826–1300); and **Wallach & Company** (107 W. Federal St., Box 480, Middleburg, VA 22117, tel. 703/687–3166 or 800/237–6615).

Lodging

Apartment and Villa Rentals Among the companies to contact are **At Home Abroad** (405 E. 56th St., Suite 6H, New York, NY 10022, tel. 212/421–9165); **Hometours International** (Box 11503, Knoxville, TN 37939, tel. 615/588–8722 or 800/367–4668); **Interhome** (124 Little Falls Rd., Fairfield, NJ 07004, tel. 201/882–6864); **Property Rentals International** (1008 Mansfield Crossing Rd., Richmond, VA 23236, tel. 804/378–6054 or 800/220–3332); **Rental Directories International** (2044 Rittenhouse Sq., Philadelphia, PA 19103, tel. 215/985–4001); **Rent-a-Home International** (7200 34th Ave. NW, Seattle, WA 98117, tel. 206/789–9377 or 800/488–7368); **Vacation Home Rentals Worldwide** (235 Kensington Ave., Norwood, NJ 07648, tel. 201/767–9393 or 800/633–3284); and **Villas and Apartments Abroad** (420 Madison Ave., Suite 1105, New York, NY 10017, tel. 212/759–1025 or 800/433–3020). Members of the travel club **Hideaways International** ($99 annually; 767 Islington St., Portsmouth, NH 03801, tel. 603/430–4433 or 800/843–4433) receive two annual guides plus quarterly newsletters and arrange rentals among themselves.

Lists of rental properties are available free of charge from the **British Tourist Authority**. Discounts of up to 50% apply during the off-season (October–March). **Heart of England Cottages, Inc.** (Box 878, Eufaula, AL 36072, tel. 205/687–9800, fax 205/687–5324) will send you a detailed brochure on the properties they handle, which start at $210 per week.

Bed-and-Breakfasts The famous *Cottages, B&Bs and Country Inns of England and Wales*, by Elizabeth H. Gundrey (Fodor's, $15), covers the waterfront and has given its author's name to the language, as in "Let's go Gundreying."

Home Exchange Principal clearinghouses include **Intervac International** ($65 annually; Box 590504, San Francisco, CA 94159, tel. 415/435–3497), which has three annual directories, and **Loan-a-Home** ($35–$45 annually; 2 Park La., Apt. 6E, Mount Vernon, NY 10552-3443, tel. 914/664–7640), which specializes in long-term exchanges.

Landmarks Want to spend your vacation in a Gothic banqueting house, an old lighthouse, or maybe in a gatehouse that sheltered Mary, Queen of Scots in 1586? Several organizations have specially adapted historic buildings to rent, most of them self-catering. Best of all is **The Landmark Trust** (Shottesbrooke, Maidenhead, Berkshire SL6 3SW, tel. 01628/825925); also try the **National Trust** (Box 101, Western Way, Melksham, Wiltshire SN12 8EA, tel. 01225/705676). All the buildings have been modernized, with due respect to their historic status, (there are no TVs in the Landmark Trust properties).

University Housing In larger cities and in some towns, universities offer their residence halls to paying visitors on a nightly basis during the vacations. The facilities are usually compact single sleeping units. For information, contact the **British Universities Accommodation Consortium** (Box 907, University Park, Nottingham NG7 2RD, tel. 01602/504571).

Mail

If you're uncertain where you'll be staying, you can arrange to have your mail sent to **American Express** (6 Haymarket, London SW1Y 4BS). The service is free to cardholders; all others pay a small fee. You can also collect letters at London's main post office. Ask to have them sent to Poste Restante, Main Post Office, London. The point of collection is the King Edward Building (King Edward St., London EC1A 1AA, tel. 0171/239–5047). Hours are Monday, Tuesday, Thursday, and Friday 8:30 AM–6:30 PM, Wednesday 9 AM–6:30 PM. You'll need your passport or other official form of identification.

Money Matters

The unit of currency in Britain is the pound sterling, divided into 100 pence (p). The bills are 50, 20, 10, and 5 pounds (Scotland has £1 bills as well). Coins are £1 and 50, 20, 10, 5, 2, and 1p.

ATMs For specific foreign **Cirrus** locations, call 800/424–7787; for foreign Plus locations, consult the **Plus** directory at your local bank.

Currncy Exchange If your bank doesn't exchange currency, contact **Thomas Cook Currency Services** (41 E. 42nd St., New York, NY 10017, or 511 Madison Ave., New York, NY 10022, tel. 212/757–6915 or 800/223–7373 for locations) or **Ruesch International** (tel. 800/424–2923 for locations).

At press time the exchange rate was about US$1.60 and C$2.10 to the pound sterling.

Wiring Funds Funds can be wired via **American Express MoneyGram**ᔆᴹ (tel. 800/926–9400 from the U.S. and Canada for locations and information) or **Western Union** (tel. 800/325–6000 for agent locations or to send using MasterCard or Visa, 800/321–2923 in Canada).

Passports and Visas

U.S. Citizens For fees, documentation requirements, and other information, call the **Office of Passport Services** information line (tel. 202/647–0518).

Canadians For fees, documentation requirements, and other information, call the Ministry of Foreign Affairs and International Trade's **Passport Office** (tel. 819/994–3500 or 800/567–6868).

Phone Matters

The country code for Great Britain is 44. For local access numbers abroad, contact **AT&T** USADirect (tel. 800/874–4000), **MCI** Call USA (tel. 800/444–4444), or **Sprint** Express (tel. 800/793–1153).

Photo Help

The **Kodak Information Center** (tel. 800/242–2424) answers consumer questions about film and photography.

Rail Travel

You can find detailed timetables of most rail services in Britain and some ferry services in the *Thomas Cook European Timetable*, issued monthly and on sale in the United States at **Forsyth Travel Library** (9154 W. 57th St., Dept. TCT, Shawnee Mission, KS 66201, tel. 913/384–3440 or 800/367–7984, fax 913/384–3553).

Discount Passes For exploring a specific part of Britain in greater detail, Regional Rail Rover unlimited travel tickets offer excellent value; there are also All Line tickets, covering the whole of Britain but the BritRail Pass bought in advance in the U.S. costs much less. Details can be obtained from any **British Rail Travel Centre** (one is at Euston Station, London NW1 1DF, tel. 0171/387-7070).

If you plan on doing a lot of traveling while in Britain, consider purchasing a BritRail Pass, which gives unlimited travel over the entire British Rail Network and will save you a great deal of money. A variety of passes are offered. The cost of a BritRail adult pass for 8 days is $230 standard and $315 first-class; for 15 days, $355 standard and $515 first-class; for 22 days, $445 and $645; and for a month, $520 and $750. The BritRail Youth Pass, for those ages 16–25, provides unlimited second-class travel and costs $189 for 8 days, $280 for 15 days, $355 for 22 days, and $415 for one month. The BritRail Senior Citizen Pass, for passengers over 60, costs $209 for 8 days (first-class $295), $320 for 15 days (first-class $479), $399 for 22 days (first-class $585), and $465 for one month (first-class $675). (These are U.S. dollar figures; Canadian ones will be a little higher.)

There are also Flexi Passes, which allow 4, 8, or 15 days of travel in one month. All BritRail Pass holders also get useful discounts on Britainshrinkers, escorted rail and coach tours of one to three days out of London to various heritage attractions. Another option is the England/Wales Pass, good for four days of unlimited travel within a month. The adult first-class ticket costs $205, standard class is $155 (children 5–15 pay half-fare). The Freedom of Scotland Travelpass allows unlimited standard-class travel for $159 (8 days), $220 (15 days), or $269 (22 days); a Scotland Flexipass allows 8 days of travel over a 15-day period for $185.

If you want the flexibility of a car combined with the speed and comfort of the train, try BritRail/Drive (from around $250 for one adult, with a $145 supplement for additional adults and $72.50 for children 5–15); this gives you a three-day BritRail FlexiPass and three vouchers valid for Hertz car rental from more than 100 locations throughout Great Britain. A 6-day rail pass with 7 days of car rental is also available (from $459, with $209 adult supplement, $104.50 children). Larger cars, automatic transmission, and first-class rail seats will cost you more. If you call your travel agency or Hertz's international desk (tel. 800/654-3131), the car of your choice will be waiting for you at the station as you alight from your train.

There is also a BritRail + Eurostar Flexipass that includes a round-trip rail journey through the Channel Tunnel to Paris; prices start from $295.

You *must* purchase your BritRail Pass before you leave home. They are available from most travel agents or from the **BritRail Travel International** office (1500 Broadway, New York, NY 10036, tel. 212/575-2667 or 800/677-8585). Note that the Eurail Pass is not valid in Britain.

Senior Citizens

Educational Travel The nonprofit **Elderhostel** (75 Federal St., 3rd Floor, Boston, MA 02110, tel. 617/426-7788), for people 60 and older, has offered inexpensive study programs since 1975. The nearly 2,000 courses cover everything from marine science to Greek myths and cowboy poetry. Fees for two- to three-week international trips—including room, board, and transportation from the United States—range from $1,800 to $4,500.

For people 50 and over and their children and grandchildren, **Interhostel** (University of New Hampshire, 6 Garrison Ave., Durham, NH 03824, tel. 603/862-1147 or 800/733-9753) runs 10-day summer programs involving lectures, field trips, and sightseeing. Most last two weeks and cost $2,125–$3,100, including airfare.

Organizations Contact the **American Association of Retired Persons** (AARP, 601 E St. NW, Washington, DC 20049, tel. 202/434–2277; $8 per person or couple annually). Its Purchase Privilege Program gets members discounts on lodging, car rentals, and sightseeing.

For other discounts on lodgings, car rentals, and other travel products, along with magazines and newsletters, contact the **National Council of Senior Citizens** (membership $12 annually; 1331 F St. NW, Washington, DC 20004, tel. 202/347–8800) and **Mature Outlook** (subscription $9.95 annually; 6001 N. Clark St., Chicago, IL 60660, tel. 312/465–6466 or 800/336–6330).

Publications *The 50+ Traveler's Guidebook: Where to Go, Where to Stay, What to Do,* by Anita Williams and Merrimac Dillon ($12.95; St. Martin's Press, 175 5th Ave., New York, NY 10010, tel. 212/674–5151 or 800/288–2131), offers many useful tips. "**The Mature Traveler**" ($29.95; Box 50400, Reno, NV 89513, tel. 702/786–7419), a monthly newsletter, covers travel deals.

Shopping

Little-known even to most Brits are the factory shops that sell directly to the public, where the savings can be as much as 50% off the normal store price. *Factory Shop Guides* are published by Gillian Cutress and Rolf Stricker (34 Park Hill, London SW4 9PB) and cost around £5.

Stately Homes and Castles

Stately homes, if still in private hands, can survive only by charging entry fees, which have rocketed over the past few years together with the owners' expenses. Many attractions now offer family tickets that cover two parents and two or three children. Luckily, most stately homes and nearly all castles belong to either the **National Trust** or to **English Heritage**. If you are visiting lots of castles or stately homes, buying an annual membership, which entitles you to free or reduced entry to member properties, can mean huge savings. Contact the National Trust **Royal Oak Foundation** (285 West Broadway, Suite 400, New York, NY 10013, tel. 212/966–6565; membership $40 for individuals, $65 for families); **English Heritage** (write for details: Box 1BB, London W1A 1BB £15 adult); **Friends of Scottish Monuments** (c/o Historic Scotland, SDD Room 306, 20 Brandon St., Edinburgh EH3 5RA, tel. 0131/668–8600; £14 adult, £28 for a family); and **Heritage in Wales** (Dept. EH, Cadw, Brunel House, 2 Fitzalan Rd., Cardiff CF2 1UY, tel. 0122/246–5511; membership £15 and £30).

Students

Groups Major tour operators include **Contiki Holidays** (300 Plaza Alicante, Suite 900, Garden Grove, CA 92640, tel. 714/740–0808 or 800/466–0610) and **AESU Travel** (2 Hamill Rd., Suite 248, Baltimore, MD 21210-1807, tel. 410/323–4416 or 800/638–7640).

Hosteling There are more than 350 youth hostels throughout England, Scotland, and Wales, many in remote and beautiful areas. These inexpensive, generally reliable digs range from very basic to almost luxurious, and usually include cooking facilities. Despite the name, there is no age restriction.

Contact **Hostelling International–American Youth Hostels** (733 15th St. NW, Suite 840, Washington, DC 20005, tel. 202/783–6161) in the United States, **Hostelling International–Canada** (205 Catherine St., Suite 400, Ottawa, Ontario K2P 1C3, tel. 613/237–7884) in Canada, and the **Youth Hostel Association of England and Wales** (Trevelyan House, 8 St. Stephen's Hill, St. Albans, Hertfordshire AL1 2DY, tel. 01727/855215 and 01727/845047) in the United Kingdom. Membership ($25 in the U.S., C$26.75 in Canada, and £9 in the U.K.) gets you access to 5,000 hostels worldwide that charge $7–$20 nightly per person.

I.D. Cards To be eligible for discounts on transportation and admissions, get the **International Student Identity Card** (ISIC) if you're a bona fide student or the **International Youth Card** (IYC) if you're under 26. In the United States, the ISIC and IYC cards cost $16 each and include basic travel accident and illness coverage, plus a toll-free travel hot line. Apply through the Council on International Educational Exchange (*see* Organizations, *below*). Cards are available for $15 each in Canada from **Travel Cuts** (187 College St., Toronto, Ontario M5T 1P7, tel. 416/979–2406 or 800/667–2887) and in the United Kingdom for £5 each at student unions and student travel companies.

Organizations A major contact is the **Council on International Educational Exchange** (CIEE, 205 E. 42nd St., 16th Floor, New York, NY 10017, tel. 212/661–1450), with locations in Boston (729 Boylston St., 02116, tel. 617/266–1926), Miami (9100 S. Dadeland Blvd., 33156, tel. 305/670–9261), Los Angeles (1093 Broxton Ave., 90024, tel. 310/208–3551), 43 college towns nationwide, and the United Kingdom (28A Poland St., London W1V 3DB, tel. 0171/437–7767). Twice a year, it publishes *Student Travels* magazine. The CIEE's Council Travel Service is the exclusive U.S. agent for several student-discount cards.

Campus Connections (325 Chestnut St., Suite 1101, Philadelphia, PA 19106, tel. 215/625–8585 or 800/428–3235) specializes in discounted accommodations and airfares for students. The **Educational Travel Centre** (438 N. Frances St., Madison, WI 53703, tel. 608/256–5551) offers rail passes and low-cost airline tickets, mostly for flights departing from Chicago. Only for air travel contact **TMI Student Travel** (100 W. 33rd St., Suite 813, New York, NY 10001, tel. 800/245–3672).

In Canada, also contact **Travel Cuts** (*see above*).

Publications See the *Berkeley Guide to Great Britain & Ireland* ($17.50; Fodor's Travel Publications, 800/533–6478 or from bookstores).

Tour Operators

Group tours and independent vacation packages can turn out to be a bargain depending on what they include (*see* Packages and Tours under Smart Travel Tips A to Z, *below*). Among the companies selling tours and packages to Great Britain, the following have a proven reputation, are nationally known, and have plenty of options to choose from.

Group Tours Budget tours are sold by **Cosmos** (*see* Globus, *above*) and by **Trafalgar Tours** (*see above*).

Packages Just about every airline that flies to Great Britain sells packages that include round-trip airfare and hotel accommodations. Carriers to contact include **American Airlines' Fly AAway Vacations** (tel. 800/321–2121); **British Airways** (*see above*); **Continental Airlines' Grand Destinations** (tel. 800/634–5555); **Delta Dream Vacations** (tel. 800/872–7786); and **United Airlines' Vacation Planning Center** (tel. 800/328–6877). Other packagers include **Certified Vacations** (Box 1525, Ft. Lauderdale, FL 33302, tel. 305/522–1414 or 800/233–7260); **CIE Tours** (108 Ridgedale Ave., Box 2355, Morristown, NJ 07962, tel. 201/292–3899 or 800/243–8687); **DER Tours** (11933 Wilshire Blvd., Los Angeles, CA 90025, tel. 310/479–4140 or 800/782–2424); and **Jet Vacations** (1775 Broadway, New York, NY 10019, tel. 212/474–8740 or 800/538–2762).

Theme Trips Theme trips are, by their nature, more expensive than a general-interest tour or package, but they still may be a better deal than arranging everything on your own.

Travel Contacts (45 Idmiston Rd., London SE27 9HL, England, tel. 011/44–81766–7868, fax 011/44–81766–6123), with 135 member operators, can satisfy virtually any special interest in Great Britain. **Great British Vacations** (4800 Griffith Dr., Suite 125, Beaverton, OR 97005, tel. 503/643–8080 or 800/452–8434) creates custom-designed itineraries that include barging, walking and visiting stately homes.

Adventure **All Adventure Travel** (5589 Arapahoe #208, Boulder, CO 80303, tel. 800/537–4025) can book hiking, walking, kayaking, skiing, and many other adventures in Great Britain.

Antiques **Travel Keys Tours** (Box 162266, Sacramento, CA 95816-2266, tel. 916/452–5200) specializes in tours to the antiques fairs and flea markets of Europe.

Barge Cruises For barge cruising through the canals of England or Scotland, contact **Le Boat** (tel. 201/342–1838 or 800/922–0291) or **Barge & Voyage** (140 E. 56th St., Suite 4C, New York, NY 10022, tel. 800/438–4748).

Bicycling Bike tours are available from **Backroads** (1516 5th St., Suite A550, Berkeley, CA 94710-1470, tel. 510/527–1555 or 800/462–2848); **Classic Adventures** (Box 153, Hamlin, NY 14464-0153, tel. 800/777–8090, fax 716/964–7297); **Euro-Bike** (Box 990-P, DeKalb, IL 60115, tel. 800/321–6060, fax 815/758–8851); and **Uniquely Europe** (2819 1st Ave., #280, Seattle, WA 98121, tel. 206/441–8682 or 800/426–3610).

Cooking **Cuisine International** (7707 Willow Vine Ct., Suite 219, Dallas, TX 75230, tel. 214/373–1161, fax 214/373–1162) has week-long cooking programs taught by famous chefs in Oxford and the Cotswolds.

Fishing Try **Rod and Reel Adventures** (3507 Tully Rd., Modesto, CA 95356, tel. 209/524–7775 or 800/356–6882) or **Francine Atkins' Scotland/Ireland/England** (Dallas/Fort Worth Metroplex, 2 Ross Ct., Trophy Club, TX 76262, tel. 817/491–1105 or 800/742–0355), which combines fishing and golfing in one vacation package.

Homes and Gardens **Coopersmith's England** (Box 900, Inverness, CA 94937, tel. 415/669–1914, fax 510/339–7135) wines and dines you with gourmet meals and books your accommodations in castles, historic country inns, and manor houses. **Expo Garden Tours** (101 Sunrise Hill Rd., Norwalk, CT 06851, tel. 203/840–1441 or 800/448–2685) visits the annual Chelsea Flower Show.

Horseback Riding **FITS Equestrian** (685 Lateen Rd., Solvang, CA 93463, tel. 805/688–9494, fax 805/688–2943) is a top horseback-riding operator with year-round departures and tours for every level of rider.

Learning Vacations **Earthwatch** (680 Mount Auburn St., Watertown, MA 02272, tel. 617/926–8200 or 800/776–0188) recruits volunteers to serve in its EarthCorps as short-term assistants to scientists or research expeditions. **The Smithsonian Institution** (1100 Jefferson Dr. SW, Room 3045, Washington, DC 20560, tel. 202/357–4700) has tours that showcase Great Britain's natural history and culture.

Music **Dailey-Thorp Travel** (330 W. 58th St., New York, NY 10019, tel. 212/307–1555; book through travel agents) specializes in classical music and opera programs throughout Europe; its packages include tickets that are otherwise very hard to get.

Tennis **Championship Tennis Tours** (9 Antigua, Dana Point, CA 92629, tel. 714/661–7331 or 800/545–7717) and **Sportstours** (6503 N. Military Trail, #207, Boca Raton, FL 33496, tel. 800/879–8647) has packages to Wimbledon, held each summer in London.

Walking **English Adventures** (803 Front Range Road, Littleton, CO 80120, tel. 303/797–2365) and **English Lakeland Ramblers** (18 Stuyvesant

Oval #1A, New York NY 10009, tel. 212/505–1020 or 800/724–8801) hike and walk the English Lake District with visits to castles and the homes of Wordsworth and Beatrix Potter. **Above the Clouds Trekking** (Box 398, Worcester, MA 01602, tel. 800/233–4499 or 508/799–4499) has walking/hiking tours through the Cotswolds, Cornwall, the Peak District, and the Shetland Islands. Cotswolds walking tours also are available from **Country Walkers** (Box 180S, Waterbury, VT 05676, tel. 802/244–1387).

In the U.K. **Countrywide Holidays** (Birch Heys, Cromwell Range, Manchester M14 6HU, tel. 0161/225–1000) organizes excursions for beginners and experienced walkers, with lodging in country houses and hotels. **Greenscape UK** (Milkaway La., Croyde, North Devon EX33 1NG, tel. 01271/890–677) has walks through the Wales, Scotland, the Cotswolds, the Bath area, the West Country, and the Yorkshire Dales. **Mountain Goat Holidays and Tours** (Victoria St., Windermere, Cumbria LA23 1AD, tel. 015394/45161) leads guided weekly walks around the Lake District and the Yorkshire Dales.

Organizations The **National Tour Association** (546 E. Main St., Lexington, KY 40508, tel. 606/226–4444 or 800/755–8687) and **United States Tour Operators Association** (USTOA, 211 E. 51st St., Suite 12B, New York, NY 10022, tel. 212/750–7371) can provide lists of member operators and information on booking tours.

Publications Consult the brochure **"On Tour"** and ask for a current list of member operators from the National Tour Association (*see* Organizations, *above*). Also get a copy of the **"Worldwide Tour & Vacation Package Finder"** from the USTOA (*see* Organzations, *above*) and the Better Business Bureau's **"Tips on Travel Packages"** (publication No. 24-195, $2; 4200 Wilson Blvd., Arlington, VA 22203).

Travel Agencies

For names of reputable agencies in your area, contact the **American Society of Travel Agents** (1101 King St., Suite 200, Alexandria, VA 22314, tel. 703/739–2782).

U.S. Government Travel Briefings

The U.S. Department of State's Overseas Citizens Emergency Center (Room 4811, Washington, DC 20520; enclose SASE) issues **Consular Information Sheets**, which cover crime, security, political climate, and health risks as well as embassy locations, entry requirements, currency regulations, and other routine matters. For the latest information, stop in at any U.S. passport office, consulate, or embassy; call the interactive hot line (tel. 202/647–5225 or fax 202/647-3000); or, with your PC's modem, tap into the Bureau of Consular Affairs' computer bulletin board (tel. 202/647–9225).

Visitor Information

Contact the **British Tourist Authority** (BTA).

In the U.S. 551 5th Ave., New York, NY 10176, tel. 212/986–2200; 625 N. Michigan Ave., Chicago, IL 60611, tel. 312/787–0490; World Trade Center, 350 S. Figueroa St., Suite 450, Los Angeles, CA 90017, tel. 213/628–3525; 280 Cumberland Pkwy., Suite 470, Atlanta, GA 30339-3909, tel. 404/432–9635.

In Canada 94 Cumberland St., Suite 600, Toronto, Ontario M5R 3N3, tel. 416/925–6326.

In Britain Thames Tower, Black's Rd., London W6 9EL; tel. 0181/846–9000.

Information on rail, coach, and air travel can be obtained (in person only) at the **British Travel Centre** (12 Regent St., London SW1 4PQ), Monday–Saturday 9–6, Sunday 10–4.

Walking

The British have a gentle name for travel on foot—"rambling." The whole country is criss-crossed by meandering trails—there are over 100,000 miles of them in England and Wales—some tiny and local, some very long and historic, like Peddlar's Way in East Anglia, or the Pennine Way in Yorkshire. For £14 you can join **the Ramblers Association** (1–5 Wandsworth Rd., London SW8 2XX, tel. 0171/582-6878) and get a bimonthly magazine and an annual yearbook with articles and a list of more than 2,000 bed-and-breakfast accommodations near rambling trails.

Given a couple of weeks' advance notice, **Walker's Britain** (part of **Sherpa Expeditions**, 131A Heston Rd., Hounslow, Middlesex TW5 ORD, tel. 0181/577-2717) will arrange inexpensive self-guided walking tours around Britain, with maps and suggested lodgings, and will send a free catalogue. You can also arrange these hikes through All Adventure Travel (*see* Packages and Tours, *above*).

The BTA (*see* Visitor Information, *above*) puts out a very useful free map, *Walking in Britain,* which gives book lists and other information for 49 named routes. The best maps for walkers to use are the Ordnance Survey Maps. A free color brochure of their range can be obtained from **Ordnance Survey** (Romsey Rd., Southampton SO9 4DH, tel. 01703/379-2765).

Weather

For current conditions and forecasts, plus the local time and helpful travel tips, call the **Weather Channel Connection** (tel. 900/932-8437; 95¢ per minute) from a touch-tone phone.

Smart Travel Tips

The more you travel, the more you know about how to make trips run like clockwork. To help make your travels hassle-free, Fodor's editors have rounded up dozens of tips from our contributors and travel experts all over the world, as well as basic information on visiting Great Britain. For names of organizations to contact and publications that can give you more information, *see* Important Contacts A to Z, *above*.

Air Travel

If time is an issue, **always look for nonstop flights,** which require no change of plane. If possible, **avoid connecting flights,** which stop at least once and can involve a change of plane, although the flight number remains the same; if the first leg is late, the second waits.

Cutting Costs
Major Airlines
The least-expensive airfares from the major airlines are priced for round-trip travel and are subject to restrictions. You must usually **book in advance and buy the ticket within 24 hours** to get cheaper fares, and you may have to **stay over a Saturday night.** The lowest fare is subject to availability, and only a small percentage of the plane's total seats are sold at that price. It's good to **call a number of airlines, and when you are quoted a good price, book it on the spot**—the same fare on the same flight may not be available the next day. Airlines generally allow you to change your return date for a $25 to $50 fee, but most low-fare tickets are nonrefundable. However, if you don't use it, you can apply the cost toward the purchase price of a new ticket, again for a small charge.

Consolidators Consolidators, who buy tickets at reduced rates from scheduled airlines, sell them at prices below the lowest available from the airlines directly—usually without advance restrictions. Sometimes you can even get your money back if you need to return the ticket. Carefully read the fine print detailing penalties for changes and cancellations. If you doubt the reliability of a consolidator, **confirm your reservation with the airline.**

Within Great Britain For trips of less than 200 miles, **take the train**—it's quicker, given the time it takes to get between city centers and airports. Flying tends to cost more, and many internal U.K. flights are scheduled primarily as feeders from provincial airports into Heathrow and Gatwick for international flights.

For trips of more than 200 miles—for example, between London and Glasgow or Edinburgh—or where a sea crossing is involved, to places such as the Isle of Man, Belfast, the Channel Islands, or the Scottish islands, air travel has a considerable time advantage. But it can be expensive.

Aloft
Airline Food If you hate airline food, **ask for special meals when booking.** These can be vegetarian, low-cholesterol, or kosher, for example; commonly prepared to order in smaller quantities than standard catered fare, they can be tastier.

Jet Lag To avoid this syndrome, which occurs when travel disrupts your body's natural cycles, try to maintain a normal routine. At night, **get some sleep.** By day, move about the cabin to **stretch your legs, eat light meals, and drink water—not alcohol.**

Smoking Smoking is banned on all flights within the U.S. of less than six hours' duration and on all Canadian flights; the ban also applies to domestic segments of international flights aboard U.S. and foreign carriers. Delta has banned smoking system-wide. On U.S. carriers flying to Great Britain and other destinations abroad, a seat in a no-smoking section must be provided for every passenger who requests one, and the section must be enlarged to accommodate such passengers if necessary as long as they have complied with the airline's deadline for check-in and seat assignment. If smoking bothers you, request a seat far from the smoking section.

Foreign airlines are exempt from these rules but do provide no-smoking sections (British Airways has banned smoking, as has Virgin Atlantic on most international flights); some nations have banned smoking on all domestic flights, and others may ban smoking on some flights. Talks continue on the feasibility of broadening no-smoking policies.

Beaches

The use of British beaches is free for the most part, with a small charge made for any changing facilities, toilets, or umbrellas. British beaches vary: Some are grossly polluted and a few are as clean as a whistle. Before going to a beach, ask if it has been awarded a European Blue Flag, granted to beaches with a high standard of water quality (they should be cleaned daily during high season) and good facilities. In 1992, 17 won the award, 10 of which were in southern Wales and the southwest. To counter the disturbing picture created by winning so few European Blue Flags, Britain has instituted its own awards, the Seaside Awards—also blue! Sixty-four of these were awarded to various beaches in 1992. The *Good Beach Guide*, produced by the Marine Conservation Society (Ebury Press, 20 Vauxhall Bridge Rd., London, England, SW1V 2SA; £6.99), will set you right on which are good, bad, or downright dangerous.

Bike Travel

Even experienced cyclists should **avoid main roads.** Bikes are banned from motorways and on most dual carriageways or main trunk roads. However, on side roads and country lanes, the bike is supreme as a way of exploring Britain. You will find the Ordnance Survey 1:50,000 *Landranger* maps, sold throughout Britain, invaluable for planning routes.

There are special bicycle routes in some towns and parts of the countryside, and public bridleways—green, unsurfaced tracks —are reserved for horses, walkers, and cyclists. Unfortunately, taking bikes on British Rail is not easy these days because of many different restrictions. So as soon as you arrive in Britain, **get a copy of the brochure covering bikes on trains** (not available in the United States) at any large rail station.

When you rent a bike, a deposit of £30–£50 is usually required; some firms will accept a credit card. If you're considering a cycling holiday in Britain, it is a good idea to **join the Cyclists' Touring Club** (*see* Bicycling *in* Important Contacts A to Z, *above*).

Also **consider a bike tour** (*see* Theme Trips *under* Tour Operators *in* Important Contacts A to Z, *above*).

Boat Travel

Rivers and lakes in Britain are not big enough to maintain regular boat or waterbus systems, with one or two notable exceptions. The Scottish Highlands offer boat services on Loch Lomond, Loch Etive, and Loch Katrine. The Lake District also has regularly scheduled boat services from April until October on the larger lakes—Windermere, Coniston, Ullswater, and Dertwentwater. These services allow passengers to alight and return on foot along the shore or by a later boat.

Business Hours

Banks   Banks are open weekdays 9:30–4:30. Some have extended hours on Thursday evenings, and a few are open on Saturday mornings.

Shops   Usual business hours are Monday–Saturday 9–5:30; on Sunday, small shops stay open all day if they wish to, and larger stores can, too, since the relaxation of the Sunday trading laws in late 1994. Outside the main centers, most shops close at 1 PM one day a week, often Wednesday or Thursday. In small villages, many also close for lunch. In large cities—especially London—department stores stay open late (usually until 7:30 or 8) one day a week. Pubs are generally open Monday–Saturday 11 AM–11 PM, Sunday noon–3 and 7–10 or 10:30. Some further relaxation of the blue laws was pending at press time.

Museums, Stately Homes, and Castles   Museum and gallery hours vary considerably from one part of the country to another, and holiday closings vary, so be sure to check. In large cities, most are open Tuesday–Saturday; many are also open on Sunday afternoons. The majority close on Monday. Many museums admit children under 6 free.

Most stately homes change their opening times at Easter and in October—or when Britain changes its clocks for summertime. Many of them close down completely from October to Easter, or to April 1, whichever is earlier. Opening and closing times can change at a moment's notice, so always phone first. Many stately homes close their doors a half-hour before the stated time, to allow the last parties time to complete their tour.

Bus Travel

Within Great Britain Britain has a comprehensive bus (short-haul) and coach (long-distance) network that offers an inexpensive way of seeing the country. Coaches cost about half the price of trains, or even less, but are generally slower. Seats are comfortable, and some coaches have toilet facilities on board.

The classic British double-decker buses still operate on many of the routes of Britain's extensive local bus network. It's difficult to plan a journey by country bus, because privatization of lines has given rise to many small companies and schedules are constantly changing. But wherever you're staying, the local bus station and the local tourist information center will have precise information. Most companies offer day or week "Explorer" or "Rover" unlimited-travel tickets, and those in popular tourist areas invariably operate special scenic tours in summer.

Cameras, Camcorders, and Computers

Laptops Before you depart, **check your portable computer's battery**, because you may be asked at security to turn on the computer to prove that it is what it appears to be. At the airport, you may prefer to **request a manual inspection**, although security X-rays do not harm hard-disk or floppy-disk storage. Also, **register your foreign-made laptop with U.S. Customs.** If your laptop is U.S.-made, call the consulate of the country you'll be visiting to find out whether or not it should be registered with local customs upon arrival. You may want to **find out about repair facilities at your destination** in case you need them.

Photography If your camera is new or if you haven't used it for a while, **shoot and develop a few rolls of film** before you leave. Always **store film in a cool, dry place**—never in the car's glove compartment or on the shelf under the rear window.

Every pass of film through an X-ray machine increases the chance of clouding. To protect it, carry it in a clear plastic bag and **ask for hand inspection at security.** Such requests are virtually always honored at U.S. airports and are usually accommodated abroad. Don't depend on a lead-lined bag to protect film in checked luggage—the airline may increase the radiation to see what's inside.

Video Also, **test your camcorder, invest in a skylight filter to protect the lens, and charge the batteries.** (Airport security personnel may ask you to turn on the camcorder to prove that it's what it appears to be). The batteries of most newer camcorders can be recharged with a universal or worldwide AC adapter charger (or multivoltage converter), usable whether the voltage is 110 or 220. All that's needed is the appropriate plug.

Videotape is not damaged by X-rays, but it may be harmed by the magnetic field of a walk-through metal detector, so **ask that videotapes be hand-checked.** Videotape sold in Great Britain is based on the PAL standard, which is different from the one used in the United States. You will not be able to view your tapes through the local TV set or view movies bought there in your home VCR. Blank tapes bought in Great Britain can be used for camcorder taping, but they are pricey. Some U.S. audiovisual shops convert foreign tapes to U.S. standards; contact an electronics dealer to find the nearest.

The Channel Tunnel

The Channel Tunnel provides the fastest route across the Channel—35 minutes from Folkestone to Calais, 60 minutes from motorway to motorway, or 3 hours from Waterloo, London to Paris, Gare du

Nord. It consists of two large 50-kilometer- (31-mile-) long tunnels for trains, one in each direction, linked by a smaller service tunnel running between them.

Le Shuttle, a special car, bus, and truck train, operates a continuous loop, with trains departing every 15 minutes at peak times and at least once an hour through the night. No reservations are necessary, although tickets may be purchased in advance from travel agents. Most passengers travel in their own car, staying with the vehicle throughout the "crossing," with progress updates via radio and display screens. Motorcyclists park their bikes in a separate section with its own passenger compartment, while foot passengers must book passage by coach. At press time, prices for a one-day round-trip ticket began at £107–£154 for a car and its occupants. Prices for a five-day round-trip ticket began at £115.

Eurostar operates high-speed passenger-only trains, which whisk riders between stations in Paris (Gare du Nord) and London (Waterloo) in three hours and between London and Brussels (Midi) in 3¼ hours. At press time, fares were $154 for a one-way, first-class ticket and $123 for an economy fare.

The tunnel is reached from Exit 11a of the M20/A20. Tickets for either tunnel service can be purchased in advance (*see* Important Contacts A to Z, *above*).

Children and Travel

Baby-sitting   For recommended local sitters, **check with your hotel desk.**

Driving   If you are renting a car, **arrange for a car seat when you reserve.** Sometimes they're free.

Flying   Always **ask about discounted children's fares.** On international flights, the fare for infants under age 2 not occupying a seat is generally either free or 10% of the accompanying adult's fare; children ages 2–11 usually pay half to two-thirds of the adult fare. On domestic flights, children under 2 not occupying a seat travel free, and older children currently travel on the lowest applicable adult fare. Some routes are considered neither international nor domestic and have still other rules.

Baggage   In general, the adult baggage allowance applies for children paying half or more of the adult fare. Before departure, **ask about carry-on allowances** if you are traveling with an infant. In general, those paying 10% of the adult fare are allowed one carry-on bag, not to exceed 70 pounds or 45 inches (length + width + height) and a collapsible stroller; you may be allowed less if the flight is full.

Safety Seats   According to the FAA, it's a good idea to **use safety seats aloft.** Airline policy varies. U.S. carriers allow FAA-approved models, but airlines usually require that you buy a ticket, even if your child would otherwise ride free, because the seats must be strapped into regular passenger seats. Foreign carriers may not allow infant seats, may charge the child's rather than the infant's fare for their use, or may require you to hold your baby during takeoff and landing, thus defeating the seat's purpose.

Facilities   When making your reservation, **ask for children's meals or free-standing bassinets** if you need them; the latter are available only to those with seats at the bulkhead, where there's enough legroom. If you don't need a bassinet, **think twice before requesting bulkhead seats**—the only storage for in-flight necessities is in the inconveniently distant overhead bins.

Lodging   Most hotels allow children under a certain age to stay in their parents' room at no extra charge, while others charge them as extra adults; be sure to **ask about the cut-off age.**

Credit Cards

The following credit card abbreviations are used in this guide: AE, American Express; DC, Diners Club; MC, MasterCard (also called Access and Eurocard in Britain); V, Visa (also called Barclaycard in Britain). Many B&Bs do not accept credit cards. If they do, the most widely accepted are MasterCard and Visa, far and away the most useful ones to have when traveling in Britain. Diners Club is the least accepted.

Customs and Duties

In Great Britain There are two levels of duty-free allowance for travelers entering Great Britain: one for goods bought outside the EU, the other for goods bought in the EU (Belgium, Greece, the Netherlands, Denmark, Italy, Portugal, France, the Irish Republic, Spain, Germany, or Luxembourg).

Of goods purchased outside the EU, you may import duty-free: 200 cigarettes or 100 cigarillos or 50 cigars or 250 grams of tobacco; two liters of table wine and, in addition, (a) one liter of alcohol over 22% by volume (most spirits), (b) two liters of alcohol under 22% by volume (fortified or sparkling wine), or (c) two more liters of table wine; 50 milliliters of perfume; ¼ liter of toilet water; and other goods up to a value of £36, but not more than 50 liters of beer or 25 cigarette lighters.

If you are entering the United Kingdom from another EU country, you no longer need to pass through customs. If you plan to bring large quantities of alcohol or tobacco, check in advance on EU limits. No animals or pets of any kind can be brought into the United Kingdom without a lengthy quarantine. The penalties are severe and strictly enforced. Similarly, fresh meats, plants and vegetables, illegal drugs, and firearms and ammunition may not be brought into Great Britain.

You will face no customs formalities if you enter Scotland or Wales from any other part of the United Kingdom, though anyone coming from Northern Ireland should expect a security check.

Back Home *In the U.S.* You may bring home $400 worth of foreign goods duty-free if you've been out of the country for at least 48 hours and haven't already used the $400 exemption, or any part of it, in the past 30 days.

Travelers 21 or older may bring back one liter of alcohol duty-free, provided the beverage laws of the state through which they reenter the United States allow it. In addition, 100 non-Cuban cigars and 200 cigarettes are allowed, regardless of your age. Antiques and works of art more than 100 years old are duty-free.

Duty-free, travelers may mail packages valued at up to $200 to themselves and up to $100 to others, with a limit of one parcel per addressee per day (and no alcohol or tobacco products or perfume valued at more than $5); outside, identify the package as being for personal use or an unsolicited gift, specifying the contents and their retail value. Mailed items do not count as part of your exemption.

In Canada Once per calendar year, when you've been out of Canada for at least seven days, you may bring in C$300 worth of goods duty-free. If you've been away less than seven days but more than 48 hours, the duty-free exemption drops to C$100 but can be claimed any number of times (as can a C$20 duty-free exemption for absences of 24 hours or more). You cannot combine the yearly and 48-hour exemptions, use the C$300 exemption only partially (to save the balance for a later trip), or pool exemptions with family members. Goods claimed under the C$300 exemption may follow you by mail; those claimed under the lesser exemptions must accompany you.

Alcohol and tobacco products may be included in the yearly and 48-hour exemptions but not in the 24-hour exemption. If you meet the age requirements of the province through which you reenter Canada, you may bring in, duty-free, 1.14 liters (40 imperial ounces) of wine or liquor *or* 24 12-ounce cans or bottles of beer or ale. If you are 16 or older, you may bring in, duty-free, 200 cigarettes, 50 cigars or cigarillos, and 400 tobacco sticks or 400 grams of manufactured tobacco. Alcohol and tobacco must accompany you on your return.

An unlimited number of gifts valued up to C$60 each may be mailed to Canada duty-free. These do not count as part of your exemption. Label the package "Unsolicited Gift—Value Under $60." Alcohol and tobacco are excluded.

Dining

With a little planning you can eat very well in Britain for a sensible price. The most ubiquitous type of feeding house is probably the good old British public house. Even villages which are too small to support their own store or post office tend to have a pub, and such places are often good and historic to boot. The typical lineup of English bar food is: ploughman's lunch (a slab of cheddar, crusty bread, relish), quiche and salad (which often only just qualifies for that description), sandwiches (heavy on the bread), sausages, pork pie (beware of mass-produced fatty, bright pink versions), and maybe steak-and-kidney pie, shepherd's pie, or lasagna. That's the average, but if you search a little, you're bound to find a place that prides itself on excellent home-cooked bar food—pot pies, soups, pâtés, stews, and apple crumble.

Ethnic food can be another excellent budget option. Italian restaurants are an obvious choice, but sometimes they rank in the slightly higher price bracket. Chinese food is good value, especially in London's and Manchester's Chinatowns. Indian restaurants are to be found throughout the country—especially in London, where Tandoori houses predominate, named after the clay *tandoor* oven in which spiced breads, fish, and meat are baked, and Birmingham, whose *balti* (a type of stew-like curry, scooped up with unleavened bread) houses are so good they're cloning elsewhere. Other common ethnic cuisines include Thai, Greek, and Vietnamese, with everything from Tibetan to Ethiopian found in London. A meal at any should cost around £15.

Most city centers have sandwich shops that cater to the office lunchtime trade. Some churches (St. James's and St. Martin-in-the-Fields in London) serve light lunches at reasonable cost, and stately homes nearly always have a tearoom attached, with home-made cakes and maybe full meals. There are useful links in burger chains all over the country; McDonald's golden arches are on every high street, and the slightly more upmarket Garfunkles in the Southeast offers good value on their well-stocked salad bars.

The item that really hikes up the check is alcohol. Always try for the house wine, by the glass, carafe, or bottle. It can be palate curling to a wine buff, but at least the cost won't be too great. There is often an inescapable cover charge in a restaurant and almost always a service charge (the fixed tip). If you opt for bar food, there should be no service charge.

What to Wear Generally, the restaurants and pubs we list are happy with informal attire. We have noted the establishments that request men to wear a jacket and tie; women should dress accordingly. Also, unless otherwise noted, it is unnecessary to book ahead.

Mealtimes In general, breakfast is served between 7:30 and 9, and lunch between noon and 2. Tea—often a meal in itself—is generally served between 4:30 and 5:30. Dinner or supper is served between 7:30 and

9:30, sometimes earlier, seldom later, except in large cities to after-theater diners. High tea, at about 6, replaces dinner in some areas.

Prices The following chart is a key to pricing symbols in the Dining sections in this guide. Prices are quoted in pounds sterling (with dollar equivalents at press time) and are based on a three-course meal for one, including tax, but excluding drinks and service.

	London and Southern England	Other Towns
££	£20–£30 (US$32–US$48)	£15–£20 (US$24–US$32)
£	£12–£20 (US$19–US$32)	£10–£15 (US$16–US$24)
¢	under £12 (US$19)	under £10 (US$16)

For Travelers with Disabilities

When discussing accessibility with an operator or reservationist, **ask hard questions.** Are there any stairs, inside *or* out? Are there grab bars next to the toilet *and* in the shower/tub? How wide is the doorway to the room? To the bathroom? For the most extensive facilities, meeting the latest legal specifications, **opt for newer accommodations,** which more often have been designed with access in mind. Older properties or ships must usually be retrofitted and may offer more limited facilities as a result. Be sure to **discuss your needs before booking.**

Discount Clubs

Travel clubs offer members unsold space on airplanes, cruise ships, and package tours at as much as 50% below regular prices. Membership may include a regular bulletin or access to a toll-free hot line giving details of available trips departing from three or four days to several months in the future. Most also offer 50% discounts off hotel rack rates. Before booking with a club, **make sure the hotel or other supplier isn't offering a better deal.**

Driving

Serving more than 55 million inhabitants and a country about the size of California, Britain's roads are among the most crowded in the world. But away from the towns and cities, you can find miles of little-used roads and lanes where driving can be a real pleasure—and adventure.

Auto Clubs If you are a member of a motoring organization, there may be reciprocal membership benefits, including breakdown assistance, with Britain's Automobile Association (AA). Check with your club; they will also be able to advise you about procedures, insurance, and necessary documentation.

Rules of the Road The most noticeable difference is that when in Britain you drive on the left. This takes a bit of getting used to, but it's easier if you're driving a British car with steering and mirrors designed for U.K. conditions. Be sure to **give yourself time to adjust.**

Speed limits are complicated, and traffic police can be hard on speeders, especially in urban areas. In those areas, the limit (shown on circular red signs) is generally 30 mph (50 kph), 40 mph (65 kph) on some main roads. In rural areas, the official limit is 60 mph (97 kph) on ordinary roads and 70 mph (113 kph) on motorways (*see* Types of

Roads *below*). The use of seat belts is obligatory in the front seat, and in the back seat where they are provided.

Types of Roads There's now a very good network of superhighways (motorways) and divided highways (dual carriageways) throughout most of Britain, though in Scotland and Wales travel is noticeably slower. Motorways (with the prefix *M*), shown in blue on most maps and road signs, are mainly two or three lanes in each direction, without any right-hand turns. Service areas are about an hour's travel time apart (or less), though some stretches (like the M11 out of London) have none at all, a circumstance helpfully announced by NO SERVICES FOR X MILES signs, when it's too late to veer off. Dual carriageways (with the prefix *A*), shown on maps as thick red lines, have both traffic lights and traffic circles, and right turns are sometimes permitted.

The vast network of lesser roads (single red *A* and narrower brown *B* lines), for the most part old coach and turnpike roads, might make your trip take twice as long and show you twice as much. Minor roads, drawn in yellow or white, unlettered, and unnumbered, are the ancient lanes and byways, a superb way of discovering the real Britain. Some of these are potholed switchbacks, littered with blind corners and cow pats, and barely wide enough for one car, let alone for two to pass. Be prepared to reverse into a passing place if you meet an oncoming car or tractor.

Gasoline Expect to pay a good deal more for gasoline than in the United States; it costs about £2.60 a gallon (60p a liter) for four-star—and up to 10p a gallon higher in remote locations—but remember that the British Imperial gallon (4½ liters) is about 20% greater in volume than the U.S. gallon. Most gas stations stock four-star (97 octane), diesel, and lead-free gas. Diesel and lead-free are both cheaper than four-star. Service stations on motorways are located at regular intervals and are usually open 24 hours a day; elsewhere they usually close from 9 PM to 7 AM and in country areas sometimes at 6 PM and all day Sunday.

Ferry Travel

Most of the islands off the coast of Britain are served by regular car ferries, usually linked to train and coach services on the mainland. For shorter crossings, reservations are not needed, but you should **reserve for the longer ferry crossings** to Ireland, the Isle of Man, and the Channel Islands. Details of most crossings will be found in either the *Thomas Cook European Timetable* or in the British Rail timetables.

Insurance

Travel insurance can protect your investment, replace your luggage and its contents, or provide for medical coverage should you fall ill during your trip. Most tour operators, travel agents, and insurance agents sell specialized health-and-accident, flight, trip-cancellation, and luggage insurance as well as comprehensive policies with some or all of these features. Before you make any purchase, **review your existing health and homeowner policies** to find out whether they cover expenses incurred while traveling.

Baggage Airline liability for your baggage is limited to $1,250 per person on domestic flights. On international flights, the airlines' liability is $9.07 per pound or $20 per kilogram for checked baggage (roughly $640 per 70-pound bag) and $400 per passenger for unchecked baggage. Insurance for losses exceeding the terms of your airline ticket can be bought directly from the airline at check-in for about $10 per $1,000 of coverage; note that it excludes a rather extensive list of items, shown on your airline ticket.

Flight You should **think twice before buying flight insurance.** Often purchased as a last-minute impulse at the airport, it pays a lump sum when a plane crashes, either to a beneficiary if the insured dies or sometimes to a surviving passenger who loses eyesight or a limb. Supplementing the airlines' coverage described in the limits-of-liability paragraphs on your ticket, it's expensive and basically unnecessary. Charging an airline ticket to a major credit card often automatically entitles you to coverage and may also embrace travel by bus, train, and ship.

Health If your own health insurance policy does not cover you outside the United States, **consider buying supplemental medical coverage.** It can reimburse from $1,000 to $150,000 to cover medical and/or dental expenses incurred as a result of an accident or illness during a trip. These policies also may include a personal-accident or death-and-dismemberment provision, which pays a lump sum ranging from $15,000 to $500,000 to your beneficiaries if you die or to you if you lose one or more limbs or your eyesight, and a medical-assistance provision, which may either reimburse you for the cost of referrals, evacuation, or repatriation and other services, or automatically enroll you as a member of a particular medical-assistance company.

Trip Without insurance, you will lose all or most of your money if you must cancel your trip due to illness or any other reason. Especially if your airline ticket, cruise, or package tour is nonrefundable and cannot be changed, it's essential that you **buy trip-cancellation-and-interruption insurance.** When considering how much coverage you need, look for a policy that will cover the cost of your trip plus the nondiscounted price of a one-way airline ticket should you need to return home early. Read the fine print carefully, especially sections defining "family member" and "preexisting medical conditions." Also **consider default or bankruptcy insurance,** which protects you against a supplier's failure to deliver. However, such policies often do not cover default by a travel agency, tour operator, airline, or cruise line if you bought your tour and the coverage directly from the firm in question.

Lodging

Budget-minded visitors should be aware that lodging in Britain is going to eat up a large chunk of their vacation cash. Hotels, especially fancy ones in big cities, are very expensive, often unjustifiably so. London's hotel rates are sky high, especially in the center of town. However, conscious of the cutthroat competition, smaller hotels are usually very careful to ensure that their prices match their services.

Be sure to **ask for reduced rates on weekends,** usually the downtime for hotels and B&Bs, when you can often stay in a normally expensive hotel for around half the mid-week rate. Also, don't hesitate to **inquire about specials deals when staying for more than one night.** Many hotels and inns offer inclusive packages (dinner, bed, and breakfast for two nights is a typical deal) that represent considerable savings over the standard rate. The English, Welsh, and Scottish tourist boards all produce annual guides on where to stay, covering B&Bs, hotels, guest houses, and inns, in every possible category.

If you're staying anywhere for a week, save money by staying in accommodations that allow self-catering, particularly off-season; the bigger the group, the bigger the saving. If you enjoy the outdoors, try spending some or all of your nights at the very affordable campsites located throughout Britain. Equipment, however, is likely to be less expensive at home, so buy what you need before you go.

Apartment If you want a home base that's roomy enough for a family and comes
and Villa with cooking facilities, **consider a furnished rental.** It's generally
Rentals cost-wise, too, although not always—some rentals are luxury properties (economical only when your party is large). Home-exchange
directories list rentals—often second homes owned by prospective
house swappers—and some services search for a house or apartment for you (even a castle if that's your fancy) and handle the paperwork. Some send an illustrated catalogue and others send
photographs of specific properties, sometimes at a charge; up-front
registration fees may apply.

Bed-and- B&Bs and guest houses—their slightly snootier cousins—will help
Breakfasts stretch your pounds. The heaviest concentrations of B&Bs are in
large holiday resorts, but they exist everywhere, even in the remot-
est countryside. All tourist offices should have lists of local B&Bs
and guest houses, and the central tourist organizations produce national lists.

The reasonable rates include breakfast, which is often solid enough
to keep you going for most of the day. Another advantage of staying
in a B&B is getting grass-roots information and a better feel of the
town from the proprietors. Don't worry if the B&B is outside the
center of town; there are almost always buses to ferry you around.
You'll find many B&Bs in large Victorian houses that were built
when huge families demanded plenty of bedrooms. Most B&Bs have
a few rooms—those being the most expensive—with bath or shower
attached (en suite), but more rooms without. Generally, three or
four rooms to a bath is fine, six or more is too many. Nowadays,
though, almost all bedrooms have washbasins.

Farmhouses Farmhouse accommodations have become increasingly popular in
recent years. Farmhouses do not offer top hotel standards, but they
do have a special appeal: the rustic, rural experience. This option
may be difficult if you are not touring by car. Prices are generally
very reasonable. Ask for the British Tourist Authority booklet
"Farmhouse Vacations."

Home If you would like to find a house, an apartment, or other vacation
Exchange property to exchange for your own while on vacation, **become a**
member of a home-exchange organization, which will send you its
annual directories listing available exchanges and will include your
own listing in at least one of them. Arrangements for the actual exchange are made by the two parties to it, not by the organization.

Prices The following chart is the key to pricing symbols in the Lodging sections in this guide. Prices are quoted in pounds sterling (with dollar
equivalents at press time) and are based on double occupancy for a
night's stay, including tax and service.

	London and Southern England	Other Towns
££	£60–£80 (US$96–US$128)	£50–£60 (US$80–US$96)
£	£40–£60 (US$64–$US$96)	£40–£50 (US$64–US$80)
¢	under £40 (US$64)	under £40 (US$64)

Mail

Airmail letters to the United States and Canada cost 41p for 10
grams; postcards 35p; aerogrammes 36p. Letters and postcards to
Europe weighing less than 20 grams, 30p (25p to EU member coun-

tries). First-class letters within the United Kingdom cost 25p, second class and postcards 19p. These rates may have increased by early 1996.

Money and Expenses

ATMs Cirrus, Plus and many other networks connecting automated-teller machines operate internationally. Chances are that you can **use your bank card at ATMs** to withdraw money from an account and get cash advances on a credit-card account if your card has been programmed with a personal identification number, or PIN. Before leaving home, **check in on frequency limits** for withdrawals and cash advances. Also **ask whether your card's PIN must be reprogrammed** for use in Great Britain. Four digits are commonly used overseas. Note that Discover is accepted only in the United States.

On cash advances you are charged interest from the day you receive the money, whether from a teller or an ATM. Although transaction fees for ATM withdrawals abroad may be higher than fees for withdrawals at home, Cirrus and Plus exchange rates are excellent because they are based on wholesale rates only offered by major banks.

Costs Naturally, the cost of visiting Britain will depend on the dollar/pound exchange at the time of your trip, and luckily for earners of dollars, there had been a swing in favor of U.S. currency after a protracted period when the United Kingdom was virtually out of reach for any budget traveler. As we went to press, however, the dollar was falling against the mark and the yen, so the exchange rate may not be in your favor.

Generally speaking, lodging and transportation are the two most expensive items on the visitor's British budget. The best way to minimize them is to **stay in B&Bs and guest houses as much as you can** and to **buy reduced-price rail tickets before you leave home.** Be sure to **compare the costs of car rentals versus train travel** in advance; rail costs can be exorbitant in the United Kingdom.

Most churches and museums even in London are still free, although this is changing. London museum admission, when it is charged, ranges from 50p (*Gipsy Moth IV*) to £8.95 (Madame Tussaud's) and is often a "suggested donation." Outside London, provincial museums that charge anything usually ask £1–£2. Bed-and-breakfast accommodations for two (outside London), £40. Budget London hotel for two, £60 (Periquito). Budget London dinner, £15 (Stockpot). Cheapest West End theater ticket, £7 (play) or £10 (musical). Coca-Cola, 80p (in budget restaurant). Cup of coffee, 90p (in budget restaurant/café). Fish-and-chips for two, £8 to eat in, £4.50 to take out (in budget restaurant). Glass of wine, £2 (in budget restaurant). London taxi, £3.50 (1 mile, plus tip). Tube ride, 90p short, £1.90 longer. Movie ticket, £6 (in London); elsewhere £3.50. *Daily National* morning newspaper, 60p. Pint of beer in pub, £1.90. Pub lunch for two, £10. Cheap-day round-trip train fare London–Bath £20 (with restrictions).

Exchanging Currency For the most favorable rates, **change money at banks.** You won't do as well at exchange booths in airports, rail and bus stations, or in hotels, restaurants, and stores, although you may find their hours more convenient. To avoid lines at airport exchange booths, **get a small amount of currency before you leave home.**

Taxes Airport An airport departure tax of £10 (£5 to EU countries) per person is charged.

VAT The British sales tax (VAT, Value Added Tax) is 17½%. The tax is almost always included in quoted prices in shops, hotels, and restaurants. Where it is quoted separately, the idea—as in the United

States—is to make the quoted price look more attractive. There is no VAT in the Channel Islands.

Foreign visitors can **get a refund of Britain's 17½% Value Added Tax (VAT)** by the Over the Counter or the Direct Export method. Most larger stores provide these services, but only if you request them, and they will handle the paperwork. For the Over the Counter method, you must spend more than £75 in one store. Ask the store for Form VAT 407 (you must have identification—passports are best), and give the form to Customs when you leave the country. (Lines at major airports are usually long, so allow plenty of time.) The refund will be forwarded to you in about eight weeks, minus a small service charge, either as a credit to your charge card or in a check, which most American banks will charge a conversion fee to cash. The Direct Export method, where the goods are sent directly to your home, is more cumbersome. VAT Form 407 must be certified by Customs, police, or a notary public when you get home and then sent back to the store, which will refund your money.

Traveler's Checks Whether or not to buy traveler's checks depends on where you are headed; **take cash to rural areas and small towns, traveler's checks to cities.** The most widely recognized are American Express, Citicorp, Thomas Cook, and Visa, which are sold by major commercial banks for 1%–3% of the checks' face value—it pays to **shop around.** Both American Express and Thomas Cook issue checks that can be countersigned and used by you or your traveling companion, and they both provide checks, at no extra charge, denominated in pounds. You can cash them in banks without paying a fee (which can be as much as 20%) and use them as readily as cash in many hotels, restaurants, and shops. So you won't be left with excess foreign currency, **buy a few checks in small denominations** to cash toward the end of your trip. Record the numbers of the checks, cross them off as you spend them, and keep this information separate from your checks. If possible, **take traveler's checks in pound sterling,** which are readily usable and which banks will cash will no fee.

Wiring Money You don't have to be a cardholder to send or receive funds through MoneyGram[SM] from American Express. Just go to a MoneyGram agent, located in retail and convenience stores and in American Express Travel Offices. Pay up to $1,000 with cash or a credit card, anything over that in cash. The money can be picked up within 10 minutes in the form of U.S. dollar traveler's checks or local currency at the nearest MoneyGram agent, or, abroad, the nearest American Express Travel Office (in London, tel. 0171/5846182). There's no limit, and the recipient need only present photo identification. The cost runs from 3% to 10%, depending on the amount sent, the destination, and how you pay.

You can also send money using Western Union. Money sent from the United States or Canada will be available for pickup at agent locations in 100 countries within 15 minutes. Once the money is in the system, it can be picked up at any one of 25,000 locations. Fees range from 4% to 10%, depending on the amount you send.

Packages and Tours

A package or tour to Great Britain can make your vacation less expensive and more convenient. Firms that sell tours and packages purchase airline seats, hotel rooms, and rental cars in bulk and pass some of the savings on to you. In addition, the best operators have local representatives to help you out at your destination.

A Good Deal? The more your package or tour includes, the better you can predict the ultimate cost of your vacation. Make sure you know exactly what is included, and **beware of hidden costs.** Are taxes, tips, and service charges included? Transfers and baggage handling? Entertainment and excursions? These can add up.

Most packages and tours are rated deluxe, first-class superior, first class, tourist, and budget. The key difference is usually accommodations. If the package or tour you are considering is priced lower than in your wildest dreams, **be skeptical.** Also, **make sure your travel agent knows the hotels** and other services. Ask about location, room size, beds, and whether it has a pool, room service, or programs for children, if you care about these. Has your agent been there or sent others you can contact?

Buyer Beware   Each year consumers are stranded or lose their money when operators go out of business—even very large ones with excellent reputations. If you can't afford a loss, take the time to **check out the operator**—find out how long the company has been in business, and ask several agents about its reputation. Next, **don't book unless the firm has a consumer-protection program.** Members of the United States Tour Operators Association and the National Tour Association are required to set aside funds exclusively to cover your payments and travel arrangements in case of default. Nonmember operators may instead carry insurance; look for the details in the operator's brochure—and the name of an underwriter with a solid reputation. Note: When it comes to tour operators, **don't trust escrow accounts.** Although there are laws governing those of charter-flight operators, no governmental body prevents tour operators from raiding the till. Next, **contact your local Better Business Bureau and the attorney general's office** in both your own state and the operator's; have any complaints been filed? Last, **pay with a major credit card.** Then you can cancel payment, provided that you can document your complaint. Always **consider trip-cancellation insurance** (*see* Insurance, *above*).

Big vs. Small   An operator that handles several hundred thousand travelers annually can use its purchasing power to give you a good price. Its high volume may also indicate financial stability. But some small companies provide more personalized service; because they tend to specialize, they may also be experts on an area.

Using an Agent   Travel agents are an excellent resource. In fact, large operators accept bookings only through travel agents. But it's good to **collect brochures from several agencies,** because some agents' suggestions may be skewed by promotional relationships with tour and package firms that reward them for volume sales. If you have a special interest, **find an agent with expertise in that area;** the American Society of Travel Agents can give you leads in the United States. (Don't rely solely on your agent, though; agents may be unaware of small-niche operators, and some special-interest travel companies only sell direct).

Single Travelers   Prices are usually quoted per person, based on two sharing a room. If you are traveling solo, you may be required to pay the full double occupancy rate. Some operators eliminate this surcharge if you agree to be matched up with a roommate of the same sex, even if one is not found by departure time.

Packing for Great Britain

Pack light because porters and baggage carts are scarce and international luggage restrictions tight.

You'll want a heavy coat for winter and a lightweight coat or warm jacket, even in summer. There's no time of year when a raincoat or umbrella won't come in handy. For the cities, pack as you would in the United States: jackets and ties for expensive restaurants and nightspots, casual clothes elsewhere. Jeans are popular in Britain and are perfectly acceptable for sightseeing and informal dining.

Tweeds and sports jackets are popular here with men. For women, ordinary street dress is acceptable everywhere.

If you plan to stay in budget hotels, bring your own soap. Many do not provide it, and some give guests only one tiny bar per room. Bring an extra pair of eyeglasses or contact lenses in your carry-on luggage, and if you have a health problem, **pack enough medication** to last the trip or have your doctor write a prescription using the drug's generic name, because brand names vary from country to country (you'll then need a prescription from a doctor in the country you're visiting). **Don't put prescription drugs or valuables in luggage to be checked,** for it could go astray. To avoid problems with customs officials, carry medications in original packaging. Also don't forget the addresses of offices that handle refunds of lost traveler's checks.

Electricity To use your U.S.-purchased electric-powered equipment, **bring a converter and an adapter.** The electrical current in Great Britain is 220 volts, 50 cycles alternating current (AC); wall outlets take plugs with three rectangular prongs and with two round prongs.

If your appliances are dual voltage, you'll need only an adapter. Hotels sometimes have 110-volt outlets for low-wattage appliances marked FOR SHAVERS ONLY near the sink; don't use them for high-wattage appliances like blow-dryers. If your laptop computer is older, carry a converter; new laptops operate equally well on 110 and 220 volts, so you need only an adapter.

Luggage Free airline baggage allowances depend on the airline, the route, and the class of your ticket; ask in advance. In general, on domestic flights and on international flights between the United States and foreign destinations, you are entitled to check two bags—neither exceeding 62 inches, or 158 centimeters (length + width + height), or weighing more than 70 pounds (32 kilograms). A third piece may be brought aboard; its total dimensions are generally limited to less than 45 inches (114 centimeters), so it will fit easily under the seat in front of you or in the overhead compartment. In the United States, the Federal Aviation Administration gives airlines broad latitude to limit carry-on allowances and tailor them to different aircraft and operational conditions. Charges for excess, oversize, or overweight pieces vary.

If you are flying between two foreign destinations, note that baggage allowances may be determined not by piece but by weight— generally 88 pounds (40 kilograms) in first class, 66 pounds (30 kilograms) in business class, and 44 pounds (20 kilograms) in economy. If your flight between two cities abroad *connects* with your transatlantic or transpacific flight, the piece method still applies.

Safeguarding Before leaving home, **itemize your bags' contents** and their worth
Your Luggage and label them with your name, address, and phone number. (If you use your home address, cover it so potential thieves can't see it.) Inside your bag, **pack a copy of your itinerary.** At check-in, **make sure that your bag is correctly tagged** with the airport's three-letter destination code. If your bags arrive damaged or not at all, file a written report with the airline before leaving the airport.

Passports and Visas

If you don't already have one, **get a passport.** While traveling, **keep one photocopy of the data page** separate from your wallet and leave another copy with someone at home. If you lose your passport, promptly call the nearest embassy or consulate, and the local police; having the data page can speed replacement.

U.S. Citizens All U.S. citizens, even infants, need a valid passport to enter Great Britain for stays of up to six months. New and renewal application forms are available at any of the 13 U.S. Passport Agency offices and at some post offices and courthouses. Passports are usually mailed within four weeks; allow five weeks or more in spring and summer.

Canadians You need a valid passport to enter Great Britain for stays of up to six months. Application forms are available at 28 regional passport offices as well as post offices and travel agencies. Whether for a first or a renewal passport, you must apply in person. Children under 16 may be included on a parent's passport but must have their own to travel alone. Passports are valid for five years and are usually mailed within two to three weeks of application.

Rail Travel

British Rail, Britain's state-owned rail system, has for many years provided an excellent—if expensive—way of exploring Britain without the stress and hassle of driving yourself around. But the long-awaited privatization raises many questions about the future. Although changes are happening far more slowly than was originally projected, by the time you read this, it is possible that everything we say about train travel in Britain may have changed.

The basic BritRail network is still one of the densest in the world, with frequent main-line service, especially on the InterCity network (*see below*). On main routes (but not on Sundays or in remote rural areas), you can expect to find a train departing within the hour. And there has been a reintroduction of vintage steam locomotives on scenic tourist routes. The *British Rail Passenger Timetable* (about £6.50), published twice a year, covers all BritRail services, including private, narrow-gauge, and steam lines, as well as special services and rail-based tourist facilities.

BritRail offers high-speed modern service on the InterCity passenger network between large cities, either on electric trains or streamlined InterCity 125 diesels (which can go 125 mph). The new 140-mph electrified route between London and Yorkshire is being extended to Newcastle and Edinburgh. London's suburban Network SouthEast is a largely electrified commuter service that extends to Brighton, northwest to Oxford, and northeast to Cambridge. Seat reservations are strongly advised on the major express routes out of London, and mandatory on some trains. You can reserve a seat (smoking or no-smoking) on any InterCity train from any main-line station or BR travel agent, at £1 for standard class, £2 for first class.

The London area has 13 major terminals, all serving both main and suburban lines, so be sure you know which station you're arriving at or leaving from. All are linked by London's Underground network.

To save money, **look into rail passes** (*see* Important Contacts A to Z, *above*). But be aware that if you don't plan to cover many miles, you may come out ahead by buying individual tickets.

Many travelers assume that rail passes guarantee them seats on the trains they wish to ride. Not so. You need to **book seats ahead even if you are using a rail pass**; seat reservations are required on some European trains, particularly high-speed trains, and are a good idea on trains that may be crowded—particularly in summer on popular routes. You will also need a reservation if you purchase overnight sleeping accommodations. BritRail can help you determine if you need reservations and can make them for you. They cost about $6 each, less if you purchase them in Europe at the time of travel.

Keep in mind that overnight rail travel saves money on accommodations. But if you decide to spend the night on a train, take the necessary precautions against thieves, such as sleeping on top of your wallet or valuables.

Renting a Car

Cutting Costs   To get the best deal, **book through a travel agent and shop around.** When pricing cars, **ask where the rental lot is located.** Some off-airport locations offer lower rates—even though their lots are only minutes away from the terminal via complimentary shuttle. You may also want to **price local car-rental companies,** whose rates may be lower still, although service and maintenance standards may not be up to those of a national firm. Also **ask your travel agent about a company's customer-service record.** How has it responded to late plane arrivals and vehicle mishaps? Are there often lines at the rental counter, and, if you're traveling during a holiday period, does a confirmed reservation guarantee you a car?

Always **find out what equipment is standard** at your destination before specifying what you want; **do without automatic transmission or air-conditioning** if they're optional. In Europe, manual transmissions are standard and air-conditioning is rare and often unnecessary.

Also in Europe, **look into wholesalers**—companies that do not own their own fleets but rent in bulk from those that do and often offer better rates than traditional car-rental operations. Prices are best during low travel periods, and rentals booked through wholesalers must be paid for before you leave the United States. If you use a wholesaler, **know whether the prices are guaranteed** in U.S. dollars or foreign currency, and if unlimited mileage is available; find out about required deposits, cancellation penalties, and drop-off charges; and confirm the cost of any required insurance coverage.

Insurance   When you drive a rented car, you are generally responsible for any damage or personal injury that you cause as well as damage to the vehicle. Before you rent, **see what coverage you already have** under the terms of your personal auto-insurance policy and credit cards. For about $14 a day, rental companies sell insurance, known as a collision damage waiver (CDW), that eliminates your liability for damage to the car; it's always optional and should never be automatically added to your bill.

Requirements   In Great Britain your own driver's license is acceptable. An International Driver's Permit, available from the American or Canadian Automobile Association, is a good idea.

Surcharges   Before picking up the car in one city and leaving it in another, **ask about drop-off charges or one-way service fees,** which can be substantial. Note, too, that some rental agencies charge extra if you return the car before the time specified on your contract. To avoid a hefty refueling fee, **fill the tank just before you turn in the car.**

Senior-Citizen Discounts

To qualify for age-related discounts, **mention your senior-citizen status up front** when booking hotel reservations, not when checking out, and before you're seated in restaurants, not when paying your bill. Note that discounts may be limited to certain menus, days, or hours. When renting a car, **ask about promotional car-rental discounts**—they can net lower costs than your senior-citizen discount.

Shopping

Throughout Britain, museum and gallery shops offer high-quality posters, books, art prints, and crafts. Both Wales and Scotland are famous for woolen products, and retail outlets sell sweaters, tartans, tweeds, scarves, skirts, and hats at reasonable prices. Traditional Celtic jewelry is also popular. The Midlands offers world-renowned china and pottery, including Wedgwood, Royal Doulton, and Royal Worcester. The factory outlet shops, prevalent in northern England, where you can buy seconds, are well worth a detour. The Southwest, especially Devon and Cornwall, is known for its edibles—homemade toffees and rich fudge.

London, with its high prices and attractive items, is often frustrating for budget travelers, but ask at your hotel or at the tourist bureau about the street markets around town.

Students on the Road

To save money, **look into deals available through student-oriented travel agencies.** To qualify, you'll need to have a bona fide student I.D. card. Members of international student groups also are eligible. *See* Students in Important Contacts A to Z, *above.*

Telephones

There are three types of public payphones: Those that accept (a) only coins, (b) only phonecards, (c) phonecards and credit cards.

(a) Insert coins *before* dialing (minimum charge is 10p). The indicator panel shows you how much money is left; add more whenever you like. If there is no answer, replace the receiver and your money will be returned.

(b) and (c) Buy BT cards from shops, post offices, or newsstands. They are ideal for longer calls, are composed of units of 10p, and come in values of £2, £4, £10 and more. An indicator panel shows the number of units used. At the end of your call, the card will be returned. Where credit cards are taken, slide the card through, as indicated.

Local Calls Each city, town, or region in Britain has its own numerical prefix, which is used only when you are dialing from outside the city. In provincial areas, the dialing codes for nearby towns are often posted in the booth, and some even list international codes. For long-distance calls within Britain, dial the area code (which usually begins with a zero–one), followed by the number. London numbers are prefixed by 0171 for inner London or 0181 for outer London. You do not need to dial either if calling from inside the same zone, but you will have to dial 0181 from a 0171 number, and 0171 from a 0181 number. Drop the zero from the prefix and dial only 171 or 181 when calling London from overseas.

All calls are charged according to the time of day. Standard rate is weekdays 8 AM–6 PM; cheap rate is weekdays 6 PM–8 AM and all day on weekends.

Long-Distance For direct dialing, dial 010, then the country code, area code, and number. For the international operator, credit card, or collect calls, dial 155. Bear in mind that hotels usually levy a hefty (up to 300%) surcharge on calls; it's better to **use the pay phones located in most hotel foyers or a U.S. calling card.**

The long-distance services of AT&T, MCI, and Sprint make calling home relatively convenient and let you avoid hotel surcharges; typically, you dial a local number. Before you go, **find out the local access codes** for your destinations.

Operators and To call the operator, dial 100; directory inquiries (information) 192; **Information** international directory inquiries, 153. A charge is made for directory inquiries.

Tipping

Some restaurants and most hotels add a service charge of 10%–15% to the bill. In this case you are not obliged to tip extra. If no service charge is indicated, add 10%–15% to your total bill. Taxi drivers should also get 10%–15%. You are not expected to tip theater or cinema ushers, elevator operators, or bartenders in pubs. Hairdressers and barbers should receive 10%–15%.

When to Go

To save money, **plan to travel during the off-season**—between November and March—**or else the shoulder season**—April, May, and mid-September through October. Although winter is the most affordable time to visit Britain, almost all stately homes, many attractions, and a lot of B&Bs in seaside resorts close from October to Easter, especially between Christmas and New Year's. Also, the cold, wet weather can make getting around by public transportation an ordeal. In summer, the most attractive regions become overcrowded and rates increase. Both spring and fall can be sheer magic, with excellent weather and the countryside in its fresh or autumnal colors. Airfares are usually more expensive on weekends, so try to travel midweek. Also, you may save money by staying in big cities over the weekend when the rates may be lower.

Climate   What follows are the average daily maximum and minimum temperatures for major cities in Britain.

Aberystwyth (*Wales*)	Jan.	44F	7C	May	58F	15C	Sept.	62F	17C
		36	2		45	7		51	11
	Feb.	44F	7C	June	62F	17C	Oct.	56F	13C
		35	2		50	10		46	8
	Mar.	49F	9C	July	64F	18C	Nov.	50F	10C
		38	4		54	12		41	5
	Apr.	52F	11C	Aug.	65F	18C	Dec.	47F	8C
		41	5		54	12		38	4

Edinburgh (*Scotland*)	Jan.	42F	5C	May	56F	14C	Sept.	60F	18C
		34	1		43	6		49	9
	Feb.	43F	6C	June	62F	17C	Oct.	54F	12C
		34	1		49	9		44	7
	Mar.	46F	8C	July	65F	18C	Nov.	48F	9C
		36	2		52	11		39	4
	Apr.	51F	11C	Aug.	64F	18C	Dec.	44F	7C
		39	4		52	11		36	2

London	Jan.	43F	6C	May	62F	17C	Sept.	65F	19C
		36	2		47	8		52	11
	Feb.	44F	7C	June	69F	20C	Oct.	58F	14C
		36	2		53	12		46	8
	Mar.	50F	10C	July	71F	22C	Nov.	50F	10C
		38	3		56	14		42	5
	Apr.	56F	13C	Aug.	71F	21C	Dec.	45F	7C
		42	6		56	13		38	4

Plymouth	Jan.	43F	6C	May	62F	17C	Sept.	65F	19C
		39	4		47	8		53	12
	Feb.	47F	8C	June	64F	18C	Oct.	58F	15C
		38	4		52	11		49	9
	Mar.	50F	10C	July	66F	19C	Nov.	52F	11C
		40	5		55	13		44	7
	Apr.	54F	12C	Aug.	67F	19C	Dec.	49F	9C
		43	6		55	13		41	5

York	Jan.	43F	6C	May	61F	16C	Sept.	64F	18C
		33	1		44	7		50	10
	Feb.	44F	7C	June	67F	19C	Oct.	57F	14C
		34	1		50	10		44	7
	Mar.	49F	10C	July	70F	21C	Nov.	49F	10C
		36	2		54	12		39	4
	Apr.	55F	13C	Aug.	69F	21C	Dec.	45F	7C
		40	4		53	12		36	2

National Holidays
For 1996: **England and Wales:** January 1; April 5 (Good Friday); April 8 (Easter Monday); May 6 (May Day); May 27 (Spring Bank Holiday); August 26 (Summer Bank Holiday); December 25, 26, 27. **Scotland:** January 1, 3; April 1; May 6 and 27; August 5; December 25, 26, 27.

Festivals and Seasonal Events
Tickets for prestigious sporting events must be obtained months in advance—check first to see if your travel agent can get them. There is a complete list of ticket agencies in *Britain Events*, free from the British Tourist Authority.

Jan. (first two weeks): London International Boat Show is the largest boat show in Europe. *Earls Court Exhibition Centre, Warwick Rd., London SW5 9TA, tel. 0178¼/473–377.*

Feb.: Jorvik Viking Festival is the occasion for a month-long celebration of Viking history. *Jorvik Viking Festival Office, 4 Clifford St., York Y01 1RD, tel. 01904/611–944.*

Feb.–Mar.: London Arts Season, showcases the city's extensive arts scene, with bargain-priced tickets and special events. *British Travel Centre, 12 Regent St., SW1Y 4PQ, tel. (for Arts Season only) 0171/839–6181.*

Mid-Apr.: London Marathon. Information from Box 262, Richmond, Surrey TW10 5JB, tel. 0181/948–7935.

May: Glasgow Mayfest. Citywide international festival of theater, dance, music, and street events. Glasgow's answer to the Edinburgh Festival. *Festival Dir., 18 Albion St., Glasgow G1 1LH, tel. 0141/552–8000.*

May–Sept.: Chichester Festival Theatre Season offers classical and contemporary plays. *Chichester Festival Theatre Box Office, Oaklands Park, Chichester, West Sussex PO19 4AP, tel. 01243/781312.*

Late May: Chelsea Flower Show, Britain's major flower show, covers 22 acres at the Royal Hospital. *Royal Hospital, Chelsea, London SW3, tel. 0171/834–4333.*

Late May–mid-June: Bath International Festival is an international celebration of music and the arts. *Box office, tel. 01225/462231.*

Early June: Derby Day is the world-renowned horse racing event at Epsom Racecourse, Epsom, Surrey. *Information from United Racecourses Ltd., Racecourse Paddock, Epsom, Surrey KT18 5NJ, tel. 01372/463072.*

Mid–late June: Aldeburgh Festival of Music and the Arts was founded in 1948 by composer Benjamin Britten. *Aldeburgh Foundation, High St., Aldeburgh, Suffolk IP15 5AX, tel. 01728/452935.*

Mid-June: Trooping the Colour is Queen Elizabeth's official birthday celebration at Horse Guards Parade, Whitehall, London. *Write for tickets early in the year to The Brigade Major, H.Q. Household Division, Chelsea Barracks, London SW1H 8RD.*

Late June–early July: Wimbledon Lawn Tennis Championship Write (Oct.–Dec. only) for Center and Number One court tickets to *All-England Lawn Tennis and Croquet Club, Church Rd., Wimbledon, London SW19 5AE, tel. 0181/946–2244.*

Early July: Henley Royal Regatta is an international rowing event and top social occasion. *Regatta House, Henley-on-Thames, Oxfordshire RG9 2LY, tel. 01491/572153.*

Early–mid-July: Llangollen International Musical Eisteddfod sees the little Welsh town of Llangollen overflow with music, costumes, and color. *Musical Eisteddfod Office, Llangollen, Clwyd LL20 8NG, tel. 01978/860236.*

Mid-July: Royal Tournament features military displays and pageantry by the Royal Navy, Royal Marines, Army, and Royal Air Force. *Earls Court Exhibition Centre, Warwick Rd., London SW5 9TA, tel. 0171/373–8141.*

Mid-July–mid-Sept.: Henry Wood Promenade Concerts are a celebrated series of concerts, founded in 1895. *Royal Albert Hall, Kensington Gore, London SW7 2AP, tel. 0171/589–8212.*

Mid-Aug.: Three Choirs Festival is an ancient choral and orchestral music festival. *John Harris, The Gables, South St., Leominster, Hereford HR6 8JN, tel. 01568/615223.*

Mid-Aug.–early Sept.: Edinburgh International Festival is the world's largest festival of the arts. Festivities include the nighttime **Edinburgh Military Tattoo.** Information from Edinburgh Festival Society, 21 Market St., Edinburgh EH1 1BW, tel. 0131/226–4001.

Nov. 5.: Guy Fawkes Day is celebrated all over the country with fireworks and bonfires, to commemorate the attempt to blow up James I and Parliament.

Early Nov.: Lord Mayor's Procession and Show coincides with the Lord Mayor's inauguration, with a procession from Guildhall to the Royal Courts of Justice. *The City of London, tel. 0171/606–3030.*

2 London

*Westminster, Covent Garden,
Knightsbridge, Kensington,
the City*

Many of London's best attractions are free. Of course, a chief pleasure for the traveler on a budget is to explore the new territory on foot, and in this city of contrasts, where glass towers border green parks and winding alleys meander around wide avenues and major thoroughfares, a stroll through the different boroughs (as the administrative areas are known) provides plenty of entertainment. London is an ancient city and its history greets you at every street corner. To gain a sense of the continuity of history in London, stand on Waterloo Bridge at sunset. To the east, the great globe of 17th-century St. Paul's Cathedral glows golden in the dying sunlight, still majestic, despite the towers of glass and steel that hem it in. To the west stand the mock-medieval ramparts of Westminster, home to the "Mother of Parliaments" that has met here, or hereabouts, since the 1250s. And beyond them both snake the swift, dark waters of the Thames, flowing as they did past the first Roman settlement here nearly 2,000 years ago.

Present-day London still largely reflects its medieval layout, a bewildering tangle of streets. Even when the city was devastated in the Great Fire of 1666, and again in the Blitz of the 1940s, it was rebuilt on its old street plan. Sir Christopher Wren's 17th-century master concept for a classical site, with vistas and crossing avenues, was turned down, and the plans for rebuilding in the 1950s again harked back to the ancient disposition of streets. A wonderful opportunity for imaginative replanning was lost.

Close-up exploration will reveal that London, like all great cities, also has its darker side: the squalor and crowds that are as much a part of every modern city as they were of medieval ones. On an icy winter's evening, when you are coming out of the warm Queen Elizabeth Hall after a concert, you will pass down-and-outs sheltering in cardboard lean-tos in the open spaces underneath the building, grateful for the mobile soup kitchen that rolls up every night at 10:30. And where crowds are concerned, London definitely has the edge on any city in western Europe. It starts with the largest population—nearly 7 million live here—and has well over the same number of visitors every year.

But in the midst of all those millions, life goes on as it has for centuries, and whether your interests center on the past or the present, on the arts, on shopping, theater, or architecture, London has it all.

Essential Information

Arriving and Departing by Plane

Airports and Airlines London is admirably served by airports. The two major ones are Gatwick, 28 miles to the south, and Heathrow, 15 miles to the west. There are also three smaller ones: Luton, 35 miles northwest, Stansted, 34 miles northeast, and London City, in the Docklands.

Heathrow is the world's busiest airport. All North American airlines that have scheduled services to Great Britain use Heathrow.

Gatwick, which has the lion's share of charter flights, has scheduled North American flights, too, among them American Airlines, Continental, Delta, Northwest, and Wardair Canada. British airlines—principally British Airways and Virgin Atlantic—use both airports, but favor Heathrow.

From the Airports to Downtown *Heathrow* The quickest and least expensive route into London is via the Underground's Piccadilly line from all terminals. Trains run every 4 to 8 minutes and the 40-minute trip costs £3.10 each way. **London Transport** (tel. 0171/222–1234) runs two Airbus services from the airport; each costs £6 one way and travel time is about an hour. The **A1** leaves for Victoria Station, with several intermediate stops, every 30 minutes from 6:40 AM to 8:15 PM. The journey is about an hour. The **A2** leaves for Russell Square, also with other stops, including Marble Arch, every 30 minutes from 6 AM to 9:30 PM.

The **390** bus departs Bay C, Heathrow Central Bus Station, for Stand 8, Buckingham Palace Road (near Victoria Station), at 6:30, 9:35, and 11:45 AM; 1:45, 3:15, 5:15, and 7:45 PM (times vary slightly on weekends). The journey takes about an hour and the fare is £5 one way.

Gatwick **Gatwick Express** trains leave for Victoria Station every 15 minutes from 5:30 AM to 9:45 PM; hourly from 10 PM to 5 AM. The 30- to 40-minute trip costs £8.90 each way. An hourly local train runs throughout the night.

Greenline's **Flightline 777** bus leaves for Victoria Coach Station every 30 minutes; journey time is about 70 minutes and the cost is £7.50 one way.

Arriving and Departing

By Train London has 15 major train stations, each serving a different area of the country, all accessible by Underground (*see* Getting Around, *below*) or bus. Since April 1994, **Railtrack** has been operating all these stations, as well as the tracks countrywide, while **British Rail** still controls all train services, until they are sold off as franchises. These major changes in the structure of Britain's railways should not affect the traveler unduly, although nobody can predict exactly what will happen to the fares.

Call for further information and schedules: South (tel. 0171/928–5100); West and the South Midlands (tel. 0171/262–6767); Northwest, East, West Midlands, Scotland, and Ireland (tel. 0171/387–7070); East, Northeast, and Scotland (tel. 0171/278–2477).

By Bus **National Express** buses—or coaches, as they are known—operate from Victoria Coach Station (Buckingham Palace Rd., tel. 0171/730–0202) to more than 1,000 major towns and cities. It's about half as expensive as the train but trips can take twice as long. **Green Line** buses (tel. 0181/668–7261) operate within a 30- to 40-mile radius of London, ideal for excursions. Their **Golden Rover** ticket allows unlimited travel for either a day or a week.

Getting Around

Though London is a rewarding city for walkers, it could not be called compact. Attractions are spread out over miles, so it's best to take a bus or tube (London's colloquialism for subway; "subway" in London means underground pedestrian crossing) close to where you're going and then start walking. It's essential to arm yourself with one of the daily, weekly, or monthly travel passes (*see* Fares, *below*), which are good for use on both bus and tube. Maps, leaflets, and route and fare information can be found at most ticket booths. Another essential for the walker is a good city map. London's layout is labyrinthine, so it's worth investing £4 (or so) in an "A–Z" guide (the one most Londoners use). Note: "Z" is pronounced "zed" by the British.

By Underground London's Underground is the most widely used form of transportation. Trains run beneath and above ground, out into the suburbs. Stations are clearly marked by London Transport's circular symbol, and all cars are one class and smoking is not allowed on board trains or in any part of any station.

There are 10 basic lines, plus the East London line and the Docklands Light Railway; several lines have branches, so be sure you know which you want. Electronic platform signs in many stations tell you the destination, route, and the time you'll have to wait for the next train.

From Monday to Saturday, trains start just after 5 AM and run until midnight or 12:30. On Sunday trains start 2 hours later and finish about an hour earlier. Frequency of trains varies, but a maximum wait should be no more than about 10 minutes in central areas.

By Bus In central London, buses are mainly the traditional bright red double- and single-deckers, though there are increasing quantities of privately owned companies with different-colored buses. Not all buses run the full length of their route at all times; check with the driver or conductor. On some buses you pay the conductor after finding a seat; on others you pay the driver upon boarding. Smoking is not allowed on board any bus.

Buses pick up and drop off only at clearly indicated stops. Main stops have a red LT symbol on a plain white background. When the word "Request" is written across the sign, you must flag the bus down. Buses are a good way of seeing the town, but don't take one if you are in a hurry. Fares start at 60p for short distances in outer zones, and increase for stops within the central zone. Rides within the central zone begin at 90p.

Fares and Travelcards London is divided into six concentric zones for both bus and tube fares: The more zones you cross, the higher the fare. There's a wide variety of ticket categories; the London Transport(LT) booklet, *Tickets*, available from Underground ticket counters, gives all the details. **One Day Travelcards** (from £2.80) are the handiest. They allow unrestricted travel on bus and tube lines after 9:30 AM and all day on weekends and national holidays. **One Day LT Cards** (from £3.90) work the same way, but have no time restrictions. Weekly and Monthly Travelcards are cheaper than several one-day passes, while **Visitor Travelcards** (£3.70) are the same as the One Day Travelcards, but with the bonus of a booklet of money-off vouchers to major at-

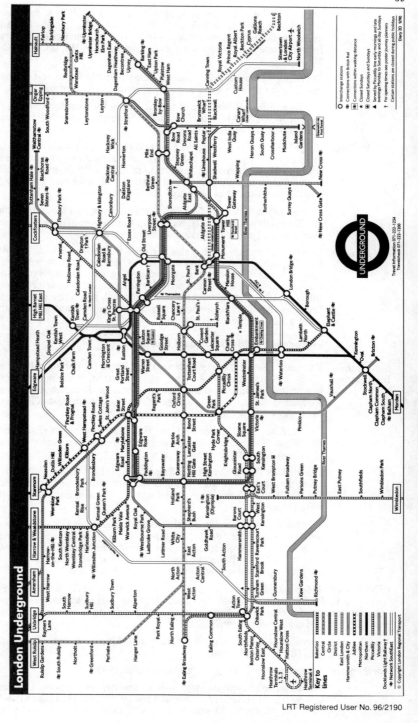

London Underground

tractions. These are also available in the United States, complete with voucher booklet at $25, $32, and $49, ($11, $13, and $21 for children ages 5–15) for three, four, and seven days, from **BritRail Travel International** (1500 Broadway, New York, NY 10036, tel. 212/382–3737).

Traveling without a valid ticket makes you liable for an on-the-spot fine (£10 at press time), so always pay your fare before you travel.

For more information, stop at the **LT Travel Information Centres** at Heathrow, Oxford Circus, Piccadilly Circus, St. James's Park, and Victoria, or call 0171/222–1234.

By Taxi Hotels and main tourist areas have taxi ranks; you can also flag them down on the street. If the yellow "for hire" sign is lit on top, the taxi is available. But drivers often cruise at night with their signs unlit to avoid unsavory characters, so if you see an unlit cab, keep your hand up and you might be lucky.

Fares start at £1 for the first 582 yards and increase by units of 20p per 291 yards or 60 seconds. Surcharges are added after 8 PM and on weekends and public holidays. Fares increase annually.

By Minicab London has countless minicab companies that operate fleets of ordinary, unmarked cars. Drivers are unlicensed, so their cars can't be flagged in the street but must be ordered by phone or in person from the minicab office. The vast majority of these services are reliable, and a minicab costs about two-thirds as much as a black taxi. Local firms are listed in the phone book; a hotel or restaurant will usually order a minicab for you if you ask.

Important Addresses and Numbers

Tourist Information The main **London Tourist Information Centre** (in-person callers) at Victoria Station provides details about London, including information on tube and bus tickets, theater, concert and tour bookings, and accommodations. It also provides information on the rest of Britain. Open weekdays and Saturday 8–7, Sunday 8–5.

Information centers located in **Harrods** (Brompton Rd.) and **Selfridges** (Oxford St.) are open store hours only; there are others at **Heathrow Airport** (Terminals 1, 2, and 3).

The **British Travel Centre** (12 Regent St., tel. 0171/730–3400) provides details about travel, accommodations, and entertainment for the whole of Britain. Open weekdays 9–6:30 and Saturday 10–4; closed Sunday.

Visitorcall is the London Tourist Board's phone service—it's a premium-rate (49p per minute; 39p off-peak) recorded information line, with different numbers for theater, events, museums, sports, getting around, etc. To access the list of options, call 01839/123456, or see the display advertisement in the city phone book.

Embassies and Consulates **American Embassy** (24 Grosvenor Sq., W1A 1AE, tel. 0171/499–9000). Located inside the embassy is the American Aid Society, a charity that helps Americans in distress. Dial the embassy number and ask for extension 570 or 571.

Canadian High Commission (McDonald House, 1 Grosvenor Sq., W1, tel. 0171/258–6600).

Emergencies For police, fire brigade, or ambulance, dial 999.

The following hospitals have 24-hour emergency sections: **Charing Cross**, tel. 0181/846–1234; **Royal Free** (Pond St., Hampstead, tel. 0171/794–0500); **St. Thomas's** (Lambeth Palace Rd., tel. 0171/928–9292).

Pharmacies Chemists (drugstores) with late hours include **Bliss Chemist** (5 Marble Arch, tel. 0171/723–6116), open daily 9 AM–midnight.

Travel Agencies **American Express** (6 Haymarket, tel. 0171/930–4411, 147 Victoria St., tel. 0171/828–7411, and 89 Mount St., tel. 0171/499–4436); **Hogg Robinson Travel/Diners Club** (176 Tottenham Court Rd., tel. 0171/580–0437); **Thomas Cook** (45 Berkeley St., Piccadilly, tel. 0171/499–4000 and 1 Marble Arch, tel. 0171/706–4188).

Money Exchange For the best exchange rate and lowest commission fees, avoid the numerous bureaus de change and stick to banks, **American Express,** and **Thomas Cook.** Bringing some of your money in sterling traveler's checks avoids even bank fees. For anyone with a card linked to the Cirrus or Plus networks, the most convenient way to get cash is at automated teller machines.

Opening and Closing Times

Banks Normally banks are open weekdays 9:30–4:30, but some branches do provide services on Saturday. Banks at major airports and train stations also have extended hours.

Museums Most museums are open Monday–Saturday 10–5 or 10–6, and Sunday 2–5 or 2–6, including most bank holidays, but are closed on public holidays such as Good Friday. Check individual listings for definite opening hours.

Pubs Since mid-1988 most pubs are open Monday–Saturday 11–11; Sunday noon–3 and 7–10 or 10:30, but hours are at the discretion of the proprietor.

Shops Usual business hours are Monday–Saturday 9–5:30 or 9–6. Some shops stay open late on Wednesday or Thursday (until 7 or 7:30 PM), and, due to recent changes in the law, many are open on Sunday.

Lodging

London offers many options to the budget traveler, including less expensive hotels, guest houses, youth hostels (not restricted to students), university halls of residence (during school vacations), and self-catering apartments, or those with kitchen facilities. Multiple-occupancy or family rooms are cheaper than single rooms and may be worth considering. Remember, however, that a bargain rate can mean sacrificing some of the facilities ordinarily taken for granted.

One way to save money is to choose an accommodation that is slightly outside the city center. London's attractions are so spread out that accommodations outside the city center are not necessarily inconvenient. We have given the nearest tube station to the hotel to help with planning a stay. North and West London are especially convenient for budget-conscious visitors because there is so much to see locally and both areas are well served by transportation to the West End (center).

The **British Tourist Authority,** which has offices in New York, Los Angeles, Chicago, and Atlanta, can help with lodging information. Ask for the free booklet *Accommodation for Budget Travellers 1994*. The **London Tourist Board** will make reservations to suit your budget if you write at least six weeks in advance to: LTB, 26 Grosvenor Gdns., SW1W 0DU. There is also an **LTB Accommodation Line** for credit card bookings (tel. 0171/824–8844).

Barclay International Group (*see* Lodging *in* Chapter 1) has more than 2,500 London housekeeping flats in elevator buildings, with color TV, and some with air-conditioning.

London Homestead Services (Coombe Wood Rd., Kingston-upon-Thames, Surrey KT2 7JY, tel. 0181/949–4455, fax 0181/549–5492) is a family-run business that arranges B&B accommodations in private homes. The majority of the more than 500 addresses are in quiet residential areas and offer first-floor bedrooms with shared bathrooms. The top rate runs about £50 a night, for which you get a room in central London and a latchkey so you can come and go as you please. There are also a few self-catering apartments in the West End beginning at £30 per person. Naturally, the homes vary greatly in decor and ambience, but they have all been evaluated by LHS staff. The minimum stay is three nights, and there is a 25% discount for children under age 12.

Uptown Reservations (50 Christchurch St., SW3 4AR, tel. 0171/351–3445, fax 0171/351–9383) lists 50 host homes in fashionable areas of central London that have rooms for rent (with bath and Continental breakfast) for about £68 double, £35 single.

If you plan to stay in a **youth hostel**, you must be a member of International Youth Hostel Federation (Dept. 863, Box 37613, Washington, DC 20013, tel. 202/783–6161). They can supply a list of London hostels, which you should book far ahead.

Camping near London is probably best left to masochists, though in summer the experience can turn out wonderfully. A few sites to try—all accessible, but well outside the center—are Hackney Camping (Millfields Rd., E5, tel. 0181/985–7656) in the East End, open summer only; Abbey Wood (Federation Rd., SE2 0LS, tel. 0181/310–2233), near Greenwich; Lea Valley Campsite (Sewardstone Rd., Chingford, E4, tel. 0181/529–5689), in a "green belt" area; and Tent City (Old Oak Common La., London W3, tel. 0181/749–9074) in Acton, west London, open June–August. Bring your own tent.

Home swapping provides the cheapest accommodation of all. UK-based agencies include: **Intervac** (6 Siddals Lane, Allestree, Derby DE3 2DY, tel. 01332/558931), **Homelink International** (84 Lees Gdns. Maidenhead, Berks SL6 4NT, tel. 01628/31951), and **Home Base Holidays** (7 Park Ave., London N13 5PG, tel. 0181/886–8752). (*See also* Essential Information, chapter 1).

For **university halls of residence,** *see* the **Lodging** section, *below.*

Dining

London's ethnic mix ensures a wide range of cuisines. For the price of a burger, fries, and coffee, you can fill up at the neighborhood Indian, Chinese, Turkish, Thai, or Greek restaurant. You might like to eschew the American-style fast-food burger and pizza chains in favor of London's caffs, or cafés, which serve huge (and often greasy) fried bangers (sausage), chips (fries), eggs, bacon, beans, or the very British fish- (deep fried in batter) and-chips. The traditional cockney dish of pie and mash is disappearing, but it still can be sampled in the East End (surviving family firms include Cooke, Goddard's, Kelly, and Manze's)—if you want stewed eels in green jello with mashed potato, that is!

Chinatown, centered in Gerrard Street in Soho, offers a concentration of mostly inexpensive restaurants, many offering an excellent dim sum. The Indian communities of Southall and Brick Lane have the least expensive, most atmospheric curry houses; the latter also boasts two bagel bakeries (Nos. 155 and 159), which sell filled bagels from about 35p and are open nearly all night. South Indian Bhel Poori houses, which serve the delicious, very inexpensive, light vegetarian dishes of Bombay, are clustered on Drummond Street, near Tottenham Court Road. Most of London's Greek, Cypriot, and Turkish expats live—and set up restaurants—in north London (Camden Town, Archway, Stoke Newington, and Islington). These informal places offer good food and good prices.

At lunchtime, you can taste the hautest of haute cuisine in many top restaurants for a set price that is far below the normal rate. At the opposite extreme, business districts usually crawl with sandwich bars. These establishments sell breads and baps (large, flat rolls) with a variety of fillings for a couple of pounds, but will probably disappoint Americans who are accustomed to more filling than bread. It may be better to construct your own sandwich from the deli counter of any supermarket (with fruit from one of the Oxford Street stalls, perhaps) and grab a park bench along the Embankment overlooking the Thames.

Exploring London

Guided Tours

If you're watching your pennies, you might prefer to wander around on foot, clutching map and guidebook, instead of forking over any money for a coach tour that may feature mostly tired commentary. Because London offers so much by way of attractions, you can easily design your own tour, especially if you study route maps and "bushop" around town on the tops of double-deckers (*see* Getting Around in Essential Information, *above*). Many guided walks are very good value, since they're often led by extrovert types who point out eccentric details in an entertaining way. River and canal trips are not expensive and are worth every penny, especially when the weather's fine.

Orientation Tours
By Bus

London Transport's London Plus guided sightseeing tours (tel. 0171/828–7395) offer passengers a good introduction to the city from double-decker buses, which are open-topped in summer. Tours run daily every half-hour, 9:30–5;30 Apr.–Oct., and on the hour 10–4 Nov.–Mar., departing Haymarket, Baker Street, Embankment, Marble Arch, and Victoria. You may board or alight at any of around 21 stops to view the sights, and then get back on the next bus. Tickets (£10 adults, £5 children) may be bought from the driver, LT Travel Information Centres, or tourist information centers. Other agencies offering half- and full-day bus tours include **Evan Evans** (tel. 0171/930–2377), **Frames Rickards** (tel. 0171/837–3111), and **Travellers Check-In** (tel. 0171/580–8284), all of which provide standard coach-and-commentary along the beaten track (Westminster Abbey, Buckingham Palace, etc.). **The Big Bus Co.** (tel. 0181/944–7810) has more original itineraries.

By River

From April to October boats cruise up and down the Thames. Most leave from **Westminster Pier** (tel. 0171/930–4097), **Charing Cross Pier** (Victoria Embankment, tel. 0171/839–3312), and **Tower Pier** (tel. 0171/488–0344). Downstream services go to the Tower of London, Greenwich, and the Thames Barrier; upstream destinations include Kew, Richmond, and Hampton Court. Trips last 1 to 4 hours, depending on the destination. **The London Waterbus Company** (tel. 0171/482–2550) and **Jason's Trip** (tel. 0171/286–3428) offer inexpensive barge cruises along the Regent's Canal.

Walking Tours

There are many walking tours from which to choose. **Citisights** (tel. 0181/806–4325), **Cockney Walks** (tel. 0181/504–9159), **Streets of London** (tel. 0181/882–3414), and **City Walks** (tel. 0171/700–6931) are just a few of the better-known firms. But **The Original London Walks** (tel. 0171/624–3978) was the first and is the best of the walking tour firms. Their professional guides are experienced and entertaining, there's a big choice of programs, groups are kept small, and rates are inexpensive. For an overall picture, peruse leaflets at the London Tourist Information Centre at Victoria Station or check *Time Out*, a weekly magazine with entertainment and arts listings. The length of walks varies, but each is generally around 2 hours and costs around £4 per person.

Excursions **London Transport, Evan Evans, Frames Rickards,** and **Travellers Check-In** all offer day excursions by bus to places within easy reach of London, or do it yourself with Brit Rail's cheap day-return (round-trip) tickets.

London for Free

London is a gift to the freeloader. But in order to enjoy the free delights of the city, you should make a very small investment in a Travelcard (*see* Getting Around in Essential Information, *above*). Once you have that, the city's your oyster.

Churches Most churches are all, or partly, free. You may have to pay to visit parts of St. Paul's and Westminster Abbey, but the main areas are still without charge. All of Wren's lovely City churches are free.

Some churches also offer free lunchtime music recitals, though a collection is usually taken. Try St. Anne and St. Agnes (Gresham St., EC2, tel. 0171/373–5566. Tube: St. Paul's), St. Martin-in-the-Fields (Trafalgar Sq., WC2, tel. 0171/976–1926. Tube: Charing Cross), St. Michael's Cornhill (Cornhill EC3, no phone. Tube: Bank), St. Bartholomew-the-Great (West Smithfield, EC1, tel. 0171/606–5171. Tube: St. Paul's), or St. James —though there's usually a charge at this one, the Baroque programs are especially fine (Piccadilly, W1, tel. 0171/734–4511. Tube: Piccadilly Circus).

Concerts Particularly worth investigating are the foyers of the National Theatre, the Royal Festival Hall, and the Barbican, which host free musical events.

Many pubs host musical performances, including rock-and-roll, traditional Irish folk music, jazz, and new bands. Often admission is free. Check listings in *Time Out*.

Galleries The commercial art galleries in and around Bond Street allow visitors to browse for free, and some will even lend you their expensive catalogues without charge. This is also true of the great auction houses, Christie's and Sotheby's, whose offerings often rival all but the topmost museums.

The atmosphere in these places tends to be decidedly snobbish, and you may feel out of place if you're not smartly dressed. For a collection of more relaxed private galleries showing mainly the work of younger artists, try Portobello Road (Anderson O'Day, No. 255, tel. 0171/221–7592; Portfolio, No. 345, tel. 0181/969–0453; Todd, No. 326, tel. 0181/960–6209. Tube: Ladbroke Grove) and the surrounding streets of Notting Hill. The Serpentine (tel. 0171/402–0343. Tube: none; Bus 9, 10, 12, 52, 88, then walk through the park) is a public gallery with interesting shows of notable modern artists.

Museums Most of the museums still have no admission fees, though there is a growing movement toward charging for entry. Among the most important ones that open their doors without charge are the British Museum, the National Gallery, the National Portrait Gallery, and the Tate Gallery.

Just a word about a money-saving way to get around all the major museums that *do* charge: The White Card costs £14 for 3 days or £23 for 7 days concentrated museum-hopping. It's available, and valid, at all three South Kensington museums, and at nine other museums and galleries, and admits you as often as you like.

Although it's in the center of town, the anthropological Museum of Mankind (Burlington Gardens, W1, tel. 0171/437–2224. Tube: Picadilly/Bond Street), one of the best of its kind, is inexplicably deserted. The collection will eventually be moved to the British Museum, however, so see it while you can in its present spacious surroundings.

Many lesser known, but fascinating museums are also free: Try Sir John Soane's Museum (*see* Tour 2), Leighton House (*see* Tour 3), the National Postal Museum (*see* Tour 4), and the Museum of Garden History (*see* Tour 5).

In addition to these museums, there are many wonderful collections that are housed in the outer areas of London (accessible by public transport) and are often virtually unknown to Londoners. In the historic, working-class East End, try the Bethnal Green Museum of Childhood (Cambridge Heath Rd., E2, tel. 0181/980–2415. Tube: Bethnal Green), which is full of Victorian dolls and their houses and accessories, puppets, and games. Also, visit the Ragged School Museum (46-50 Copperfield Rd., E3, tel. 0181/980–6405. Tube: Mile End), whose exhibits reconstruct the life and times of children at Dr. Bernardo's famous school for orphans. The quaint and intimate Geffrye Museum (Kingsland Rd., E2, tel. 0171/739–8368. Tube: Old Street) displays reconstructed furnished living rooms from Elizabethan times to the 1950s, all housed in 14 18th-century almshouses.

Even farther out, find the Horniman Museum (London Rd., Forest Hill, SE23, tel. 0181/699–2339. Station: Forest Hill Brit Rail, Bus 12, 63, 122, 124, 171, 176, 185, 194), much loved for its anthropological collections, including tribal masks, costumes, and musical instruments; its new aquatic gallery; and its colony of honey bees that is displayed inside glass walls.

Parks The great parks are a summer vacation in themselves. To lie on the grass in Hyde Park or by the Serpentine, or to wander among the deer in the park of Hampton Court Palace, is to enjoy the best of country life in the middle of the city. Spend a few dollars on a picnic, and you can relax for hours.

To the north lies Hampstead Heath, a spreading parkland with views over the city. It also boasts Kenwood House (Hampstead La., NW3, tel. 0181/348–1286. Tube: Golders Green, then take Bus 210/ Finsbury Park), a lovely mansion designed by Robert Adam and containing the important Iveagh bequest art collection. In summer, there are free open-air concerts around the lake.

Regent's Park (Tube: Regent's Park, Baker Street, or Camden Town) in summer becomes overrun with people playing softball, from the most casual pick-up games (which you'd be welcome to join) to serious, uniformed league matches. Even British baseball leagues play in London. First-division games are listed in *Time Out*.

In the center of town, St. James's Park (Tube: Victoria) is a haven whose lake teems with bird life. Don't sit on the hundreds of deck chairs unless you're prepared to pay a small fee for the privilege. Battersea Park (take British Rail from Victoria Station to Battersea), south of the river, plays host to sports and has a large boating lake. On the north side is the Buddhist Peace Pagoda.

The more beautiful of the the lesser-known parks include Holland Park (No phone. Tube: Holland Park), with its peacocks and formal rose gardens; Gunnersbury Park (tel. 0181/992–1612. Tube: Acton Town), with a museum; and Waterlow Park (Swains La., N6, tel. 0181/340–1834. Tube: Archway), which abuts the atmospheric and beautiful Highgate cemetery, where Karl Marx is buried, and which offers guided tours for a well-spent £2.50. All three have reasonably priced cafés (unlike the ridiculously expensive one in Regent's Park).

Speakers' Corner, in Hyde Park, close to Marble Arch, has been a source of free fun for decades. Here, anyone with a soapbox and an opinion can air his or her views on any subject under the sun. Though the entertainment on a Sunday morning is not as freewheeling and bizarre as it used to be, it can still provide the occasional thought- or mirth-provoking performance.

People-Watching London and its weather were not designed for this favorite spectator sport, but when the sun does come out or on balmy evenings, Covent Garden Piazza (Tube: Covent Garden) stands as the centerpiece for this activity. Enjoy the street performers' shows, market stalls, and occasional fairground rides, but be wary of "minimum charge" levies in the open-air cafés: You could be charged as much as £5 for a coffee.

Fast overtaking Covent Garden for crowds is the youth mecca of Camden Lock (Tube: Camden Town), which has been developed into a complex of cafés, pubs, and stalls (*see* Street Markets in Shopping, *below*). Beware: On a sunny Sunday, it may be too crowded here to move, but you could always escape along the towpaths of the Grand Union Canal—Camden Lock is still a working, water-level-regulating lock, after all.

Views The following list suggests some glimpses of London that you may want to capture: Westminster Bridge at sunset, preferably when it's foggy (Tube: Westminster); Primrose Hill on a clear day, when the whole city is spread at your feet (Tube: Chalk Farm); over the canal at Blomfield Road, affectionately called Little Venice (Tube: Warwick Ave.); the northeast corner of Regent's Park looking west over the big skyline toward the golden dome of the mosque (Tube: Camden Town); Riverside Walk by the National Film Theatre Café or any South Bank Complex walkway (Tube: Waterloo).

Above all, London herself is a free show. You can wander the streets, explore the tiny alleys and lanes, search out historic houses where famous people have lived—all without spending a cent.

Orientation

Traditionally, central London has been divided between the City to the east, where its banking and commercial interests lie; Westminster to the west, the seat of the royal court and the government; and the mainly residential areas that surround them both. That distinction still holds, as our itineraries show. "The City" route covers London's equivalent of New York's Wall Street, while the "Westminster and Royal London" exploration roves past royal palaces and surveys the government area in and around Parliament Square. Part of another walk, "Legal London, Covent Garden, and Bloomsbury," explores the capital's legal center, a lively, rejuvenated shopping district, and its university and literary quarter.

London expanded from Westminster during the 17th and 18th centuries. Elegant town houses sprang up in St. James's and Mayfair, and later in Bloomsbury, Chelsea, Knightsbridge, and Kensington. Today these are pleasant residential districts, and elegant, if pricey, shopping areas. London also enjoys unique "lungs"—its stupendous parks—thanks to past royalty who reserved these great tracts of land for their own hunting and relaxation. The two largest of them, now administered by the government, feature in the "Around Two Royal Parks—Knightsbridge and Kensington" walk.

The area along the Thames, once London's most important highway, is currently enjoying a renaissance. The "South Bank" walk takes you along the river's traditionally less fashionable south side, while the last exploring section, "Up and Down the Thames," covers out-of-town riverside attractions, old and new.

Tour 1: Westminster and Royal London

Westminster is by far the younger of the capital's two centers, post-dating the City by some 1,000 years. Edward the Confessor put it on the map when he packed up his court from its cramped City quarters and went west a couple of miles, founding the abbey church of Westminster—the minster west of the City—in 1050. Subsequent kings continued to hold court here until Henry VIII decamped to Whitehall Palace in 1512, leaving Westminster to the politicians. And there they still are, not in the palace, which was burned almost to the ground in 1834, but in the Victorian mock-Gothic Houses of Parliament, whose 320-foot Clock Tower is as much a symbol of London as the Eiffel Tower is of Paris.

Trafalgar Square is the obvious place to start exploring for several reasons. It is the center of London, by dint of a plaque on the corner of the Strand and Charing Cross Road from which distances on U.K. signposts are measured. It is the home of the National Gallery and of one of London's most distinctive landmarks, Nelson's Column; also of many a political demonstration, a raucous New Year's party, and the highest concentration of bus stops and pigeons in the capital. In short, it is London's most famous square.

Numbers in the margin correspond to points of interest on the London map.

❶ Keeping watch from his 145-foot granite perch is E. H. Baily's 1843 statue of Admiral Lord Horatio Nelson, one of England's favorite heroes. Around the foot of **Nelson's Column,** three bas-reliefs depict his victories at Cape St. Vincent, the Battle of the Nile, and Copenhagen, and a fourth his death at Trafalgar itself in 1805; all four were cast from cannon he captured. The four majestic lions, designed by the Victorian painter Sir Edwin Landseer, were added in 1867.

★ ❷ The north side of the square is filled by the low, gray, colonnaded neo-classical facade of the **National Gallery.** The institution was founded in 1824, when George IV and a connoisseur named Sir George Beaumont persuaded a reluctant government to spend £57,000 on part of the recently deceased philanthropist John Julius Angerstein's collection. These 38 paintings, including works by Raphael, Rembrandt, Titian, and Rubens, were augmented by 16 of Sir George's own and exhibited in Angerstein's Pall Mall residence until 1838, when William Wilkin's building was completed. By the end of the century, enthusiastic directors and generous patrons had turned the National Gallery into one of the world's foremost collections, with works from painters of the Italian Renaissance and earlier, from the Flemish and Dutch masters, the Spanish school, and of course the English tradition, including Hogarth, Gainsborough, Stubbs, and Constable. *Trafalgar Sq., tel. 0171/839–3321; 0171/ 839–3526 (recorded general information); 0171/389–1773 (recorded exhibition information). Admission free; admission charge for special exhibitions. Free 1-hr guided tours start at the Sainsbury Wing weekdays at 11:30 and 2:30, Sat. 2 and 3:30. Open Mon.–Sat. 10–6, Sun. 2–6; June–Aug., also Wed. until 8; closed Good Friday, May Day, Dec. 24–26, Jan. 1.*

❸ Around the corner, at the foot of Charing Cross Road, is the **National Portrait Gallery,** which contains portraits of celebrated (and not so-well-known) Britons, including monarchs, statesmen, and writers. This newly remodeled and expanded gallery is a lot more interesting than you might expect: The collection extends beyond painted portraits to busts, photographs, and even cartoons. *2 St. Martin's Pl., tel. 0171/930–1552. Admission free. Open weekdays 10–5, Sat. 10–6, Sun. 2–6.*

❹ Across from the entrance to the portrait gallery is the church of **St. Martin-in-the-Fields,** built in 1724, set off by its elegant spire. The

London

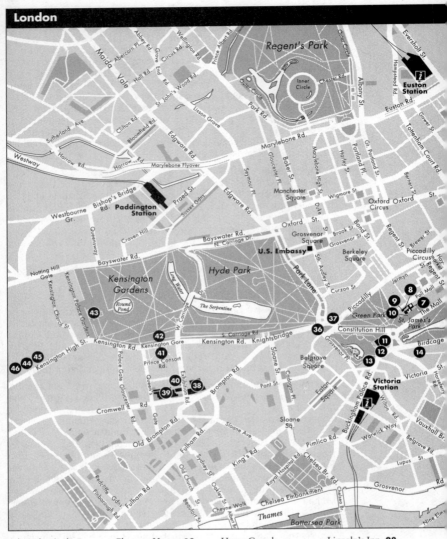

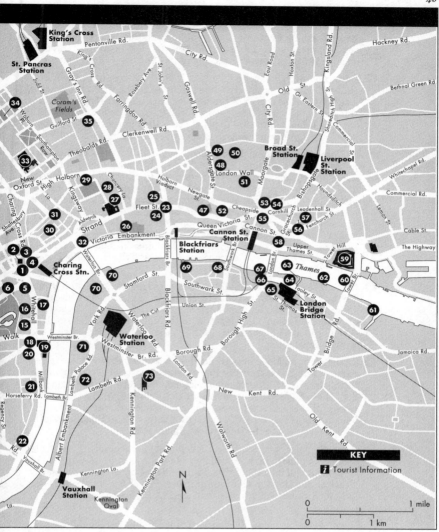

National Postal Museum, **49**	Queen's Gallery, **12**	South Bank Arts Complex, **70**	Tate Gallery, **22**
Natural History Museum, **39**	Royal Albert Hall, **41**	Southwark Cathedral, **66**	Tower Bridge, **60**
Nelson Column, Trafalgar Square, **1**	Royal Courts of Justice, **27**	St. Bride's Church, **24**	Tower of London, **59**
Old St. Thomas's Hospital, **65**	Royal Exchange, **54**	St. James's Palace, **7**	Victoria and Albert Museum, **38**
Palace of Westminster, (Houses of Parliament), **19**	Royal Mews, **13**	St. John's, **21**	Wellington Barracks, **14**
	Royal Opera House, **31**	St. Mary-le-Bow, **52**	Wellington Museum (Apsley House), **37**
Parliament Square, **18**	Science Museum, **40**	St. Martin-in-the-Fields, **4**	Westminster Abbey, **20**
Percival David Foundation of Chinese Art, **34**	Shakespeare Globe Museum, **68**	St. Paul's Cathedral, **47**	York House, **8**
	Sir John Soane's Museum, **29**	St. Thomas's Hospital, **71**	

KEY

🛈 Tourist Information

celebrated Academy of St. Martin-in-the-Fields was founded here. Look for notices announcing free lunchtime concerts. At the **London Brass Rubbing Centre** in the crypt you can take impressions from replica brass tombs. *Trafalgar Sq., tel. 0171/437–6023. Fee from £1, according to size of rubbing. Open Mon.–Sat. 10–6, Sun. noon–6.*

⑤ Admiralty Arch, near the Royal Navy headquarters in the Admiralty Building, marks the entrance to **The Mall,** the great promenade leading from one corner of Trafalgar Square past St. James's Park to Buckingham Palace. The present Mall (pronounced to rhyme with "pal") was laid out in 1904 to provide a stately approach to Buckingham Palace, replacing a more modest avenue dating from 1660.

★ **St. James's Park** is small but handsome and, like most of London's parks, has royal origins. In ancient times the Thames spread far and wide, and the marshes here were drained by Henry VIII to be used as a playground for his deer. Charles II employed Le Nôtre, the famous French landscape gardener, to reshape it and in 1829 it was given its present look by John Nash, the prolific architect and friend of George IV. Meticulously maintained flower beds and many varieties of waterfowl make the park a beautiful place for a stroll, especially on a summer's evening, when illuminated fountains cascade and, beyond the trees, Westminster Abbey and the Houses of Parliament are floodlit.

⑥ On the other side of the Mall, you'll pass the imposing **Carlton House Terrace,** built in 1827–32 (also by Nash), with a gleaming white stucco facade and massive Corinthian columns. The column at the head of the steps is topped by a statue of the duke of York, George III's second son and commander in chief of the British forces during the French Revolution.

⑦ To the right up Marlborough Road is **St. James's Palace,** the earliest parts of which date from the 1530s. The palace has declined in importance since 1837, when Queen Victoria moved to Buckingham Palace. It is the London residence of the Prince of Wales, and some royal officials still work here, and court functions are occasionally held in the state rooms. All foreign ambassadors to Britain are officially accredited to the Court of St. James's.

Across from Friary Court on Marlborough Road is the exquisite **Queen's Chapel.** It was built by Inigo Jones in the 1620s for Henrietta Maria, wife of Charles I, and was one of the first purely classical buildings in the country. *The chapel is open for services only on Sunday mornings at 8:30 and 11:15 from Easter to the end of July.*

Turn left at the end of Marlborough Road along Cleveland Row, past **⑧** **York House,** the London home of the duke and duchess of Kent. Another left turn onto Stable Yard Road brings you to **Lancaster House,** built for the duke of York by Nash in the 1820s and now used for government receptions and conferences. On the other side of Stable **⑩** Yard is **Clarence House,** built by Nash in 1825 for the duke of Clarence, who later became King William IV. Restored in 1949, it is now the home of the Queen Mother (i.e., Queen Elizabeth's mother).

⑪ Buckingham Palace (Tube: St. James's Park) stands at the end of the Mall, behind a huge traffic circle edged with flower beds. When the queen is in residence (generally on weekdays except in January, August, September, and part of June), the royal standard flies over the east front. Inside, there are dozens of splendid state rooms used on formal occasions; offices for the royal staff; and, in the north wing, the private apartments of the queen and Prince Philip. Behind the palace lie 40 acres of secluded garden. Until recently the interior was off limits to the public, but a 1992 fire at Windsor Castle created an urgent need for cash. And so Buckingham Palace is now being opened to tourists—on something of an experimental basis through

1997—for eight weeks in August and September, when the royal family is away. *Buckingham Palace Rd., tel. 0171/799–2331. Admission: £8 adults, £5.50 senior citizens, £4 children. Call for hours; they had not been set at press time.*

That most celebrated of all London ceremonies, the **Changing of the Guard,** takes place in front of the palace daily from April through July, and on alternate days the rest of the year. The guard marches from Wellington Barracks (*see below*) at 11 AM to the palace. The ceremony itself begins promptly at 11:30, but arrive early for a good view; the base of the Queen Victoria Memorial in the traffic circle provides a convenient grandstand.

The palace was originally Buckingham House, built in the early 18th century for the duke of Buckingham. George III bought it in 1762. In 1824, Nash remodeled it for George IV, at which time it acquired palace status. The east end, which faces the public, does not represent Nash's work, though. The 1913 remodeling of the wing rendered it dull and heavy.

⑫ The former palace chapel, bombed during World War II and rebuilt in 1961, has been converted into the **Queen's Gallery,** where exhibitions from the royal art collections are held. *Buckingham Palace Rd., tel. 0171/799–2331. Admission: £3 adults, £2 senior citizens, £1.50 children. Open Tues.–Sat. 10–5, Sun. 2–5.*

⑬ **The Royal Mews,** farther along the road, house the queen's horses and the gilded state coaches. *Buckingham Palace Rd., tel. 0171/799–2331. Admission: £3 adults, £2 senior citizens, £1.50 children. Combined ticket for Queen's Gallery and Royal Mews: £5 adults, £3.50 senior citizens, £2.20 children. Open Oct.–Mar., Wed. noon–4; Apr.–Oct., Tues.–Thurs. noon–4; closed Mar. 25–29, Oct. 1–5, Dec. 23–Jan. 5.*

⑭ **Birdcage Walk,** once the site of the royal aviaries, runs along the south side of St. James's Park past **Wellington Barracks,** the regimental headquarters of the Guards Division. The elite troops that guard the sovereign and mount the guard at Buckingham Palace live here. The **Guards Museum** relates their history; many conflicts, including the Falklands campaign, are represented. Battle paintings, uniforms, and a cat o' nine tails are among the displays. *Wellington Barracks, Birdcage Walk, tel. 0171/930–4466, ext. 3271 and 3253. Admission: £2 adults, £1 senior citizens and children under 16. Open Sat.–Thurs. 10–4.*

⑮ On Birdcage Walk and still following the perimeter of St. James's Park, turn left onto Horse Guards Road. Between the massive bulks of the Home Office and the Foreign Office nestles the **Cabinet War Rooms,** a labyrinth of underground offices used by the British high command during World War II and worth the cost of entry if you're interested in the Britain of that period. Many strategic decisions were made here. You can see the Prime Minister's Room, where Winston Churchill made some of his inspiring wartime broadcasts, and the Transatlantic Telephone Room, used when he spoke directly to President Roosevelt. *Clive Steps, King Charles St., tel. 0171/930–6961. Admission: £3.90 adults, £3 senior citizens, £1.90 children under 16. Open daily 10–5:15.*

⑯ Continue along Horse Guards Road to the mid-18th-century Horse Guards Building, overlooking **Horse Guards Parade.** Originally the tilt yard (a place for jousting contests) of Whitehall Palace, the square is now the site of the **Trooping the Colour** each June, the great military parade marking the queen's official birthday. (Her real birthday is April 21.) The "Colour" (or flag) displayed identifies the battalion selected to provide the monarch's escort for that year. Cross the parade ground and walk through the arch.

The queen's Life Guards—cavalrymen in magnificent uniforms— stand duty on the facade overlooking Whitehall. The guard changes here at 11 AM Monday through Saturday, and at 10 AM on Sunday.

⑰ The **Banqueting House,** across from Whitehall, survived the White- hall Palace fire of 1698; Charles I was beheaded here in 1649. The Banqueting House was built by Inigo Jones in 1625; the main hall's magnificent ceiling frescoes, painted by Rubens for Charles I in 1630, honor the house of Stuart. Charles and his father, James I, as- sume a godlike stance—typical of the attitude that led to Charles's downfall at the hands of Cromwell and the Parliamentarians. *White- hall, tel. 0171/930–4179. Admission: £2.90 adults, £2.20 senior citi- zens, £1.90 children under 16. Open Mon.–Sat. 10–5, closed Sun.*

Walking toward Parliament Square, you pass on the right the en- trance to **Downing Street,** a terrace of three unassuming 18th-centu- ry houses. No. 10 has been the official residence of the prime minister since 1732. The cabinet office, the hub of the British system of government, is on the ground floor; the prime minister's private apartment is on the top floor. The chancellor of the exchequer, the chief finance minister, occupies No. 11. Downing Street is cordoned off, but you should be able to catch a glimpse of it from Whitehall.

The **Cenotaph,** in the center of Whitehall, commemorates the dead of both world wars. On Remembrance Day in November the sovereign lays a tribute of silken Flanders poppies here, symbolic of the blood- red flowers that grew on the killing fields of World War I. A statue of

⑱ Winston Churchill dominates traffic-beleaguered **Parliament Square** (Tube: Westminster), at the foot of Whitehall.

Other statues in the square are mostly of 19th-century prime minis- ters, but Abraham Lincoln is here, too, and outside the Houses of Parliament are Richard I (Richard the Lionheart) and Oliver Crom- well, Lord Protector of England during the country's sole, brief re- publican period in the 1650s.

⑲ The only remaining part of the original **Palace of Westminster** (still the official name of the complex) is the 240-foot-long **Westminster Hall,** built at the end of the 11th century; the fine hammer-beam roof was added by Richard II in 1397. The hall, where the country's early parliaments met and which once housed the law courts, is now used only on ceremonial occasions. The rest of the palace, extended and altered over the centuries, was destroyed by fire in 1834. It was re- built in mock-medieval Gothic style with an ornate interior by archi- tect Augustus Pugin, whose many delightful touches include Gothic umbrella stands. Parts of this building, notably the Chamber of the House of Commons, were badly damaged by bombing in 1941, but were reconstructed on virtually identical lines, though with modern amenities incorporated.

The palace contains the debating chambers and committee rooms of the two Houses of Parliament, the Commons (whose members are elected) and the Lords (which contains a mixture of appointed and hereditary members), plus offices and libraries. The public is admit- ted only to the public gallery of each House; note that the line for the Lords is generally much shorter than for the Commons, but the de- bates to be heard there are a lot less dramatic.

The most famous features of the palace are the towers at each end. At the south end is the recently restored 336-foot **Victoria Tower.** At the other end is **St. Stephen's Tower,** better known as **Big Ben** after the 13-ton bell in the tower, which strikes the hours. It is thought to have been named after Sir Benjamin Hall, commissioner of works when the bells were installed in the 1850s. A light shines from the top of the tower when Parliament meets at night.

★ **⑳** **Westminster Abbey** is the most ancient of London's great churches. Britain's monarchs have been crowned here since the coronation of

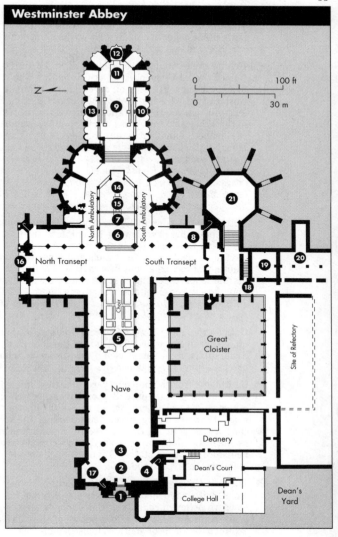

Westminster Abbey

William the Conqueror on Christmas Day 1066. There has almost certainly been a church here since the 6th century, and some historians believe the site was a place of pagan worship long before Christianity reached Britain. The present abbey is a largely 13th- and 14th-century rebuilding of the 11th-century church founded by Edward the Confessor. Two notable later additions are the Henry VII Chapel, built in the early 1500s, and the 18th-century twin towers over the west entrance. Early morning is a good time to catch something of the abbey's sacred atmosphere and to avoid the hordes of visitors; better still, attend a service.

There is space here to mention only a few of the abbey's many memorials. **Winston Churchill's** is just inside the west door (he is buried near Blenheim Palace, where he was born). The **Tomb of the Unknown Warrior** contains the body of a nameless World War I soldier buried in earth brought from France with his corpse; nearby hangs the **U.S. Congressional Medal** awarded to him symbolically. Among the many other nonroyal people commemorated in the abbey are

Robert Baden-Powell, founder of the Boy Scout movement, and the Wesleys, pioneers of Methodism. **Poets' Corner** memorializes an idiosyncratic collection of British writers, including Geoffrey Chaucer, Ben Jonson, and Alfred Tennyson.

Behind the high altar, the **Chapel of St. Edward the Confessor** contains Edward I's primitive oak Coronation Chair, and just beyond lies the **Henry VII Chapel,** an exquisite example of the rich Late Gothic style—the last riot of medieval design in England. Binoculars will help you spot the statues high up on the walls and the details of the abbey's stained glass. Striking effigies adorn the royal tombs of Elizabeth I and her sister, "Bloody" Mary; Mary, Queen of Scots; Henry V; Richard II and his wife, Anne of Bohemia; and many more. *Broad Sanctuary, tel. 0171/222–5152. Admission to nave free; to Poets' Corner and Royal Chapels: £4 adults, £2 students and senior citizens, £1 children under 15 (Royal Chapels free Wed. 6–8 PM). Open Mon., Tues., Thurs., Fri. 9–4; Wed. 9–7:45; Sat. 9–2, 3:45–5; Sun. for services only; closed to visitors during weekday services.*

The Norman **Undercroft,** just off the **Cloisters,** houses a museum on the abbey's history. Among its exhibits are lifelike royal effigies that used to be carried in funeral processions. The **Pyx Chamber** next door displays silver vessels and other treasures. The **Chapter House,** where Parliament first met, was built in the 1240s and is remarkable for its feeling of space and its daring design. A single column, like a frozen fountain, supports the roof. *Tel. 0171/222–5152. Joint admission to museum and Chapter House: £1.90 adults, £1.40 senior citizens, 90p children under 16. Open daily 10:30–1:45.*

Outside the abbey's west front an archway leads to **Dean's Yard,** a quiet, green courtyard. This side of the abbey was once the monks' living quarters; it's now used by **Westminster School,** a prestigious private ("public") school on the abbey grounds.

Continue through the courtyard and turn immediately left, then take the first right into Barton Street, which leads via Cowley Street and Lord North Street to Smith Square, one of London's most attractive Georgian residential areas. The splendidly classical ㉑ church of **St. John's** (1729) has been deconsecrated and now functions as one of London's favorite small concert halls (try the inexpensive **Footstool** café downstairs). Turn left back onto Millbank then right to follow the river to the Tate.

★ ㉒ The **Tate Gallery** (Tube: Pimlico) is Britain's most important museum of British and modern art. Its new director has instituted an innovative policy of rehanging the whole gallery every nine months. While a rotation like this does put all of the extensive collection on exhibit at one time or another, it also means that favorite pieces may not be on view when you are visiting. Another new development is the emphasis put on the British holdings. The Clore Gallery, with the magnificent (J.M.W.) Turner Bequest, including 100 of his finished oil paintings, has escaped the changes. A major new Tate is being built in the old Bankside Power Station on the Thames South Bank, opposite St Pauls. *Millbank, tel. 0171/821–1313 or 0171/821–7128 (recorded information). Admission free; fee for special exhibitions. Open Mon.–Sat. 10–5:50, Sun. 2–5:50; closed Good Friday, May Day holiday, Dec. 24–26, Jan. 1.*

Tour 2: Legal London, Covent Garden, and Bloomsbury

This walk explores three diverse areas that exemplify London's rich history: the Inns of Court, where the country's top lawyers have had their chambers or offices for centuries; Covent Garden, the former monastery garden turned marketplace; and literary Bloomsbury.

㉓ Start at **Ludgate Circus** (Tube: Blackfriars), a drab traffic circle west of St. Paul's Cathedral, where **Fleet Street,** once the traditional home of Britain's newspaper industry, begins. High operating costs have driven the newspapers to other parts of London, and not one is now left here.

24 Walk west along Fleet Street. On the left stands **St. Bride's Church,** rebuilt by Christopher Wren following the Great Fire of 1666 and restored again after it was bombed in 1940. The spire was added in 1703 and became the model for multitiered wedding cakes. The crypt's small museum contains Roman and later antiquities found in the area. *Tel. 0171/353-1301. Admission free. Open daily 9-5.*

25 Around the corner, on Gough Square, is **Dr. Johnson's House,** where the famous 18th-century lexicographer compiled his dictionary. *17 Gough Sq., tel. 071/353-3745. Admission: £3 adults, £2 senior citizens and those under 18. Open May-Sept., Mon.-Sat. 11-5:30; Oct.-Apr., Mon.-Sat. 11-5.*

The Inns of Court—there are four in all, and this walk visits three— were founded at different times during the Middle Ages to provide food and lodging for lawyers; as the centuries passed, they became more or less permanent residences and offices combined. Their atmosphere is reminiscent of Oxford or Cambridge colleges, hardly surprising since they were founded in the same era as places for serious study. The Inns of Court retain an important educational role: Aspiring lawyers, or barristers, must pass a series of examinations held here. More quirkily, they must establish their attendance by eating a certain number of dinners in the Hall of the Inn to which they are attached.

26 The **Inner** and **Middle Temples** (Tube: Temple) lie immediately south of Fleet Street; note that there never was an Outer Temple. Enter through the **Old Mitre Court** passageway to see one of the finest groupings of unspoiled historic buildings in London. The two Temples derive their names from the land on which they stand, once owned by the Knights Templar, the chivalric order founded during the first Crusade in the 11th century. The following century, the Knights built the **Temple Church** here, one of only three round churches in Britain. The worn tombs of the Knights can still be seen on the floor. About 1250, the choir was extended in Early English style, a particularly pure form of Gothic; this is probably the country's finest example. *The Temple, tel. 0171/353-8462. Admission free. Open daily 10-4.*

The **Inner Temple Hall** is not open to the public, but the superb Elizabethan **Middle Temple Hall** may be freely visited (unless in use by the Inn). *Tel. 0171/353-4355. Admission free. Open weekdays 10-noon, 3-4.*

Return to Fleet Street through the **Inner Temple Gateway.** At the entrance is an early Jacobean half-timbered building inside which is **Prince Henry's Room,** with oak paneling and an elaborate plasterwork ceiling. It is named after the eldest son of James I, who became Prince of Wales in 1610, but died before he could succeed his father. *17 Fleet St. Admission free. Open weekdays 1:45-5, Sat. 1:45-4.*

27 Across the way, on the left, stand the **Royal Courts of Justice** (Tube: Aldwych), where important civil cases are heard. Though it looks medieval, the building dates from the 1870s. The magnificent main hall—238 feet long and 80 feet high—dwarfs the bewigged and gowned figures that scurry through it. *Strand, tel. 0171/936-6000. Admission free. Open weekdays 9-4:30; closed national holidays.*

Now walk up **Chancery Lane,** to the **Public Record Office** on the right, where a small museum displays historic documents such as the Domesday Book of 1085. *Tel. 0181/876-3444. Admission free. Open weekdays 9:30-4:45.*

28 **Lincoln's Inn** (Tube: Chancery Lane), probably the most beautiful of the Inns and the one least damaged during World War II, lies left of Chancery Lane. The buildings date from various periods beginning with the late 15th-century **Old Hall** and **Old Buildings. New Square** is the only intact 17th-century square in London. The chapel was remodeled by Inigo Jones in 1619–23. *Chancery La., tel. 0171/405–1393. Gardens open daily 8–7, chapel open weekdays 12:30–2:30; the public may also attend 11:30 Sunday service in the chapel during legal terms. Guided tours are available in summer; for information, tel. 0171/405–1393.*

The adjoining **Lincoln's Inn Fields** is the capital's largest and oldest square—more like a small park—surrounded by handsome buildings. The magnificent 1806 portico on the south side fronts the Royal

29 College of Surgeons. The square's great attraction, however, is **Sir John Soane's Museum,** one of the most idiosyncratic and fascinating museums in London. Sir John Soane, whose home this was from 1790 to 1831, was the famous architect of the Bank of England, among other things, and an avid collector who left his house to the nation on condition that it stayed this way—for which every visitor is thankful, since his taste was eccentric and exuberant. The exhibits include Hogarth's series of paintings, *The Rake's Progress*, and the sarcophagus of the Egyptian pharaoh Seti I, which Soane bought for £2,000 after the British Museum refused it. *13 Lincoln's Inn Fields, tel. 0171/405–2107. Admission free. Open Tues.–Sat. 10–5.*

Southwest of Lincoln's Inn Fields at 13 Portsmouth Street is the 16th-century antique shop that Dickens reputedly used as the model for his *Old Curiosity Shop.*

★ **30** **Covent Garden** (Tube: Covent Garden) lies about half a mile to the west. The original "Covent Garden" produced fruit and vegetables for the 13th-century Abbey of St. Peter at Westminster. The fruit, flower, and vegetable market established in the later 1700s flourished until 1974, when its traffic grew to be too much for the narrow surrounding streets and it was moved south of the Thames.

Since then, the area has been transformed through small-scale projects rather than massive redevelopment, making Covent Garden one of the most appealing areas of London for adults and children alike. The 19th-century **Market Building** is now an elegant shopping arcade. On the south side is the lively **Jubilee open-air market** where crafts and flea-market goods are sold from open stalls. Open-air entertainers perform under the portico of **St. Paul's Church,** where George Bernard Shaw set the first scene of *Pygmalion* (reshaped as the musical *My Fair Lady*). The church, entered from Bedford Street, is known as the actors' church; inside are numerous memorials to theater people.

On the east side of the market area are two of London's newer museums. The **London Transport Museum** houses a steam locomotive, a tram, and a modern underground car among other relics of London's transport. This really is a "hands-on" museum: Visitors are positively encouraged to operate many of the exhibits. *39 Wellington St., tel. 0171/379–6344. Admission: £3.95 adults, £2.50 senior citizens and children 5–16. Open daily 10–6.*

On the same block, the **Theatre Museum** holds a comprehensive collection on the history of English theater—not just drama, but also opera, music hall (vaudeville), pantomime, and musical comedy. Scripts, playbills, costumes, props, and memorabilia of stars are displayed. *Russell St., tel. 0171/836–7891. Admission: £3 adults, £1.50 senior citizens and children 5–14. Open Tues.–Sat. 11–8, Sun. 11–7.*

The streets around the central market are packed with history. Garrick Street is home to the **Garrick Club,** London's equivalent of New York's Players Club. Actors and publishers are among today's members; in the 19th century, Dickens, Thackeray, and Trollope were on the club's roster. Long Acre, along with Neal Street and surrounding streets to the north, is lined with shops of all natures, making the whole neighborhood a prime—and not overpriced—consumer playground.

③ Bow Street is famous for the **Royal Opera House,** home of both the Royal Ballet and the Royal Opera Company. The theater is the third on this site; its interior is all rich Victorian gilt and plush seats, with excellent acoustics. The **Magistrates Court,** opposite the theater, was established in 1749 by Henry Fielding, magistrate, journalist, and—most notably—novelist. He employed a band of private detectives, the "Bow Street Runners," and paid them out of the fines imposed in the court. They were the forefathers of the modern police force.

Bloomsbury is a semiresidential district north of Covent Garden that contains a number of elegant 17th- and 18th-century squares; it is home to the British Museum and the University of London. The Bloomsbury Group, once based here, was a coterie of writers and painters that included the novelists E. M. Forster and Virginia Woolf; Woolf's husband, Leonard; the poet Rupert Brooke; Bertrand Russell, the philosopher; and J. M. Keynes, the economist.

③② South of Bow Street, by the end of Waterloo Bridge and on the Strand, is the new home of the **Courtauld Institute Galleries** (Tube: Aldwych). This collection of paintings has moved into the majestic rooms of Somerset House from its former hidden galleries in Woburn Square. Here you can see some of the best French Impressionist work anywhere, with Manets, Van Goghs, and Gauguins supported by dozens of old masters. But the more convenient location means that there can be long lines. *Somerset House, The Strand, tel. 0171/873–2526. Admission: £3 adults, £1.50 children. Open Mon. and Wed–Sat. 10–6, Tues. 10–8, Sun. 2–6.*

★ **③③** Museum Street, lined with print and secondhand book shops, leads to the **British Museum** (Tube: Tottenham Court Road or Holborn) on Great Russell Street, a monumental, severely Greek edifice built in the first half of the 19th century. The vast collection of treasures here includes Egyptian, Greek, and Roman antiquities; Renaissance jewelry, pottery, coins, and glass; and drawings from virtually every European school since the 15th century. It's best to concentrate on one area that particularly interests you. Some of the highlights are the Elgin Marbles, sculptures from the Parthenon in Athens; the Rosetta Stone, which helped archaeologists decipher Egyptian hieroglyphics; and the Mildenhall Treasure, a cache of Roman silver found in East Anglia in 1842. The King's Library, part of the **British Library,** contains illuminated and printed books, including many from the earliest days of printing. Within the next couple of years, the British Library will move to its controversial new home on Euston Road, King's Cross. *Great Russell St., tel. 0171/636–1555 or 0171/580–1788 (recorded information). Admission free. Open Mon.–Sat. 10–5, Sun. 2:30–6.*

The university area lies to the north of the British Museum. Behind **University College** (at the north end of Gower Street), Gordon Square contains restored 19th-century town houses and, at No. 53, **③④** the **Percival David Foundation of Chinese Art** (Tube: Euston Square), a collection of Chinese ceramics from the 10th to the 19th centuries. *53 Gordon Sq., tel. 0171/387–3909. Admission free. Open weekdays 10:30–5 (sometimes closed 1–2 for lunch).*

Turn right onto Tavistock Place, then take the second right into Woburn Place and continue until you see Guildford Street on your left.

Go past Coram's Fields (on your left), and continue until you come to the fourth road on the right, Doughty Street. A little way down is the **Dickens Museum** (Tube: Russell Square) at No. 48, the house where Charles Dickens lived from 1837 to 1839. During this fertile period he finished *Pickwick Papers,* wrote all of *Oliver Twist,* and started *Nicholas Nickleby.* The house now boasts a fascinating collection of Dickens memorabilia related in particular to his early life and novels. *Tel. 071/405–2127. Admission: £3 adults, £1 children under 16. Open Mon.–Sat. 10–5; closed Sun.*

Tour 3: Around Two Royal Parks— Knightsbridge and Kensington

Hyde Park and Kensington Gardens together form a great swath of green that cuts across the heart of London. They are bordered on one side by opulent Knightsbridge and Kensington and their glamorous shopping and restaurant districts. This walk includes fewer "must-see" landmarks of British history than the others, although there are some excellent museums en route.

Start at traffic-clogged **Hyde Park Corner** (Tube: Hyde Park Corner). On the central island is the triumphal **Wellington Arch,** originally intended to adorn the back gate of Buckingham Palace. The original statue of the duke of Wellington, victorious at the Battle of Waterloo against the French in 1815 and later prime minister, was moved to Aldershot and replaced by *Peace in Her Chariot* in 1912. The mansion standing by the park entrance is **Apsley House,** built in the 1770s by celebrated Scottish architect Robert Adam. The London home of the first duke of Wellington for some 30 years, it is now the **Wellington Museum.** The interior is much as it was in the Iron Duke's day, full of heavy, ornate pieces; there's also a fine equestrian portrait of Wellington by Goya. *149 Piccadilly, tel. 0171/499– 5676. Admission: £3 adults, £1.50 senior citizens and children. Open Tues.–Sun. 11–5.*

★ **Hyde Park** (361 acres) was originally a royal hunting ground, while **Kensington Gardens** (273 acres), which adjoins it to the west, was once the park of Kensington Palace. Both contain fine trees— though many were lost during the 1987 windstorm—and a surprisingly large variety of wildlife; almost 100 species have been recorded, including cormorant, heron, and little grebe.

Enter the park through the **Decimus Burton Gateway** beside Apsley House. Almost immediately you reach **Rotten Row,** the long sandy avenue used for horseback riding that runs along the bottom of the park. The odd name derives from *route du roi* ("the King's Way"), a route William III and Queen Mary took from their home at Kensington Palace to the court at St. James's.

To the north is an artificial, crescent-shaped lake called the **Serpentine** in Hyde Park and **Long Water** in Kensington Gardens, formed in 1730 by damming a river that used to flow here. The Serpentine has its own atmosphere: festive in the summer, with its deck chairs, rowboats, and swimmers; melancholy on windy winter days.

Leave the park on the south side via **Park Close** for **Knightsbridge.** The high rise to the right is the Hyde Park Barracks, headquarters of the Household Cavalry; the soldiers often exercise their horses in the park. At precisely 10:28 every morning (9:28 on Sunday) you should be able to see the mounted Guards leaving for the Changing of the Guard ceremony at the Horse Guards Building (*see* Tour 1, *above*).

Brompton Road takes you to **Harrod's** (Tube: Knightsbridge)—the famed department store—and the museums of South Kensington.

38 Beyond **Brompton Oratory,** an Italianate, late 19th-century church, stands the massive **Victoria and Albert Museum** (Tube: South Kensington), crowned with cupolas, and the first of the great museums strung along Cromwell Road, all of which are well worth the cost of admission. The V&A, as it is known, originated in the 19th century as a museum of ornamental art, and has extensive collections of costumes, paintings, jewelry, musical instruments, and crafts from every part of the globe. The collections from India, China, Japan, and the Islamic world are especially dazzling. If you can afford only one museum, you may want to choose this one, because it's so huge and varied and there's something for everyone. *Cromwell Rd., tel. 071/938–8500 or 071/938–8349 (recorded information). Suggested contribution: £4.50 adults, £1 senior citizens and children. White Card (see London for Free, above), also valid at 12 other museums and galleries, available at this museum. Open Mon. noon–5:50, Tues.–Sun. 10–5:50*

39 Next to the V&A are two museums devoted to science. The **Natural History Museum** occupies an ornate late-Victorian building with modern additions; note the little animals carved into the cathedral-like entrance. The collections are excellent (and don't miss the full-size model of a blue whale), especially in the areas of human biology and evolution. The Earth galleries, including the popular earthquake simulator, are all that remain of the former Geological Museum. As part of the massive renovation project, new exhibits are being added. *Cromwell Rd., tel. 0171/938–9123. Admission: £5 adults, £2.50 senior citizens and children under 17, £13.50 family (2 adults, 4 children). Admission free weekdays 4:30–5:50, weekends 5–5:50. Open Mon.–Sat. 10–5:50., Sun. 11–5:50.*

40 The **Science Museum** concerns itself with everything from locomotives to space technology, the history of medicine to computers. Working models and "hands-on" exhibits are informative and fun (great for children). *Cromwell Rd., tel. 0171/938–8000. Admission: £4.50 adults, £2.40 senior citizens and children 6–14. Open Mon.–Sat. 10–6, Sun. 11–6.*

Exhibition Road runs back toward the parks past the Imperial College of Science (part of the University of London). At the center of the campus is the **Queen's Tower**—the only survivor of the original 1890s Imperial Institute demolished in the 1960s. The tower has been closed to the public recently.

41 On the left off Exhibition Road stands the grandiose bulk of the **Royal Albert Hall,** named after Queen Victoria's consort. It is the venue of the summer Promenade Concerts, which you can attend for about £3.50 (bring your own cushion—seating is on the floor), and choral and symphony concerts throughout the year. Note the pseudo-Greek frieze called "The Triumph of Arts and Letters" that runs round its exterior below the dome.

42 Across the road in **Kensington Gardens** is the **Albert Memorial,** the expression of Queen Victoria's obsessive devotion to her husband's memory. The monument, epitomizing high Victorian taste, commemorates Albert's many interests. For instance, the statue holds the catalogue of the Great Exhibition of 1851, which took place in the Crystal Palace (destroyed in a 1936 fire) in Hyde Park. The memorial is in a bad way physically, and is frequently shrouded in scaffolding and fencing while work is carried out.

43 From the **Flower Walk,** strike across Kensington Gardens to the **Round Pond,** a favorite place for children and adults to sail toy boats, and then head for **Kensington Palace,** a royal home since the late 17th century; Princess Margaret now has an apartment here. It was a simple country house until William III bought it in 1689. The interior was remodeled by leading architects Wren, Hawksmoor, Vanbrugh, and William Kent during the 18th century. Eighteen-year-old Princess Victoria was living here when, on June 20, 1837, she learned that her uncle William IV had died, which meant her accession to the throne. Some of the state apartments have remained virtually unchanged since the 1830s when young Victoria lived here with her dominating mother and governess, and are currently being restored to resemble their original selves. *Kensington Gardens. Palace closed for major refurbishment.*

Immediately behind the palace is **Kensington Palace Gardens** (called Palace Green at the south end), a wide, leafy avenue of mid-19th century mansions. This is one of the few private roads in London with uniformed guards at each end; there are several foreign embassies here, including the Russian Embassy.

Just west, past the towering modern Royal Garden Hotel, **Kensington Church Street** (Tube: High Street Kensington) runs up to the right. **St. Mary Abbotts Church** on the corner looks medieval but was built in the 1870s. This is rich territory for antiques enthusiasts: The street's shops (all the way up to Notting Hill) carry everything from Japanese armor to Victorian commemorative china, but are for browsing only, since prices are fearsome. Tucked away behind the church is **Kensington Church Walk,** a pretty lane lined with tiny shops (go down Holland Street, take the second left).

If you follow **Kensington High Street** (another flourishing shopping street) westward, you'll come to the **Commonwealth Institute**, recognizable by its blue walls and huge, tentlike copper roof. The institute focuses on the cultures of Commonwealth countries with frequent exhibitions, concerts, and film shows. *230 Kensington High St., tel. 0171/603–4535. Admission £1 adults, 50p senior citizens and children. Open Mon.–Sat. 10–5, Sun. 2–5.*

On the eastern side of the Commonwealth Institute is **Linley Sambourne House,** built and furnished in the 1870s by Mr. Sambourne, for more than 30 years the political cartoonist for the satirical magazine *Punch*. Full of pictures, furniture, and ornaments, it provides a marvelous insight into the day-to-day life of a prosperous, cultured family in late Victorian times. Some of the scenes from the movie *A Room with a View* were shot here. *18 Stafford Terr., tel. 0171/994–1019. Admission: £3 adults, £1.50 children under 16. Open Mar.–Oct., Wed. 10–4, Sun. 2–5.*

A little way past the Commonwealth Institute, on the right, is **Melbury Road**, which leads to **Holland Park Road**. Lord Leighton, the Victorian painter par excellence, lived at No. 12. The exotic richness of late 19th-century aesthetic tastes is captured in **Leighton House**, especially the Arab hall, which is lavishly lined with Persian tiles and pierced woodwork. The rest of the property has been somewhat neglected, but thanks to the generosity of John Paul Getty III, the house is now being set to rights. This neighborhood was one of the principal artists' colonies of Victorian London. If you are interested in domestic architecture of the 19th century, wander through the surrounding streets. *12 Holland Park Rd., tel. 0171/602–3316. Admission free. Open Mon.–Sat. 11–5 (weekdays 11–6 during exhibitions).*

Tour 4: The City

The City, the traditional commercial center of London, is the capital's oldest quarter, having been the site of the great Roman city of Londinium. Over the past 2,000 years the City has been continually renewed. The wooden buildings of the medieval City were destroyed in the Great Fire of 1666, and rebuilt in brick and stone. There were waves of reconstruction in the 19th century, and again after World War II, to repair the devastation wrought by air attacks. Since the '60s, modern office towers have completely changed the City's skyline, as the great financial institutions indulged in conspicuous construction.

Throughout these changes, the City has preserved its unique identity. It is governed by the Lord Mayor and the Corporation (city council) of London, as it has been for centuries. Commerce remains the City's lifeblood, but with banking now ascendant over trade. Until the first half of the 19th century, merchants and traders who worked in the City also lived there. Now, despite a huge work force, scarcely 8,000 people actually live within the City's 677 acres. Try, therefore, to explore on a weekday. On weekends, the streets are empty, and most of the shops—even some of the churches—are closed.

❹ **St. Paul's Cathedral** (Tube: St. Paul's) was rebuilt after the Great Fire of 1666 by Sir Christopher Wren, the architect who designed 50 other City churches to replace those lost in the Fire. St. Paul's is Wren's greatest work and fittingly, he is buried in the crypt, his epitaph composed by his son: *Lector, si monumentum requiris, circumspice*—Reader, if you seek his monument, look around you. The cathedral has been the scene of many state pageants, including Winston Churchill's funeral in 1965 and the wedding of the Prince and Princess of Wales in 1981. Fine painting and craftsmanship abound—the choir stalls are by the great 17th-century wood carver Grinling Gibbons—but overall the atmosphere is somewhat austere and remote. Perhaps this is because Wren's design was based on Italian Renaissance style rather than the English medieval tradition. The fact that the church was built in just 35 years also helps to account for its unusually unified quality.

The cathedral contains dozens of monuments and tombs. Among those commemorated are two national heroes: Nelson, victor over the French at Trafalgar in 1805; and Wellington, who defeated the French on land at Waterloo 10 years later. The essayist and lexicographer Dr. Johnson (another notable here) and even George Washington have their places. In the ambulatory (the area behind the high altar) is the **American Memorial Chapel**, a memorial to the 28,000 Americans stationed in Britain during World War II who lost their lives in active service. Henry Moore's sculpture *Mother and Child*, donated by the artist in 1984, stands near the entrance to the ambulatory.

The cathedral's crowning glory is its dome. It consists of three distinct shells: an outer timber-framed dome covered with lead; the interior dome, built of brick and decorated with frescoes of the life of St. Paul by the 18th-century artist Sir James Thornhill; and, in between, a brick cone that supports and strengthens both. There is a stunning view down to the body of the church from the **Whispering Gallery**, high up in the inner dome. The gallery's name comes from its remarkable acoustics: Words whispered at one point can be heard clearly on the opposite point 112 feet away.

Above the Whispering Gallery are the **Stone Gallery** and the **Golden Gallery**, both commanding fine views across London from the cathedral's exterior. These galleries also afford close views of the flying buttresses and western tower. The steps to the Golden Gallery just below the lantern, ball, and cross, though safe, are very steep; from them you can see the brick cone that divides the inner and outer domes. *Tel. 0171/248–2705. Cathedral open Mon.–Sat. 7:30–6, Sun. 8–6. Admission to ambulatory (American Memorial Chapel), Crypt, and Treasury: £2.50 adults, £1.50 children; to galleries: £2.50 adults, £1.50 children. Ambulatory, Crypt, and galleries open weekdays 10–4:15, Sat. 11–4:15. Guided tours of the cathedral weekdays at 11, 11:30, 2, and 2:30. Cost: £5 adults, £2.50 children.*

A short walk north of the cathedral to **London Wall**, so called because it follows the line of the wall that surrounded the Roman settlement, brings you to the **Museum of London**. Its imaginative

★ **❽**

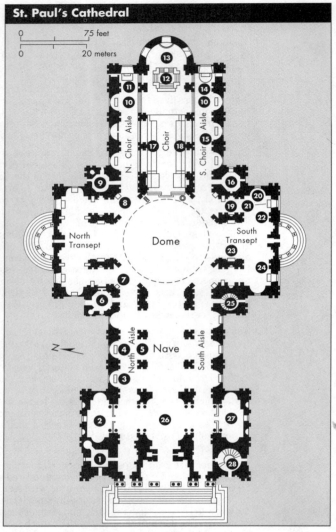

St. Paul's Cathedral

0   75 feet
0   20 meters

- All Souls' Chapel, **1**
- The American Memorial Chapel, **13**
- Bishop's Throne, **18**
- Chapel of Modern Martyrs, **11**
- Chapel of St. Michael & St. George , **27**
- Collingwood, **21**
- Crypt, **19**
- Dean's Vestry, **16**
- The Donne Effigy, **15**
- Dr. Johnson, **8**
- General Gordon Mon., **4**
- Geometric Staircase, **28**
- High Altar & Baldachino, **12**
- Howe, **20**
- Lady Chapel, **14**
- Lord Leighton Monument, **3**
- Lord Mayor's Stall, **17**
- Lord Mayor's Vestry, **6**
- Minor Canons' Vestry, **9**
- Nelson, **23**
- Reynolds by Flaxman, **7**
- St. Dunstan's Chapel, **2**
- St. Paul's Watch Mem. Stone, **26**
- Sanctuary Screens, **10**
- Sir John Moore, **24**
- Staircase, **25**
- Turner, **22**
- Wellington, **5**

displays bring London to life from Roman times to the present. Among the highlights are the Lord Mayor's Ceremonial Coach, a reenactment of the Great Fire, and the Cheapside Hoard—jewelry hidden during an outbreak of plague in the 17th century and never recovered by its owner. The 20th-century exhibits include a Woolworth's counter and elevators from Selfridges; both stores (founded by Americans) had considerable impact on the lives of Londoners. *London Wall, tel. 0171/600–3699. Admission: £3.50 adults, £1.75 senior citizens and those under 18, £8.50 family ticket, White Card available; free Tues.–Fri. 4:30–6. Open Tues.–Sat. 10–6, Sun. 2–6; closed national holidays.*

49 The **National Postal Museum** is housed in the General Post Office and contains one of the world's most important collections of postage stamps, philatelic archives, and an extensive reference library. *King Edward Bldg., King Edward St., tel. 0171/239–5420. Admission free. Open Mon.–Thurs. 9:30–4:30, Fri. 9:30–4; closed national holidays.*

50 The **Barbican** (Tube: Barbican or Moorgate) is a vast residential complex and arts center built by the City of London that takes its name from the watchtower that stood here in the Middle Ages, just outside the City walls. The arts center contains a concert hall, where the London Symphony Orchestra is based, two theaters, an art gallery for major exhibitions, a cinema, a library, a café, and a restaurant. The Royal Shakespeare Company, which stages the plays of Shakespeare, other classics, and more modern works, has its London base here. *Silk St., tel. 0171/638–4141. Admission free. Open Mon.–Sat. 9 AM–11 PM, Sun. noon–11 PM. Barbican art gallery: admission varies according to exhibition; open Mon.–Sat. 10– 6:45, Sun. noon–5:45.*

Almost the only building in this area to survive even partially the German bombings of 1940 and 1941 is **St. Giles without Cripplegate,** St. Giles being the patron saint of cripples. Today it is the parish church of the Barbican, and stands just south of the main complex, forlornly swamped by its towering modern neighbors. Only the church tower and walls are original; the remainder was rebuilt in the 1950s.

51 On the south side of London Wall stands the **Guildhall** (Tube: Bank), the home of the Corporation of London, which elects the Lord Mayor of London here each year with great ceremony. The building dates from 1410, with much reconstruction over the centuries. *King St., tel. 0171/606–3030. Admission free. Great Hall open weekdays 9:30–5 unless a function is being held. Library open weekdays 9:30– 4:45.*

Now walk south to **Cheapside.** This was the chief marketplace of medieval London (the Old English word *ceap* meant market), as the area's street names indicate: Milk Street, Ironmonger Lane, Bread Street, etc. Many of them still follow the medieval layout. The **52** church of **St. Mary-le-Bow** on Cheapside was rebuilt by Wren after the Great Fire, and again after it was bombed in World War II; it is said that to be a true Cockney you must be born within the sound of Bow bells.

A short walk east along Cheapside brings you to a seven-way inter- **53** section. The **Bank of England,** Britain's treasury, is the huge building on the left. A new museum here highlights the history of the bank and its role in the world economy. *Bartholomew La., tel. 0171/ 601–4444. Admission free. Open Good Friday–Sept., Mon.–Sat. 10–6, Sun. 2–6; Oct.–Good Friday, weekdays 10–6.*

54 At right angles to the Bank is the **Royal Exchange,** originally built in the 1560s for merchants and traders to conduct business. The present building, opened in 1844 (the third on the site), is now unoccupied.

55 The third major building at this intersection is the **Mansion House,** the official residence of the Lord Mayor (not open to the general public).

Continue east along Cornhill, site of a Roman basilica and a medieval grain market. Turn right onto Gracechurch Street and left onto **56** **Leadenhall Market.** There's been a market here since the 14th century; the glass and cast-iron building here dates from 1881.

Just behind the market is one of the most striking examples of con- **57** temporary City architecture: the headquarters of **Lloyd's of London** (Tube: Monument) designed by Richard Rogers and completed in 1986. Its main feature is a 200-foot-high barrel vault of sparkling glass that looks "alive" in all weather; it encloses a great atrium ringed with 12 tiers of galleries used largely as offices. Since its founding in the 19th century, Lloyd's has earned its fame by underwriting every kind of risk imaginable: ships, aircraft, oil rigs, Betty

Grable's legs. Its luck finally began to fail in 1993, when it was forced to extract huge sums of money from the individuals who underwrote it. It has yet to recover. *1 Lime St., tel. 0171/623–7100. It is sometimes possible to visit. Groups of 10 or more from relevant organizations must apply in writing on letterhead paper at least one week in advance.*

58 The **Monument** (Tube: Monument), to the south, is a massive column of white stone designed by Wren and erected in 1667 to commemorate the Great Fire. It stands 202 feet high, with its base exactly 202 feet from the site of the small bakery shop in Pudding Lane where the fire started. At the summit is a gilt urn with flames leaping from it, 311 steps up from the street. *Monument St., tel. 0171/626–2717. Admission: £1 adults, 25p children. Open Mon.–Sat. 9–2.*

★ **59** The **Tower of London** (Tube: Tower Hill) is one of London's most popular (hence, crowded) sights. Visit as early in the day as possible, and join one of the excellent free 1-hour tours given by the Yeoman Warders of the Tower (the "Beefeaters"), who wear a picturesque Tudor-style uniform. Tours start from the Middle Tower (near the entrance) about every 30 minutes.

The Tower served as both fortress and palace in medieval times; every British sovereign from William the Conqueror (11th century) to Henry VIII (16th century) lived here, and it is still officially a royal palace. The Tower has such a long history and its buildings have known so many uses that it can be difficult to grasp the overall story. The **History Gallery** is a useful walk-through display that answers most questions about the Tower and its inhabitants.

The **White Tower** is the oldest and most conspicuous building in the entire complex. When it was completed in about 1097, it dominated the whole settlement, forcing home the power of England's new Norman overlords. Inside, the austere **Chapel of St. John** is one of the Tower's few unaltered structures, a Norman chapel of great simplicity, almost entirely lacking in ornamentation. In the basement are displayed the Tower's instruments of torture, including the block and axe.

The **Royal Armouries,** England's national collection of arms and armor, occupies the rest of the White Tower. Sixteenth- and 17th-century armor is predominant, including four personal armors of Henry VIII (one with a matching horse armor) and an all-gilt armor that belonged to Charles I. The **New Armouries** house examples of almost every weapon made for British forces from the 17th to the 19th centuries.

Surrounding the White Tower are structures dating from the 11th to the 19th centuries. Sir Walter Raleigh was held prisoner in the **Bloody Tower** (originally the Garden Tower) in relative comfort between 1603 and 1616; he passed the time writing his *History of the World.* The young princes, sons of Edward IV, supposedly murdered on the orders of their uncle Richard III, lived and probably died in the Bloody Tower. Next door stands the **Wakefield Tower,** where Henry VI was allegedly murdered in 1471 during the Wars of the Roses, England's medieval civil war.

Tower Green was the site of the executioner's block. It was a rare honor to be beheaded inside the Tower in relative privacy; most people were executed outside on Tower Hill, where the crowds could get a better view. Important prisoners were held in the **Beauchamp Tower** to the west of Tower Green; its walls are covered with graffiti and inscriptions carved by prisoners.

The **Crown Jewels** are now housed in the **Duke of Wellington's Barracks,** which can accommodate 20,000 visitors per day, reducing the fearsome line for this most popular of exhibits. The Jewels are a breathtakingly impressive collection of regalia, precious stones, gold, and silver. The Royal Sceptre contains the largest cut diamond in the world. The Imperial State Crown, made for Queen Victoria's coronation in 1838, is studded with 3,000 precious stones, mainly diamonds and pearls. *Tower Hill, tel. 0171/709–0765. Admission: £7.95 adults, £5.95 senior citizens, £5.25 children under 15, family ticket (up to 2 adults, 3 children) £21.95. Open Mar.–Oct., Mon.– Sat. 9:30–5, Sun. 2–5; Nov.–Feb., Mon.–Sat. 9:30–4. Free Yeoman Warder guides' tours leave about every half hour from the Middle Tower; last tour 3:30 in summer, 2:30 in winter.*

To the west of the Tower is a new development, where various shops and food outlets surround the entrance to **Tower Hill Pageant,** London's first dark-ride museum. Automated cars take visitors past mock-ups of scenes from the past, complete with "people," sound effects, and smells. There's also an archaeological museum with finds from the Thames. *Tower Hill Terrace, tel. 0171/709–0081. Admission: £5.45 adults, £3.45 senior citizens and children under 16. Open Apr.–Oct., daily 9:30–5:30; Nov.–Mar., daily 9:30–4:30. Closed Dec. 25.*

60 **Tower Bridge** (Tube: Tower Hill) may look medieval, but it was built from 1885 to 1894. It is the only Thames bridge that can be raised to allow ships to pass, although with the virtual extinction of London's shipping trade and the movement of big ships on the Thames, the complex lifting mechanism is used only four or five times a week. To celebrate the bridge's 100th birthday this year, a new exhibition has opened. An elevator in the North Tower takes you up to an audiovisual journey through the history, construction, and raison d'être of what for many people is the very symbol of London. The show uses compact disc interactive technology to superimpose skylines of past ages over the magnificent views from the bridge's walkways, and includes models and dramatizations of Victorian London, and an animatronic tour guide. The tour ends in the engine room with a recreation of the 1894 Royal Opening ceremony. *Tel. 0171/407–0922. Admission: £5 adults, £3.50 senior citizens and children under 16. Open Apr.–Oct., daily 10–6:30; Nov.–Mar., daily 10–5:15.*

Tour 5: The South Bank

Southwark, on the south bank of the Thames, has long been neglected. Full of derelict 19th-century warehouses, it seemed a perfect location for Jack the Ripper movies. Now ambitious new building complexes with stylish museums and stores are turning it into a riverside center of activity again.

The first settlement here was Roman. Across the river from the City proper, and thus outside its jurisdiction, by the Middle Ages Southwark had acquired a reputation for easy living. Londoners used to go there to enjoy a night in one of the many inns—Southwark was famous for good, strong beer—or to sample the pleasures of the Southwark "stews" (brothels, not casseroles!). Bear-baiting and the theater were other forms of entertainment here. Shakespeare was both actor and shareholder at the Elizabethan Globe Theatre, and his plays were staged regularly.

61 Start at **Butler's Wharf** (Tube: Tower Hill, then walk across bridge), a short distance downstream (east) of the south end of Tower Bridge. This was originally a large warehouse, and has been converted into a residential and commercial complex. Until 1982 there was a brewery here; its tower is all that remains. The **Design Museum** focuses on the history and evolution of mass-produced goods and services. Films, sound recordings, posters, and other advertising material help place the exhibits in their contemporary social and cultural context. Permanent displays of "classic" design are combined with temporary theme exhibitions that emphasize how mass-produced consumer goods are developed. There is also a riverside café. *Butler's Wharf, tel. 0171/403-6933. Admission: £4.50 adults, £3.50 senior citizens and those under 18. Open daily 10:30-6:30.*

62 Upstream of Tower Bridge lies **HMS *Belfast*** (Tube: London Bridge; or take the Riverbus to London Bridge City Pier), the largest and one of the most powerful cruisers ever built for the Royal Navy (a ferry runs between it and the Tower of London). The *Belfast* stood off Normandy on D-Day in 1944, protecting the landing beaches, and after the war served in the Far East. When its service career ended in 1963, the vessel was saved from the scrapyard by the Imperial War Museum. Naval and World War II enthusiasts will want to tour the *Belfast;* the armaments, mess decks, punishment cells, operations room, and engine room are open to view. Others can admire it from the riverside. *Symon's Wharf, Vine Lane, Tooley St., tel. 0171/407-6434. Admission: £4 adults, £3 senior citizens, £2 children under 16. Open mid-Mar.-Oct., daily 10-5:20; Nov.-early Mar., daily 10-4.*

63 **Hay's Galleria** is a shopping mall housed beneath a dramatic 100-foot-high, 300-foot-long glass barrel-vault roof. In the center is a massive kinetic sculpture, *Navigators,* by David Kemp. Shaped like a huge comic boat, parts of which move under the water jets, it recalls the history of Hay's Wharf, one of London's oldest, dating from 1651. Planners had hoped that the Galleria would develop into a Covent Garden on the Thames but so far this has not happened, perhaps due to the recession.

Walking westward from the Galleria, follow the riverside path past the Cottons building, with its offices overlooking a 100-foot-high atrium and water garden, to **London Bridge.**

64 On **Tooley Street,** below Hay's Galleria, is the **London Dungeon,** which re-creates scenes of medieval torture, execution, disease, and persecution, as well as the Great Fire of 1666. The dungeon is expensive, but it's a fun exhibit that far outdoes Madame Tussaud's Chamber of Horrors for wonderful goriness. *28-34 Tooley St., tel. 0171/387-1405. Admission: £6.95 adults, £5.50 senior citizens, £4 children under 14. Open daily 10-4:30.*

65 **Old St. Thomas's Hospital,** on St. Thomas Street (over the railway viaduct from Tooley Street), provides an insight into hospital life of only a few generations ago. This operating theater dates from 1821 and has been restored to its original state. Surgeons at the time worked in aprons stained with blood from previous operations, washing facilities scarcely existed, and a sawdust box underneath the table caught patients' blood; when it was full, the surgeon called for more sawdust. The herb garret next door, where medicinal herbs were dried and stored, has also been restored. *St. Thomas St., tel. 071/806-4325. Admission: £1.50 adults, £1 senior citizens and children under 16. Open Mon., Wed., Fri. 12:30-4, other times by appointment.*

66 **Southwark Cathedral** is the largest Gothic church in London after Westminster Abbey—building began on it in 1220. The chief feature of interest for American visitors is the Harvard Chapel. It commemorates John Harvard, founder of the great American university, baptized here in 1608. Shakespeare's younger brother Edmund is buried here.

Around the corner, **St. Mary Overie Dock** is an office development built on the site of the London palace of the bishops of Winchester; the massive west wall of the great hall has been preserved, and you **67** can see the outline of a rose window. The ***Kathleen & May,*** one of the last surviving wooden three-masted schooners, is permanently moored here. She was one of hundreds of schooners that plied the coasts of Britain in the early 20th century. On board is a maritime exhibition including a rare film of the *Kathleen & May* under sail. *St. Mary Overie Dock, tel. 0171/403–3965. Closed at press time. Call for details.*

Now walk west along Clink Street, where one of Southwark's several prisons stood, past the Bankside pub and under Cannon Street Railway Bridge and Southwark Bridge. On the left, a narrow street
68 called Bear Gardens leads to the **Shakespeare Globe Museum.** For more than two decades, until he died in 1993, the American actor and film director Sam Wanamaker worked ceaselessly to raise funds for this ambitious project, an exact replica of Shakespeare's open-roofed Globe Playhouse (built in 1599; incinerated in 1613). Until the theater is completed, there's a fascinating tour to be had, showing the construction in progress. Once finished, the Globe will be a celebration of the great bard's life and work, an actual rebirth of his "Great Wooden O" (see *Henry V*), where his plays will be presented in natural light (and sometimes rain), to 1,000 people on wooden benches in the "bays," plus 500 "groundlings," standing on a carpet of filbert shells and clinker, just as they did nearly four centuries ago. For any theater buff, this stunning project should not be missed. *New Globe Walk, Bankside., tel. 0171/928–6406. Admission: £4 adults, £3 senior citizens, £2.50 those under 18. Open daily 10–5.*

The riverside path passes Cardinal's Wharf and then continues along Bankside toward **Blackfriars Bridge.**

On the way to the bridge is **Coin Street** (Tube: Waterloo), a residen-
69 tial enclave that has been preserved from development. At **Gabriel's Wharf** there are crafts shops, studios, and a crafts market.

A short walk along the new embankment promenade—look for the display panels that identify the buildings across the river—brings you to the **National Theatre,** the first of the concrete buildings look-
70 ing like giant bunkers that make up the **South Bank Arts Complex.** The foyers, open to the public six days a week, are full of activity, with bookshops, bars, cafés, exhibitions, and free performances. The National Theatre Company plays here regularly in three auditoriums, each with its distinct character. Although performances can be uneven, its best work is electrifying. *South Bank, tel. 0171/ 928–2252. Open Mon.–Sat. 10 AM–11 PM. 1-hr tours of the theater 5 times daily, between 10:15 and 6; cost: £3.50 adults, £2.50 senior citizens, children, actor's union members.*

Underneath Waterloo Bridge nearby are the **National Film Theatre** (N.F.T.) and the **Museum of the Moving Image (MOMI).** MOMI celebrates every aspect of the moving image, from Chinese shadow plays of 2,500 BC to the latest fiber optics and satellite images; cinema and television take center stage, however. This is very much a hands-on museum, with the emphasis on participatory displays, especially of film and television-making processes. *South Bank, tel. 0171/401–2636. Admission: £5.50 adults, £4 senior citizens and children, £4.70 students. Open daily 10–6; last admission 5 PM.*

The rest of the arts complex, on the far side of Waterloo Bridge, consists of three concert halls and the **Hayward Gallery,** which hosts large-scale art exhibitions. The next stretch of the embankment affords photogenic views across the river to Big Ben and the Houses of Parliament.

The river frontage on the far side of **Westminster Bridge** is occupied
71 by **St. Thomas's Hospital** (Tube: Lambeth North). In early 1989 St. Thomas's became the site of the **Florence Nightingale Museum,** dedicated to the famous nurse's life and work and also featuring the evolution of modern nursing techniques. *Gassiot House, 2 Lambeth*

Palace Rd., tel. 0171/620-0374. Admission: £2.50 adults, £1.50 senior citizens and children under 16. Open Tues.-Sun. 10-4.

72 Beyond St. Thomas's stands **Lambeth Palace,** the London residence of the Archbishop of Canterbury—the senior archbishop of the Church of England—since the early 13th century. It's rarely open to the public, but you can admire the fine Tudor gatehouse.

Beside the palace, in the yard of the now-deconsecrated **St. Mary's Church,** are buried the two John Tradescants, father and son, who were royal gardeners in the 17th century. They traveled widely in Europe and America, bringing back plant specimens not previously known in this country; their garden in Lambeth became a pioneer nursery. St. Mary's Church now houses the Tradescant Trust's **Museum of Garden History.** This unique collection includes a duplication of a 17th-century knot garden (the name describes its shape) containing only plants grown in the 17th century, especially those grown by the Tradescants. *St. Mary-at-Lambeth, Lambeth Palace Rd., tel. 0171/261-1891. Admission free; donations welcome. Open early Mar.-early Dec., weekdays 11-3, Sun. 10:30-5.*

73 The **Imperial War Museum** lies a short walk inland from Lambeth Palace, down Lambeth Road. Its holdings constitute the country's principal collection of 20th-century war artifacts. Among the hardware on display are a Battle of Britain Spitfire, a World War I tank, and a German V1 pilotless flying bomb, a type dropped on London in 1944-45. The "Blitz Experience" gives you the sights, sounds, and smells of London during the World War II bombing, while "Operation Jericho" is a flight simulator that re-creates the famous raid over France. *Lambeth Rd., tel. 0171/416-5000. Admission: £3.90 adults, £2.90 senior citizens, £1.95 children. Open daily 10-6.*

Tour 6: Up and Down the Thames

The River Thames unites the oldest and the newest areas of London. It's spanned by bridges of different design. The earliest, Richmond, dates from 1774, and the most recent, London Bridge, from 1973—the former London Bridge having been sold and rebuilt in Arizona. The river has played an important role in the history of London and from it the familiar historic buildings and sites take on a new and dramatic perspective. Points of interest, such as Greenwich, the Thames Barrier, Hampton Court Palace, and Kew, are serviced by BritRail. Suggested BritRail stops for the following tour have been noted in the text. Also, boat excursions can be taken in either direction from piers at Westminster, Charing Cross, and Tower Bridge. Another option is to take the high-speed catamaran Riverbus, which stops at Chelsea Harbour, Charing Cross, South Bank, London Bridge City, Swan Lane, West India Dock, and Greenwich. Call Riverbus (tel. 0181/858-0891 or 0171/515-0909) for information. *Tel. 0171/730-4812 for the recorded Riverboat Information Service.*

Greenwich Downstream, a few miles past the imposing bulk of the Tower of London, lies **Greenwich** (BritRail: Greenwich). At its heart are the late-17th-century buildings of the **Royal Naval College,** once an old sailors' home; the college has been here since 1873. The buildings are the work of Sir Christopher Wren and his two assistants, Hawksmoor and Vanbrugh, later celebrated architects in their own right. You can visit the grand **Painted Hall,** the college dining hall, dramatically decorated with huge frescoes by Sir James Thornhill, who also painted the dome in St. Paul's Cathedral. It was here that Nelson's body lay in state at Christmas of 1805, after the Battle of Trafalgar. Across from the Painted Hall is the **College Chapel.** The airy 18th-century interior is a delight of pastel shades and intricate, delicate detail. The pulpit maintains the naval theme; it's made from the top deck of a three-decker sailing ship. *Royal Naval College:*

King William Walk, tel. 0181/858–2154. Admission free. Open Fri.–Wed. 2:30–4:30.

Two dry-docked boats alongside the river are the **Cutty Sark,** the last of the 19th-century clipper ships, and the tiny **Gipsy Moth IV,** which Sir Francis Chichester sailed single-handedly around the world in 1966. *Cutty Sark: King William Walk, tel. 0181/858–3445. Admission: £3.25 adults, £2.25 senior citizens and children under 16. Open Mon.–Sat. 10–5, Sun. noon–5.* Gipsy Moth IV: *King William Walk, tel. 081/853–3589. Admission: 50p adults, 30p senior citizens and children. Open Apr.–Oct., Mon.–Sat. 10–6, Sun. noon–6.*

The **National Maritime Museum** (BritRail: Maze Hill) charts Britain's illustrious maritime heritage through maps, paintings, and models. Among the highlights are the original royal barges, displayed in the **Barge House.** *Romney Rd., tel. 0181/858–4422. Admission: £4.95 adults, £3.95 senior citizens, £2.95 children. Open Mon.–Sat. 9–6, Sun. noon–6.*

On the hill behind the museum and the Naval College, in **Greenwich Park,** is the **Old Royal Observatory,** founded in 1675 by Charles II, who was a great patron of the sciences. Many original telescopes and astronomical instruments are on display here. The world's prime meridian (zero degrees longitude) runs through the courtyard: Straddle the line and you'll have a foot in each hemisphere. *Greenwich Park, tel. 0181/858–1167. Admission to all the above (except Cutty Sark and Gipsy Moth IV), including one free return visit: £4.95 adults, £3.95 senior citizens, £2.95 children.*

A crafts market takes place on weekends in the Victorian covered market, and there's also an antiques market at the foot of Crooms Hill most weekend mornings.

Thames Barrier A major attraction just a few miles downriver is the Thames Barrier. Constructed between 1975 and 1982, it is the world's largest movable flood barrier, designed to prevent the Thames from overflowing its banks into extensive parts of central and south London. You can take BritRail to Silvertown and City Airport, or you can take the boats that depart frequently from Greenwich Pier to visit this awesome piece of civil engineering. Also here is **Hallett's Panorama,** an incongruous re-creation, with oils and sculpture, of the city of Bath, and the Soviet navy's largest submarine, the 1967-vintage **U-475 Foxtrot,** moored at nearby Long's Wharf. *Unity Way, off Woolwich Rd., tel. 0181/854–1373. Admission (including Hallett's Panorama): £2.50 adults, £1.55 senior citizens and children. Open weekdays 10:30–5, weekends 10:30–5:30; closed Dec. 25–26, Jan. 1. Russian submarine, admission: £3.95 adults, £2 children. Open daily 10–6.*

Hampton Court Palace ★ A series of royal palaces and grand houses line the Thames west of central London, built as aristocratic country residences close to the capital when the river was the primary means of travel. The most celebrated is **Hampton Court Palace** (BritRail: Hampton Court), surrounded by rolling parkland, some 20 miles upstream. It was begun in 1514 by Cardinal Wolsey, taken from him by Henry VIII, and expanded 150 years later by Sir Christopher Wren for William and Mary. Steeped in history and hung with priceless paintings and tapestries, Hampton Court provides a magical trip out of town, especially if you are able to go on a sunny day from spring through to the fall, to see the gardens and the famous maze at their colorful best. *East Molesey, tel. 0181/977–8441. Admission: state apartments and maze, £7 adults, £5.30 senior citizens, £4.70 children under 16; maze only, £1.75 adults, £1.10 senior citizens and children; grounds free. State apartments open Apr.–Sept., daily 10–6; Oct.–Mar., daily 10–4:30. Tudor tennis court open Apr.–Sept. only; grounds open daily 8–dusk.*

Richmond **Richmond** is an old, wealthy suburb of London with elegant 18th-century houses fronting its green; **Richmond Hill** has many good antiques shops. **Richmond Park** is one of the last vestiges of the vast medieval forests and hunting grounds that once pressed in on London; deer still roam here.

Kew **The Royal Botanic Gardens** at **Kew** (Tube or BritRail: Kew Gardens) are the headquarters of the country's leading botanical institute as well as a public garden of 300 acres and more than 60,000 species of plants.

Kew Palace, on the grounds, was home to George III for much of his life. Its formal garden has been redeveloped on a 17th-century pattern. The 19th-century greenhouses, notably the **Palm House** and the **Temperate House,** are among the highlights here. In the ultra-modern Princess of Wales Conservatory, opened in 1987, there are 10 climatic zones, their temperatures all precisely controlled by computer. *Royal Botanic Gardens, tel. 0181/940–1171. Admission: £4 adults, £2 senior citizens, £1.50 children 5–16. Gardens open daily 9:30–6:30, greenhouses 10–6:30 (both open Sun. and national holidays until 8); in winter, closing times depend on the light, usually 4 or 5. Kew Palace, tel. 0181/940–3321. Admission: £1.20 adults, 90p senior citizens, 80p children under 16. Open Apr.–Sept., daily 11–5:30.*

Regent's Park The **Gardens of the Zoological Society of London,** known simply as the Zoo, were founded more than 150 years ago, and are one of London's major tourist attractions. Although financial problems have been a constant threat in recent years, £1 million from the Emir of Kuwait, among other private benefactors, plus the proceeds of the "Save Our Zoo" campaign have kept the wolves from the door (so to speak), and now an ambitious 10-year improvement plan is under way. Major attractions include (1) the Mappin Terraces, which were built some 70 years ago as a natural habitat for animals such as goats, pigs, and bears; (2) the remodeled Children's Zoo; (3) the Snowdon Aviary, designed by Lord Snowdon in 1965 when he was married to Princess Margaret; (4) the Lion Terraces; (5) the Elephant and Rhino Pavilion, an oddly delicate name for such a massive, castlelike structure; (6) the Small Bird House; and (7) the Tropical House, with its darting hummingbirds. One fascinating and unique exhibit is the Moonlight World, on the lower floor of the Charles Clore Pavilion. Here night conditions are simulated so that visitors can watch nocturnal animals during the day. The process is reversed at night, when the cages are lit, and the animals take up their daytime activities. *Regent's Park, tel. 071/722–3333. Admission £6.95 adults, £5.95 senior citizens, £4.95 children under 4–14. Open daily 9–6.*

Shopping

Shopping is just as much a priority in London as sightseeing, but you have to know where and when to go to pick up a bargain. Generally, sale seasons occur in January and June (although they seem to start earlier every year), when the department stores as well as boutiques and chain stores reduce everything from 25% to as much as 75%, to make room for the next season's goods.

You'll find the best deals on clothing—especially leather jackets, designer labels, and knitwear. Although they can be expensive, china and glass may be worth the investment because they are often high quality. Many shops offer "export schemes," wherein the 17½% VAT is waived on goods you take back to the United States with you.

Districts Chelsea, Knightsbridge, Mayfair, Bond Street, Piccadilly, Regent Street, and St. James's are pricey, making them terrific areas for window shopping. Even during the sales (especially tempting in top couture and designer clothes on Knightsbridge's Sloane Street, Beauchamp Place, and Walton Street), reductions are relative to the original prices. Liberty, on Regent Street, has one of the best sales on textiles and accessories and is a perennial favorite. Camden Town and Upper Street, Islington, both in north London, and the streets around Portobello Road, west London, are lined with shops selling clothes, jewelry, antiques, ceramics, and books at affordable prices. Covent Garden's Neal Street and its open-air and Jubilee Hall markets are worth checking out for clothing and household items. Around once-famous Carnaby Street and into Soho, a wealth of unusual boutiques have sprung up, mostly selling youthful clothing from T-shirts and athletic shoes to designer outfits and jewelry at reasonable costs.

Specialty Stores There is space to include only a few London specialty stores, but note their locations: Stores selling the same wares are often grouped together.

Antiques Prime areas are the Camden Passage Market (*see* Street Markets, *below*) and Bermondsey Market, where a bargain can still be found, but arrive early as the best buys go quickly. Portobello Road and Kensington Church Street have antiques of every description, but you can expect high prices in the latter. Stores worth a visit include:

Gray's Antique Market (58 Davies St., and around the corner **Gray's Mews**, at 1–7 Davies Mews, tel. 0171/629–7034) is a gaggle of smaller places all selling curios and collectibles. Prices are not the lowest, but they are fair, and Gray's guarantees that every piece is genuine.

Books Charing Cross Road is London's book country, with a couple of dozen stores there or thereabouts. Especially large—if confusing and chaotic—is **Foyles** (No. 119, tel. 0171/437–5660). **Dillons** (82 Gower St., WC1, tel. 0171/636–1577), near the British Museum, and **Hatchards** (187–188 Piccadilly, tel. 0171/437–3924) not only have a huge stock, but both employ a well-informed staff to help you choose.

Among the secondhand meccas are **Quinto** (83 Marylebone High St., tel. 0171/935–9303), with a fascinating galleried section at the back, and **Bell, Book and Radmall** (4 Cecil Ct., tel. 0171/240–2161), which specializes in modern first editions, and is just one of more than 30 specialist bookstores in this pedestrians-only lane.

China and Glass All of London's department stores carry classic Wedgwood or Minton and their less expensive competitors.

Thomas Goode (19 South Audley St., tel. 0171/499–2823) carries enormous lines of crystal and china. Their very best is very expensive, but their range is fairly wide.

General Trading Co. (144 Sloane St., SW1, tel. 0171/730–0411). With a dozen departments, it sells French glass, Indian crafts, Italian lighting fixtures, Chinese toys, and English bone china. Although you can spend as little as £5 and feel you've got something special, every debutante has her wedding present list here, and that's who General Trading really caters to.

Clothing Most leading international houses have major branches in London, and most department stores have fashion floors; Harvey Nichols sells practically nothing but, and has a permanent sale department. Simpson's, and Liberty's provide more traditional, good quality clothes. London is still renowned for men's clothing, especially for the exquisite tailoring of the Savile Row masters, who rightly charge stratospheric amounts. For cut-rate, quality clothing with a British look, shop where even many Savile Row patrons get their underwear: Marks & Spencer. London's strength also lies in streetwise clothes—try the ubiquitous chainstore, Warehouse (*see below*), and especially the markets and boutiques where young designers start out.

Womenswear **Browns** (23–27 South Molton St., tel. 0171/491–7833 and 6C Sloane St., tel. 0171/493–4232) offers the most unmissable sale of all for the fashion victim. (See *Evening Standard* listings for times of this and other sales.) Here you'll find Azzedine Alaïa, Romeo Gigli, Jean Muir, Donna Karan, Jasper Conran, Claude Montana, Rifat Ozbek, Sonia Rykiel . . . and just about every designer you've ever coveted.

Labels for Less, opposite, is where slow-selling lines are decanted for major discounts.

Designer Sale Studio (241 King's Rd., tel. 0171/351–4171, and branches) stocks samples by mainly Italian designers such as Gianni Versace, Byblos, Erreuno, and Valentino. Prices are at least a third lower than list and, needless to say, turnover is high.

Hennes (481 Oxford St., tel. 0171/493–8557; 123 Kensington High St., tel. 0171/937–3329) is a Swedish chain with up-to-the-minute versions of what's on the catwalk at very low prices. Check out the children's department, too.

Venus (19 Shorts Gardens, tel. 0171/379–1426) has an amazing selection of the more eccentric and avant-garde British designers' samples and surplus: Westwood, Galliano, Hamnett—all the greats.

Warehouse (16–21 Argyll St., tel. 0171/437–7101) is where every thrifty yet hip girl shops for essential runway looks at good prices.

Whistles (12–14 St. Christopher's Pl., tel. 0171/487–4484). This small chain of high-fashion stores caters to the older, richer sister of the Warehouse customer, with a higher cost, higher quality selection. However, the house label of each season's stylish basics are competitively priced. Check out the sale shop opposite.

Menswear **Marks & Spencer** (458 Oxford St., tel. 0171/935–7954), with its famous food department, women's lingerie, and clothing and articles for the home, is by no means just for menswear, but quality is excellent and styles are timeless. Knitwear is a strength, and fashion gets better every year, as top designers are hired anonymously to add a piece or two.

Paul Smith (41–44 Floral St., tel. 0171/379–7133) appears to be every well-dressed man's favorite shop, whether he can afford the fairly high prices or not. Perhaps he takes advantage of the fabulous sales. Smith designs witty, modern suits, shirts, knitwear, ties, and accessories.

Sam Walker (41 Neal St., tel. 0171/240–7800) provides a refined way to buy secondhand clothing. Most of the stock is pre–World War II, with nostalgia in every fold and pocket.

Crafts A revived interest in traditional crafts has meant a new wave of stores devoted to selling fine craftwork. Here are a couple:

Combined Harvest (128 Talbot Rd., just off Portobello Rd., tel. 0171/221–4870) markets the work of some 50 craftsworkers at reasonable prices. Commissions are accepted.

Craftsmen Potters Shop (7 Marshall St., tel. 0171/437–7605) is a cooperative carrying a wide spectrum of the potter's art.

Gifts A catch-all category, admittedly, but you have to buy something for friends back home. London's department stores are good for gift hunting, as are the major museum shops, most of which sell books, posters, and reproductions of items in their collections. Below are some other places you might look:

Camden Lock (Chalk Farm Rd., NW1, tel. 0171/485–7963) is where cost-conscious Londoners do their Christmas shopping. Now that they've been rehoused in the new village by the canal, there are more stalls and shops than ever, selling everything from wrought-iron candlesticks to vast amounts of vintage clothing, boots, and jeans. Be warned: This is a youth shantytown, which can resemble a slackers' meatmarket on weekends.

Hamleys (188–196 Regent St., tel. 0171/734–3161) has six floors of toys and games for both children and adults, ranging from teddy bears to computer games and all the latest space-age gimmickry.

Neal Street East (5 Neal St., tel. 0171/240–0135). The "East" in the name refers to the Orient. This is a colorful labyrinth of Far Eastern goods.

The Tea House (15A Neal St., tel. 0171/240–7539). You'll find gifts galore at this refreshing store devoted to everything concerning the British national drink.

Prints Prints are another London specialty. Below are two of many print stores in Central London. If you know what you want, scour the markets for bargains.

CCA Galleries (8 Dover St., tel. 0171/499–6701) offers an interesting range of work by contemporary printmakers. Their prices are reasonable, and their knowledgeable staff is helpful.

Grosvenor Prints (28–32 Shelton St., tel. 0171/836–1979). Grosvenor Prints sells antiquarian prints—especially of London buildings and dogs! Its eccentricity and wide selection virtually guarantee a find.

Department Stores **Harrods** (87 Brompton Rd., tel. 0171/730–1234), one of the world's most famous department stores, can be forgiven its immodest motto, *Omnia, omnibus, ubique* ("everything, for everyone, everywhere"), since there are more than 230 departments, and it's nearly true. Although it's now perhaps less exclusive than its former self, it is still a British institution. The food halls are stunning, and yield perhaps the most acessible wares for the low-budget shopper.

John Lewis (278 Oxford St., tel. 0171/629–7711) claims as its motto, "Never knowingly undersold." This is perhaps the most traditional of English department stores, with a good selection of dress fabrics and drapes.

Liberty (200 Regent St., tel. 0171/734–1234). Famous principally for its fabrics, Liberty's is also known for an improving fashion floor, costume jewelry and accessories, and its original merchandise, Oriental goods.

Selfridges (400 Oxford St., tel. 0171/629–1234). This is London's mammoth upmarket version of Macy's. **Miss Selfridge,** with its Duke Street entrance, is their outpost for trendy, affordable young women's clothes. (Check the phone book for other branches.)

Street Markets Street markets are mainly a weekend happening, and because many of them are open Sunday morning, they provide diversion during an otherwise quiet time in London. A morning in the markets, followed by a hearty lunch and an afternoon in a park or museum, is as much a Londoner's kind of Sunday as it is a tourist's.

Bermondsey (Tower Bridge Rd., SE1), Fri. 4:30 AM–noon. This is one of London's largest markets, and the one the antique dealers frequent, which gives you an idea of its scope. Take Bus 15 or 25 to Aldgate, then Bus 42 over Tower Bridge to Bermondsey Square; or take the tube to London Bridge and walk.

Camden Lock (NW1). Stores: Tues.–Sun. 9:30–5:30, stalls on weekends 8–6 (approximately). This sprawling market in the area of London with the highest concentration of single under-20s is now mostly housed in renovated warehouses on the canal banks, but is still good for cheap and secondhand clothing, music, books, crafts, and jewelry. Canal trips begin here, too; check at the Regent's Canal (Camden Lock) Information Centre. Take the tube to Camden Town.

Camden Passage (Islington, N1). Wed. and Sat. 8:30 AM–3 PM. Hugged by curio stores, the passage drips with jewelry, silverware, and antiques. On days when the stalls aren't up, only some stores are open. Bus 19 or 38 or the tube to Angel will get you there.

Petticoat Lane/Brick Lane (Middlesex St., E1). Sun. 9–2. Petticoat Lane is the familiar name of this famous market on Middlesex Street. You'll find bargain leather goods, clothes, bric-a-brac, antiques, CDs, cameras, videos, and stereos. Liverpool Street, Aldgate, or Aldgate East tubes are the closest.

Portobello Market (Portobello Rd., W11). Fruit and vegetables Mon.–Wed., Fri.–Sat. 8–5, Thurs. 8–1; antiques Sat. 8–5; flea-market Fri.–Sat. 8–5. The Notting Hill Gate end is far and away the most expensive, but the farther you walk, the more realistic the prices become and the more basic the goods on sale are. At the Westway (north) end, you'll find a good flea market. It's a fun place to explore. Take Bus 52 or the tube to Ladbroke Grove or Notting Hill Gate.

Lodging

Although it is not recommended to do so if you're looking to save money on your hotel bill, if you do arrive in London without a room, the **London Tourist Board Information Centres** at Heathrow and Victoria Station forecourt (no telephone reservations) will help, or you can make credit card (MC, V) bookings on the **LTB Accommodation Line** (tel. 0171/824–8844), which charges a small fee. (*See also* Lodging, Chapter 1, *above*.)

Highly recommended establishments are indicated by a star ★.

All prices are for two people sharing a double room and include service, VAT, and sometimes breakfast.

££
Bayswater
★
Commodore. This peaceful hotel of three converted Victorians has some amazing (especially for the price) rooms—as superior to the regular ones (which usually go to package tour groups) as Harrods is to Woolworths. Twenty are mini-duplexes, with sleeping gallery, and all have the full deck of tea/coffeemakers, hair dryers, and TVs with pay movies. One (No. 11) is a real duplex, entered through a secret mirrored door, with thick-carpeted, *very* quiet bedroom upstairs and its toilet below. It's getting very popular here, so book ahead. *50 Lancaster Gate W2 3NA, tel. 0171/402–5291, fax 0171/262–1088. 90 rooms with bath. Facilities: lounge, bar, business center. AE, MC, V. Tube: Lancaster Gate.*

££
★
London Elizabeth. Steps from Hyde Park, Lancaster Gate tube, and rows of depressing cheap hotels, is this family-owned gem. Foyer and lounge are crammed with coffee tables and chintz drapery, lace antimacassars, and little chandeliers, and this country sensibility persists through the freshly decorated bedrooms. Some rooms lack a full-length mirror, but they do have TV, direct dial phone, and hair dryer, and they're serviced by an exceptionally charming Anglo-Irish staff. *Lancaster Terrace, W2 3PF, tel. 0171/402–6641, fax 0171/224–8900. 55 rooms. Facilities: 24-hour room service, restaurant, bar, lounge. AE, DC, MC, V. Tube: Lancaster Gate.*

££
Bloomsbury
Academy. These three adjoining Georgian houses, boasting a little patio garden and a fashion-conscious wood-floored, mirrored basement bar/brasserie, supply the most sophisticated and hotel-like facilities in the Gower Street "hotel row." The comfortable bedrooms have TVs (with no extra channels), direct-dial phones, and tea/

coffeemakers, and the two without bathrooms are £30 per night cheaper. *17–21 Gower St., WC1E 6HG, tel. 0171/631–4115, fax 0171/ 636–3442. 33 rooms, 25 with bath/shower. Facilities: patio garden, restaurant/bar, lounge. AE, DC, MC, V. Tube: Russell Square.*

£𝙁 **Fielding.** Tucked away in a quiet alley by the Royal Opera House
Covent Garden (what a location!), this small hotel is adored by its regulars. There
★ are rather a lot of stairs in this labarynthine conversion, and no elevator. But the atmosphere is homey and welcoming; bedrooms are all different and, though some are very small, all are comfortable. *4 Broad Ct., Bow St., WC2B 5QZ, tel. 0171/836–8305, fax 0171/497– 0064. 26 rooms, 1 with bath, 23 with shower. Facilities: bar, breakfast room. AE, DC, MC, V. Tube: Covent Garden.*

£𝙁 **La Gaffe.** Italian Bernardo Stella has been welcoming the same
Hampstead guests back to these early 18th-century shepherds' cottages, a short walk from the Hampstead tube, for over a decade. Make no mistake, rooms are tiny, and the predominantly pink and beige decor isn't luxurious, but the wine bar, with (naturally) Italian food, is yours to lounge around in at all hours—there's a shelf of assorted books to borrow. Between the two "wings" is a raised patio for summer, and each room has a TV and phone. *107–111 Heath St., NW3 6SS, tel. 0171/435–8965, fax 0171/794–7592. 14 rooms with shower. Facilities: restaurant, wine bar/café. AE, MC, V. Tube: Hampstead.*

£𝙁 **Kensington Close.** This is a rarity—a reasonably priced hotel in Lon-
Kensington don that boasts a full health club with a gym, squash courts, and a large pool. There's a garden, too. Standard rooms are small but quiet, freshly decorated, and well equipped, and the hotel is easily accessible. Ask about the Leisure Break, when rooms are £10–£15 less per night and include a full English breakfast (normally not included). There is sometimes an additional 30% discount if you book your reservation 30 days in advance. *Wrights Lane, W8 5SP, tel. 0171/937–8170, fax 0171/937–8289. 532 rooms with bath. AE, DC, MC, V. Tube: High Street Kensington.*

£𝙁 **Bryanston Court.** Three 18th-century houses have been converted
West End into this traditional English family-run hotel, with an open fire and leather wing chairs in the lounge, creaky floors, and pink drapes in the small bedrooms. *56–60 Great Cumberland Pl., W1H 7FD, tel. 0171/262–3141, fax 0171/262–7248. 56 rooms with bath or shower. Facilities: restaurant, bar, lounge, satellite TV. AE, DC, MC, V. Tube: Marble Arch.*

£ **Columbia.** The public rooms in these five adjoining Victorians are as
Bayswater big as museum halls, painted in icy hues of powder blue and butter-
★ milk, or panelled in dark wood. At one end of the day they contain the most hip band du jour doing alcohol; at the other, there are sightseers sipping coffee. Rooms are clean, high-ceilinged, and sometimes very large (especially those with three or four beds), boasting park views and balconies; all have hair dryers, tea/coffeemakers, TVs, and direct dial phones. It's just a shame that teak veneer, khaki-beige-brown color schemes, and avocado bathroom suites haven't made it back into the style bible yet. *95–99 Lancaster Gate, W2 3NS, tel. 0171/402–0021, fax 0171/706–4691. 103 rooms with bath. Facilites: bar, restaurant, lounge, conference rooms. AE, MC, V. Tube: Lancaster Gate.*

£ **Morgan.** This Georgian row-house hotel, family-run, has charm and
Bloomsbury panache. Rooms are small and functionally furnished, but cheerful. The tiny, paneled breakfast room is straight out of a dollhouse. There are also four apartments with eat-in kitchens and their own phone lines. *24 Bloomsbury St., WC1B 3QJ, tel. 0171/636–3735, fax 071/323–1662. 14 rooms with shower, 4 apartments. No credit cards. Tube: Tottenham Court Road or Russell Square.*

£ **Ridgemount.** The kindly owners, Mr. and Mrs. Rees, make you feel at home. The public areas, especially the family-style breakfast

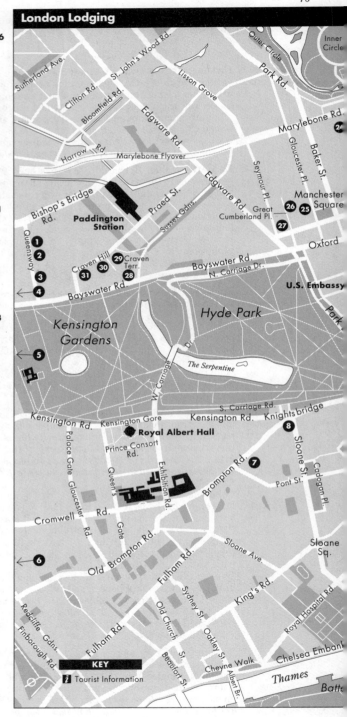

London Lodging

KEY

🛈 Tourist Information

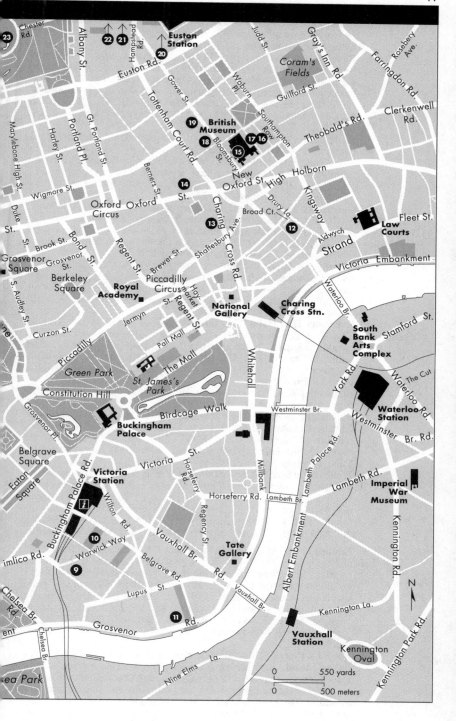

room, have a friendly, cluttered Victorian feel. Some rooms overlook a leafy garden. *65 Gower St., WC1E 6HG, tel. 0171/636–1141. 15 rooms, none with bath. Facilities: lounge. No credit cards. Tube: Tottenham Court Road.*

£ **Ruskin.** Immediately opposite the British Museum, this family-owned hotel is both pleasant and quiet—thanks to its double-glazed windows. Rooms are clean, though somewhat lacking in character; back rooms overlook a pretty garden. Notice the country-scene mural (c. 1808) in the lounge. *23–24 Montague St., WC1B 5BN, tel. 0171/636–7388, fax 0171/323–1662. 35 rooms, 7 with shower. AE, DC, MC, V. Tube: Russell Square.*

£ **St. Margaret's.** Set in a tree-lined Georgian street, this hotel has
★ been run by a friendly Italian family for many years. Its spacious rooms, towering ceilings, and prime location by Russell Square are highlights. The back rooms have a garden view. *24 Bedford Pl., WC1B 5JL, tel. 0171/636–4277. 64 rooms, 10 with bath or shower. No credit cards. Tube: Russell Square.*

£ **Gate Hotel.** This tiny B&B, at the top of the famous Portobello Road,
Kensington/ is friendly and clean, with reasonably sized rooms with modern fur-
Notting Hill nishings that include refrigerators, TVs, and phones. *6 Portobello
Gate Rd., W11 3DG, tel. 0171/221–2403. 8 rooms, 5 with bath/showers, 1 with shared bathroom. V. Tube: Notting Hill Gate.*

£ **Vicarage.** A family concern for nearly 30 years, the Vicarage feels
★ like a real home. It's beautifully decorated, and quiet, overlooking a garden square near Kensington's shopping streets. *10 Vicarage Gate, W8 4AG, tel. 0171/229–4030. 19 rooms, without bath. No credit cards. Tube: High Street Kensington.*

£ **Lancaster Hall Hotel.** This modest place is owned by the German
Paddington YMCA, which guarantees efficiency and spotlessness. There's a bargain 20-room "youth annex" offering basic rooms with shared baths. *35 Craven Terr., W2, tel. 0171/723–9276, fax 0171/224–8343. 100 rooms, 80 with bath or shower. Facilities: restaurant, bar. MC, V. Tube: Paddington.*

£ **Elizabeth Hotel.** This little hotel, set on a quiet, pretty, early 19th-
Victoria century garden square, offers little in the way of facilities but has a convenient location and some rooms with pleasant views. The Elizabeth is situated right next to Victoria Station and is easily accessible. *37 Eccleston Sq., SW1V 1PB, tel. 0171/828–6812. 25 rooms, 7 with bath/shower, 6 shared bathrooms. No credit cards. Tube: Victoria.*

£ **Windermere Hotel.** A two-minute walk from Victoria, this porticoed white stucco corner house offers not only a convenient location but a few facilities as well. Each bedroom has a TV and a phone, and evening meals are available. Reduced-rate packages are sometimes offered. *142-144 Warwick Way, SW1V 4JE, tel. 0171/834–5163, fax 0171/630–8831. 24 rooms, 20 with bath. AE, MC, V. Tube: Victoria.*

£ **Edward Lear.** This Georgian town house, former home of the author
West End of *The Owl and the Pussycat,* is a good value because of the central location. The owner takes pride in the place and keeps the bright breakfast room and all the guest rooms spotless. Some of the triple and family rooms are huge, and rooms in the back are especially quiet; all include a sink, TV, phone, and tea/coffeemakers. *28–30 Seymour St., W1H 5WD, tel. 0171/402–5401, fax 0171/706–3766. 32 rooms, 12 with bath/shower, 7 shared bathrooms. MC, V. Tube: Marble Arch.*

£ **Hotel La Place.** This small, friendly B&B, near Sherlock Holmes's Baker Street, just across from Madame Tussaud's, is centrally placed in a quiet residential area. Although this property is on the high end of the category, a few bargain rooms in the basement are available. The French-born owner/chef and his staff convey a pleasantly European feel. All rooms are equipped with TV and minibar, and spacious twin rooms have two double beds. The wine bar/restaurant serves guests 24 hours. *17 Nottingham Pl., W1M 3FB, tel.*

0171/486–2323, fax 0171/486–4335. 24 rooms with bath. AE, DC, MC, V. Tube: Baker Street.

£ **Wigmore Court Hotel.** This centrally located lodging, situated practically next to Marble Arch, offers some small double rooms at a cheaper rate. Regardless of the size of your room, you're still getting a good value; all units have a private bathroom, TV, and phone. Rooms that face the front have double-pane windows to reduce the traffic noise. *23 Gloucester Pl., W1H 3PB, tel. 0171/935–0928, fax 0171/487–4254. 16 rooms with bath. MC, V. Tube: Marble Arch.*

¢ **Central London Accommodations.** From their personally inspected
B&Bs pool of private-home B&Bs, Peter and Vera Forrest will select one within your budget, and in the area you prefer, and handle the booking. Calling to discuss your requirements is a good idea. Their own B&B, Forrest House, is perennially full of repeat guests who have become virtual family. *83 Addison Gardens, W14 0DT, tel. 0171/ 602–9668, fax 0171/602–5609. B&Bs in most neighborhoods. Facilities vary. AE, MC, V.*

¢ **Central Club.** This YWCA is slightly more expensive than the aver-
Bloomsbury age, but considering the amenities, the rates are actually quite reasonable. Included in the cost is free access to the excellent sports facilities, such as the large pool, gym equipment, and aerobics, yoga, and martial arts classes. Also, the "central" in the name is no misnomer: This facility is a short walk from theaters, shops, and the British Museum. Rooms are clean, if basic, and a coffee shop, laundry, and hairdresser are on the lower floors. Boarders must be at least 18 years old. *16–22 Great Russell St., WC1B 3LR, tel. 0171/ 636–7512 (ask for Reservations Manager), fax 0171/636–5278. 104 rooms, 25 shared bathrooms. No credit cards. Tube: Tottenham Court Road.*

¢ **John Adams Hall.** This group of Georgian houses has been converted into student accommodations that are available at bargain rates during school vacations. There is nothing luxurious about it, but it's a short walk to the British Museum, and Euston Station is across the street. *15–23 Endsleigh St., WC1H 0DH, tel. 0171/387–4086 or 4796 (ask for Ms. S. Waller), fax 0171/383–0164. 148 rooms (of which 126 are singles), 28 shared bathrooms. No credit cards. Closed Feb., May, Oct.–Nov. Tube: Euston.*

¢ **Primrose Hill B&B.** Members of this small B&B believe "traveling
Hampstead shouldn't be a rip-off" and invite guests into their very beautiful homes at reasonable rates to prove it. All houses are in and around Primrose Hill and Hampstead, and guests receive a latchkey. Booking well ahead is essential. Phone or write for more details. *Contact Gail O'Farrell, 14 Edis St., NW1 8LG, tel. 0171/722–6869. Approximately 15 rooms with varying facilities. No credit cards.*

¢ **Holland House.** Though this is a proper youth hostel, complete with
Holland Park an 11 PM curfew, a 68-year-old man was staying here when we visited. Based in a historic Jacobean manor (plus a modern extension), Holland House is in one of London's prettiest parks. The set-up is dormitory-style, with 10–26 beds per room, and you are required to be out from 10 AM to 5 PM, so the setting is clearly this hostel's draw. Rates are as low as £14 per person. *Holland Walk, W8 7QU, tel. 0171/937–0748, fax 0171/376–0667. 186 beds: 13 dormitory rooms, 1 double room, 38 bathrooms. No credit cards. Tube: Holland Park.*

¢ **Regents College.** The nicest thing about this converted Regency
Regent's Park mansion is that it's right in the middle of green and glorious Regent's Park, which at least half the rooms overlook. Again, this is an off-duty student accommodation, so it's all somewhat communal, with bunk beds in many rooms and eight showers per bathroom. On the plus side, the college has its own café, bar, cafeteria, tennis courts, and weight room. In the summer, the park is the center of London softball, so bring your mitt. *Inner Circle, Regent's Park, NW1 4NS, tel. 0171/487–7483. 82 rooms, 9 shower rooms, 5 bathrooms. No credit cards. Closed Oct.–Nov. and Feb.–Apr. Tube: Baker Street.*

Splurges

Knightsbridge **Basil Street.** This gracious Edwardian hotel has been family-run for nearly eight decades. Each room is different—antiques-filled, and amazingly quiet—and the smaller doubles without bath are affordable at around £80. This is a good choice for families because children under 16 stay free in their parents' room and family suites are not prohibitively priced. You can write letters home in the peaceful Gallery, which has polished wooden floors and fine Turkish carpets. This is a true "period" hotel. *Basil St., SW3 1AH, tel. 0171/581–3311, fax 0171/581–3693. 92 rooms. 72 with bath. Facilities: restaurant, wine bar. AE, DC, MC, V. Tube: Knightsbridge.*

Notting Hill Gate ★ **Portobello.** In London's most vibrant, arty neighborhood is this very special 25-year-old hotel. Inside is a dream of a Victorian fantasy, cross-pollinated with a Moroccan souk. It's always attracted hip Hollywood people, lots of music biz (including the stars), and, of course, the fashion pack adore it—for the never-closed bar as much as the damask duvets and round-bedded suite. Think Mick Jagger in *Performance*, and you'll be on the right track. The "cabin" rooms are minute, but are bargains at £60; doubles start at £100. *22 Stanley Gardens, W11 2NG, tel. 0171/727–2777, fax 0171/792–9641. 25 rooms with bath. Facilities: restaurant, bar. AE, DC, MC, V. Closed 10 days over Christmas. Tube: Notting Hill Gate.*

Pimlico **Dolphin Square.** This unique Art Deco quadrangle, situated by the Thames has peaceful, modern, self-catering apartments starting at £130. A studio apartment (with kitchenette) costs around £25 less than a two-room unit. Features include a large swimming pool and bar, a tennis court, a very stylish brasserie, and a row of shops. The Dolphin Square is a five-minute drive from Westminster and a five-minute walk from the tube. *Dolphin Sq., SW1V 3LX, tel. 0171/834–3800, fax 0171/798–8735. 152 apartments with bath. AE, DC, MC, V. Tube: Pimlico.*

South Kensington **Claverley.** As gorgeous to look at as it is friendly, the Claverley's rates are most reasonable for the neighborhood. They include a gargantuan English breakfast, and an exuberant decorating style— some rooms have four-posters, or *toile de Jouy* walls and drapes set off by colors of coral and teal and dove, with Georgian prints and mahogany bureaus. *13–14 Beaufort Gardens, SW3 1PS, tel. 0171/589–8541, fax 0171/584–3410. 31 rooms with bath. AE, V. Tube: South Kensington.*

West End **Hazlitt's.** It's an open secret that Hazlitt's is a disarmingly friendly place, full of personality. Robust antiques are everywhere, assorted prints crowd every wall, and every room has a Victorian claw-foot bath in its bathroom. Book way ahead—this is the London address of media people and antiques dealers everywhere. *6 Frith St., W1V 5TZ, tel. 0171/434–1771, fax 0171/439–1524. 23 rooms with bath. AE, DC, MC, V. Tube: Tottenham Court Road/Leicester Square.*

Dining

The following selection of eating places, from modest cafés to celebrated restaurants, has been chosen for their value.

Unless otherwise noted, reservations are not needed. In general, casual chic or informal dress is acceptable in most establishments. Highly recommended restaurants are indicated by a star ★.

Prices are per person for a three-course meal, excluding drinks, service, or VAT.

££ **Bertorelli's.** Right across from the stage door of the Royal Opera
Bloomsbury House, Bertorelli's is quietly chic, the food better than ever with
and Covent Maddalena Bonnino (formerly of 192, *see below*) in charge. Poached
Garden cotechino sausage with lentils; monkfish ragout with fennel, tomato
★ and olives; and garganelli with French beans, cob nuts, and Parmesan are typical dishes. Downstairs is a very relaxed, inexpensive
wine bar serving a simpler menu of pizza, pasta, salads, and a few
big dishes and daily specials. *44A Floral St., tel. 0171/836–3969.
Reservations required. AE, DC, MC, V. Closed Christmas. Tube:
Covent Garden.*

££ **Joe Allen's.** This well-known, brick-walled basement follows the
★ style of its New York counterpart, and is similarly frequented by
theater folk. The ribs these days come with trendy wilted greens
and black-eyed peas, but you can still order great burgers and fries,
plus brownies and ice cream. *13 Exeter St., tel. 0171/836–0651. Reservations required. No credit cards. Closed Dec. 25–26. Tube: Covent Garden.*

££ **Museum Street Café.** This convenient restaurant near the British
Museum serves impeccably fresh dishes, charged prix fixe. The evening menu might feature chargrilled, maize-fed chicken with pesto,
followed by a rich chocolate cake; at lunchtime you might choose a
sandwich of Stilton on walnut bread and a big bowl of soup. Repeat
customers, prepare for a shock—the place has doubled in size, and
you no longer have to bring your own wine, but there's still an atypi-
cal (for London) ban on smoking. *47 Museum St., tel. 0171/405–
3211. Reservations required for dinner. No credit cards. Closed
weekends, public holidays. Tube: Holborn.*

££ **Porters.** Good British food (really), an Olde Worlde public house interior, a nob owner (the Earl of Bradford), and a reasonable check,
with vegetables and service included—no wonder Americans invariably like this place. Pies star on the menu—lamb-and-apricot or
chicken-and-chili alongside the traditional fish or steak-and-kidney—with steamed sponges and custard for dessert. *17 Henrietta
St., WC2, tel. 0171/836–6466. Reservations required for weekend
dinner. AE, MC, V. Closed Christmas. Tube: Covent Garden.*

££ **Quality Chop House.** At the very bottom of this price range, this
City trendy little place in a beautifully restored Victorian café has
reinvented caff food for refined palates. The bangers and mash
might be homemade veal sausages accompanied by perfect, fluffy
creamed potatoes, and wine is offered instead of stewed tea. The oak
pews are not comfortable, but the jolly atmosphere is. *94
Farringdon Rd., tel. 0171/837–5093. Reservations advised. No
credit cards. Closed Sun., Mon. dinner, Sat. lunch, public holidays. Tube: Farringdon.*

££ **St. John.** This former smokehouse (ham, not cigars) of soaring white
★ walls, stone floors, and plain wooden chairs would be bleak, but for
the nattering crowds. They're here for the buzz and the achingly
trendy food—roast bone marrow and parsley salad; smoked eel,
beetroot, and horseradish; deviled crab—which is practically a par-
ody of Britishness, often looks shockingly nude and lumpen, but
tastes great. An all-French wine list has plenty of affordable bottles, service is efficiently matey, and the pastry chef's chocolate
slice belongs in the brownie hall of fame. *26 St John St., EC1, tel.
0171/251–0848. Reservations required. AE, MC, V. Closed Sun.
dinner, Christmas. Tube: Farringdon.*

££ **192.** A noisy, buzzy wine bar/restaurant just off the Portobello Road,
Kensington and this is as much a social hangout for the local media mafia as anything.
Notting Hill Food likes to keep ahead of fashion, and is best on the appetizer
Gate list—many people order two of these instead of an entrée (try the
risottos, the seasonal salad, the fish—sea bass with fennel, lemon,
and rosemary—or whatever sounds unusual), which also lowers the
check. *192 Kensington Park Rd., W11, tel. 0171/229–0482. Reservations required. AE, MC, V. Closed Sun. dinner, national holidays.
Tube: Notting Hill Gate.*

££ **Lou Pescadou.** Walking into this Provençal restaurant is like cross-
Knightsbridge ing the Channel to France. As befits the heavily boat-theme decor,
and South fish is the specialty. Typical dishes are *petite bouillabaisse* (fish
Kensington soup), or poached red mullet in tarragon sauce. *241 Old Brompton
Rd., tel. 0171/370–1057. AE, DC, MC, V. Closed Sun., Aug.,
Christmas. Tube: South Kensington.*

PJ's Bar and Grill. A very friendly place, PJ's has polo memorabilia
on the white walls, wooden floorboards, and stained-glass windows.
Eat large amounts of all-American specialties, such as soft-shell
crab, gumbo, steak, and salads, and wash them down with any cocktail ever invented, mixed by expert bartenders. *52 Fulham Rd., tel.
0171/581–0025. Reservations advised on weekends. AE, DC, MC,
V. Closed Christmas. Tube: South Kensington.*

££ **Quaglino's.** Glamour, taste (in every sense) and a check that just
St. James's squeezes into an "Affordable" guide, this famous pre–World War II
★ restaurant was resurrected in '93, bigger and better than ever, by
Sir Terence Conran of Habitat, Bibendum, and Pont de la Tour fame.
Eat fashionable pan-European food (rabbit with prosciutto and
herbs; plateau de fruits de mer); stare; be stared at; enjoy. *16 Bury
St., SW1, tel. 0171/930–6767. Reservations required. AE, DC, MC,
V. Tube: Green Park.*

££ **Bistrot Bruno.** A star chef in affordable guise, the former Four Sea-
Soho sons' 3-Michelin-starred Bruno Loubet here offers his justly famous
★ *cuisine de terroir.* Nonfoodies should steer clear of fromage de tête
(brawn, or pig's head in aspic) and tripe niçoise (cow's stomach), and
try, perhaps, duck leg confit with crushed potato and cepe sauce. *63
Frith St., W1, tel. 0171/734–4545. Reservations required. Closed
Sat. lunch, Sun., Christmas. Tube: Leicester Square.*

££ **dell'Ugo.** Chef/restaurateur Antony Worrall Thompson has a knack
for knowing what London wants to eat—and at this arty, three-
floor Soho place, that means Mediterranean dishes like bruschetta;
spicy sausages with white bean casserole; crunchy chicken with garlic potatoes; overstuffed deli sandwiches (at around £6); or just a kir
and garlic bread. The ground floor's a café/wine bar. *56 Frith St.,
W1, tel. 0171/734–8300. Reservations advised for restaurant. AE,
MC, V. Closed Sun., Christmas. Tube: Leicester Square.*

££ **Fung Shing.** This comfortable, mint green restaurant is a cut above
the Chinatown crowd in service and ambience, as well as food preparation. The standard offerings are supplemented by unusual dishes,
such as fried intestines (better than they sound!) and the delicious
salt-baked chicken. *15 Lisle St., tel. 0171/437–1539. Reservations
advised. AE, DC, MC, V. Closed Christmas. Tube: Leicester
Square.*

££ **Soho Soho.** Stuck on a corner and apparently built of glass, you can't
miss this lively place. The ground floor is a café-bar with a rotisserie
at the rear (upstairs is a formal restaurant) that serves flavorsome
Provençal-influenced food that matches the decor. Omelets, charcu-
terie, and cheeses supplement the main menu, which includes wild
mushroom risotto with shaved Parmesan and Provençal beef stew.
*11–13 Frith St., tel. 0171/494–3491. Reservations required for up-
stairs restaurant. AE, DC, MC, V. Closed Sun., Christmas. Tube:
Leicester Square.*

£ **Camden Brasserie.** Brick walls, wood floors, and spotlights set the
Camden Town tone in this exemplary, relaxed brasserie popular with media folk.
Try charbroiled beef brochette marinated in ginger and lime, or the
fresh fish of the day. Downstairs is **The Underground Café,** a pastel-
colored, modern basement dining room serving regional Italian
fare. The location is very near Camden Lock. *214–216 Camden High
St., tel. 0171/482–2114. Reservations advised. MC, V. Closed public
holidays. Tube: Camden Town.*

££ **The Hermitage.** The French owners at this homey coffee house–
Covent Garden cum-restaurant make you feel welcome, even if you don't want a full
and meal. For those who do, good regional dishes and daily specials are
Bloomsbury offered. Near various branches of the University of London, it's pop-

ular with both students and their professors, and children are welcome. *19 Leigh St., tel. 0171/387–8034. Reservations advised. MC, V. Closed Christmas. Tube: Russell Square.*

££ **Maxwell's.** Not to be confused with its Hampstead sister, which was London's first-ever burger place, this new dive under the Opera House does the kind of food you're homesick for—quesadillas and nachos, Buffalo wings, barbecued ribs, Cajun chicken and shrimp, chef's salad, and a real New York City Reuben. *8–9 James St., WC2, tel. 0171/836–0303. Reservations advised weekends. AE, DC, V. Closed Christmas. Tube: Covent Garden.*

££ **Bistrot 190.** Another place to enjoy the robust, vivid European peasant cooking of Antony Worrall Thompson (*see* dell'Ugo, *above*) this light, attractive dining room, adorned with hundreds of prints, is not far from the museums and is especially convenient if you're coming from or going to the Albert Hall. **Downstairs at 190** (guess where it is; tel. 0171/581–5666) is also Thompson's, and is for fish and seafood fiends. Watch the check, or you'll make it bust this price range. *190 Queensgate, tel. 0171/581–5666. Reservations advised. AE, MC, V. Closed public holidays. Tube: High Street Kensington.*

Kensington, South Kensington, Knightsbridge, Notting Hill Gate

££ **Daquise.** It's possible to spend considerably less than £20 for a meal at this corner of South Ken that is forever Warsaw. Daquise has been serving filling Polish staples, such as kielbasa (garlic sausage) and pierogi (a kind of ravioli), and tea and cakes for more than 40 years. It's not smartly decorated, but it is much loved and convenient to the museums. *20 Thurloe St., tel. 0171/589–6117. Reservations advised. No credit cards. Closed Christmas. Tube: South Kensington.*

££ **Khan's.** An institution, this spacious north Indian restaurant is always packed. Upmarket decor of trompe l'oeil skies and palms and downmarket prices ensure its popularity. The rich and delicious butter chicken is a favorite dish. *13-15 Westbourne Grove, tel. 0171/727–5420. Reservations advised. AE, DC, MC, V. Closed Christmas. Tube: Bayswater.*

£ **Luba's Bistro.** Russian cuisine, such as chicken Kiev and beef Stroganoff, is served at long wooden tables; bring your own wine. *6 Yeoman's Row, tel. 0171/589–2950. Reservations advised. MC, V. Closed Sun., Christmas, national holidays. Tube: Knightsbridge.*

Soho

£ **Melati.** A gigantic menu features great Malaysian food, with lots of options for vegetarians, such as the *tahu telor* (bean curd omelet). Londoners find this place in their student days and they never give it up, so there are usually big groups around the pine tables, with corresponding amounts of noise and merriment. *21 Great Windmill St., tel. 0171/437–2745. Reservations advised. AE, DC, MC, V. Closed Christmas. Tube: Leicester Square.*

West End

£ **Café Fish.** This bustling restaurant has a wonderful selection of fish, from trout and halibut to turbot and shark, arranged on the menu according to cooking method—meunière, steamed, broiled, or baked; smoked fish pâté and crusty bread are included with the cover charge, and there's often a pianist. *39 Panton St., tel. 0171/930–3999. Reservations advised. AE, DC, MC, V. Closed Sat. lunch, Sun., Christmas. Tube: Piccadilly Circus.*

£ **Chicago Pizza Pie Factory.** An inexpensive, Chicago-style place serving enormous deep-dish pies with the usual toppings, in a wood-floored basement, loud with the sounds of WJMK, the Windy City's oldies station. The rest rooms are labeled "Elton John" and "Olivia Newton John." *17 Hanover Sq., tel. 0171/629–2669. Reservations advised for lunch. No credit cards. Closed for Christmas. Tube: Oxford Circus.*

£ ★ **Criterion.** This palatial neo-Byzantine mirrored marble hall, which first opened in 1874, is now back on the map with an unpretentious "nouveau Brit" menu (grilled squid on spinach with lemon vinaigrette; cod and crab cakes; sticky toffee pudding), and a generous attitude toward set-priced dining: About half the dishes on the main menu are offered at £10 for two courses, any time. *Piccadilly Cir-*

cus, W1, tel. 0171/925–0909. Reservations advised. AE, DC, MC, V. Closed Christmas. Tube: Piccadilly.

£ **Down Mexico Way.** Here's an atmospheric place that's decorated with beautiful Spanish ceramic tiles and serves better-than-average Mexican food. Try fish in almond-chili sauce with spiced spinach. Avoid weekend evenings if you want a quiet night out. *25 Swallow St., tel. 0171/437–9895. Reservations advised evenings. AE, MC, V. Closed Christmas. Tube: Piccadilly Circus.*

£ **L'Artiste Musclé.** This charming wine bar/restaurant, where dining rooms occupy two cozy levels, is in the style of a Parisian bistro. The *cuisine bourgeoise* menu features steak with baked potato, stews, and casseroles. The tone is friendly and fun. *1 Shepherd Market, tel. 0171/493–6150. Reservations for parties of 6 or more. AE, MC, V. Closed Sun. lunch, public holidays. Tube: Green Park.*

¢ **North Sea Fish Restaurant.** This is the place for good old British
Bloomsbury fish-and-chips—battered and deep-fried whitefish with thick-cut fries. It's a bit tricky to find—head south down Judd Street 3 blocks from St. Pancras station. *7–8 Leigh St., tel. 0171/387–5892. Reservations advised. AE, DC, MC, V. Closed Sun., Christmas, national holidays. Tube: Russell Square.*

¢ **Pizza Express.** London's best pizza chain, with many branches, serves the usual toppings on a thin, crispy, authentic Italian base. Also offered are a few uninteresting salads. *30 Coptic St., tel. 0171/636–3232. Reservations advised. AE, DC, MC, V. Closed Christmas. Tube: Tottenham Court Road.*

¢ **Wagamama.** London's gone wild for Japanese noodles, and this ul-
★ tra-popular, high-tech café does them best. Ramen, in soup, topped with meat or fish, are supplemented by rice dishes, and curries, plus "raw energy" dishes for the jaded. Canteen-style, you will have to share a table, and stand on a fast-moving line to get in. *4 Streatham St., WC1, tel. 0171/323–9223. No reservations. No credit cards. Closed Christmas. Tube: Tottenham Court Road.*

¢ **Bar Gansa.** This award-winning Camden Town tapas bar can be
Camden Town packed and noisy, but that's because the *patatas bravas* (spiced potato), *boquerones* (marinated anchovies), *tortilla* (potato omelet), and other little Spanish dishes are so good. *2 Inverness St., tel. 0171/267–8909. MC, V. Closed public holidays. Tube: Camden Town.*

¢ **The Eagle.** Excellent Italian food is served in this comfortable pub.
City Food and ambience here are as good as at the swanky, trendy places popping up everywhere, but at a fraction of the price. *159 Farringdon Rd., tel. 0171/837–1352. No credit cards. Closed Christmas. Tube: Farringdon Road.*

¢ **Diana's Diner.** This very popular café serves generous portions of ri-
Covent Garden sotto, grills (broiled meat), roasts, and stuffed baked potatoes. There are tables outside for alfresco dining at lunchtime. Diana's closes at 7 PM. *39 Endell St., tel. 0171/240–0272. No credit cards. Closed Sun. dinner, public holidays. Tube: Covent Garden.*

¢ **Fatboy's Diner.** One for the kids, this is a 1941 trailer transplanted from the banks of the Susquehanna River in Pennsylvania. Fifties jukebox raves accompany the dogs, burgers, and fries. *21 Maiden La., WC2, tel. 0171/240–1902. No reservations. No credit cards. Closed Christmas. Tube: Covent Garden or Leicester Square.*

¢ **Food for Thought.** The lines outside this self-service vegetarian café attest to the quality and quantity of the imaginative hot dishes, salads, and cakes. Come here for a quick meal, though, as it's not an especially comfortable place to sit around. Food for Thought closes at 8 PM. *31 Neal St., tel. 0171/836–0239. No credit cards. Closed Sun., public holidays. Tube: Covent Garden.*

¢ **Stockpot.** The older sister of the Panton Street branch (*see below*),
Knightsbridge this one is just as popular. It retains a peculiarly '60s feel. *6 Basil St., tel. 0171/589–8627. No credit cards. Closed public holidays. Tube: Knightsbridge.*

¢ **Geales.** Here you'll find some of the best fish-and-chips in London,
Notting Hill though not the cheapest, since this is a proper restaurant, with some
Gate outdoor tables. *2 Farmer St., tel. 0171/727–7969. Reservations advised. MC, V. Closed Sun. and Mon., public holidays. Tube: Notting Hill Gate.*

¢ **Tootsies.** Good burgers are cheerfully served in a dark restaurant brightened by vintage advertisements and vintage rock. Big salads, BLTs, chicken, and chili are also on the menu; pies and ice cream for dessert. *120 Holland Park Ave., tel. 0171/229–8567. No reservations. MC, V. Closed Christmas. Tube: Holland Park.*

¢ **Ed's Easy Diner.** This '50s-style, all-glass pit stop is another favorite
Soho burger spot (along with its three other branches). Cheese fries, brownies, and a Bud might make homesick Americans feel at home. *12 Moor St., tel. 0171/439–1955. No credit cards. Closed public holidays. Tube: Leicester Square.*

¢ **Lorelei.** This tiny, dark café serves the best pizza in town for the price. Other dishes are also of good value. Bring your own wine. *21 Bateman St., tel. 0171/734–0954. No credit cards. Closed Sun., public holidays. Tube: Leicester Square.*

¢ **Pollo.** A favorite haunt for hip club animals and fashion students, this is the place for both great pasta and people-watching. Come for lunch and stick to soup, pasta, or risotto; the meat dishes aren't so reliable. *20 Old Compton St., tel. 0171/734–5917. No credit cards. Closed Sun., public holidays. Tube: Leicester Square.*

¢ **Tai Wing Wa.** This does good dim sum for beginners—that is, there's a menu, *and* it's in English, *and* the waiters are friendly. *7–9 Newport Pl., W1, tel. 0171/287–2702. Reservations advised. AE, DC, MC, V. Closed Sat., Christmas. Tube: Leicester Square.*

¢ **The Fountain.** Pastel shades set the cool tone at this elegant restau-
West End rant at the back of Fortnum and Mason's, which offers light meals,
★ toasted snacks, sandwiches, and ice cream sodas. Go for Welsh rarebit or cold game pie by day, fillet steak by night; great for pretheater meals or ice cream sundaes after Royal Academy or Bond Street window-shopping. *181 Piccadilly, tel. 0171/734–4938. Reservations accepted for dinner only. AE, DC, MC, V. Closed Sun., national holidays. Tube: Green Park.*

¢ **The Granary.** This superior self-service restaurant offers hearty casseroles, vegetarian dishes, large salads, and satisfying desserts. In the summer you can sit at a table outside, and there is takeout year-round. It gets very crowded at lunchtime, and it closes at 8 PM. *39 Albermarle St., tel. 0171/493–2979. No reservations. No credit cards. Closed Sat. dinner, Sun., public holidays. Tube: Green Park.*

¢ **Stockpot.** In the evening, this otherwise basic place fills up with theater people who come for one of the best bargain dinners around. Food is plentiful, unpretentious, hot, and cheap: Choose among items such as moussaka, chicken casserole, or shepherd's pie for lunch; broiled steak, fish, or veal for dinner. There are other Stockpots at 18 Old Compton St. (tel. 071/287–1066) and 273 King's Rd. (tel. 071/823–3175). *40 Panton St., tel. 0171/839–5142. Reservations advised. No credit cards. Closed public holidays. Tube: Piccadilly Circus.*

Splurges

Covent **The Ivy.** An unpretentious, stylish hangout with generous portions
Garden of updated classic dishes from practically everywhere. For under £40 you'll get a three-course dinner with drinks. Enjoy fashionable food from around the world, such as black tagliatelle, roast grouse, shrimp gumbo, or braised oxtail, in the company of sophisticated gossip-column fillers. *1 West St., W1, tel. 0171/836–4751. Reservations required. AE, DC, MC, V. Closed national holidays. Tube: Leicester Square.*

Holland Park **The Belvedere.** There can be no finer setting for a summer's evening supper or a sunny Sunday brunch than a window table—or a balcony one if you luck out—at this stunning restaurant in the middle of Holland Park. The menu is big on shaved Parmesan, sun-dried tomatoes, and arugula, which suits the conservatorylike room, but both food and service do occasionally miss the target. Still, with a view like this, who cares about water glasses or bland chicken? *Holland Park, off Abbotsbury Rd., W8, tel. 0171/602–1238. Reservations required weekends. AE, DC, MC, V. Closed Sun. dinner, Christmas.*

Kensington **Kensington Place.** The local glitterati make this high-tech palace a noisy and chic setting for some of London's most fashionable food—grilled foie gras with sweet-corn pancake, for instance. On the average, a three-course dinner and wine costs under £40. *201 Kensington Church St., tel. 0171/727–3184. Reservations advised. MC, V. Closed bank holidays, Christmas. Tube: Notting Hill Gate.*

Tower Bridge **Le Pont de la Tour.** This '30s liner-style riverside restaurant—Sir Terence Conran's previous pièce de résistance (before Quaglino's, that is)—comes into its own in summer, when the outside tables are heaven. Fish and seafood (lobster salad; roast halibut with aioli), and meat and game (venison fillet with port and blueberry sauce) feature heavily; vegetarians are out of luck. An à la carte meal here could set you back £45, but the set lunch is a mere £26.50. Or else, an impeccable salade niçoise in the adjacent Brasserie is about £9. *36D Shad Thames, Butler's Wharf, SE1, tel. 0171/403–8403. Reservations required for lunch, weekend dinner. MC, V. Closed Christmas. Tube: Tower Hill.*

Pubs

Pubs are a great option if you're traveling on a budget. You can often get hearty portions of typical English fare, such as shepherd's pie or a ploughman's lunch (bread, cheese, and pickles), at inexpensive prices, as well as fairly inexpensive ales and beers. Also, these establishments sometimes have live entertainment that's free to the patron. Remember, however, that most pubs do not accept credit cards.

Black Friar. A step from Blackfriars tube, this pub has an arts-and-crafts interior that is entertainingly, satirically ecclesiastical, with inlaid mother-of-pearl, wood carvings, stained glass, and marble pillars all over the place, and reliefs of monks and friars poised above finely lettered temperance tracts. Regardless of all this, there are six beers on tap. *174 Queen Victoria St., EC4, tel. 0171/236–5650. Tube: Blackfriars.*

Dove Inn. Read the list of famous ex-regulars, from Charles II and Nell Gwynn (mere rumor, but a likely one) to Ernest Hemingway, as you line up for ages for a beer at this very popular, very comely 16th-century riverside pub by Hammersmith Bridge. If it's *too* full, stroll upstream to the Old Ship or the Blue Anchor. *19 Upper Mall, W6, tel. 0181/748–5405. Tube: Hammersmith.*

French House. In the pub where the French Resistance convened during World War II, Soho hipsters and eccentrics rub shoulders now. More than shoulders, actually, because this tiny, tricolor-waving, photograph-lined pub is always full to bursting. There's an excellent restaurant upstairs. *49 Dean St., W1, tel. 0171/437–2799. Tube: Leicester Square.*

George Inn. The inn sits in a courtyard where Shakespeare's plays were once performed. The present building dates from the late 17th century and is central London's last remaining galleried inn. Dickens was a regular—the inn is featured in *Little Dorrit.* Entertainments include Shakespeare performances, medieval jousts, and morris dancing. *77 Borough High St., SE1, tel. 0171/407–2056. Tube: Borough.*

The Lamb. Another of Dickens's locals is now a picturesque place for a summer pint, when you can drink on the patio. *94 Lamb's Conduit St., WC1, tel. 0171/405–0713. Tube: Holborn.*

Lamb and Flag. This 17th-century pub was once known as "The Bucket of Blood," because the upstairs room was used as a ring for bare-knuckle boxing. Now, it's a trendy, friendly, and entirely bloodless pub, serving food (at lunchtime only) and real ale. It's on the edge of Covent Garden, off Garrick Street. *33 Rose St., WC2, tel. 0171/836–4108. Tube: Covent Garden.*

Mayflower. An atmospheric 17th-century riverside inn, with exposed beams and a terrace, this is practically the very place from which the Pilgrims set sail for Plymouth Rock. The inn is licensed to sell American postage stamps alongside its superior pub food. *117 Rotherhithe St., SE16, tel. 0171/237–4088. Tube: Rotherhithe.*

Museum Tavern. Across the street from the British Museum, this gloriously Victorian pub makes an ideal resting place after the rigors of the culture trail. With lots of fancy glass—etched mirrors and stained glass panels—gilded pillars, and carvings, the heavily restored hostelry once helped Karl Marx to unwind after a hard day in the Library. He could have spent his capital on any one of six beers available on tap. *49 Great Russell St., WC1, tel. 0171/242–8987. Tube: Tottenham Court Road.*

Pheasant and Firkin. David Bruce single-handedly revived the practice of serving beer that's been brewed on the premises (then sold the thriving business), and this is one of his jolly microbrewery/pubs, all named the something and Firkin (a small barrel), serving beers called "dogbolter" or "rail ale," and selling T-shirts printed with *bons mots* like "I had a Pheasant time at the Firkin pub." Students like this a lot. *166 Goswell Rd., EC1, tel. 0171/235–7429. Tube: Old Street.*

Sherlock Holmes. This pub used to be known as the Northumberland Arms, and Arthur Conan Doyle popped in regularly for a pint. It figures in *The Hound of the Baskervilles,* and you can see the hound's head and plaster casts of its huge paws among other Holmes memorabilia in the bar. *10 Northumberland St., WC2, tel. 0171/930–2644. Tube: Charing Cross.*

Ye Olde Cheshire Cheese. Yes, it is a tourist trap, but this most historic of all London pubs (it dates from 1667) deserves a visit anyway, for its sawdust-covered floors, low wood-beamed ceilings, the 14th-century crypt of Whitefriars' monastery under the cellar bar, and the set of 17th-century pornographic tiles upstairs. This was the most regular of Dr. Johnson's and Dickens's *many* locals. *145 Fleet St., EC4, tel. 0171/353–6170. Tube: Aldwych.*

Wine Bars

★ **Archduke.** This is one of the few places convenient for post–South Bank dinners. It's built into the railway arches under Hungerford Bridge beside the Festival Hall. The food ranges from substantial hot meals to salad bar standards and is pretty good; sausages from many countries are a specialty. *153 Concert Hall Approach, tel. 0171/928–9370. Tube: Waterloo.*

Truckles of Pied Bull Yard. This is a wine bar, but with a difference. There's plenty of outdoor seating, ideal for summer visitors to the British Museum nearby who want to have their lunch in the sun. *Pied Bull Yard, off Bury Pl., tel. 0171/404–5334. AE, DC, MC, V. No dinner Sat. Closed Sun. Tube: Holborn.*

Afternoon Tea

The best excuse to dress up and stuff yourself with cakes is to partake of a glamourous afternoon tea. You get a five-star experience for the price of a pub lunch.

Claridges is the real McCoy, with liveried footmen proffering sandwiches, a scone, and superior patisseries (£12.50) in the palatial yet genteel Foyer, to the sound of the resident "Hungarian orchestra" (actually a string quartet). *Brook St., W1, tel. 0171/629–8860. Tea served daily 3–5. Tube: Bond St.*

Fortnum & Mason's. Upstairs at the queen's grocer's, three set teas are ceremoniously offered: standard Afternoon Tea (sandwiches, scone, cakes, £9.50), old-fashioned High Tea (the traditional nursery meal, adding something more robust and savoury, £11.50), and Champagne Tea (£13). *St James's Restaurant, 4th fl. 181 Piccadilly W1, tel. 0171/734–8040. Tea served Mon.–Sat. 3–5:20. Tube: Piccadilly Circus.*

Harrods. One for sweet-toothed and greedy people, the Georgian Room at the ridiculously well-known department store has a serve-it-yourself afternoon tea *buffet* that'll give you a sugar rush for a week. *Brompton Rd. SW3, tel. 0171/730–1234. Tea served Mon.–Sat. 3–5:30. Tube: Knightsbridge.*

The Ritz. The Ritz's new owners have put the once-peerless Palm Court tea back on the map, with proper tiered cake stands and silver pots, a harpist and Louis seize chaises, plus a leisurely four-hour time slot. A good excuse for a glass of champagne. Reservations are taken only to 50% capacity. *Piccadilly W1, tel. 0171/493–8181. Tea served daily 2–6. Tube: Green Park.*

Savoy. The glamorous Thames-side hotel does one of the pleasantest teas, its triple-tiered cakestands packed with goodies, its tailcoated waiters thrillingly polite. *The Strand WC2, tel. 0171/836–4343. Tea served daily 3–5:30. Tube: Aldwych.*

The Arts and Nightlife

The Arts

For a schedule of London arts events, consult the weekly magazine *Time Out*, good for both mainstream and fringe—London's equivalent to Off-Broadway—events. The *Evening Standard* carries listings, as do the major Sunday papers, the daily *Independent* and *Guardian*, and Friday's *Times*.

Generally speaking, tickets for West End (equivalent to Broadway) theaters are horribly expensive, though prices do not always reflect the quality of the production. Musicals are the most expensive, followed by first-run plays with star actors; shows at the Royal Shakespeare Company, Royal National Theatre, and Old Vic can be seen for relatively modest outlays and tend to be good bets. Student standby seats are not always just for students. These are returned or unsold tickets that go on sale at a discount either shortly before curtain time, or first thing in the morning. Costs vary and some theaters keep a block in reserve for students, too. Check listings for the best deals.

Theater Most theaters have a matinee twice a week (Wednesday or Thursday and Saturday) and nightly performances at 7:30 or 8, except Sunday. Prices vary; expect to pay from £6 for an upper balcony seat to at least £20 for the stalls (orchestra) or dress circle. Reserve tickets at the box office, over the phone by credit card (numbers in the phone book or newspaper marked "cc" are for credit card reservations), or through ticket agents such as **First Call** (tel. 0171/240–7941 or 0171/497–9977). To reserve before your trip, use **Ticketmaster's** U.S. booking line (tel. 800/775–2525).

Half-price, same-day tickets are sold (subject to availability) from a booth on the southwest corner of Leicester Square. Open Monday–Saturday noon–2 for matinees, 2:30–6:30 for evening shows. There is always a long line. Larger hotels have reservation services, but add hefty service charges.

Beware the scalpers! They not only charge outrageous prices and corrupt ticket availability; they sometimes sell forged tickets. The only extra you should ever pay is a nominal booking charge.

The **Fringe** can provide a more exciting theatrical experience than the West End. Numerous small theaters in back rooms of pubs mount productions you can see for a couple of pounds. Then there are the bigger venues, such as the **Almeida** in Islington, the **Royal Court Upstairs,** the **Lyric Studio Hammersmith,** the **Young Vic,** and the **ICA,** all of which show innovative and challenging work as well as more mainstream shows, often with known actors. They also play host to companies from around the world. Fringe is as much a part of London's theater scene as the famous West End. In fact, you could say it's the most lively part. The best thing about it is that you can see three Fringe shows for the price of one West End extravaganza.

Concerts Ticket prices for symphony orchestra concerts are relatively moderate, ranging from £5 to £15. International guest appearances usually mean higher prices; you should reserve well in advance for such performances. Those without reservations might go to the hall half an hour before the performance for a chance at returns (tickets that people return to the box office when they can't use them).

The London Symphony Orchestra is in residence at the **Barbican Arts Centre,** although the Philharmonia and the Royal Philharmonic also perform here. The **South Bank Arts Complex,** which includes the **Royal Festival Hall, Queen Elizabeth Hall,** and the small **Purcell Room,** forms another major venue. Between the Barbican and South Bank, there are concert performances every night of the year. The Barbican also features chamber music concerts with such smaller orchestras as the City of London Sinfonia.

For a chance to experience a great British institution, try the **Royal Albert Hall** during the Promenade Concert season lasting eight weeks from July to September. Special "promenade" (standing) tickets are usually around £3 and are available at the hall on the night of performance. Other summer pleasures are the outdoor concerts by the lake at **Kenwood** (Hampstead Heath) or **Holland Park.**

Numerous lunchtime concerts take place across London in smaller concert halls and churches, many of them free (*see* London for Free *in* Essential Information, *above*). They feature string quartets, vocalists, jazz ensembles, or gospel choirs. **St. John's,** Smith Square, and **St. Martin-in-the-Fields** are two of the more popular locations. Performances usually begin about 1 PM and last an hour.

Opera The classiest venue for opera in London is the **Royal Opera House** (Covent Garden), where international casts appear. Tickets range from £5 in the upper slips to well over £100. Performances are divided into booking periods and sell out early.

English-language operas are staged at the **Coliseum,** St. Martin's Lane, home of the English National Opera Company. Prices here are generally lower than at the Royal Opera House (from around £4 to £50-plus), and productions are unconventional and often a lot more exciting. The cheapest upper balcony seats here, known as "the gods," are better than those at the Royal: You can see from these seats. This is where opera glasses come in handy; for 20p rent a pair from the holder on the seat back. Both houses offer returns at a third or less of the regular price, if you're prepared to wait on line. Competition is keen for these seats, especially for new productions of Mozart, Verdi, Puccini, and Rossini.

Ballet The Royal Opera House is also the home of the world-famous **Royal Ballet.** Prices are slightly lower for the ballet than for the opera, but tickets go faster; reserve ahead. The **English National Ballet** (formerly the Festival) and visiting international companies perform at the Coliseum from time to time. **Sadler's Wells Theatre** hosts various ballet companies—including the Royal and the Rambert—as well as regional ballet and international modern dance troupes. Again, prices here are much lower than at Covent Garden.

Opera and Ballet Box Office Information   Contact the following for ticket information. **Coliseum** (St. Martin's La., WC2N 4ES, tel. 0171/836–3161). **Royal Opera House** (Covent Garden, WC2E 9DD, tel. 0171/240–1066). **Sadler's Wells** (Rosebery Ave., EC1R 4TN, tel. 0171/278–8916).

Movies   Despite the video invasion, West End movies still thrive. Most of the major houses (**Odeon, MGM,** etc.) are found in the Leicester Square/Piccadilly Circus area, where tickets average £7. Monday and matinees are sometimes better buys at £3–£4; lines are also shorter. Using your Travelcard (*see* Getting Around *in* Essential Information, *above*), you might consider catching movies away from the center of town, where tickets cost £1–£4 less.

The shrinking selection of **Cinema clubs** and repertory houses screen a wider range of movies: classics, Continental, and underground, as well as rare or underrated masterpieces. Some charge a nominal membership fee. The best is the **National Film Theatre** (in the South Bank Arts Complex, tel. 0171/928–3232), which screens big past hits, plus work neglected by the more ticket-sales-dependent houses, since it comes under the auspices of British Film Institute. The main events of the annual London Film Festival take place here in the fall; there are also lectures and presentations by visiting celebrities. Temporary daily membership costs 40p.

The **Institute of Contemporary Art** (ICA; the Mall, 0171/930–3647) presents a repertory program and various museums and galleries also have occasional screenings. Check listings for screenings at the principal repertory houses: the **Everyman, Prince Charles, Rio, Ritzy,** and **Riverside.**

Nightlife

Cabaret   **Comedy Store.** The Comedy Store Players' famous improvised show is now showing at the bigger, brighter, new-look premises, with bar and food. *Haymarket House, Oxendon St., near Piccadilly Circus, tel. 01426–914433 (recording). Admission: £8–£9. Shows Tues.–Sun. 8 PM, Fri.–Sat. also at midnight.*
Madame Jo Jo's. Luxurious and civilized, this may be the most fun of any cabaret in London. There are two outrageous drag shows nightly. *8 Brewer St., tel. 0171/734–2473. Admission: £5–£12.50. Shows at 12:15 AM and 1:15 AM.*

Discos   **Hippodrome.** This features lots of sparkly black and silver, several tiers of expensive bars, a restaurant, and much enthusiastic lighting around a large downstairs dance floor. Very middle-of-the-road. *Cranbourne St., tel. 0171/437–4311. Admission: Wed. £6–£15, half price for diners. Open Mon.–Sat. 9 PM–3 AM. AE, DC, MC, V.*

Jazz   **Jazz Café.** London's coolest jazz emporium, in a flashily converted bank in Camden Town, hosts excellent lineups. *5–7 Parkway, tel. 0171/284–4358. Admission: £6–£15, depending on the band. Open Sun.–Thurs. 7:30–midnight; Fri. and Sat. 7:30 PM–2 AM. Reservations advised. AE, MC, V.*
Ronnie Scott's. The legendary Soho jazz club has always drawn a host of international talent—and audiences. *Frith St., tel. 0171/439–0747. Admission: £10–£15 nonmembers. Open Mon.–Sat. 8:30 PM–3 AM, Sun. 8 PM–11:30 PM. Reservations advised; essential some nights. AE, DC, MC, V.*
The Vortex. In the wilds of Stoke Newington is this showcase for the healthy British jazz scene, with the emphasis on advanced, free, and

improvised work. *Stoke Newington Church St., N16, tel. 0171/254–6516. Admission £4–£6. Open most nights 8–11PM.*

Nightclubs **Camden Palace.** A young crowd still turns out at this recently re-modeled, big, multitiered, laser-lit cavern, which has weathered fashion. American-style food is served. *1A Camden High St., tel. 0171/387–0428. Admission: £2–£10. Open Tues.–Sat. 9 PM–3 AM. No credit cards.*

Legends. This sleek club attracts a different age range and style of clientele according to the night. Downstairs is a large, cool dance floor with a central bar. *29–30 Old Burlington St., W1, tel. 0171/437–9933. Admission: £4–£15. Open Mon., Tues., Fri., Sat. 9 PM–3 AM. AE, DC, MC, V.*

Rock **The Astoria.** Very central and quite hip, this place hosts bands that there's a buzz about, plus late club nights. *157 Charing Cross Rd., W1, tel. 0171/434–0403. Admission about £8–£12. Check listings for opening times.*

Forum. An ex-ballroom with balcony and dance floor that consist-ently attracts the best medium-to-big performers—and crowds. It's right by Kentish Town tube. *9–17 Highgate Rd., NW5, tel. 0171/284–2200. Admission: about £8. Open most nights 7–11 PM.*

For Singles **The Limelight.** Owned by New York Limelighter Peter Gatien and housed, like its New York counterpart, in an old church, this offers lots of one-nighter shows and special events. *136 Shaftesbury Ave., tel. 0171/434–0572. Admission: £5–£12. Open Mon.–Sat. 9:30 PM–3 AM. AE, DC, MC, V.*

3 The Southeast

Canterbury, Dover, Tunbridge Wells, Brighton

The historic towns of the Southeast lie only an hour to 90 minutes from London along the dense Network SouthEast rail lines. They make easy excursions from the capital for travelers with limited time and money who want to see more of England than just London. Chichester still carries traces of the early Roman occupation of Britain; at Battle, near Hastings, lies the site of the decisive Norman victory in 1066; the cathedral city of Canterbury echoes with the footsteps of Thomas à Becket and Chaucer. The area's proximity to London has also ensured the popularity of its seaside resorts: Margate; Ramsgate, including Broadstairs; and, of course, Brighton, whose raffish modern attractions are centered on the exotic fantasy of the Prince Regent's Royal Pavilion. Travelers bound for the Continent will most likely pass through this area, too, because the English Channel is at its narrowest here, and the busy ports of Newhaven, Folkestone, Ramsgate, and Dover have been gateways to the rest of Europe for many centuries. The Channel Tunnel, which is currently under construction between Dover and Folkestone, will end Britain's isolation from the Continent forever. It was due for completion in mid-1993, but last-minute delays mean that it is unlikely to be operational until at least mid-'94.

Four counties—Surrey, Kent, and East and West Sussex—make up the Southeast. The northern parts of Surrey and Kent have been overrun by the suburban sprawl of London, and now mainly consist of bedroom communities. Yet Kent's abundant apple orchards have earned it the title of "Garden of England." Kent is also known for its undulating chalk hills and distinctive oast houses: tall, cylindrical brick buildings with conical tops, where hops are dried for English beer. Sussex abounds with deep, narrow lanes leading to small, quiet villages, each with its ancient church and public house.

Essential Information

Lodging   Prices tend to be below London levels, but the area's popularity with British vacationers as well as international tourists means that you must search for hotel bargains. Local tourist offices have lists of B&Bs and guest houses. The seaside resorts have plenty of lodgings, but these can get booked up at the height of the season, especially in towns such as Brighton and Eastbourne, which are also popular conference centers. B&Bs in Brighton are notoriously difficult to find. Rely on a taxi to get you to your destination or call once you reach town for specific directions. Highly recommended establishments are indicated by a star ★.

Dining   Around the coast, seafood—much of it locally caught—is a specialty. You'll find not just the ubiquitous fish-and-chips (though they are often at their best in the Southeast), but also local dishes, as well as good international fish cuisine. In the larger towns, especially Brighton, trendy restaurants tend to spring up for a time and then disappear, making the town an ideal place for culinary experimentation.

Unless otherwise noted, dress is casual, and reservations are not necessary. Highly recommended restaurants are indicated by a star ★.

Shopping   The Southeast has a wide range of sophisticated shops with London prices, so this may not be the best place to shop if you are on a budget. Most of the major chains are represented in this area (even upmarket stores such as Liberty's), so it is possible to cash in on sales. The region is rich in crafts shops and artists' studios, and several of the main towns have ancient shopping areas that, like Brighton's Lanes, make a fascinating hour or two of productive wandering.

Biking   The gently undulating coastal landscape is good for getting around on a bike, but in this densely populated part of the country, cyclists must cope with a lot of traffic on roads near the larger towns. Here are some bike shops located in main centers: in Brighton, **Sunrise Cycle Hire** (West Pier Promenade, tel. 01273/748881), deposit £50; in Canterbury, **Canterbury Cycle Mart** (23 Lower Bridge St., tel. 01227/761488), £48 deposit required; in Dover, **Andy Cycles** (156 London Rd., tel. 01304/204401), deposit £50. Most bike shops will accept a deposit on a credit card or an ID card; if this is your preference, be sure to ask before laying out cash.

Hiking   The South Downs is ideal hiking country: If you're looking for a short stroll, walk to the edge of one of the small towns, such as Lewes, and wander along the turf of the rolling hills. More serious treks are also possible. The **South Downs Way** (106 miles) runs from Eastbourne to Winchester, to the west; the **North Downs Way** (141 miles) follows the ancient Pilgrim's Way (of Chaucer's *Canterbury Tales* fame) in places, and parts are open to cyclists; the **Downs Link** (30 miles) connects the two longer routes, which run south from near Guildford to near Brighton, and has some of the Southeast's best views. Details of these walks can be obtained from the local tourist offices.

Beaches   This entire area is fringed with beaches, although many of them (Brighton included) have pebbles underfoot instead of sand. Some of the beaches and waters are polluted, and their conditions constantly change, so take local advice before you swim. The water in the Channel is cold, except in the hottest summer weather.

The Arts and   This is an excellent area for drama and music, with regular theaters
Nightlife   at all the main seaside towns, especially Brighton. Some local orchestras play here as well. One of the world's great opera houses is

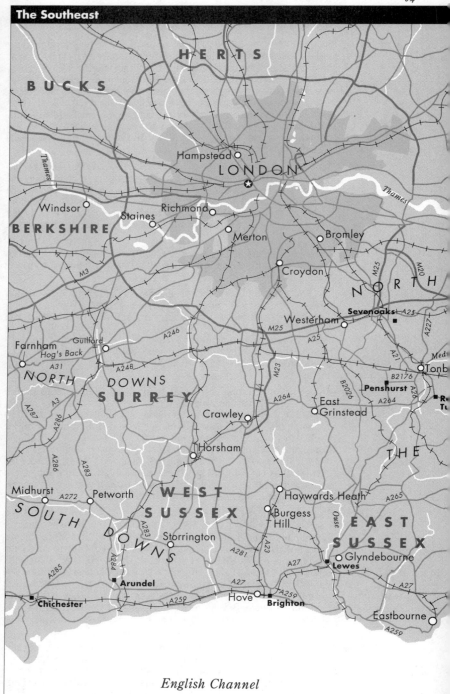

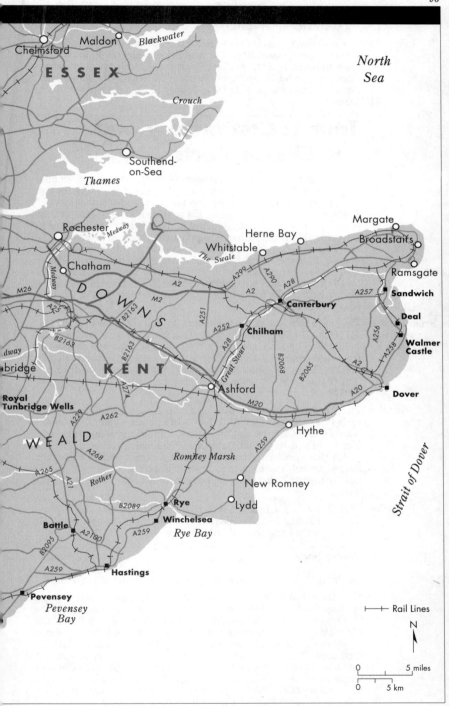

North
Sea

ESSEX

Chelmsford
Maldon
Blackwater

Crouch

Southend-
on-Sea

Thames

Margate
Broadstairs

Rochester
Medway

Herne Bay
Whitstable
The Swale
Ramsgate

Chatham
A299
A290
A28
A257
Sandwich

D
A2
M2
A2
O
W
N
S
Canterbury
Deal

M26
A251
A252
Chilham
A256
Walmer
Castle

A25
B2163
A28
A2

B2163
Great Stour
B2068
B2065
A258

dway
B2163
A20
Dover

bridge
KENT
Ashford
M20

Royal
Tunbridge Wells
A274
A259
Hythe

A229
A262

WEALD
A268
Romney Marsh
New Romney

A265
A21
Rother
Lydd

B2089
Rye
Winchelsea
Rye Bay

Battle
A2100
A259

B2095
A259

Hastings

Pevensey
*Pevensey
Bay*

Strait of Dover

⊢——⊣ Rail Lines

N

0   5 miles
0   5 km

at Glyndebourne, hidden in the downs near Lewes, although it is way out of the affordable bracket.

Festivals Because this region is easy to reach from London, festivals here can attract international attention in addition to local audiences. Apart from the season at the **Festival Theatre** at Chichester, and **summer opera** at Glyndebourne, there are major festivals in Brighton (May), Arundel (late summer), and Canterbury (fall), among other smaller locales.

Tour 1: Canterbury and the Cinque Ports

The hub of this tour is the cathedral city of Canterbury, 59 miles southeast of London. Frequent coastal train service connects Canterbury East station with the ancient Cinque (pronounced "sink") Ports lining the nearby coast. These harbor towns were granted considerable powers and privileges in the Middle Ages in return for guarding the English Channel against the threat of invasion, especially by the French. The ports, originally five in number (hence *cinque*, from the Norman French), were Sandwich, Dover, Hythe, Romney, and Hastings (*see* Tour 2, *below*). These towns are clustered close together, so travelers can base themselves in any one and visit the others by using the convenient train services or the inexpensive local bus.

From London There are two routes to Canterbury by rail: London/Victoria (tel. *By Train* 0171/928–5100) to Canterbury East, or from London/Charing Cross (0171/928–5100) to Canterbury West. The stations are equidistant from the center of town. The service to Canterbury East is slightly quicker (1 hour, 25 minutes) and more frequent, but some trains require a change at Faversham. For local train information, call 01732/ 770111.

By Bus The **National Express** Bus 007, bound for Dover, leaves London/Victoria Coach Station (tel. 0171/730–0202) 10 times daily, and takes 1 hour, 50 minutes to reach Canterbury. Canterbury is included in the National Express "Great Days Out from London" scheme. The Explorer ticket, priced about £5.40, gives a day's worth of almost unlimited travel on bus routes around Canterbury, Hastings, and nearby towns. Tickets may be bought from a ticket office or on the bus.

By Car The M2/A2 runs a direct 55-mile route from London to Canterbury; another 16 miles on the same road will take you to Dover. The A258 travels up the coast to Deal and Sandwich.

Canterbury

Canterbury tourist office: 34 St. Margaret's St., tel. 01227/766567.

The city of **Canterbury,** cradled in the rolling Kent countryside on the banks of the River Stour, is just 59 miles from London and is the undisputed star of the southeast region. Iron Age capital of the kingdom of Kent, headquarters of the Anglican church, and center of international pilgrimage, Canterbury offers a wealth of historic treasures. It also maintains a lively day-to-day atmosphere, a fact that has impressed visitors since 1388, when poet Geoffrey Chaucer wrote *The Canterbury Tales*, chronicling the journey from London to the shrine of St. Thomas à Becket. Canterbury was one of the first cities in Britain to pedestrianize its center, bringing a measure of tranquility to its streets that is best felt in the morning before the tour buses arrive, or in the evening after they depart.

Numbers in the margin correspond to points of interest on the Canterbury map.

From Canterbury West station, turn left onto St. Dunstan's Street. Keep straight ahead through the Westgate to St. Peter's, High, and St. George's streets. From Canterbury East, follow the city wall to the bus station, take St. George's Lane right, and then turn left onto St. George's Street. From this end you will see a lone church tower

❶ marking the site of **St. George's Church**—the rest of the building was destroyed in World War II—where playwright Christopher Marlowe was baptized in 1564. Continuing up St. George's Street,

❷ just before you reach the modern **Longmarket** shopping center, you will come to Butchery Lane and the colorful **Roman Pavement.** This ancient mosaic floor and hypocaust, the Roman version of central heating, were excavated in the 1940s, just one of the many long-hidden relics that were laid bare by German bombs. Displays and reconstructions of Roman buildings and of the marketplace help to create an atmosphere of antiquity. *Canterbury Roman Museum, Butchery La., tel. 01227/785575. Admission: £1.50 adults, 90p children. Open June–Oct., Mon.–Sat. 10:30–5, Sun. 1:30–5; Nov.–May, Mon.–Sat. 10:30–5.*

Mercery Lane, with its medieval-style cottages and massive, overhanging timber roofs, runs right off the High Street and ends in the

★ ❸ ❹ tiny **Buttermarket.** Here the immense **Christchurch Gate,** built in 1517, marks the entrance to the cathedral close.

★ ❺ **Christchurch Cathedral,** a living textbook of medieval architecture, is the first of England's great Norman cathedrals. The building was begun in 1070, demolished and begun anew in 1096, and then systematically expanded over the next three centuries. When the original choir burned to the ground in 1174, it was replaced by a new one designed in the Gothic style, with high, pointed arches. Don't be surprised to find a play or concert taking place in the nave; in recent years the dean and Chapter (the cathedral's ruling body) have revived the medieval tradition of using the cathedral for occasional secular performances. In the Middle Ages, only the presbytery (the area around the high altar) was considered sacred, and the nave was often used as a meeting place, or even a market.

The cathedral was only a century old, and still relatively small in size, when Thomas à Becket, the archbishop of Canterbury, was murdered here. Becket, an uncompromising defender of ecclesiastical interests, had angered his friend Henry II, who was heard to exclaim, "Who will rid me of this troublesome priest?" Thinking they were carrying out the king's wishes, four knights burst in on Becket in one of the side chapels and killed him, on December 29, 1170. Two years later Becket was canonized, and Henry II's subsequent submission to the authority of the church and his penitence helped establish the cathedral as the sole center of English Christianity.

Becket's tomb—destroyed by Henry VIII in 1538 as part of his campaign to reduce the power of the church and confiscate its treasures—was one of the most extravagant shrines in Christendom. It lay in **Trinity Chapel,** where you can still see a series of 13th-century stained-glass windows illustrating Becket's miracles. So hallowed was this spot that in 1376, Edward the Black Prince, warrior son of Edward III and a national hero, was buried near it. Over Edward's copper-gilt effigy hang replicas of his colorful surcoat, helmet, gauntlets, and a variety of other accoutrements. The faded originals are displayed in a glass case on the left.

The actual site of Becket's murder is down a flight of steps just to the left of the nave. Here you will see a modern commemorative altar, jagged and dramatic in design. A nearby plaque tells of the meeting between Pope John Paul II and Archbishop Robert Runcie, who knelt here together in prayer on May 19, 1982. In the corner, a

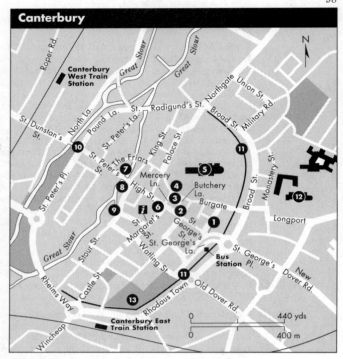

second flight of steps leads down to the enormous Norman undercroft, or vaulted cellarage, built in the early 12th century. The room has remained virtually unchanged since then. Its roof is supported by a row of squat pillars whose capitals dance with fantastic animals and strange monsters.

If time permits, be sure to explore the **Cloisters** and other small monastic buildings to the north of the cathedral. The 12th-century octagonal water tower is still part of the cathedral's water supply. As you pass through the great gatehouse back into the city, look up at the sculpted heads of two young figures: Prince Arthur, elder brother of Henry VIII, and the young Catherine of Aragon, to whom he was betrothed. After Arthur's death, Catherine married Henry, but her failure to produce a male heir led to Henry's decision to divorce her after 25 years of marriage, creating an irrevocable breach with the Catholic church that altered the course of English history.

The cathedral has undergone massive renovation in recent years. In 1993 the paving in most of the interior was relaid, and while it was open, foundations of earlier buildings, back to the Romans, were discovered.

As you leave the cathedral, cross the High Street and turn onto St. Margaret's Street. Here, in a disused church, you will find the unique and vivid **Canterbury Tales Exhibition.** This is a dramatization not only of Chaucer's *Canterbury Tales,* but also of 14th-century English life. First you will encounter Chaucer's pilgrims at the Tabard Inn near London, the starting point of their travels. Next you will come to a series of tableaux illustrating five of the tales. Then, passing through a reconstruction of the city gate, you may enter the marketplace. Don't be surprised if one of the figures comes to life: An actor dressed in period costume often forms part of the scene. The visit ends at a replica of Becket's shrine. *St. Margaret's St., tel. 01227/454888. Admission: £4.75 adults, £3.95 senior* citizens, £3.50 children, £14 family ticket. Open Nov.–Feb., Sun.–Fri. 10–4:30, Sat. 9:30–5:30; Mar.–Oct., daily 9:30–5:30.

Return to the High Street and turn left. Just past where the High Street crosses the river, you will see a distinctive group of half-timbered cottages known as the **Weavers' Houses,** built in the 16th century. These were occupied by Huguenot weavers who settled in Canterbury after escaping religious persecution in France. Before you cross the bridge over the river, stop in at the 12th-century **Eastbridge Hospital** (which we would now call a hostel), which once lodged poor pilgrims who came to pray at the tomb of Thomas à Becket. The infirmary hall, the chapel, and the crypt are open to the public. *25 High St. Admission free. Open Mon.–Sat. 10–5, Sun. 11–5.*

Just before the High Street becomes St. Peter's Street, you will see Stour Street running off to the left. Follow this a few blocks southwest until you arrive at the medieval **Poor Priests' Hospital,** now the site of the comprehensive **Canterbury Heritage Museum,** whose exhibits provide an excellent overview of the city's history and architecture. It can get crowded, so it's a good idea to visit early in the day. *20 Stour St., tel. 01227/452747. Admission: £1.50 adults, £1 senior citizens, 75p children, £3.50 family ticket. Open Mon.–Sat. 10:30–4.*

St. Peter's Street runs to Westgate, Canterbury's only surviving city gate house, which now contains the **Westgate Museum of Militaria.** Climb to the roof to catch a magnificent view of the city spires before following the landscaped, riverside gardens along the walls. *Tel. 01227/452747. Admission: 90p adults, 50p children. Open Oct.–Mar., Mon.–Sat. 2–4; Apr.–Sept., Mon.–Sat. 2–5.*

For a panoramic view of the town, follow the circuit of the **medieval city walls,** built on the line of the original Roman walls. Those to the south survive intact, towering some 20 feet high; a broad walkway runs along the top. Follow the walkway clockwise along Broad Street and you will pass the ruins of **St. Augustine's Abbey,** the burial place of Augustine, England's first Christian missionary, who was sent here from Rome in AD 597. The abbey was later seized by Henry VIII, who destroyed some of the buildings and converted others into a royal manor for his fourth wife, Anne of Cleves. Farther on, just opposite the Canterbury East train station, you will see the **Dane John** Mound, originally part of the city defenses.

From Canterbury West, grab a seat on a train (hourly departures) for the 10-minute ride to the hilltop village of **Chilham.** The village square is filled with textbook examples of English rural architecture, and the 14th-century **church** contains an old school desk covered with the carved initials of bored schoolchildren from the early 18th century onward. On public holidays in the summer, the **Chilham Castle Gardens** are the setting for medieval jousting and displays of falconry. *Tel. 01227/730319. Admission: £3 adults, £1.50 children; Mon. and Fri. (no falconry displays), £2.60 adults, £1.30 children. Open Apr.–mid-Oct., daily 11–5.*

The **White Horse,** a 16th-century inn nestled in the shadow of the church, offers wholesome evening and afternoon meals, a pleasant beer garden, and, in winter, a log fire.

Energetic visitors may want to return to Canterbury on foot along the **Pilgrim's Way,** a well-marked walking path that traces the traditional route to the cathedral. Look for signposts at the eastern end of the village; the walk is about 6 miles. Chilham is on the main rail line from London, so you can catch one of the trains that stop there and walk into Canterbury.

Lodging **Pointers.** This friendly B&B in a Georgian building is within easy
£ walking distance of the cathedral and city center (straight out be-

yond Westgate). *1 London Rd., CT2 8LR, tel. 01227/456846. 13 rooms, 11 with bath or shower. Facilities: restaurant, bar, parking. AE, DC, MC, V. Closed Dec. 24–mid-Jan.*

£ **St. Stephens Guest House.** Built in mock-Tudor style and surrounded by a stone-walled garden, this hotel offers a pleasant ambience and privacy. Its location, on the northwest edge of town, is within walking distance of the center. The rooms in the original building are comfortable, though on the simple side; the smaller rooms in the rear extension are more modern. *100 St. Stephens Rd., CT2 7JL, tel. 01227/462167. 12 rooms, 3 with shower. MC, V.*

¢ **Zan Stel Lodge.** Canterbury has plenty of choices when it comes to economical B&Bs, and this is one of the best values. Situated right next to Kent county cricket ground, and backed by a 150-foot walled garden, tranquility is assured. The house itself (which is nonsmoking) is spick-and-span, and has some lovely examples of stained glass. The only drawback might be the 15-minute walk into town. *140 Old Dover Rd., CT1 3NX, tel 01227/453654. 4 rooms, 2 with bath or shower. Facilities: garden. No credit cards.*

Splurge **Thanington Hotel.** This imposing, upmarket B&B was built sometime around 1810 as a farmhouse; 20 years later it was given an addition; more extensions have been built recently. It's just south of Canterbury East rail station, and close to the center of town. All the bedrooms have baths, TVs, and tea/coffeemaker. *140 Wincheap, CT1 3RY, tel. 01227/453227, fax 01227/453225. 10 rooms with bath. Facilities: indoor pool, snooker room, parking. AE, DC, MC, V.*

Dining **Il Vaticano.** Pilgrims with a yen for pasta should try this cheerful,
£ modern pasta parlor. It has an attractive walled garden and is lo-
★ cated in the center of town. The variety of freshly made sauces ++and toppings?++ includes grilled prawns and mushrooms in garlicky cheese. Italian ice creams round off the calorific feast. *35 St. Margaret's St., tel. 01227/765333. AE, DC, MC, V.*

¢ **Alberry's Wine Bar.** This popular eaterie makes a good place to sit and recharge your batteries. Easy to find (on the same street as the tourist office), Alberry's offers a wide selection of cheap and hearty soups, salads, and pies. Items change daily, and all are conscientiously prepared, using fresh ingredients. Sample the venison casserole, if it's offered, or the turkey and ham pie. Gammon steak is a regular. A three-course set-price menu is available for under a fiver. *38 St. Margaret St., tel. 01227/452378. AE, MC, V. Closed Sun.*

Shopping The **National Trust Shop** (24 The Burgate) stocks the National Trust line of household items, which make ideal gifts.

The Arts and Canterbury has two main theaters. The **Gulbenkian Theatre** (Giles
Nightlife La., tel. 01227/769075), is part of the University of Kent and mounts a full range of plays, particularly experimental works. The **Marlowe** (St. Margaret's St., tel. 01227/787787) is named after the Elizabethan playwright, atheist, and spy, who was born in Canterbury.

Festival The **Canterbury Festival** (tel. 01227/452853) is a prestigious three-week arts festival held every October in venues all over town.

Dover

There is a train at least once an hour directly to Dover from London/Victoria station (tel. 0171/928–5100). (Charing Cross trains also run frequently to Dover/Western Docks, but this station is mostly for travelers connecting with Channel ferries.) Twice-hourly trains from Canterbury East station take about a half hour to Dover Priory. National Express buses depart from London and stop in towns en route to Dover. Tourist office: Townwall St., tel. 01304/205108.

Many people find **Dover** disappointing as both the savage bombardments of World War II and the shortsightedness of postwar develop-
★ ers have left their scars on the city center. But the spectacular **Dover**

★ **Castle**—once one of the mightiest medieval castles in Western Europe—towers high above the chalk ramparts of the famous **White Cliffs** and is well worth a visit. The first building on the site was the Roman Pharos, or lighthouse, which still remains, casting its long shadow over the encircling walls. The castle, most of which dates back to Norman times, was begun by Henry II in 1181, but incorporates additions from almost every succeeding century, a testament to the skill of the ancient builders: It was still in use as a defense during World War II. The massive keep (central structure), with dense walls 17–22 feet thick in places, is the most imposing area of the castle. A museum here offers an interesting range of exhibits, with objects dating back to the 12th century. One of the most intriguing displays is a large-scale model of the Battle of Waterloo. Under the castle are the **Hellfire Caves** (included in admission fee), a network of tunnels that were, until recently, a military secret. They were dug when Napoleon threatened, and served as headquarters for the evacuation of British troops from Dunkirk in 1940. To rest your feet, stop in at the efficient, modern restaurant within the castle grounds, where you can get tasty meals at reasonable prices. *Castle Rd., tel. 01304/201628. Admission: £5.50 adults, £4.10 senior citizens, £2.80 children. Open Apr.–Sept., daily 10–6; Oct.–Mar., Wed.–Sun. 10–4.*

Before you leave Dover, visit the 14th-century **Maison Dieu Hall,** located in the town hall and founded in 1221 as a hostel for pilgrims traveling from the Continent to Canterbury. A museum houses a varied collection of flags and armor, while the stained-glass windows tell the story of Dover through the ages. *Biggin St., tel. 01304/201200. Admission free. Open summer, Mon.–Sat. 10–4:30, Sun. 2–4:30; winter, Wed.–Sat. 10–4:30, Sun. 2–4:30.*

Lodging **Gateway Hovertel.** As its name suggests, this is a cross between an
£ old hotel and a modern motel, located near the hoverport. It offers special rates for extended stays: If you lodge here for two nights, you save £10; three nights gets you the third half-price! (As the offer does not apply in July and August, confirm it before you book.) Another plus is the convenient location if you plan to cross the Channel, but it's also very busy and can be a bit noisy. *Snargate St., CT17 9BZ, tel. 01304/205479, fax 01304/211504. 27 rooms with bath or shower. Facilities: bar, parking. AE, DC, MC, V.*

¢ **Number One.** This attractive corner terrace home, built at the start
★ of the 19th century, is a cozy guest house that boasts a walled garden with a view of the castle, reasonably priced rooms with TVs, tea/coffeemaker, and breakfast served in your room. *1 Castle St., CT16 1QH, tel. 01304/202007. 5 rooms with shower. No credit cards.*

¢ **Tower Guest House.** What was once a water tower is now an unusual B&B in a quiet section close to the center of town and the Priory rail station. Its small size allows the staff to pay special attention to guests. Comfortably modern rooms include TVs and tea/coffeemakers, and there's a garden for the summer. *98 Priory Hill, CT17 0AD, tel. 01304/208212. 5 rooms, 3 with bath or shower. No credit cards.*

Dining **Britannia.** One of Dover's claims to fame is the fish special called
£ Dover sole, named after the town and served here. The refurbished pub, with wooden floors and a log fire in winter, also offers other local fish at a reasonable price (upstairs). The nautical theme and hearty portions keep this place busy. At lunch, only bar snacks are available. *Townwall St., tel. 01304/203248. MC, V.*

£ **Dino's.** Frankly, budget eating in Dover is no great shakes, but this friendly central spot is an exception to the rule. Acceptable, standard Italian food and a willing staff make Dino's reliable. *58 Castle St., tel. 01304/204678. AE, MC, V. Closed Mon.*

Walmer

To reach Walmer, 15 minutes away, take the train from Dover Priory.

A noted attraction is **Walmer Castle,** another of Henry VIII's fortifications. Converted in 1730 into the official residence of the Lord Warden of the Cinque Ports, it now has the atmosphere of a cozy country house. Among the famous former Lord Wardens were the Duke of Wellington, a hero of the Battle of Waterloo, who lived here from 1829 until his death in 1852 (there's a small museum of Wellington memorabilia), and Sir Winston Churchill. The present Lord Warden is the Queen Mother, though she rarely stays here. After you have seen the castle chambers, take a stroll in the gardens, and notice the moat, which has been converted to a grassy walk flanked by flower beds. *Tel. 01304/364288. Admission: £3.50 adults, £2.60 senior citizens, £1.80 children. Open Apr.–Sept., daily 10–6; Oct.–Mar., Wed.–Sun. 10–4.*

Deal

Hourly trains depart from Dover Priory for the 18-minute journey to Deal. Tourist office: Town Hall, High St., tel. 01304/369576.

North of Dover is the seaside town of **Deal,** where Caesar's legions landed in 55 BC during the invasion of Britain. From here William Penn set sail in 1682 on his first journey to America. **Deal Castle,** erected in 1540 and built in an intricate design of concentric circles, is the largest of the coastal defenses built by Henry VIII. Cannons perched on the battlements overlook the gaping moat. The castle museum offers a range of exhibits on prehistoric, Roman, and Saxon Britain. *Victoria Rd., tel. 01304/372762. Admission: £2.50 adults, £1.90 senior citizens, £1.30 children. Open Apr.–Sept., daily 10–6; Oct.–Mar., Wed.–Sun. 10–4.*

Sandwich

Hourly trains depart from the Dover Priory for Sandwich, 23 minutes away.

The Tudor town of **Sandwich** is 6 miles north of Deal. One of the town's oldest surviving buildings is the 16th-century barbican (gate house), beside the toll bridge, and another is the **Guildhall**—open to visitors when the court is not in session—also 16th-century, with a small museum of local history.

Tour 2: Tunbridge Wells and Environs

This tour follows the main train route from London through the 18th-century spa of Royal Tunbridge Wells to the southernmost of the Cinque Ports, Hastings, then changes to a local line for an excursion to Rye and Winchelsea (perched above Romney Marsh), two of southeast England's most atmospheric towns.

From London
By Train Trains depart at least every half hour from London/Charing Cross (tel. 0171/928–5100). Change at Hastings for hourly service to Winchelsea and Rye.

By Bus There is no National Express bus service to Tunbridge Wells. The **National Express** Bus 066 leaves London/Victoria Coach Station (tel. 0171/730–0202) twice a day for Hastings; the journey time is a bit more than 3 hours. For information on local services, contact Kent (tel. 0800/696996) or the East Sussex county offices (tel. 01273/

474747). Bus service links all the towns of this region, but trains are faster, more frequent, and no more expensive.

By Car The A21 more or less parallels the train route from London to Hastings, a 65-mile trip. Turn off at A2028 for Sevenoaks, at A26 for Tunbridge Wells, and at A2100 for Battle. From Hastings, take the A259 along the coast to Winchelsea and Rye.

Sevenoaks

The fast train takes 30 minutes from London to Sevenoaks. Sevenoaks tourist office: Buckhurst La., tel. 01732/430305.

An optional first stop on the journey southeast from London is **Sevenoaks.** In the center of town is **Knole,** which has been the home of the Sackville family since 1603. Begun in the 15th century, Knole, with its vast complex of courtyards and buildings, resembles a small town itself: You'll need most of an afternoon to explore it thoroughly. The house is famous for its collection of tapestries and embroidered furnishings, and paintings on display which include a series of portraits by 18th-century artists Thomas Gainsborough and Sir Joshua Reynolds. The house is set in a 1,000-acre deer park. *Tel. 01732/450608. Admission: £4 adults, £2 children; admission free to grounds. Open Apr.–Oct., Wed. and Fri.–Sun. 11–5, Thurs. 2–5. Last admission 4 PM.*

Tunbridge Wells

The fast train from London to Tunbridge Wells takes 50 minutes (20 minutes from Sevenoaks). Tunbridge tourist office: The Old Fish Market, The Pantiles, tel. 01892/515675.

This city, officially known as **Royal Tunbridge Wells** (not to be mistaken with nearby Tonbridge), owes its prosperity to the 17th- and 18th-century passion for spas and mineral baths, initially as medicinal treatments, and later as social gathering places. In 1606, a spring of chalybeate (mineral) water was discovered here, drawing legions of royal visitors from the court of King James I. From Easter to September each year it is still possible to drink the waters when a "dipper" (the traditional water dispenser) is in attendance at the spring. Tunbridge Wells reached its zenith in the mid-18th century, when Richard "Beau" Nash presided over its social life. Today it is a pleasant town and home to many London commuters.

The Pantiles, a promenade near the spring, derives its odd name from the Dutch "pan tiles" that originally paved the area. Now bordered on two sides by busy main roads, The Pantiles remains a tranquil oasis.

Across the road from The Pantiles is the **Church of King Charles the Martyr,** built in 1678 and dedicated to Charles I, who was executed by Parliament in 1649 following the English Civil War. Its plain exterior belies its splendid interior; take special note of the beautifully plastered ceiling. The people of the fashionable world came to the church to enhance their spiritual health after ministering to their bodies with mineral treatments in the 1700s. A network of alleyways behind the church leads back to the High Street.

The buildings at the lower end of the High Street date from the 18th century, but as the street climbs the hill, changing its name to Mount Pleasant Road, the buildings become more modern. Here, above the library, you'll find the **Tunbridge Wells Museum and Art Gallery,** which houses a fascinating jumble of local artifacts, prehistoric relics, and Victorian toys, as well as a permanent exhibition of interesting Tunbridge ware pieces: small, wood-carved items inlaid with different-colored wooden fragments. *Mount Pleasant, tel. 01892/526121, ext. 317. Admission free. Open Mon.–Sat. 9:30–5.*

Lodging **6 Arundel.** This solid Victorian building offers convenient accommo-
¢ dation in one of the quietest areas of Tunbridge. Tucked away in a
cul-de-sac near a public park, the B&B is just five-minutes' walk
from the train station and the High Street, and a stone's throw from
a handful of amenable pubs. Rooms have TVs and are adequately
furnished. *6 Arundel Rd., TN1 1TB, tel. 01892/525675. 3 rooms, 2
with bath or shower. No credit cards.*

Splurge **Kingswood Hotel.** This large, mock-Tudor house stands in its own
grounds within walking distance of the town center. Rooms run £60
for a night, but all have a TV and a tea/coffeemaker, and the restaurant offers reasonably priced, fairly rich dishes. Try the duck in
Cointreau. Less expensive bar meals are also available. *Pembury
Rd., TN2 3QS, tel. 01892/511269, fax 01892/513321. 15 rooms with
bath. Facilities: restaurant. AE, DC, MC, V.*

Dining **Downstairs at Thackeray's.** This friendly little bistro, set in a 1660
££ house where, later, the Victorian novelist William Makepeace
Thackeray lived, offers at more reasonable prices the same food
you'll find at Thackeray's House, the gourmet restaurant on the first
floor. Chef-owner Bruce Wass insists on fresh ingredients and cooks
them with great flair. There are good-value set menus for lunch
(£6.75) and dinner (£7.50). *85 London Rd., tel. 01892/537559. Reservations advised. MC, V. Closed Sun., Mon., and Christmas week.*

£ **Mount Edgcumbe Bar.** This is the bar and brasserie in the Mount
★ Edgcumbe House Hotel and a great place for special bar food. You
can have baguettes with a range of fillings, or something spicier
such as chicken tikka or a stir fry. More expensive fare can be
brought down from the restaurant upstairs, including Dover sole.
*Mount Edgcumbe House Hotel, The Common, tel. 01892/526823.
AE, MC, V.*

Penshurst

*Getting to this town proves an exception to the usefulness of South-
East rail. To go from Tunbridge Wells to Penshurst means a change
at Tonbridge; you would be better off on a bus: No. 233 leaves the
Tunbridge Wells war memorial at lunchtime; No. 231 leaves the rail
station for Penshurst every hour.*

The main reason to visit **Penshurst** is to tour **Penshurst Place,** one of
England's finest medieval manor houses. Elizabethan poet and soldier Sir Philip Sidney was born here in 1554, and it is still the home of
the Sidney family. The **Baron's Hall,** built in 1341, even retains its
original timber roof. Items on view include an impressive collection
of tapestries and family portraits. There is a convenient coffee shop.
*Tel. 01892/870307. Admission to house and grounds: £4.95 adults,
£4.50 senior citizens, £2.75 children; grounds only: £3.50 adults, £3
senior citizens, £2.25 children. Open Apr.–Sept., daily noon–5:30,
and Mar. and Oct., weekends noon–5:30; grounds open 11–dusk.*

Dining **Spotted Dog.** This pub first opened its doors in 1520, and today
£ tempts visitors with an inglenook fireplace, imaginative lunchtime
and evening meals, and a splendid view of Penshurst Place. *Smarts
Hill, tel. 01892/870253. MC, V.*

Battle

*Back on the main train route, Battle is 30 minutes from Tunbridge
Wells; 1 hour, 22 minutes from London/Charing Cross. Battle tourist office: 88 High St., tel. 014246/773721.*

Not surprisingly, **Battle** takes its name from the crucial Battle of
Hastings that took place here in 1066, giving William the Conqueror
and his Norman warriors control of England. The ruins of **Battle Abbey,** the great Benedictine abbey William erected after his victory,
are worth the trip. The high altar stood on the spot where the last

Saxon king, Harold II, was killed. Though the abbey was demolished in 1539 during Henry VIII's destructive binge, you can wander across the battlefield and see the remains of many of the domestic buildings. The **Abbot's House** (closed to the public) is now a girls' school. *High St., tel. 01424/773792. Admission to ruins: £3.20 adults, £2.40 senior citizens, £1.60 children. Open Apr.–Sept., daily 10–6; Oct.–Mar., daily 10–4.*

Hastings

Another 14 minutes past Battle by train will take you to Hastings. Hastings tourist office: 4 Robertson Terr., tel. 01424/781111 and 0800/181066.

Hastings, headquarters of the Norman invasion of 1066, is now a large, slightly run-down seaside resort. A visit to the old town provides an interesting overview of 900 years of English maritime history. Along the beach the tall wooden huts called **Net Shops,** which are unique to the town, are used for drying local fishermen's nets. In the town hall you'll find the famous **Hastings Embroidery,** made in 1966 by members of the Royal School of Needlework to mark the 900th anniversary of the battle. The nearly 250-foot-long piece depicts legends and great moments from British history. *Queen's Rd., tel. 01424/781113. Admission: £1.25 adults, 75p senior citizens and children. Open Oct.–Apr., weekdays 11:30–3:30; May–Sept., Mon.–Sat. 10–5.*

All that remains of **Hastings Castle,** built by William the Conqueror in 1069, are fragments of the fortifications, some ancient walls, and a number of gloomy dungeons. Nevertheless, it is worth a visit—especially for the excellent aerial view it provides of the chalky cliffs, the coast, and the town below. *West Hill, tel. 01424/718888. Admission: £2.50 adults, £2 senior citizens, £1.75 children. Open Apr.–Sept., daily 10–5, Feb.–Mar., daily 11–4.*

Lodging **Eagle House.** This well-regarded guest house, in a large, detached
£ Victorian building, stands in its own attractive garden. The house is
★ located in St. Leonard's, the western section of Hastings, within easy reach of the town center. The rooms are spacious and comfortable, and the kitchen uses fresh produce from local farms. *12 Pevensey Rd., St. Leonard's TN38 0JZ, tel. 01424/430535. 19 rooms with bath. Facilities: restaurant, garden. AE, DC, MC, V.*

Dining **Restaurant 27.** This eatery, set in the pedestrianized part of the Old
£ Town, is a good place to come if you have a hankering for French cooking. Try the salmon *en croûte* (salmon wrapped in pastry). Impressionist-style paintings on the walls and gentle French jazz enhance the atmosphere. *27 George St., tel. 01424/420060. Reservations advised. AE, MC, V. Closed lunch and Mon.*

¢ **First in Last Out.** This popular pub, with another branch in the Old Town, is prized by the locals for its beer, which is brewed on the premises. Lunchtime prices are affordable, particularly if you order the tasty bar food, and in the summer you can sip a drink in the small courtyard. Try the strong Cardinal beer. *14 High St., Old Town, tel. 01424/425079. No credit cards.*

Winchelsea and Rye

Winchelsea is 18 minutes by local train from Hastings. The Marsh Link line runs from Hastings to Ashford, passing through Romney Marsh, and taking in both Winchelsea and, 4 minutes later, Rye. Rye tourist office: The Heritage Centre, Strand Quay, tel. 01797/ 226696.

★ Perched atop its own small hill, **Winchelsea** is one of the prettiest villages in the region. The town was built on a grid system devised in

1283, after the sea destroyed an earlier settlement at the foot of the hill. Some of the original town gates still stand.

Sitting high above **Romney Marsh**—reclaimed from the sea and famous for its sheep and, at one time, its ruthless smugglers—is the ★ town of **Rye**. Over the years the sea has receded, and this former port is now nearly 2 miles inland, its steep hill providing dramatic views of the surrounding countryside. The medieval **Landgate,** one of three city gates, and the 13th-century **Ypres Tower**—part of the original 13th-century fortifications—remain intact. The tower, also known as Rye Castle, contains the town's **museum,** which has a collection of local prints, drawings, and pottery, as well as one of the oldest fire engines in the world. *Gungarden, tel. 01797/226728. Admission: £1.50 adults, £1 senior citizens, 50p children. Open Apr.– Oct., daily 10:30–5:30; Nov.–Mar., weekends 11:30–3:30.*

If you follow Mermaid Street, you can get to the site of the ancient port. While you are in the area, be sure to visit the **Rye Town Model,** a huge scale model of the town incorporating an imaginative, historical *son-et-lumière* (sound-and-light) show. *Strand Quay, tel. 01797/ 226696. Admission: £2 adults, £1.50 senior citizens, £1 children. Open daily Apr.–Oct., 10–5:30; Nov.–Feb., 11–1; Mar. 1–12, 10–2; Mar. 13–31, 10–4 (shows on the half-hour).*

Another interesting museum is **Lamb House,** an early Georgian structure that has housed several well-known writers. The most famous was the American Henry James, who lived here from 1898 to 1916. The ground-floor rooms contain some of his furniture and personal belongings. There is also a pretty walled garden. *West St., tel. 01892/890651. Admission: £2 adults, £1 children. Open Apr.–Oct., Wed. and Sat. 2–6.*

Lodging **Jeake's House.** This lovely old house (1689), on the same cobblestone
£ street as The Mermaid (*see* Dining, *below*), has cozy bedrooms furnished with antiques and views of the town. Breakfast is served in a former chapel. *Mermaid St., TN31 7ET, tel. 01797/222828, fax 01797/222623. 12 rooms, 10 with bath or shower. MC, V.*

Dining **Old Forge.** Housed in an imaginatively adapted old forge, this res-
£ taurant on the western edge of town is known for its seafood, which is caught by local fishermen. If you prefer meat, go for the chargrilled steaks. In the winter the ambience is enhanced by a large open fire. *24 Wish St., tel. 01797/223227. Reservations advised Sat. night. MC, V. Closed Wed. lunch and all day Sun. and Mon.*

¢ **Fletcher's House.** Near St. Mary's Church, this establishment, built in 1490, is a good place for a light lunch. Shakespeare's contemporary, the Elizabethan dramatist John Fletcher (for whom the restaurant was named), was born here in 1579. If you're taking tea here, sample some of the homemade cakes—the nutty Warm Treacle Tart is a show-stopper. *2 Lion St., tel. 01797/223101. MC, V.*

£ **The Mermaid.** Once the headquarters of a notorious smuggling gang that ruled the Romney Marsh area—The Mermaid is one of the classic old inns of England. It serves this ancient town as it has for six centuries, and its age can be seen in every nook and cranny; the sloping, creaky floors; oak beams and low ceilings; and the huge open hearth in the bar. Lodging here may be pricey, but a meal at the bar is relatively inexpensive. Every detail in this inn will make the seeker of atmosphere very happy. But be warned, the Mermaid is *very* popular with tourists. *Mermaid St., tel. 01797/223065. No reservations in bar. AE, DC, MC, V.*

£ **Ypres Castle.** This pub is not as classic as The Mermaid, but it does have its advantages. Overlooking the confluence of the rivers Brede and Rother, and situated on the hill near the Ypres Tower, this lodging boasts wonderful views. There is good beer on tap, and hearty pub food. *Gungarden, tel. 01797/223248. AE, DC, MC, V.*

Tour 3: Brighton to Chichester

The hub of this tour is Brighton, one of England's most cosmopolitan seaside resorts. From here, travelers can take train jaunts to nearby places of interest: Lewes, a virtual outdoor museum of architectural styles; Arundel; Chichester Cathedral; and Fishbourne Roman Palace.

From London
By Train

Trains for Brighton leave every half hour from London/Victoria Station (tel. 0171/928–5100), with the fastest ones taking just less than an hour. Gatwick airport lies on the main line, halfway between London and Brighton, and is regularly served by trains in both directions. For train information in Brighton, call 01273/206755.

By Bus

National Express has seven buses (No. 064) departing daily from London/Victoria Coach Station (tel. 0171/730–0202). The trip to Brighton takes 1 hour, 45 minutes. The local number for information is 01403/241757. Other regular buses leave from the Victoria Coach Station as well, but they lack the amenities of the National Express line, and the seats are not as comfortable.

By Car

The M23/A23 runs directly south from London to Brighton, a distance of 52 miles. The coastal road, A27, links Brighton with all the other sites on this tour; Arundel is about 20 miles west of Brighton, and Chichester about 31 miles west.

Brighton

Brighton tourist office: 10 Bartholemew Sq. (next to the Town Hall), tel. 01273/323755.

An article in Britain's *Independent* newspaper summed up the attractions of **Brighton** this way: "Pleasing decay is a very English taste. It is best indulged in at the seaside, especially off-season, when wind and rain enhance the melancholy romance of cracked stucco, rusting ironwork, and boarded-up shops. Brighton is a supreme example, with its faded glamour combined with raucous vulgarity." Unfortunately, with the recession, Brighton's decay has accelerated and is a lot less pleasing.

Numbers in the margin correspond to points of interest on the Brighton map.

Brighton, which owes its modern fame and fortune to the supposed medicinal virtues of seawater, was mentioned in the *Domesday Book* as Brighthelmstone in 1086, when it paid the annual rent of 4,000 herrings to the Lord of the Manor; it changed its name in the 18th century. In 1750, physician Richard Russell published a book recommending seawater treatment for glandular diseases. The patient was directed not only to swim in seawater, but to drink it— warm, and laced with such ingredients as vipers' eyes! The fashionable world flocked to Brighton to take Dr. Russell's "cure," and sea bathing became a popular pastime. Russell became known as "Dr. Brighton." When you visit the promenade across from the Palace Pier, notice the comfortable old pub called Dr. Brighton's Tavern, where his patients used to stay.

The next windfall for the town was the arrival of the Prince of Wales (later George IV), who acted as Prince Regent during the madness of his father, George III. "Prinny," as he was called, created the Royal Pavilion, an extraordinary pleasure palace (*see below*) that attracted London society. The influx of visitors triggered a wave of villa building and, fortunately, this was one of the greatest periods in English architecture. The elegant terraces of Regency houses, most of them built to the east of the Pavilion, on the seafront and on the streets and squares leading off it, are today among the town's greatest attractions.

The coming of the railroad set the seal on Brighton's popularity: One of the most luxurious trains in the country, the Pullman *Brighton Belle*, brought Londoners to the coast within an hour. They expected to find the same comforts and recreations they had in London and, as they were prepared to pay for them, Brighton obliged. This helps to explain the town's remarkable range of restaurants, hotels, and pubs. Horse racing was—and still is—another strong attraction.

Although fast rail service to London has made Brighton an important base for commuters, the town has unashamedly set itself out to be a pleasure resort. In the 1840s it featured the very first example of that peculiarly British institution, the amusement pier. Although ❶ that first pier is gone, the recently restored **Palace Pier** follows the great tradition. The original mechanical amusements, including the celebrated flipcard device "What the Butler Saw," are now museum exhibits, but you can still admire the handsome ironwork in its original setting.

❷ The heart of Brighton is the **Steine** (pronounced "steen"), the large open area close to the seafront, which was a river mouth until the Prince of Wales had it drained in 1793. One of the houses here was the home of Mrs. Maria Fitzherbert, later the prince's wife. The most remarkable building on the Steine, perhaps in all Britain, is ★ ❸ unquestionably the **Royal Pavilion,** the Prince of Wales's extravagant fairy-tale palace. First planned as a simple seaside villa and built in the fashionable classical style of 1787, the pavilion was rebuilt between 1815 and 1822 for the Prince Regent, who favored an exotic, eastern design with Chinese interiors. When Queen Victoria came to the throne in 1837, she so disapproved of the palace that she stripped it of its furniture and planned to demolish it. Fortunately, the Brighton city council bought it from her, and it is now lovingly preserved and recognized as unique in Europe. After a lengthy process of restoration, the pavilion looks much as it did in its magnificent heyday. The interior is once more filled with quantities of period furniture and ornaments, some given or lent by the present royal family. The two great set pieces are the **Music Room,** styled in the form of an Oriental pavilion, and the **Banqueting Room,** with its enormous flying-dragon "gasolier," or gaslight chandelier, a revolutionary new invention in the early 19th century. The upstairs rooms (once used as bedrooms) contain a selection of cruel caricatures of the Prince Regent, most produced during his lifetime, and illustrations of the pavilion at various stages of its construction. There is also a coffee shop on this floor. Following the decade-long renovation of the palace, attention has now turned to the gardens, which are being restored to something like their old elegance. *Old Steine, tel. 01273/603005. Admission: £3.75 adults, £2.75 senior citizens, £2.10 children. £5.85 and £9.60 family tickets. Open Oct.–May, daily 10–5; June–Sept., daily 10–6.*

❹ The grounds of the pavilion contain the **Brighton Museum and Art Gallery.** The buildings, which were originally designed as a stable block for the prince's horses, are almost as interesting as the collection they house. The museum has especially interesting Art Nouveau and Art Deco collections. *Church St., tel. 01273/603005. Admission free. Open Mon., Tues., Thur.–Sat. 10–5, Sun. 2–5.*

❺ Just west of the Old Steine lies **The Lanes,** Brighton's oldest section. This maze of alleys and passageways was once home to legions of fishermen and their families, and was the poorest part of town. It is said that the name "Lanes" actually refers to their fishing lines. Today The Lanes section is filled with restaurants, boutiques, and, es-

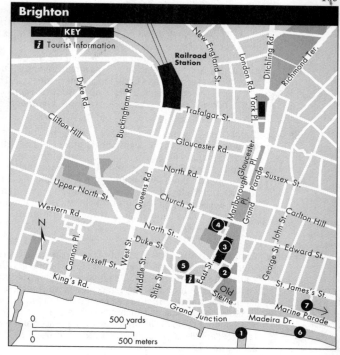

pecially, antiques shops. Vehicular traffic is barred from the area, and visitors may wander at will. Across North Street is the North Lanes, a network of streets that houses simpler, but still pleasing, shops to browse through.

The heart of The Lanes is Market Street and Square, lined with fish and seafood restaurants. The large **Pump House** pub was once an actual pumping station, bringing seawater up from the beach and distributing it to Brighton's many bathing establishments. The nearby **Bath House Arms** was just such an establishment. You can spend an hour or so wandering through The Lanes, for the architecture—largely comprised of former fishermen's cottages—is as varied as the merchandise on sale.

If you feel an urge to escape Brighton's summer crowds, take **Volk's Electric Railway** along the Marine Parade to the **Marina**. The railroad, built by inventor Magnus Volk in 1883, was the first public electric railroad in Britain. For nearly 200 years the city of Brighton has struggled to build a sophisticated harbor and marina. What they have achieved is well short of the dream.

Lodding   **The Dove.** Here you'll find a well-converted Regency house where
££   you will receive a warm welcome from its husband-and-wife owners. There is one large room with a balcony facing the sea for £78 a night, but for budget purposes, be sure to ask for the less expensive quarters, some with a sideways sea view from their bow windows, priced at £38–£68 a night. There is a 20% discount if you stay more than one night. There is no restaurant, but an à la carte breakfast is available. *18 Regency Sq., BN1 2FG, tel. 01273/779222, fax 01273/746912. 10 rooms with bath. AE, DC, MC, V.*

££   **Claremont House.** The Claremont is in Hove, Brighton's twin town to the west, but still within easy walking distance of Brighton's attractions. Hove has the advantage of being a lot less raffish, and this guest house is in an elegant Victorian building that harmonizes with its surroundings. The rooms are comfortably sized, and each has a TV and a tea/coffeemaker. Dinners are available on request. *34 2nd Ave., Hove, BN3 2LL, tel. 01273/735161, fax 01273/324764. 12 rooms with bath or shower. AE, DC, MC, V.*

¢ **Cavalaire House.** Brighton has dozens of B&Bs, each virtually indistinguishable from the others. This small, friendly one is two blocks from the waterfront and close to the town center. All bedrooms have a TV and tea/coffeemaker. *34 Upper Rock Gardens, BN2 1QF, tel. 01273/696899, fax 01273/600504. 9 rooms, 3 with bath or shower. AE, DC, MC, V.*

Splurge **Topps.** Two Regency houses have been turned into this attractive hotel, run by the owners, Paul and Pauline Collins. All the rooms are appealing and well equipped, with lush bathrooms, and the atmosphere is relaxed, friendly, and highly recommended, if you're looking to spend about £80 for a night's stay. The basement restaurant (dinner only, closed Sun., Wed., and Jan.) is worth a visit even if you're not staying at the hotel. The interesting English menu is prepared by Pauline Collins, and, as the place is small, reservations are a must. *17 Regency Sq., BN1 2FG, tel. 01273/729334, fax 01273/203679. 15 rooms with bath. Facilities: restaurant. AE, DC, MC, V.*

Dining **Langan's Bistro.** This is a spin-off from the late, eccentric restaura-
££ teur's London eatery. There are French prints and drawings on the walls, and a friendly staff. The food is imaginative with an emphasis on fish and game. Try the partridge with lentils and lardons, the rump of lamb, the fillet of sea bass with fennel, or the grilled brill. Fixed-price menus at lunch are offered at £12.50 for two courses, £14.50 for three. It is located east of the center of town. *1 Paston Pl., tel. 01273/606933. Reservations required. AE, DC, MC, V. Closed Mon., Sat. lunch, Sun. dinner.*

£ **Browns.** If you're wandering the Lanes, you may want to stop by this popular, noisy spot for lunch. Imaginative dishes, which change regularly, are on offer; the spaghetti is always good. Brown's has opened a bar three doors away on Duke Street. *3–4 Duke St., tel. 01273/323501. AE, MC, V.*

£ **Donatello.** This is a fairly new Italian restaurant in the heart of The Lanes shopping quarter. It has a brick wall and pine decor, with plants and checked cloths. The food is standard Italian, with an emphasis on pizzas. Donatello is a brother eatery to Pinocchio's, close to the Theatre Royal. *3 Brighton Pl., tel. 01273/775477. Reservations advised in summer. AE, DC, MC, V.*

¢ **Bedford Tavern.** Brighton has more than its share of pubs: In some places there are several to a block. This friendly neighborhood hangout serves huge sandwiches at lunch—an excellent value for the money. Order the smoked salmon. *30 Western St., tel. 01273/739495. No credit cards.*

Splurge **English's Oyster Bar.** Buried in the heart of The Lanes, this more
★ than 200-year-old family business is one of the few genuinely old-fashioned seafood havens left in England. You can either eat succulent oysters and other seafood dishes at the counter, or get a table in the restaurant section. It's ideal for lunch after a morning of antiques hunting; you can get a full, fabulous meal for two, including wine, for under £40. *29–31 East St., tel. 01273/327980. Reservations advised. AE, DC, MC, V.*

Shopping The main shopping area to head for is **The Lanes,** especially if you are interested in antiques or jewelry, and this cluster of alleys and tiny squares also has clothing boutiques, coffee shops, and pubs. Across North Street from the Lanes lie the **North Lanes,** a network of narrow streets full of interesting little stores, less glossy than those in the Lanes, but sometimes more interesting—there are even street stalls on weekends. Items in this part of town tend to be cheaper than those found at the Lanes.

Holleyman and Treacher (21A Duke St., at the western edge of The Lanes, tel. 01273/28007) is a book collector's dream, with a wealth of books on all subjects, and many on Brighton and Sussex. It also has a large stock of antique prints at all prices.

Pecksniff's Bespoke Perfumery (45/46 Meeting House Lane, tel. 01273/328904) has an original approach to the art of fragrance. In a room full of wooden drawers and brown glass bottles, an assistant will mix and match the ingredients to suit you. The results are very attractive and far from expensive.

The Arts and Nightlife Brighton has several theaters. **The Dome** (tel. 01273/674357), beside the Pavilion, was converted into an auditorium from the Prince Regent's stables in the 1930s, and today it stages classical and pop concerts. The **Theatre Royal** (New Rd., tel. 01273/28488), close to the Pavilion, is a very attractive Regency building with a period gem of an auditorium. It is a favorite venue for shows on their way to or from London's West End, and ticket prices are about half the cost of London's. The **Gardner Centre for the Arts** (tel. 01273/685861), on the campus of Sussex University, a few miles northeast at Falmer, presents plays, concerts, and cabaret.

Festival The **Brighton Festival** (tel. 01273/676926), an international event held every May, covers drama, music from classical to rock, dance, visual arts, and literature.

Lewes

The local trains for Lewes leave every 20 minutes from Brighton, and take 15 minutes. Lewes is also on a direct line from London/Victoria, and the quickest trains take a little more than an hour. Lewes tourist office: 187 High St., tel. 01273/483448.

★ **Lewes** is a town so rich in architectural history that the Council for British Archaeology has named it one of the 50 most important English cities. The **High Street** is lined with old buildings of all descriptions, dating from the late Middle Ages onward, including a timber-frame house once occupied by Thomas Paine, author of *Common Sense*.

Towering over the town, high above the valley of the River Ouse, stand the majestic ruins of **Lewes Castle,** an early Norman edifice, begun in 1100. For a panoramic view of the surrounding region, climb the keep and look out from the top. The **Living History Centre** has been moved inside the castle. You can also stop in at Barbican House, just opposite the 14th-century Barbican Gate, to see the **Town Model**. *169 High St., tel. 01273/474379. Admission: £2.40 adults, £2.20 senior citizens and students, £1.25 children. £7.70 family ticket. Open Mon.–Sat. 10–5, Sun. 11–5. Closed Christmas.*

Dining and Lodging **White Hart Hotel.** This ancient hotel, in the center of town, is now **££** part of the Best Western chain. Lodging rates are beyond our range (under £80), but the White Hart has a fairly reasonable restaurant where you can eat for less than £20. The back half of the paneled dining room is a bright conservatory, perfect for summer eating. There are usually roasts on a carving trolley, and there is a separate coffee shop for snacks. *55 High St., tel. 01273/476676, fax 01273/476695. 48 rooms, 33 with bath or shower. Facilities: gym, indoor pool, restaurant (reservations advised) AE, DC, MC, V.*

Lodging **Millers.** In the 17th century this old house was the Rose Inn. A later **£** occupant, John Sicklemore, a miller, sold flour from the front room, and there is still a millstone in the garden. Millers is three doors up the hill from the Shelleys Hotel. The interior has plenty of old wood paneling, and one of the bedrooms has a Victorian four-poster. The bedrooms are big, and all have TVs. Smoking is not allowed, nor are young children. *134 High St., BN7 1XS, tel. 01273/475631. 2 rooms with bath or shower. No credit cards.*

¢ **Weighed Inn.** This restaurant is at the bottom of the steep High Street, just across the bridge over the River Ouse, on the right-hand side. It has all the usual kinds of bar food, but a restaurant setting. Try the shepherd's pie or the quiche. There are several antiques markets nearby for after-lunch browsing. *Bear La., Cliffe High St., tel. 01273/477737. AE, MC, V. Closed Sun. and evenings.*

Shopping **The Old Needle Makers** (12 Flitcroft St.) is in a setting of huge beams and cobbled floors, in the shell of an old candle and needle factory, just off the High Street. Twenty small, craft-based shops sell kitchenware, flowers and baskets, cosmetics, tops, and fire grates and fire accessories.

Arundel

Arundel is a little more than an hour from Brighton by rail. Take the hourly Chichester train and change at Ford, with a 15-minute wait. Arundel tourist office: 61 High St., tel. 01903/882268.

Arundel, 23 miles west of Brighton, is a tiny hilltop town dominated by an 11th-century castle that was home to the dukes of Norfolk for more than 700 years, and an imposing **Roman Catholic cathedral**— the duke is Britain's leading Catholic peer.

The ceremonial entrance to **Arundel Castle** is at the top of the High Street, but visitors can enter at the bottom, close to the parking lot. The keep, rising from its conical mound, is as old as the original castle, while the barbican (gate house) and the Barons' Hall date from the 13th century. The interior of the castle was reconstructed in the then-fashionable Gothic style of the 19th century and is rather musty. Among the treasures on view are the rosary and prayer book used by Mary, Queen of Scots, at her execution. As is so often the case with a British historic property still in private hands, Arundel Castle has a slightly shabby air about it. The spacious grounds are open to the public, and there is a restaurant. *Tel. 01903/883355. Admission: £5 adults, £4.50 senior citizens, £3.50 children. Open Apr.–Oct., Sun.–Fri. noon–5 (gates close at 4).*

Lodging **Swan Hotel.** The Swan was a going concern by the 1780s. Refurbished in Victorian style, and centrally sited at the bottom of the High Street, it also offers friendly management. The rooms have a TV and a tea/coffeemaker. The Swan has bar food and a good restaurant, both serving hearty country dishes made with fresh local produce. *27–29 High St., BN18 9AG, tel. 01903/882314, fax 01903/733381. 15 rooms with bath or shower. Facilities: restaurant. AE, DC, MC, V.*

Dining **Black Rabbit.** This newly renovated 18th-century pub is a gem (and ¢ you must persevere along Mill Road in order to find it). Its location ★ by the river, with views of the castle and the bird sanctuary, is ideal for a summer lunch. The bar food is good and affordable, and there's a proper fish restaurant if you want something more substantial. *Mill Rd., tel. 01903/882828. No credit cards.*

Chichester

The trains from Brighton to Chichester run hourly and take 55 minutes for the trip. From London/Victoria you can go directly to Chichester in an hour and 40 minutes. Chichester tourist office: 29A South St., tel. 01243/775888.

Chichester, capital city of West Sussex, founded by the Romans, sits on the low-lying plains between the wooded south downs and the sea. Though it boasts its own giant cathedral and has all the trappings of a large, commercial city, Chichester is not much bigger than many of the provincial towns around it. The city walls and major streets follow the original Roman plan; the intersection of the four principal streets is marked by a 15th-century cross. The Norman **cathedral,** near the corner of West and South streets, also stands on Roman foundations. Inside, a glass panel reveals a group of Roman mosaics uncovered during recent restoration efforts. Other treasures include two of the most important Norman sculptures in Britain: *The Raising of Lazarus* and *Christ Arriving in Bethany,* both in the choir aisle. You will also see some outstanding modern works by artists John Piper, Marc Chagall, and Graham Sutherland.

There are more substantial traces of Chichester's Roman origins at **Fishbourne Roman Palace,** just a half-mile out (4-minute train ride). There you can take a good look at the largest Roman villa in Britain. Probably built as a residence for Roman emperor Tiberius Claudius Cogidubnus, the villa contains a remarkable range of mosaics. Sophisticated bathing and heating systems remain, and the gardens have been laid out much as they were in the 1st century AD. *Salthill Rd., Fishbourne, tel. 01243/785859. Admission: £3.50 adults, £2.80 senior citizens, £1.60 children, £8.70 family ticket. Open Mar.–July and Sept., daily 10–5; Aug., daily 10–6; Nov.–mid-Dec., Feb. 13–28, daily 10–4. Christmas period open Sun. only.*

Lodging **26 King's Avenue.** There is limited capacity in this B&B so advance
£ reservations are essential. It is a charming, well-tended cottage in a cul-de-sac, conveniently close to the center of town and two minutes from the rail station, but also easy to reach for drivers coming off the A27 by-pass. Chichester's historic canal is also nearby. Rooms have a TV and a tea/coffeemaker, and service is affable and homey. *26 King's Avenue, PO19 2EA, tel. 01243/782794++fax?++. 2 rooms with bath. No credit cards.*

Dining **Comme Ça.** This former pub is on the north side of town, near the
£ Festival Theatre. As you'd expect with a name like this, the menu is French and uses fresh local ingredients. Try any of the fish dishes, such as *moules marinière* (mussels in onion sauce) or turbot. There is a more expensive dining room, with dried flowers and hops hung from the ceiling, but the bar serves light meals. You can eat before or after festival performances. *67 Broyle Rd., tel. 01243/788724. Reservations advised. AE, MC, V. Closed Sun. and Mon.*

The Arts and **The Festival Theatre,** Chichester (tel. 01243/781312), presents mid-
Nightlife dle-of-the-road productions of classics and modern plays for the undemanding theatergoer from May through September. Like Glyndebourne, it has an international reputation and can provide the evening focus for a relaxed day out of London. There is also a theater restaurant, geared to the timing of performances.

4 The South

Winchester, Salisbury, Stonehenge, Poole

The south coast of England has been central to the country's history for more than 4,000 years. From the sheltered bays and river estuaries, Britain's fleets have long set sail for war: American and British forces departed from ports along this coast for Normandy on D-Day, British troops left from here for the Falklands and, most recently, to fight in the Persian Gulf. In peacetime, all the great Atlantic liners have docked here.

Inland, the fertile river valleys and rolling hills have seen prehistoric man give way to the Celts, Romans, and Saxons. Salisbury Plain has hundreds of prehistoric remains, with Stonehenge the most renowned. Winchester, the lovely cathedral city located just 64 miles southwest of London, was the capital of Wessex, one of the original seven Anglo-Saxon kingdoms, and home to several rich prince-bishops. For centuries the noble landowners of the area invested in building magnificent homes for themselves. Other points of interest include the wild, scenic expanse of the New Forest, ancient hunting preserve of William the Conqueror, and the Dorset coastline, immortalized in the novels of Thomas Hardy and John Fowles.

The South is made up of the counties of Hampshire (Hants), Dorset, and Wiltshire. The public transport network is one of the best in the country, and bus routes link all the towns and most of the villages, though very careful planning is necessary if you want to take in several sights on the same day. All the local bus companies issue budget tickets specifically designed to help the visitor get around cheaply. Main train lines to the Southwest run from London/Waterloo, taking in Winchester, Salisbury, and Bournemouth.

Essential Information

Lodging   Among the coast's popular holiday spots are Bournemouth and Poole—big, old-fashioned seaside towns that offer a wide range of accommodations. When booking for summer months (make reservations in advance), you may find that guest houses will be reluctant to take one-nighters and many may require you to eat at least one main meal on the premises each day. Highly recommended establishments are indicated by a star ★.

Dining Fertile soil, well-stocked rivers, and a long coastline ensure excellent farm produce and a plentiful stock of fish throughout the South. Try fresh-grilled river trout or sea bass poached in brine, or dine like a king on the New Forest's famous venison. Unless otherwise noted, reservations are not needed and dress is casual. Highly recommended restaurants are indicated by a star ★.

Shopping In the South these days, well-known chain stores are being increasingly challenged by newly established, independent specialist stores. These are now so numerous as to constitute a specialty in their own right and a boon to the visitor—not only as outlets for such local crafts as jewelry and ceramics, but also as the first choice of shoppers with discriminating tastes in everything from food to furniture.

Open-air markets are an almost daily event throughout the South (a complete list is available from the Southern Tourist Board). Among the best are Salisbury's traditional city market (Tuesday and Saturday) and a general country market (Wednesday) at Ringwood, near Bournemouth.

Biking This is a fairly level region, with easy but often busy roads for the cyclist. Areas with lots of hidden lanes, such as the New Forest, are suited for leisurely exploration. Some stores where bikes can be rented (mainly in summer) are in Bournemouth: **Bicycle World** (244 Charminster Rd., tel. 01202/520289) and **Pedals** (290 Holdenhurst Rd., tel. 01202/301683); in Dorchester: **Dorchester Cycles** (31B Great Western Rd., tel. 01305/268787); in Poole: **Bikes** (431–433 Poole Rd., Branksome, tel. 01202/769202); in Salisbury: **Hayball's Cycle Shop** (26–30 Winchester St., tel. 01722/411378).

Hiking The **Dorset Coast Path** runs from Lyme Regis to Poole, 72 miles in all. You can walk all or only a part of the route. There are some highlights along the way, especially Golden Cap, the highest point on the south coast, with spectacular views; the swannery at Abbotsbury; Lulworth Cove; and Chesil Bank. Details are available from the local tourist offices.

The **Solent Way** runs for 60 miles along the coast from Milford on Sea to Emsworth, passing through the New Forest, Buckler's Hard, Beaulieu, Portsmouth, and Southsea. The walk is especially good for anyone interested in ships and the historic harbors.

The **New Forest** offers opportunities for all types of walkers. For details of trails, visit the Information Centre at Lyndhurst.

Festivals The South is host to numerous music and crafts festivals, particularly in the spring and summer months. Among other towns, Salisbury has a particularly active schedule.

Tour 1: Winchester and Portsmouth

The main sights of Winchester lie close together and can be visited easily in a few hours. This tour makes a decent day trip from London, or you can plan to stop here en route to another base city such as Salisbury.

From London Winchester is on the London/Southampton line, with trains running
By Train at least every hour. The average journey takes 1½ hours. For sched-

The South

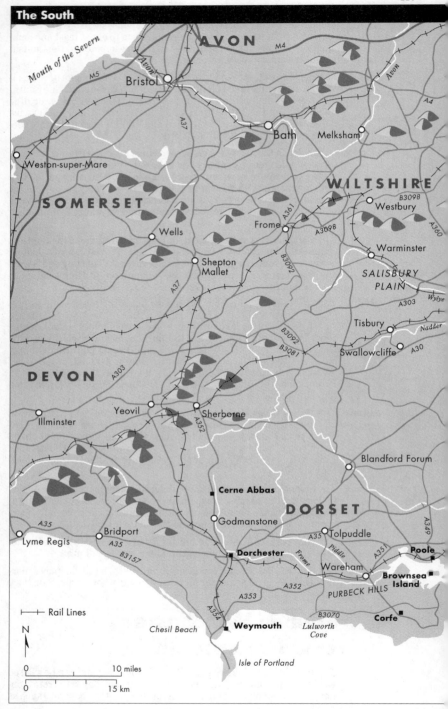

Mouth of the Severn

AVON

M4

Avon

Bristol

M5

Bath

Melksham

Avon

A37

A4

Weston-super-Mare

WILTSHIRE

B3098

SOMERSET

Westbury

A360

Wells

Frome

A361

A3098

Warminster

Shepton Mallet

A37

B3092

SALISBURY PLAIN

A303

Wylye

Tisbury

Nadder

B3092

DEVON

A303

B3081

Swallowcliffe

A30

Illminster

Yeovil

Sherborne

A352

Blandford Forum

Cerne Abbas

A35

A349

Lyme Regis

Bridport

A35

B3157

Godmanstone

DORSET

Tolpuddle

A35

A351

Poole

Dorchester

Frome

Piddle

Wareham

Brownsea Island

A352

PURBECK HILLS

A353

A354

B3070

Corfe

Chesil Beach

Weymouth

Lulworth Cove

Isle of Portland

├──┤ Rail Lines

N

0 _____ 10 miles

0 _____ 15 km

ules call London/Waterloo information (tel. 0171/928–5100) or Winchester rail information (tel. 01703/229393).

By Bus **National Express** coaches make the 2-hour trip to the Winchester bus station (on Broadway, near the cathedral, tel. 01962/853129), leaving every 2 hours from the London/Victoria Coach Station (tel. 0171/730–0202).

By Car The M3 from southwest of London goes directly to Winchester, 72 miles away.

Winchester

Winchester tourist office: The Guildhall, The Broadway, tel. 01962/840500.

Winchester is among the most historic of English cities, and as you walk its graceful, unspoiled streets, a sense of the past envelops you. Though it is now merely the county seat of Hampshire, for more than four centuries Winchester served as England's capital. Here, in AD 827, Egbert was crowned first king of England, and his successor Alfred the Great held court until his death in 899. After the Norman Conquest in 1066, William I ("the Conqueror") had himself crowned in London, but took the precaution of repeating the ceremony in Winchester. The city remained the center of commercial and political power until the 13th century. Medieval Winchester was also the ecclesiastical center of England, renowned throughout Europe for its illuminated manuscripts, some of which you can still see in the cathedral library.

Numbers in the margin correspond to points of interest on the Winchester map.

★ ❶ Start your tour at the **cathedral,** the city's greatest monument. Begun in 1079 and consecrated in 1093, the cathedral's original Norman structure was altered several times during the Middle Ages. In the cathedral's tower, transepts, and crypt, as in the core of the great nave, you can see some of the world's best surviving examples of Norman architecture. Other features, such as the arcades, the clerestory (the wall dividing the aisles from the nave), and the windows, are Gothic alterations carried out during the 12th and 13th centuries. The remodeling of the nave in the Perpendicular style was not completed until the 15th century. Little of the original stained glass has survived, thanks to Cromwell's Puritan troops, who ransacked the cathedral in the 17th century during the English Civil War.

Among the many important people buried in the cathedral are William the Conqueror's son, William II (Rufus), mysteriously murdered in the New Forest in 1100; Izaak Walton, author of *The Compleat Angler*, whose memorial window in Silkestede's Chapel was paid for by "the fishermen of England and America"; and Jane Austen, whose memorial window can be seen in the north aisle of the nave. In the retro-choir, look for the statuette of William Walker, the diver, "who saved this cathedral with his two hands." This curious inscription refers to Walker's heroic underpinning of the building's flooded foundations (1906–12), when the medieval ones had proved too shallow.

❷ Behind the cathedral is the **Close,** an area containing the Deanery, Dome Alley, and Cheyney Court. On the right, as you enter
❸ Cheyney Court, you will see the **King's Gate,** built in the 13th century, one of two gates remaining from the original city wall. **St. Swithun's** church is built over the King's Gate.

Turn left onto College Street and proceed to No. 8, the house where Jane Austen died on July 18, 1817, three days after writing a comic poem (copies are usually available in the cathedral) about the legend

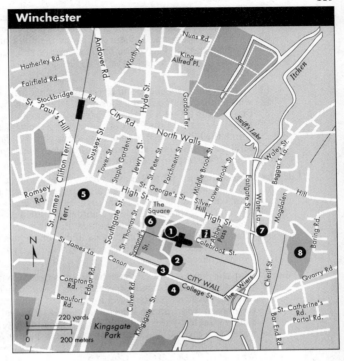

Winchester

of St. Swithin's Day—a remarkable testimony to her unfailing cheerfulness.

❹ Continue along College Street to **Winchester College,** founded in 1382, and probably England's oldest "public" (that is, private) school. Among the original buildings still in use is Chamber Court, center of college life for six centuries. Keep an eye out for "scholars"—students holding academic scholarships—clad in their traditional gowns. *College St., tel. 01962/886–8778. Admission: £2 adults, £1.50 senior citizens and children. Guided tours last about an hour (must be booked in advance) Apr.–Sept., Mon.–Sat. 11:15, 2:15, and 3:30, Sun. 2:15 and 3:30.*

❺ A few blocks west of the cathedral is another of Winchester's important historical sites, the medieval **Great Hall,** which is all that remains of the city's castle. It has witnessed many historic events: The English Parliament met here for the first time in 1246; Sir Walter Raleigh was tried for conspiracy against King James I and condemned to death here in 1603 (though he wasn't beheaded until 1618); and Dame Alice Lisle was sentenced here by the infamous Judge Jeffreys to be burned at the stake for sheltering a fugitive, following Monmouth's Rebellion in 1685. (King James II, in a rare act of mercy, commuted her sentence to beheading.) On the west wall of the hall hangs what is said to be the tabletop of King Arthur's Round Table, with places for 24 knights and a portrait of Arthur, which bears a remarkable resemblance to King Henry VII. In fact, the table is a Tudor forgery; the real Arthur was probably a Celtic cavalry general who held off the invading Saxons following the fall of the Roman Empire. Henry VII revived the Arthurian legend for political purposes. He named his eldest son Arthur, though the boy did not live to inherit the throne. *Castle Hill, tel. 01962/846476. Admission free. Open Apr.–Oct., daily 10–5; Nov.–Mar., daily 10–4.*

Retrace your steps along High Street to **The Square,** across from the cathedral, and have a look at Winchester's past through the exhibits ❻ in the **City Museum.** Objects on display include Celtic pottery, Roman mosaics, and Saxon coins. *The Square, tel. 01962/848269. Admission free. Open weekdays 10–5, Sat. 10–1, 2–5, Sun. 2–5 (closed Mon. Oct.–Mar.).*

❼ For a change of scenery and era, visit the **City Mill,** an 18th-century ❽ water mill situated at the foot of **St. Giles's Hill,** just east of High Street. You'll find a National Trust gift shop and a café at the Mill that are open all year. Part of the building is used as a youth hostel. Climb the hill for a panoramic view of the city. *Bridge St., tel. 01962/ 870057. Admission: 90p adults, 45p children. Open Apr.–Sept., daily 11–4:45; Mar. and Oct., weekends noon–4.*

Lodding **Stratton House.** This Victorian home, situated on a hill just beyond £ St. Giles Park, is located in a quiet area on the east side of town. In addition to its placid surroundings, Stratton has an attentive and friendly staff that tends to the comfortably furnished and fairly spacious bedrooms. Tea/coffeemakers and TVs are among the amenities offered, and an evening meal is available on request. *Stratton Rd., SO23 8JQ, tel. 01962/863919, fax 01962/842095. 6 rooms with bath or shower. No credit cards.*

Dining **Nine the Square.** You can have budget food at the wine bar or select £ from the regularly changing restaurant menu, which might include salmon, duck, or chicken, and a variety of glamorous desserts. To accompany your dinner, there's a fine list of wines, some of which can be bought by the glass. While you're here, take in views of the majestic cathedral that towers outside the windows. *9 Great Minster St., The Square, tel. 01962/864004. Reservations required for restaurant. AE, DC, MC, V. Closed Sun.*

¢ **The Eclipse.** The 14th-century Eclipse, Winchester's smallest pub, ★ has all the trappings of age, including wood beams that tilt every which way, oak settles (like high-backed pews), and a collection of mugs hanging from the ceiling. The one sour note is the Muzak (definitely not medieval!). Filling and tasty bar food features homemade steak-and-kidney or game pies, ploughman's lunches, and a variety of sandwiches. In the summer there are tables and chairs placed out front. It is very close to the cathedral. *The Square, tel. 01962/ 865676. No reservations. No credit cards.*

¢ **Wykeham Arms.** This old inn is centrally located, near both the cathedral and the college. During lunchtime, traditional, low-budget fare is served at the four busy, happily cluttered bars that are adorned with everything from old sports equipment to pewter mugs; in the winter, a log fire blazes. At night the presentation is fancier (with prices to match), beginning with house specials such as venison in port, monkfish brochettes, and fresh grilled Alresford trout. To round out the meal, pick from an award-winning wine list, with more than 20 selections available by the glass. *75 Kingsgate St., tel. 01962/853834. Reservations advised for dinner (last orders 8:30). AE, DC, MC, V.*

Shopping The **Antiques Market** (King's Walk, tel. 01962/862277) sells crafts and gift items, as well as antiques. A complete list of local antique stores is available from Winchester Tourist Information Center (tel. 01962/840500).

H. M. Gilbert, an antiquarian bookseller, is located at 19 The Square (tel. 01962/226420), in a network of ancient streets. His shop is housed in five medieval cottages, with the antiquarian section in a 15th-century hall.

The Arts and The **Theatre Royal** in Winchester (Jewry St., tel. 01962/843434), **Nightlife** with a splendidly ornate Edwardian interior, houses mainly touring shows.

Portsmouth

Portsmouth lies 25 miles southeast of Winchester. Regular trains make the one-hour journey hourly between the two cities each day. Bus 69 does the trip hourly in one hour and 40 minutes. The **Guide Friday** *(tel. 01789/826722) tour operator offers guided tours of Portsmouth from the end of May to mid-September in open-top buses (£5.50 adults, £4 senior citizens, £1.50 children). Portsmouth tourist office: The Hard, tel. 01705/826722; Clarence Esplanade, Southsea, tel. 01705/832464 (Easter–Oct.)*

The city of Portsmouth is England's naval capital and the principal port of departure for British forces. The harbor covers about 7 square miles and has the world's first dry dock (built in 1495) and extensive defenses, including **Portchester Castle,** founded more than 1,600 years ago. The castle has the most complete set of Roman walls (constructed in the 3rd century) still existing in northern Europe. The keep's central tower affords a sweeping view of the harbor and coastline. *Near Fareham, tel. 01705/378291. Admission: £2 adults, £1.50 senior citizens, £1 children under 16, children under 5 free. Open Apr.–Sept., daily 10–6; Oct.–Mar., daily 10–4.*

Portsmouth Naval Base has an unrivaled collection of ships on display, of which the most outstanding is Nelson's flagship.

★ **HMS *Victory*.** She has been painstakingly restored to appear as she did at the time of her last and most famous battle at Trafalgar (1805). You can inspect the cramped gun-decks, visit the cabin where Nelson entertained his officers, and stand on the spot where he was mortally wounded by a French sniper. The four main sights in the Portsmouth Naval Base, HMS *Victory*, the *Mary Rose*, HMS *Warrior*, and the Royal Naval Museum, are all run by the Portsmouth Heritage Trust (tel. 01705/839766). *Admission: to each of the three ships when visited separately—(HMS Victory includes the museum)—£4.75 adults, £4.25 senior citizens, £3.50 children. 2-ship and 3-ship and family tickets are also available. Open Mar.–June and Sept.–Oct., daily 10–6; July–Aug., daily 10–7; Nov.–Feb., daily 10–5:30.*

★ In 1982, a much-publicized exercise in marine archaeology succeeded in raising the **Mary Rose,** flagship of the Tudor navy, which capsized and sank in the harbor in 1545 while heading out to attack French warships. The *Mary Rose*, which was described at the time as "the flower of all the ships that ever sailed," is now housed in a specially constructed enclosure, where her timbers are continuously sprayed with water to prevent them from drying out and breaking up. Thousands of remarkably well-preserved objects—including tools, weapons, pots, and surgical instruments—were found on board during the excavation, and a selection can be seen in the museum located in the same complex. The exhibition is one of the most dramatic and fascinating archaeological displays in the world.

HMS *Warrior*, another of Portsmouth's great ships, is now berthed near HMS *Victory* and the *Mary Rose*. The *Warrior* was built in 1860 as Britain's first armored battleship—the fastest, longest (over 400 feet), and most powerful warship of her day. She spent her active life guarding the Channel against foreign attack. Close by is the **Royal Navy Museum,** with its fine collection of painted figureheads, relics of Nelson's family, and galleries of paintings and mementos recalling different periods of naval history.

The even more popular **D-Day Museum,** near the corner of Southsea Common, tells the complex story of D-Day. A variety of exhibits vividly reconstructs the many stages of planning, the communications and logistics involved in the maneuver, as well as the actual invasion. The centerpiece of the museum is the **Overlord Embroidery,** a 272-foot-long tapestry with 34 panels illustrating the history of

World War II, from the Battle of Britain in 1940 to D-Day itself (June 6, 1944) and the first days of the liberation. It is modeled on the Bayeux Tapestry. *Clarence Esplanade, Southsea, tel. 01705/ 827261. Admission: £3.50 adults, £2 senior citizens and children, £9 family ticket. Open Apr.–Sept., daily 9:30–7:30; Oct.–Mar., daily 10:30–5.*

Dining **Bistro Montparnasse.** Candles, prints, and pink tablecloths help fos-
£ ter the intimate atmosphere of a traditional French restaurant. Among the dishes featured are mussels in saffron sauce, and a refreshingly sharp lemon soufflé. *103 Palmerston Rd., Southsea, tel. 01705/816754. Reservations advised. AE, MC, V. Closed Sun. and Mon. lunch, and 3 weeks over Christmas and Jan.*

£ **Sally Port.** This big 16th-century pub, recently redecorated with a nautical theme, is located close to the Dockyard Heritage Center, making it a convenient stop for a bar-food lunch after viewing the *Victory* or the *Mary Rose,* or a more expensive meal from the à la carte menu in the restaurant. There are also 10 rooms available (under £60). *High St., Old Portsmouth, tel. 01705/821860. AE, DC, MC, V.*

Tour 2: Salisbury and Stonehenge

The public associates Salisbury with artist John Constable's paintings of the town's remarkable cathedral and with scenes from the film *The French Lieutenant's Woman.* Hordes of visitors are drawn to these romantic settings, turning an otherwise quiet country village into anything but quiet. Salisbury is an excellent exploring base for a fascinating region that includes Stonehenge, Dorchester, and several fine, stately homes. It is a nexus for dozens of busy bus routes, mostly run by the Wilts and Dorset company, which open up the surrounding countryside to the budget tourist. Sightseers can cash in on some excellent deals offered by the bus company.

From London The fastest trains from London/Waterloo (tel. 0171/928–5100) take a
By Train little more than 1½ hours with two stops. For schedules and rail information in the area, tel. 01703/229393.

By Bus Three **National Express** buses (No. 005) run daily from London/Victoria Coach Station (tel. 0171/730–0202) to Salisbury. The trip takes just under three hours. The **Wilts and Dorset** company offers a seven-day Busabout sightseeing ticket for £18.25 for adults and £10 for children. For schedules and the price of other budget tickets, call Salisbury bus information (tel. 01722/336855).

By Car From London, take the M4, M25, and M3 sequence of motorways west; go as far as junction 8 on the M3, then take the A303 and A34, turning west onto A30 for the last 22 miles into Salisbury. The total length of the trip is 91 miles.

Salisbury

Salisbury tourist office: Fish Row, just off Market Sq., tel. 01722/ 334956.

Numbers in the margin correspond to points of interest on the Salisbury map.

Salisbury's old stone buildings—shops and houses—grew up in the shadow of its great cathedral. Unlike Winchester, Salisbury did not become important until the 13th century, when the diocese of Old Sarum (the original settlement 2 miles to the north) was transferred here. The cathedral at Old Sarum was razed (today only ruins remain), and **Salisbury Cathedral** was built. The local people relocated

★ ❶

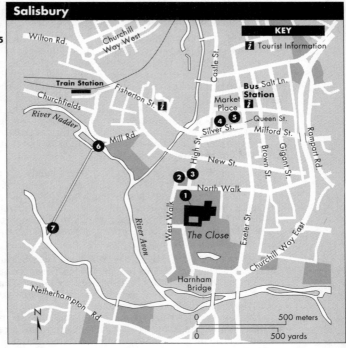

Salisbury

along with the ecclesiastical center, and the city of Salisbury was born. In the 19th century, novelist Anthony Trollope based his tales of ecclesiastical life, notably *Barchester Towers,* on life in Salisbury, although his fictional city of Barchester is really an amalgam of Winchester and Salisbury.

Salisbury is dominated by its towering cathedral, a soaring hymn in stone. It is unique among medieval British cathedrals in that it was conceived and built as a whole in the amazingly short span of only 38 years (1220–58). The spire, which commands the surrounding countryside, was added in 1320 and is a miraculous feat of medieval engineering—even though the point, 404 feet above the ground, is 2½ feet off vertical. For a fictional, keenly imaginative reconstruction of the human drama underlying this achievement, read William Golding's novel *The Spire.*

The interior of the cathedral is remarkable for its lancet windows and the sculpted tombs of crusaders and other medieval heroes. The clock in the north aisle—probably the oldest working mechanism in Europe, if not the world—was made in 1386. The spacious cloisters are the largest in England, and don't overlook the octagonal **Chapter House,** which contains a marvelous 13th-century frieze showing scenes from the Old Testament. Here you can also see one of the four original copies of the **Magna Carta,** the charter of rights that the English barons forced King John to accept in 1215; it was sent here for safekeeping in the 13th century.

The **Cathedral Close** (grounds) appears much as it did when it was first laid out, with its wide lawns flanked by historic houses, some of which are open to the public. One of these is the impressive **Mompesson House** on the north side, which boasts some fine original paneling and plasterwork, as well as a fascinating collection of 18th-century drinking glasses, and an attractive walled garden. *Tel.*

01722/335659. Admission: £3 adults, £1.50 children. Open Apr.–Oct., Sat.–Wed. noon–5:30.

❸ Leaving the close on the north side will take you through **High Street Gate**—one of the four castellated stone gateways built to separate the close from the rest of the city—and into the heart of the modern town. Turn right into Silver Street, and you will find one of

❹ Salisbury's best-known landmarks, the **Poultry Cross.** This little hexagonal structure is the last of the four original market crosses, and market dealers still set up their stalls beside it. A narrow side

❺ street links it to **Market Square,** site of one of southern England's most popular markets, held on Tuesday and Saturday. Permission to hold an annual fair here was granted in 1221, and that right is exercised for three days every October.

Many medieval cities in England boast handsome half-timbered houses, but Salisbury has more than most. A particularly fine example can be found close to Market Square, at No. 8 Queen Street. This house, originally the home of a successful wool merchant, is now a store that sells fine china and glassware. You can browse here and see the old staircase, the fireplaces of local Chilmark stone, and the Jacobean oak paneling.

Just west of High Street lies Mill Road, which leads you across

❻ Queen Elizabeth Gardens to **Long Bridge.** Cross the bridge and continue on the town path; the view from here inspired a classic 19th-century painting, John Constable's *Salisbury Cathedral,* now hung in the Constable Room of London's National Gallery. Continue farther along the town path in the same direction until you come to the

❼ **Old Mill,** dating from the 12th century. It is now a restaurant and coffee shop under the same management as the Old Mill Hotel next door.

Lodging **County Hotel.** This mellow, 100-plus-year-old stone Victorian man-

£ sion, a member of the Berni hotel chain and conveniently located in the city center, offers river views and boasts its own ghost. The reasonably sized bedrooms have TVs and tea/coffeemakers. *Bridge St., SP1 2ND, tel. 01722/320229, fax 01722/414313. 31 rooms with bath. Facilities: restaurant, parking. AE, MC, V.*

¢ **Byways House.** Friendly service, good value for the money, and a

★ quiet location are some of the reasons the century-old hotel is popular with visitors. Ask for a room with a view of the cathedral. *31 Fowlers Rd., SP1 2QP, tel. 01722/328364, fax 01722/322146. 23 rooms, 19 with bath. Facilities: large garden. MC, V.*

¢ **Glen Lyn.** This large, Victorian house is located in a peaceful cul-de-sac on the east side of town, just a few minutes' walk from the town center. The comfortable rooms have a TV and a tea/coffeemaker, and dinner is available on request. Smoking is not permitted on the premises. *6 Bellamy La., Millford Hill, SP1 2SP, tel. 01722/327880. 9 rooms, 4 with bath or shower. No credit cards.*

Dining **Harper's.** This is a spacious, airy, second-floor restaurant overlook-

£ ing the marketplace. Its cuisine mingles English and French dishes with such specialties as boeuf bourguignon and fillet of salmon. There is a good-value Shopper's Special lunch. The friendly staff makes dining here a pleasure. *7 Ox Row, Market Pl., tel. 01722/333118. Reservations advised weekends. AE, DC, MC, V. Closed Sun. in winter.*

¢ **George and Dragon.** This family-run pub that dates to the 16th century offers a wide variety of beers, including real ale. Roasts and daily specials highlight the menu, and the summertime barbecues on the riverside garden are real treats. *85 Castle St., tel. 01722/333942. AE, DC, MC, V.*

¢ **Haunch of Venison.** Quite a bit of history is contained in this pub,

★ parts of which date to 1430. In the wood-paneled restaurant upstairs (mind your head on the beams) is a fireplace that's more than 500

years old, and in a niche is a mummified hand holding some 18th-century playing cards. The downstairs bar, with timbered walls and black-and-white tile floors, is small, noisy, and comfortable and serves simpler fare than the upstairs restaurant. *1 Minster St., tel. 01722/322024. Reservations required for upstairs. AE, DC, MC, V.*

¢ **Sunflowers.** The bright decor in this vegetarian restaurant provides a pleasant ambience for a good lunchtime snack or something more substantial. Soups are simple and appetizing, while sandwich fillings include cheddar, apple, and walnut; hummus and roasted pepper; and stilton and cucumber. Tortillas, Indian pancakes, and vegetable pie are also on the menu, which is rounded off by a good choice of mousses, meringues, and gâteaux. Wine, beer, and cider are available. *2–4 Ivy St., tel. 01722/333948. No reservations. MC, V. Closed Sun. and lunch Mon.–Wed.*

The Arts and Nightlife

The **Salisbury Playhouse** (Malthouse Lane, tel. 01722/320333) presents high-caliber drama year-round and is the focus for the Salisbury Festival.

The **Salisbury Festival** (tel. 01722/323883), held in May, features excellent classical concerts, recitals, and plays.

Wilton

Wilton is very close to Salisbury with regular local bus services: Buses X4, 25, 26, 27, 60, and 61 cover the route in about 12 minutes, and leave from New Canal in the city center.

About 3 miles along the valley of the River Nadder is the ancient town of **Wilton,** from which the county takes its name. A traditional market is held here every Thursday, but the main attraction is

★ **Wilton House and Gardens,** home of the 17th Earl of Pembroke. The original Tudor house burned down in 1647, and the present mansion, which replaced it, was designed by Inigo Jones, Ben Jonson's stage designer and the architect of London's Banqueting House. The house contains a superb collection of paintings by Rubens, Breughel, and Van Dyke, among others, as well as family treasures such as Napoleon's pearl-inlaid dispatch box and a lock of Queen Elizabeth I's hair. The main focus of interest, however, is the building itself. Among the staterooms are a Single Cube Room (designed as an exact 30-foot cube) and a Double Cube Room (twice the length), both elaborately decorated with moldings of fruit and flowers, gilded in different shades of gold, and sumptuously furnished with 18th-century sofas and chairs upholstered in red velvet. It was in the Double Cube Room that Eisenhower prepared some of his plans for the Normandy invasion. Reconstructions of a Tudor kitchen and a Victorian laundry have been added to the attractions, as well as a collection of toy "Wareham Bears." The gardens have a number of magnificent old cedars and an imposing Palladian bridge which was built in 1737. *Tel. 01722/743115. Admission: £5 adults, £4.50 senior citizens, £3.50 children, £15 family ticket; grounds only: £2 adults, £1.50 children. Open Easter–mid-Oct., daily 11– 4:45. Restaurant opens at 11.*

Stonehenge

*The Wilts and Dorset Bus 3 departs from the Salisbury bus station for Stonehenge via Amesbury, five times daily, for the 40-minute journey. Stonehenge can be visited in about a half-hour, and you can catch the next Bus 3 for the return. Every coach tour stops at Stonehenge, including **Guide Friday** (tel. 01225/444102), for a fee of £11.50 adults, £9.50 senior citizens, £5 children. Fee includes entrance to the site.*

★ **Stonehenge** looks small because of its lonely isolation on the wide sweep of Salisbury Plain. The barriers around the great circle of stones have been installed to keep back the relentless throngs of tourists. During the summer solstice, Stonehenge becomes the target of the feeble remnants of the Alternate Society, who embark on an annual struggle with the police to celebrate, in the monument's imposing shadow, a barely understood pagan festival. But if you visit in the early morning, when the crowds have not yet arrived, or in the evening, when the sky is heavy with scudding clouds, you can experience Stonehenge as it once was: a magical, mystical, awe-inspiring place.

Stonehenge was begun around 2800 BC, enlarged between 2100 and 1900 BC, and altered yet again by 150 BC. It has been excavated and rearranged several times over the centuries. The medieval phrase "Stonehenge" means "hanging stones." (Interestingly enough, the use of "henge" to denote a circular arrangement of stone or wooden elements seems to have come from Stonehenge itself—an example of what wordsmiths call back-formation.) The monument, however, did not start out with great stones at all, but with the ditch and bank that still encircle the site. The first stone to be added was probably the Heel Stone, which stands outside the circle, near the main road.

Many of the huge stones that ringed the center were brought here from great distances. The original 80 bluestones (dolerite), which made up the two internal circles, were transported from the Preseli Mountains, near Fishguard on the Atlantic coast of Wales, presumably by raft on sea and river. Next they were dragged on rollers across country—a total journey of 130 miles as the crow flies, but closer to 240 by the easiest route. Later, great blocks of sarsen stone were quarried in north Wiltshire, dressed, and fitted together with primitive joints. The labor involved in quarrying, transporting, and carving these stones is astonishing, all the more so when you remember that it was begun before the major pyramids of Egypt were built.

We still do not know why the great project at Stonehenge was undertaken in the first place. It is fairly certain that it was a religious site, and that worship here involved the cycles of the sun; the alignment of the stones to point to sunrise at midsummer and sunset in midwinter makes this clear. One thing is certain: The Druids had nothing to do with the construction. The monument had already been in existence for nearly 2,000 years by the time they appeared.

There has been speculation that Stonehenge may have been a kind of neolithic computer, with a sophisticated astronomical purpose. Such theories are, of course, pure guesses, but fascinating nonetheless. *Stonehenge Decoded* by Gerald S. Hawkins is but one of many intriguing books on the subject.

As you can't get very close to the monoliths, and then only along one section of the site, it's a good idea to take a pair of binoculars to make out the details more clearly. The visitors' amenities at Stonehenge are rather squalid, but there are grandiose plans to improve them. *Near Amesbury (tel. 01980/623108). Admission: £3 adults, £2.30 senior citizens, £1.50 children++any age cut-off?++. Open Apr.– May and Sept., daily 9:30–6; June–Aug., daily 9–7; Oct.–Mar., daily 9:30–4.*

Tour 3: Bournemouth, Poole, Dorchester, and Weymouth

Like many towns swallowed by the endless south coast development, Bournemouth and Poole run together, although they still manage to maintain something of their original identities. These popular summer resorts, with a number of budget accommodations, make good bases for exploring the surrounding area: They are the center of a radiating local bus network, mainly run by the Wilts and Dorset company.

From London One train an hour makes the 90-minute journey daily from London/
By Train Waterloo (tel. 0171/928–5100) to Bournemouth; two other trains hourly take about 2¼ hours. Call Bournemouth rail information (tel. 01202/292474) for schedules.

By Bus The **National Express** *Rapide* Bus 515 from London/Victoria Coach Station (tel. 0171/730–0202) stops in both Bournemouth and Poole. There are 10 departures a day and the traveling time is 2 hours, 40 minutes to Bournemouth; about 3 hours to Poole.

By Car Take the motorway M33 southwest past Winchester to join with M27 at junction 4. Take M27 west to junction 1, then take A31 to the outskirts of Bournemouth.

Bournemouth

Wilts and Dorset buses (tel. 01202/673555) make stops throughout the area. Bournemouth tourist office: Westover Rd. (overlooking the bandstand), tel. 01202/789789.

Bournemouth has a relatively short and uneventful history. It was founded in 1810 by Lewis Tregonwell, an ex-army officer who had taken a liking to the area when stationed here some years before. He settled near what is now **The Square** and planted the first pine trees in the steep little valleys—or chines—cutting through the cliffs to the famous Bournemouth sands. The scent of fir trees was said to be good for consumption (tuberculosis) sufferers, and the town grew steadily as more and more people came for prolonged rest cures. Today Bournemouth is one of the south coast's most popular vacation destinations.

The Square and the beach are linked by gardens laid out with flowering trees and lawns. This is an excellent spot to relax and listen to stirring music wafting from the **Pine Walk bandstand**. Regular musical programs take place at the **Pavilion** and at the **Winter Gardens** (home of the Bournemouth Symphony Orchestra) nearby. There are also regular shows at the **Bournemouth International Centre** (tel. 01202/297297) on Exeter Road, which includes a selection of restaurants and bars and a swimming pool.

On the corner of Hilton Road stands **St. Peter's** parish church, easily recognizable by its 200-foot-high tower and spire. Lewis Tregonwell is buried in the churchyard. Here, too, you will notice the elaborate tombstone of Mary Shelley, author of *Frankenstein* and wife of the great Romantic poet Percy Bysshe Shelley, whose heart is buried with her. Admirers of Shelley will want to visit the **Casa Magni Shelley Museum** in Boscombe (on the west side of Bournemouth), with its touching collection of Shelley memorabilia. *Boscombe Manor, Beechwood Ave., tel. 01202/303571. Admission free. Open June–Sept., Mon.–Sat. 10:30–5; Oct.–May, Thurs.–Sat. 10:30–5.*

In Bournemouth, itself, you will find the interesting **Russell-Coates Art Gallery and Museum.** This late-Victorian mansion, perched on top of East Cliff, overflows with Victorian paintings and miniatures, cases of butterflies, and treasures from the Far East, including an exquisite suit of Japanese armor. *Tel. 01202/551009. Admission: £1 adults, 50p senior citizens and children, free on weekends. Open Tues.–Sun. 10–5.*

Lodging **Kiwi Hotel.** Like many of Bournemouth's accommodation choices,
£ this is a somewhat staid place, occupying the corner of a quiet street. Its main advantages are that it remains open all year, it is conveniently located for trips to the center (a five-minute walk), and represents excellent value, with discounts in low-season. The reasonably sized bedrooms are equipped with a TV and a tea/coffee-maker, and there is an airy nonsmoking dining room. *West Hill Rd., BH2 5EG, tel. 01202/555889. 45 rooms, 41 with bath or shower. Facilities: 2 bars, restaurant. AE, MC, V.*

£ **San Remo.** This well-built Victorian hotel is near the sea and the town center. The entire hotel has been refurbished, with cheerful flower-patterned wallpaper in the bedrooms, all of which have TVs. Dinner is available at 6 PM for £7.50 (bring your own wine). *7 Durley Rd., BH2 5JQ, tel. 01202/290558. 18 rooms, 14 with bath or shower. Closed Oct.–Easter.*

Dining **Sophisticats.** As the name suggests, there's a lot of felinity in the de-
££ cor here. This small (seats 34) restaurant, hidden in a shopping mall just outside the center of town, is especially adept with seafood, though there's Javanese fillet steak on the menu, too. *43 Charminster Rd., tel. 01202/291019. Reservations advised. No credit cards. Open Mon.–Sat., dinner only.*

£ **Coriander.** Throughout the ground-floor Cantina bar and the main restaurant upstairs the Mexican theme prevails, from the menu to the decor. Featured dishes include guacamole, nachos, tacos, quesadillas, and coriander soup (hence the restaurant's name). Gringo specials are offered for the fainthearted. *14 Richmond Hill, tel. 01202/552202. Reservations advised. MC, V. Closed Sun. lunch.*

Festivals **Bournemouth** holds a **Music Festival** during June and July with choirs, brass bands, and orchestras, some visiting from overseas (for information, tel. 01202/291718).

Poole

Wilts and Dorset buses (tel. 01202/673555) make stops throughout the region, and trains from London (Waterloo) stop here frequently on their way from Bournemouth. Poole tourist office: The Quay, tel. 01202/673322.

The fast-growing modern town of **Poole** has one of the largest natural harbors in the world, with more than 90 miles of serrated coastline harboring a myriad of bays, inlets, and islands. Ferries make regular trips to **Brownsea Island,** which belongs to the National Trust and is open to visitors who enjoy roaming the woods, relaxing on the beach, and observing rare waterfowl. *Boats from Poole Quay and Sandbanks (tel. 01202/666226) leave about every 30 minutes. Round-trip from Poole Quay: £3.50 adults, £3.15 senior citizens, £2.50 children; from Sandbanks: £2.10 adults, £1.90 senior citizens, £1.50 children; Landing charge: £2.20 adults, £1.10 children, £5.20 family ticket (available only Apr.–June and Sept.). Operates Apr.–Sept., daily 10–8 (or dusk).*

Lodging **Harmony Hotel.** This friendly B&B is in a quiet, residential area.
£ The comfortable bedrooms have TV and tea/coffeemaker, and evening meals are available on request. Reduced prices are offered for a two-night stay. *19 St. Peter's Rd., BH14 ONZ, tel. 01202/747510, fax 01202/731030. 11 rooms, 8 with bath, 1 with shower. V.*

£ **Sheldon Lodge.** Set in the Branksome Park area of Poole, this guest house, surrounded by trees, has such amenities as billiards, a bar, and a solarium. The sunny bedrooms have a private bathroom, TV, and tea/coffeemaker. *22 Forest Rd., Branksome Park, BH13 6DH, tel. 01202/761186, fax 01202/769891. 14 rooms with bath or shower. Facilities: bar. MC, V.*

Dining **Allan's Seafood Restaurant.** Though this excellent restaurant is ded-
£ icated to seafood, other dishes, including steak and chicken, are
★ available as well. The fresh fish, prepared simply for the regularly changing menu, is often included among the choices for the fixed menu, which costs £10.75 for two courses, £12.75 or £19.75 for three. *8 Bournemouth Rd., Lower Parkstone, tel. 01202/741489. MC, V.*

¢ **The Guildhall Tavern.** This small, atmospheric pub is just the place to go for tasty fresh fish. The bar food features a range of seafood at reasonable prices (the menu depends on the day's catch), and there is also a good selection of house wines. It is close to the Guildhall and is easy to find. *Market St., tel. 01202/671717.*

Shopping **Poole Pottery** (The Quay, tel. 01202/666200) has a shop that sells the creamy-colored ware that has been popular in Britain for many years, and you can watch demonstrations of the pottery being made and decorated.

Lyndhurst

To get to Lyndhurst from Poole it is necessary to take any of the frequent bus services to Bournemouth (X3, 101, 102, 103, or 105). Bus X1 goes from Bournemouth to Lyndhurst six times daily, and takes 1 hour, 20 minutes. Lyndhurst tourist office: The Main Car Park, tel. 01703/282269.

Lyndhurst is known as the "capital of the New Forest." Alice Hargreaves (*née* Liddell), Lewis Carroll's Alice, is buried in the churchyard here. The town provides an excellent base for travelers exploring this beautiful wooded region. This is also a good, easy area for hiking. Ask the **Tourist Information Center** (tel. 01703/282269) in the main parking lot for details of local walks.

The New Forest consists of 145 square miles of mainly open, unfenced countryside interspersed with dense woodland. It is the largest area of open countryside in southern Britain and a natural haven for herds of free-roaming deer, cattle, and hardy New Forest ponies. The forest was "new" in 1079, when William the Conqueror cleared the area of farms and villages and turned it into his private hunting forest. He left it unfenced so as not to hinder the free run of deer, the main quarry of the royal hunting parties. Three centuries ago large numbers of oaks were cut down to build houses and ships, but otherwise the landscape has not changed much over the past 1,000 years. Although some favorite spots can get crowded in summer, there is ample room to accommodate the many visitors who use the parking lots, picnic grounds, and campgrounds as hiking bases. Miles of walking trails crisscross the region. Although minor roads pass through the forest, the best way to explore the area is on foot.

Beaulieu

Buses 56 and 56A connect Lyndhurst with Lymington, on the coast. Bus 112 leaves Lymington several times a day, stopping at the Beaulieu Motor Museum. At other times it stops nearby in Beaulieu village. Travel time is 35 minutes. There is no Sunday service. Beaulieu tourist office: John Montagu Bldg., tel. 01590/612345.

Six miles southeast of Lyndhurst is the village of **Beaulieu** (pronounced "Bewley"), which offers three major attractions (and one ticket gets you into all of them). First there are the ruins of **Beaulieu Abbey,** established by King John in 1204 for the Cistercian order of monks, who gave their new home its name, which means "beautiful place." Three centuries later, during the reign of Henry VIII, it was badly damaged, leaving only the cloister, the doorway, the gate-house, and two buildings, one of which today contains a well-planned exhibition re-creating daily life in the monastery. The gate house has been incorporated into **Palace House,** home of the Montagu family since 1538, one of Britain's most popular stately homes. Here, you can see drawing rooms, dining halls, and a number of very fine family portraits. The present Lord Montagu is noted for his work in establishing the **National Motor Museum,** which traces the development of motor transport from 1895 to the present with more than 200 classic cars, buses, and motorcycles. Museum attractions include a monorail, audiovisual presentations, and a trip in a 1912 London bus. *Beaulieu, near Southampton, tel. 01590/612345. Admission: £7.60 adults, £6.50 senior citizens, £5.25 children, £25 family ticket. Open Easter–Sept., daily 10–6; Oct.–Easter, daily 10–5.*

Among local places of interest is **Buckler's Hard,** an almost perfectly restored 18th-century hamlet of 24 brick cottages, leading down to an old shipyard on the river Beaulieu. Nelson's favorite ship, H.M.S. *Agamemnon,* was built here of New Forest oak, as recalled in the fascinating **Maritime Museum.** *Beaulieu, tel. 01590/616203. Admission: £2.60 adults, £2.10 senior citizens, £1.75 children, £7.10 family ticket. Open Mar.–May, daily 10–6; Jun.–mid.-Sept., daily 10–9; mid.-Sept.–Feb., daily 10–4:30.*

Corfe

Corfe can be reached in about 50 minutes from the Poole bus station by Bus 142, 143, 144 and, in summer only, Bus X36.

Corfe is actually due south of Poole, but the road travels the long way around the vast harbor and its inlets. **Corfe Castle** ruins rise majestically on a hill that overlooks the pretty village. The castle site guards a gap in the surrounding range of hills, and has been fortified from very early times. The present ruins of the castle date from 1105, when the great central keep was erected, and the 1270s, when the outer walls and towers were built. It owes its ramshackle state to Cromwell's soldiers, who blew it up in 1646 during the Civil War. This is one of the most impressive ruins in Britain, and will stir the imagination of all history buffs. It is looked after by the National Trust, which runs a coffee shop at the entrance. *Tel. 01929/481294. Admission: £3 adults, £1.50 children under 16. Open early Feb.–Mar., daily 10–4:30; Apr.–Oct., daily 10–5:30; Nov.–early Feb., daily noon–3:30.*

Dining **The Fox.** For lunch in Corfe try the Fox, an atmospheric old pub hidden behind the church. The backyard garden, with views of the castle, makes a wonderful setting. A fresh crab sandwich or steak-and-kidney pie could be followed by a luscious homemade pudding. *West St., Corfe Castle, tel. 01929/480449. No credit cards.*

Dorchester

*Bus 187 travels west from Poole to Dorchester three times daily; the journey takes 1 hour, 15 minutes. Dorchester is also a stop on the Salisbury–Weymouth route of Buses 184 and 185; three to five buses depart on weekdays and one to two on Sunday for the trip that takes about 90 minutes. The first half of this route runs through the superb scenery of Cranborne Chase, the remnants of an ancient royal hunting forest. Hourly trains also run from London/Waterloo (tel. 0171/928–5100) to Dorchester South station, and take 2 hours, 25 minutes. One or two daily **National Express** bus services from London to Weymouth (Bus 515) stop at Dorchester. This trip takes 3 hours, 50 minutes or 4½ hours. Tourist office (1 Acland Rd., tel. 01305/267992).*

Dorchester is in many ways a traditional southern country town. To appreciate its character, visit the local Wednesday market in the **Market Square,** where you can find Dorset delicacies such as Blue Vinney cheese (which some connoisseurs prefer to Blue Stilton) and various handcrafted items, which are also available at the **Dorset Crafts Guild Shop.**

Dorchester owes much of its fame to its connection with Thomas Hardy, whose bronze statue looks westward from a bank on **Colliton Walk.** Born in a cottage (now preserved by the National Trust) in the hamlet of Higher Brockhampton, about 3 miles northeast of Dorchester, Hardy attended school in the town and was apprentice to an architect here. Later he had a house, Max Gate (not open to the public), built to his own design on the edge of Dorchester. Hardy's study there has been reconstructed in the **Dorset County Museum,** which houses a diverse and fascinating collection. Exhibits range from ancient Celtic and Roman remains to a vicious, 19th-century mantrap, used to snare poachers. It was this very trap that Hardy had in mind when writing the mantrap episode in *The Woodlanders. High West St., tel. 01305/262735. Admission: £2.35 adults, £1.20 senior citizens and children. Open Sept.–June, Mon.–Sat. 10–5; July–Aug., daily 10–5.*

Dorchester's popular **Dinosaur Museum** has life-size models and various interactive displays. *Icen Way, off High East St., tel. 01305/269880. Admission: £3.50 adults, £2.75 senior citizens, £2.25 children, £9.95 family ticket. Open daily 9:30–5:30.*

Roman history and artifacts abound in Dorchester. The town was laid out by the Romans around AD 70, and if you walk along **Bowling Alley Walk, West Walk,** and **Colliton Walk,** you will have followed the approximate line of the original Roman town walls. On the north side of Colliton Park lies an excavated **Roman villa** with a marvelously preserved mosaic floor. Possibly even more interesting is **Maumbury Rings,** the remains of a Roman amphitheater on the edge of town. The site was later used as a place of execution. (Hardy's *Mayor of Casterbridge* contains a vivid evocation of the Rings.) As late as 1706, a girl was burned at the stake here.

Lodging   **Casterbridge Hotel.** The Georgian building (1790) reflects its age
£   with period furniture and old-world elegance—it's small but full of
★   character. *49 High East St., DT1 1HU, tel. 01305/264043, fax 01305/ 260884. 16 rooms with bath. Facilities: bar, conservatory, courtyard garden. AE, DC, MC, V. Closed Dec. 25–26.*

£   **Wessex Royale.** Originally built as a town house for the earls of Ilchester in the 1600s, the Wessex Royale hotel sounds a lot grander than it actually is. It has, however, undergone considerable renovation, making it a comfortable, central base for touring the area around Dorchester. Three of the bedrooms have four-poster beds, all rooms have TVs and blow dryers, and there's a large restaurant in the hotel. *32 High West St., DT1 1UP, tel. 01305/262660, fax 01305/251941. 23 rooms with bath. Facilities: restaurant. AE, DC, MC, V.*

£   **Westwood House.** Centrally located on High West Street, this up-
★   scale B&B is in a gracious Georgian house that has been tastefully decorated with comfortable furniture and antiques. The bedrooms have a TV and a tea/coffeemaker. *29 High West St., DT1 1UP, tel. 01305/268018, fax 01305/250282. 7 rooms, 5 with bath. MC, V.*

Dining   **Judge Jeffreys Restaurant.** Situated in the original beamed building
£   where Judge Jeffreys held his notorious Bloody Assizes in 1685, this restaurant is an interesting spot for morning coffee or afternoon tea, as well as for lunch or dinner. The lunchtime specials change daily, and the prices are moderate. *6 High West St., tel. 01305/264369. Reservations advised. MC, V. Closed all day Sun., Mon.–Thur. dinner in winter, Mon.–Tues. dinner in summer.*

Cerne Abbas

The local Bus 216, from Dorchester to Sherborne, passes through
Cerne Abbas (except on Sunday).

The village of **Cerne Abbas,** 6 miles north of Dorchester, is worth a
short exploration on foot. Appealing Tudor houses line the road beside the church, and nearby you can also see the original village
stocks. If you pass through the graveyard, you will arrive at a shallow pool known as **St. Augustine's Well.** Legend holds that the saint
created it by striking the ground with his staff, thereby ensuring a
regular supply of baptismal water. Tenth-century **Cerne Abbey** itself is now a ruin, with little left to see except its old gateway,
though the nearby Abbey House is still in use.

Cerne Abbas's main claim to fame is the colossal **figure of a giant,** cut
in chalk on a hillside overlooking the village. The 180-foot-long giant
with a huge club bears a striking resemblance to Hercules, although
he probably originated as a tribal fertility symbol long before the
Romans appeared. His outlines are formed by two-foot-wide
trenches, regularly cleared of overgrowth by local people.

Lodging   **Lamperts Cottage.** Here's an idyllic little B&B, about 3 miles from
¢   Dorchester. It has a stream front and back (so you have to cross a
little bridge to reach it), a thatched roof, and it is covered with summer roses. The house dates from the 16th century, has exposed
beams, fireplaces, and is very comfortable, though small. You can be
sure of a warm welcome, and if you call in advance, the owner will
pick you up from the bus route or the Maiden Newton station.
Dorchester Rd., Sydling St. Nicholas, DT2 9NU, tel. 01300/341659.
3 rooms with washbasins, 2 hall baths. No credit cards.

Weymouth

Weymouth is just 8 miles south of Dorchester and is well served by
Buses 184, 185, 186, and 187. The trip is 25 minutes. The town is also
on the rail line from Bournemouth, and takes less than an hour.
Weymouth tourist office: Pavilion Complex, The Esplanade, tel.
01305/785747, and The King's Statue, The Esplanade, tel. 01305/
765221, accommodations tel. 0800/765223.

About 8 miles south of Dorchester is **Weymouth,** Dorset's main
coastal resort, known both for its wide, safe, sandy beaches and its
royal connections. King George III took up sea-bathing here for his
health in 1789, setting a trend among the wealthy and fashionable
people of his day. Their influence has left Weymouth with many fine
period buildings, including the Georgian row houses lining the esplanade. Historical details clamor for your attention: A wall in **Maid-
en Street,** for example, still holds a cannonball that was embedded in
it during the Civil War. Nearby, a **column** commemorates the
launching of the American forces from Weymouth on D-Day, June 6,
1944.

A 5-mile-long peninsula jutting south from Weymouth leads to the
Isle of Portland, the eastern end of the unique geological curiosity
known as **Chesil Beach**—a 200-yard-wide, 30-foot-high bank of pebbles that decrease in size from east to west. The beach extends for 18
miles along the shore. Here a powerful undertow makes swimming
dangerous. Tombstones in local churchyards attest to the many shipwrecks the beach has caused.

Lodging   **Streamside Hotel.** Quiet and cozy, this hotel on the outskirts of town
££   always graces its tables with fresh flowers and candles. There are 15
★   comfortable rooms available for less than £80, and the hotel, with
award-winning gardens, is only 200 yards from the beach. The cuisine at the restaurant is English, with specialties such as smoked
salmon with melon and steak in cream and brandy sauce. *29 Preston*

Rd., Overcombe, DT3 6PX, tel. 01305/833121, fax 01305/832043. 15 rooms with bath or shower. Facilities: restaurant. AE, DC, MC, V.

£ **Bay Lodge.** Situated near the beach, shops, and harbor, this tasteful Victorian hotel makes a good base for the town and surrounding area. The well-equipped bedrooms are enhanced by sympathetic decor, while the oak-paneled reading and games room, open fires, and glass dome over the staircase help to create a tranquil, welcoming environment. Self-catering guests are also accommodated, but if you stay in the main building, choose a room with a sea view, for which there is no extra charge. *27 Greenhill, DT4 7SW, tel. 01305/786514, fax 01305/782828. 12 rooms with bath or shower. AE, DC, MC, V.*

Dining **Perry's.** This fairly basic restaurant, with simple dishes of the best
£ local seafood, is right by the harbor. Try roast sea bass with an olive oil and citrus dressing. The meat dishes, such as venison with cassis, or rack of lamb, are tasty, too. *The Harbourside, 4 Trinity Rd., tel. 01305/785799. Reservations advised. MC, V. Closed Mon. and Sat. lunch, and Sun. dinner in winter.*

£ **Sea Cow.** At this quayside restaurant, you can enjoy the very freshest seafood and seasonal game dishes. In summer, you can snack on tapas and light meals based on shellfish and other marine delicacies, in addition to the regular menu. *7 Custom House Quay, tel. 01305/783524. Reservations required weekends. MC, V. Closed Sun. eve. in winter.*

5 The Southwest

Wells, Plymouth, Penzance

The Southwest of England, the West Country, is a winning juxtaposition of rugged moorlands, gorges and caves, unspoiled woods, towering sea cliffs, lush river valleys, popular coastal resorts, sandy beaches, and ancient market towns. This part of the country, most associated with the legendary King Arthur, includes Glastonbury, where myth places his tomb.

Three counties make up the Southwest—Somerset, Devon, and Cornwall. Somerset, the most easterly, is characterized by miles of rolling green countryside, some of England's most fertile farmland, the cave-hollowed Quantock and Mendip Hills, boggy Sedgemoor, and the heather-covered expanse of Exmoor. Devon, the home of Drake and other Elizabethan seadogs, is famed for its wild moorland and its large coastal towns, while Cornwall, which is warmed by the Gulf Stream, is England's mildest county. The northern shore is jagged and dramatic, while the south coast offers delightful beaches and sunny coves, and it is not uncommon to see palm trees growing here. In this county you are never more than 20 miles from the sea.

Unfortunately, the Southwest is badly served by railways; only one main line runs along the south coast. But for visitors on a budget and locals alike, the bus network is best because it connects all the main points. As we have said elsewhere, however, if you travel by bus, allow plenty of time so you can take full advantage of the region. Bus riders should look for the Badgerline specials offered in and around Wells.

Essential Information

Lodging With the growth of the tourist industry, many farmhouses in rural areas have begun renting out rooms. However, the best-value farm accommodations are difficult to reach unless you are traveling by car. Seaside towns have plenty of B&Bs, but they fill up quickly during the summer, when the natives take their holidays. Tourist offices keep lists of available accommodations. Highly recommended establishments are indicated by a star ★.

Dining Most of the regional specialties are fairly inexpensive. Somerset is the home of Britain's most famous cheese, the ubiquitous Cheddar, from the Mendip Hills village. If you are lucky enough to taste real farmhouse Cheddar, made in the traditional "truckle," you may find it hard to return to processed cheese. The calorie-conscious should beware of Devon's cream teas, which traditionally consist of a pot of tea, homemade scones, and lots of "clotted" cream and strawberry jam. "Clotted," that is, specially thickened, cream is a regional specialty; it's sometimes called "Devonshire cream."

Cornwall's specialty is the "pasty," a pastry shell filled with chopped meat, onions, and potatoes. The pasty was originally devised as a handy way for miners to carry their dinner to work. The modern pasty may bear little resemblance to its tasty original, but excellent local pasties can still be found.

"Scrumpy," a homemade dry cider available throughout the Southwest, is refreshing, but deceptively mild. English wine, which is similar to German wine, is available in Somerset, while in Cornwall you can get mead made from local honey. Highly recommended restaurants are indicated by a star ★.

Shopping The Southwest is a rich area to explore if you are interested in crafts, especially pottery. Whole groups of artists and craftspeople have settled here, in Devon and Cornwall especially, to pursue their calling in the warm air of this attractive region. Ancient crafts, such as the making of baskets and shoes, are still practiced here as well. Glastonbury has a market every Tuesday, and Wells on Wednesday and Saturday. If you buy directly from the workshops, as opposed to the boutiques, you'll get much better prices on crafts.

Biking Although you'll have to cope with a lot of hilly ground, the great tracts of isolated, scenic countryside in the Southwest are ideal biking territory. Be aware, though, that roads can be windy and the high hedges can make it difficult to see oncoming traffic; this is especially true in Cornwall. Stores where you can rent bikes are in Glastonbury, **Pedalers Cycle Shop** (8 Magdalene St., tel. 01458/831117); in Penzance, **Blewett & Pender** (Albert St., tel. 01736/64157); and in Plymouth, **Plymvale Mountain Bikes** (Queen Anne's Battery, tel. 01752/268328).

Hiking Of the many magnificent walks in the Southwest, one of the very best is a coastal clifftop hike from Hartland Quay down to Lower Sharpnose Point. This 10-mile walk along some of the highest cliffs in Britain, provides breathtaking views. The coast below Bude is also ideal for walking, especially in the section around Tintagel. Almost all of the 600 miles of coast around the southwest peninsula can be walked: local routes are available from tourist offices, or contact the **South West Way Association** (Windlestraw, Penquit, Ermington, Devon PL21 OLU, tel. 01752/896237), which supplies current information on tides, transportation, accommodation, and wildlife, and publishes a book with detailed itineraries.

Dartmoor is not for the unwary, but with sufficient local advice, hikers may find many walks of great interest. The areas around Widgery Cross, Becky Falls, and the Bovey Valley, and—for the really energetic and adventurous—Highest Dartmoor, south of Okehampton, are all worth considering.

A much shorter—but no less spectacular—walk is along the Lydford Gorge (*see* Tour 2, *below*).

The Saints Way, a 26-mile walk in Cornwall, stretches from coast to coast. Originally a Bronze Age trading route, and later used by Celt-

ATLANTIC OCEAN

Woolacombe

Bideford Bay

Hartland Quay

Sharpnose Point

Bude

Bude Bay

A39

B3254

A388

B3263

A39

Tintagel

B3314

Launceston

A30

BODMIN MOOR

Tamar

B3276

Bodmin

A38

Newquay

A30

Fal

A391

Perranporth

Plymouth

C O R N W A L L

St. Ives

A30

Truro

A390

Mevagissey

B3306

B3289

Trelissick

Carrick Roads

Penzance

St. Michael's Mount

A394

Falmouth

Sennen Cove

A394

Helston

B3291

Land's End

B3315

A3083

GOONHILLY DOWNS

B3293

Kynance Clover

Well within the grounds of the Bishop's Palace. Spring water has run through the High Street since the 15th century.

The ancient **Market Place** in the city center is surrounded by 17th-century buildings. William Penn was arrested here in 1695 for preaching without a license at the Crown Hotel (*see* Dining, *below*). Though the elaborate fountain at the entrance to the square is only 200 years old, it's on the same spot as the lead conduit that brought fresh, but undrinkable, spring water to the market in medieval times.

★ The great west towers of the famous **Cathedral Church of St. Andrew** are visible for miles. To appreciate the elaborate west front facade, approach the building on foot from the cathedral green, which is accessible from Market Place through a great medieval gate called "penniless porch" (named after the beggars who once waited here to collect alms from worshipers). The cathedral's west front is twice as wide as it is high and is adorned with some 300 statues. Begun in the 12th century, it is the oldest surviving English Gothic church; the vast inverted arches were added in 1338 to stop the central tower from sinking to one side. Erosion currently is cause for a great deal of anxiety, and a restoration program is under way. The cathedral also has a rare medieval clock, consisting of the seated figure of a man named Jack Blandiver who strikes a bell on the quarter hour while mounted knights circle in mock battle. Near the clock you will find the entrance to the chapter house—a small, wooden door opening onto a great sweep of stairs worn down on one side by the tread of pilgrims over the centuries. Every capital (column top) and pillar in the church has a carving; look for the ones of a man with a toothache and another with a thorn in his foot.

The second great gate leading from Market Place, the Bishop's Eye, takes you to the **Bishop's Palace.** Most of its original 12th- and 13th-century residences remain, and you can also see the ruins of a late 13th-century great hall, which lost its roof in the 16th century because Edward VI needed the lead! The palace is surrounded by a moat, fed from wells, which is home to a variety of waterfowl, including swans. *Market Pl., tel. 01749/678691. Admission: £2.50 adults, £2 senior citizens, children under 16 free. Open Easter–Oct., Tues.–Thurs. 10–6, Sun. 2–6; Aug., daily and national holidays, 10–6.*

North of the cathedral is **Vicar's Close,** Europe's oldest street, with two terraces of handsome 14th-century houses. A tiny medieval chapel at the end is still in use.

Lodging **Bekynton House.** Here's a family-run guest house, located near the
£ cathedral in the oldest part of town—and that's *old!* The architecture combines a stone facade and parts of a converted barn. Bedrooms are comfortably furnished and include TVs and tea/coffeemakers. There's no restaurant, but the breakfasts here will lay down a solid foundation for the day's sightseeing. *7 St. Thomas St., BA5 2UU, tel. 01749/672222, fax 01749/672222. 8 rooms, 6 with bath or shower. MC, V.*

£ **Tor Guest House.** This reconditioned 17th-century building is set on lovely grounds and offers magnificent views overlooking the cathedral. Bedrooms have both TVs and tea/coffeemakers. Lunch and dinner are available. *20 Tor St., BA5 2US, tel. 01749/672322. 8 rooms, 5 with bath. MC, V.*

Dining **Ancient Gate House.** Traditional Italian dishes made largely from lo-
£ cal produce are the specialty here. An English set-price lunch menu is offered for only £5.20. *20 Sadler St., tel. 01749/672029. Reservations advised weekends. AE, DC, MC, V.*

£ **Crown Hotel.** This hotel has been a landmark in Wells since the Middle Ages; William Penn was arrested here in 1695 for illegal preaching. There's a delightful period atmosphere to the place, but the

Penn Bar and Eating House facilities are quite modern. The menu, however, lists traditional items such as steak-and-kidney pie. Dine at one of the tables outside in the summer. *Market Pl., tel. 01749/ 673457. AE, DC, MC, V.*

£ **Fountain Inn and Boxers Restaurant.** In this fine Georgian building, located next to the cathedral, you can choose between bar food and fuller meals in the restaurant upstairs. Dishes use mostly local ingredients: The lamb with rosemary and red currants is particularly satisfying. A wide selection of local cheeses gives you a chance to taste some you might not otherwise find; also try the farm cider. *1 St. Thomas St., tel. 01749/672317. AE, MC, V.*

¢ **Cloister Restaurant.** This eatery in the cathedral cloisters is the perfect place to relax. It's an ideal spot for morning coffee or afternoon tea, though lunch is also offered. Everything is homemade and tasty. *Wells Cathedral, tel. 01749/676543. No credit cards. Open Mon.–Sat. 10–5, Sun. 2–5.*

Glastonbury

Glastonbury is only 5 miles southwest of Wells. There are several local buses that make the 18-minute run, among them No. 376, which runs hourly. It is on the direct Wells–Taunton route. Glastonbury tourist office: The Tribunal, 9 High St., tel. 01458/ 832954; open Apr.–Sept., Sun.–Thurs. 10–5, Fri.–Sat. 10–5:30; Oct.–Mar., closes 1 hour earlier.

Five miles southwest of Wells is **Glastonbury,** a town steeped in history, myth, and legend, much of it contradictory. The town lies at the foot of **Glastonbury Tor,** a grassy hill rising 520 feet. In legend, Glastonbury is identified with Avalon, the paradise into which King Arthur was reborn after his death. It is also said to be the burial place of Arthur and Guinevere, his queen. And according to Christian tradition, it was to Glastonbury, the first Christian settlement in England, that Joseph of Arimathea brought the Holy Grail, the chalice used by Christ at the Last Supper. At the foot of the Tor is **Chalice Well,** the legendary burial place of the Grail. It's a stiff climb up the Tor, but you'll be rewarded by the view across the Vale of Avalon. At the top stands a ruined tower, all that's left of **St. Michael's Church,** which collapsed after a landslide in 1271. The tor is now owned by the National Trust, and is open free to the public.

In the town below lie the ruins of the great **Abbey of Glastonbury.** According to legend, this is the site upon which Joseph of Arimathea built a church in the 1st century; a monastery had certainly been erected here by the 9th century. The present ruins are those of the abbey, completed in 1524 and destroyed shortly thereafter, during Henry VIII's dissolution of the monasteries in 1539. *Tel. 01458/ 832267. Admission: £2 adults, £1 children, £1.50 senior citizens. Open June–Aug., daily 9–6; Sept.–May, daily 9:30–dusk.*

While you are in Glastonbury, visit the Abbey Barn, which now houses the **Somerset Rural Life Museum.** This 14th-century tithe barn stored the portion of the town's produce due the church (one-tenth of the total harvest) and is more than 90 feet long. *Chilkwell St., tel. 01458/831197. Admission: £1.50 adults, £1 senior citizens, 40p children. Open Apr.–Oct., weekdays 10–5, weekends 2–6; Nov.–Mar., weekdays 10–5, Sat. 11–4.*

Lodging **No. 3.** This Georgian house next to the abbey ruins has log fires in
££ the winter and a terrace for summer evenings. Bedrooms are at-
★ tractive and well equipped, and the house's ambience is elegant yet relaxed. But the best reason to stay here is to experience the gastronomic delights of the dining room, which has always been a renowned restaurant in its own right. The French-style cuisine features mainly seafood; try the Cornish lobster in season, and any of

the superb ice creams. *3 Magdalene St., tel. 01458/832129. 5 rooms with bath. Facilities: restaurant, garden. MC, V.*

Dining **George and Pilgrims.** Immediately striking is the ornately carved fa-
¢ cade of this rambling, 15th-century inn. Try the unusual (and cheaper) bar food or the fancier fare in the recently opened brasserie,
which offers a three-course menu for £9.50. You might also like to
sample the local white wine. *1 High St., tel. 01458/831146. AE, DC,
MC, V.*

Shopping Somerset is sheep country, and sheepskin products abound
throughout the region. One of several good outlets is **Morlands Factory Shop** (2 miles out of town on A39 to Street [a village], tel. 01458/
835042), which sells a range of goods, including coats, slippers, and
rugs; there is also a history center. Another outlet, **Draper's Factory
Shop** (Chilkwell St., tel. 01458/831118), produces everything in
sheepskin from coats to soft toys and additionally sells leather
goods, knitwear, and walking sticks.

Wookey Hole

*Bus 172 connects Wells and Wookey Hole. Buses depart hourly, and
the trip takes only 8 minutes.*

★ Signs in Wells town center will direct you 2 miles north to **Wookey
Hole,** a fascinating complex of limestone caves reaching deep into
the Mendip Hills, which may have been the home of Iron Age people.
In addition to a geological and archaeological museum, there is a
large underground lake and several newly opened chambers to explore, plus a working paper mill and a display of Madame Tussaud's
early waxwork collection dating from the 1830s. *Tel. 01749/672243.
Admission: £5.20 adults, £4.50 senior citizens, £3 children. Open
Mar.–Oct., daily 9:30–5:30; Nov.–Feb., daily 10:30–4:30. Closed 1
wk before Christmas.*

Cheddar Caves

*Badgerline Buses 126, 127, and 826 between Wells and Weston-su-
per-Mare (No. 126 hourly) stop at Cheddar Village.*

Six miles north of Wookey Hole lie the **Cheddar Caves.** This beautiful, subterranean world of stalactites, stalagmites, and naturally
colored stone is enhanced by holograms and stunning man-made optical effects. Evidence in the caves, discovered in the 19th century,
suggests that they were occupied during the Stone Age. *Cheddar
Gorge, tel. 01934/742343. Admission: £4.90 adults, £2.90 children,
£14.50 family ticket. Open summer, daily 10–5:30; winter, daily
10:30–4:30.*

Shopping **Cheddar Gorge Cheese Company,** situated only 200 yards from the
bottom of the gorge, produces cheese spreads, in addition to the
breads and cakes that are made daily in the bakery. Samples of the
products are available. *The Cliffs, tel. 01934/742810. Admission:
£2.45 adults, £1.95 senior citizens, £1.45 children. Open daily 10–5
(final admission: 4:30).*

Tour 2: Plymouth

Plymouth, the Pilgrim Fathers' last landfall in England, makes a
useful base for exploring some of the Southwest's most interesting
historic houses. For those with the time, Plymouth can also be a
good base for exploring Dartmoor, which we do not include in the
Southwest Exploring section.

From London The rail time to Plymouth from London/Paddington (tel. 0171/262–
   By Train 6767) ranges from 3 to 4 hours. For schedules, call train information
in Plymouth (tel. 01752/221300).

   By Bus **National Express** has good *Rapide* services, Nos. 500, 501 and 504,
direct to Plymouth from **London/Victoria Coach Station** (tel. 0171/
730–0202). The trip takes about 4 hours, 25 minutes. The route has
just one stop, at Heathrow, and after Plymouth it continues on to
the tip of Cornwall, at Penzance. For details, call National Express
information in Plymouth (tel. 01752/671121).

   By Car The fastest way to travel the 218 miles from London to Plymouth is
by the M4 and M5 motorways to Exeter and then by A38 (46 miles).

Plymouth

*Plymouth tourist office: Island House, 9 The Barbican, tel. 01752/
264849.*

*Numbers in the margin correspond to points of interest on the
Plymouth map.*

Plymouth has long been linked with England's commercial and maritime history, but it didn't attain the status of a city until 1914, when
the three separate towns of Plymouth, Stonehouse, and Dock (later
renamed Devonport) were amalgamated.

❶ From the **Hoe,** a wide, grassy esplanade with crisscrossing walk-
❷ ways high above Plymouth—and especially from **Smeaton's Tower**—
you can get a magnificent view of the many inlets, bays, and harbors
that make up Plymouth Sound. At the end of the Hoe stands the
❸ huge **Royal Citadel,** built by Charles II in 1666. A **visitor center** displays exhibits on both old and new Plymouth.

❹ The **Barbican,** which lies east of the Royal Citadel, is the oldest surviving section of Plymouth (much of the city center was destroyed
by air raids in World War II). Here, Tudor houses and warehouses
rise from a maze of narrow streets leading down to the fishing docks
and harbor. Many of these buildings have become antiques shops,
★ art shops, and bookstores. By the harbor you can visit the **Mayflower**
❺ **Steps,** where the Pilgrims embarked in 1620; the **Mayflower Stone**
marks the exact spot. Plymouth was the last port visited by the
Mayflower before the crossing to North America. Nearby, on St.
❻ Andrew's Street, the largely 18th-century **Merchant's House** has a
museum of local history. *33 St. Andrew's St., tel. 01752/668000, ext.
4383. Admission: 80p adults, 20p children. Open weekdays 10–1
and 2–5:30, Sat. 10–1 and 2–5.*

❼ The **Royal Naval Dockyard,** on the west of town, was begun in the
late 17th century by William III. It is still a navy base and, though
much is hidden behind the high dock walls, parts of the 2-mile-long
frontage can be seen from pleasure boats that travel up the River
Tamar. *Plymouth Boat Cruises Ltd., Millpool House Head,
Millbrook, Torpoint, Cornwall, tel. 01752/822797; also Tamar
Cruising, Penhellis, Maker La., Millbrook, Torpoint, Cornwall,
tel. 01752/822105. Both companies run 1-hour boat trips around the
sound and the dockyard, leaving every 40 minutes from Phoenix
Wharf and the Mayflower Steps in the Barbican. Cost: £3 adults,
£1.50 children. Service available Easter–Oct., daily 10–4.*

From Plymouth, hop on one of the Plymouth Citybuses (Nos. 20A,
21, 22A, or 51) to the Plymouth Road/Plympton Bypass junction.
From there, follow the ¾-mile footpath to **Saltram House,** a lovely
18th-century house built around the remains of a late-Tudor mansion. It has two fine rooms designed by Robert Adam and paintings
by Sir Joshua Reynolds, first president of the Royal Academy of
Arts, who was born nearby in 1723. The house is set in a beautiful
garden adorned with rare trees and shrubs. There is a restaurant in

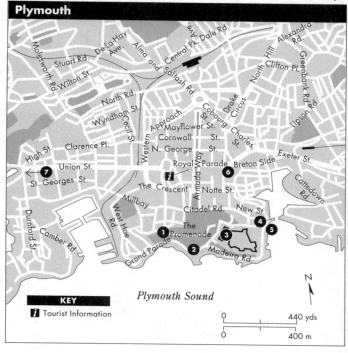

Plymouth

Plymouth Sound

KEY

i Tourist Information

0 ——— 440 yds
0 ——— 400 m

N

the house and a cafeteria in the Coach House. *Plympton, tel. 01752/ 336546. Admission: £5 adults, £2.50 children; garden only, £2.20 adults, £1.10 children. Open Apr.–Oct., Sun.–Thurs. 12:30–5:30 (to 5 in Oct.); garden only, as house but from 10:30.*

Lodging
£

Bowling Green Hotel. Set in a completely refurbished Victorian house overlooking Sir Francis Drake's bowling green on Plymouth Hoe, this hotel is centrally located for both shopping and sightseeing. Ask for the room with the view of the bowling green. All of the fairly large rooms have TVs and tea/coffeemakers, and locked garages are available for guests' use. *9–10 Osborne Pl., Lockyer St., PL1 2PU, tel. 01752/667485, fax 01752/255150. 12 rooms with private bath or shower. AE, DC, MC, V.*

¢
Georgian House. Another pleasant, small hotel in the vicinity is this family-owned and -run lodging. The comfortable rooms include TVs, tea/coffeemakers, and trouser presses. There is also a candlelit public restaurant—the **Fourposter**—a small and intimate place with an interesting menu. *51 Citadel Rd., The Hoe, PL1 3AU, tel. 01752/ 663237, fax 01752/253953. 10 rooms with bath or shower. Facilities: restaurant. AE, DC, MC, V.*

Dining
££
★

Chez Nous. This French—*very* French—restaurant is worth searching for among the rows of stores in the shopping district. Fresh local fish is served, and the atmosphere is pleasant and relaxed. Although the price of a meal may be a little high, with set menus at £28.50, it's certain to be money well spent. *13 Frankfort Gate, tel. 01752/266793. Reservations advised. AE, DC, MC, V. Closed Sun., Mon., national holidays, and first 3 weeks in Feb. and Sept.*

£
Piermaster's. Fresh fish landed at nearby piers is served here. Located in the Barbican, the Piermaster has "basic seafront" decor, with a tiled floor and wooden tables. *33 Southside St., Barbican, tel. 01752/229345. Reservations advised. AE, DC, MC, V. Closed Sun.*

£ **Trattoria Pescatore.** This trattoria may have slightly substandard murals, but the freshest, most deliciously prepared seafood is served here. Although it's located a little away from the town center (near the ferry harbor), it's worth seeking out. Try the bouillabaisse or the crayfish thermidor. *36 Admiralty St., Stonehouse, tel. 01752/ 600201. Reservations advised. MC, V. Closed Sat. lunch and Sun.*

Buckland Abbey

Buckland can be reached by Buses 83, X83, and 84 from Plymouth to Yelverton, then by Bus 55.

Although it will cost you time to catch two buses to this destination, ★ **Buckland Abbey** is a worthwhile place to go for a day's outing. The 13th-century Cistercian monastery became the home of Sir Francis Drake in 1581. Today it is full of mementos of Drake and the Spanish Armada. The abbey has a licensed restaurant. *Yelverton, tel. 01822/ 853607. Admission: £4 adults, £2 children, £10 family ticket; gardens only, £2 adults, £1 children. Open Apr.–Oct., Fri.–Wed. 10:30–5:30; Nov.–Mar., weekends 2–5.*

Morwellham Quay

Bus 186 runs on Wednesday and Sunday from Plymouth to the museum. In summer, there is British Rail service to Bere Alston with a connecting coach link.

Morwellham Quay Openair Museum was England's main copper exporting port in the 19th century, and it has been restored as a working museum, with quay workers and coachmen in costume, and a copper mine open to visitors. *Tel. 01822/832766 or 01822/833808 (recorded information). Admission: £6.50 adults, £5.50 senior citizens, £4.50 children. Open Apr.–Oct., daily 10–5:30 (last admission at 4); Nov.–Mar., daily 10–4 (last admission at 2:30).*

Lydford Gorge

The gorge can be reached by bus from Plymouth to Tavistock. Downs Bus 118 from Tavistock.

★ **Lydford Gorge,** a spectacular chasm carved into the rock by the River Lyd, is now looked after by the National Trust. Two long paths, above and below, lead along the gorge, past gurgling whirlpools and waterfalls with names such as the Devil's Cauldron and the White Lady. Refreshments are available at the main entrance. *Lydford, tel. 01822/82–441. Admission: £2.80 adults, £1.40 children. Open Apr.–Oct., daily 10:30–5:30; Nov.–Mar., daily 10:30–3 (walk restricted to main waterfall).*

Tour 3: Penzance and Land's End

The hub of this tour is Penzance, which makes a good base for exploring the western tip of Cornwall. Located around Penzance are Land's End and St. Ives—haunt of artists and craftspeople—as well as St. Michael's Mount, Helston, and Falmouth. All these towns are served by local buses whose winding routes enable you to visit other places along the way. Penzance has long been a popular holiday resort, as reflected by its many B&Bs and guest houses.

From London Penzance is on a direct line via Plymouth from London/Paddington
By Train (tel. 0171/262–6767), taking about 5½ hours. For schedules, call Truro rail information (tel. 01872/76244).

By Bus **National Express** has five coaches daily to Penzance from London/ Victoria Coach Station (tel. 0171/730–0202), via Plymouth and Truro. The journey time is 7 hours, 25 minutes on the fastest run. To save some time, take one of the buses that travels through the night. For schedule information call National Express in Camborne (tel. 01209/719988).

By Car The fastest route is to take the M4 from London to the M5 in Exeter and take the A30 to Penzance.

Penzance

Penzance tourist office: Station Rd., tel. 01736/62207.

Penzance owes its popularity as a seaside resort both to its mild climate and to its attractive architecture. During the 16th century, Spanish raiders destroyed most of the original town, and the majority of old buildings you see date from as late as the 18th century. The main street is called Market Jew Street, a folk mistranslation of the Cornish expression "Marghas Yow," which actually means "Thursday Market." Look for **Market House,** constructed in 1837, an impressive, domed granite building that is now a bank.

One of the prettiest streets in Penzance is **Chapel Street,** formerly the main street. It winds from Market House down to the harbor, its predominantly Georgian and Regency houses suddenly giving way to the extraordinary **Egyptian House,** whose facade is an evocation of ancient Egypt. Built around 1830 as a geological museum, today it houses a National Trust shop. Across the street is the 17th-century **Union Hotel** (*see* Lodging, *below*), where in 1805 the death of Lord Nelson and the victory of Trafalgar were first announced from the minstrels' gallery in the assembly rooms. Nearby is one of the few remnants of old Penzance, the **Turk's Head,** an inn said to date from the 13th century.

The town's **Maritime Museum,** also on Chapel Street, simulates the lower decks of a four-deck man-of-war, and exhibits items salvaged from shipwrecks off the Cornish coast. *19 Chapel St., tel. 01736/ 68890. Admission: £1.50 adults, 75p children, £4 family ticket. Open Easter–mid-Oct. (season may be extended), Mon.–Sat. 10–5.*

Lodging **Union Hotel.** Spanish pirates burned the Union down in 1597; it was
£ also here that the victory at Trafalgar and the death of Nelson in 1805 were first announced. The present building dates from the 17th century, and over the years it has been tastefully refurbished. *Chapel St., TR18 4AE, tel. 01736/62319. 28 rooms, 21 with bath. AE, DC, MC, V.*

¢ **Blue Seas.** Situated in a Regency house near the Promenade, this B&B is especially convenient if you are thinking about a trip to the Scilly Isles; the boat is within a two-minute walk. Simple bedrooms feature color TV, and tea/coffeemakers. *13 Regent Terr., TR18 4DW, tel. 01736/64744. 10 rooms with bath or shower. MC, V.*

¢ **The Willows.** A Georgian house with patio and garden, this B&B was once used as a coach staging post. Today it's run by a friendly husband-and-wife team. Each room is equipped with tea/coffeemakers, and evening meals are available on request. *Cornwall Terr., TR18 4HL, tel. 01736/63744. 6 rooms with private bath or shower. No credit cards.*

Dining **Admiral Benbow.** Once a smugglers' inn, this 15th-century gem is
¢ now full of seafaring bric-a-brac, including a brass cannon, model
★ ships, figureheads, and ropes everywhere. The popular pub serves good, solid bar food at low prices, or you can sit down to a more serious meal in the restaurant. Try the steak and Guinness pie. *Chapel St., tel. 01736/63448. MC, V.*

¢ **Richmonds.** Right in the middle of historic Chapel Street, this stop is a good place for coffees, teas, and homemade cakes, as well as some excellent hot dishes at lunchtime, and a full, reasonably priced à la carte menu in the evening. Steak, pasta, seafood, and vegetarian dishes are always available, and there is a scrumptious selection of puddings. *Chapel St., tel. 01736/63540. MC, V. Closed Sun.*

Splurge **Harris's.** Tucked away off Market Jew Street, Harris's provides an elegant refuge for the travel-weary, even though the decor may be a shade overpowering. A good range of meat and fish recipes are cooked sensitively and are well presented. Try the corn-fed chicken breast in pastry with apple and calvados sauce, or Crab Florentine, grilled on a bed of spinach with cheese sauce. Main courses average out at £14. *46 New St., tel. 01736/64408. Dinner reservations preferred. AE, MC, V. Closed Sun., Mon. lunch (all day Mon. in winter), 2 weeks in Nov., 1 week in Feb.*

The Arts and Nightlife A theater peculiar to this area is the open-air **Minack Theatre** (tel. 01736/810181) in Porthcurno near Penzance. It was begun in the early 1930s, using the natural slope of the cliff to form an amphitheater, and terraces and bench seats have since been added. With the sea as a backdrop, plays are performed here throughout the summer, ranging from classical dramas to modern comedies. Ticket prices are minimal.

St. Ives

*Regular buses make the 35-minute run from Penzance Bus Station to St. Ives (Nos. 16, 17, and 17A). The buses follow different routes, so you could take the No. 16 one way and one of the others back. Also, some of the **National Express** coaches make the run in 15 minutes. In summer, there is a bus that will take you on from St. Ives to Land's End. St. Ives tourist office: The Guildhall, Street-an-Pol, tel. 01736/796297.*

The fishing village of **St. Ives,** 10 miles northeast of Penzance, is named after St. Ia, a 5th-century, female Irish missionary said to have arrived on a floating leaf. The town has attracted artists and tourists for more than 100 years, and is now a well-established artists' colony. The **Tate Gallery St. Ives** opened in spring 1993. The four-story gallery, set on a cliff with dramatic sea views, houses the work of artists who lived and worked in St. Ives, mostly from 1925 to 1975, drawn from the rich collection of the Tate Gallery in London. This is the latest move in the Tate's plan to spread its artistic wealth outside the capital. *Porthmeor Beach, tel. 01736/796226. Admission: £2.50 adults, £1.50 senior citizens, £10 family tickets. Open Sept.–May, Tues. 11–9, Wed.–Sat. 11–5, Sun. 1–5; June–Aug., Mon.–Sat. 11–7, Tues. and Thurs. 11–9, Sun. 1–7.*

One of the most famous artists who lived in St. Ives was Dame Barbara Hepworth, a resident for 26 years. She pioneered abstract sculpture in England and died tragically in a fire in her studio in 1975. Her house and garden, now the **Barbara Hepworth Museum and Sculpture Garden,** run by the Tate, are fascinating to visit. *Trewyn Studio, Barnoon Hill, tel. 01736/796226. Admission is included in the Tate Gallery admission fee. Open June–Aug., Mon. 11–7, Tues. and Thurs. 11–9, Sun. 1–7; Sept.–May, Tues.–Sat. 11–5, Sun. 1–5.*

Examples of other artists' work can be found at the St. Ives Society of Artists in the **Old Mariner's Church** (tel. 01736/795582) in Norway Square. *Admission: 20p.*

Dining **Sloop Inn.** Built in 1312, this inn, situated beside St. Ives harbor, is ¢ one of England's oldest watering holes. Inexpensive pub lunches are available Monday–Saturday in the handsome, wood-beamed rooms. *Beside St. Ives harbor, tel. 01736/796584. No credit cards.*

Shopping St. Ives is full of crafts stores, and one of the better ones is the **Sloop Craft Market** by the harbor; here a variety of goods, ranging from watercolor paintings to leather bags and belts and ships in bottles, are sold. Many of the artisans have shops here, so it is often possible to watch them at work.

Land's End

Buses 1 and 4 run weekdays, five times daily, from Penzance Bus Station to Land's End in just under an hour.

★ **Land's End** is exactly what its name says, the western tip of England. Although the point draws tourists from all over the world, and a multimillion-dollar glitzy theme park has been added, its savage grandeur remains undiminished. The sea crashes against its rocks and lashes ships battling their way around it. Approach it from one of the coastal footpaths for the best panoramic view. Over the years, sightseers have caused some erosion of the paths, but new ones have recently been built, and Cornish "hedges" (granite walls covered with turf) planted to prevent future erosion.

St. Michael's Mount

Bus 2 from Penzance Bus Station will take you to Marazion for St. Michael's Mount in 10 minutes.

★ About 3 miles east of Penzance is one of Cornwall's greatest natural attractions, **St. Michael's Mount,** a spectacular granite and slate island rising out of Mount's Bay just off the coast. What was originally the site of a Benedictine chapel founded by Edward the Confessor is now a 14th-century castle perched at the highest point, some 200 feet above sea level. In its time, the structure on the Mount has been a church, a fortress, and a private home. The Mount is surrounded by fascinating gardens, where a great variety of plants flourish in micro-climates—snow can lie briefly on one part while it can be 70° in another. To get there, follow the causeway or, when the tide is in, take the ferry (it runs only during the summer months). As the number of visitors is restricted on the Mount, expect delays. There is a handy restaurant at the harbor. *Marazion, tel. 01736/710507. Admission: £3 adults, £8 family ticket. Open Apr.–Oct., weekdays 10:30–4:45; Nov.–Mar., Mon., Wed., Fri. by guided tour only at 11, noon, 2, 3.*

Helston

Bus 2 departs from Penzance Bus Station for the 37-minute trip to Helston.

The attractive Georgian town of **Helston** is most famous for its annual "Furry Dance" (a corruption of "floral"), which takes place on Floral Day, May 8 (unless the date is a Sunday or Monday, when it's on the nearest Saturday). The whole town is decked with flowers for the occasion, and dancers weave their way in and out of the houses following a 3-mile route. To see more of the coastline, explore from
★ Helston down the **Lizard Peninsula,** the southernmost point in mainland Britain and an officially designated Area of Outstanding Natural Beauty. In winter this flat heathland can look bleak, but in summer tourists flock here. The huge, eerily rotating dish antennae of the **Goonhilly Satellite Communications Earth Station** are visible from the road as it crosses Goonhilly Downs, the backbone of the peninsula. The National Trust owns much of the Lizard coastline, so this spectacular coastal area is protected from development.

Dining **Blue Anchor.** What used to be a 15th-century monastery rest house
¢ is now a thatched pub with an inglenook fireplace, small rooms with flagstone floors, and bare stone walls. Mellow beer brewed on the

premises is featured: Try the Spingo Special. There is some bar food and a hidden terrace for summer drinking. *50 Coinagehall St., tel. 01326/562821. No credit cards.*

Falmouth

Bus 2 travels from Penzance Bus Station to Falmouth in 40 minutes. Falmouth tourist office: 28 Killigrew St., tel. 01326/312300.

To the northeast is **Falmouth,** site of one of the finest natural harbors in the country. It's a combination of busy resort town, fishing harbor, yachting center, and commercial port, and its bustle adds to its charm. The oldest section is on the eastern side of the Pendennis peninsula, while the western (seaward) side is lined with modern hotels. In the 18th century, Falmouth was a mailboat port, and in Flushing, a village across the inlet, are the slate-covered houses built by prosperous mailboat captains. A ferry service now links the two towns. On Falmouth's quay, near the early 19th-century **Customs House,** is the **King's Pipe,** an oven in which seized contraband was burned.

At the end of the Pendennis peninsula stands formidable **Pendennis Castle,** built by Henry VIII in the 1540s and later improved by his daughter Elizabeth I. From here there are sweeping views over the English Channel and across the stretch of water known as the Carrick Roads to St. Mawes Castle on the Roseland peninsula, which was designed as a companion fortress to guard the roads. *Pendennis Head, tel. 01326/316594. Admission: £2 adults, £1.50 senior citizens, £1 children. Open Apr.–Sept., Tues.–Sun. 10–6; Oct.–Mar., Tues.–Sun. 10–4.*

Lodging **Gyllyngvase House.** This hotel is centrally sited near the seafront.
£ The rooms are small but brightly furnished, and there is a garden at the back. *Gyllyngvase Rd., TR11 4DJ, tel. 01326/312956. 15 rooms, 12 with bath or shower. No credit cards. Closed Nov.–Mar.*

¢ **Chellowdene.** This B&B has a slight fairytale air about it, with white walls, high gables, and a pretty garden. It is located close to the beach and the seafront—ideal for a family stay. The rooms are very comfortable, with a TV and a tea/coffeemaker. *Gyllyngvase Hill, TR11 4DN, tel. 01326/314950. 6 rooms with bath. Open May–Sept. No credit cards.*

Dining **Pandora Inn.** This thatched pub, with both a patio and a moored pon-
£ toon for summer dining, combines maritime memorabilia and fresh flowers. You can eat either in the bar or in the candlelit restaurant. The backbone of the menu is fresh seafood—try the seafood Stroganoff or crab thermidor. *Restronguet Creek, Mylor Bridge, tel. 01326/72678. Reservations advised. MC, V. Closed Sun. in winter.*

£ **The Seafood Bar.** The window of this restaurant on the quay is a fish
★ tank, and beyond it is the very best seafood. Try the thick crab soup; the turbot cooked with cider, apples, and cream; or the locally caught lemon sole. *Quay St., tel. 01326/315129. Reservations advised. MC, V. Dinner only. Closed Sun. and Mon.*

6 The Thames Valley

Windsor, Henley-on-Thames, Oxford

The River Thames snakes its way from the outskirts of London, past Windsor, to distant Oxford. It meanders through meadows, drowned in early morning mist, and is overlooked by ranges of beech-clad hills. It's not surprising that some of England's most evocative literature has been created here: This is *Wind in the Willows* country, after all. Today, Londoners come to the multitudinous marinas that fringe the most accessible riverside towns. On weekends, especially in the summer, cars jam the roads, beautiful riverside spots are packed with people, and the riverside pubs are crowded. In spite of this, the Thames Valley is still one of England's most attractive areas to explore.

The splendid medieval bulk of Windsor Castle is the first point to visit on the river after it leaves the immediate area of Greater London. Despite a terrible fire in 1992, there will still be a lot to see, including much of the queen's fabulous art collection. Nearby is Runnymede, where, on a riverside greensward in 1215, King John's barons forced him to sign the Magna Carta.

Henley-on-Thames and Marlow are representative Thames-side towns, both famous for high-profile boating events that figure importantly in the social calendar. In summer the river at Henley is choked with shiny cabin cruisers. Marlow, a quieter place, is surrounded by wooded hills and has a magnificent suspension bridge. Both are central points from which the countryside can be visited easily on budget tickets offered by local bus companies. Farther upstream lies Oxford, where generations of the country's ruling elite have been educated. Unlike Cambridge, deep in the fen country, Oxford is a busy modern city, with major industry on its outskirts. The colleges manage with difficulty to maintain their scholarly calm in the middle of clamorous traffic and tides of tourists.

We treat the Thames Valley in this chapter as days-out-from-London territory. When you are planning to visit the area, make a careful

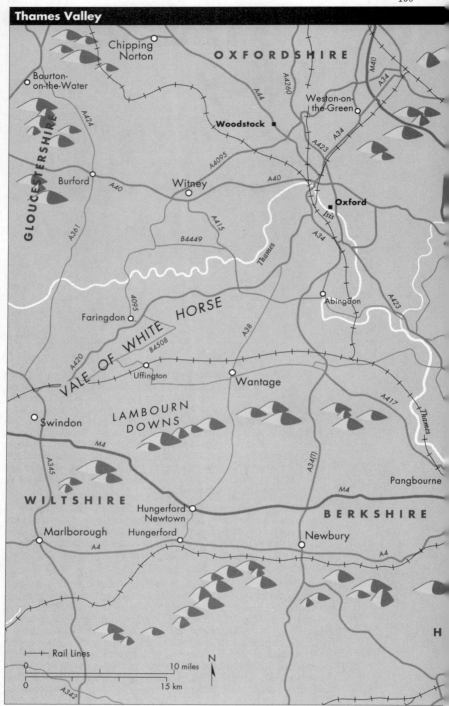

Thames Valley

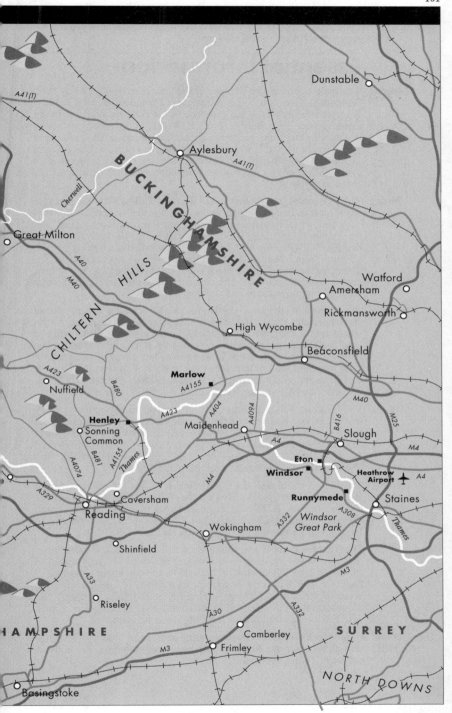

comparison between the advantages of train and bus. Both offer budget tickets, but you'd be wise to use the train where you can because you will save valuable time.

Essential Information

Lodging The main towns in the Thames Valley can be visited in a day from London, so there is no need to stay over. Formal hotels here are fairly expensive, but there are guest houses and B&Bs available in the larger towns, especially Oxford. However, many accommodations are outside the center of town, necessitating bus trips. Oxford has lots of rooms available when students are away on vacation. We have included a few listings in Oxford in case you choose to make it an overnight excursion. Highly recommended establishments are indicated by a star ★.

Dining The pub comes into its own in the Thames Valley: Fine old inns lace the region and many—sited on the banks of the Thames—offer outdoor dining in the summer. All pubs serve bar food at lunchtime, and some have flourishing restaurants attached for leisurely, more formal meals. Generally both types of facilities are reasonably priced. The area also has some of the priciest and best restaurants in England, but be careful; the check could top £100 for two. You're best advised to go to the ones with reasonable set menus. Highly recommended restaurants are indicated by a star ★.

Shopping The towns and villages of the Thames Valley offer a wide selection of small specialty stores, branches of chain stores, and markets. As the whole area is relatively prosperous, you can expect to find a range of quality British goods, from antiques to clothing. Generally the stores are geared to serve local people, but shops specializing in gifts may be found in popular stops, such as Windsor and Henley. Antiques are worth looking for in most towns—particularly Eton, Windsor, and Dorchester-on-Thames—but will be pricey.

Biking The Thames Valley is especially attractive biking country. Lazy lanes that loop and meander beside the river make the perfect path for two-wheel exploration, especially in the spring when the air is fresh and the world, a new, vivid green. Bikes can be hired in Oxford from **Denton's** (294 Banbury Rd., tel. 01865/53859) and **Pennyfarthing** (5 George St., tel. 01865/249368).

Hiking For long-distance walkers, the **Oxfordshire Way** runs 60 miles from Henley-on-Thames to Bourton-on-the-Water, on the eastern edge of the Cotswolds. A 13-mile ramble starts in Henley, runs north through the **Hambleden Valley**, takes in Stonor Park, and returns to Henley via the Assendons, Lower and Middle.

The Thames Path, a long-distance walking route, 180 miles long, throughout the Thames Valley region, is due to be inaugurated in the fall of 1996. Meanwhile, it is possible to walk along almost all of the river as it winds its way from the suburbs of London, through Windsor, Henley-on-Thames, Oxford, and finally through the Gloucestershire countryside to its source near Cirencester. Check with the local tourist offices for route plans for each area.

The Arts and Nightlife Oxford is the focus for the performing arts in the Thames Valley, although Windsor and Reading both have lively theaters. *See* individual tours, *below*, for details.

Tour 1: Windsor and Environs

Windsor and Eton together provide the archetypal day out from London. Strangely enough, Windsor is very badly linked by public transport to the surrounding area, which rules it out as an exploring base. But the two towns and nearby Runnymede can spark quite enough interest for a busy day of sightseeing.

From London
By Train

Windsor has two rail stations, Central and Riverside. Although both are near the castle, Central is the nearest and is served by trains from London/Paddington (tel. 0171/262–6767) with a change at Slough. The journey time to Slough is 20 to 40 minutes; from Slough to Windsor, 6 minutes. Windsor Riverside has direct service from London/Waterloo (tel. 0171/928–5100); the journey time is 40 minutes. During most of the day, two trains run per hour. Train information is available in Windsor (tel. 01753/538621).

By Bus

Take the **Green Line** bus from the Colonnades bus station, off Eccleston Bridge, immediately behind Victoria train station. The direct service, Bus 700, takes about 90 minutes, leaving roughly every hour (£5.20 adults, £2.60 children!!any age cutoff here & throughout text?!!). The nondirect service, Bus 702, also leaves hourly, and the trip takes more than an hour; in addition to boarding at Victoria, you can catch the 702 at Hyde Park Corner, Kensington High Street, and Hammersmith. In Windsor the bus leaves from the Castle Hotel. In summer, the less frequent Bus 718 stops at Runnymede on its way to Windsor.

By Car

Take the M4 motorway west from London, past Heathrow airport. Get off at Exit 6 south, to Windsor and Eton. The distance is 28 miles.

Windsor

Guide Friday *has open double-deck buses that make tours of Windsor, taking in all the main sights and including the castle and Eton. The tickets are valid all day, and you can get on and off the buses as you please, which will save you a lot of walking. The service operates from March to November and costs £5.50 adults, £4 senior citizens, £1.50 children under 12. For information, call Central Station (tel. 01753/855755). Windsor tourist office: Central Station, Thames St., tel. 01753/852010.*

Windsor is just 21 miles west of London. The principal attraction is the castle, rising majestcally on its bluff above the Thames, visible for miles around. But the city itself, with its narrow streets brimming with shops and ancient buildings, is well worth a visit on its own account.

★ The most impressive view of **Windsor Castle** is from the southern approach to the town. Settlements here have included a Roman villa, but the present castle was begun by William the Conqueror in the 11th century, and was transformed and extended by Edward III in the mid-1300s. One of his largest contributions was the enormous and distinctive **round tower**. Finally, between 1824 and 1837, George IV transformed what was essentially still a medieval castle into the fortified royal palace you see today. In all, work on the castle was spread over more than eight centuries, with most of the kings and queens of England demonstrating their undying attachment to it. In fact, Windsor is the only royal residence that has been in continuous use by the royal family since the Middle Ages.

The terrible fire of November 1992, which started in the queen's private chapel, totally gutted some of the State Apartments. Miracu-

Windsor Castle

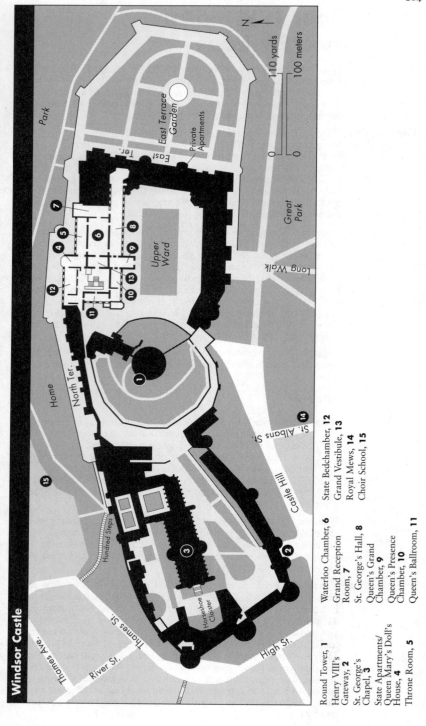

East Terrace Garden

Private Apartments

East Ter.

Park

Great Park

Upper Ward

Long Walk

Home

North Ter.

Hundred Steps

Horseshoe Cloister

Thames Ave.

River St.

Thames St.

High St.

Castle Hill

St. Albans St.

N

0   110 yards
0   100 meters

Round Tower, **1**
Henry VIII's
 Gateway, **2**
St. George's
 Chapel, **3**
State Apartments/
Queen Mary's Doll's
 House, **4**
Throne Room, **5**

Waterloo Chamber, **6**
Grand Reception
 Room, **7**
St. George's Hall, **8**
Queen's Grand
 Chamber, **9**
Queen's Presence
 Chamber, **10**
Queen's Ballroom, **11**

State Bedchamber, **12**
Grand Vestibule, **13**
Royal Mews, **14**
Choir School, **15**

lously, a swift rescue effort meant that hardly any works of art were lost. At press time, only two of the state rooms previously visitable are still closed and all of the other public areas are open. It is hoped that most of the restoration work will be completed by 1999, but in the meantime visitors will be able to watch some of the expert work of restoration in progress. A lot about the art of restoration could be learned after the fire a few years back at Hampton Court Palace.

As you enter the castle (*see* Windsor Castle plan, *below*), **Henry VIII's gateway** leads uphill into the wide castle precincts, where visitors are free to wander. Directly opposite the entrance is **St. George's Chapel,** where the queen invests new knights at the colorful Order of the Garter ceremonies in June, and where several of her predecessors, including her father, George VI are buried. One of England's finest churches, built in the 15th- and 16th-century Perpendicular style, the chapel features elegant stained-glass windows; a high, vaulted ceiling; and intricately carved choir stalls. The heraldic banners of the Knights of the Garter hang in the choir, giving it a richly medieval look (the knights have been installed at Windsor for more than 640 years). Members of the choir live close by in the 15th-century timbered buildings of the **Horseshoe Cloister.**

The **North Terrace** provides especially good views across the Thames to Eton College (*see below*). From the terrace, you enter the **State Apartments** (*see above*), a sequence of splendid rooms containing priceless furniture, including a magnificent Louis XVI bed; Gobelin tapestries; and paintings by Canaletto, Rubens, Van Dyck, Holbein, Dürer, and Andrea del Sarto. A high point of the tour is the **Waterloo Chamber,** where Sir Thomas Lawrence's portraits of Napoleon's victorious foes line the walls. You can also see a collection of arms and armor, much of it exotic.

Queen Mary's Doll House, on display to the left of the entrance to the State Apartments, is a perfect palace-within-a-palace, with functioning lights, running water, and even a library of Lilliputian-size books specially written by famous authors of Queen Mary's day (the 1920s). You may also want to see an exhibition from the **Queen's Collection of Master Drawings,** which contains works by Leonardo da Vinci, plus 87 Holbein portraits, and many others.

Just outside the bounds of Windsor Castle, on St. Albans Street, you'll find the **Royal Mews,** where the royal horses are kept, with carriages, coaches, and splendid red and gold harnesses. The highlight is the Scottish State Coach, used for the 1981 wedding of the Prince and Princess of Wales. *Tel. 01753/868286. Admission: £8 adults, £5.50 senior citizens, £4 children, 18 family ticket (these fees cover the Precincts, the State Apartments, the Gallery, St. George's Chapel, and the Albert Memorial Chapel). Doll's House or Royal Mews, viewable for extra £1 on the ticket price, or separately £1.60 adults, £1.40 senior citizens, 80p children. Open Mar.–Oct., daily 10–5:30 (last admission at 4); Nov.–Feb., daily 10–4 (last admission 3).*

Only a small part of old Windsor has survived. Opposite the castle entrance you can explore tiny Church Lane and Queen Charlotte Street, both narrow and cobbled. The old buildings now house antiques shops or restaurants. Around the corner, on High Street, stands the colonnaded **Guildhall** built in the 1680s by Sir Christopher Wren, who designed London's St. Paul's Cathedral (his father was dean of Windsor). Wren also built himself a fine house overlooking the river in Thames Street, now the Sir Christopher Wren's House Hotel.

Just south of Windsor Castle, stretching for some 8 miles (about 5,000 acres), is **Windsor Great Park,** the remains of an ancient royal hunting forest. Much of it is open to the public and can be explored by car or on foot. Focal points include the 3-mile **Long Walk;** the **Roy-**

al **Mausoleum** at Frogmore, where Queen Victoria and her husband Prince Albert are buried (open only two days a year, in May); **Virginia Water**, a 2-mile-long lake; and the **Savill Garden**, which offers a huge variety of trees and shrubs. *Wick Lane, Englefield Green, Egham, tel. 01753/860222. Admission (garden): £3.30 adults, £2.80 senior citizens, children under 16 free. Open Mar.–Oct., daily 10–6, Nov.–Feb., daily 10–4.*

Dining

¢ **The Courtyard.** The idyllic setting, near the river and castle, makes this a pleasant spot for light lunches and teas. *8 King George V Pl., tel. 01753/858338. No credit cards.*

¢ **The Dôme.** Proximity to the castle, budget prices, and a varied French menu are reasons to come here for lunch. Specialties include *croque-monsieur,* quiche, pâté, and salads. *5 Thames St., tel. 01753/ 864405. AE, MC, V.*

¢ **Two Brewers.** Set on a Georgian side street near the castle (off the High Street, next to the Royal Mews), this agreeable pub serves ample helpings of bar food from the counter near the entrance. In the summer there are benches for outdoor eating. *Park St., no phone. No credit cards.*

The Arts and Nightlife

Windsor's **Theatre Royal** (Thames St., tel. 01753/853888), where productions have been staged for nearly 200 years, is one of Britain's leading provincial theaters. It stages a range of plays and musicals throughout the year, frequently starring leading actors and actresses. A traditional pantomime is staged for six weeks after Christmas. As with most provincial theaters, tickets are very reasonably priced.

Festival

The **Windsor Festival** (tel. 01784/432618) is usually held in early fall, September or October, with occasional events taking place in the castle itself. A concert in the Waterloo Room is quite an event to attend.

Eton

For transportation information, see *Windsor,* above.

A footbridge across the Thames links Windsor with its almost equally historic neighbor, **Eton,** perhaps the most famous of Britain's exclusive "public" boys' schools. With its single main street leading from the river to the famous school, Eton is a much quieter town than Windsor and retains an old-fashioned charm. The splendid ★ redbrick, Tudor-style buildings of **Eton College,** founded in 1440 by King Henry VI, border the north end of the High Street; drivers are warned of "Boys Crossing." During the college semesters, the schoolboys are a distinctive sight, dressed in their pinstripe trousers, swallow-tailed coats, top hats, and white collars. The oldest buildings, grouped around a quadrangle called School Yard, include the **Lower School,** which is one of the oldest schoolrooms in use in Britain. The Gothic **chapel** rivals St. George's at Windsor in both size and magnificence. Beyond the cloisters are the school's famous playing fields where, according to the duke of Wellington, the Battle of Waterloo was won, since so many of his officers had learned discipline in their school days there. The **Museum of Eton Life** has displays on the school's history, and there are guided tours of the Lower School and chapel. *Brewhouse Yard, tel. 01753/671177. Admission: £2.30 adults, £1.60 children; with tour, £3.40 adults, £2.80 children. Open during term, daily 2–4:30; out-of-term, daily 10:30–4:30; guided tours Mar.–Oct., daily at 2:15 and 3:15.*

Dining

¢ **Watermans Arms.** Reflecting its proximity to the river and the Eton Rowing Club, this establishment is decorated with boating bits and pieces. It has an airy conservatory, partially uncovered for summer eating. The bar food—ploughman's lunches, pies, omelets, and salads—is hearty fare for anyone intending to spend the afternoon on the river. *Brocas St., tel. 01753/861001. No credit cards.*

Shopping Eton has a reputation for excellent antiques shops, most of them along the High Street. **Turk's Head Antiques** (at No. 98, tel. 01753/863939) has jewelry, silver, and Victoriana.

Runnymede

The Green Line Bus 718, an hourly service, stops at Runnymede on the London route. See Windsor, above, for details.

★ Directly southeast of Windsor is **Runnymede,** a tiny island in the middle of the Thames where King John, under his barons' compulsion, signed the Magna Carta in 1215, affirming the individual's right to justice and liberty. On the wooded hillside, in a meadow given to the United States by Queen Elizabeth in 1965, stands a **memorial to President John F. Kennedy.** Nearby is another memorial, in the style of a classical temple, erected by the American Bar Association to commemorate the 750th anniversary of the signing of the Magna Carta.

Tour 2: River Trips

By far the best way to see the Thames Valley is from the river itself. During the summer months the choice of river trips ranges from half-hour outings to full-day excursions. Among the boat firms offering such excursions are:

Hobbs and Sons (Station Rd., Henley-on-Thames, tel. 01491/572035), which offers trips along the Henley Reach and also rents rowboats and self-drive motorboats.

Salter Brothers (Folly Bridge, Oxford, tel. 01865/243421), probably the largest company operating on the river. Boarding points for daily steamer cruises (mid-May–mid-Sept.) include Windsor (Thameside), Abingdon, Henley-on-Thames, Marlow (Higginson Park), Reading, and Oxford (Folly Bridge).

Thames River Cruises (Piper's Island, Bridge St., Caversham Rd., Reading, tel. 01734/481088), which conducts outings from Caversham Bridge (Easter–Sept.).

Windsor Boat Co. (The Clewer Boat Yard, Clewer Court Rd., Windsor, tel. 01753/862933), which operates 35-minute and 2-hour river trips from The Promenade in Windsor (Easter–Sept.).

Tour 3: Henley-on-Thames and Marlow

Henley and Marlow epitomize the River Thames lifestyle. Henley's wide main street is lined with Georgian inns and houses, and this stretch of water is almost always busy with boats, especially at regatta time. The elegantly decorated, five-arch bridge acts as a vantage point for viewing up- and downstream. Even more attractive is Henley's near neighbor, Marlow. You can visit both in a day. Take the bus from Henley to Marlow, and you will see just a snatch of the appeal of the Thames. A visit here can be a gentle wandering through the village, with a budget meal in an ancient inn.

From London Reading, not a very attractive town in itself, is the transport hub of
By Train the Thames Valley. You'll have to change here to get to Henley by train. Trains to Reading from London/Paddington (tel. 0171/262-6767) are frequent, but not quite so frequent from London/Waterloo (tel. 0171/928–5100). The best journey time from Paddington is 23

minutes. There are hourly connecting trains from Reading to Henley via Twyford, and this trip takes 12 minutes. Henley rail station is in the center of town.

By Bus Thames Transit service Bus 390 leaves eight times a day from Stand 8 on Buckingham Palace Road, Victoria, stopping at Henley on its way to Oxford. Journeys take about 90 minutes, with day-return tickets costing £7.

By Car Take the M4 motorway due west out of London to Maidenhead, then the A423 for 6 more miles to Henley (for a total trip of 40 miles), or take the A415 to Marlow (about 32 miles).

Henley-on-Thames

Henley tourist office: Town Hall, Market Pl., tel. 01491/578034.

Henley, set in a broad valley between gentle hillsides, about 8 miles from Reading and 36 miles from central London, has been an important river crossing since the 12th century. The handsome Henley bridge, its keystones carved with personifications of the Thames and Isis rivers, is more than 200 years old. Now, unfortunately, the bridge is a serious traffic bottleneck, especially on weekends.

Henley's many historic buildings, including one of Britain's oldest theaters, are all within a few minutes' walk. Half-timbered cottages and inns abound. Many have courtyards that once witnessed the brutal sport of bear-baiting, where tethered bears were tormented to death by hungry dogs. There is also an interesting selection of small antiques and gift shops, and several historic pubs.

Just beside the bridge you will see the **Red Lion Hotel,** built in mellow terra-cotta brick. This inn has been the town's focal point for nearly 500 years. Kings, dukes, and authors have stayed here, including Charles I in 1632 and 1642, and the duke of Marlborough, who used the hotel as a base during the building of Blenheim Palace in the early 18th century (he even had a room furnished to his specifications). The biographer James Boswell and the 18th-century poet William Shenstone also stayed here.

Overlooking the bridge is the 16th-century "checkerboard" tower of **St. Mary's Church** on Hart Street. The building is made of alternating squares of local flint and white stone. If the church's rector is about, you will be able to climb to the top and enjoy the superb views up and down the river and around the countryside. The **Chantry House,** connected to the church by a gallery, was built as a school for poor boys in 1420. It is an unspoiled example of the rare timber-frame design, with upper floors jutting out. *Hart St., tel. 01491/ 577340. Admission free. Open Thurs. and Sat. 10–noon.*

Mention Henley to Britons, and even those who have scarcely seen a boat will conjure up idyllic scenes of summer rowing. Indeed, Henley Royal Regatta, held in early July each year on a long, straight stretch of the River Thames (1 mile, 550 yards), has made the charming little riverside town famous throughout the world. For four days each year a group of large tents is erected, especially along both sides of that unique straight stretch, and every surrounding field becomes a parking lot. The most prestigious place for spectators is the stewards' enclosure, but admission is by invitation only and, however hot, men must wear jackets and ties and ladies in trousers are refused entry. Fortunately, there is plenty of space on the public towpath to see the early stages of the races.

Townspeople launched the Henley Regatta in 1839, initiating the Grand Challenge Cup, the most famous of its many trophies. After 1851, when Prince Albert, Queen Victoria's consort, became its patron, it was known as the Royal Regatta. Oarsmen compete in crews of eight, four, or two, or as single scullers. For many of the spectators, however, the social side of the event is far more important. Elderly oarsmen wear brightly colored blazers and tiny caps, businesspeople entertain wealthy clients, and everyone admires the range of ladies' fashions on parade.

Another traditional event, in the third week of July, is Swan-Upping. This activity dates back 800 years. Most of the swans on the Thames are owned by the Queen, though a few belong to two City of London companies, the Dyers and the Vintners, descendants of the medieval crafts guilds. Swan markers in Thames skiffs start from Sunbury-on-Thames, catching the new cygnets and marking their beaks in order to establish ownership. The Queen's swan keeper, dressed in scarlet livery, presides over this colorful ceremony, complete with festive banners.

Across the river, on the eastern side, follow the towpath north along the pleasant, shady banks to **Temple Island,** a tiny, privately owned island with trailing willows and a solitary house. This is where the Regatta races start. On the south side of the town bridge, a riverside promenade passes **Mill Meadows,** where there are gardens and a pleasant picnic area. Along both stretches, the river is alive with boats of every shape and size, from luxury "gin palace" cabin cruisers to tiny rowboats.

Edged by the gently sloping Chiltern Hills and in a wide horseshoe-shaped valley, the Thames meanders from Henley through a cluster of small country towns and villages. Main roads follow the river on both sides, but it is along the narrow lanes that the villages and wooded countryside—generally prettiest north of the river—are best explored. Plan to enjoy the area at a leisurely pace, stopping for morning coffee, a pub lunch, or a cream tea at one of the ancient inns overlooking the river, and then visit shops or stroll along the river towpath to visit a lock. For more serious sightseers, the region offers a wide range of earthworks, churches, and stately homes.

Dining

£ **Little Angel Inn.** Housed in a quaint building over 500 years old, this is an associate of the French Routier chain of restaurants, which are known for their good value and no-nonsense food. Specialties include fish and duck. We are not recommending it for its main restaurant, which would fit the *Splurge* category, but for the less expensive meals, served in the bistro/bar, which is open even when the restaurant is closed. *Remenham (¼ mi from Henley), tel. 01491/574165. Reservations advised. AE, DC, MC, V. Closed Sun. dinner and Mon.*

¢ **Argyll.** There's an exotic touch of Scotland inside this black-and-white pub, complete with a tartan carpet in the lounge and Highland pictures on the walls. However, the thoroughly English menu includes such favorites as home-cooked ham, quiche, Lancashire hot pot, and a roast of the day (there's food only at lunchtime). *Market Pl., tel. 01491/573400. V.*

¢ **Three Tuns.** You are never more than a few steps from an interesting
★ pub in Henley, a town where beer has been brewed for about 200 years. This pub, dating back to the late 16th century, is one of the most popular and features a buttery with massive beams and a small terrace. The bar food is reasonably priced and filling—hot salt beef, savory pancakes, sandwiches—all meant to be savored with good local beer. *5 Market Pl., tel. 01491/573260. AE, MC, V.*

Festivals **Henley Festival** takes place during the week following the regatta each year. All kinds of open-air concerts and events are staged, making a popular summer occasion for both local people and tourists. *Henley Festival, Festival Yard, 42 Bell St., Henley, tel. 01491/411353.*

Marlow

Marlow lies about 20 minutes (by bus) northeast of Henley on the Thames. The Bee Line (Buses 325, 328, 329) follows a scenic route along the winding of the river; the trip is spectacular in the fall. Return to Henley for the trip back to London. Tourist office: Garden Leisure Complex, Pound Lane, tel. 01628/483597.

★ As you enter **Marlow**, take particular note of its unusual **suspension bridge**, which William Tierney Clark built in 1831. (His better-known creation is the bridge over the Danube linking Buda with Pest.) Marlow has a number of striking old buildings, particularly the stylish, privately owned Georgian houses along Peter and West streets. In 1817, the Romantic poet Percy Bysshe Shelley stayed with friends at 67 West Street and then bought **Albion House** on the same street. His second wife, Mary, completed her Gothic novel *Frankenstein* here. Marlow Place, in Station Road, dates from 1721, and has been lived in by several princes of Wales.

Dining **Two Brewers.** Pubs in this part of the world tend to have been around
¢ for a long time, and this one, founded in 1742, is no exception. This large, popular place on the riverbank near Marlow bridge has low beams and black woodwork. In addition to the bar food, more serious dishes, such as grilled plaice, mussels marinière, and steak, are offered. You can sit in a courtyard or out front with a view of the Thames. *St. Peter St., tel. 01628/484140. AE, MC, V.*

Tour 4: Oxford and Blenheim Palace

Oxford makes a full and interesting day trip from London. If you get an early enough start, and if you hustle, you'll have some time to see Blenheim Palace. However, you may be better off staying overnight in Oxford if you want to take a thorough tour of the palace.

From London Oxford is well served by **British Rail** from London/Paddington (tel.
By Train 0171/262–6767). Although journey times vary, the average is about 90 minutes. The Oxford station (tel. 01865/722333) is within easy walking distance of the center of town.

By Bus The **X90 Citylink** runs from Victoria Coach Station, London, to Oxford every 20 minutes (tel. 0181/668–7261 or 01865/711312). The trip takes about 1 hour and 40 minutes and costs £6 round-trip. You can also board at Grosvenor Gardens, Marble Arch, and Baker Street. The **Oxford Tube** (tel. 01865/772250) departs from Grosvenor Gardens, Victoria, with the same frequency, travel time, and cost. Other boarding points are Marble Arch, Notting Hill Gate, and Shepherd's Bush (outside the Kensington Hilton).

By Car Oxford is 57 miles northwest of London by the M4 and M40 motorways. The journey time on a clear road (very rare) is a bit more than an hour.

Oxford

Guide Friday offers a tour of Oxford on an open-top bus, which you can get on and off as you please to visit special points. Cost: £7 adults, £4.50 senior citizens, £2 children under 12. Information: Oxford Rail Station (tel. 01865/790522). Daily themed walks are also organized by Oxford tourist office: Gloucester Green, tel. 01865/726871.

The most picturesque approach to **Oxford** is from the east, over **Magdalen Bridge** (pronounced "Maudlin"), which leads you directly into the broad, gently curving High Street, flanked by ancient colleges.

★ Among the ancient honey-colored buildings and elegant spires, you will see the 15th-century tower of **Magdalen College,** famous for its May Day carol service.

In Oxford the rarefied air of academia and the bustle of modern life compete with each other, for in addition to its historic university, Oxford is home to two major industrial complexes: the Rover car factory and the Pressed Steel works. In the city center, "town and gown" merge as modern stores sit side by side with centuries-old colleges and their peaceful quadrangles. With its tremendous historical and architectural wealth—no fewer than 653 buildings are designated as having "architectural or historical merit"—Oxford deserves a serious visit. Keep in mind, however, that congested sidewalks jammed with students, townspeople, tourist groups, and legions of foreign schoolchildren can be hell to negotiate.

Newcomers are surprised to learn that the University of Oxford is not one unified campus, but a collection of many colleges and buildings, new as well as old, scattered across the city. Altogether there are 40 different colleges where undergraduates live and study. Most of their grounds are open to tourists, including the magnificent dining halls and chapels, though the opening times (displayed at the entrance lodges) vary greatly. Some colleges are open only in the afternoons during university semesters, when the undergraduates are in residence.

Numbers in the margin correspond to points of interest on the Oxford map.

❶ Let's begin with **Magdalen College,** one of the largest and most impressive, founded in 1458. Its ancient vaulted cloisters, overhung with wisteria, enclose a serene quadrangle. Beyond this, a narrow stone passage leads through to a large, open park with grazing deer and a cluster of imposing classical buildings, and the sleepy Cherwell River. At the foot of Magdalen Bridge you can rent a punt (C. Howard and Son, tel. 01865/61586; £6 per hour), a shallow-bottom boat that is poled slowly up the river. Students punting on summer afternoons sprawl on cushions, dangling champagne bottles in the water to cool them.

❷ Farther along the High Street is **St. Edmund Hall,** one of the smallest and oldest colleges (founded c. 1220). Its tiny quadrangle, entered through a narrow archway off Queen's Lane, has an ancient
❸ well in the center. Up Queen's Lane you will see the far grander **New College** (founded in 1379), with its extensive gardens overlooking part of the medieval city wall. This was the home of the celebrated Dr. Spooner, known for his tongue-twisting "spoonerisms." He is reputed to have told a dilettante student, "You have hissed your mystery lectures and tasted a whole worm."

❹ The 14th-century tower of the **University Church** (St. Mary's), a bit farther on, provides a splendid view of the city's famous skyline— the pinnacles, towers, domes, and spires which span every architectural style since the 11th century. *Tel. 01865/243806. Admission to tower: £1.40 adults, 70p children. Open daily 9:15–7, 9:15–4:30 in winter.*

Immediately opposite the church is one of the largest domes in Brit-
❺ ain, that of the **Radcliffe Camera.** This building contains part of the
❻ **Bodleian Library,** an important collection begun 300 years ago. It holds more than 2 million volumes.

❼ The university's ornate **Sheldonian Theatre** is where the impressive graduation ceremonies (conducted entirely in Latin) are held. Built in 1663, it was the first building designed by Sir Christopher Wren. Semicircular like a Roman amphitheater, it has pillars, balconies, and an elaborately painted ceiling. There is an impressive view from the top. Outside, beige stone pillars are topped by the massive stone

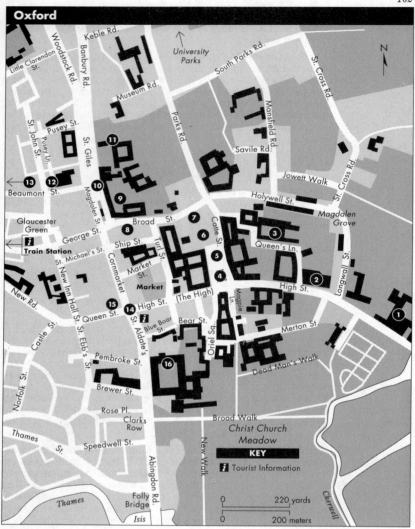

Ashmolean, **12**
Balliol College, **9**
Bodleian Library, **6**
Carfax, **14**
Christ Church
College, **16**
Magdalen College, **1**
Martyrs' Memorial, **10**

New College, **3**
Oxford Story
Exhibition, **8**
Radcliffe Camera, **5**
St. Edmund Hall, **2**
St. John's College, **11**
St. Martin's
Church, **15**
Sheldonian
Theatre, **7**
University Church, **4**
Worcester College, **13**

heads of 18 Roman emperors, sculpted in the 1970s to replace the originals that had been rendered faceless by air pollution. *Tel. 01865/277299. Admission: 50p adults, 25p children. Open Mon.– Sat. 10–12:45 and 2–4:45; mid-Nov.–Feb., closes 3:45.*

Broad Street, known to undergraduates as "the Broad," is a wide, straight thoroughfare lined with colleges and bow-fronted, half-timbered shops. Among them is **Blackwell's,** a family-run bookstore offering one of the largest selections of books in the world. It has been in business since 1879.

❽ While you are on Broad Street, stop in at the **Oxford Story Exhibition,** situated in a converted warehouse. The imaginative presentation makes 800 years of Oxford life come alive with models, sounds, and smells. Visitors ride through the exhibition in small cars shaped like medieval students' desks. *Tel. 01865/728822. Admission: £4.50 adults, £3.95 senior citizens, £3.25 children, £14 family ticket. Open Apr.–June, Sept., Oct., daily 9:30–5; July and Aug., daily 9:30–7; Nov.–Mar., daily 10–4.*

Broad Street leads westward to **St. Giles,** reputed to be the widest **❾** street in Europe. At the corner is prestigious **Balliol College** (1263). The wooden doors between Balliol's inner and outer quadrangles still bear scorch marks from 1555 and 1556, during the reign of Mary I ("Bloody Mary"), when Bishops Latimer and Ridley and Archbishop Cranmer were burned on huge pyres in Broad Street for their Protestant beliefs. A small cross on the roadway marks the actual **❿** spot. The three men are also commemorated by the tall **Martyrs' Me-**
⓫ **morial** in St. Giles. A little farther up St. Giles, step inside **St. John's College** (1555), whose huge gardens are among the city's loveliest.

Beaumont Street, running west from St. Giles, is the site of the **⓬** **Ashmolean,** Britain's oldest public museum. Among its priceless collections (all university-owned) are a large number of Egyptian, Greek, and Roman artifacts, most uncovered during archaeological expeditions conducted by the university. Michelangelo drawings, antique silver, and a wealth of important paintings are also on display. *Beaumont St., tel. 01865/278000. Admission free. Open Tues.–Sat. 10–4, Sun. 2–4.*

⓭ Beaumont Street leads on to **Worcester College** (1714), noted for its wide lawns, colorful cottage garden, and large lake. It was built on the site of a former college, founded in 1283 by the Benedictines.

A side trip into the southern part of town should begin in **Cornmarket,** Oxford's main shopping street. As you pass through **⓮ ⓯** **Carfax,** where four roads meet, you will see the tower of **St. Martin's Church,** where Shakespeare once stood as godfather for William Davenant, who himself became a playwright. Continue south on St. **⓰** Aldate's to reach **Christ Church College** (1546), referred to by its members as "The House." Christ Church boasts Oxford's largest quadrangle, "Tom Quad," named after the huge bell (6¼ tons) that hangs in the gate tower. Its clock is stubbornly set to its own time, calculated by its distance from the Greenwich Meridian. The vaulted, 800-year-old chapel in one corner has been Oxford's cathedral since the time of Henry VIII. The college's medieval dining hall contains portraits of many famous alumni, including John Wesley, William Penn, and 14 of Britain's prime ministers. *Admission: £2.50 adults, £1 senior citizens and children. Open Mon.–Sat. 9:30–4:30, Sun. noon–4:30.*

The **Canterbury Quadrangle** offers a fine picture gallery exhibiting works by Leonardo, Michelangelo, Rubens, Dürer, and other old masters. *Tel. 01865/276172. Admission: £1 adults, 50p senior citizens and children. Open Mon.–Sat. 10:30–1 and 2–4:30 (5:30 in summer), Sun. 2–4:30 (5:30 in summer).*

Beyond the quadrangle lies the extensive **Christ Church Meadow,** where the wide, tree-lined paths are as quiet and green as the depths of the countryside. On its journey through here, the Thames takes on a new name—the Isis. During university terms it is always busy as college "eights" practice their rowing.

Lodging **River Hotel.** Reasonably priced accommodations in the center of Oxford are few and far between. However, this family-run hotel, which overlooks the Thames at Osney Bridge, is within a comfortable walk of the colleges and main sights. Rooms cost about £65 a night for two. All bedrooms have TVs and tea- and coffee-making appliances, and there is a restaurant on the premises. *17 Botley Rd., OX2 0AA, tel. 01865/243475, fax 01865/724306. 24 rooms, 18 with bath or shower. Facilities: restaurant. MC, V.*

££

£ **Cotswold House.** This popular B&B lies in the north of town, on the main road to Banbury. Inside the stone building are comfortable, refurbished rooms with attractive modern furniture. The owners, who really know the area, are pleased to help with touring advice. Enjoy the well-kept garden on the grounds. If asking for directions to the Cotswold House, do not confuse this property with the much more expensive Cotswold Lodge. *363 Banbury Rd., OX2 7PL, tel. 01865/310558, fax 01865/310558. 7 rooms with shower. No credit cards.*

£ **Norham Guest House.** This simple lodging, in a Victorian building, is located in a conservation area, and thus is very peaceful. The rooms are tastefully decorated and comfortable, all with TVs and tea/coffeemakers. As with many guest houses now, smoking is not permitted on the premises. Norham Guest House is on the north side of town, within an easy 15-minute walk of the center. *16 Norham Rd., OX2 6SF, tel. 01865/515352. 8 rooms, 7 with bath or shower. No credit cards.*

£ **Pickwicks.** Pickwicks is located 1½ miles east of the town center, off the main London road. This quietly run hotel, situated on the corner and standing in its own garden, features standard rooms with TVs and tea and coffee making appliances. Things run smoothly here, and evening meals are available on request. *17 London Rd., OX3 7SP, tel. 01865/750487/69413, fax 01865/742208. 14 rooms, 10 with bath or shower. AE, MC, V.*

Dining **Browns.** So popular is this restaurant with both undergraduates and local people that you may have to wait for a table. The wide choice of informal dishes includes steak, mushroom and Guinness pie, and hot chicken salad. Potted palms and mirrors give the otherwise plain rooms a cheery atmosphere. *5–11 Woodstock Rd., tel. 01865/511995. No reservations. MC, V.*

£ **Cherwell Boathouse.** About a mile north of town, this is an ideal spot for a meal in a riverside setting. The menus change weekly, but could include mussels in white wine and cream, loin of lamb with red wine, lime and garlic, or tagliatelle with fennel and cashew nuts. It's a very friendly spot, so be prepared to linger. There is a good set menu as well. *Bardwell Rd. (off Banbury Rd.), tel. 01865/52746. Reservations suggested. Closed Mon., Tues. lunch, and Sun. dinner. AE, DC, MC, V.*

£ **Fifteen North Parade.** Just outside the city center, this intimate restaurant is decorated with attractive cane furniture and plants. Try the lobster ravioli, potted partridge, rib-eye steak, or one of the many dishes with wild mushrooms. You may have to be a bit selective when choosing, but getting a reasonably priced meal is possible. There are set menus for lunch and dinner at about £16. *15 North Parade, tel. 01865/513773. Reservations advised. MC, V. Closed Sun. dinner, Mon., and 2 weeks in Aug.*

£ ★ **Munchy Munchy.** In spite of the dreadful name, this is a fine place, offering spicy Malaysian dishes that change three times a week, as well as a good selection of fish and fresh vegetables. The surroundings are unpretentious and the prices very reasonable. *6 Park End*

St., tel. 01865/245710. MC, V. Closed Sun., Mon., 2 weeks in Aug./ Sept., and 2 weeks in Dec./Jan.

¢ **Eagle and Child.** If you are in St. Giles around midday, stop for lunch at this friendly, old-fashioned pub. The narrow interior leads to a conservatory (smoking is not permitted) and a small terrace. The Eagle and Child was once the meeting place for J.R.R. Tolkien and his friends, the "Inklings." The bar food is fairly basic, but good value. *St. Giles, tel. 01865/58085. No credit cards.*

The **Perch** at Binsey (tel. 01865/240386) and the **Trout** at Godstow (tel. 01865/54485) are two excellent Thameside pubs on the northern edge of Oxford. Connoisseurs go to the thatched Perch at lunchtime to enjoy its wide lawn, unusual sandwiches, and cooing doves. In the evening, they go to the creeper-covered Trout for a meal or a drink and to watch its peacocks strutting back and forth beside the weir.

Shopping As a major shopping location, Oxford has improved recently with the arrival of several malls within easy walking distance of Carfax, at the city center. Cornmarket and Queen Street are lined with small shops, while the Clarendon and Westgate centers which lead off them have branches of several nationally known stores. A particularly good selection of specialty stores is gathered around Golden Cross, a cobbled courtyard with pretty window boxes, between Cornmarket and the excellent covered food market. Broad Street, parallel to High Street, is famous for its bookstores, including **Blackwell's,** whose Norrington Room (tel. 01865/792792) boasts the largest selection on sale in one room anywhere in the world. **Culpepers** (7 New Inn Hall St., tel. 01865/249754) is an herbalist specializing in natural toiletries and soaps.

The Arts and Nightlife **The Apollo** (George St., tel. 01865/244544) is Oxford's main theater. It stages a varied program of plays, opera, ballet, pantomime, and concerts, and is the recognized second home of both the Welsh National Opera and the Glyndebourne Touring Opera.

During university terms, many undergraduate productions are staged in the colleges or local halls. In the summer, there are usually some outdoor performances in ancient quadrangles or college gardens. Posters, with details of how to obtain tickets, appear in store windows or on college bulletin boards. Also, check with *Daily Information* (a newssheet posted up in shops, pubs, and the tourist office) for current events.

Oxford Coffee Concerts is a program of chamber concerts performed on Sunday at the Holywell Music Room, Holywell Street, Oxford. String quartets, piano trios, and solo performers present a variety of Baroque and classical pieces in this venerable old hall, dating from 1748. Tickets are very reasonably priced, available from Blackwell's Music Shop, Holywell Street (tel. 01865/261384) or can be booked direct by calling 01295/810683.

Music at Oxford is a highly acclaimed series of weekend classical concerts performed from mid-September to June in such illustrious surroundings as Christ Church Cathedral and Sir Christopher Wren's Sheldonian Theatre. The music is performed by musicians and orchestras from all over the world, as well as from both Oxford and Cambridge. Information and tickets are available from Music at Oxford (Elms Court, Botley, Oxford OX2 9LP, tel. 01865/242865.) Tickets are generally inexpensive.

Woodstock

Blenheim Palace (at Woodstock) can be reached by Bus 20 from Oxford, leaving from the depot every 30 minutes, for the 30-minute trip.

★ The village of **Woodstock,** site of **Blenheim Palace,** Britain's largest
stately home and the birthplace of Sir Winston Churchill, is 8 miles
from Oxford. A classical-style mansion built by Sir John Vanbrugh
in the early 1700s, Blenheim Palace stands in 2,000 acres of parkland
and gardens landscaped by Capability Brown. Queen Anne gave the
land and money to build the palace to General John Churchill, first
duke of Marlborough, after his victory over Louis XIV's armies in
1704 at the Battle of Blenheim. It is now the home of the 11th duke.
Winston Churchill, who was born at the palace in 1874 (his father
was the younger brother of the then-duke), wrote that the unique
beauty of the Blenheim estate lay in its perfect adaptation of an English parkland to an Italian palace. In addition to paintings, tapestries, and furniture, it houses an exhibition devoted to Winston
Churchill, including some of his own paintings. Both a restaurant
and a cafeteria, which is by far the best budget bet, can be found at
the palace. *Woodstock, tel. 01993/811091. Palace admission: £7
adults, £4.90 senior citizens, £3.50 children. Open mid-Mar.–Oct.,
daily 10:30–5:30. Park admission free. Open daily 9–4:45.*

Dining **The Feathers.** If you do not have lunch at Blenheim, try this lovely
££ old Cotswold hotel. It's a 17th-century building that was recently
refurbished by the new owners. In the restaurant's luxurious,
wood-paneled rooms, you can enjoy a set-price, two- or three-course
menu for £19.50 and £24.50, respectively. You can also have lunch in
the attractive courtyard, where there's a wide variety of bar food,
including tomato and basil soup, flat mushroom fritter with spinach
and nutmeg mayonnaise, or chargrilled fillet of salmon. Rooms are
also available here. *Market Sq., Woodstock, tel. 01993/812291. Reservations advised. AE, DC, MC, V.*

7 The Heart of England

Stratford-upon-Avon, Warwick, Birmingham, the Cotswold Hills, the Forest of Dean, Bath, Bristol

The Heart of England is a name we have borrowed from the tourist powers-that-be—and by which they mean the heart of *tourist* England, so immensely popular are its attractions. Here it means the three counties of west-central England—Warwickshire (pronounced Worrick), Gloucestershire (pronounced Gloster . . .), and Avon. Together they make up a sweep of land stretching from Shakespeare country in the north down through Bath to the Bristol Channel in the south.

If you have time to tour only one part of England, the Heart of England is probably your best choice. It has everything: a countryside that has been cultivated for centuries, but has retained traces of the ancient forest; magnificent architecture such as Warwick Castle and Gloucester; Stratford, with its internationally acclaimed theater; the elegant Regency terraces of Bath; some of the country's best Roman remains around Cirencester; and an off-the-beaten-track prehistoric stone circle at Stanton Drew. In addition to all this, the Heart has quiet, attractive villages hidden in a countryside that has remained virtually unchanged for centuries.

The one snag is that this part of England is upscale and can be costly for visitors. The Cotswolds are popular with rich commuters and well-heeled retirees, so there are plenty of expensive hotels and restaurants. Fortunately, the budget traveler will find a variety of B&Bs and pubs that offer good bar food, and the tourist offices work hard to accommodate and welcome all visitors.

Stratford, Warwick, and Bath figure on almost every coach operator's "Days Out from London" program, and day trips are a good way to see the area if you are in a hurry, though you don't get more than a quick taste. If you opt to travel at your own pace, consider using the cities of Stratford-upon-Avon, Cheltenham, and Bath as your bases for exploring. Stratford acts as the focus for a fairly tight group of villages and also as a springboard for a straight trip to Cov-

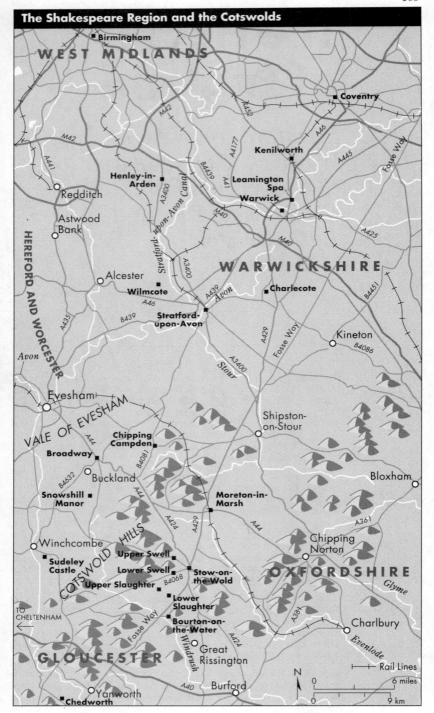

The Shakespeare Region and the Cotswolds

- Birmingham
- **WEST MIDLANDS**
- Coventry
- Kenilworth
- Henley-in-Arden
- Redditch
- Leamington Spa
- Warwick
- Astwood Bank
- **WARWICKSHIRE**
- Alcester
- Charlecote
- Wilmcote
- Stratford-upon-Avon
- Kineton
- *Avon*
- *Stour*
- Evesham
- Shipston-on-Stour
- **VALE OF EVESHAM**
- Chipping Campden
- Bloxham
- Broadway
- Buckland
- Moreton-in-Marsh
- Snowshill Manor
- Chipping Norton
- Winchcombe
- **COTSWOLD HILLS**
- **OXFORDSHIRE**
- Sudeley Castle
- Upper Swell
- Lower Swell
- Stow-on-the-Wold
- Upper Slaughter
- Lower Slaughter
- Bourton-on-the-Water
- TO CHELTENHAM
- Charlbury
- *Glyme*
- *Evenlode*
- Great Rissington
- *Windrush*
- **GLOUCESTER**
- Yanworth
- Chedworth
- Burford

N

0 — 6 miles
0 — 9 km

Rail Lines

HEREFORD AND WORCESTER

Fosse Way

entry, taking in Warwick en route, and another side trip to Birmingham, which is making every effort to change its image from one of civic horror to a place with a vibrant cultural identity. Cheltenham is centrally placed between the Cotswolds and the Forest of Dean. Bath, like Stratford, is a self-contained destination, and from there you can also see Bristol and the countryside.

Essential Information

Lodging The Heart of England attracts many tourists annually, and there are upscale lodgings and B&Bs to meet travelers' needs. A somewhat inexpensive option for most of the region is the large Victorian, or Edwardian, houses that were built for large families, but are now guest houses with decent-size rooms and large public areas. Unfortunately, however, once you reach the Cotswolds, the situation changes: The large houses are there, certainly, but you will have trouble finding affordable lodgings in the smaller towns of this plush region. You would be well advised to stay in a larger place and visit the rest of the area on day trips.

Whenever you make a reservation, ask about accommodations with restaurants on the premises, and also inquire about two- and three-day packages and half-board (a room and one main meal) policies. The tourist offices have lists of available rooms, so you don't have to book ahead, except in the height of the summer season. Highly recommended establishments are indicated by a star ★.

Dining The steady flow of tourism to this area has created the need for good restaurants—a need that largely has been met, although the distribution is patchy. Local chefs have no problem finding excellent produce for their kitchens. Apart from easy access to fresh vegetables, there are salmon from the Rivers Severn and Wye, local lamb, and venison from the Forest of Dean. Game, including pheasant, partridge, quail, and grouse, is also in seasonal abundance. Finding a good, reasonably priced meal is no problem. The entire region is filled with attractive old pubs and inns that serve first-class homemade food. Unless otherwise noted, reservations are not needed and dress is casual. Highly recommended restaurants are indicated by a star ★.

Shopping This is an excellent region for shopping, with both Bath and Stratford full of interesting stores to explore. Both, too, have branches of the popular national chains, and souvenir shops, not all of which are tacky. All the Cotswold villages have craft shops, and you may well find exquisite pottery hidden away in a most unexpected spot; but perhaps the chief reason for shopping here is the hundreds of small antiques shops that line every high street—and most back streets, too. The trade in antiques has reached the level of a major industry in the Cotswolds, so don't expect to find many bargains.

Markets in this region are very popular. In **Stratford-upon-Avon,** there is an open market every Friday in the Market Square. In **Cheltenham** there is a market every Sunday at the racecourse, a produce market every Thursday morning on Market Street, and undercover stalls Tuesday through Saturday on Winchcombe Street.

Markets are held in Moreton-in-Marsh on Tuesday and in Chipping Norton on Wednesday.

Biking This is a good area for cycling on the back roads, but the main ones are very busy and can be dangerous. On a bicycle you'll be able to see some of the many stately homes that are not reached easily by public transport. Here are a few of the shops where you can rent bikes: in Bath, **Avon Valley Cyclery** (in the rail station car park, tel. 01225/ 461880); in Cheltenham, **Crabtrees** (50 Winchcombe St., tel. 01242/ 515291) and **Cotswold Bicycle Company** (48 Shurdington Rd., tel.

01242/250642); in Chipping Campden, **Cotswold Country Cycles**
(Longlands Farm Cottage, between Chipping Campden and
Hidcote, tel. 01386/438706); in Bourton-on-the-Water, **Pritchard's
Cycle Hire** (2 Lamberts Field, tel. 01451/821415); in Stratford,
Knotts (15 Western Rd., tel. 01789/205149).

Hiking This part of England offers glorious yet gentle countryside to ramble through. Extending from Chipping Campden to Bath is the 100-
mile-long **Cotswold Way.** Among the firms that provide guided walking tours in the area is **Cotswold Walking Holidays** (10 Royal Parade,
Bayshill Rd., Cheltenham GL50 3AY, tel. 01242/254353).

The Arts and Stratford is, of course, the main theater town in the region, offering
Nightlife world-class productions of Shakespeare and other playwrights. Birmingham has its own brand-new Symphony Hall, the second-string
company of the Royal Ballet, and a lively repertory theater. Bath
has a lovely old theater, too, which mainly houses touring shows.
Bristol has two main theaters and a lively cultural scene. You are
likely to come across concerts and recitals throughout the region, so
keep an eye open for posters in your hotel.

Festivals There's a wide variety of festivals in this part of the country, several
of which date back a very long way. The chief ones are an annual **literary** wingding and an **international music** festival in Cheltenham;
an early summer **arts** festival in Bath; the **Three Choirs Festival,** the
oldest musical festival in the world and still one of the best, held every third year in Gloucester; and the **Shakespeare Birthday celebrations,** held in Stratford every April. The **Birmingham International
Jazz Festival** stars some of the best British and international jazz talent in July.

Tour 1: Stratford-upon-Avon and the Shakespeare Region

From London Although the train service to Stratford is not terribly convenient, it
By Train is a feasible means of transport. From London/Paddington (tel.
0171/262–6767) it takes about 2¼ hours with a change at
Leamington Spa, though on some trains you may have to change at
Oxford, too. The Stratford station is within easy walking distance of
the town center. On winter Sundays, when the station is closed,
you'll have to bus in from Leamington. Considering the time involved, you may want to stay overnight and see a play.

By Bus The trip to Stratford by **National Express** from London/Victoria
Coach Station (tel. 0171/730–0202) is considerably cheaper than by
train, but takes 25–45 minutes longer and there are just three departures a day. There are direct services from Oxford run by the
Oxford Bus Company (tel. 01865/711312).

By Car Take the M40 motorway from London past Oxford to junction 15,
then take A46 and A439 to Stratford. The distance from London is
96 miles.

Stratford-upon-Avon

*If you want a guided tour of Stratford, you should latch on to **Guide
Friday** (The Civic Hall, 14 Rother St., tel. 01789/294466). They do
tours year-round in open-top double-decker buses for £7 adults,
£4.50 senior citizens, £2 children. They also run tours to Warwick
Castle. Stratford tourist office: Bridgefoot, tel. 01789/293127.*

Its connections with Shakespeare have made **Stratford-upon-Avon** a
mecca for tourists from all over the world. But it is conceivable that

the town would have attracted a fair number of tourists even without its famous son. By Elizabethan times (16th century), this was a prosperous market town with thriving guilds and industries. Its characteristic half-timbered houses from this era have been preserved over the centuries, set off by the charm of such later architecture as the elegant Georgian storefronts on Bridge Street, with their 18th-century porticoes and arched doorways.

Yet Stratford is far from a museum piece. It has adapted itself well to the rising tide of visitors, and though the town is full of souvenir shops—every back lane seems to have been converted into a shopping mall, with boutiques selling everything from sweaters to china models of Anne Hathaway's Cottage—Stratford isn't particularly strident in its search for the quick buck. If you prefer to seek out traces of its history in peace, try to hit the place out of season, or at a time of day either before the bus tours arrive or after they leave.

Numbers in the margin correspond to points of interest on the Stratford-upon-Avon map.

★ ❶ Start your tour at the **Shakespeare Centre** on Henley Street (Stratford-upon-Avon CV37 6QW, tel. 01789/204016), home of the Shakespeare Birthplace Trust, which has five properties in the area. This modern building was erected in 1964 as a 400th-anniversary tribute to the playwright; it contains a small BBC Television **Shakespeare Costume Exhibition.** Next door, and reached from the Centre, is ❷ **Shakespeare's Birthplace,** a half-timbered house typical of its time, although much altered and restored since Shakespeare lived here. Half the house has been furnished to reflect Elizabethan domestic life, the other half contains an exhibition illustrating Shakespeare's professional life and work. *Henley St., tel. 01789/204016. Admission: Shakespeare's Birthplace only, £2.60 adults, £1.20 children; Town Heritage Trail (3 town properties), £5.50 adults, £5 senior citizens, £2.50 children; joint ticket for all 5 Shakespeare Trust properties, £8 adults, £7 senior citizens, £3.60 children, £21 family ticket. Open mid-Mar.–mid-Oct., Mon.–Sat. 9–6, Sun. 9:30–6; mid-Oct.–mid-Mar., Mon.–Sat. 9:30–4:30, Sun. 10–4:30. Jan. 1, 1:30–4:30, Good Friday 1:30–6; last admissions 30 minutes before closing. Closed Dec. 24–26.*

Walk down Henley Street and its continuation, Bridge Street, to find the new, custom-built **tourist office** beside the river. The staff will be able to advise you further about your visit to the town and general area. *Bridgefoot, tel. 01789/293127.*

❸ Back up Bridge Street, turn left onto the High Street, where next to the Garrick Inn you will find **Harvard House,** the half-timbered, 16th-century home of Catherine Rogers, mother of the John Harvard who founded Harvard University in 1636. *Open May–Sept. Contact the Shakespeare Centre for hours.*

❹ Across the street and down a block is **Nash's House,** home of Thomas Nash, who married Shakespeare's granddaughter, Elizabeth Hall. Heavily restored, the house has been furnished in 17th-century style, and it also contains a local museum. On the house's grounds, which include an intricately patterned Elizabethan "knot" garden, are the foundations of **New Place,** the house in which Shakespeare died in 1616, aged 52. New Place, built in 1483 for a Lord Mayor of London, was Stratford's grandest piece of real estate when Shakespeare bought it in 1597 for £60. Unfortunately, the original building was torn down in 1759. *Chapel St., tel. 01789/293455. Admission: £1.90 adults, 90p children. Open mid-Mar.–mid-Oct., Mon.–Sat. 9:30–5:30, Sun. 10–5:30; mid-Oct.–mid-Mar., Mon.–Sat. 10–4:30, Sun. 10:30–4:30; Jan. 1 1:30–4:30, Good Friday 1:30–5:30; last admissions 30 minutes before closing. Closed Dec. 24–26.*

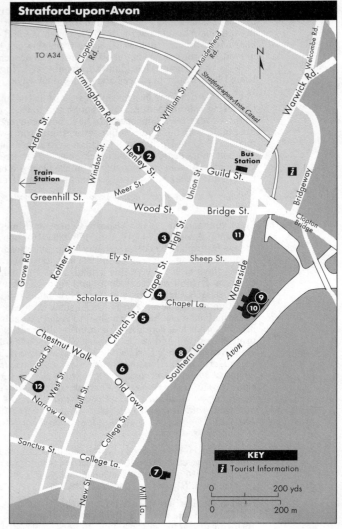

Stratford-upon-Avon

Anne Hathaway's Cottage, **12**

Guildhall and Grammar School, **5**

Hall's Croft, **6**

Harvard House, **3**

Holy Trinity Church, **7**

Nash's House and New Place, **4**

The Other Place, **8**

Royal Shakespeare Theatre, **9**

Shakespeare Centre, **1**

Shakespeare's Birthplace, **2**

Swan Theatre, **10**

World of Shakespeare, **11**

KEY

i Tourist Information

0   200 yds

0   200 m

5 Continue on to Church Street. On your left are poorhouses built by the Guild of the Holy Cross in the early 15th century. On the second floor of the adjoining **Guildhall** is the **Grammar School,** which Shakespeare probably attended as a boy and which is still used as a school. *Tel. 01789/293351. Open Easter and summer school vacations, daily 10–6.*

6 Turning left at the end of Church Street into Old Town (a street), you will see **Hall's Croft,** one of the finest surviving Tudor town houses, with a walled garden behind. This was the home of Shakespeare's elder daughter, Susanna, and her husband, Dr. John Hall, whose dispensary is on view, along with the other rooms, all containing heavy oak Jacobean furniture. *Tel. 01789/292107. Admission: £1.90 adults, 90p children. Open mid-Mar.–mid-Oct., Mon.–Sat. 9:30–5:30, Sun. 10–5:30; mid-Oct.–mid-Mar., Mon.– Sat. 10–4:30, Sun. 10:30–4:30; Jan. 1 1:30–4:30, Good Friday 1:30– 5:30; last admission 30 minutes before closing. Closed Dec. 24–26.*

❼ At the end of Old Town is the 13th-century **Holy Trinity Church,** in which are buried William Shakespeare, his wife Anne, his daughter Susanna, his son-in-law John Hall, and his granddaughter's husband, Thomas Nash. The bust of Shakespeare in the church is thought to be an authentic likeness, executed a few years after his death. *The church charges a small fee to enter the chancel where Shakespeare's grave is.*

From the church, walk either along Southern Lane or through the
❽ gardens along the river Avon to the recently rebuilt **The Other Place,** on Southern Lane, where experimental theater is performed.
❾ Continue on to the **Royal Shakespeare Theatre,** where the Royal Shakespeare Company (RSC) stages plays from late March to late
❿ January. At the rear is the new **Swan Theatre,** created in the only part of the Victorian theater to have survived a fire in the 1930s. It was built with the financial backing of an Anglophile American philanthropist, Frederick Koch. The theater follows the lines of Shakespeare's original Globe and is one of the most exciting acting spaces in Britain. Beside the Swan is an art gallery where you can see the RSC's exhibition of costumes and props, and where you can book tours of the theater, preferably well in advance. *Southern La., tel. 01789/296655. Tours weekdays except matinee days at 1:30, 5:30; matinee days 5:30 and after show; 4 tours Sun. afternoon (hours vary seasonally). Cost: £3.80 adults, £2.60 students and senior citizens, £12 family ticket (Sun. only). Exhibition open Mon.–Sat. 9:15–8, Sun. noon–4:30. Admission: £1.70 adults, £1.20 students and senior citizens, £3.50 family ticket.*

Across the small park in front of the theater is the Heritage Thea-
⓫ tre's **World of Shakespeare,** a glorified waxworks show, using recorded dialogue and dramatic lighting to re-create the "royal progress" of Queen Elizabeth I from London to Kenilworth, where she was lavishly entertained by her favorite, the earl of Leicester, in 1575. Some will consider it a mite pricey for just under half an hour's show. *13 Waterside, tel. 01789/269190. Admission: £4 adults, £3 students, senior citizens, and children, £10 family ticket. Open daily 9:30–5; performances every half hour. Closed Dec. 25.*

⓬ The most picturesque of the Shakespeare Trust properties is **Anne Hathaway's Cottage,** family home of the woman Shakespeare married in 1582, in what was evidently a shotgun wedding. The Hathaway "cottage," actually a beautiful and substantial farmhouse, with a thatched roof and large garden, is in the village of Shottery, now a western suburb of Stratford. The best way to get there is to walk, especially in late spring when the hawthorns and apple trees are in blossom. *Tel. 01789/292100. Admission: £2.30 adults, £1.10 children. Open mid-Mar.–mid-Oct., Mon.–Sat. 9–6, Sun. 10–5:30; mid-Oct.–mid-Mar., Mon.–Sat. 9:30–4:30, Sun. 10–4:30. Jan. 1 1:30–4:30, Good Friday 1:30–6; last admission 30 minutes before closing. Closed Dec. 24–26.*

Lodging **Caterham House.** Built in 1830, this landmark building is in the cen-
£ ter of town, close to the theater: You may spot an actor or two among
★ the guests. Its bedrooms are individually decorated in early 19th-century style, featuring brass beds and antique furniture. The French proprietor and his wife have recently opened a restaurant on the premises, **Le Bonaparte,** which is quickly establishing a good reputation. *58 Rother St., CV37 6LT, tel. 01789/267309, fax 01789/414836. 10 rooms with bath or shower. Facilities: restaurant. MC, V.*

£ **Moonraker House.** This distinctly upmarket B&B, in the northwest section of town and near the rail station, is actually a complex of three white suburban houses. Rooms range in both size and price, so you should be able to find something here even if you are on a tight budget. All rooms have TVs, hair dryers, and tea/coffeemakers, and all guests are invited to use the garden. *40 Alcester Rd., CV37 9DB, tel. 01789/299346, fax 01789/295504. 19 rooms with bath. MC, V.*

¢ **Penryn House.** The convenient location of this lodging—halfway between the city center and Ann Hathaway's Cottage and within an easy walk of both—makes it a good value. Comfortably furnished rooms have TVs, hair dryers, tea/coffeemakers, and an unlimited supply of hot water (the system was recently installed). *126 Alcester Rd., CV37 9DP, tel. 01789/293718. 8 rooms, 6 with bath or shower. AE, DC, MC, V.*

Dining **The Opposition.** The Opposition is located on Sheep Street, just up
£ from the theater. It offers pre- and post-theater dining in a converted 16th-century building. The American and Continental food—with regularly changing dishes—is also popular with the locals, always a good sign. Try the Cajun chicken or the courgette and eggplant lasagne. *13 Sheep St., 01789/269980. Reservations advised. MC, V.*

£ **Vintner Wine Bar.** A real find, this bar/restaurant, located just up the hill from the theater, serves imaginative food from a menu that changes daily. A typical dish might be chicken breast stuffed with Parma ham with a delicious apricot sauce. To accompany your meal, choose one of the excellent wines by the glass. The restaurant gets crowded with out-of-town visitors before curtain time and after performances. *5 Sheep St., tel. 01789/297259. AE, MC, V.*

¢ **River Terrace.** There's informal cafeteria dining right at the theater, where the meals and snacks are crowd-pleasers. Dishes include lasagna, shepherd's pie (minced beef and potato), salads, sandwiches, and cakes, with wine or beer available. *Royal Shakespeare Theatre, Waterside, tel. 01789/293226. No credit cards. Closed when theater is closed.*

Splurge **Box Tree Restaurant.** This elegant dining spot in the Royal Shake-
★ speare Theatre overlooks the River Avon and has some of the very best food in town. You will be veering into Splurge territory if you dine à la carte, but set-price menus are currently available at £15.75 (lunch) and £23.50 (dinner) excluding drinks, and if you're looking for a striking setting, it's worth eating here, even if you're not taking in a play. Specialties include *noisettes* of lamb, and fillet of Scottish beef. *Waterside, tel. 01789/293226. Reservations required. AE, DC, MC, V. Closed when theater is closed.*

Shopping **Robert Vaughan** (20 Chapel St., tel. 01789/205312), the best of Stratford's many secondhand bookshops, has a large stock and is especially good on books about Shakespeare and the theater, as you very would expect.

Once a Tree (8 Bard's Walk, tel. 01789/297790) is a thoroughly "green" setup, selling only items crafted from sustainable wood sources—animal figures, bowls, and dozens of imaginative articles. It's ideal for presents or for finding just the thing you never knew you needed. It's in a small shopping mall that runs from Henley Street to Wood Street.

The Arts and The **Stratford-upon-Avon Shakespeare Birthday Celebrations** take
Nightlife place on the weekend nearest to April 23, when ambassadors and diplomats join townspeople and tourists in colorful receptions and processions. There are lectures, a special performance of one of the plays, and a church service, as well as fringe events such as morris (folk) dancing. Details are available from the Shakespeare Centre (Henley St., Stratford-upon-Avon CV37 6QW, tel. 01789/204016).

The **Royal Shakespeare Theatre** (Stratford-upon-Avon CV37 6BB, tel. 01789/295623) usually features five of Shakespeare's plays in a season lasting from March to January each year. In the excitingly designed **Swan Theatre** at the rear, plays by Shakespeare contemporaries, such as Christopher Marlowe and Ben Jonson, and Restoration comedies are staged. In **The Other Place** some of the RSC's experimental work is produced. Reserve seats for all three auditoriums well in advance. "Day of performance" tickets are often available, and it is always worth asking if there are any returned tickets.

Wilmcote

There is an infrequent local bus, No. 228, to Wilmcote from Stratford, though trains leaving every two hours take only 5 minutes to get there. Alternatively, you might choose to see Wilmcote with a Guide Friday or other tour.

Three miles northwest of Stratford, at the village of **Wilmcote,** is the fifth Shakespeare Birthplace Trust property, **Mary Arden's House.** The authentic Tudor farmhouse was the family home of Shakespeare's mother and it, combined with the adjoining glebe (church-owned farm), forms the **Shakespeare Countryside Museum,** offering exhibitions of rural crafts and, among other things, a remarkable 16th-century dovecote. *Tel. 01789/293455. Admission: £3.20 adults, £1.40 children, £8 family ticket. Open mid-Mar.–mid-Oct., Mon.–Sat. 9:30–5:30, Sun. 10–5:30; mid-Oct.–mid-Mar., Mon.–Sat. 10–4:30, Sun. 10:30–4:30; Jan. 1 1:30–4:30, Good Friday 1:30–5:30; last admission 30 min before closing; closed Dec. 24–26.*

Henley-in-Arden

Henley is easily reached either by local Bus X20 in 16 minutes or by the Birmingham train (13 minutes), both from Stratford.

The village of **Henley-in-Arden** has a wide main street lined with buildings dating from the past six centuries. The 15th-century guildhall and some of the coaching inns, especially the **Blue Bell,** will provide worthwhile photo opportunities and, in the latter case, a good pub lunch. Henley is in the area that was once the Forest of Arden, where Shakespeare set *As You Like It.*

Charlecote

Charlecote is a half-hour bus ride from Stratford in the direction of Warwick on the Stratford Blue Bus 18.

Queen Elizabeth I is known to have stayed at **Charlecote Park,** and this Tudor manor house of the Lucy family was extensively renovated in neo-Elizabethan style in the 19th century. According to tradition, soon after his marriage, Shakespeare was caught poaching deer here and forced to flee to London. Years later he is supposed to have retaliated by portraying Charlecote's owner, Sir Thomas Lucy, as the foolish Justice Shallow in *Henry IV, Part 2.* A restaurant in the Orangery is open for morning coffee, light lunches, and teas. *Tel. 01789/470277. Admission: £4 adults, £2 children (under 5 free), family ticket £11. Open Apr.–Oct., Fri.–Tues. and national holiday Mon. 11–1 and 2–6. Closed Good Friday.*

Warwick

Warwick is about 27 minutes from Stratford by a little two-carriage diesel train (the station is closed Sunday in winter); 26 minutes by Bus X16 (also X18 on Sun.); 52 minutes by Bus 18 via Charlecote. Warwick tourist office: The Court House, Jury St., tel. 01926/492212.

Warwick, the county seat of Warwickshire, is an interesting architectural mixture of Georgian redbrick and Elizabethan half-timbering. Much of the town center has been spoiled by unattractive postwar development, but find the 15th-century **Lord Leycester Hospital,** which has been a home for old soldiers since the earl of

Leicester dedicated it to that purpose in 1571. *High St., tel. 01926/ 492797. Admission: £2.25 adults, £1.50 senior citizens, £1 children. Open Apr.–Sept., Tues.–Sun. 10–5; Oct.–Mar., Tues.–Sun. 10–4. Closed Good Friday and Dec. 25.*

Well worth visiting, too, is the **Collegiate Church of St. Mary,** on Church Street, especially for the florid Beauchamp Chapel, burial chapel of the earls of Warwick. Its gilded, carved, and painted tombs are the very essence of late medieval and Tudor chivalry.

St. John's House, one of the three museums that make up the Warwickshire Museum, presents a social history of the county and includes a Victorian school classroom, costumes, and scenes of domestic life. *St. John's, tel. 01926/412021. Admission free. Open Tues.–Sat. 10–12:30 and 1:30–5:30, Sun. and national holiday Mon. (May–Sept. only) 2:30–5.*

★ The city's chief attraction is **Warwick Castle,** the finest medieval castle in England, which is built on a cliff overlooking the Avon. Its most powerful commander was the 15th-century earl of Warwick, known during the Wars of the Roses as "the Kingmaker." He was killed in battle near London in 1471 by Edward IV, whom he had just deposed in favor of Henry VI. Warwick Castle's monumental walls now enclose one of the best collections of medieval armor and weapons in Europe, as well as historic furnishings and paintings by Rubens, Van Dyck, and other old masters. Twelve rooms are devoted to an imaginative Madame Tussaud's wax exhibition, "A Royal Weekend Party—1898." Below the castle, along the Avon, strutting peacocks patrol 60 acres of grounds landscaped by Capability Brown in the 18th century. There is a restaurant in the cellars, for lunch during your visit. *Tel. 01926/495421. Admission: £8.75 adults, £6.25 students, £5.95 senior citizens, £4.95 children, £20 family ticket. Open Apr.–mid-Oct., daily 10–6 (7 weekends Aug. and national holiday Mon.): mid-Oct.–Mar., daily 10–5. Closed Dec. 25.*

Lodding **Tudor House Inn.** In spite of its name, part of this inn—built in
£ 1472—predates the Tudors. The building's age shows, but in a comfortable, charming way: The whole place is filled with creaky timbers, some of them salvaged from ancient warships. While you can hear the bedrooms settling, be assured that the plumbing is definitely post-Tudor. For a moderate price, you can take in a hearty meal served in the Hall with its huge fireplace. In the summer you can sit in the attractive garden. *West St., CV34 6AW, tel. 01926/ 495447, fax 01926/492948. 11 rooms, 8 with bath. AE, DC, MC, V.*

Kenilworth

Kenilworth is 25 minutes beyond Warwick by Bus X16 (also X18 on Sun.). Kenilworth tourist office: The Library, 11 Smalley Pl., tel. 01926/52595.

The next stop after Warwick is at the great, red ruins of **Kenilworth Castle.** Founded in 1120, this castle remained one of the most formidable fortresses in England until it was finally dismantled by Oliver Cromwell after the Civil War in the mid-17th century. Its keep (central tower), with 20-foot-thick walls, its great hall, and its "curtain" walls (low outer walls forming the castle's first line of defense) are largely intact. Here the earl of Leicester, one of Queen Elizabeth I's favorites, entertained her four times, most notably in 1575 with 19 days of sumptuous feasting and revelry. *Tel. 01926/52078. Admission: £2 adults, £1.50 senior citizens, £1 children. Open Apr.–Oct., daily 10–6; Nov.–Mar., daily 10–4. Closed Dec. 24–26.*

Dining **Restaurant Bosquet.** This attractive, small restaurant serves set
££ menus (during the week) which are presently just below £20, though you must pay more to sample some of the regularly changing à la carte selections, all cooked by the French patron. Try the boned ox-

tail wrapped in lettuce leaves, or breast of duck with fig sauce. The desserts are mouth-watering. It is mainly a dinner spot, though lunch is available on request. *97A Warwick Rd., tel. 01926/52463. Reservations advised. AE, MC, V. Closed Sun. and lunch Mon.*

¢ **Clarendon Arms.** This recently refurbished pub is an ideal spot for lunch after a visit to the castle. Excellent home-cooked food is offered at the small bar downstairs, and at the larger, slightly pricier restaurant upstairs (open evenings only), you can sink your teeth into big, charcoal-grilled steaks. *44 Castle Hill, tel. 01926/52017. AE, DC, MC, V.*

Coventry

You can easily reach Coventry direct from London/Euston in about 1¼ hours; from Stratford, Bus X16 takes 1 hour, 17 minutes (also X18 on Sun.). Coventry tourist office: Bayley Lane, tel. 01203/832303.

As a testament to history, **Coventry's** original 1,000-year-old **cathedral,** destroyed by air raids in 1940 and 1941, has been left as a bombed-out shell next to the magnificent new cathedral. The new building contains the best of modern religious art in Britain at the time (1954–62), including an engraved glass screen by John Hutton; a tapestry by Graham Sutherland, who painted Churchill's 80th birthday portrait; stained-glass windows by John Piper; and various pieces by Sir Jacob Epstein, the New York–born sculptor. The visitor center beneath the cathedral uses audiovisual aids and holograms to show the history of Coventry and its old and new cathedrals. About the rest of Coventry, which contains some of the worst postwar rebuilding to be seen in Britain, the less said the better. *Priory Row, tel. 01203/227597. Admission free; tower, £1 adults, 50p children; visitor center, £1.25 adults, 75p senior citizens and children, £3 family ticket. Open Apr.–Sept., daily 9–7:30; Oct.–Mar., 9–5:30. Closed during services.*

Dining £ **Corks Wine Bar.** The menu in this intimate bistro, near the Odeon cinema, carries a range of international dishes, including Mexican. It's a friendly spot, open Monday–Saturday for lunch and dinner and just dinner on Sunday. *4/5 Whitefriars St., tel. 01203/223628. AE, DC, MC, V.*

The Arts and Nightlife The **Belgrade Theatre** (Corporation St., tel. 01203/553055) hosts drama and dance performances and stages its own productions.

Tour 2: Birmingham

Birmingham is within easy reach of London. Trains leave London/Euston (tel. 0171/387–7070) at least twice an hour. The express trains take 1 hour, 45 minutes, arriving in Birmingham at New Street Station. For rail information in Birmingham, call 0121/643–2711. Fifteen National Express Rapide buses from Victoria Coach Station (tel. 0171/730–0202) take 2 hours, 40 minutes. With a slightly shorter journey time, the London Express service runs up to seven times a day from Victoria Coach Station with a pick-up point at Marble Arch (tel. 0121/333–3232). For all travel information in Birmingham, call 0121/200–2700. From Stratford-upon-Avon you can catch the local train (except Sun.), which stops frequently and takes just over 50 minutes to cover the 25 miles before it arrives at Snow Hill Station. The hourly Midland Red Bus X20 gives you a chance to see the countryside at leisure; trip time is 1 hour, 5 minutes. Birmingham tourist office: Convention and Visitor Bureau, 2 City Arcade, Birmingham B2 4TX, tel. 0121/643–2514.

Numbers in the margin correspond to points of interest on the Birmingham map.

Birmingham is England's second-largest city, but one that was grossly disfigured by injudicious planning and building in the period after World War II. Mercifully, in the past few years the city leaders have adopted a new policy of humanizing the areas that their immediate predecessors had ruined. Much has been accomplished and future plans include pulling down many of the worst buildings.

The city flourished in the boom years of the Industrial Revolution, and at one time it could boast some of the finest Victorian buildings in the country, built from the wealth that its inventive, hard-working citizens accumulated. Birmingham started with iron and steel industries and was a major center of arms manufacture in both world wars. But 20th-century civic "planning" managed to destroy much of the city's hard-won riches. There are still architectural treasures to be found, but to find them requires a dedicated search, carefully negotiating the city's impossible road network. While most communities manage to keep their manic motorways on the edge of town, Birmingham's inner ring road twists through the city center. But this is all changing: City planners are making Birmingham "pedestrian-friendly" by replacing the ring road with a network of local access roads and by turning the downtown shopping area into pedestrian arcades and buses-only streets.

Birmingham is at the center of a system of waterways built during the Industrial Revolution to connect inland industries to rivers and seaports—by 1840 the canals extended more than 4,000 miles throughout the British Isles. The canals in Birmingham have been restored. Contact the Convention and Visitor Bureau for maps of walkway routes along the canal towpaths and for details on canal barge cruises.

❶ Start your visit in the heart of the city at the new **International Convention Centre,** where there is also a good tourist information desk. The main atrium of this high-tech building is dominated by a network of blue struts and gleaming air ducts, partly softened by banks of indoor plants. Above the entrance is a straggling neon sculpture of birds in flight, adding, so to speak, a light touch.

★ ❷ Next door to the International Convention Centre—and part of the same brand-new building—is the **Symphony Hall.** This auditorium has been hailed as an acoustical triumph and is a significant addition to English musical life. Attending a concert here is definitely a good reason for visiting Birmingham. The internationally recognized City of Birmingham Symphony Orchestra, which has won awards for its recordings with its young conductor Simon Rattle, has found a very welcome home here (*see* The Arts and Nightlife, *below*).

❸ Once outside the Convention Centre, you are in **Centenary Square,** a sort of miniature Lincoln Center. It is paved with a pattern of bricks of various shades, like an Oriental carpet, created by artist Tess Jaray. She was responsible for all the square's landscaping, designing the benches, bins, and planted areas as well as the unusual paving, which echoes the fancy brickwork that Victorian architects so ❹ favored. To one side stands the **Birmingham Repertory Theatre,** which houses one of England's oldest and most esteemed theater companies (*see* The Arts and Nightlife, *below*).

In the middle of Centenary Square is a group sculpture by a Birmingham artist, Raymond Mason, called *Crowd Scene*. It celebrates Birmingham's past with a bursting crowd of people, backed by factories belching smoke. Behind the *Crowd Scene* is a small, modern bronze fountain embodying Birmingham's civic virtues of Enterprise, Industry, and Learning.

❺ On the other side of the square from the Convention Centre you will find the octagonal **Hall of Memory,** a war memorial built in the 1920s in remembrance of those who died in World War I. Inside there is a

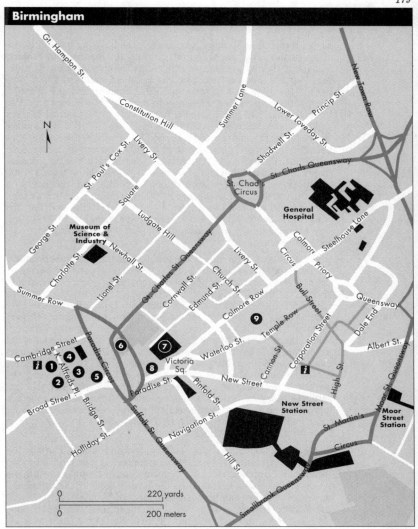

Birmingham

Birmingham Cathedral
(St. Philip's), **9**

Birmingham Repertory
Theatre, **4**

Centenary Square, **3**

Central Library, **6**

City Museum and Art
Gallery, **7**

International
Convention Centre, **1**

Hall of Memory, **5**

Symphony Hall, **2**

Town Hall, **8**

book containing the names of the fallen. *Admission free. Open Mon.–Sat., 10–4.*

Leave the Hall of Memory, go through the building beyond (Paradise Forum), and you will find yourself in **Chamberlain Square,** which was the city's central square before the construction of Centenary Square. The two now comprise a linked complex. The Chamberlain family were civic leaders of Birmingham, and one, Neville, was prime minister in 1939 when war broke out with Germany. The building you have just passed through houses the **Central Library** and has been described by Prince Charles as looking "like a place where books are incinerated." It used to be bare concrete, but now boxes of flowers and plants attempt to soften its facade. In any case, the treasures are inside the building. The library houses a **Shakespeare Memorial Room** on the sixth floor, the survivor from a previous library. There are around 50,000 books and thousands of illustrations about Shakespeare in the collection. Also in this complex of buildings are the Adrian Boult Concert Hall and the Birmingham School of Music. *Chamberlain Square, tel. 0121/235–4511. Admission free. Open weekdays 9–8, Sat. 9–5. Shakespeare room open only on request.*

In the middle of the square is the ornate Victorian **Chamberlain Memorial Fountain** (1881), which looks rather forlorn and is dwarfed by the modern architecture behind it. Across the square from the library is the **City Museum and Art Gallery,** a huge place that contains a magnificent collection of Victorian art, especially by the Pre-Raphaelites. All the big names are here—Ford Madox Brown, Holman Hunt, Edward Burne-Jones (who was born in Birmingham), Dante Gabriel Rossetti, and many more. One room houses the Arthurian *Holy Grail* tapestries, designed by Burne-Jones and executed by the William Morris Arts Workers' Guild. The collection reflects the enormous wealth of 19th-century Birmingham and the taste of its industrialists. Also in the museum are African tribal art, natural history collections, and imaginative displays tracing the history of the city. There is an excellent crafts shop, a museum shop, and a café. *Chamberlain Sq., tel. 0121/235–2834. Admission free. Open Mon.–Sat. 11–5, Sun. 11–5:30.*

Turn right when you leave the gallery, and on your right will be the **Town Hall,** surrounded by classical columns. It was built over two decades in the middle of the 19th century and is a copy of the Temple of Castor and Pollux in Rome. As the former home of the symphony orchestra, it heard the first performances of Mendelssohn's *Elijah* and Elgar's *Dream of Gerontius,* among others. Town Hall now hosts concerts and exhibitions. *Victoria Sq., tel. 0121/235–3942. Opening times vary; call ahead.*

Now turn left through the newly renovated Victoria Square, and walk down Colmore Row. Three blocks will bring you to **Birmingham Cathedral** (St. Philip's) on your right, which is the Anglican cathedral. The paths around the cathedral are edged with the square cobblestones that used to pave the roads of the city. The early 18th-century building is undergoing a major restoration and preservation program at the moment, so it is shrouded in scaffolding. The gilded Georgian interior is very elegant, with lovely plasterwork. Striking windows behind the altar seem to glow with a garnet light. They were designed by Burne-Jones and made by William Morris. At the end of the south aisle is a vivid modern tapestry representing God's creative energy, and in front of it stands the font made from phosphor bronze in 1982.

One of the finest small art collections in England can be found on the outskirts of Birmingham in **The Barber Institute of Fine Arts,** at the University of Birmingham. The Barber Institute was founded in 1932 by the wife of a leading Birmingham real-estate developer. It is a superb collection, including works by Canaletto, Guardi, Poussin, Murillo, Gainsborough, Turner, Whistler, Renoir, Gauguin, and Van Gogh. The original terms of the bequest forbade the purchase of 20th-century work, but they have been changed to take in the paintings of Redon, Magritte, and other artists of the early years of the century. The Barber also owns collections of miniatures, watercolors, and sculptures (notably by Roubiliac, Degas, and Rodin), making it an art lovers' paradise. *Take the Cross City Line train from New Street Station south to University Station, or Buses 61, 62, or 63 from the city center. The Barber Institute is off Edgbaston Park Rd., near the east gate of the university. Tel. 0121/472–0962. Admission free. Open Mon.–Sat. 10–5, Sun. 2–5.*

Lodging **Beech House.** Most B&Bs are outside the city center, and this is no
£ exception. Beech House—a large Edwardian house in mock-Tudor design—is on the A5127, close to Exit 6 of the M6 motorway. The bedrooms are comfortably furnished, and there are two lounges, one for nonsmokers. *21 Gravelly Hill North, Erdington, B23 6BT, tel. 0121/373–0620. 9 rooms, 4 with bath. Facilities: lounges. MC, V.*

£ **Willow Tree.** This friendly guest house is family-run and within easy reach of the city center by bus. There are TVs and tea/coffeemakers in all rooms, as well as trouser presses and hair dryers. There's a restaurant and a large garden. *759 Chester Rd., B24 OBY, tel. 0121/373–6388. 7 rooms, 5 with bath or shower. Facilities: restaurant, garden. MC, V.*

Dining **Henry's.** One of a pair of Cantonese restaurants, Henry's is located
£ in the jewelry district, making it a good bet for lunch during a shopping spree. The menu is immense, with more than 100 dishes, and as with all westernized Cantonese restaurants, vegetarians should have no difficulty finding satisfaction. *27 St. Paul's Sq., tel. 0121/200–1136. Reservations advised. AE, DC, MC, V. Closed Sun.*

£ **Lopez.** This is a little corner of Spain in the heart of Birmingham. It's a small restaurant, but all the friendlier for that. Try the paella valenciana or the king prawns or one of the French dishes that are also offered. There's live music some nights. *73 Cornwall St., tel. 0121/236–2724. Reservations advised. AE, MC, V. Closed Sun.*

Splurge **Sloans.** This unexpectedly good restaurant is located in a shopping precinct in the southeast of the city (most of the best things in Birmingham are hidden on the outskirts). It is managed by a father-and-son team. The menu is fairly large, with an interesting range of dishes—try the veal and mushrooms with a leek and truffle sauce, or ballottine of chicken, and finish with a mouth-watering lime soufflé. *27–29 Chad Sq., Hawthorne Rd., tel. 0121/455–6697. Reservations advised. AE, DC, MC, V. Closed Sat. lunch and Sun.*

Shopping A 10-minute walk north from the city center is the **Jewelery Quarter,** with more than 200 manufacturing jewelers and 50 silversmiths. The area is much as it was in Victorian times. The quarter can trace its beginnings back to 1460, when work with precious metals was first recorded here. There are still more than 100 shops that sell gold and silver handcrafted jewelry, clocks, and watches. Most of them will undertake special commissions or repairs. The city has its own Assay Office, with an anchor as its silver mark. For those interested in the history of the neighborhood and the craft of the jeweler, a **Discovery Centre** opened in 1992. *77–79 Vyse St., tel. 0121/554–3598. Admission: £2 adults, £1.50 students, senior citizens, and children; £5 family ticket. Open weekdays 10–4, Sat. 11–5.*

The Arts and Birmingham is the second city for the performing arts after London.
Nightlife But if you base yourself in Stratford-upon-Avon, you will have to make do with matinees, as the last bus and train leave around 7 and 9 in the evening, respectively.

The second company of the Royal Ballet, which was based at Sadler's Wells in London, has moved to the city to become the **Birmingham**

Royal Ballet. It is based at the **Hippodrome Theatre,** where it performs for at least six weeks a year, touring the rest of the time. The Hippodrome also hosts visiting performances of such prestigious companies as the Welsh National Opera. *Hippodrome, Hurst St., tel. 0121/622–7486.*

The **City of Birmingham Symphony Orchestra** (CBSO) performs regularly in the new **Symphony Hall,** which is also the venue for visiting recital artists. *Symphony Hall, International Convention Centre, tel. 0121/212–3333.*

The **Birmingham Repertory Theatre** was founded in 1913 in an earlier building and has maintained an international reputation ever since. The company is equally at home in modern or classical work. There is a restaurant on the ground floor. *Centenary Sq., Broad St., tel. 0121/236–4455.*

The **Alexandra Theatre,** home to the D'Oyly Carte Opera Company, is also a leading fixture for touring theater companies, welcoming them on their way to London's West End or after they complete their run there. *Station St., tel. 0121/643–1231.*

Festival The Birmingham **International Jazz Festival** stars some of the best British and international jazz talent for a week in July.

Tour 3: Cheltenham and the Cotswold Hills

Occupying the eastern and largest part of Gloucestershire, these wooded hills and valleys brim with small towns and villages, built of golden Cotswold stone. The following sequence is a selection of some of the main points of interest, arranged in a counterclockwise direction, beginning with Cheltenham.

From London The fastest train from London/Paddington (tel. 0171/262–6767)
By Train reaches Cheltenham in about 2 hours. Other trains, which change at Swindon, take slightly longer to complete the journey; most also serve Gloucester. For schedules, call Gloucester rail information (tel. 01452/529501).

By Bus **National Express** (tel. 0171/730–0202) from London/Victoria Coach Station calls at Gloucester, takes 2½ hours, and has more daily services than the train. For schedule information, call the station in Cheltenham (tel. 01242/584111).

By Car The most direct route from London (99 miles) is via M40 to Oxford, then A40 to Cheltenham.

Cheltenham

*All the Cotswold villages that follow can be visited by local bus, but you'll have to plan carefully and allow yourself plenty of time, as some of the smaller towns see only one bus a week. The Gloucestershire County Council produces free bus maps of its area. The North Cotswold Bus and Tourism Guide will help you with the places mentioned in Tours 2 and 3. To obtain a guide, visit the Cheltenham or Gloucester tourist office or call 01452/425543. An easier way to tour the Cotswold villages is with one of the local coach companies. Two major ones are **Pulham's** (Station Road Garage, Bourton-on-the-Water, tel. 01451/820369) and **Barry's Coaches** (Pool Garage, Moreton-in-Marsh, tel. 01608/650876). **Guide Friday** (Stratford-upon-Avon, tel. 01789/294466) runs tours in open-top buses, mid-April–early September, on an irregular schedule. Cheltenham tourist office: 77 Promenade, tel. 01242/226554.*

If you visit the historic health resort of **Cheltenham** in the spring or summer, you may find it difficult to decide which is more attractive, its profusion of flower gardens or its architecture. The flowers cover even traffic circles, while the town's elegantly laid-out avenues, crescents, and terraces, with their characteristic row houses, balconies, and iron railings, make Cheltenham an outstanding example of the Regency style of architecture and town planning.

Although it can't compare either in fame, history, or scale with Bath, **Cheltenham Spa** has been a popular health resort since the visit of George III and his consort Queen Charlotte in 1788. During the Regency period Cheltenham's status was assured by the visits of the duke of Wellington, the national hero who defeated Napoleon at Waterloo in 1815. A stroll around the town will reveal many of its most interesting Regency features. The **Rotunda** building on Montpellier (street)—now a bank—contains the spa's original "pump room," that is, the room in which the mineral waters were on draft; such rooms, as in Bath, often evolved into public drawing rooms of polite society. Parallel to Montpellier Street is Montpellier Walk, where more than 30 statues, like the caryatids in Athens, adorn the storefronts. Wander past **Imperial Square,** with its intricate ironwork balconies; past the ornate Neptune's Fountain and along the elegant Promenade; and continue through Lansdown toward Pittville Park.

A 20-minute walk from the town center brings you to the **Pittville Pump Room,** built in the late 1820s, where the mineral waters can still be tasted. The pump room, which is surrounded by parkland, now houses the **Gallery of Fashion,** which tells the history of the town through displays drawn from an extensive costume collection. *Albert Rd., Pittville Park, tel. 01242/523852. Admission: £1.50 adults, 50p senior citizens and children, £2.25 family ticket. Open May–Sept., Wed.–Mon. 11–4:30; Oct.–Apr., Wed.–Mon. 11–4.*

Lodging **Lypiatt House.** This splendid Victorian house is an award-winning
££ B&B, and only a short walk from central Cheltenham. Comfortable
★ rooms cost just under £70 for a double, but are a nice size and have modern bathrooms. There's a small dining room and attentive service from the husband-and-wife team who took over the Lypiatt in 1992. Young children are not accommodated. *Lypiatt Rd., GL50 2QW, tel. 01242/224994, fax 01242/224996. 10 rooms with bath or shower. MC, V.*

£ **Regency House.** This attractive guest house is quite exceptional—it's beautifully furnished with antiques and period-style wallpaper. The front rooms have views of trees in the square, and the back ones look out at a garden. All rooms have TVs, tea/coffeemakers, and hair dryers. *50 Clarence Sq., Pittville, GL50 4JR, tel. 01242/582718, fax 01242/262697. 7 rooms with bath. AE, MC, V.*

Dining **Below Stairs, The Seafood Restaurant.** This seafood dive, located on
£ the Promenade in the heart of Cheltenham, really is in the cellar. It's an ideal place for a sightseeing break during lunch. The seafood is caught fresh daily and cooked to your liking. *103 Promenade, tel. 01242/234599. AE, DC, MC, V. Closed Sun.*

¢ **Old Swan.** This is a comfortable old pub with plenty of elbowroom. The fairly standard bar food is homemade, plentiful, and attractively served. Tea, coffee, and scones are available all day, and there's a relaxing conservatory in which to sit. *37 High St., tel. 01242/584929. No credit cards.*

Festivals Cheltenham's annual **International Festival of Music** (July) highlights new compositions, often conducted by the composer, together with classical repertory pieces. The town's **Festival of Literature** (October) brings together world-renowned authors, actors, and critics. Tickets for both festivals are reasonably priced. The range for the music festival is £7–£19; for the literature festival it's up to £10, with discounts for early booking. *For details of both events con-*

tact Festival Office, Town Hall, Imperial Sq., Cheltenham GL50 1QA, tel. 01242/521621.

Cirencester

Cirencester tourist office: Corn Hall, Market Place, tel. 01285/ 654180.

Cirencester (usually pronounced "Sirensester") has been the hub of the Cotswolds since Roman times, when it was called Corinium and stood at the intersection of two strategic Roman roads, the Fosse Way and the Ermin Way. Cirencester is a lovely old market town, full of mellow stone buildings—take a stroll down Dollar Street to see the bow-fronted stores—and has a magnificent parish church, St. John the Baptist. The whole town is built on ancient Roman remains, and the **Corinium Museum** offers an excellent collection of Roman artifacts, as well as full-scale reconstructions of local Roman interiors—kitchen, dining room, and workshop. *Park St., tel. 01285/655611. Admission: £1.50 adults, £1.25 senior citizens and students, 75p children, £3.75 family ticket. Open Mon.–Sat. 10–5, Sun. 2–5. Closed Mon. Nov.–Mar.; closed last 2 weeks of Dec.*

★

Lodding **King's Head.** Here's a good example of a very old coaching inn that
Splurge has been modernized without losing its period charm. Under new ownership since 1992, the King's Head is run to solid standards, providing comfortable bedrooms with sensible bathrooms en suite. You do, however, pay for the modern amenities, at £80 per night for a double, though discounts are available. The restaurant specializes in moderately priced English cooking and offers some tasty homemade soups. *Market Pl., GL7 2NR, tel. 01285/653322, fax 01285/655103. 60 rooms, all with bath. Facilities: restaurant. AE, DC, MC, V.*

Dining **Slug and Lettuce.** This pub has pine furniture, flagstones, cheery log
¢ fires, interesting antique knickknacks, and a menu that is a step up from normal bar fodder. Try the homemade salmon fish cakes or chicken liver pâté with Cointreau. In summer you can eat at tables in the secluded courtyard. *West Market Pl., tel. 01285/653206. MC, V.*

Chedworth

★ **Chedworth Roman Villa,** surrounded by woodland and overlooking Cotswold Hills, is the best-preserved Roman villa in England. Thirty-two rooms, including two complete bath suites, have been identified. The visitor center and museum give a picture of Roman life in Britain. *Yanworth, tel. 01242/890256. Admission: £2.70 adults, £1.35 children, £7.40 family ticket. Open Mar.–Oct., Tues.–Sun. and national holiday Mon. 10–5:30; Nov., Wed.–Sun. 11–4. Closed Dec.–Feb. and Good Friday.*

Bourton-on-the-Water

Bourton-on-the-Water, on the eastern edge of the Cotswold Hills, is deservedly famous as a classic Cotswold village. The little River Windrush, crossed by low stone bridges, runs through Bourton. This village makes a good touring base because of its facilities as well as its central location in Gloucestershire. Be warned, however, that in summer Bourton, like Stratford and Broadway, is overcrowded with tourists, and at that time you will find a quieter, more typical Cotswold atmosphere in nearby villages with such evocative names as Upper Slaughter, Lower Slaughter, Upper Swell, and Lower Swell, all of which lie to the north.

A stroll through Bourton takes you past Cotswold cottages, many now converted to little stores and coffee shops. Follow the rushing stream and its ducks to the end of the village and the old mill, now the **Cotswold Motor Museum and Exhibition of Village Life.** In addition to 30 vintage motor vehicles and the largest collection of old advertising signs in Britain, this museum offers an Edwardian store, a blacksmith's forge, a wheelwright's shop, a country kitchen, and a huge collection of children's toys. *The Old Mill, tel. 01451/821255. Admission: £1.40 adults, 70p children, £3.95 family ticket. Open Feb.–Nov., daily 10–6.*

Behind the Old New Inn Pub is a **Model Village,** an outdoor working replica of Bourton village, built in 1937 to a scale of one-ninth. Choir music can be heard from the church and there is even a model of the model, scaled down again to one-ninth. *The Old New Inn, tel. 01451/ 820467. Admission: £1.30 adults, £1.10 senior citizens, 90p children. Open Apr.–Sept., daily 11–5:30; Oct.–Mar., weekends only 11–5. Closed Dec. 25.*

Lodging **Coombe House.** This centrally located small guest house with an at-
£ tractive garden is run by Graham and Diana Ellis, who will help you plan your route and steer you to the best local food. The bedrooms all have TV and tea/coffeemakers. *Rissington Rd., GL54 2DT, tel. 01451/821966, fax 01451/810477. 7 rooms with bath. AE, MC, V.*

Dining **Rose Tree Restaurant.** English and French food is served with Old-
£ World style here, overlooking the River Windrush and the village. The chef has an especially light touch with fish and such specialties as beef Wellington in brandy sauce. *Riverside, tel. 01451/820635. Reservations advised. AE, MC, V. Closed Sun. evening and Mon.*

Shopping The **Cotswold Perfumery** (Victoria St., tel. 01451/820698) has a wide range of perfumes that are manufactured here. While deciding what to buy, visit the **Exhibition of Perfumery** and the **Perfumed Garden** (admission to exhibition: £1.30 adults, £1 senior citizens and children). Perfume bottles, jewelry, and porcelain dolls are also on sale.

Stow-on-the-Wold

Stow-on-the-Wold, 3 miles north of Bourton, is another exemplary Cotswold town, with imposing golden stone houses built around a wide square. Many of these have now been discreetly converted into quality antiques stores. Look for the Kings Arms Old Posting House, its wide entrance still seeming to wait for the stagecoaches that once stopped here on their way to Cheltenham. At 800-feet elevation, Stow is the highest, as well as the largest, town in the Cotswolds. It's also an antiques-hunter's paradise, and, like Bourton, a convenient touring base.

Lodging **The Limes.** This large, friendly B&B, surrounded by gardens, is
¢ conveniently located close to the center of town. All rooms have a TV and tea/coffeemakers, and one has an early Victorian four-poster. *Tewkesbury Rd., GL54 1EN, tel. 01451/830034. 4 rooms, 3 with shower. No credit cards.*

Dining **Queen's Head.** This is an excellent spot for a pub lunch. In the winter
¢ the inside, with a large fireplace, flagstone floors, and wood beams, is cozy. During the summer you can sip a drink in the courtyard out back or in the front on a bench, under a climbing rose bush. *The Square, tel. 01451/830563. No credit cards.*

Moreton-in-Marsh

Moreton-in-Marsh, 5 miles north of Stow, has fine views across the hills. In Moreton the houses have been built not around a central square but along a street wide enough to accommodate a market every Tuesday.

Chipping Campden

Chipping Campden tourist office: Woolstaplers Hall Museum, High St., tel. 01386/840289. (Open Apr.–Oct., daily; Nov.–Dec., weekends only.)

Northwest of Moreton-in-Marsh lies **Chipping Campden,** a lovely Cotswold market town, its broad High Street lined with houses in an attractive variety of styles, many the product of medieval wealth from the wool trade. In the center is the **Market Hall,** a gabled, Jacobean structure built by Sir Baptiste Hycks in 1627 "for the sale of local produce." *High St. Admission free. Always open.*

One of the oldest buildings in Chipping Campden, built in the 14th century, is **Woolstaplers Hall.** As well as the local tourist information center, it houses the local museum, a 1920s movie theater, and collections of medical equipment. *High St., tel. 01386/840289. Admission: £1 adults, 50p children. Open Apr.–Oct., daily 10–5; Nov.–Dec., weekends 10–5.*

Lodging **King's Arms.** This characterful inn is slap in the middle of Chipping
£ Campden, on the central square. The homey place, with comfortable old furniture, a huge fireplace in the Saddle Room (combined bar and restaurant), and a garden, also provides lots of friendly service. It is a reasonable place to stay, and a good place to eat. Set menus range from £5 for lunch to £12 for dinner. *The Square, GL55 6AW, tel. 01386/840256. 14 rooms, with bath. MC, V.*

Dining **Greenstocks.** This cottage brasserie and tea shop, set in the middle
¢ of town, is just the place for a morning coffee or a delicious lunch. If you need an afternoon break from sightseeing, try the tea with cinnamon toast or homemade scones and Jersey cream. *Cotswold House Hotel, The Square, tel. 01386/840330. MC, V.*

Broadway

On the way to **Broadway** you can glimpse the distant Malvern Hills to the west in Worcestershire. Named for its wide main street, Broadway offers many shops and one of the most renowned hotels in the Cotswolds, the **Lygon Arms.** This hotel's striking facade dates from 1620, but the building has been restored and has several modern extensions. Experienced travelers tend to avoid Broadway in the summer, when it is clogged with tourists' cars and buses.

Dining **Buckland Manor.** As an alternative to the razzmatazz of Broadway,
Splurge try this exceptional hotel 2 miles southwest, just off B4632. Parts of
★ the building date back to Jacobean times and there are gracious old pictures and fine antiques everywhere. The garden is lovely, and the place is so peaceful you can hear a swan's feather drop. Although the hotel is definitely out of the budget price range, the restaurant, which offers a table d'hôte for less than £25, is well worth the splurge. *Near Broadway, WR12 7LY, tel. 01386/852626. AE, MC, V.*

Snowshill Manor

South of Broadway is **Snowshill Manor,** whose 17th-century facade hides the house's Tudor origins. It contains a delightful clutter of musical instruments, clocks, toys, bicycles, weavers' and spinners' tools, and much more. Children love it. *Snowshill, tel. 01386/852410. Admission: £5 adults, £2.50 children, £13.75 family ticket; grounds only £2 adults, £1 children!!any age cut-off?!!. Open Apr. and Oct., Wed.–Mon. 1–5; May–Sept., Wed.–Mon. 1–6; grounds open from noon; closed Good Friday. (National holidays and summer Sun. overcrowded.)*

Sudeley Castle

★ Seven miles southwest of Broadway lies **Sudeley Castle,** the home and burial place of Catherine Parr (1512–48), Henry VIII's sixth and last wife, who outlived him by one year. The castle was once at the center of great affairs of state; today its peaceful air belies its turbulent history. The magnificent grounds are the setting for outdoor theater, concerts, and other events in the summer. *Winchcombe, tel. 01242/602308. Admission: £4.95 adults, £4.55 senior citizens, £2.75 children, £13 family ticket. Grounds open Apr.–Oct., daily 10:30–5:30; castle open 11–5.*

Tour 4: Gloucester and the Forest of Dean

West of the Cotswolds there are two main sections to Gloucestershire—the rather urbanized axis connecting Gloucester, the county seat, with the resort town of Cheltenham, and westward, the low-lying Forest of Dean, bordered by the Wye and Severn rivers, which is only 8 miles away. Regular local bus and train service runs between Gloucester and Cheltenham. For more transportation information, *see* Tour 2, *above.*

Gloucester

Gloucester tourist office: St. Michael's Tower, The Cross, tel. 01452/421188.

Although much of **Gloucester's** ancient heritage has been lost to nondescript modern stores and offices, the **Gloucester Folk Museum** will give you a very good idea of its past. Housed in a row of fine Tudor and Jacobean half-timbered houses, the museum presents displays of the social history, folklore, crafts, and industries of the county. *99–103 Westgate St., tel. 01452/526467. Admission free. Open Oct.–June, Mon.–Sat. 10–5; July–Sept., Mon.–Sat. 10–5, Sun. 10–4.*

★ Across Westgate Street is **Gloucester Cathedral,** originally a Norman abbey church, consecrated in 1100. The exterior soars in elegant lines, while the interior of this magnificent building has largely been spared the sterilizing attentions of modern architects who like to strip cathedrals down to their original bare bones. The place is a mishmash of periods, and the clutter of centuries mirrors perfectly the slow growth of ecclesiastical taste, be it good or bad. The interior is an almost complete Norman carcass, with the massive pillars of the nave left untouched since their completion. The fan-vaulted roof of the cloisters is the finest in Europe. The cloisters enclose a peaceful garden, where one can easily imagine medieval monks thoughtfully pacing around. Look, too, for the tomb of Edward II—to your left as you stand in the choir facing the high altar—who was imprisoned and murdered in Berkeley Castle in 1327. *Westgate St., tel. 01452/528095. Donation of at least £3 per adult requested. Open daily 8–6, except during services and special events.*

A short walk from the Cathedral, at the end of Westgate Street, along the canal, are the historic **Gloucester Docks.** The docks still function, though now on a much reduced scale. The vast Victorian warehouses are being restored, and new buildings of shops and cafés are being added to bring the area back to life. Tours, starting at the **Mariner's Chapel** by the Southgate Street entrance to the docks, are conducted every Friday in July and August at 2:30.

One of the restored warehouses holds **The National Waterways Museum.** Outside are examples of canal houseboats and barges; inside is the national canal and waterway exhibition. *Llanthony Warehouse,*

Gloucester Docks, tel. 01452/318054. Admission: £4.25 adults, £3.25 senior citizens and children, £9.95 family ticket. Open Apr.–Sept., daily 10–6; Oct.–Mar., daily 10–5.

Lodging
¢ **New Inn.** Right in the center of town, the "New" Inn is quite old. In the 15th century, it was a hostel for pilgrims visiting Edward II's shrine in the cathedral. In 1553, Lady Jane Grey was proclaimed queen here; seven months later she lost her head. Although the inn has been modernized, with TV and tea/coffeemakers in each room, there are still plenty of period touches about, including a cobbled courtyard. There are also two suites with four-posters. *Northgate St., GL1 1SF, tel. 01452/522177, fax 01452/301054. 9 rooms with bath or shower. Facilities: restaurant, bar. AE, MC, V.*

Dining
£ **College Green.** With a keen notion of the right meal in the right place, this upstairs restaurant, with views out over the cathedral, serves classic English cooking—beef casserole, duck with apricot sauce—accompanied by a respectable wine list. *7 College St., tel. 01452/520739. AE, MC, V. Closed Sun.*

¢ **Dick Whittington House.** The name of this pub commemorates one of Gloucester's most famous sons, who, during the Middle Ages, was Lord Mayor of London for three terms. Near the cathedral, this is a handy spot to break for lunch, a snack, or a local beer straight from the barrel. In the summer there are garden barbecues. *100 Westgate St., tel. 01452/502039. No credit cards.*

Shopping
The **Antique Centre** (tel. 01452/529716) can be found in one of the recently restored Victorian warehouses at Gloucester Docks. Next to the Cathedral Gate is the house Beatrix Potter chose for the tailor in her story *The Tailor of Gloucester*. It is now the **Beatrix Potter Gift Shop** (College Court, tel. 01452/422856). Gifts for children and other Potter fans are on sale, and there are also exhibits of the author's life and work.

Forest of Dean

By its very nature, the Royal Forest of Dean isn't easy to explore by public transport, but it is possible to get around. Many bus routes run only one day a week, so plan ahead. For information call Gloucestershire County Council Public Transport Information (tel. 01452/527516). The main Forest of Dean tourist office in Coleford (27 Market Pl., tel. 01594/836307), as well as smaller branches in Newent (tel. 01531/822145), Cinderford (tel. 01594/823184), and Lydney (tel. 01594/844894), have information and leaflets on walking, fishing, places to eat, scenic drives, activities, events, and accommodation in the forest and surrounding areas.

★ The mysterious, prehistoric **Forest of Dean** covers much of western Gloucestershire in the valley between the Rivers Severn and Wye. Although the first-growth forest has long since been cut down and replanted, the landscape here remains one of strange beauty, hiding in its folds and under its hills deposits of iron, silver, and coal that have been mined for thousands of years.

Of the original royal forest established in 1016 by King Canute, 27,000 acres are preserved by the Forestry Commission. It's still an important source of timber, but parking lots and picnic grounds have been created and eight nature trails marked. One trail links sculptures, commissioned by the Forestry Commission, around **Speech House,** the medieval verderer's court in the forest's center. The verderer was the royal officer responsible for the enforcement of the forest laws. It was usually a capital offense to kill game or cut wood without royal authorization.

The Dean Heritage Centre at Soudley, based in a restored mill building in a wooded valley, tells the history of the forest, and displays reconstructions of a mine and a miner's cottage, a water wheel, and a "beam engine" (a primitive steam engine used to pump water from flooded coal mines). Outside the center is a tiny farm with pigs and poultry, as well as natural history exhibitions. Watch craftspeople at work in the outbuildings. *Tel. 01594/822170. Admission: £2.75 adults, £2.50 senior citizens and students, £1.60 children. Open Feb.–Mar., daily 10–5; Apr.–Oct., daily 10–6; Nov.–Jan., weekends only 10–4.*

The area around **Coleford** is a maze of weathered and moss-covered rocks, huge ferns, and ancient yew trees—a shady haven on a summer's day. Underground iron mines, worked continuously from Roman times to 1945, can be visited at **Clearwell Caves.** *Tel. 01594/ 832535. Admission: £3 adults, £2.50 senior citizens, £2 children. Open Mar.–Oct. daily 10–5. Dec., Christmas workshops, admission £3, open weekdays 2–6, weekends 10–5.*

Tour 5: Bath and Beyond

One of the delights of basing yourself in Bath is living amid the magnificent 18th-century architecture, a lasting reminder of the elegant world described by Jane Austen. Bath suffered slightly from World War II bombing and even more from unattractive postwar urban renewal, but the damage was halted before it could ruin the center of the city. Bath is not a museum. It is a lively and interesting place, offering dining and entertainment, excellent art galleries, and a thriving cultural center, with theater and music throughout the year. It is also a city of civic pride, and the streets are filled with lavish flower displays in summer.

From London You can reach Bath by **InterCity** trains in about 1 hour, 25 minutes
By Train from London/Paddington (tel. 0171/262–6767; in Bath, tel. 0117/ 929–4255). At least one train makes the 107-mile journey every hour.

By Bus The **National Express** Bath service from London/Victoria Coach Station (tel. 0171/730–0202; in Bath tel. 01225/464446) runs nine times daily; the trip takes 3 hours.

Bath

*Bath tourist office: 27 The Colonnades, 11–13 Bath St., tel. 01225/ 462831. **Guide Friday** (tel. 01225/464446) operates tours of Bath year-round in open-top double-decker buses. Cost: £6 adults, £4.50 senior citizens, £2 children.*

★ The **Pump Room,** described by Jane Austen, is Bath's primary watering hole. People still gather here to drink the mineral waters— which taste revolting—and to socialize. The baths as such are no longer in use, and this magnificent Georgian building now houses a tourist information desk, a souvenir store, and a restaurant. Almost the entire Roman bath complex has been excavated, and you can see the remains of swimming pools, saunas, and Turkish baths, as well as part of the temple of Minerva itself, with the bronze head of the

The Romans first put **Bath** on the map when they built a temple here in honor of the goddess Minerva. They also built a sophisticated network of baths that make full use of the curative springs that gush from the earth at a constant temperature of 116°F. Much later, 18th-century society took the city to its heart, and Bath became the most fashionable spa in Britain. The architect John Wood (1704–54) created a harmonious city from the same local stone used by the Romans, with beautifully executed terraces, crescents, and Palladian villas.

Numbers in the margin correspond to points of interest on the Bath map.

❶ The **Pump Room,** described by Jane Austen, is Bath's primary watering hole. People still gather here to drink the mineral waters— which taste revolting—and to socialize. The baths as such are no longer in use, and this magnificent Georgian building now houses a tourist information desk, a souvenir store, and a restaurant. Almost the entire Roman bath complex has been excavated, and you can see the remains of swimming pools, saunas, and Turkish baths, as well as part of the temple of Minerva itself, with the bronze head of the

The Forest of Dean and Bath Environs

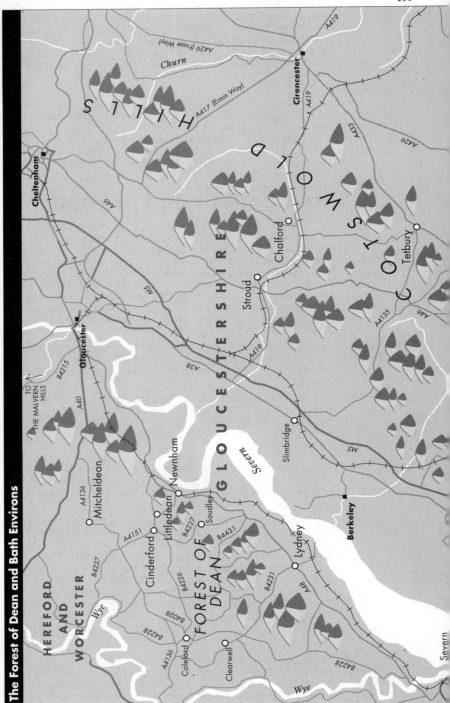

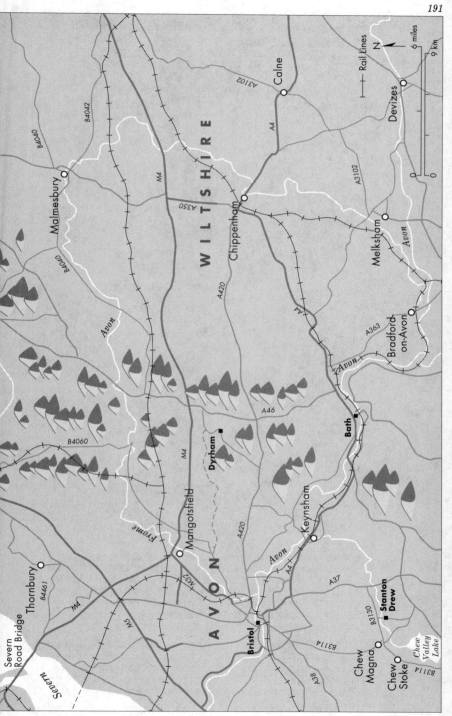

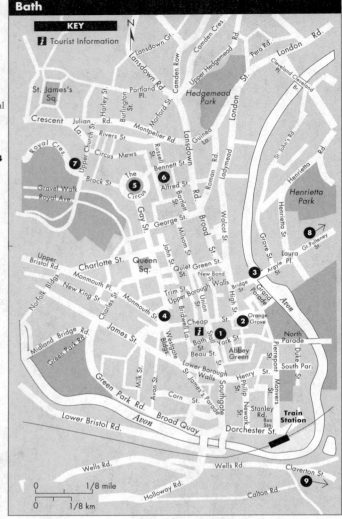

goddess and votive offerings left by worshipers nearly 2,000 years ago. *Abbey Churchyard, tel. 01225/477000, ext. 2783. Admission: £5 adults, £3 children, £13 family ticket; combined ticket for Roman Baths and Costume Museum (see below), £6.60 adults, £3.50 children, £16 family ticket. Pump Room only, free; open Apr.–Sept. daily 9–6 (and Aug. 8–10 PM), Oct.–Mar., Mon.–Sat. 9:30–5, Sun. 10:30–5.*

2 Next to the Pump Room is the **Abbey,** dating from the 15th century. It was built in the Perpendicular (English Gothic) style on the site of a Saxon abbey, and has superb, fan-vaulted ceilings in the nave. *Abbey Churchyard. Voluntary offering requested. Open most times, though visitors are asked not to enter during services.*

Off Abbey Churchyard, where a rich variety of buskers (strolling musicians) perform, are tiny alleys leading to little squares of stores, galleries, and eating places. Walk up Stall and Union streets—the main shopping center—toward Milsom Street, and you'll find nu-

merous alleyways with fascinating small stores. Work your way east
3 toward Bridge Street and the 18th-century **Pulteney Bridge,** which
spans the river Avon, and which is lined with little shops. Head back
4 along Upper Borough Walls to find the **Theatre Royal,** one of the finest Georgian theaters remaining in England. Next door is the former home of the dandy, Richard "Beau" Nash—the dictator of
fashion for mid-18th-century society in Bath—and his mistress Juli-
ana Popjoy. This is now a restaurant called Popjoy's (*see* Dining, below).

Turning north will take you to the Georgian houses of Queen
5 Square, Gay Street, and **The Circus,** its three perfectly proportioned Georgian terraces outlining the round garden in the center.
"Circus," as in London's Piccadilly Circus, means a circular inter-
change of streets, an arrangement popular with Georgian town
6 planners. Turn east from The Circus to the **Assembly Rooms,** which
figure in Jane Austen's novel *Persuasion.* This classical-style building, once a social center like the Pump Room, now houses the **Museum of Costume,** which has been completely redesigned. It displays
costumes from Beau Nash's day up to the present, in lavish settings.
*Bennett St., tel. 01225/477000, ext. 2785. Admission: £3.20 adults,
£2 children, £9 family ticket. Open Mon.–Sat. 10–5, Sun. 11–5.*

Turn west from The Circus and you'll arrive at Royal Crescent, the
crowning glory of architecture in Bath, and much used as a location
for period films. At the center is Bath's most elegant hotel, the Roy-
7 al Crescent. On the corner, **Number 1, Royal Crescent** has been
turned into a museum and furnished as it might have been when
Beau Nash and his circle strutted around the crescents of Bath. The
museum crystallizes a view of the English class system in its 18th-
century setting: "Upstairs" is all gentility and elegance; "downstairs" is the servants' world, with a fascinating kitchen museum.
*Tel. 01225/428126. Admission: £3 adults, £2.50 senior citizens, stu-
dents, and children. Open Mar.–Oct., Tues.–Sun. 10:30–5; Nov.–
mid-Dec., Tues.–Sun. 10:30–4.*

Across the Avon by the Pulteney Bridge, in an elegant 18th-century
8 building, is the **Holburne Museum and Crafts Study Centre,** which
houses a small but superb collection of 17th- and 18th-century fine
art and decorative crafts. There is also work by 20th-century
craftspeople in the study center. *Great Pulteney St., tel. 01225/
466669. Admission: £3.50 adults, £3 senior citizens, £1.50 children,
£7 family ticket. Open Easter–mid-Dec., Mon.–Sat. 11–5, Sun.
2:30–5:30; mid-Feb.–Easter, Tues.–Sat. 11–5, Sun. 2:30–6. Closed
mid-Dec.–mid-Feb.*

The local Bus 25 goes directly (May–Sept., Tues.–Sun.) from the
9 Bath bus station to **Claverton Manor,** situated high above the city
and just 2½ miles southeast on the Warminster road. The Greek re-
vival mansion houses the first museum of Americana to be established outside the United States, quietly sponsored by an American
millionaire, Dallas Pratt. A series of furnished rooms portrays
American domestic life from the 17th to the 19th centuries. The fine
parkland includes a replica of George Washington's garden and an
arboretum. You can even have tea with American cookies.
*Claverton Down, tel. 01225/460503. Admission: £5 adults, £4.50
senior citizens and students, £2.50 children. Open Easter–Oct.,
Tues.–Sun. 2–5, national holidays and preceding Sun. 11–5.*

Lodging **Paradise House.** This worthwhile but expensive (from £48 to £65 per
££ night) B&B is about a 10-minute, uphill walk from the town center.
From the upstairs windows of this 1720 house, you will be rewarded
with great views of Bath. Cheerfully decorated in cool green and
white, it has been restored and has open fires in the winter and a
garden in the summer. You can request one of the less expensive
rooms (which share a bath). Although there is no restaurant, a full

breakfast is offered, and all rooms are equipped with TVs. *88 Holloway, BA2 4PX, tel. 01225/317723, fax 01225/482005. 9 rooms, 7 with private bath or shower. AE, MC, V.*

££ **Villa Magdala Hotel.** This solid mid-Victorian house—named after a 1868 battle in Ethiopia—offers attractive views of Henrietta Park, across the road. Rooms cost from £58 up a night, and some have four-poster beds; all have color TVs and phones. *Henrietta Rd., BA2 6LX, tel. 01225/466329, fax 01225/483207. 17 rooms with bath or shower. AE, MC, V. Closed Jan.*

£ **Tasburgh Hotel.** A mile from the city center, this refurbished Victorian mansion with two acres of gardens boasts views over the valley and a canal at the bottom of the grounds. Attentive service is provided by the owner/managers, Mr. and Mrs. Archer. A night's stay costs about £55 for two. *Warminster Rd., tel. 01225/425096, fax 01225/463842. 10 rooms with bath. AE, DC, MC, V.*

Dining **Popjoy's Restaurant.** The home of the mistress of Beau Nash pro-
££ vides an elegant setting for a fine, after-theater dinner. Meals run a
★ bit more than £25 per person, but for a special occasion, this is a special place. On the other hand, you could economize by supping at Nashville's Brasserie downstairs, where meals from the same kitchen cost about £10 a head less, though here the monochrome decor is no substitute for the sumptuous Georgian ambience of the restaurant. *Sawclose, tel. 01225/460494. Reservations advised, required after theater and weekends. AE, MC, V. Closed Sun. and Mon.*

£ **Number Five.** Just over the Pulteney Bridge from the center of town, this airy bistro, with its plants, framed posters, and cane-backed chairs, is an ideal spot for a light lunch or supper. The regularly changing menu includes tasty homemade soups, and such dishes as seafood terrine. You can bring your own bottles of wine to the restaurant on Monday and Tuesday. *5 Argyle St., tel. 01225/444499. DC, MC, V. Closed Mon. lunch and Sun.*

£ **Rascals.** This is a good spot, close to the Abbey, for a meal on a sight-seeing day. In a network of small and snug cellar rooms, you can choose from either the set menu or the daily specials. As the dishes change regularly, it's difficult to recommend specialties, but all are attractively presented, and the desserts are rich and delicious. There's a very good wine list. *8 Pierrepont Pl., tel. 01225/330201. Reservations advised. MC, V. Closed Sun. lunch.*

Shopping The **Bath Antiques Market** is a wonderful place for the collector to browse. Ninety dealers have stalls here, and there is a restaurant, too. *Guinea Lane. Open Wed. only, 6:30 AM–2:30 PM.*

A crafts shop well worth visiting is **Beaux Arts Ceramics** (York St., tel. 01225/464850), which carries the work of prominent potters and holds six solo exhibitions a year.

The Arts The **Theatre Royal** in Bath, opened in 1805 and restored in 1982, is now one of the finest Georgian theaters in England. Its year-round program often includes pre- or post-London tours. You have to reserve the best seats well in advance, but you can line up for same-day standby seats or standing room. Check the location of your seats at the box office—the theater dates from the days when the public went to be seen, rather than to see the performance, and sightlines can be poor. *Box Office, Sawclose, Bath BA1 1ET, tel. 01225/448844.*

Festival The **Bath International Festival** is 47 years old in 1996 (2 weeks in May/June). Concerts, dance, and exhibitions will be held in and around Bath. Some take place in the Assembly Rooms and the Abbey, and opening night festivities are held in Royal Victoria Park, near the Royal Crescent. *Bath Festival Office, Linley House, 1 Pierrepont Pl., Bath BA1 1JY, tel. 01225/462231.*

Dyrham

There are no public transport links to Dyrham except for a Ryan's Coach 729 from the Bath bus station on Friday and Saturday, which makes the trip in about 30 minutes.

Eight miles north of Bath in **Dyrham** lies **Dyrham Park,** a late-17th-century country house with paneled interiors and a deer park, which is the setting for occasional open-air concerts in the summer. *Dyrham, tel. 0117/937–2501. Admission: £4.80 adults, £2.40 children; park only: £1.60 adults, 80p children. House and garden open Apr.–Oct., Sat.–Wed. noon–5:30; park open daily noon–5:30 or dusk if earlier. Closed Dec. 25.*

Bristol

Bristol has two main rail stations, Parkway and Temple Meads, both on the InterCity network of British Rail, with hourly trains from London/Paddington station. Parkway is on the outskirts of town (though with frequent bus connections), so you should opt for trains to Temple Meads, from which it is a 5-minute bus ride to the center. The trip time to Bristol/Temple Meads is 1 hour, 40 minutes. Call Bristol rail information (tel. 0117/929–4255) for schedules. You can reach Bristol direct from London/Victoria Coach Station by National Express (tel. 0171/730–0202); the bus trip takes 2 hours, 20 minutes. Call for National Express bus information in Bristol (tel. 0117/954–1022). Bristol is also easily reached by a good local bus and train service from Bath, 13 miles away. Bristol tourist office: St. Nicholas Church, St. Nicholas St., tel. 0117/926–0767.

Bristol, on the River Avon, has been a major city since medieval times. In the 17th and 18th centuries, it was an important port for the North American trade, but now that the city's industries no longer rely on the docks, the historic harbor has been largely given over to pleasure craft. The quayside offers an arts center, movie theaters, museums, stores, pubs, and restaurants; carnivals, speedboat races, and regattas are held regularly.

On view in the harbor is the **SS *Great Britain,*** the first iron ship to cross the Atlantic. Built by the great English engineer Isambard Kingdom Brunel in 1843, it remained in service until the end of the century, first on the North American route and then on the Australian. *Great Western Dock, off Cumberland Rd., tel. 0117/926–0680. Admission: £3.40 adults, £2.30 senior citizens and children (under 5 free). Open Apr.–Sept., daily 10–6; Oct.–Mar., daily 10–5. Closed Dec. 24–25.*

Bristol is also the home of the **Church of St. Mary Redcliffe,** called "the fairest in England" by Queen Elizabeth I. It features rib-vaulting and dates from the 1300s, when it was built by Bristol merchants who wanted a place in which to pray for the safe (and profitable) voyages of their ships. *Redcliffe Way, a five-minute walk from Temple Meads train station toward the docks.*

Those who dissented from the Church of England also found a home in Bristol; John Wesley built the first Methodist church in England here in 1739, the **New Room.** Its austerity contrasts sharply with the ornate Anglican churches. *Broadmead. Admission: £2 adults, £1 children. Open Mon.–Sat. 10–1, 2–4; closed Wed. in winter.*

If you cross the Avon Gorge via Clifton Suspension Bridge, opened in 1864 (also built by Brunel), you will reach the **Bristol Zoo,** where more than 1,000 species of animals live in 12 acres of landscaped gardens. *Clifton, tel. 0117/973–8951. Admission: £5.50 adults, £4 senior citizens, £2.50 children (under 3 free). Open Apr.–Sept., daily 10–6; Oct.–Mar., daily 9–5. Closed Dec. 25.*

Lodging **Clifton Hotel.** The Clifton is in a pleasant neighborhood opposite the
££ church on St. Paul's Road, beyond the university but still within
easy reach of the town center. The hotel also features **Racks,** a restaurant and wine bar. Compact bedrooms include modern amenities, along with tea/coffeemakers and TVs. Prices range from £45 to
£64 for a double room, including a full, filling breakfast. *St. Paul's
Rd., BS8 1LX, tel. 0117/973–6882, fax 0117/974–1082. 60 rooms, 48
with private bath or shower. Facilities: restaurant. AE, DC, MC, V.*

¢ **Oakdene Hotel.** This Georgian-style B&B, situated on a tree-lined
street, has its own garden and is central to the major sights of Bristol. The comfortable bedrooms have TV and tea/coffeemaker. Evening meals are available on request. *45 Oakfield Rd., Clifton, BS8
2BA, tel. 0117/973–5900. 14 rooms, 7 with bath. No credit cards.*

Dining **Bell's Diner.** Though it's a Bristol institution, this bistro is rather
£ hidden—drive or take a bus up the A38 (Stokes Croft) north, then
turn right onto Picton Street, which will lead you to York Road—a
10-minute walk from the bus station. Bell's is in a converted corner
shop, with Bristol prints on its pale gray walls, polished wooden
floors, and open fires. The inventive menu changes regularly, with
light dishes and toothsome desserts. Smoking is not permitted. *1
York Rd., Montpelier, tel. 0117/924–0357. Reservations advised.
MC, V. Closed Tues.–Sat. lunch, Sun. dinner (and Sun. lunch
May–Sept.), Mon., and Aug. 30–Sept. 8.*

£ **Bouboulina's.** It is not often one finds in England a highly recommended Greek restaurant, but here's one, as the friendly, busy atmosphere and repeat clientele attest. The menu is standard Greek
and Cypriot, but the difference is that many of the dishes are charcoal-grilled. Four set-price menus are offered, including one vegetarian. It is located in the Clifton village quarter of town, near the
Suspension Bridge, and outdoor tables are available for summer
dining. *9 Portland St., Clifton, tel. 0117/973–1192. AE, DC, MC, V.
Closed Sat., Sun., and Mon. lunch.*

The Arts The local tourist office produces an ***Entertainment Bulletin,*** which
covers what's on in the city, particularly in Bristol's active theater
scene, or you can buy the local listings magazine for Bristol and
Bath, *Venue.* The **Bristol Old Vic,** an offshoot of London's classic
theater and one of the country's best repertories, has two auditoriums, and the main one is in the beautiful old **Theatre Royal** (King St.,
tel. 0117/987–7877). In the same building, the **New Vic** concentrates
on new and experimental productions. The **Hippodrome** (St.
Augustine's Parade, tel. 0117/929–9444) is a large old-fashioned
touring house, with musicals, dance, and opera performances. Generally, ticket prices are half those in London.

Stanton Drew and Chew Valley Lake Area

*Buses 673 and 674 run from Bristol to the Chew Valley Lake area.
For bus information in Bristol, tel. 0117/955–5111; Chew Region
tourist office: tel. 01761/412221.*

The area south of Bristol is worth visiting for its scenery, its villages, and the Bronze Age circles found here. **Chew Valley Lake,** a
modern reservoir in a drowned valley surrounded by woods, boasts
240 recorded species of birds. Nearby, photogenic villages include
Chew Magna and **Chew Stoke.** Among the most notable ancient
buildings is the Chew Magna church, with lots of gargoyles on its
tower. **Stanton Drew** is another such village, and near it are the
Stanton Drew Circles, where three stone circles, two avenues of
standing stones, and a burial chamber make up one of the grandest
and most mysterious monuments of its kind in the country. The site
lies in a field reached through a farmyard, so you'll need suitable
shoes for a visit. *The stones stand on private land, though they are*

supervised by English Heritage. The landowner charges a small admission fee. Open Mon.–Sat. until sunset.

Dining There are two possible places for lunch during your visit to the at-
¢ tractive village of Chew Magna, both on South Parade and both ancient hostelries. The **Bear and Swan** (tel. 01275/332577) serves hot bar food on weekdays, cold on weekends. The **Pelican Inn** (tel. 01275/332448) has a choice of either hot or cold dishes every day. They are both good value. *South Parade. No credit cards.*

Berkeley

Berkeley and its castle can be reached by the Badgerline Bus 308 from either Bristol or Gloucester (in Bristol tel. 0117/955–5111). The trip time is 42 minutes from Gloucester; 1 hour, 10 minutes from Bristol.

★ **Berkeley Castle,** in the sleepy little village of **Berkeley** (pronounced "Barkley"), is a perfectly preserved building, everyone's ideal castle. It was the setting for the gruesome murder of King Edward II in 1327—the cell can still be seen. He was deposed by his French consort, Queen Isabella, and her paramour, the earl of Mortimer. They then connived at his imprisonment and subsequent death. The castle was begun in 1153 by Roger De Berkeley, a Norman knight, and has remained in the family ever since. It vies with Windsor as the oldest inhabited castle in the country. The state apartments here are furnished with magnificent pieces, and with tapestries and pictures. The surrounding meadows, now the setting for pleasant Elizabethan gardens, were once flooded to make a formidable moat. Light lunches are available between May and September. *Berkeley, tel. 01453/810332. Admission: £4 adults, £3.20 senior citizens and students, £2 children, £11 family ticket. Open May–Sept., Tues.–Sat. and national holidays 11–5, Sun. 2–5; Apr., Tues.–Sun. 2–5; Oct., Sun. 2–4:30.*

Dining **Mariner's Arms.** For an ancient village, an ancient pub. Originally
¢ built in the 15th century, it serves excellent homemade bar food, with tables outside for summer lunching. *Salter St., tel. 01453/811822. No credit cards.*

8 The Welsh Borders

Worcester, Hereford, Shrewsbury, Manchester, Buxton

Behind the high hedges and under the wooded hills of this region time seems to have stood still: Brooding medieval castles loom above the old towns, suggesting that today's air of sleepy tranquillity has not always been so. This was a troubled borderland across which the medieval English and Welsh eyed each other with ill-disguised hostility; they built fortresses to enforce a shaky peace. The border with the principality stretches from Chepstow on the Severn Estuary in the south to Chester in the north, edging the counties of Worcester and Hereford, Shropshire, and part of Cheshire.

For the last 500 years or so, the people of this border country have enjoyed a more peaceful existence, with little to disturb the traditional patterns of country life. In the 18th century, however, one small corner of Shropshire heralded the birth of the Industrial Revolution, for it was here, in a pretty, wooded stretch of the Severn Gorge, that the first coke blast furnace was invented and the first iron bridge was erected (1774).

Herefordshire, in the south, is a county of rich, rolling countryside and river valleys, gradually opening out in the high hills and plateaus of Shropshire. North of the Shropshire hills, the gentler Cheshire plain stretches toward the great industrial cities of Liverpool and Manchester. This is dairy country, dotted with small villages and market towns, many rich in the 13th- and 14th-century black-and-white, half-timbered buildings so typical of northwestern England. These are the legacy of a forested countryside, where wood was easier to come by than stone. In the market towns of Chester and Shrewsbury, the more elaborately decorated half-timbered buildings are monuments to wealth, dating mostly from the early Jacobean period at the beginning of the 17th century.

Although Buxton and the Peak District of Derbyshire (pronounced "Darbyshire") are not part of the Welsh Borders, trains and buses make this region accessible, and so it is treated in this chapter as an

The Welsh Borders

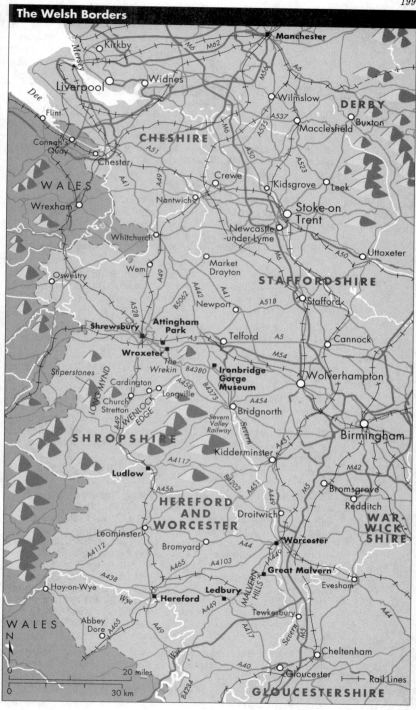

Manchester

Kirkby

Liverpool
Widnes
Wilmslow
DERBY
Dee
Flint
Buxton
A537
Macclesfield
Connah's
Quay
CHESHIRE
A51
Chester
A523
WALES
Crewe
Kidsgrove
Leek
Wrexham
Nantwich
Stoke-on
Trent
Whitchurch
Newcastle
-under-Lyme
A50
Uttoxeter
Wem
Market
Drayton
STAFFORDSHIRE
Oswestry
B5062
A442
A61
A518
Stafford
A528
Newport
A49
Shrewsbury
**Attingham
Park**
A5
Telford
A5
Cannock
Wroxeter
The
Wrekin
B4380
M54
Stiperstones
Cardington
A458
B4373
**Ironbridge
Gorge
Museum**
A454
Wolverhampton
Longville
Church
Stretton
WENLOCK
EDGE
Bridgnorth
LONG MYND
Severn
Valley
Railway
Birmingham
SHROPSHIRE
Kidderminster
A4117
A451
Ludlow
A456
B4202
A451
M42
Bromsgrove
A449
Redditch
**HEREFORD
AND
WORCESTER**
Droitwich
**WAR-
WICK-
SHIRE**
Leominster
M5
A4112
Bromyard
A44
Worcester
A465
A4103
A449
Hay-on-Wye
A438
Great Malvern
MALVERN
HILLS
Evesham
Wye
Ledbury
Hereford
A449
Abbey
Dore
A465
A49
A417
Tewkesbury
A44
WALES
N
Wye
Severn
M5
Cheltenham
0   20 miles
A40
+ + + Rail Lines
0   30 km
Gloucester
GLOUCESTERSHIRE

excursion from Manchester. The Peaks offer an affordable alternative, one that is immensely popular with hikers and those who love the great outdoors. This is a wilder, grander part of England, a region of open spaces, wide horizons, and hills that seem to rear violently out of the plain.

Essential Information

Lodging The Welsh Borders are full of ancient inns and elegant, Regency-style houses converted into hotels. Though British hotels are pricey, bargains can be found in small-town pubs with a few rooms to let. You may find that you have to put up with asthmatic plumbing and creaking beams that masquerade as period atmosphere, but it's usually worth the savings. Highly recommended establishments are indicated by a star ★.

Dining This is rich farming country where, for centuries, the orchards have produced succulent fruit, especially apples. Hereford cider, for example, is popular because it tastes much sweeter than the cider brewed farther south in Devon. The meat and milk products, which come from the local black-and-white breed of cattle, are second to none here.

Although many of the fine restaurants grow their own produce, the prices tend to be expensive. Your best deals will be found in the local pubs that offer homemade food at a reasonable cost, but, for the most part, you will not be able to use your credit cards.

Unless otherwise noted, reservations are not needed and dress is casual. Highly recommended restaurants are indicated by a star ★.

Shopping The rural counties of the borderlands have few specialized shopping areas. Most towns, however, are good for antiques hunting: Sometimes there are roadside signs that advertise a shop or outlet.

Several towns of the Welsh Borders have markets on select days during the week. Chester's market is every day except Wednesday. Hereford offers a different type of market each day—food, clothing, livestock—located on New Market Street. In Shrewsbury, there is a market on Tuesday, Wednesday, Friday, and Saturday, and Worcester holds a street market every day except Sunday and Monday in Angel Place, near the bus station, and an indoor market Monday–Saturday in the Shambles.

Biking The Borders make ideal country for biking, although you should be sure to get a bike whose gears can cope with the hilly terrain. About 10 miles outside Shrewsbury, **Longmynd Cycles** (Sandford Court, Sandford Ave., Church Stretton, tel. 01694/722367) rents mountain bikes, helmets, and other accessories (weekends by prior arrangement), and in Worcester, bikes can be rented from **Peddlers** (46 Barbourne Rd., tel. 01905/24238). Near Ross-on-Wye, **Pedalaway** (Trereece Barn, Llangarron, tel. 01989/770357) arranges rentals and individually tailored cycling holidays. A mile outside Ludlow, try **Pearce Engineering** (Fishmore, tel. 01584/876106) for rentals and bike routes, or, farther out of town, **Wheely Wonderful Cycling Co.,** (Petchfield Farm, Elton, Ludlow, tel. 01568/770755), which also arranges excursions and longer vacations.

Hiking In the **Malvern Hills** there are climbs and walks of varying lengths and difficulty. The best places to start are Great Malvern and Ledbury. The route has been designated the "Elgar Way," running for 45 miles, but, of course, you don't need to do the whole thing.

One of Britain's major long-distance hikes lies mostly within this area: the **Offa's Dyke Path**, so called after the earthwork built by an 8th-century king to mark the boundary between England and Wales. The whole route runs 168 miles, starting at Sedbury Cliffs, south of Chepstow, and finishing at the seafront of Prestatyn, on the north coast of Wales, but only about 60 miles of this walk is along the actual dike. For details contact local tourist centers or **The Offa's Dyke Association** (Offa's Dyke Centre, West St., Knighton, Powys LD7 1EW, tel. 01547/528753).

The winding 172-mile **Shropshire Way** takes in Shrewsbury, Ludlow, Ironbridge, and plenty of hilly scenery. Check with the local tourist offices for route information.

Festivals   The **Ludlow Festival** is staged against the town's dramatic castle, an especially exciting backdrop for Shakespearean plays such as *Macbeth*. The **Three Choirs Festival,** the grandpappy of all musical events, moves every year on its inexorable round of Worcester, Gloucester, and Hereford cathedrals, as it has for a couple of centuries. Strengthened by visiting orchestras and soloists, the local choirs perform an incredible range of music, often pieces written for the festival, which takes place in August. The **Shrewsbury** and **Malvern festivals** are both small scale, but they carry a lot of tradition.

Tour 1: Worcester to Hereford

This tour of the border region starts in the ancient Severn Valley city of Worcester, renowned for its proud cathedral and fine bone china. From here we travel south and west, along the lovely Malvern Hills, taking in the peaceful spa town of Great Malvern before stopping in the prosperous agricultural city of Hereford, on the banks of the River Wye. On the way north from here to Shrewsbury, the tour suggests visiting Ludlow, an architectural jewel of a town.

From London   The average journey time from London/Paddington (tel. 0171/262–
By Train   6767) is about 2½ hours, and trains run almost every hour, but about half of them require a change at either Oxford or Swindon. Worcester's two stations are Shrub Hill (the main one) and Foregate (the most central). Call rail information in Worcester (tel. 01452/29501) for schedules.

By Bus   The **National Express** route to Worcester from London/Victoria Coach Station (tel. 0171/730–0202) is 511. It follows scenic roads through the Cotswolds, taking in Broadway and Chipping Campden. The trip takes 3½ hours, and departs once a day at 5:30 PM. Alternatively, take the 1:30 PM bus to Birmingham (No. 522), where you can change onto a bus to Worcester, arriving there at about 6.

By Car   M4/M5 from London take you to Worcester in just under 3 hours. The more direct route (120 miles) on M40 via Oxford to A40 across the Cotswolds is prettier but takes longer because it is only partly motorway.

Worcester

Worcester tourist office: The Guildhall, High St., tel. 01905/726311.

Worcester (pronounced "Wooster") is situated on the Severn River in the center of Worcestershire, 118 miles northwest of London. It is an ancient city proud of its history. Its nickname, "The Faithful City," refers to its steadfast allegiance to the crown during the English Civil War. Worcester played an important role in this conflict between the king and Parliament, and two major battles were waged here. The second one, the decisive Battle of Worcester in 1651, resulted in the exile of Charles II. More recently the town's name has become synonymous with the fine bone china produced here.

The city suffered considerable "modernization" during the 1960s, but happily some of medieval Worcester remains. This ancient section forms a convenient and pleasant walking route around the great cathedral.

★ There are few more quintessentially English sights than that of **Worcester Cathedral**, its towers overlooking the green expanse of the county cricket ground, its majestic image reflected in the swift-flowing—and frequently flooding—waters of the River Severn. The cathedral stands on one of the most ancient sites of English Christianity; there has been a cathedral here since the year 680. Later centuries saw considerable rebuilding, and much of what remains dates from the 13th and 14th centuries. Notable exceptions are the Norman crypt (built in the 1080s), the largest in England, and the ambulatory, a cloister built around the east end. The most important tomb in the cathedral is that of King John (1167–1216), one of the country's least admired monarchs, who alienated his barons and subjects through bad administration and heavy taxation, and was eventually forced to sign the Magna Carta, the great charter of liberty, in 1215. The cathedral's most beautiful decoration is in the vaulted **chantry chapel of Prince Arthur**, Henry VII's elder son, whose body was brought to Worcester after his death at Ludlow in Shropshire in 1502. (Chantry chapels were endowed by wealthy families to enable priests to sing masses there for the souls of the deceased.) *Tel. 01905/28854. Open daily 7:30–6:30.*

South of the cathedral (follow Severn Street) is the **Royal Worcester Porcelain Factory**, where you can browse through the showrooms or rummage in the "seconds" store; especially good bargains can be had in the January and July sales. Forty-five-minute tours of the factory take you through the processes of porcelain-making, from raw materials to finished pieces. Reserve in advance to be sure of getting on a tour. Another part of the factory is the **Dyson Perrins Museum,** which houses one of the finest and most comprehensive collections of rare Worcester porcelain, with examples that date from the start of manufacturing in 1751 to the present day. *Severn St., tel. 01905/ 23221. Admission: £1.50 adults, £1 children; tours of factory, weekdays, ¾ hour (must book in advance), £3.25 adults, £2.25 children; Connoisseur Tours 2 hours, £10 adults, £8 children. Open weekdays 9:30–5, Sat. 10–5; tours Mon.–Thurs. 10:30–3:30, Fri. 10:30–2:30.*

Across the road from the porcelain factory is **The Commandery,** a cluster of 15th-century half-timbered buildings, originally built as a poorhouse, but serving as the headquarters of the royalist troops during the Battle of Worcester. Now a museum, it presents a colorful, audiovisual presentation about the Civil War in the magnificent, oak-beamed great hall. *Sidbury, tel. 01905/355071. Admission: £3.15 adults, £2.15 senior citizens and children, £8.50 family ticket. Open Mon.–Sat. 10–5, Sun. 1:30–5:30.*

Between The Commandery and the cathedral lies **Friar Street,** one of Worcester's most notable medieval streets. As you walk toward the Cornmarket, there are several buildings of particular interest, among them the **Tudor House,** a museum of domestic and social history, and **King Charles's House,** where the beleaguered Charles II hid before his escape from the city. The latter is now a restaurant. *Tudor House, tel. 01905/20904. Admission: £1.50 adults, 75p students, senior citizens, and children, £3.25 family ticket. Open Mon.–Wed., Fri. and Sat. 10:30–5.*

Follow High Street, closed to traffic and pleasant for walking, back toward the cathedral. Set on the right behind ornate iron railings is the **Guildhall,** with an 18th-century facade that features gilded statues of Queen Anne, Charles I, and Charles II, as well as a smaller carving of Cromwell's head pinned up by the ears—a savage addition by the royalist citizens of Worcester.

At the end of High Street stands a statue of Sir Edward Elgar (1857–1934), who spent his early childhood in his parents' music store just a few yards from the cathedral. Elgar was one of Britain's best-known composers of choral and orchestral works, noted particularly for his *Enigma Variations,* his oratorio *The Dream of Gerontius,* and the *Pomp and Circumstance* marches.

If you walk down Deansway, you can turn left into the riverside gardens and work your way back along the river below the cathedral and porcelain factory.

Lodging **40 Britannia Square.** Set in a quiet, elegant, Georgian square, this
£ guest house is half a mile from Foregate Street Station and downtown. *40 Britannia Sq., WR1 3DN, tel. 01905/611920, fax 01905/ 27152. 3 rooms with bath or shower. No credit cards. Closed Dec. 25– Jan. 1.*

£ **Ye Old Talbot Hotel.** The Old Talbot was originally a courtroom belonging to the cathedral, which stands close by. The hotel has been refurbished, and there are modern extensions to the 16th-century core of the building. *Friar St., WR1 2NA, tel. 01905/23573, fax 01905/612760. 29 rooms with bath. Facilities: restaurant. AE, DC, MC, V.*

Dining **Il Pescatore.** An authentic Italian restaurant located in a timber-
££ frame ex-tearoom in the heart of Worcester may be something of a cultural clash, but the oddness is quickly forgotten as you are seduced by the best Italian food in town, if not in the whole county. Italian staples are served, but there are also some unexpected delights on the daily-changing menu, and the desserts are out of this world: Try the hot passion-fruit soufflé. The setting is formal, but there are some good-value set-price menus available—lunch at £11.50, dinner at £16.50, both three-course. *34 Sidbury, tel. 01905/ 21444. Reservations advised evenings. MC, V. Closed Sun., Mon. lunch.*

¢ **Farriers Arms.** This 17th-century pub, close to the cathedral, serves very reasonable bar food, with tasty beef-and-mushroom pie, and a vegetarian dish that changes daily. It has a beamed bar with a tall case clock, and a terrace for outdoor summer eating. *Fish St., tel. 01905/26929. No credit cards.*

Shopping **Bygones** has two stores in Worcester, one right beside the cathedral at 32 College Street (tel. 01905/25388), and the other a few hundred yards away at 55 Sidbury (tel. 01905/23132), near the Commandery. Both have finely crafted antiques from various periods; they specialize in Worcester porcelain, and they always have a selection of small silver, glass, and porcelain items suitable for gifts.

Lovers of fine china should not forget the shops at the Worcester Porcelain Factory (*see above*), where seconds are available.

Great Malvern

Worcester is linked to Hereford by a direct National Express Bus 308, which makes the 1-hour trip, with stops at Malvern and Ledbury, once daily. A network of local buses connects the four towns: Worcester to Malvern (Buses 44, 45, 46); Malvern to Ledbury (Bus 675); Ledbury to Hereford (Bus 476). Regular trains make the trip from Worcester to Malvern and to Hereford in about 20 and 50 minutes, respectively. Malvern tourist office: Winter Gardens Complex, Grange Rd., tel. 01684/892289.

If you travel southwest from Worcester, you will soon see the **Malvern Hills,** their long, low purple profile rising starkly from the surrounding plain. The Malverns shelter a string of communities that stretch from the village of North Malvern to Little Malvern at the southwestern end of the range. The main town is **Great Malvern,** a Victorian spa town about 7 miles south of Worcester, whose architecture has changed little since the mid-1800s. Exceptionally pure spring water is still bottled here and exported all over the world— the queen never travels without a supply. Many of the large hotels built during the spa days remain hotels, while others have been converted into "public" (that is, private) schools. Great Malvern is known today both as an educational center and as a great place for old folks' homes. The town also has a Winter Gardens complex with a theater, movie theater, and gardens, but it is the **Priory** that dominates the steep downtown streets. This early Norman Benedictine abbey in Perpendicular style is decorated throughout with vertical lines of airy tracery, but it's also of interest for its large quantity of fine 15th-century glass and some local wall tiles of the same period. *Entrance opposite the church. Admission free. Open daily 8 AM–dusk.*

The most striking feature of Great Malvern, however, is the gentle hills that rise above it and are ideal for leisurely hiking. The hilltops provide magnificent views of the Welsh Black Mountains to the west and the contrasting patchwork of the Severn plain as it stretches eastward toward the Cotswold Hills in Gloucestershire.

Lodging **Sidney House.** In addition to the great views, this dignified Georgian
£ hotel is also near the town center. It has been restored and is run by a friendly husband-and-wife team. Bedrooms are comfortably sized (and include TVs and tea/coffeemakers), making the Sidney House a good value for people traveling on a budget. *40 Worcester Rd., WR14 4AA, tel. 01684/574994. 8 rooms, 5 with bath or shower. AE, MC, V.*

Festivals Malvern has historical connections with George Bernard Shaw, who premiered many of his plays here, as well as with Sir Edward Elgar. The **Malvern Festival** was originally devoted to their works, although now it also offers a wide variety of new music and drama. The **Malvern Fringe Festival** has an exceptional program of alternative events. Both festivals run for two or three weeks from the end of May to early June. *Details from Malvern Tourist Information Centre, Winter Garden Complex, Grange Rd., Hereford & Worcester WR14 3HB, tel. 01684/892289.*

Ledbury

To reach Ledbury, take the National Express Bus 308 from Worcester, which runs once daily and takes about 35 minutes. If you're coming from Malvern, take the local Bus 675 for the 30-minute ride. Ledbury tourist office: 1 Church La., tel. 01531/636147.

Leaving Great Malvern, you'll travel southwest about 10 miles through Malvern Wells and Little Malvern to the market town of **Ledbury**, where you will see some exceptional black-and-white half-timbered buildings. Take special note of the **Feathers Hotel**, the **Talbot Inn** (both late 16th century), and the 17th-century **market house**, perched on 16 oak columns. On Saturday you can still buy a variety of produce from the market stalls. Look for the cheesemaker, and be sure to sample his very rare Gloucester, which is tasty and far less rich and oily than the traditional orange-red Double Gloucester.

Almost hidden behind the market hall is a cobbled lane leading to the church, with medieval, half-timbered buildings crowded together leaning into the narrow road from either side. One of them is the **Old Grammar School**, now a heritage center that traces the history of some of the local industries, and features some displays on two literary celebrities linked to the area, John Masefield and Elizabeth Barrett Browning. *Tel. 01531/635680. Admission free. Open May–Sept., daily 10:30–4; Easter–May, weekends 10:30–4 (opening hours may vary and should be confirmed).*

Dining **Feathers Hotel.** You can eat very reasonably in this centrally located
¢ 1565 coaching inn, with its dazzling black-and-white beamed facade.

Perfect vacations.
Some assembly required.

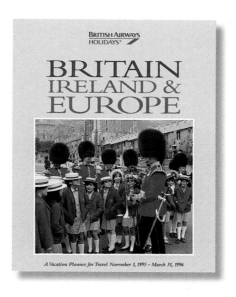

Who better to design your dream vacation than you? Especially with our Britain Ireland & Europe vacation planner.

It covers everything.

Like places to stay in the city and the country, theatre tickets, sightseeing and auto rentals, to name a few.

So call your travel agent or give us a ring at 1-800-AIRWAYS. You'll make the choices, we'll make it happen.

Reality check. Call home.

——— *AT&T USADirect® and World Connect®. The fast, easy way to call most anywhere.* ———

Take out AT&T Calling Card or your local calling card.** Lift phone. Dial AT&T Access Number for country you're calling from. Connect to English-speaking operator or voice prompt. Reach the States or over 200 countries. Talk. Say goodbye. Hang up. Resume vacation.

Austria⁺⁺⁺....................022-903-011	Luxembourg 0-800-0111	Turkey*..........................00-800-12277
Belgium*.........................0-800-100-10	Netherlands*..................06-022-9111	United Kingdom................0500-89-0011
Czech Republic*..............00-420-00101	Norway 800-190-11	
Denmark 8001-0010	Poland⁺♦◇...............0◇010-480-0111	
Finland 9800-100-10	Portugal⁺........................05017-1-288	
France 19-0011	Romania*.....................01-800-4288	
Germany...........................0130-0010	Russia*⁺(Moscow)...............155-5042	
Greece*.........................00-800-1311	Slovak Rep.*..................00-420-00101	
Hungary*.....................00◇-800-01111	Spain●............................900-99-00-11	
Ireland 1-800-550-000	Sweden 020-795-611	
Italy*..................................172-1011	Switzerland*......................155-00-11	

AT&T
Your True Choice

**You can also call collect or use most U.S. local calling cards. Countries in bold face permit country-to-country calling in addition to calls to the U.S. World Connect® prices consist of USADirect® rates plus an additional charge based on the country you are calling. Collect calling available to the U.S. only. *Public phones require deposit of coin or phone card. ⁺May not be available from every phone. ⁺⁺⁺Public phones require local coin payment during call. ♦Not available from public phones. ◇Await second dial tone. ‡Dial 010-480-0111 from major Warsaw hotels. ●Calling available to most European countries. ©1995 AT&T.

For a free wallet sized card of all AT&T Access Numbers, call: 1-800-241-5555.

From Monday to Saturday sample the Fuggles Bar's daily specials, such as Ledbury sausages or venison casserole, which often include local ingredients. For the ploughman's lunch, you cut your own wedge of cheese. Quills Restaurant offers similar fare with trimmings and higher prices. If you decide to sleep here (it gets noisy at night), be prepared to pay relatively high rates for creaking plumbing and ancient floorboards. *High St., HR8 1DS, tel. 01531/635266. AE, DC, MC, V.*

Hereford

You can reach Hereford from London by train and bus via Worcester (see From London, *above), or from Ledbury on local Bus 476; journey time is about 40 minutes. Hereford tourist office: 1 King St., tel. 01432/268430.*

Hereford is a busy country town and the center of a wealthy agricultural area known for its cider, fruit, and cattle—the white-faced Hereford breed has spread across the world. It is also an important cathedral city, its massive Norman cathedral towering proudly over the River Wye. Before 1066, Hereford was the capital of the Anglo-Saxon kingdom of Mercia and, earlier still, the site of Roman, Celtic, and Iron Age settlements. Today, tourists come primarily to see the cathedral, but quickly discover the charms of a town that has changed slowly but fairly unobtrusively with the passing centuries.

The small town center's attractive old buildings remain, but the stores are generally unremarkable, many of them members of chains. However, **Buttermarket,** in High Town, is a good place for local produce, while the **cattle market** provides an unmistakable glimpse of English country life. Livestock auctions are held every Wednesday, but there are special auctions and market stalls here virtually every day.

★ **Hereford Cathedral,** built of local red sandstone with a massive central tower, has some fine 11th-century Norman carvings, but like many of England's early churches, it suffered considerable "restoration" in the 19th century, which spoiled the nave and other examples of skillful work by earlier craftsmen. Inside, the greatest glories include the 14th-century **bishop's throne;** some fine **misericords** (the elaborately carved undersides of choristers' seats); and the extraordinary **Mappa Mundi,** Hereford's own picture of the medieval world. This great map, which dates to 1290 and is thought to have been the center section of an altarpiece, shows the Earth as flat, with Jerusalem at its center. The dean of the cathedral caused a furor in 1988 when he began negotiations with Sotheby's to put the piece on the market, in an attempt to raise funds to help pay the costs of the cathedral's upkeep and restoration. Britain suddenly realized that the rich heritage of art treasures held by the Church, mostly in cathedrals, might be under threat, and the map was withdrawn from sale.

Best of all the cathedral's attraction is the library, containing some 1,500 chained books. Among the most valuable volumes is an 8th-century copy of the four gospels. Chained libraries are extremely rare: There are only six of them in the country, dating from medieval times when books were as precious as gold. A gallery built especially for Mappa Mundi and the chained library is expected to open in mid-1996. *Tel. 01432/359880. Cathedral admission free. Open Mon.–Sat. 8:30–5:30, Sun. 12:30–3:30. Mappa Mundi admission fee includes an audiovisual display: £3 adults, £2 senior citizens and children. Chained library admission: 80p adults, 10p children. Open Apr.–Oct., Mon.–Sat. 10:30–12:30 and 2–4; Nov.–Mar., Mon.–Sat. 11–12 and 2:30–3:30.*

Leave the cathedral by the north door and walk down Church Street to find the town's more unusual stores: jewelers, bookstores, and crafts and antiques shops, all of which stock unique, high-quality products.

From Church Street, cross East Street and follow the passageway into **High Town**, a large pedestrian square in the corner of which stands a fine example of domestic Jacobean architecture. Called simply **The Old House**, it is furnished on three floors in 17th-century style and is the only building remaining from the original Butchers' Row. *Tel. 01432/268121, ext. 225. Admission: £1 adults, 50p senior citizens and children. Open Apr.–Sept., Mon. 10–1, Tues.–Sat. 10–1 and 2–5:30, Sun. 10–4; Oct.–Mar., Mon. and Sat. 10–1, Tues.–Fri. 10–1 and 2–5:30.*

On the west side of High Town is the 13th-century **All Saints Church**, which contains another 300 chained books, as well as canopied stalls and fine misericords.

From All Saints, walk down the pedestrian Eign Gate, go under the ring road using the pedestrian underpass, and proceed down Eign Street, which continues as Whitecross Road. At the traffic lights turn left into Grimmer Road and bear right for the **Cider Museum,** which traces the story of cider-making through the ages. A farm cider-house and a cooper's (cask maker's) workshop have been re-created here, and you can tour ancient cider cellars that date to Napoleonic times and house huge oak vats. Apple brandy (applejack) has recently been made here for the first time in hundreds of years, and the museum has its own brand for sale. *Pomona Pl., off Whitecross Rd., tel. 01432/354207. Admission: £2 adults, £1.50 senior citizens and children. Open Apr.–Oct., daily 10–5:30; Nov.–Mar., Mon.–Sat. 1–5.*

Lodging   **Castle Pool.** Hereford's massive castle has virtually disappeared,
££   but part of its moat has survived. The 1850 building, once the bishop's residence, is now a hotel that features blandly furnished but comfortable and quiet bedrooms, with TVs and tea/coffeemakers for under £65 a night. A restaurant on the property serves an intriguing mix of dishes, including some Moroccan and Egyptian specials. In the summer, join guests for a barbecue in the garden. *Castle St., HR1 2NR, tel. 01432/356321. 27 rooms with bath. Facilities: restaurant, garden, parking. AE, DC, MC, V.*

£   **Ferncroft Hotel.** This small, family-run hotel is decorated in Victorian style, with some antique furniture. The restaurant serves local produce, thoughtfully prepared. *144 Ledbury Rd., HR1 2TB, tel. 01432/265538. 11 rooms, 6 with shower. MC, V. Closed 2 wks at Christmas.*

¢   **Hopbine Hotel.** The Hopbine is a mile from the center of town, in the
★   direction of Leominster, but worth the jaunt. It is a Victorian guest house, set on 2 acres. The very comfortable, quiet rooms come equipped with TV and tea/coffeemakers. Evening meals are available. This is a simple place, but very friendly. *Roman Rd., HR1 1LE, tel. 01432/268722, fax 01432/268722. 12 rooms with bath. No credit cards.*

Dining   **Orange Tree.** This is a refurbished, wood-paneled pub at the junction
£   of King and Bridge streets, near the cathedral. A comfortable place to stop after sightseeing, the Orange Tree offers good, solid bar food at lunchtime. *16 King St., tel. 01432/267698. No credit cards.*

Shopping   **The Hereford Book Shop** (tel. 01432/357617) on Church Street has new and secondhand books. There is also a large selection of local guidebooks, maps, and unusual greeting cards.

The **Hereford Society of Craftsmen** (tel. 01432/266049) is based in Capuchin Yard, off 29 Church Street. In this small yard, you can see a violin-maker at work, as well as a potter. Aside from the usual crafts, knitwear, posters, and watercolors are also for sale.

Ludlow

It is possible to make the long jump northward from Hereford to Shrewsbury (see Tour 2, below) by both bus and train. Among the buses between the two cities are the Midland Road 192 from Hereford to Ludlow (trip time: 1 hour, nine times daily), and 435 from Ludlow to Shrewsbury, five times a day, taking 1 hour, 20 minutes. The direct train ride takes less than 1 hour. Ludlow tourist office: Castle St., tel. 01584/875053.

★ **Ludlow** has often been described as the most beautiful small town in England, with its mix of medieval, Georgian, and Victorian buildings. Cross the river and climb **Whitcliff** for the spectacular view. The town centers around the cathedral-like bulk of the **Church of St. Lawrence,** and is dwarfed by the massive, ruined, red sandstone **castle.** The latter dates from 1085 and was a vital stronghold in this part of the border country. It was the seat of the Marcher Lords who ruled this area, and whose name derived from the local name for the border region, "the Marches." It is still privately owned by the earl of Powys. Follow the terraced walk around the castle for a lovely view. *Tel. 01584/873947. Admission: £2.50 adults, £2 senior citizens, £1.50 children, £7.50 family ticket. Open Feb.–Apr. and Oct.–Dec., daily 10:30–4; May–Sept., daily 10:30–5.*

If you take the time to wander around the town, look for the **Feathers Hotel,** to admire its extravagantly decorated half-timbered facade.

Lodging **The Church.** This centrally located pub, just behind Buttercross, of-
£ fers rooms to let: Those on the side of the church next door are the quietest. Parts of the building date to the 13th century, lending even more to the interesting ambience. If you choose to dine here, you can eat either in the bar, for about £6 a head, or more expensively in the restaurant. In either case the food is home cooked and very tasty: Try fresh trout or a steak. *Church St., SY8 1AW, tel. 01584/872174. 9 rooms with bath. MC, V.*

Dining **Dinham Hall.** Dinham Hall is a newly converted merchant's 1792
££ town house near Ludlow castle. The owners have managed to combine the original historic elements in the house with modern comforts. The hotel part tends to be a bit pricey for the cost-conscious traveler, but the menu is priced more reasonably. The dining room serves imaginative dishes, such as salmon with wild mushrooms and venison with noodles. Set menus are priced at £24.50 for four courses, £19.50 for three, and afternoon teas are served in the walled garden in summer. *Off Market Sq., tel. 01584/876464. Reservations advised. Jacket and tie. AE, DC, MC, V.*

£ **Eagle House.** This good-value eatery has a regularly changing menu of home-cooked dishes made with local produce. Apart from the reliable food, the draw here is the adventurous selection of wines. It's a place for a wine buff to experiment without breaking the bank. *17 Corve St., tel. 01584/872325. Reservations advised. No credit cards.*

Festivals The **Ludlow Festival,** starting at the end of June, sums up all that is English: Shakespeare is performed in the open air, against the romantic backdrop of the ruined castle, to an audience armed with cushions, raincoats, lap robes, and picnic baskets, as well as hip flasks. Reservations are accepted starting in early May. *Details from: The Festival Box Office, Castle Sq., Ludlow, Shropshire SY8 1AY, tel. 01584/872150.*

Tour 2: Shrewsbury and the Ironbridge Gorge Museums

This tour begins in the handsome medieval city of Shrewsbury, then moves through the Roman town of Wroxeter to the cluster of Ironbridge museums—living memorials to an area that was responsible for much of Britain's industrial preeminence in the 18th and 19th centuries.

From London
By Train
Direct trains and some with a change at Wolverhampton travel from London/Euston (tel. 0171/387–7070) to Shrewsbury in about 3 hours. Call for train information in Shrewsbury (tel. 0345/350761).

By Bus
National Express coaches (Nos. 520, 521, and 522) for Shrewsbury leave the London/Victoria Coach Station (tel. 0171/730–0202) three times daily at 1:30, 3:30 and 5:30 and go via Birmingham, taking about 4 hours, 40 minutes.

By Car
From London, take M1 north to junction 19, then turn onto M6 to Walsall. From there take M54 to Telford and A5 to Shrewsbury. The total distance is 150 miles, and during the latter part of the journey you may run into a lot of traffic. There are other more attractive routes on back roads through the Cotswolds and the Welsh Borders, but they will be much slower.

Shrewsbury

Shrewsbury tourist office: The Music Hall, The Square, tel. 01743/350761.

Shrewsbury (usually pronounced "Shrose-bury"), the county seat of Shropshire, is strategically located within a great horseshoe loop of the Severn, with only one landward entrance. One of England's most important medieval towns, Shrewsbury has a wealth of well-preserved, 16th-century half-timbered buildings as well as many elegant ones from later periods. The market square forms the natural center of the town; leading off it are narrow alleys overhung with timbered gables. These alleys, called "shuts," were designed to be closed off at night to afford their residents greater protection. The town is especially proud of its flower displays, for which it has won many national awards. In the summer, window boxes and hanging baskets are a riot of color, providing a vivid contrast to the stark black-and-white buildings.

Numbers in the margin correspond to points of interest on the Shrewsbury map.

Shrewsbury is best seen on foot, because its narrow, traffic-congested streets are not pleasant to drive in. Indeed, some of the most historic streets have been pedestrianized. A good starting point for a walking tour is the small square between **Fish Street** and **Butchers Row**. These streets are little changed since medieval times, when some of them took their names from the principal trades carried on

❶ ❷ there. Nearby are **St. Alkmund's** (the only church in England to be named after a Saxon saint) and **St. Mary's** churches. Both are worth a visit for their iron-framed stained glass (an indication of the proximity of the Ironbridge Gorge). **Bear Steps,** a cluster of restored half-timbered buildings, links Fish Street with Market Square.

❸ Here the most notable building is **Ireland's Mansion,** a massive merchant's house. An outstanding example of elaborate Jacobean architecture, this house boasts heavy timbering, richly decorated with quatrefoils (openings carved in the timbers in the shape of four-leaf moldings or foils).

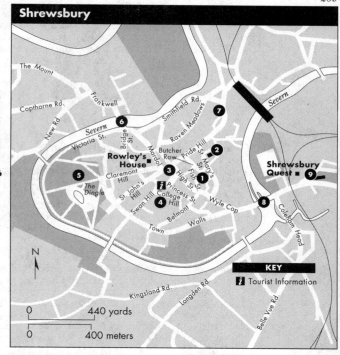

Castle and Shropshire Regimental Museum, **7**

Clive House, **4**

English Bridge, **8**

Ireland's Mansion, **3**

Quarry Park, **5**

St. Alkmund's, **1**

St. Mary's, **2**

Shrewsbury Abbey Church, **9**

Welsh Bridge, **6**

Shrewsbury

KEY

i Tourist Information

0 ——— 440 yards

0 ——— 400 meters

Nearby, in Barker Street, stands the magnificent 16th-century timber-framed warehouse and the adjoining brick and stone mansion of 1618 that is now **Rowley's House Museum,** containing Roman finds and other items of local history, costume, Shropshire pottery and ceramics, and regular exhibitions. *Barker St., tel. 01743/361196. Admission: £2 adults, £1 senior citizens, 50p children. Open Tues.–Sat. 10–5, Sun. in summer and national holidays 10–4. Inclusive ticket for Rowley's House, Clive House, and Castle: £3 adults, £2 senior citizens, £1 children.*

❹ Princess Street leads from the square to College Hill and **Clive House,** the home of Sir Robert Clive when he was Shrewsbury's member of Parliament in the mid-18th century. Better known as "Clive of India," this soldier-statesman was especially famous for winning the Battle of Plassey in 1757, thereby avenging the atrocity of the Black Hole of Calcutta, in which 146 Britons were imprisoned overnight in a stifling Indian dungeon, with only 23 surviving until morning. The house contains rooms furnished in Clive's period and striking displays of fragile Staffordshire pottery, particularly pieces from the Caughley and Coalport factories. The house was burgled in 1992 and a lot of valuable silver was stolen, but there is still more in storage than can be displayed. *College Hill, tel. 01743/354811. Admission: £1 adults, 50p children. Open Tues.–Sat., Sun. in summer and national holidays 10–4.*

❺ Below Swan Hill (turn left out of Clive House, then left again) you will see the manicured lawn of **Quarry Park** sloping down to the river. In a sheltered corner is the Dingle, a colorful garden offering changing floral displays through the year. St. John's Hill in the Mardol, another of Shrewsbury's strangely named streets, will take
❻
❼ you back into town, or you can head for **Welsh Bridge** and stroll along the river bank. As the river loops away, the **castle** rises up on the right. The originally Norman-style fortress was dismantled during the Civil War and later rebuilt by Thomas Telford, the distinguished

Scottish engineer who designed a host of notable buildings and bridges at the beginning of the 19th century. The castle now houses the **Shropshire Regimental Museum,** providing an interesting reflection on 200 years of the county's past. You need not be a military history buff to appreciate what's inside. It was this regiment that was responsible for burning down the White House in Washington in 1814. The museum suffered badly from an IRA bomb in 1992, only reopening after extensive restoration in the spring of 1995. *Shrewsbury Castle, tel. 01743/358516. Admission: £2 adults, £1 senior citizens, 50p children. Open Tues.–Sat., Sun. in summer, and national holidays 10–4:30.*

8 9 If you cross the river by the **English Bridge,** you'll reach **Shrewsbury Abbey Church,** almost all that remains of the monastery that stood here from 1083. The abbey figures in a series of popular medieval whodunits by Ellis Peters, which feature the detective Brother Cadfael and provide an excellent idea of life in this area during the Middle Ages. The Abbey Restoration Project has developed an intriguing series of medieval walking tours. *Details from Restoration Project Office, 1 Holy Cross Houses, Abbey Foregate, Shrewsbury SY2 6BS, tel. 01743/232723.*

Opposite the Abbey Church, devotees of Brother Cadfael won't be able to resist the **Shrewsbury Quest,** opened in 1994 and presenting a re-creation of monastic life in the Middle Ages, complete with a scriptorium, library, cloisters, and even a trail of clues to help solve a medieval mystery. Children will be particularly interested, even without a knowledge of the sandaled sleuth. *Abbey Foregate, tel. 01743/243324. Admission: £3.50 adults, £2.80 senior citizens, £2 children. Open daily 10–5 or dusk.*

Lodding **Sandford House.** The Jones family warmly welcomes guests into
£ their large Georgian B&B, which is near the river and close to the
★ town center. Clean and functional bedrooms, a spacious blue-and-white breakfast room, and a pleasant rear garden make this house unique. *St. Julian's Friars, SY1 1XL, tel. 01743/343829. 10 rooms, 8 with bath or shower. MC, V.*

£ **Sydney House.** Here's a sensible B&B, situated in the northern part of the city but still within easy walking distance of the center. The Edwardian building boasts sizable, modernized bedrooms and a restaurant that serves a home-cooked four-course meal from a set menu. To accompany your meal, choose from the long, reasonably priced wine list. *Coton Crescent, Coton Hill, SY1 2LJ, tel. 01743/354681. 7 rooms, 4 with shower. Facilities: restaurant. AE, MC, V.*

Dining **Peach Tree.** This small restaurant beside the abbey, housed in an at-
£ tractive 16th-century building, has lots of beams and is decorated with stenciled peach trees. The traditionally English fare, with imaginative touches, is presented on a set menu that is a good value for lunch (about £10). If calories aren't a concern, try the rich, old-fashioned trifle for your dessert. *21 Abbey Foregate, tel. 01743/355055. Reservations advised. MC, V. Closed Sun. and lunch Mon.*

£ **Traitor's Gate.** Traitor's Gate is an atmospheric restaurant installed in a series of 13th-century vaulted brick cellars. The freshly prepared, reasonably priced meals make a perfect break in a day's sightseeing. The restaurant is near the castle and gains its name from an incident in the Civil War, when a young Roundhead lieutenant ransacked the Cavalier-held fortress. He was later executed as a traitor. Lunch from £3.50, dinner from £11; very friendly service. *St. Mary's Water La., tel. 01743/249152. AE, MC, V. Closed Sun. and Mon. (also Tues. and Wed. evening in winter).*

Shopping **Manser & Son** (53–54 Wyle Cop, tel. 01743/351120) displays quality antiques, and sells furniture, silver, lighting, pictures, and jewelry of the 17th to 20th centuries—items may cost as little as £5, or as much as £10,000.

St. Julian's Craft Centre (High St., tel. 01743/353516) is worth visiting for a ceramic, wooden, or jewelry gift to take home. Housed in a deconsecrated church, it's quite unlike any craft center you've seen before, with work from all over Shropshire on view. Open Mon.–Sat. 10–5 (closed Thurs.).

Festivals During the **Shrewsbury International Music Festival,** the town vibrates to traditional and not-so-traditional music by groups of performers from America, western Europe, and sometimes eastern Europe. It is held in early July. *Details from: Concertworld (UK) Ltd., 150 Waterloo Rd., London SE1 8BD, tel. 0171/401–9941.*

Attingham Park and Wroxeter

To get to Attingham Park, at Atcham, take Bus 81, 82, 96, or X96 from Shrewsbury; the trip takes 15 minutes.

The rural scenery around Shrewsbury is among England's loveliest, with small towns, stately homes, and evocative museums scattered across the wide, open landscape. Four miles southeast of Shrewsbury is **Attingham Park,** a mansion built in 1785 by George Stuart, who designed the round church of St. Chad's in Shrewsbury. It has an impressive three-story portico, with a pediment carried on four tall columns, which dominates a wide sweep of parkland. The deer park was landscaped by Humphrey Repton. Inside are painted ceilings, delicate plasterwork, and a collection of 19th-century Neapolitan furniture. *Tel. 01743/709203. Admission: £3.50 adults, £1.75 children, £8.70 family ticket; park and grounds only, £1.40 adults, 70p children. Open Apr.–Sept., Sat.–Wed. 1:30–5, national holiday Mon. 11–5; Oct., weekends 1:30–5; park and grounds open daily until dusk.*

One mile farther east on Buses 96 and X96 route is **Wroxeter,** originally the Roman city of Viroconium, which flourished around AD 150 and was the fourth-largest city in Roman Britain. Excavations beginning in 1863 revealed the foundations of the shattered pillars of the forum and fragments of the town walls. A complex of buildings around the forum has now been unearthed, providing a clear impression of the original town plan. Your imagination is helped along by an artist's reconstructions placed all over the site. The small museum houses the Roman artifacts found in the past 100 years. *Tel. 01743/761330. Admission: £2 adults, £1.50 senior citizens. £1 children. Open Apr.–Sept., daily 10–6, Oct., daily 10–4, Nov.–Mar., Wed.–Sun. 10–4.*

Ironbridge

The Ironbridge museums cover a wide area. To get from Shrewsbury to the center, take Bus 96, X96, 819, or 836; the trip takes 30 minutes to one hour. Before you go, confirm routes and schedules with both local bus information (tel. 01345/056785 Mon.–Sat.) and Iron bridge Gorge Museum Trust (tel. 01952/433522). Ironbridge tour ist office: The Wharfage, tel. 01952/432166.

If you take the southeastward-bound bus from Shrewsbury, you will see, rising on the left, the **Wrekin,** a strange, conical-shaped extinct volcano. A few miles farther on you will enter the wooded gorge of the Severn River. Here sits the world's earliest iron bridge (1774), a monument to the discovery of how to smelt iron ore using coke, rather than charcoal, the technological breakthrough that led Britain to glory as the leading industrial nation and workshop of the world.

★ The **Ironbridge Gorge Museum** has been established around a unique series of industrial sites and monuments spread over 6 square miles and has six component sections: Museum Visitors Center, Museum of Iron, The Iron Bridge, Jackfield Tile Museum, Blists Hill Open-Air Museum, and the Coalport China Museum. Enthusiasts could spend a couple of days here but a good half-day is enough time to take in the major sites. You can also spend a pleasant half hour strolling around the famous bridge, perhaps hunting for Coalport china in the stores that cluster around it. To put this seemingly sleepy little place into its proper 18th-century perspective, start at the **Severn Warehouse,** which has a good selection of literature and an audiovisual show on the gorge's history.

In the summer the museum provides transportation to Coalbrookdale and the **Museum of Iron.** Iron has been produced on this site since the 17th century, and you can see the original blast furnace built by Abraham Darby, who developed the coke process in 1709. The museum in the adjoining Great Warehouse explains the production of iron and steel through a series of displays, models, and exhibits.

Retrace your steps along the river until the graceful arches of the **Iron Bridge** come into view. Although it is now closed to traffic, you can still walk onto the bridge to enjoy the sight of the river snaking through the gorge. The tollhouse on the far side houses an exhibition on the bridge's history and restoration.

Hop on one of the complex's buses to the **Coalport China Museum,** located just a mile farther along the river. Production of Coalport china was transferred many years ago to Stoke-on-Trent, 50 miles to the north, but the 19th-century factory buildings and the bottle-shaped kilns remain here. Inside are exhibits of some of the factory's most beautiful wares, and craftspeople demonstrate their skills.

Above Coalport is **Blists Hill Open-Air Museum,** where you can see old mines, the remains of two enormous furnaces built into the hillside, and the only surviving wrought-iron works in the Western world. But this 42-acre site is particularly fascinating for its re-creation of a Victorian town: There's the doctor's office, the gruesome dentist's chair, the sweet-smelling bakery, the candlemaker's, the sawmill, the printing shop, and the candy store—exactly as they would have appeared in an industrial town in the 19th century.

Although these are the major sites in Ironbridge, there are several more, including **Jackfield Tile Museum,** once the home of Maw & Co., the largest maker of ceramic wall tiles in the world; the **Tar Tunnel,** still oozing natural bitumen; **Rosehill House,** home of the Darby family of ironmasters; and **Rose Cottages.**

For details on all these museums, contact Ironbridge Gorge Museum Trust, Ironbridge, Telford, Shropshire TF8 7AW, tel. 01952/ 433522. Admission ticket to all sites: £8 adults, £7 senior citizens, £5 children, £25 family ticket, valid until all sites have been visited once. Open daily 10–5 (July and Aug. closes at 6).

Lodging
£

Library House. This small hotel, nestled into the hillside in a central location for the Ironbridge museums, was refurbished in 1993. The former darkness is gone; the attractive Victorian style remains. Rooms are well-equipped, and there is a no-smoking policy. *11 Severn Bank, TF8 7AN, tel. 01952/432299, fax 01952/433967. 3 rooms with bath. No credit cards.*

Dining
¢
★

New Inn. So that it could be part of an open-air museum, this Victorian building was moved to Blists Hill from Walsall, 22 miles away. It is a fully functioning pub, with gas lamps, sawdust on the floor, and traditional ales served from the cask. For an inexpensive meal, you can try a ploughman's lunch, a pasty from the antique-style bakery, or a pork pie from the butcher's store next door. *Blists Hill Museum, tel. 01952/453522. No credit cards.*

Tour 3: Manchester

Covering 43 miles and with a population of 450,000, Manchester (at the heart of the much larger Greater Manchester) is a relatively big city. What was once the textile manufacturing center of the world is now a tribute to what civic pride and financial acumen can do. In recent years, the city center has undergone a remarkable transformation, with heavy investment in a new transportation system and impressive sporting and leisure facilities. In part, these changes resulted from successive attempts to bring the Olympic Games to the city: Manchester bid unsuccessfully for the 1996 and, most recently, the 2000 Games (losing out to Sydney, Australia). But despite the great local disappointment at not securing the games for Britain, the bequest to the people of Manchester has been a fine set of civic and sports amenities.

In addition to the city center, where modern developments have been interspersed with lovingly preserved Victorian buildings, Manchester offers a vigorous cultural life, with some of the best theater in the country, as well as Britain's oldest leading orchestra, the Hallé (founded in 1857).

One, or at the most two, full days will allow you to see most of Manchester, and to anyone with an interest in history, art, and urban planning, it will be time well spent.

From London Manchester is amply served by rail links with the whole of Britain.
By Train From London/Euston (tel. 0171/387–7070) there is at least one **InterCity** train every hour; the journey takes 2 hours, 30 minutes. Keep in mind that the main Manchester station is called Piccadilly, which can make things confusing. Call for rail information (tel. 0161/832–8353).

By Bus **National Express** runs six buses a day from London/Victoria Coach Station (tel. 0171/730–0202) to Manchester Coach Station (Chorlton St., tel. 0161/228–3881). Travel time is a little more than 4 hours. There is also a *Rapide* link from Gatwick and Heathrow airports to Manchester and Manchester airport, but it takes well over 6 hours.

By Car To reach Manchester from London, take M1 north to M6, leaving M6 at exit 21a and joining M62 east, which becomes M602 as it enters Greater Manchester. The distance is 185 miles, and driving time is 3 to 3½ hours.

Manchester

Manchester Visitor Centre: Town Hall Extension, Lloyd St., tel. 0161/234–3157.

The mechanization of the cotton industry—the first cotton mill powered by steam opened in 1783—caused the rapid growth of **Manchester;** then, in 1894, the opening of the Manchester Ship Canal turned the world's cotton capital into a major inland port. Until only a few years ago, Manchester was a blackened, forbidding city, unlovely and unloved. But now it has been spruced up, and the once-begrimed buildings in the center of town, masterpieces of sturdy Victorian architecture, have been cleaned. Severe damage caused by World War II bombing has been remedied by modern development, not all of it attractive, and the visitor now sees an expansive center city, which has managed to hang onto at least some of its architectural heritage.

Numbers in the margin correspond to points of interest on the Manchester map.

Within just a few blocks you can visit most of the important sights.
❶ Start at the **City Art Gallery,** a striking neoclassical building hous-

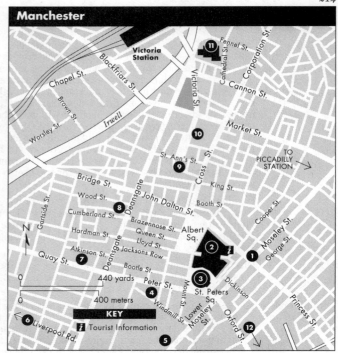

ing a fine collection. Many Manchester industrial barons of the 19th century spent some of their vast wealth buying paintings, and their interests are reflected in the art on display here. Apart from a large collection of Pre-Raphaelites, there are works by Gainsborough, Samuel Palmer, Turner, Claude Lorrain, and Bellotto. A re-creation of the living room and studio of L. S. Lowry—the popular Manchester artist who died in 1976—adds a touch of local interest. *Mosley St., tel. 0161/236–5244. Admission free. Open Mon.–Sat. 10–5:45, Sun. 2–5:45. Free guided tours, weekends at 2:30 PM.*

The City Art Gallery also manages several other exhibit spaces in Manchester, including the **Atheneum Gallery,** next door, a showcase for changing contemporary shows, and the **Gallery of English Costume,** south of the center at Platt Hall in Rusholme. Details of events and exhibitions are available from the City Art Gallery (*see above*).

❷ Two blocks northwest of the Art Gallery is the **Town Hall,** a magnificent Victorian Gothic building (1867–76), with extensions added just before World War II. The Great Hall, with its soaring hammerbeam roof, is decorated with murals of the city's history, painted between 1852 and 1865 by the Pre-Raphaelites' contemporary, Ford Madox Brown. As the Town Hall is used for meetings a great deal, the murals are sometimes covered up to protect them. *Free guided tours Mon., Wed., and Thurs. 10 AM; Wed. 2:30 if there are no meetings in progress.*

❸ To one side of the Town Hall is the **Central Library,** with the Library Theatre (*see* The Arts, *below*) as part of the complex. Turn right at the library onto Peter Street and two blocks down you will find the ❹ **Free Trade Hall,** restored after World War II damage; it has been the home of the Hallé Orchestra for more than a century. The orchestra will soon have a custom-built auditorium of its own. (*see* The Arts, *below*).

❺ South of the Free Trade Hall is the **G-Mex Centre,** formerly the central railroad station, now the city's biggest and brightest exhibition and events center. Follow Great Bridgewater Street and Liverpool Road west, and you'll come to the district of Castlefield, site of an early Roman fort and later the heart of Manchester's first canal and railroad developments. The district has now been restored as **Castlefield Heritage Park.** The gate to the Roman fort has been re-

❻ constructed, and the 7-acre site contains the excellent **Museum of Science and Industry,** which displays in separate buildings (including the world's oldest train station) marvellous collections relating to Manchester's industrial past and present. To walk through a reconstructed Victorian sewer and to examine the world's largest collection of working steam-mill engines is a real thrill. *Castlefield, tel. 0161/832–1830. Admission: £3.50 adults, £1.50 children. Open daily 10–5.*

Walk back down Liverpool Road to Deansgate and head north, and

❼ you'll find the **Opera House** on Quay Street, an ornate refurbished building that hosts major dance and opera companies (*see* The Arts,

❽ *below*). Four blocks north on Deansgate is the **John Rylands Library,** named after a rich weaver whose widow spent his money founding it. Built in a late-Gothic style in the 1890s, the library, which became part of the University of Manchester in 1972, houses one of Britain's most important collections—priceless historic documents and charters, bibles in more than 300 languages, manuscripts dating from the dawn of Christianity, and fine bindings. There are always exhibitions from the collection. *150 Deansgate, tel. 0161/834–5343. Admission free. Open weekdays 10–5:15, Sat. 10–1.*

Up Deansgate toward the River Irwell and on the right, down St.

❾ Ann's Street, you will come upon **St. Ann's Church,** a handsome 1712 building, with *The Descent from the Cross*, a painting by Annibale Carracci (1561–1609). North of the church, on the right side of St.

★ ❿ Ann's Square, is the **Royal Exchange,** once the cotton market, and built with impressive panache. In its echoing bulk it now houses one of the most imaginative theaters in Britain (*see* The Arts, *below*).

To complete this stroll around downtown Manchester, continue

⓫ north up Victoria Street to the **cathedral,** beside the river. Originally the medieval parish church of the city, it became a cathedral in 1847. It's a strange shape, very broad for its length, and contains a few attractive items: early 16th-century choir stalls, with intriguing misericord seats; paintings of the Beatitudes by Carel Weight (1908–89); a sculpture by Eric Gill (1882–1919), famed for the typeface that he designed and which bears his name; a fine brass of Warden Huntingdon, who died in 1458; and an octagonal chapter house from 1485. *Admission free. Open daily 8–6.*

One of the most interesting places to visit outside the center of Man-

⓬ chester is the university-run **Whitworth Gallery,** southeast of town in an area called Moss Side. At the Piccadilly bus depot ask for a bus to the Manchester Royal Infirmary, which is just across the road from the Whitworth. The collections in the gallery are especially strong in British watercolors, old master drawings, and Postimpressionism. Its captivating rooms full of textiles—Coptic and Peruvian cloths, Spanish and Italian vestments, tribal rugs, and contemporary fabrics—are just what you might expect in a city built on textile manufacture. There's the Gallery Bistro for light meals and a good gallery shop. *Oxford Rd., tel. 0161/273–4865. Admission free. Open Mon.–Wed., Fri.–Sat. 10–5, Thurs. 10–9.*

Lodging Most of the hotel accommodation in the city center falls way out of our price range, though there are plenty of guest houses and hotels in the suburbs that lie on good bus routes. First stop should be Manchester Visitor Centre, where personal callers only can use their room-booking service. Apart from the youth hostel (*see below*), the cheapest downtown accommodation available is in one of the city center's pubs (about £20 single, £36 double, B&B); the few small downtown hotels start at £55 double, though the Visitor Centre may be able to find you a standard room, without en-suite facilities, for as little as £30 double, depending on the season. In all cases, the rooms have been inspected by the Visitor Centre; and you pay a 10% deposit on the first night's accommodation, deducted from your final bill.

££ **Willowbank Hotel.** From the outside, the odd-looking architecture is half Victorian stately and half modern cubic; inside it is uniformly comfortable. Situated in a southern neighborhood, with trees and grounds, and near the university, the location is relaxing and appealing. The bedrooms have a modern country look, with lots of wood and plain fabrics; a rolling program of decoration keeps them fresh and bright. Both set menus (lunch £7.50, dinner £10) and à la carte are offered in the restaurant, which features Scottish beef and lamb dishes. Ask for special discounts off room rates on weekends. *340 Wilmslow Rd., Fallowfield, M14 6AF, tel. 0161/224–0461. 10 rooms with bath. Facilities: restaurant, in-house movies. AE, DC, MC, V.*

¢ **Ebor Hotel.** This suburban guest house 3 miles south of the center of town, is situated on good bus routes, and is also convenient for the little pubs around Chorlton Green. The converted Edwardian home offers comfortable-size rooms with TVs and tea/coffeemakers ensuite rooms cost £5 more than standard ones. *402 Wilbraham Rd., Chorlton-cum-Hardy, M21 0UH, tel. 0161/881–1911 or 0161/881–4855. 16 rooms, 8 with showers. MC, V.*

¢ **Manchester Youth Hostel.** The cheapest available downtown accommodation is in Manchester's new youth hostel, but banish any thoughts of institutional deprivation. The purpose-built hostel—in the heart of the city's Castlefield urban heritage district—offers superior budget accommodation in smart, if small, rooms; doubles are available for £12 per person, or you can share 4- or 6-bedded rooms for even less, ideal if you're travelling with a family. *Potato Wharf, off Liverpool Rd., Castlefield, M3 4NB, tel. 0161/839–9960, fax 0161/835–2054. 150 beds. Facilities: café, laundry, games room. No credit cards.*

Dining Manchester has a huge number of restaurants, serving modern British, Continental, and various ethnic cuisines. The city has one of Britain's most vibrant Chinatowns, featuring excellent Cantonese cuisine, while locals and students set great store in the 20-odd Asian restaurants along Wilmslow Road, in the suburb of Rusholme, a few miles south of the city center (easily accessible by bus from Piccadilly). Here you can enjoy Bangladeshi, Pakistani, and Indian food in places ranging from simple cafés where no alcohol is served (though often BYOB) to smart designer restaurants serving rich curries and tandoor-baked breads.

££ **Market Restaurant.** This unpretentious, dinner-only spot is the
★ place to taste some very original British recipes, as well as other interesting in-house creations. Its menu changes monthly with an emphasis on vegetarian dishes; desserts are always inventive. The proprietor, a beer enthusiast, maintains an excellent selection of international bottled beers, as well as an interesting wine list. *104 High St., tel. 0161/834–3743. Reservations essential. Open Wed.–Sat., evenings only; closed Easter, Aug., and 1 week at Christmas. AE, DC, MC, V.*

££ **Yang Sing.** One of Manchester's good Cantonese restaurants, it's popular with Chinese families, always a good sign, but *so* popular that you must reserve ahead. The *dim sum* is always a good bet, and don't forget to ask about the daily specials—they're often only listed in Chinese on the menu. There is also a slightly cheaper offshoot, **Little Yang Sing** (17 George St., tel. 0161/228–7722). This was Manchester's original Yang Sing restaurant; it has a rather cramped basement setting but still serves fine Cantonese food. *34 Princess St., tel. 0161/236–2200. Reservations required. AE, MC, V.*

£ **Café Istanbul.** This is an authentic Turkish place, where you can find Turkish coffee, Turkish pastries, even Turkish wine. It is always popular and has recently expanded its premises. The *meze* are inexpensive and there's a special *meze* menu for those who like to fill up on the multitude of little dishes—*hummus*, stuffed grape leaves, cheese-filled pastries, *taramasalata,* and other treats. *79 Bridge St., tel. 0161/833–9942. Reservations advised. MC, V. Closed Sun.*

£ **Indian Cottage.** While most of Rusholme's many Asian eateries pack diners in for quick (though admittedly excellent) meals, this more upscale, first-floor restaurant, with separate bar area, allows you plenty of time to explore a menu strong on tandoor-baked dishes and breads. A central rock pool and lavish decoration add some spice, but it's the food, among the best in town, that makes the difference. *501 Claremont Rd., corner of Wilmslow Rd., Rusholme, tel. 0161/ 224–0376. Reservations advised. MC, V.*

¢ **Dmitri's.** Set in a covered Victorian arcade, in an old market building, this attractive tapas bar-taverna dispenses its dishes with good cheer to a trendy Manchester set. It's interesting, hybrid menu ranges from Greek and Mediterranean snack dishes to pasta, mixed grills, rice pilafs, and salads. Only the Greek meat and fish specials will take you over the £10 a head mark, but most meals cost well under that; or just come for a glass of wine and a snack. *Campfield Arcade, Tonman St., Deansgate, tel.0161/839–3319. Reservations advised. No credit cards.*

Shopping   The **Manchester Crafts Centre** (17 Oak St., tel. 0161/832–4274) is made up of 18 workshops-cum-retail outlets where you can see potters, jewelers, hatters, theatrical costumers, and metal enamelers at work, and where you can buy the fruits of their labors.

The **Whitworth Art Gallery** (Oxford Rd., tel. 0161/273–4865) has a fine shop that specializes in handmade cards, postcards, and prints. They also sell stationery, art books, jewelry, and ceramics; from time to time there is a potter on the premises. Along the same lines, the **Manchester University Museum shop** (Oxford Rd., tel. 0161/275–2000) offers a similar selection, but specializes in books and imaginative toys for children.

The **Royal Exchange Crafts Centre** (St. Ann's Square, tel. 0161/833–9333), an unusual glass structure in the foyer of the Royal Exchange Theatre, specializes in jewelry, ceramics, glassware, and textiles produced throughout the country. Next door, in the **Royal Exchange Shopping Centre,** the first-floor **Design Centre** stores feature the creations of young fashion designers.

For retro and antique clothing, and cheap and cheerful jewelry and accessories, visit the trendy **Affleck's Palace** (52 Church St., tel. 0161/834-2039), with stores on four floors.

Manchester also has branches of **Hatchards, Waterstones,** and **Dillons** chain booksellers.

The Arts   Manchester has an enviable reputation in the performing arts. Local productions are excellent and inexpensive. Visiting companies—opera and ballet, especially—offer plenty of budget-priced tickets. There are three main theaters in town: the **Opera House** (tel. 0161/ 831–7766), the **Library Theatre** (tel. 0161/236–7110), which stages mostly classic and serious drama, and the **Royal Exchange Theatre** (tel. 0161/833–9333), an extremely inventive acting space with a reputation for daring productions. The airy, tubular steel-and-glass structure, set down in the middle of the vast echoing spaces of this Victorian building, is like a space ship delicately parked in a great cathedral.

The **Hallé Orchestra** performs at the Free Trade Hall (Peter St.), usually between October and May, though it will eventually have its own auditorium; for now, the box office is in Albert Square (tel. 0161/834-1712).

Tour 4: Excursion to Buxton and the Peak District

Although this area is not in the Welsh Borders, it can be easily reached from Manchester (or London). The hub of the tour is the Georgian spa town of Buxton, gateway to the Peak District. Local bus service connects Buxton to the many historic sites in the area. An excellent travel bargain is the Wayfarer ticket, which gives a single day's unlimited travel on buses and trains throughout the region (including greater Manchester) for less than £5.90 and a discount on entry fees to many top attractions. If you'd like to combine a trip to Buxton and its environs with visits to Liverpool, Manchester, Chester, and the North Wales coast, then a seven-day Coast & Peaks Rail Rover ticket (£43) is another money-saving option.

The Peak District National Park is internationally recognized for its conservation activities. The national park centers at Castleton and Edale offer maps and guides covering everything from short strolls to day-long hikes. You can also join a guided hike led by an experienced ranger with detailed knowledge of the region's local and natural history. Also, rambling clubs such as the **Derbyshire County Council** (Programme of Guided Walks, Countryside Section, County Offices, Matlock, tel. 01629/580000) offer organized walks.

From London Take the Manchester train from London's Euston station (tel. 0171/
By Train 387–7070) and change at Stockport for Buxton. Trains depart every hour on the hour, Monday–Saturday, and there is a connecting train hourly from Stockport to Buxton. The total journey time is just under 4 hours.

By Bus **National Express** (tel. 0171/730–0202) serves the region from London's Victoria Coach Station, with one direct departure to Buxton daily at 2 PM. The journey takes a little more than 4 hours.

By Car The principal route north from London, the M1, gets you to the region in about three hours. For the Peak District, leave M1 at Exit 29, then head toward Buxton via the A617/A619/A6020/A6, passing through Chesterfield.

Buxton

Buxton tourist office: The Crescent, tel. 01298/25106. The office is normally open Monday–Saturday 9:30–5:30.

★ **Buxton**'s sheltered position in a great, natural bowl of hills gives it a surprisingly mild climate, considering its altitude: At more than 1,000 feet, it's the second-highest town in England.

The Romans arrived in AD 79 and named Buxton *Aquae Arnemetiae*—loosely translated as "The Waters of the Goddess of the Grove." The mineral springs, which emerge from 3,500 to 5,000 feet below ground at a constant 82°F, were believed to cure a variety of ailments, and in the 18th century established the town as a popular spa, a minor rival to Bath. You can still drink water from the ancient St. Anne's Well (across from The Crescent), and it's also bottled and sold throughout Britain; it's excellent with a good malt whiskey.

Buxton's spa days have left a legacy of 18th- and 19th-century buildings, parks, and open spaces that now give the town an air of faded

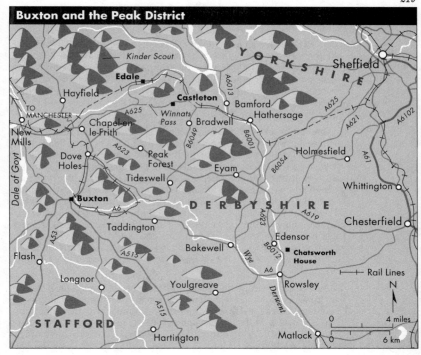

grandeur. A good place to start exploring is **The Crescent** on the northwest side of The Slopes park (the town hall is on the opposite side); almost all out-of-town roads lead toward this central green. The three former hotels that make up the Georgian-era Crescent, with its arches, Doric colonnades, and 378 windows, were built in 1780 by John Carr for the fifth duke of Devonshire (of nearby Chatsworth House). The splendid ceiling of the former assembly room now looks down on the town's public library, and the thermal baths at the end of The Crescent house look out on a shopping center.

The Devonshire Royal Hospital, behind The Crescent, also built by Carr, was originally a stable with room for 110 of the hotel guests' horses. In 1859 the circular area where horses were once exercised was covered with a massive 156-feet-wide dome and incorporated into the hospital.

The Buxton Museum, on the eastern side of The Slopes, has a collection of the rare Blue John stone (amethystine spar; the unusual name is a local corruption of French **bleu-jaune**), a semiprecious mineral found only in the Peak District. In The Crescent itself, **The Buxton Micrarium,** an unusual natural-history museum, features microscopic displays of insects, plants, and other specimens. *The Buxton Museum: Terrace Rd., tel. 01298/24658. Admission £1 adults, 50p senior citizens and children. Open Tues.–Fri. 9:30–5:30; Sat. 9:30–5. The Buxton Micrarium: The Crescent, tel. 01298/78662. Admission: £2.50 adults, £2 senior citizens, £1.50 children. Open 1 wk in mid-Mar. and early Apr.–late Oct., daily 10–5.*

Adjacent to The Crescent and The Slopes on the west is the **Octagon** (part of the Pavilion) with its ornate iron-and-glass roof. The venue, which was erected in the 1870s, is still a lively place, with a conservatory, several bars, a restaurant, and a cafeteria. The surrounding

25 acres of well-kept Pavilion gardens are pleasant to stroll in on a summer's day.

The Parish Church of St. John the Baptist, on St. John's Road, bordering the Pavilion gardens on the north, is in a handsome, Regency-Tuscan-style building dating from 1811, with some extremely fine mosaic and stained glass. A good deal more architecturally exuberant is the **Opera House** on the same road (Water St. end); built in 1903, it's a massive marble structure bedecked with carved cupids and is the center for Buxton's annual festival.

If you follow the Broad Walk through the Pavilion gardens and continue southwest along Temple Road for about half an hour, you'll come to **Poole's Cavern,** a large limestone cave far beneath the 100 wooded acres of Buxton Country Park. Named after a legendary 15th-century robber's lair, the cave was inhabited in prehistoric times and contains, in addition to the standard stalactites and stalagmites, the source of the River Wye, which flows through Buxton. Poole's Cavern was also known to the Romans, who built baths nearby; a display of Roman archaeology as well as a nature trail and visitor center are outside. *Green La., tel. 01298/26978. Admission (including tour): £3.40 adults, £2.70 senior citizens, £1.70 children. Country Park and visitor center free. Open Easter–Nov., daily 10–5. Closed Wed. in Apr., May, and Oct.*

If you're still feeling energetic, walk southeast from Poole's Cavern up to Grin Low. Here **Solomon's Temple,** a Victorian folly—the technical name for a fanciful building, a popular way of dramatizing the landscape—offers panoramic views. (There's a trail, too, from the south side of town, but it's much steeper.) Access to the temple is unrestricted.

Lodging **Lakenham Guest House.** This large Victorian house with a sweeping
¢ garden has been converted into a comfortable, friendly guest house.
★ Bedrooms all enjoy excellent views. The house has a number of attractive pieces of antique furniture, and there's ample parking for guests. *11 Burlington Rd., SK17 9AL, tel. 01298/79209. 6 rooms, 5 with bath. MC, V.*

¢ **Stoneridge Guest House.** The pleasant Victorian building, in a quiet spot near the town center, features modern facilities and evening meals with home cooking. *9 Park Rd., SK17 6SG., tel. 01298/79488. 4 rooms with bath. No credit cards. Closed Christmas.*

Dining **Hay-Way.** Decorated with Victoriana, and with a pretty indoor gar-
£ den area with fountain, The Hay-Way offers a choice of English and French cuisine, such as chicken in a cheese and herb croute. Kids are welcome, and they do a delicious afternoon tea. *35 High St., tel. 01298/78388. Reservations advised. AE, DC, MC, V. Closed Wed. lunch and tea.*

Shopping Buxton is well-stocked with antiques shops and jewelers. **Ratcliffe's** (7 Cavendish Circus, tel. 01298/23993) specializes in, among other things, fine silver cutlery and items made out of the rare Blue John stone.

The Arts Buxton's Opera House, Water St. (tel. 01298/72190) is the focal point of the town's renowned **Festival of Music and the Arts** (Festival Office, 1 Crescent View, Hall Bank, tel. 01298/70395), held during the second half of July and the beginning of August each year. It includes opera, drama, classical concerts, jazz, recitals, and lectures. An amateur drama festival also takes place at the opera house during the summer.

Chatsworth

It is not easy to get to Chatsworth from Buxton by bus, although it is only 16 miles. Take the R1 (running every 2 hours) to Bakewell, and then the 170 (every hour) toward Baslow and ask to be let off at The Cutting so that you can walk through the Chatsworth park, a very pretty stroll on a fine day.

Chatsworth House, ancestral home of the dukes of Devonshire, is one of England's greatest country houses. As you approach, the expanse of parkland, on which graze deer and sheep, opens before you to set off the Palladian elegance of "the Palace of the Peak." Originally an Elizabethan residence, altered by various dukes over several generations starting in 1686, Chatsworth was conceived on a grand, even monumental, scale. It is surrounded by woods, elaborate colorful gardens, greenhouses, rock gardens, cascading water, and terraces—all designed by two great landscape artists, Capability Brown and, later, Joseph Paxton, an engineer as well as a brilliant gardener. Paxton was responsible for most of the eye-catching waterworks. Plan at least half a day to explore the grounds properly, and avoid going on Sunday, when the place is very crowded. A brass band plays in the grounds from June to August.

Inside, the 175 rooms are filled with treasures: intricate carvings, Van Dyck portraits, Rembrandt's *Portrait of an Oriental*, sculptures, tapestries, superb furniture, and china. The magnificent condition of much of the furnishings and decorations is largely due to the dowager duchess, who supervises an ongoing program of in-house repair and restoration. Home-cooked refreshments are available in the Coach Drivers' Rest Room. *Bakewell, tel. 01246/582204. Admission: £5.75 adults, £5 senior citizens, £3 children, £15 family ticket; Garden only: £3 adults, £2.25 senior citizens, £1.50 children, £8 family ticket. Open late Mar.–late Oct., daily; house 11–4:30, garden 11–5. Jun.–Aug garden open 10:30–5.*

Castleton

Buses run from Buxton to Castleton on Tuesday, Thursday, and Friday afternoons, but there is no return service until the next morning. On Sunday and bank holiday Mondays buses make the 40-minute journey several times daily each way May–September.

Castleton, a town in the Hope Valley, which also tends to be crowded in the peak season, is somewhat commercialized, but is worth a visit if only to see the ruins of **Peveril Castle** on a crag to the south of town. Built in the late-12th century, there are superb views of the Peak District from here. *Tel. 01433/620613. Admission: £1.30 adults, £1 senior citizens. 70p children. Open Apr.–Oct., daily 10–6; Oct.–Mar. daily 10–4.*

Another interesting natural feature is the massive **Peak Cavern** (under the castle), where rope has been made on a great ropewalk for more than 400 years. A prehistoric village has been excavated here as well. *Tel. 01433/620285. Admission: £3 adults, £1.75 senior citizens and children. Open Apr.–Oct., daily 10–5; Nov.–Mar., Tues.–Sun. 10–5.*

Castleton has a number of other caves and mines open to the public, including some former lead mines and Blue John mines. Try to visit the **Speedwell Cavern** at the bottom of Winnats Pass, two miles west of Castleton, the only mine in England you can tour by boat, traveling 840 feet below ground through great illuminated caverns to reach the "Bottomless Pit." There is also an exhibition and a store selling Blue John jewelry. *Tel. 01433/620512. Admission: £4.50 adults, £3.50 senior citizens, £2.75 children under 14. Open daily 9:30–5:30 (Nov.–Mar. to 4:30). Closed Christmas Day.*

Lodging **Ye Olde Nags Head Hotel.** This Old World hotel has lovely rooms,
££ three with four-poster beds and one with a spa bathroom. Open log fires blaze in the public bar, which serves a selection of ales and bar food, and the dining room is open to nonguests for lunch and dinner.

*S30 2WH, tel. 01433/620248, fax 01433/621604. 8 rooms with bath.
Facilities: restaurant/bar, coffee lounge. AE, DC, MC, V.*

Edale

*Buses run frequently from Castleton bus station to Bamford (about
20 minutes away), where hourly trains will take you on the 10-minute trip to Edale.*

If you're interested in hiking, make your way to **Edale,** a sleepy village in the shadow of Mam Tor and Lose Hill, and the moorlands of
Kinder Scout. This extremely popular walking center is the starting
point of the 250-mile Pennine Way. The Edale information center
has maps, guides, and information on walks in the area. *Tel. 01433/
70207. Open Easter–Oct., daily 9–1 and 2–5:30; Nov.–Mar., daily
9–1 and 2–5.*

Lodging **Stonecroft Hotel.** This charming, licensed country-house style hotel
£ is situated at the start of the Pennine Way and has a no-smoking policy. Well-furnished, pretty bedrooms, with TVs, are complete with
armchairs to enjoy the wonderful views. The owners are specialists
in walking and cycling holidays. Meals—with many good vegetarian
options—are hearty and home-cooked; they're ideal for filling up after a long walk. The hotel will also happily cater to those with special diets, if informed in advance. Dinner costs £12.50. *Grindsbrook,
S30 2ZA, tel. 01433/670262. 3 rooms, none with bath. Facilities: dining room, bar, lounge. MC, V. Closed Christmas.*

¢ **Rambler Inn.** This attractive, stone hotel, located above a pub next
to the railway station, is in an ideal central location for those enjoying a walking holiday. The simple rooms have TVs, and evening
meals are available in the dining room. Breakfast costs extra but is
well worth the outlay: £3.95 for a fine full English breakfast, vegetarian if you prefer. *Lane Head Green, S30 2ZA, tel. 01433/670268. 8
rooms, none with bath. AE, MC, V.*

9 Wales

Cardiff, Aberystwyth, Llandudno, Beaumaris

Fewer than 5% of American visitors to Britain take in Wales, and many of those do so only on their way to the ferry for Ireland. But to neglect Wales is to miss some of Britain's most dramatic scenery and most hospitable people. Though often compared to England or Scotland, Wales is unique, with its own startling landscapes at every turn, and impressive, spirited personalities in every character you'll meet.

Despite being dominated by England for centuries, Wales has managed to conserve its Celtic essence by clinging to its history, legends, and language with fierce, stubborn pride. The Welsh will not thank you for confusing their country with England and doing so is one of the worst insults you can offer them. As Wales has a prince all its own—Prince Charles—it is called a principality, the only section of Britain to be so named.

Welsh History The Welsh are a Celtic race. Although the Romans made sporadic attempts to subdue Wales, the people were never Romanized as, later, they were never Anglicized. When, toward the middle of the first millennium AD, the Anglo-Saxons spread through Britain, they pushed the indigenous Celts farther back into their Welsh mountain holds. (In fact, "Wales" comes from the Saxon word "Weallas," which means "strangers," the impertinent name given by the new arrivals to the natives. The Welsh, however, have always called themselves "Y Cymry," "the companions.") The Normans made attempts to extend their influence over Wales in the 11th century, but it was not until the fearsome English king Edward I (1272–1307) waged a brutal and determined campaign to conquer Wales that English supremacy was established. Welsh hopes were finally crushed with the death in battle of Llywelyn ap Gruffudd, the last native prince of Wales, in 1282. Dreams of nationhood were revived under the brilliant and popular leadership of Owain Glyndwr between 1400 and 1410. He ruled virtually the whole of Wales at one point, but English might prevailed again.

Crewe

Liverpool
Wallasey
Birkenhead
Hoylake
Ellesmere Port
Chester
R. Mersey

Wrexham
Ellesmere
Wem
Shrewsbury
Severn

Llangollen
Chirk
B5000

Welshpool
Montgomery
Church Stretton
A483

Talacre
Prestatyn
Rhyl
Holywell
R. Dee
A55

Denbigh
Ruthin
A525
A542
Corwen
Glyn Ceiriog
Ceiriog
Tanat
Llanfyllin
Powis Castle
Newtown
Bishop's Castle

Llandudno
Colwyn Bay
Abergele
Bodnant Garden
Conwy
A470
Betws-y-Coed
Brenig Res.
A5
A525
B4501
A5
Bala
Llanhaeadr ym Mochnant
B4391
B4580
Llanidloes
A44
A470

Irish Sea

Conwy Bay
Bangor
Snowdonia National Park
A5
Capel Curig
A4086
Blaenau Ffestiniog
A212
Trawsfynydd
A470
Llyn Tegid/Bala Lake
Lake Vyrnwy
B4394
A458
MOUNTAINS
Dolgellau
Dovey
A44

Caernarfon
Llanberis
Snowdon
Ffestiniog
B5013
A4573
B4391
A496
Snowdonia National Park
Cadair Idris
A493
Machynlleth
A487

Beaumaris
Menai Strait
ISLE OF ANGLESEY
A5
Penygroes
A499

Portmeirion
Porthmadog
Tremadog Bay
Harlech
Barmouth
Barmouth Bay
Tywyn
Borth

Amlwch

Holyhead

Caernarfon Bay

LLYN PENINSULA
Pwllheli
A497

Cardigan Bay

Aberystwyth

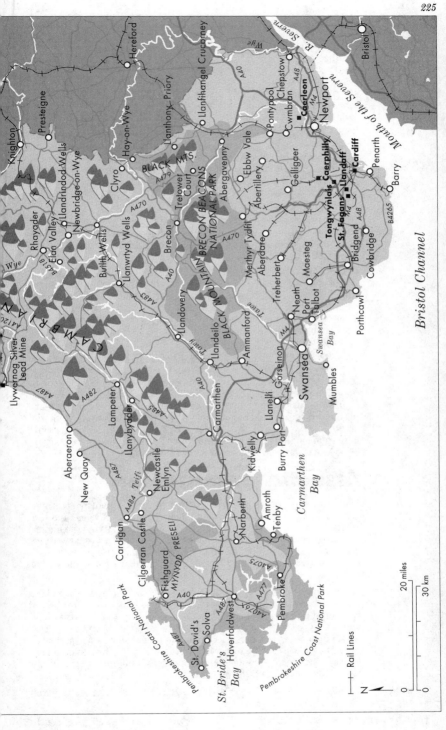

Bristol Channel

Mouth of the Severn

Rail Lines

20 miles

30 km

N

In the 15th and 16th centuries, the Tudor kings Henry VII and Henry VIII continued England's ruthless domination of the Welsh, principally by attempting to abolish their language. Ironically it was another Tudor monarch, Elizabeth I, who ensured its survival by authorizing a Welsh translation of the Bible in 1588. Today, many people still say they owe their knowledge of Welsh to the Bible. The language is spoken by only a fifth of the population, but it still flourishes, especially in parts of the north, where you'll find it's the first language, if not the only one, spoken. Signs are bilingual, too.

The Welsh Language The language is just one key to Wales's distinctiveness. English speakers—the vast majority of the country's 2.75 million inhabitants—regard themselves as being just as Welsh as anyone else, which sometimes leads to differences of opinion, mainly about cultural affairs. But, despite the disputes over language, there exists a deep-rooted attachment to Wales and a widespread sense of identity.

Pronouncing Welsh correctly can be tongue-twisting, although since it is almost entirely phonetic, it's not as difficult as it looks. The best way to learn is to ask a friendly local—your interest will be appreciated.

One useful—and interesting—feature of the language is the way in which place-names often tell you a great deal about the physical surroundings and, sometimes, their historical associations. Many, for example, begin with *aber*, which means "rivermouth or confluence." Thus Aberystwyth means mouth of the river Ystwyth. Another very common place-name component is *llan*, which means "church or enclosure," so Llandudno means "The church of St. Tudno."

Other Welsh terms that crop up frequently in place-names include *bach* or *fach* (small), *blaen* (head, end, source), *bryn* (hill), *bwlch* (pass), *cefn* (ridge), *craig* or *graig* (rock), *cwm* (valley), *cymer* (meeting of rivers), *dyffryn* (valley), *eglwys* (church), *glyn* (glen), *llyn* (lake), *llys* (court, hall), *maen* (stone), *mawr* or *fawr* (great, big), *merthyr* (church, burial place), *moel* or *foel* (bare hill), *mynydd* or *fynydd* (mountain, moorland), *pen* (head, top, end), *pentre* (village, homestead), *plas* (hall and mansion), *pont* or *bont* (bridge), *sarn* (causeway, old road), and *ystrad* (valley floor).

Essential Information

Unfortunately, getting around Wales by public transport is not easy. The regular trains run around the edges, as it were, and the Little Trains of Wales (*see* Train Travel, *below*) penetrate the mountains, but do not connect with each other, making it necessary to use other means of transport as well. There are major bus routes around the principality, but you will need to plan in advance and allow a lot of time.

By Car Wales may be the exception to the Affordable Guide rule of public transportation. This is a part of Britain where the cost of renting a car would be amply repaid by having the ability to explore at will and reaching the remoter parts that public transport cannot. A car would also allow you access to some of the farmhouse accommodations that are off the beaten track but inexpensive (breakfast and a hearty dinner may be included in room fees) and quite representative of the scenery and the people.

Car-Rental Agencies **Cardiff: Avis,** 14–22 Tudor St., tel. 01222/342111; **Hertz,** 9 Central Sq., tel. 01222/224548.

Train Travel British Rail's **Regional Railways** service covers the valleys of south Wales, west Wales, central Wales, the Conwy Valley, and the north Wales coast (for details tel. 01222/228000). Many of these regional lines are highly scenic: the **Cambrian Coast Railway,** for example (70 mi, between Aberystwyth and Pwllheli), and the **Heart of Wales** line (95 mi, Swansea–Craven Arms, near Shrewsbury). You can buy three-day and seven-day unlimited-travel **Rail Rover** tickets for All-Wales and north and mid-Wales, which include travel on some of Wales's Great Little Trains and certain bus services.

Wales is undoubtedly the best place in Britain for narrow-gauge steam railways. The **Great Little Trains of Wales,** for instance, operate during the summer months through the mountains of Snowdonia and central Wales. Many of these lines wind through landscapes of extraordinary grandeur; for example, the **Ffestiniog Railway,** which links two British Rail lines, Blaenau climbs the mountainside in an ascending loop more reminiscent of the Andes than rural Britain. Tiny, copper-knobbed engines, panting fiercely, haul narrow carriages packed with tourists through deep cuttings and along rocky shelves above ancient oak woods through the heart of the Snowdonia National Park from the little harbor of Porthmadog to the old slate town of Blaenau Ffestiniog; other lines include: the **Talyllyn,** following a deep valley from the coastal resort of Tywyn; the **Vale of Rheidol Railway,** from Aberystwyth to Devil's Bridge; the **Welshpool and Llanfair Light Railway,** between Welshpool and Llanfair Caereinion; the **Welsh Highland Railway** from Porthmadog; the **Brecon Mountain Railway** from Merthyr Tydfil; and the **Llanberis Lake Railway.**

Wanderer tickets are available for unlimited travel on the Great Little Trains of Wales: four days, £24; eight days, £33; children, half price. Full details, including summary timetables, are available from **Great Little Trains of Wales** (c/o The Station, Llanfair Caereinion, Powys SY21 0SF, tel. 01938/810441).

Snowdonia also has Britain's only Alpine-style steam rack railway, the **Snowdon Mountain Railway,** where little sloping boilered engines on rack-and-pinion track push their trains 3,000 feet up from Llanberis to the summit of Snowdon, Wales's highest mountain. Details of services can be obtained from **Snowdon Mountain Railway** (Llanberis, Caernarfon, Gwynedd, tel. 01286/870223).

Bus Travel Although the overall pattern is a little fragmented and service is sometimes infrequent, most parts of the country are accessible by bus. The main operators include: **Cardiff Bus** (tel. 01222/396521), **Newport Transport** (tel. 01633/262914), **Red and White** (tel. 01633/265100), and **South Wales Transport** (tel. 01792/475511) for south Wales; **Crosville Wales** (tel. 01492/592111) for mid- and north Wales.

Crosville offers **Day Rover** and **Weekly Rover** tickets and also operates long distance. Its main **TrawsCambria** service runs daily between Cardiff and Bangor, calling at Swansea, Carmarthen, Aberystwyth, Dolgellau, and Caernarfon. Another route connects Wrexham and Aberystwyth, calling at Llangollen, Corwen, Bala, Dolgellau, and Machynlleth.

A good way of seeing Wales is by local tour bus. In summer, there's a large choice of day and half-day excursions to most parts of Wales. Ask at a tourist information center or bus station for details.

Lodging A 19th-century dictum, "I sleeps where I dines" still holds true in Wales. Good hotels and good restaurants mostly go together, and since conversion is the rage, castles, country mansions, farmhouses, and even workhouses and small railroad stations are being transformed into hotels and restaurants. Traditional inns remain the country's pride, but they tend to be off the beaten track and you will need a car or bicycle to make the most of them. Probably one of the nicest experiences you'll have in Wales will be if you lodge in a farmhouse (many are working farms), where you'll be invited to take your meals with the family and other guests.

Cardiff and the other large towns are well supplied with bed-and-breakfasts, which are friendly and very reasonably priced. Indeed, generally speaking, lodging in Wales is among the best value in Britain. For the lowest rates of all, consider youth hostels (YHA, 1 Cathedral Rd., Cardiff, CF1 9HA, tel. 01222/396766). Highly recommended establishments are indicated by a star ★.

Dining In recent years there has been a revolution in dining out in Wales. Many restaurants now are of an extremely high standard and usually are not as expensive as those across the border. Salmon from local rivers, seafood, and Welsh lamb are all cooked in the traditional way, and there is often an emphasis on fresh, home-produced food. Imaginative appetizers and an amazing range of desserts are also served. Look for the sign "Blas ar Cymru" ("A Taste of Wales"), which means that the establishment produces traditional Welsh specialties. Unless otherwise noted, reservations are not needed and dress is casual. Highly recommended restaurants are indicated by a star ★.

Biking Anyone desiring to cycle in Wales should certainly consult the tourist board, which will tell you how to obtain a copy of the *Activity Wales* magazine listing information on a wide range of sports, activities, and pastimes. Tourist Information Centers should be good sources of advice for suitable and scenic cycling routes, together with details of local bike rentals. If you're a serious cyclist, you won't want to miss the beauty and challenge of biking through Snowdonia National Park. Because much of the principality is mountainous, it should be tackled only by experienced bikers. The rewards, though, are tremendous, with breathtaking views. If you really want to get off the beaten track, mountain biking is now a very popular pastime in Wales. Rhayader and Llanwrtyd Wells, two mid-Wales towns surrounded by wild uplands, are particularly good centers.

Hiking The **Ramblers' Association** (Ty'r Cerddwyr, High St., Gresford, Wrexham, Clwyd LL12 8PT, tel. 01978/855148) can supply you with information on walking in Wales. Local tourist information centers have information on guided walks; those in **Snowdonia National Park** (tel. 01766/770274) are among the most spectacular, although also the most dangerous. One of the longest (and hardest) official trails in Wales is **Glyndwr's Way,** 121 miles from Knighton to Welshpool, with some spectacular panoramic views along the route. The **Pembrokeshire Coast Path** starts 2 miles northwest of St. Dogmael's and stretches 180 miles around the **Pembrokeshire Coast National Park** (tel. 01437/764591) to Amroth, which is near Saundersfoot, right back in Carmarthen Bay. You can join or leave the path at several points, mostly where inns are available for overnight stops, and there is also a special bus service linking the particularly interesting stretches. Rolling hills and open moorlands await hikers in the **Brecon Beacons National Park,** a 519-square-mile area containing some of the most beautiful scenery in southeast Wales. Contact the **Brecon Beacons Mountain Centre** (tel. 01874/623366) for suggested routes and further information. Another good walk is the **Offa's Dyke Footpath** (tel. 01547/528753), which follows the 8th-century border between Wales and England.

Beaches Wales has some of the best and cleanest beaches in Britain. Much of the coast of the **Isle of Anglesey** and around **Llandudno** in the north, the **Llŷn Peninsula,** the mouth of the **River Dyfi** on the west coast, the south coast near Dylan Thomas's **Laugharne,** and the **Gower Peninsula** west of Swansea have sandy beaches, some of them golden. Many of the beaches in the popular north and south coast resorts are crowded in summer, and in several areas, such as the section of coast east of Colwyn Bay in the north, you will see miles of unattractive trailer parks, where families keep their caravans all year.

The Arts and Nightlife Wales has two of the best-regarded theater companies in Britain: The **Theatr Clwyd** performs repertory drama of a very high standard at Mold, east of Denbigh, and the **Welsh National Opera** mounts internationally famed productions at its home in Cardiff and tours them around the principality and in England. It's also possible that you'll come upon this company performing in a movie theater in the boondocks, where tickets will be cheaper than in the bigger centers.

The Welsh are essentially a musical people and an evening spent listening to a local choir can be unexpectedly thrilling and certainly inexpensive.

Festivals One of Britain's leading festivals, the **Llangollen International Musical Eisteddfod** (eisteddfod means "gathering"), attracts performers from all over the world to this pretty borderland town in July.

The **Royal National Eisteddfod** of Wales is an important annual event that will take place August 3–10 in 1996. Every aspect of the arts is represented, including modern dance, ballet, and folk dancing; competitions for solo voice and choral singing; nightly concerts by various orchestral groups, including the BBC Welsh Symphony Orchestra and the Welsh Youth Orchestra; poetry readings and literature competitions; and crafts displays including Welsh pottery. The festival will be held in Llandeilo, Dyfed, tel. 01222/763777.

Tourist Information The tourist information offices are trying to encourage travel to Wales, and they will likely be most helpful with any matters you may present to them. In the United States, consult the **Wales Tourist Board** through the British Tourist Authority (*see* Before You Go *in* Chapter 1). There is a major Welsh information office in London: **The Wales Bureau** (The British Travel Centre, 12 Lower Regent St., Piccadilly Circus, London, SW1 4PQ, tel. 0171/409–0969). In Cardiff contact **The Wales Tourist Board** main administrative office (Brunel House, 12th Fl., 2 Fitzalan Rd., Cardiff, CF2 1UY, tel. 01222/499909) and **Cadw: Welsh Historic Monuments** (Brunel House, 2 Fitzalan Rd., Cardiff, CF2 1UY, tel. 01222/465511). These two offices are administrative headquarters and do not encourage personal callers. For drop-in information, try the city **Tourist Information Center** (Central Station, Cardiff, tel. 01222/227281). If you are interested in history and intend visiting a few Welsh castles, it is well worth purchasing the **Cadw Explorer Pass,** which allows unlimited access to most of Wales's historic sites. The seven-day pass costs £12 (single adult), £17 (two adults) or £21 (family ticket); the three-day pass costs £7, £12, and £17 respectively. Passes are available from Cadw sites.

Tour 1: Cardiff and Environs

Cardiff is the most Anglicized of Wales's two cities, and you will rarely hear Welsh spoken here. It is a lively, interesting place with plenty to see, and you should make it your first port of call, especially if you opt to use only public transportation. However, don't make the mistake of visiting Cardiff without taking in any other parts of the principality—the coast or inland—the city alone does not offer a true picture of Wales. Cardiff is easy to get to from London and has an excellent range of museums and bookshops with lots of information on Wales. Additionally, as the Welsh capital city it is the obvious place to begin your tour of the rest of the country.

If you stay overnight, there are plenty of B&Bs, especially along Cathedral Road, a long stretch of large Victorian houses that leads from the center of town toward the suburb of Llandaff. The buses in and around Cardiff are much cheaper than those in most of England, and the suburban rail network is efficient.

From London There is an excellent **InterCity** service to Cardiff Central from Lon-
By Train don/Paddington (tel. 0171/262–6767), with 20 trains daily making the trip in under 2 hours. There are also **Regional Railways** services that operate from other parts of the country, including Birmingham, Brighton, Bristol, Liverpool, Manchester, Portsmouth, and Southampton. For more information, call the recorded information service in Cardiff (tel. 01222/228000).

By Bus **National Express** has a *Rapide* Bus 509 that departs from London/Victoria Coach Station (tel. 0171/730–0202) and stops off at Cardiff Central. The buses run the trip (which takes about 3½ hours) six or seven times daily. Another *Rapide* Bus, No. 201, links Cardiff with Heathrow and Gatwick airports. For information call the office in Cardiff (tel. 01222/344751).

By Car The M4 due west from London (155 miles) passes just north of Cardiff. The motorway network feeds into M4 from other parts of the country.

Cardiff

Cardiff is well served by bus companies, with frequent trips on all routes and low fares. Most of the buses originate at the Bus Station (tel. 01222/396521 for Cardiff Bus) on Wood Street. A Capital Ticket (£3 adults, £1.80 children) gives you unlimited travel for one day around the city and its environs. A family ticket, for weekends and public holidays, costs £4. All the attractions in and around Cardiff can be easily reached by local bus.

Cardiff has been the Welsh capital since 1956. Although the city's history is long—it was settled by the Romans and used by the Normans as a strategic fortress—it wasn't until the Industrial Revolution and the arrival of the railroad in the 19th century that the city suddenly began to expand. As heavy industry declined in this century, Cardiff diversified as an administrative and commercial center. It is now a city of office blocks, not bustling docklands, though the old waterfront is undergoing an ambitious restoration.

Begin your exploration at Cardiff's **castle**, easily the city's oldest central building, which is located in Bute Park—one section of Cardiff's hundreds of acres of parkland. The castle is a mishmash of periods: Parts of the walls are Roman, the solid keep is Norman, and the whole complex was restored more than 100 years ago by the third marquess of Bute. Bute employed William Burges (1827–81), an architect obsessed by the Gothic period, to carry out the work, and Burges transformed the castle inside and out into an extravaganza of medieval color and detailed craftsmanship. It's well worth a visit. *Tel. 01222/822083. Admission: guided tour of the castle, £3.50 adults, £1.70 senior citizens and children, £6.60 family ticket (not available high season); grounds only, £2.20 adults, £1.10 senior citizens and children, £4.40 family ticket. Open May–Sept., daily 10–6; Mar., Apr., Oct., daily 10–5; Nov.–Feb., daily 10–4:30.*

Two blocks east of the castle is Cardiff's **Civic Centre**, a well-designed complex of civic buildings that boast impressive Portland stone facades. City Hall, the National Museum of Wales, the Law Courts, the Welsh Office (seat of government), and the university campus are all located here. The city tourist office organizes walking tours of the Civic Centre throughout the summer.

The **National Museum of Wales** could take several hours to explore properly. It sets out to tell the story of Wales through its plants, rocks, archaeology, art, and industry, and also has a fine collection of modern European art, especially Postimpressionist works. Don't miss *La Parisienne* by Renoir. The museum has a convenient cafeteria on the top floor. *Main Building, Cathays Park, tel. 01222/ 397951. Admission: £2.50 adults, £1.85 senior citizens, £1.25 children, £6.25 family ticket. Open Tues.–Sat. 10–5, Sun. 2:30–5.*

South of the Civic Centre, with its tree-lined avenues, are the shopping and business areas of Cardiff. Here you will find a large, modern shopping mall that includes **St. David's Hall.** One of Europe's best modern concert halls, with outstanding acoustics, St. David's hosts performances in classical music, jazz, rock, ballet—even snooker championships. This popular spot also includes a coffee bar and a restaurant.

The **Welsh Industrial and Maritime Museum** (tel. 01222/481919) is located in the old dockland, amid the waterfront redevelopment. There's also an interesting hands-on science and technology center here, known as **Techniquest** (tel. 01222/460211).

Lodging **Clare Court.** This small, recently refurbished family-run hotel is
  £ within strolling distance of the city center and quite close to the Cardiff Central rail station. Bedrooms are equipped with TVs and tea/coffee-making facilities. You may request an evening meal. *46–48 Clare Rd., CF1 7QP, tel. 01222/344839, fax 01222/665856. 8 rooms with bath. AE, MC, V.*

  £ **Ferrier's Hotel.** Larger than most B&Bs, this newly refurbished,
  ★ family-run guest house on Cathedral Road—where every other house seems to take in guests—stands out. If mobility is a problem, ask for one of the seven ground-floor bedrooms. All the guest rooms have TVs and tea/coffee-making facilities. There is also a well-stocked bar, and light meals are available. *130–132 Cathedral Rd., CF1 9LQ, tel. and fax 01222/383413. 26 rooms, 6 with bath or shower. AE, DC, MC, V.*

  £ **Town House.** Gregarious American couple Bart and Iris Zuzik run
  ★ this immaculate guest house, the best B&B in Cardiff, on Cathedral Road within walking distance of the city center. Their tall Victorian home has been tastefully converted, with neat, well-equipped bedrooms. Guests enjoy traditional British or American breakfasts in the beautifully appointed dining room. No evening meals are served. *70 Cathedral Rd., Cardiff, S. Glamorgan CF1 9LL, tel. 01222/ 239399, fax 01222/223214. 6 rooms with bath. No credit cards.*

  £ **Wynford Hotel.** The drawing card of this hotel is its central location
  ★ and friendly atmosphere. It may be a little noisy for some, but you have the luxury here of an on-site bistro, a restaurant, and two bars. The bedrooms have TVs. *Clare St., CF1 8SD, tel. 01222/371983, fax 01222/340477. 29 rooms with bath. MC, V.*

Dining **Armless Dragon.** A windowfront full of plants enlivens this bright,
  ££ friendly restaurant, popular with the university crowd. Seafood dishes are always a good bet here; much of the fish comes from local waters. For an even more uniquely Welsh flavor, try a laverburger, made out of seaweed. *97 Wyeverne Rd., Cathays, tel. 01222/382357. Reservations advised. Closed Sat. lunch, Sun. and Mon. AE, DC, MC, V.*

  ££ **Blas ar Gymru.** If you want to immerse yourself in Welsh ambience,
  ★ this is the place to go. Aptly named (it translates to "A Taste of Wales"), this is one of the leading restaurants in the principality to offer a Welsh menu. Waitresses in traditional costume further the nationalistic theme. Your meal could begin with laverbread (made with seaweed) and bacon, then continue with a main course of Lady Llanover salt duck with onion sauce, lean Welsh lamb cooked in honey cider and ginger, or a poacher's pie, a delicious beef, rabbit, chicken, and game dish served in a rich wine sauce and topped with flaky pastry. To round the meal off there is a wide selection of Welsh cheeses, including ewe's cheese marinated in mead. Welsh wines and Welsh whisky are served, too. For the budget-conscious, there's a

three-course lunchtime menu for about £10. *48 Crwys Rd., tel. 01222/382132. Reservations advised. AE, MC, V. Closed Sun. and Sat. lunch.*

££ **Le Cassoulet.** A genuinely French restaurant, decorated with
★ touches of red and black, Le Cassoulet sits in the maze of Victorian streets west of Cathedral Road. Try the namesake cassoulet for a filling meal. The patron/chef also creates a very tasty fish soup. Try the good-value lunchtime menu (dinner is more expensive). *5 Romilly Cres., tel. 01222/221905. Reservations advised. Closed Sat. lunch, Sun., and Mon. AE, MC, V.*

Shopping The central shopping area of Cardiff is bright, busy, and brash, with branches of almost all the main British chain stores and a few specifically Welsh shops. Pedestrianized Queen Street runs centrally through the area, with several large shopping malls leading off it, among them: **St. David's Centre, Queen's West Centre, Capitol Exchange,** and the **Queens Arcade.** This latter complex, the latest addition to the shopping scene, is in architectural terms a modern interpretation of the beautiful Victorian arcades of Cardiff—traditional canopied thoroughfares lined with small shops that weave their way through the modern center. A traditional indoor **Central Market** on St. Mary Street—full of local color—is worth a visit. For traditional souvenirs, look for the **Lovespoon Gallery** (Castle St.) and **Things Welsh** (3–7 Duke St. Arcade). Drop by the **Old Library Craft Centre** at The Hayes (close to St. David's Hall) for modern crafts, which range widely in price.

The Arts In addition to St. David's Hall, Cardiff has many venues for the arts. The **New Theatre** (Park Pl., tel. 01222/394844), an Edwardian building, is the home of the **Welsh National Opera** and host to touring shows as well. **Sherman Theatre** (Senghennydd Rd., tel. 01222/230451) stages a wide range of productions in its two auditoriums. Tickets here are generally very reasonable. The informal, lively **Chapter Arts Centre** (Market Rd., Canton, tel. 01222/396061) has movie houses, galleries, a theater, and bars.

Llandaff

From Cardiff Central, take Bus 21A, 33, or 133, which run daily every 30 minutes, to Llandaff, 2 miles away (restricted Sunday service).

Just across the River Taff is the suburb of **Llandaff,** which retains its original village atmosphere. It can be reached by bus, but is also a pleasant 40-minute walk from Cardiff. Cross the river and follow Cathedral Road for about 2 miles. This part of Cardiff has maintained much of its individuality, with a village green and some pretty houses, and is worth wandering around in for an hour. Take the flight of steps that runs up through the trees from the side of the **Llandaff Cathedral,** which was completely renovated after serious bomb damage in World War II. Inside is an overwhelming statue by Jacob Epstein (1880–1959), entitled *Christ in Majesty.* The massive figure on a great cylinder is supported high over the center of the nave on a freestanding arch. The cathedral also has some Pre-Raphaelite works.

St. Fagans

Bus 32 leaves Cardiff's central bus station for St. Fagans (4 miles away) at irregular intervals throughout the day.

★ At the open-air **Welsh Folk Museum** in **St. Fagans,** on 100 acres of parkland and gardens, lie farmhouses, cottages, and terraced houses that show the evolution of Welsh building styles. Visitors can also view an Elizabethan mansion, built within the walls of a Norman castle. There are craft workshops, a saddler, cooper, blacksmith, and woodturner; demonstrations of these country skills are given during the summer. Special events are held during the year to highlight ancient rural festivals—May Day, Harvest, and Christmas among them. There is a cafeteria, a coffee tavern, restaurants, and a museum shop. *Tel. 01222/569441. Admission: £4 adults, £3 senior citizens, £2 children, £10 family ticket. Open daily 10–5.*

Castell Coch in Tongwynlais

Buses 26 and 136 depart from Cardiff's central bus station for the village of Tongwynlais, just 6 miles away. It's a short walk up to the castle.

★ On a hill above the village of Tongwynlais is **Castell Coch,** the Red Castle. It was built on the site of a medieval castle in the 1870s around the time that Ludwig of Bavaria was creating his fantastic dream castles, and it could almost pass for one of them. But the castle was actually a collaboration of the third marquess of Bute and William Burges, whose work can be seen at Cardiff Castle. Here Burges re-created everything—architecture, furnishings, carvings, murals—in a remarkable exercise in Victorian-Gothic whimsy. *Tel. 01222/810101. Admission: £2 adults, £1.50 senior citizens and children. Open late Mar.–late Oct., daily 9:30–6:30; late Oct.–late Mar., Mon.–Sat. 9:30–4, Sun. 2–4.*

Caerphilly

Caerphilly can be reached by frequent trains from Cardiff Central in about 19 minutes. Caerphilly Tourist Information Center: Old Police Station, Park Lane, tel. 01222/851378.

Standing in 30 acres of grounds, 5 miles northeast of Castell Coch, are the substantial ruins of one of Britain's biggest and most impres-
★ sive medieval fortresses. **Caerphilly Castle** was the height of defensive design when it was built (and rebuilt after swift destruction) in the 13th century. The moat has survived, as well as one Pisa-like leaning tower. There are two exhibitions to visit: "Castles of Wales" in the northwest tower, and a display on the history of Caerphilly in the outer gate. *Tel. 01222/883143. Admission: £2 adults, £1.50 senior citizens and children. Open late Mar.–late Oct., daily 9:30–6:30; late Oct.–late Mar., Mon.–Sat. 9:30–4, Sun. 2–4.*

Caerleon

Situated just 2 miles away from Newport, this town can be reached by the Newport Transport (tel. 01633/262914) Bus 2 from Newport Bus Station. From Cardiff take a train to Newport (just 15 minutes away), or you can catch one of several buses. Caerleon Tourist Information Center: High St., tel. 01633/430777.

Caerleon, east of Cardiff, was built over the ruins (dating to AD 75) of a major Roman military base, then known as Isca. It was the headquarters of the Second Augustan Legion, heavy infantry, for more than 200 years. The remains to be seen here are the Fortress Baths, whose concrete vaults once stood 60 feet high; the Amphitheatre, which was originally designed to seat 5,000 spectators; the Barracks, the only one on view anywhere in Europe; and a museum that displays objects found at the site. *Tel. 01633/422518. Admission: Amphitheatre and Baths each £1.50 adults, £1 children and senior citizens. Open late Mar.–late Oct., daily 9:30–6:30; late Oct.–late Mar., Mon.–Sat. 9:30–4, Sun. 2–4.*

Dining **Bagan Tandoori Restaurant.** Tandoori and Indian regional curries
£ are served here, as well as English dishes. It is an attractive and comfortable restaurant, and all meals are well cooked and presented: Lobster Dilruba is the house specialty, and Indian wines are

available. *2 Cross St., tel. 01633/430086 or 01633/422489. AE, MC, V.*

Tour 2: Cardiff to Bangor, the West Coast

As we have said, getting around Wales by public transport isn't easy. The western side north of Carmarthen has no rail routes at all, except for the Cambrian Coast Line in mid- and north Wales, which runs from Aberystwyth northward along the coast to Pwllheli, and the Little Trains, which chug their way into the scenic mountains. There is, however, a daily **Crosville/Traws Cambria** Bus 701, which runs from Cardiff up the west coast to end in Bangor, near the Isle of Anglesey and the resort of Llandudno (*see* Tour 3). This bus continues on to Holyhead for the ferries across the Irish Sea to Dublin/Dun Laoghaire. It leaves daily at 9 AM from the central station in Cardiff and arrives in Bangor at 5:05 PM; tickets cost £31.90 round-trip, £17.70 one-way, with 25% off for children under 16. Bus 94A/2 runs four times daily between Aberystwyth and Caernarfon in north Wales via Dolgellau; you can get off the bus anywhere and rejoin it later. A ticket costs £4.20. This is certainly one way of seeing a lot of Wales in one short budget burst.

In this tour we list a few of the places you will see en route, with special emphasis on Aberystwyth—the halfway point—where you might wish to break your journey. For the first 2 hours, 25 minutes the bus travels westward along the well-settled south coast, passing through **Swansea** (Abertawe in Welsh), part of whose docks have been converted into a stylish new Maritime Quarter, and reaching **Carmarthen,** the legendary birthplace of Merlin.

From Carmarthen the bus turns north to **Llanybydder,** situated in peaceful countryside that was once Wales's main textile-producing area, and then follows the River Teifi northeast for about 15 minutes to reach **Lampeter.** Bus 701 then turns northwest to reach the coast at **Aberaeron,** 3 hours, 35 minutes into the trip. The town was nearly all built in Georgian style in the early 19th century, lending a pleasing sense of harmony and coherence. There is an interesting display of the Cardigan Bay coastline in the tourist information center on the quay, and an unusual honey-bee exhibition in the harborside café.

In the only part of the journey that follows a true coastal road, the bus next turns northeast to arrive at **Aberystwyth** in a half hour.

Aberystwyth

Aberystwyth Tourist Information Center: Terrace Rd., tel. 01970/ 612125.

The seaside resort of **Aberystwyth** on hill-sheltered Cardigan Bay is an ideal vacation center for exploring mid-Wales. Being a resort, it has plenty of hotels and guest houses, good bus and rail service, a once-elegant seafront promenade with a bandstand, and the King's Hall for summer shows. Aberystwyth, which came to prominence as a Victorian watering hole, is also a university town and a major shopping center.

Numbers in the margin correspond to points of interest on the Aberystwyth map.

A fine, curving beach edges the bay, with the university at the southern end and Constitution Hill on the northern. The modern ❶ **university campus,** on the hill above the town, includes the National Library of Wales, an arts center with galleries, a theater, concert

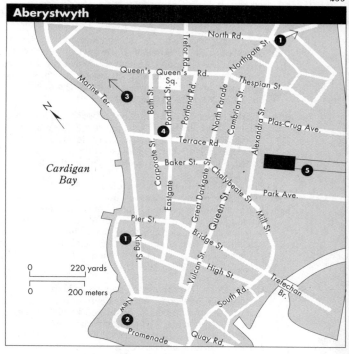

hall, and crafts shop—all open to visitors. The original university, founded in the 19th century, stands on the seafront. *The Library, tel. 01970/623816. Admission free. Open weekdays 9:30–6, Sat. 9:30–5.*

② The **castle,** at the southern end of the bay, built in 1277 and rebuilt in 1282 by Edward I, was one of several strongholds to fall, in 1404, to the Welsh leader Owain Glyndwr. Recaptured by the English, it became a mint in the 17th century, using silver from the Welsh hills. Today it is a romantic ruin on a headland separating the north shore from the harbor shore.

Long before its resort days, Aberystwyth was a major fishing port and shipbuilding center. The names of many small inns, such as **Ship and Castle,** reflect its origins.

③ At the end of the promenade, **Constitution Hill** offers the energetic a zigzag cliff path/nature trail to the view from the top. But it's more fun to travel up by the **Aberystwyth Cliff Railway,** the longest in Britain. Opened in 1896, to great excitement—520 passengers used the new attraction on its first day—it has been refurbished without diminishing its Victorian look. It takes you up 430 feet to the **Great Aberystwyth Camera Obscura,** a modern version of a Victorian amusement: Its massive 14-inch lens gives a bird's-eye view of more than 1,000 square miles of sea and scenery, including the whole of Cardigan Bay and 26 Welsh mountain peaks, Snowdon among them. *Tel. 01970/617642. Admission to Camera Obscura free; railway £1.95 adults, £1.75 senior citizens, £1 children. Open Easter–Oct., daily 10–6 (mid-July–Aug., 10–9).*

④ Back in town, the excellent **Ceredigion Museum** in an old theater on Terrace Road displays coins minted at the castle and many items of folk history. There is also a fascinating **Aberystwyth Yesterday** collection in the town (above the British Rail station), which shows 19th-century fashions, furniture, toys, and photographs.

Ceredigion Museum, Terrace Rd., tel. 01970/617911. Admission free. Open Mon.–Sat. 10–5.

At Aberystwyth Station you can hop on the narrow-gauge steam-operated **Vale of Rheidol Railway** (tel. 01970/625819 or 01970/615993). The terminus, an hour's ride away, is **Devil's Bridge,** where the Rivers Rheidol and Mynach meet in a series of spectacular falls. The walk down to the lowest bridge, "the devil's," is magnificent, but strictly for the surefooted!

Lodging **Four Seasons.** Located in Aberystwyth's town center, this family-
££ run hotel has a relaxed atmosphere and friendly staff. The spacious rooms are simply and attractively decorated, and the restaurant serves excellent meals at reasonable prices. *50–54 Portland St., Dyfed, SY23 2DX, tel. 01970/612120, fax 01970/627458. 14 rooms, 11 with bath. AE, MC, V.*

£ **Sinclair Guest House.** An excellent budget find, the Sinclair is well
★ under £50 (current prices are about £40). From the outside, it looks like any of the many small guest houses in Aberystwyth, but within, friendly owners Lester and Sarah Ward have transformed the rooms with an accent on neatness and style. The bedrooms are surprisingly spacious and well equipped. The Sinclair is a nonsmoking property. Advance booking is recommended. *43 Portland St., Dyfed SY23 2DX, tel. and fax 01970/615158. 3 rooms, 2 with bath, 1 with shower. No credit cards.*

Splurge **Groves Hotel.** Family-owned and in the heart of town, the hotel has comfortable bedrooms with tea/coffee-making facilities; a paneled lounge bar; and Welsh, English, and French dishes on the menu in the two restaurants. For an inexpensive meal, try the bar snacks. *44–46 N. Parade, Dyfed, SY23 2NF, tel. 01970/617623, fax 01970/627068. 9 rooms with bath. Facilities: restaurant, bar, sea fishing and pony trekking arranged. AE, MC, V.*

Dining **Connexion.** This simple traditional bistro, decorated with the work
£ of local artists, offers bistro fare made on the premises, including Italian chicken and apple tart. Other dishes, such as paella, locally caught lobster, and a variety of pastas, are offered as well. *19 Bridge St., tel. 01970/615350. Reservations advised. MC, V.*

£ **Gannets.** Another simple bistro, Gannets specializes in locally sup-
★ plied meat, fish, and game, which are transformed into hearty roasts and pies. Organically grown vegetables and a good French house wine are further draws for a university crowd. *7 St. James's Sq., tel. 01970/617164. Reservations advised. MC, V. Closed Sun. and Tues.*

Cadair Idris

Traveling northeast from Aberystwyth, the bus strikes inland to the village of **Tre'r-ddol** and starts to pass through some of the most striking scenery of the whole trip. After the town of **Machynlleth** on the River Dyfi (Dovey in English) comes the **Dyfi Forest,** and soon
★ the menacing bulk of **Cadair Idris** (2,927 feet) looms into view. The name means "the Chair of Idris," though no one is completely sure just who Idris was—probably a warrior bard. It is said that anyone sleeping for a night in a certain part of the mountain will awaken either a poet or a madman. The Talyllyn narrow-gauge railway (tel. 01654/710472) runs from Tywyn on the coast to the foothills of Cadair Idris. There are several routes up Cadair Idris. Be sure to check at the Dolgellau tourist center for the best one for you. For those strong of foot and head there is the famous Precipice Walk in the hills to the north of the town, which has spectacular views over the winding Mawddach estuary.

What to do when your *money* is done traveling before you are.

Don't worry. With **MoneyGram**,^{SM} your parents can send you money in usually 10 minutes or less to more than 19,000 locations in 80 countries. So if the money you need to see history becomes history, call us and we'll direct you to a **MoneyGram**^{SM} agent closest to you.

USA: **1-800-MONEYGRAM**
Germany: **0130-8-16629**

Canada: **1-800-933-3278**
England: **0800-89-7198**
or call collect **303-980-3340**

France: **05-905311**
Spain: **900-96-1218**

Dolgellau

Dolgellau Tourist Information Center: Eldon Sq., tel. 01341/ 422888.

Dolgellau (pronounced "Doll-geth-lee"), north of Cadair Idris, is a solidly Welsh market town with handsome old coaching inns and attractive dark buildings with slate roofs. Lying as it does at the foot of the mountain and with the **Snowdonia National Park** stretching to the north, Dolgellau is a popular spot for foot travelers who want to explore the surrounding area. The town was at the center of a gold rush in the 19th century, and you can take a trip from here by bus to an authentic gold mine where you can participate in an underground guided tour (tel. 01341/423332). Dolgellau is a very busy place in summer. After it departs from town, the TrawsCambria bus service strikes due north through the southern part of Snowdonia to **Trawsfynydd,** on the lake of the same name, created in 1930 as part of a hydroelectric scheme. There is a decommissioned nuclear power station here.

Lodding **Clifton House.** The hotel, with its very comfortable rooms and gar-
£ den, is in the center of town and is small enough to give friendly personal service. The restaurant (which was a jail in the 18th century) uses the best local produce. *Smithfield Sq., Gwynedd, LL40 1ES, tel. 01341/422554. 7 rooms, 4 with bath. Reservations recommended for restaurant. MC, V.*

¢ **Tyddynmawr Farmhouse.** This beautifully restored 18th-century farmhouse, nestled at the foot of Cadair Idris, has superb mountain views. Other area attractions include waterfalls, slate mines, caves, and fishing on the mountain lake on the farm. This is a good place to find peace, tranquillity, and seclusion. *Islawrdref, Cadair Rd., Gwynedd, LL40 1TL, tel. 01341/422331. 2 rooms, 1 with bath, 1 with shower. No credit cards.*

Porthmadog

Porthmadog Tourist Information Center: High St., tel. 01766/ 512981.

At **Maentwrog,** past the north shore of the lake, the bus turns west to reach the coast at **Porthmadog,** a little town that's the gateway to Llŷn, an unspoiled peninsula of beaches, wildflowers, and country lanes. Within the town is the Porthmadog British Rail Station, which provides relatively easy access along the Cambrian Coast Line (with two changes) back to London's Euston Station. But don't leave the resort before taking in some of the activities around the harbor, including the **Maritime Museum** (tel. 01766/513736). In the busy town are boutiques and crafts shops.

The **Ffestiniog Railway,** oldest of the Welsh narrow-gauge railways, was built in the mid-19th century to bring slate from the Blaenau Ffestiniog quarries down to the harbor at Porthmadog. Now you can take the train through Snowdonia National Park for great views. *Tel. 01766/512340. Open Mar.–Nov., also Christmas. Call for schedules.*

Beyond the embankment across the river mouth known as "The Cob" (the small toll charge goes to charity) is **Portmeirion,** a tiny fantasy Italianate village built in 1926 by architect Clough Williams-Ellis, complete with hotel, restaurant, and town hall. He called it his "light opera approach to architecture," and the result is an odd, pretty, though distinctly un-Welsh tourist attraction. The cult '60s TV series "The Prisoner" was filmed here, and the shop in the complex, called The Prisoner Shop, sells only items related to the series. Other shops include antiques and food stores. *Tel. 01766/770228. Ad-*

mission: £3 adults, £2.50 senior citizens, £1.50 children. Open daily 9:30–5:30.

Lodging **Trefaes Guest House.** It's worth making the short detour of a few
£ miles to Criccieth, a pretty Victorian resort with a ruined castle, to
★ stay at Pat Clayton's immaculate guest house. The rooms are tastefully decorated and spotless, and Pat makes special efforts to look
after her guests. Rates are very reasonable—much nearer £40 than
£50. *Y Maes, Criccieth, Gwynedd LL52 OAE, tel. 01766/523204, fax
01766/523013. 3 rooms with bath. No credit cards.*

From Porthmadog, Bus No. 701 cuts due north across the base of the
Llŷn Peninsula to **Penygroes** and **Caernarfon.**

Caernarfon

*Caernarfon Tourist Information Center: Oriel Pendeitsh, Castle
St., tel. 01286/672232.*

The town of **Caernarfon,** on the Menai Strait, 13 miles southwest of
★ Beaumaris (*see* Tour 3) is dominated by **Caernarfon Castle,** begun in
1283. The castle towers, unlike those of Edward I's other castles, are
polygonal and patterned with bands of different-colored stone. According to tradition, it was here, in 1301, that the first English
Prince of Wales was presented to the Welsh people. Their conquer-
or, Edward I, had promised them a prince who did not speak English—and duly offered his baby son, later Edward II. The tradition
that the first-born son of the monarch shall become Prince of Wales
continues, and in July 1969, Caernarfon glowed with pageantry
when Elizabeth II presented her eldest son, Prince Charles, to the
people of Wales as their prince. This was the first time the ceremony
had been held for 58 years—since 1911, in fact, when Prince
Edward, the late duke of Windsor, was presented by his father,
George V. In the Queen's Tower, an intriguing museum charts the
history of the local regiment, the Royal Welch Fusiliers. *Tel. 01286/
677617. Admission to castle: £3.50 adults, £2.50 senior citizens and
children, £10 family ticket. Open late Mar.–late Oct., daily 9:30–
6:30; late Oct.–late Mar., Mon.–Sat. 9:30–4, Sun. 2–4.*

A wander through Caernarfon takes you back centuries. Even the
new administrative complex is built in a moderately convincing
medieval style. Don't miss the garrison church of **St. Mary,** built into
the city walls. A half mile outside the town is the extensive excavation site of the **Roman fortress of Segontium** and the **Museum of the
Legions,** a branch of the National Museum of Wales. It contains material found on the site, one of Britain's most famous Roman forts.
*Tel. 01286/675625. Admission: £1 adults, 60p senior citizens and
children. Open Mar.–Oct., Mon.–Sat. 9:30–5:30 (until May 6–
Sept.), Sun. 2–5; Nov.–Feb., Mon.–Sat. 9:30–4, Sun. 2–5.*

Caernarfon Airport (at the end of Dinas Dinlle beach road) operates
Pleasure Flights in light aircraft (including a vintage Rapide) over
Snowdon, Anglesey, and Caernarfon. The airport also contains the
Caernarfon Air World museum. *Tel. 01286/830800. From £17 per
seat. Flights daily, year-round.*

Lodging **Hafoty.** Located off the beaten track a few miles from Caernarfon,
¢ Hafoty is a good value. The 18th-century farmhouse, on a hillside
with spectacular views of Caernarfon Castle and the sea, has been
modernized to provide extremely comfortable accommodations.
Guests also enjoy a warm Welsh welcome and good food.
*Rhostryfan, near Caernarfon, Gwynedd LL54 7PH, tel. 01286/
830144. 4 rooms with bath. No credit cards.*

¢ **Pengwern Farm.** Sited between the mountains and the sea, this
charming, spacious farmhouse boasts breathtaking views of
Snowdonia National Park, and for naturalists, there's much bird life
around this land near Foryd Bay. Evening meals make the most of

farm produce and beef and lamb, and children are welcome. There's fishing and horseback riding nearby. *Saron, Llanwnda, near Caernarfon, Gwynedd, LL54 5UH, tel. 01286/830717. 3 rooms with bath. No credit cards.*

Dining **Courtney's Bistro.** Welcoming, informal, and unpretentious,
£ Courtney's is an excellent value. All the food is home-cooked with changing menus based on local availability of produce. The bistro serves an eclectic range of dishes, including vegetarian choices. *9 Segontium Terr., tel. 01286/677290. Reservations recommended. MC, V. Closed Sun. (also Mon. and Tues. in winter).*

Tour 3: Llandudno and the North

Llandudno is a relaxed seaside town, very popular as a summer resort and full of B&Bs. There are good bus services around the region, and from Llandudno you can visit the glorious gardens at Bodnant, Beaumaris on the Isle of Anglesey, and Caernarfon (*see* Tour 2), with its magnificent castle and the Roman fortress of Segontium. You can then travel southward into Snowdonia National Park, and southeast to Denbigh, Ruthin, and Llangollen.

From London **BritRail** has no direct trains to Llandudno, but from London/Euston
By Train (tel. 0171/387–7070) you can pick up a train that will require a change at Crewe, Chester, or Llandudno Junction (which is only a few miles from the resort itself). The average journey time via Crewe is more than 4 hours. From Llandudno Junction, the trip takes about 3½ hours. Call rail information in Llandudno (tel. 01492/585151) for details.

By Bus There are three **National Express** *Rapide* buses (No. 545) departing daily from London/Victoria Coach Station (tel. 0171/730–0202) for Llandudno. The route is via Birmingham and Chester and takes 6 hours, 30 minutes. There are also occasional direct services with a slightly shorter journey time.

By Car Take M1 from London to Exit 19, then M6 and M54 to Telford. From there the quick route will take you by A442 to Whitchurch, A525/A541 to Queensferry on the coast at the Welsh border, then A55 west to Llandudno. For the more scenic, mountainous route, go west from Telford on A5 to Shrewsbury. From Shrewsbury you have a wide choice of northwestern roads, all with great views. The distance from London is about 243 miles.

Llandudno

Tourist Information Center: Chapel St., tel. 01492/876413.

Llandudno is a charming, old-fashioned resort town, with pleasant Victorian houses and a dignified approach to life. Its name comes from a 6th-century saint, Tudno, who lived and preached here. The town lies at the base of the **Great Orme,** a steep limestone headland, mostly a Country Park now, which dominates the skyline. There is a 90-year-old tramway that climbs the Orme in San Francisco style, or you can take a mile-long trip on a cable car from the Happy Valley entertainment area.

Although we have chosen Llandudno for its function as a base, there's quite a lot to see and do in the resort. The **Mostyn Art Gallery** (Vaughan St., tel. 01492/879201) has monthly exhibits and acts as an arts center; the **Alice in Wonderland Visitor Centre** (Trinity Sq., tel. 01492/860082) celebrates Llandudno's links with Charles Dodgson, alias Lewis Carroll; **Llandudno Museum** (Gloddaeth St., tel. 01492/876517) contains a wide range of exhibits, including Roman artifacts, pictures, furniture, and an authentic Welsh kitchen; the **Great Orme Mines** (Great Orme, tel. 01492/870447) is an underground attraction that shows how copper was mined in ancient times; and **Ski Llandudno** (Great Orme, tel. 01492/874707), is a popular dry-ski and toboggan slope. No Victorian seaside resort would be complete without a pier, and the one at Llandudno is 2,296 feet long. A major attraction for vacationers here has always been the beaches, which are wide and safe. The resort's imaginatively designed **North Wales Theatre** is an excellent new venue for all kinds of entertainment, from classical concerts to comedy.

Lodging

££
★ **Bryn Derwen Hotel.** A short distance from the seafront, this excellent hotel is well worth seeking out. It's family run, and personal service is a strong point. So too is the food, prepared by the proprietor, who is one of north Wales's top chefs. The rooms are beautifully decorated, combining comfort and style. Bedrooms have TVs and tea/coffee-making facilities. The Bryn Derwin is a first-class seaside hotel. *34 Abbey Rd., Gwynedd LL30 2EE, tel. 01492/876804. 9 rooms with bath. MC.*

£ **Belle Vue Hotel.** Set on the seafront near the pier, this hotel offers great views across the bay (try for a front room). All the bedrooms have TVs, in-house videos, and tea/coffee-making facilities. On the property is a sun terrace, the Fisherman's Bar, and a restaurant that also has sea views. Some rooms may be over £50. *26 N. Parade, Gwynedd, LL30 2LP, tel. 01492/879547. 17 rooms with bath. DC, MC, V. Closed Nov.–Mar.*

¢
★ **Britannia Hotel.** Overlooking the bay, with views of the Great Orme, this is another small seafront hotel. The bedrooms (some costing about £30 a night) have TVs and tea/coffee-making facilities, and there is a restaurant for evening meals during the summer season. *15 Craig-y-Don Parade, Gwynedd, LL30 1BG, tel. 01492/877185. 9 rooms, 7 with bath or shower. No credit cards.*

¢ **Mayfair Private Hotel.** This small, family-run hotel is known for its cuisine, comfort, and cleanliness. It is well situated within walking distance of the town center. *4 Abbey Rd., Gwynedd, LL30 2EA, tel. 01492/876170. 12 rooms, 9 with bath. No credit cards.*

Dining

£ **Casanova Restaurant.** The lively and bustling atmosphere of this town-center Italian restaurant is one of its biggest draws. The other highlight is a fine menu, on which you'll find *calamari fritti* (fried squid) and *filetto ai funghi* (beef filet with mushrooms). *18 Chapel St., tel. 01492/878426. Reservations advised. MC, V. Closed lunch.*

Splurge
★ **Bodysgallen Hall.** Set in wide, walled gardens 2 miles out of town, the Hall is part 17th, part 18th century, full of antiques, comfortable chairs by cheery fires, pictures, and polished wood. The set-price dinner (£27.50 for three courses, £32 for a gourmet menu) matches the Hall's incredible setting and high standard, and is worth it if you have a special occasion to spend in excess of your budget. The restaurant serves fine traditional meals, with an emphasis on local produce such as lamb and locally smoked salmon. *Gwynedd, LL30 1RS, tel. 01492/584466. Reservations advised. Jacket and tie required for restaurant. AE, DC, MC, V.*

Splurge **Garden Room.** This is the restaurant of the St. Tudno Hotel, where Alice Liddell, the model for Lewis Carroll's Alice, stayed in 1861. At lunchtime, there's good bar food at reasonable prices and set menu meals for about £15. The restaurant, one of the best in Wales, is painted to give the room a conservatory effect. The food at dinner can be on the rich side, with plenty of sauces, but there's a good choice of dishes (rack of Welsh lamb in a minted butter sauce, for example) and also lighter entrées, all served with fresh local vegetables. Set menus (above the budget range) are available, though a two-course option costs £20. *St. Tudno Hotel, tel. 01492/874411. Reservations advised. AE, MC, V.*

From Llandudno, you can take a scenic trip along the coast on an old-fashioned open-top double-decker bus, the Happy Dragon Bus No. 100. In summer this service makes the 35-mile run from Conwy to Talacre daily at half-hour intervals, calling at Colwyn Bay and Rhyl. Sit upstairs as long as the weather's fine, and enjoy the views.

Beaumaris

To reach Beaumaris take Bus 5 (runs throughout the day, mostly at 30-minute intervals; journey time: just over 1 hour) from Llandudno to Bangor. Change for Bus 57 (runs every hour in winter, more frequently in summer; journey time: 30 minutes) to Beaumaris.

Beaumaris, which means "beautiful marsh," is on Anglesey, the largest island off the shore of either Wales or England. It is linked to the mainland by the Britannia road and rail bridge, and by Thomas Telford's remarkable chain suspension bridge built in 1826 over the dividing Menai Strait. An elegant town of simple cottages, Georgian terraces, and bright shops, Beaumaris looks across the strait to the magnificence of Snowdonia, the dramatic range of north Wales mountains. The town dates from 1295, when Edward I, the English
★ invader, commenced work on the **castle** that guards the entrance to the Menai Strait, the last and largest link in an "iron ring" of fortifications around north Wales, built to contain the Welsh. The castle that stands at the far end of the town is solid and symmetrical, with arrow slits and a moat, and it is acknowledged as one of the finest examples of medieval defensive planning in Britain. Look for the mooring rings on the southern side, a reminder that the sea once slapped against the castle walls. *Tel. 01248/810361. Admission: £1.50 adults, £1 senior citizens and children. Open late Mar.–late Oct., daily 9:30–6:30; late Oct.–late Mar., Mon.–Sat. 9:30–4, Sun. 2–4.*

Opposite the castle is the **courthouse,** built in 1614, which houses the oldest court in Britain that still hears cases. A plaque depicts one view of the legal profession: Two farmers pull a cow, one by the horns, one by the tail, while a lawyer sits in the middle milking. Many people were transported from here to convict colonies in Australia—one woman, in 1773, for stealing goods worth less than a shilling. *Tel. 01286/679098. Joint admission ticket for court and gaol (see below): £3.15 adults, £2.15 senior citizens and children, £7 family ticket. Open Easter; weekends in May; and end of May–end of Sept., weekdays 11–5, weekends 2–5, except when court is in session.*

Just beyond is the **Museum and Memorabilia of Childhood,** an Aladdin's cave of music boxes, magic lanterns, trains, cars, toy soldiers, rocking horses, and mechanical savings banks. *1 Castle St., tel. 01248/712498. Admission: £2.50 adults, £1.25 senior citizens and children. Open Mar.–Oct., Mon.–Sat. 10–5:30, Sun. noon–5.*

Nearby, in Castle Street, is **The Tudor Rose,** a house dating back to 1400, and an excellent example of Tudor timberwork.

Turning right up Steeple Lane brings you to the old **gaol** (jail), built in 1829 by Joseph Hansom, who was also the designer of the hansom cab. It was considered a model prison, the best in Britain at the time, but an exhibition shows what life there was really like. You can wander the corridors, be locked in the soundproof punishment cell or the condemned cell, and see the country's only working treadmill, where prisoners trudged hopelessly around like hamsters in a cage. *Tel. 01286/679098. Joint admission with Beaumaris Courthouse (see above).*

Opposite the jail is the 14th-century **parish church.** In 1862 an innocent man was hanged on the gibbet outside the prison wall—to give the crowd a good view—and he cursed the clock on the church tower. Locals say that the clock never kept good time from that day, although a successful overhaul in 1980 slightly spoils the legend.

Dining and Lodging
££
★

Llwydiarth Fawr. The Hughes family, which owns and runs this working farm (with over 4,000 sheep), offers guests a real Welsh experience with a stay in their luxurious Georgian farmhouse. The room costs about £50 a night with breakfast for two, and most people are glad to spend the £12 a night for a delicious home-cooked dinner. The living room, with TV and books, has a huge picture window that overlooks green fields dotted with sheep. Margaret Hughes prepares the tasty and filling meals and has a wealth of information about Beaumaris and the Isle of Anglesey. The bedrooms, fully equipped with TV, etc., are better than those found at most hotels. This accommodation is some way from Beaumaris—it is a good base from which to explore all of Anglesey—but you'll need a car to get here. *Llanerchymedd, Isle of Anglesey, LL71 8DF, tel. 01248/ 470321. 3 rooms with bath. No credit cards.*

¢ **Plas Cichle.** This 200-acre working farm is close to Beaumaris, the beaches, and other area attractions, making it an ideal base from which to tour. Morning and evening meals and packed lunches, including vegetarian choices, are available. Riding and fishing opportunities are nearby. Hosts also give a discount for children. *Contact: Mrs. Roberts, Beaumaris, Isle of Anglesey, Gwynedd, LL58 8PS, tel. 01248/810488. 3 rooms with bath. No credit cards.*

Splurge **Ye Olde Bull's Head.** This old coaching inn, which dates to 1472 and has had such famous guests as Dr. Johnson and Charles Dickens, is an exceptional place to stay the night or just to take in a meal. All guest rooms (double: £73, including breakfast) are cheerfully decorated à la Laura Ashley, and each is uniquely furnished. Oak beams across the low ceilings enhance the homey atmosphere. The mostly French menu features a variety of warm salads, such as pigeon breast with hazelnut oil, and is also renowned for its seafood. Don't overlook the back bar of this property, where locals and guests converse over tall glasses of ale. *Castle St., Isle of Anglesey, Gwynedd, LL58 8AP, tel. 01248/810329, fax 01248/811294. 15 rooms with bath. Facilities: restaurant, garden, bar, game room. AE, DC, MC, V.*

Dining
¢
Liverpool Arms. At the opposite end of Castle Street from the castle is this nautically decorated pub that is popular with the locals. Emphasizing inexpensive seafood, the Liverpool Arms does a good job with the crab sandwiches. *Castle St., tel. 01248/810362. MC, V.*

Snowdonia National Park

Snowdonia National Park encompasses 840 square miles that stretch from Snowdon in the north to Machynlleth in mid-Wales. The mass boasts dramatic scenery at every turn, including a lush wilderness estuary, unforgiving mountain peaks, and green carpeted pastures filled with sheep.

There are several tours you can take from Llandudno south into Snowdonia. One of the easiest and best is on a regular **Crosville/ Wales** Bus 19, which leaves every two hours for Llanberis. The journey time is nearly two hours (four hours round-trip), but if you have a Rover ticket, you can leave the bus, explore **Llanberis,** and catch a later bus back.

Llanberis

Llanberis Tourist Information Center: High St., tel. 01286/870765.

The village of **Llanberis** is the starting point for the steep **Snowdon Mountain Railway**—some of its track at a gradient of 1 in 5—which terminates within 70 feet of the 3,560-foot summit. **Snowdon, Yr**

Wyddfa in Welsh, is the highest peak south of Scotland. From the summit on a clear day you can see as far as the Irish Wicklow Mountains, about 90 miles away. *Tel. 01286/870223. Maximum round-trip fare, £13.20 adults, £9.50 children. Open (weather permitting) Mar.–Oct., daily from 9 AM. The train usually climbs all the way to the summit terminus (weather permitting) May–Sept.*

Also in Llanberis is the **Museum of the North,** another branch of the National Museum of Wales, which sets out to interpret the historical, geological, and social history of the Snowdonia area. The museum also features a "Power of Wales" theme, and offers guided tours of the awesome underground world that has been created in Llanberis's mountainsides as part of a mammoth scheme to generate hydroelectricity. *Tel. 01286/870636. Admission: £3.50 adults (+ £1.50 to visit power station), £2.60 senior citizens (+ £1.15), £1.75 children (+ 75p). Open June–mid-Sept., daily 9:30–6; Mar.–May and mid-Sept.–Oct., daily 10–5; Feb. and Nov., daily 10:30–4.*

Across the lake, the workshops of the old Dinorwig slate quarry now house the **Welsh Slate Museum.** *Dinorwig Quarry, tel. 01286/ 870630. Admission: £1.50 adults, £1.20 senior citizens, 80p children, £3.80 family ticket. Open Easter–Sept., daily 9:30–5:30.*

Try a lakeside ride on the **Llanberis Lake Railway,** which once transported the slate (tel. 01286/870549).

Conwy

Conwy, about a mile south of Llandudno, can be easily reached by several local buses or by train to Conwy Station. Conwy tourist office: Conwy Castle Visitor Centre (at the castle entrance), tel. 01492/ 592248.

The walled town of **Conwy** is presently the focus of a conservation project in which the once-cobbled roads are being restored and the storefronts of historic buildings are being redesigned or preserved to reflect their original architectural character. The town is celebrating the completion of a new tunnel that has been built under the Conwy estuary, thus removing heavy traffic that once ran through the town center. It's a pleasant town to walk around and have tea in, especially since the project has given a fresh look to a fine medieval town that is no longer strangled by the motor car.

One of the most striking aspects of Conwy is its castle, another of Edward I's. If you travel to Llandudno by rail, you will see the castle from the train, with a dramatic Victorian suspension bridge leading to it. Conwy is a solid castle built on a narrow thrust of rock, with eight massive towers and a barbican at either end. It is clearly a building of great military strength and manages, even today, to look magnificently proportioned. *Tel. 01492/592358. Admission: £2.90 adults, £1.80 senior citizens and children, £8 family ticket. Open late Mar.–late Oct., daily 9:30–6:30; late Oct.–late Mar., Mon.– Sat. 9:30–4, Sun. 2–4.*

On the quay beside the castle is what is said to be the smallest house in Britain, furnished in mid-Victorian Welsh style; it can hold only a few people at a time. Another outstanding historic feature of Conwy is its ring of amazingly well-preserved medieval town walls. It's a most exhilarating experience to walk above the rooftops along sections of these walls, which are over three-quarters of a mile in length, with 22 towers and three original gateways.

Bodnant Garden

Bus 25 takes a circular scenic route beside the River Conwy, from Llandudno south to Bodnant Gardens, seven times a day; the trip takes about 25 minutes. Also, a train runs every two hours on the Conwy Valley line to Tal-y-Cafn.

★ Beautiful **Bodnant Garden,** a National Trust property, features terraces, lawns, thickets of magnolias, and Himalayan rhododendrons, with the mountains of Snowdonia forming a complementary backdrop. What's unique about this estate—owned by Lord Aberconway and managed by Martin Puddle (whose father and grandfather previously were head gardeners)—is that there are no formal tours or guides. Instead, guests are invited to walk the grounds at their own pace, much the way they would appreciate their own gardens. The views and careful landscapes are awe-inspiring. *Tal-y-Cafn, tel. 01492/650460. Admission: £3.90 adults, £1.95 children. Open mid-Mar.–Oct., daily 10–5.*

Denbigh

From Llandudno take Bus 13 or 16 to Rhyl (15-minute frequencies; journey time: about 1 hour, 15 minutes) then change to Bus 51 (every 30 minutes; journey time: 40 minutes).

Head southeast 20 miles for **Denbigh,** which is served by A55 and A525. This market town (Wednesdays) was much admired by Dr. Samuel Johnson, who stayed on Pentrefoelas Road at Gwaenynog Hall, where he designed two rooms. A walk along the river bank at nearby Lawnt, a spot he loved, brings you to a monumental urn placed in his honor. Not that it pleased him: "It looks like an intention to bury me alive," thundered the great lexicographer.

Denbigh Castle is known as "the hollow crown" because it is not much more than a shell set on high ground, dominating the town. A tiny museum inside is devoted to Denbigh native son H. M. Stanley, the 19th-century journalist and explorer who found Dr. Livingstone in Africa. *Tel. 01745/813979. Admission: £1.50 adults, £1 senior citizens and children. Open May–Sept., daily 10–5.*

Below the castle are the ruins of "Leicester's Folly," a church begun but never finished by Elizabeth I's favorite, Robert Dudley, earl of Leicester.

Ruthin and Llangollen

Bus 51 from Rhyl continues on a short distance from Denbigh to Ruthin. To get to Llangollen is more difficult—stay on No. 51 to Corwen, then take No. 94—a total of 2½ hours from Rhyl.

From Denbigh it is just 8 miles (A525) southeast to **Ruthin,** the capital of Glyndwr country, where the 15th-century Welsh hero Owain Glyndwr lived and ruled. Its well-preserved black-and-white buildings date from the 16th to the 19th centuries. Ruthin also has elegant shops, good inns, and a crafts center where a number of artisans are based. Since the 11th century, they have been ringing the curfew here each evening at 8. Popular Medieval banquets are held nightly at the Ruthin Castle Hotel.

The spectacular **Horseshoe Pass** (on A525, then A542), 14 miles southeast of Ruthin, leads past the substantial ruins of the Cistercian **Abbey of Valle Crucis** to **Llangollen,** home each July to the International Musical Eisteddfod. The tradition of the *eisteddfod,* held throughout Wales, goes back to the 12th century. Originally gatherings of bards, the *eisteddfodau* of today are more like competitons or festivals. While you are in Llangollen, visit **Plas Newydd,** home from 1778 to 1828 of the eccentric Ladies of Llangollen, who set up a scandalous single-sex household, collected curios and magnificent wood carvings, and entertained celebrated guests, among them William Wordsworth, Sir Walter Scott, and the Duke of Wellington. The Ladies had a servant with the delightful name of "Mollie the Basher."

Hill St., tel. 01691/773291 (ask for curator). Admission: £1.70 adults, 75p children. Open Apr.–Oct., daily 10–5.

From the **Canal Museum** on the wharf, you can take a horse-drawn boat along the Shropshire Union Canal. *Tel. 01978/860702. Museum admission: £1.50 adults, £1.10 senior citizens, £1 children. Open daily Easter–Oct., 10–5:30; 45-min boat trip: £2 adults, £1.50 children.*

Llangollen's bridge, over the River Dee, a 14th-century stone structure, is named in a traditional Welsh folk song as one of the "Seven Wonders of Wales." The Bishop Trevor Tearooms, by the bridge, are cheerful and traditional. Near the bridge is the terminus of the **Llangollen Railway,** a restored standard-gauge, steam-powered line. It runs for a few miles along the scenic Dee Valley. *Tel. 01978/860951. Round-trip fare: £5 adults, £2.50 children. Open Mar.–Nov., daily 10–5.*

There are easy walks along the banks of the River Dee or along part of **Offa's Dyke path.** The 167-mile-long dyke, a defensive wall whose earthen foundations still stand, was built along the border with England in the 8th century by King Offa of Mercia to keep out Welsh raiders.

Dining and Lodging
££

Eyarth Old Railway Station. This Victorian railway station was closed for 17 years before being converted in 1981 to an award-winning bed-and-breakfast, which also serves evening meals. (In 1988 it was voted "Best Bed-and-Breakfast Establishment in Wales" by the Worldwide B&B Association.) The bedrooms are spacious, with large windows looking out onto breathtaking rural scenery. *Llanfair Duffryn Clwyd, near Ruthin, Clwyd LL15 2EE, tel. 01824/703643, fax 01824/707464. 6 rooms with bath. Facilities: bar, pool. MC, V.*

10 The Lake District

Windermere, Ambleside, Grasmere, Keswick

The Lake District is the largest and most popular national park in Britain. In 1951 the 35 square miles of lakes, mountains, and fells (moorland) were officially so designated, but the district's popularity dates back much further. Its attractions were first etched into the popular imagination in the 19th century by the vivid descriptions of the Romantic poets. William Wordsworth, for one, was born in the area in 1770 and lived in Grasmere, on the banks of Rydal Water. Other writers who popularized the Lake District include Dorothy Wordsworth, Samuel Taylor Coleridge, Thomas De Quincey, John Ruskin, and Matthew Arnold. Artists, too, have brought to the public the intense images of the region, capturing the severe grays and browns of the peaks, the brilliant blaze of the fall colors, and the contrasting whites and blues of the winter snows on their canvases.

Unfortunately, tourism has disturbed the tranquility that so motivated these artists: It's estimated that annually at least 4 million people visit the area, and consequently the most popular hill tracks are completely worn away by the tramp of thousands of feet—damage that costs more than £1 million a year to repair. July and August are the most crowded months; in the spring and fall the lakes are at their best.

For the person traveling on a budget, this is a convenient and affordable destination. A plethora of guest houses and bed-and-breakfasts offer reasonable accommodations; taking in the natural beauty is free; and the busy bus network is geared to the needs of the visitor. Many companies offer explorer-type tickets for periods of varying length: A one-day go-anywhere ticket, for example, costs £5 for an adult, £3.75 for a child or senior citizen, £9.99 for a family; a four-day ticket costs £13 for an adult and £9 for a child. Contact Cumberland Motor Services (tel. 01946/63222) for details.

Essential Information

Lodging The Lake District has attracted tourists for more than 200 years and has built up a reputation for taking good care of its guests. Medium-size, family-run hotels can offer the best value and plenty of comfort and hospitality, but even those can be costly. Bed-and-breakfasts (B&Bs), however, provide the cheapest, simplest accommodations, and come in every shape and size, from the house on Main Street renting out one room to farmhouses with an entire wing to spare. You can expect to pay about £15–£20 per person.

If you're really looking to save money, you'll do best to stay in the Lake District's network of youth hostels, which are, in fact, open to anyone with a membership card from their home country's hostel association. Some hostels are located on specific hiking routes, or in strategic walking areas, and though they can be fairly basic, keen walkers will find them invaluable. They are very inexpensive—the most you'll pay is about £10 per person per night—but you must book well in advance for summer travel. Local tourist information centers have all the relevant details—some of the most popular hostels are those at Ambleside, Windermere, Grasmere, Kendal, Coniston, Hawkshead, and Derwentwater.

Summer is the busiest season here—and that means *very* busy indeed. You *must* book ahead. At other times of the year you can travel easily and more inexpensively without advance reservations, choosing your accommodations once you're actually in the region. Highly recommended establishments are indicated by a star ★.

Dining Cumbria is noted for its good country food. Dishes center on the abundant local supply of lamb, beef, game, and fish, especially salmon and river and lake trout. Cumberland sausage, a thick, meaty pork sausage which is a meal in itself, is another regional specialty, as are the bread, cake, pastries, gingerbread, and scones.

Cumbria also offers health food and vegetarian restaurants as well as some excellent Continental ones. Standards vary, so it's worth doing a little research. Pubs often give the best value at lunchtime, offering appetizing bar lunches at prices beginning as low as £4. Unless otherwise noted, reservations are not necessary and dress is informal. Highly recommended restaurants are indicated by a star ★.

Shopping The huge influx of visitors to the Lake District has proved a spur to shopkeepers in general, and craft workshops in particular. Jewelry and knitted wear are particularly widespread here, while items made from horn and wood, together with pottery and glassware, are featured all over the area.

The town center in Kendal holds a market on Wednesday and Saturday. Keswick's market is on Saturday; Ambleside, on Wednesday; Penrith, on Tuesday; Cockermouth, on Monday.

Biking You have to be a dedicated cyclist to attack the Lake District on two wheels, but the superb scenery will more than reward you for your aching calf muscles, and you will find that a bike is an "open sesame" to places that are otherwise difficult to reach. Among the stores where you can rent bikes are, in Braithwaite, **Braithwaite House** (near Keswick, tel. 017687/78273), no deposit but ID needed; in Windermere, **Windermere Cycles** (South Terr., Bowness, tel. 015394/44479), deposit and ID required; **Lakeland Leisure** (opposite Windermere rail station, tel. 015394/44786), ID and deposit needed. **Biketreks** (tel. 015394/31245), based in Ambleside, offers guided bike rides for about £25 a day, with routes that are custom-made for interest and ability. They also organize days for women only.

Hiking There are walks of every length and difficulty throughout the Lake District, around lake shores, up the valleys, and over the fields.

The Lake District

Beacon Pike

M6   A6

Penrith

Shap Fell

Pooley
Bridge

Dalemain

A592

Hawewswater

Aira Force

Ullswater

Patterdale

Brockhole
National Park
Centre

Ridge of
Blencathra

A5091

Helvellyn

Rydal
Mount

Ambleside

A66

Grasmere

A591

Castlerigg
Stone Circle

B5322

Thirlmere

Rydal Water

Mt.
Skiddaw

Keswick

A591

Langdale Fell

Ellerwater

Mt.
Latrigg

B5289

Derwent
water

Lodore

Scafell
Pike

C U M B R I A

B5292

Bassenthwaite
Lake

Grange

Sectoller

Cockermouth

A66

Buttermere

West Water

B5289

Crummock
Water

Ennerdale
Water

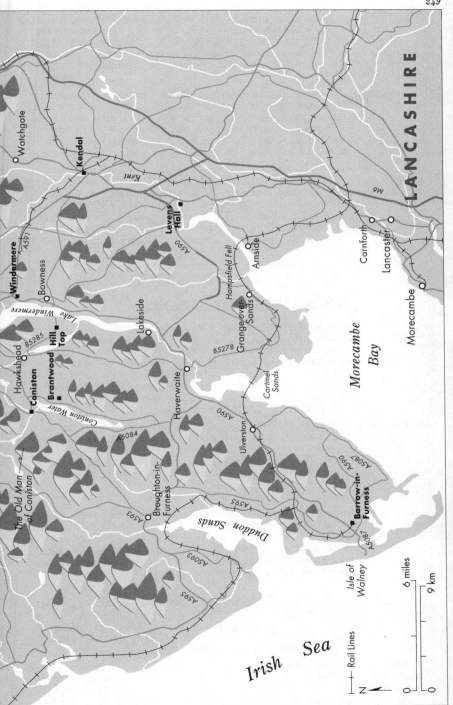

Some of the easier ones tend to be overcrowded and can be more like busy city sidewalks than quiet country paths. The longest structured walk, the **Cumbria Way** (70 miles), crosses the whole of the area over mountains and around lakes, starting at the market town of Ulverston and finishing at Carlisle, near the border with Scotland.

Guides   The **National Park Authority** (tel. 015394/46601) at Brockhole near Windermere has an advisory service that puts you in touch with members of the Blue Badge Guides, who are experts on the area. From Easter to October they will take you on half-day or full-day walks, and introduce you to the history and natural beauty of the Lake District. The Authority has nine information offices throughout the district.

Rock climbing, except for the experienced, should be undertaken only with a guide. **Mountain Adventure Guides** (Eel Crag, Melbecks, Braithwaite, west of Keswick, CA12 5TL, tel. 017687/78517), and **Summitreks** (14 Yewdale Rd., Coniston, LA21 8DU, tel. 015394/41212) coordinate climbing trips for either individuals or groups on a daily or weekly basis, and accommodations are arranged where needed.

Tour 1: Windermere and the Southern Lakes

The Lake District is compact, with basically two main base towns—Windermere and Keswick—as the focal points for the extensive network of bus routes that crisscrosses the entire area. Both towns have a variety of reasonably priced accommodations, but because they are so convenient, they can be packed and noisy in summer, displaying some of the worst traits of Coney Island. Following are the main points of interest that can be reached easily by bus from Windermere, together with the Southern Lakes.

From London
By Train   **British Rail** serves the region from London's Euston Station (tel. 0171/387–7070). Take an InterCity train bound for Carlisle, Edinburgh, or Glasgow and change at Oxenholme for the branch line service to Kendal and Windermere. Schedules vary, but trains run weekdays from 6:25 AM to 7:25 PM and Saturday from 6:15 AM to 7:15 PM. Sunday service is infrequent. Average travel time to Windermere (including the change) is 4½ hours.

By Bus   **National Express** (tel. 0171/730–0202) serves the region from London's Victoria Coach Station, with two departures daily, at 10:30 AM and 12:30 PM. Average travel time to Kendal is a little more than 7 hours; to Windermere, 7½ hours; and to Keswick, 8¼ hours. If you want to reach the Lake District from the east, **Mountain Goat** (tel. 015394/45161) runs a bus service between York and Keswick (Apr.–Oct.).

By Car   To get to the Lake District from London, take M1 north to M6, getting off either at Exit 36 and joining A591 west (around the Kendal bypass to Windermere) or at Exit 40, joining A66 direct to Keswick and the northern lakes region. Travel time to Kendal is about 4 hours; to Keswick, allow about 5 to 6 hours.

Traveling within the Lake District
By Bus   There are several bus and coach companies serving the Lake District. Two of the main ones are **Mountain Goat** (Victoria St., Windermere, tel. 015394/45161), which runs a local Lake District minibus service linking Keswick, Grasmere, Ambleside, Windermere, and Kendal, and **Cumberland Motor Services** (tel. 01946/63222), which crisscrosses the area—call for up-to-date bus timetables and suggestions for bus excursions. During the winter bus

schedules are restricted, though you should still be able to reach all the main destinations by public transportation.

By Train   If you're heading for Keswick, you can either take the train to Windermere and continue from there by Cumberland bus (70 minutes' journey), or stay on the main London–Carlisle train line as far as Penrith station (4 hours), from which point Cumberland buses to Keswick take 45 minutes. Train connections are good around the edges of the Lake District, especially on the Oxenholme–Kendal–Windermere line and the Furness and West Cumbria branch lines from Lancaster to Grange-over-Sands, Ulverston, Barrow, and Ravenglass. Note that services on these lines are reduced, or nonexistent, on Sunday.

Seven-day regional **North West Rover** tickets (£43) are good for unlimited travel within the area (including trips on the scenic Carlisle–Settle line running just east of the Lake District).

The **Lakeside & Haverthwaite Railway Co.** (tel. 015395/31594) runs vintage steam trains in summer on the branch line between Lakeside and Haverthwaite along Lake Windermere's southern tip.

Ravenglass & Eskdale Railway (tel. 01229/717171) offers a steam train service covering the 7 miles of glorious countryside between Ravenglass and Dalegarth. There is daily service from April to October, and a reduced service in winter.

By Boat   An assortment of boats and ferries travel up and down the larger lakes and can be an enjoyable way to see the region.

Bowness Bay Boating Co. (tel. 015394/43360) runs small vessels around Lake Windermere and to Brockhole National Park Centre.

Keswick-on-Derwentwater Launch Co. (tel. 017687/72263) conducts cruises on vintage motor launches around Derwentwater, leaving from Keswick.

Ullswater Navigation & Transit Co. (tel. 01539/721626) sends its oil-burning 19th-century steamers the length of Lake Ullswater between Glenridding and Pooley Bridge (Apr.–Oct. only).

Windermere Iron Steamboat Co. (tel. 015395/31188) employs its handsome fleet of vintage cruisers in a regular service between Ambleside, Bowness, and Lakeside on Lake Windermere.

Windermere

Many of the region's buses pass through Windermere; in addition, the most popular local destinations—Ambleside, Brockhole, and Bowness Pier—are connected by Bus W1, which operates hourly Monday–Saturday 7–6. The regional tourist office for the Lake District is the Cumbria Tourist Board: Ashleigh, Holly Rd., Windermere, Cumbria LA23 2AQ, tel. 015394/44444; local Windermere tourist office: Victoria St., tel. 015394/46499.

Windermere is a natural touring base for the southern half of the Lake District, with its wealth of tourist facilities and good transportation links. The name "Windermere" applies both to the lake and to the main town nearby. The town was a hamlet originally called Birthwaite, but when the railroad was extended here from Kendal in 1847, local officials named the new station Windermere in order to cash in on the lake's reputation, already well established thanks to William Wordsworth and the other Romantic poets. Later, another village by the lake, **Bowness-on-Windermere**, 1½ miles away, was swallowed by the new town.

Today the part of town around the station is known as Windermere, while the lakeside area is still called **Bowness**, definitely the more attractive hamlet. Hop on one of the minibuses that link the two towns and visit the 15th-century parish church of **St. Martins** (in Bowness), which has an Anglo-Saxon font, chained Bibles, original stained-glass windows, and an unusual wooden sculpture of St. Martin. One of the stained-glass windows shows the striped coat of arms of John Washington, ancestor of George; the design is said to have been the original source of the stripes in the American flag.

Although Windermere's marinas and piers have some charm, you can bypass the busier stretches of shoreline (and in summer they can be packed solid) by walking beyond the boathouses. Here, from among the pine trees, is a fine view across the lake. The **car ferry** (which also carries pedestrians) crosses the water at this point to reach Far Sawrey and the road to Hawkshead and Hill Top (*see below*); ferries depart frequently with crossings every 20 minutes Monday–Saturday 6:50 AM–9:50 PM; Sunday 9:10 AM–9:50 PM, winter until 8:50 PM (cars £1.50, passengers 20p).

On the other side of the promenade, beyond the main cluster of hotels in Bowness, is the **Windermere Steamboat Museum,** which exhibits a remarkable collection of steam- and motor-powered yachts and launches. The *Dolly*, built about 1850, is one of the two oldest mechanically powered boats in the world. She was raised from the bottom of Ullswater in 1962, having lain there for 70 years. *Rayrigg Rd., tel. 015394/45565. Admission: £2.80 adults, £2.50 senior citizens, £1.40 children, £7.50 families. Open Easter–Oct., daily 10–5.*

The lake itself, which is 11 miles long, 1½ miles wide, and 200 feet deep, fills a rocky gorge between steep, thickly wooded hills. Its waters make for superb fishing, especially for char, a rare kind of reddish lake trout prized by gourmets. During the summer, Lake Windermere is alive with all kinds of boats and a **boat trip** —particularly the round-trip from Bowness to Ambleside and down to Lakeside (*see* Traveling within the Lake District, *above*)—remains a wonderful way of spending a few summer hours.

For a memorable view of Lake Windermere—at the cost of a rigorous climb along the rough, uphill track—follow signs near the Windermere Hotel (across from the station) to **Orrest Head.** Eventually you will see a stile on your right; climb over it and continue up the path to a rocky little summit where you can sit on a bench and enjoy a breathtaking, unobstructed view. The walk back is only a mile, but it takes most people at least an hour.

Lodging

£ £ ★ **Archway.** This is a centrally located Victorian guest house on a quiet street, with some terrific mountain views. Inside the building are solid Victorian furnishings and comfortable bedrooms, all of which are designated non-smoking. The home cooking is notably good; breakfasts include local Cumberland sausages and dinner is a very reasonable £11. *13 College Rd., Windermere, LA23 1BY, tel. 015394/45613. 5 rooms with bath. AE, MC, V.*

£ £ ★ **The Hawksmoor.** This small, attractive, ivy-clad guest house lies between Bowness and Windermere in an ideally quiet location, with a garden and woodland behind it. The rooms are tastefully decorated with matching wallpapers and fabrics, and all have TVs and tea/coffeemakers. If you'd like a room with a four-poster bed (the most expensive option), request this when booking. *Lake Rd., Windermere, LA23 2EQ, tel. 015394/42110. 10 rooms with bath or shower. Facilities: restaurant. MC, V. Closed Dec. and Jan.*

£ £ **Oakbank Hotel.** Right in the center of Bowness, the hillside Oakbank provides very comfortable rooms, some with views over the lake, and all tastefully decorated in pale colors. Each room has a TV and tea/coffeemakers, too. The management is friendly and welcoming. The breakfast room overlooks the town and lake; Bowness's restaurants are within easy walking distance. *Helm Rd., Bowness-on-Windermere, tel. 015394/43386. 11 rooms with shower. MC, V.*

£ **Holly Park House.** This stone-built, Victorian guest house in a quiet neighborhood has large, comfortably furnished rooms, and the resident owners are friendly and attentive. It is handily located near shops and transportation facilities. Note that on summer bank holiday weekends, the price increases by £2 per person. *1 Park Rd., Windermere, LA23 2AW, tel. 015394/42107. 6 rooms with bath. No credit cards. Closed Nov.–Feb.*

Dining **Miller Howe Café.** This excellent eating place, in rather unexpected
££ surroundings near the train station, serves inspired local food at extremely reasonable prices. The café was originally established by John Tovey, proprietor of the more famous Miller Howe hotel and restaurant, and dishes here continue to show the flair for which he is known—there's game when in season, and all manner of warming soups and tempting desserts. *Alexandra Buildings, Station Precinct, Windermere, tel. 015394/46732. Reservations advised. MC, V. Open 9–5.*

££ **Roger's.** This is a centrally located restaurant, small and darkly decorated, with a menu that contains the best French food in the region. There may be suckling pig with apricot sauce or fillet of salmon with sorrel sauce offered, and always there's a good selection of cheeses, some very rich desserts, and a short but interesting wine list. *4 High St., Windermere, tel. 015394/44954. Reservations necessary. AE, DC, MC, V. Dinner only. Closed Sun.*

£ **Rastelli.** This friendly Italian restaurant has an assured touch, serving fine pizzas from a wood-fired pizza oven as well as other classic Italian dishes—try the calzone (stuffed pizza), which comes with a tomato and garlic sauce topping. It's a cheery, informal restaurant, where a filling meal with wine can be had for around £15. *Lake Rd., Bowness-on-Windermere, tel. 015394/44227. MC, V. Dinner only. Closed Wed. and Feb.*

¢ **Hole in t'Wall.** This fine old pub is decorated with farming equipment, games machines, and a jukebox. The music can be noisy, but in summer you can avoid the din by opting to dine in the flagstone courtyard. Traditional Cumbrian ales are offered with the meat pies and Cumbrian sausages that make simple, filling, and inexpensive lunches. *Fallbarrow Rd., Bowness-on-Windermere, tel. 015394/43488. No credit cards.*

¢ **Terrace Cafeteria Restaurant.** Conveniently located in Brockhole Centre, this is an ideal place for morning coffee, lunch, or afternoon tea. Don't leave without trying one of the local fattening goodies—Helvellyn tarts, rum butter, or Cumbrian courting cake. *Brockhole Visitor Centre, Windermere, tel. 015394/46601. No credit cards.*

Splurge **Porthole Eating House.** Located in an 18th-century house in the cen-
★ ter of Bowness, the restaurant has a French and Italian menu featuring homemade pasta and excellent fish dishes, including fresh salmon and (when available) Windermere char. Other nice touches include homemade bread and petit fours served with coffee. In winter a large open fire adds to the ambience, and the friendly staff is knowledgeable about the massive wine list—which includes some excellent German wines. *3 Ash St., Bowness-on-Windermere, tel. 015394/42793. Reservations advised. AE, DC, MC, V. Dinner only. Closed Tues., mid-Dec.–Feb.*

Shopping You'll find the best range at the Bowness end of town on Lake Road and around Queen's Square: clothing stores, craft shops, and souvenir stores of all kinds.

The Horn Shop (Crag Brow, tel. 015394/44519) is one of the last British firms to practice the craft of horn-carving; its craftspeople make a remarkable variety of goods, including jewelry, utensils, mugs, and walking sticks with elaborately carved handles.

Lakeland Jewellers (Crag Brow, tel. 015394/42992) has the local experts setting semiprecious stones in necklaces, pendants, rings, bracelets, earrings, and brooches.

The Lakeland Sheepskin Centre (Lake Rd., tel. 015394/44466), which also has branches in Ambleside and Keswick, offers moderately priced leather and sheepskin goods, as well as woolens and knitting wool.

Mansion House (Queen's Sq., tel. 015394/42568) has an outstanding range of English cut glass and fine bone china, including Royal Brierly, Wedgwood, Royal Doulton, and Crown Derby.

Festival The **Windermere Festival** (contact the tourist office) takes place in early July, with boating events on the lake, Westmoreland wrestling contests, folk music, and dancing.

Hill Top

Cumberland Bus 505, known as The Coniston Rambler, runs daily from Ambleside (see below) to Hill Top, April–October. The trip takes 45 minutes. Call 01946/63222 for more details.

It is difficult to escape literary associations in the Lake District, as so many writers have been inspired by its landscape or have sought a quiet refuge here. One you may not want to miss, especially if you're traveling with young people, is **Hill Top,** home of children's author and illustrator Beatrix Potter. Now run by the National Trust, Hill Top is a popular—and often crowded—spot. Try to avoid visiting on summer weekends and during school vacations. *Near Sawrey, Ambleside, tel. 015394/36269. Admission: £3.30 adults, £1.75 children. The cottage is so small that admission is limited at peak periods. Open Apr.–Oct., Sat.–Wed. 11–4:30.*

Brockhole National Park Centre

Cumberland Bus 555/556 runs hourly from Windermere train station to Brockhole National Park Centre, a seven-minute ride away. The service operates Monday–Saturday 7:33 AM–7:03 PM; on Sunday, Bus 557 operates on the same route, departing from the train station roughly every two hours from 10:03 AM to 5:03 PM. You can also get there by boat; see Traveling within the Lake District, above.

From Windermere, it's easy to reach most of the Lake District's attractions, especially the southern part of the national park and the Furness area. **Brockhole National Park Centre,** three miles northwest from Windermere station on A591, makes a good starting point; it's easily accessible by bus and boat. A magnificent lakeside mansion with terraced gardens sloping down to the water houses the official visitor center for the Lake District National Park. In addition to tourist information, the center offers a fine range of exhibits: geological, agricultural, industrial, wildlife, and literary. The gardens are at their best in the spring, when floods of daffodils cover the lawns and the azaleas are bursting into bloom. Park activities include lectures, guided walks, and demonstrations of such lakeland crafts as dry-stone-wall building. *Ambleside Rd., near Windermere, tel. 015394/46601. Admission free; £2 parking fee each car. Open Easter–late Oct., daily 10–4.*

Ambleside

The hourly Cumberland Bus 555/556 from Windermere train station has the most frequent service from Windermere to Ambleside, about 17 minutes away. The service operates Monday–Saturday 7:33 AM–7:03 PM; on Sunday, Bus 557 operates on the same route, de-

parting from Windermere train station roughly every two hours from 10:03 AM to 5:03 PM.

Four miles north of Brockhole, lying in the green valley of River Rothay, which empties into Windermere at the head of the lake, is the town of **Ambleside,** a popular center for Lake District excursions. One of the town's most unusual features is **Bridge House,** a tiny 17th-century cottage perched on an arched stone bridge spanning Stock Beck. ("Beck" is the local word for stream.) The building now houses a National Trust shop and information center, open daily from Easter through November.

North of Ambleside the road winds around the lakeside edges of Rydal Water and Grasmere, through a delicate landscape of birch and oak woods, carpeted with wild daffodils in the spring. Here, the craggy mountain summits form a dramatic backdrop.

Dining and **Britannia Inn.** Hikers won't want to miss staying the night at this
Lodging splendid family-owned inn in the heart of some of the region's best
££ walking country. The inn itself has quaint little rooms, outdoor seat-
★ ing, and excellent, hearty homemade food. The modern guest rooms are very comfortable. Cumberland Bus 516 runs three times daily (not Sunday) from Ambleside to the inn; otherwise it's a 4-mile walk west of Ambleside on B5343. Room prices, especially those without private facilities, are usually well under £60 double, but even en-suite rooms in high summer don't go more than a few pounds over our limit. Excellent four-course dinners are under £20; bar meals are very reasonably priced. *Elterwater, Ambleside, LA22 9HP, on B5343, 4 mi west of Ambleside, tel. 015394/37210, fax 015394/37311. 13 rooms, 7 with bath. Facilities: restaurant (reservations essential), bar. MC, V.*

Rydal Mount

Just 3 miles north of Ambleside on the Cumberland Bus 555 route is Rydal Mount. See Ambleside, above, for hours of service.

After about 3 miles, heading north, you'll pass two places closely associated with William Wordsworth. First you'll come to **Rydal Mount,** where he lived from 1813 until his death 37 years later. Wordsworth and his family moved to these grand surroundings when he was nearing the height of his career, and his descendants still live here, surrounded by his furniture, portraits, and the 4½-acre garden laid out by the poet himself. *Rydal Mount, Ambleside, tel. 015394/33002. Admission: £2.50 adults, £1 children. Open Mar.–Oct., daily 9:30–5; Nov.–Feb., Wed.–Mon. 10–4. Closed Jan. 10–Feb. 1.*

Grasmere

The Cumberland Bus 555/556 continues from Rydal Mount for 2½ miles to Grasmere. Journey time from Windermere is 26 minutes.

★ Just before entering Grasmere, you'll reach Wordsworth's earlier home, **Dove Cottage.** A much humbler place than Rydal Mount, it was the poet's home from 1799 (he moved here when he was 19) until 1808. This tiny house, formerly an inn, still contains much of his furniture and many personal belongings. There's also a coffee shop and restaurant.

Dove Cottage is also the headquarters of the **Centre for British Romanticism,** which documents the contributions Wordsworth and his remarkable associates (sometimes called the Lake Poets) made to world literature. Among the associates were his sister Dorothy, Samuel Taylor Coleridge, Thomas De Quincey, and Robert Southey, the last of whom Wordsworth succeeded as poet laureate in 1843. The museum places this outburst of creative genius in its historical, social, and regional context, exhibiting portraits, watercolors, letters, and memorabilia. Poems can be heard on headphone sets in front of display cases of the poets' original manuscripts. The center holds residential summer study conferences on Wordsworth and the Romantics, as well as winter study schools. *The Wordsworth Trust, Dove Cottage, Grasmere LA22 9SH, tel. 015394/35544. Admission to Dove Cottage: £3.90 adults, £1.95 children. Open mid-Feb.–mid-Jan., daily 9:30–5.*

Although Wordsworth was born in Cockermouth, northwest of Keswick, it is Grasmere, with its tiny, wood-fringed lake, that is most closely associated with him. Among his American guests here were the American authors Ralph Waldo Emerson and Nathaniel Hawthorne. Grasmere is sometimes overwhelmed in summer by tourists and cars, but it is worth braving the crowds to explore the interesting shops, cafés, and galleries. Wordsworth, his wife Mary, his sister Dorothy, and his daughter Dora are buried in Grasmere churchyard.

Dining **The Swan.** The accommodations at this lovely, 300-year-old former
££ coaching inn on the main road just outside the village are expensive,
★ but set meals in the comfortable Waggoner restaurant are a treat and more affordable. The four-course meals incorporate local, traditional dishes—to sit and eat in an inn where Wordsworth was a regular visitor won't cost more than £20, excluding drinks. *Grasmere, tel. 015394/35551. Reservations advised. AE, DC, MC, V.*

Coniston

Coniston is on the Bus 505 route via Ambleside, with service Monday–Saturday two to three times a day. Coniston tourist office: 16 Yewdale Rd., tel. 015394/41533.

Formerly a copper-mining village, **Coniston,** with its lake—**Coniston Water**—is now a small resort and boating center. Tracks lead up from the village past an old mine to the **Old Man of Coniston;** you can reach its peak (2,635 feet) in about two hours. Many world speedboat records have been set on the lake here, and sadly, one attempt ended in tragedy: A stone seat in the village commemorates Sir Donald Campbell's death here in 1967. His body was never recovered after his boat crashed.

Lodging **Shepherd's Villa Guest House.** This B&B in a stone country house
¢ has a prime location on the edge of the village. From here you can take in wonderful views of the lake and forested hills; packed lunches are available for hikers. The rooms are large and comfortable, and there is a garden for summer relaxing. *Tilberthwaite Ave., LA21 8EE, tel. 015394/41337. 10 rooms, 5 with bath or shower. No credit cards.*

Brantwood

Bus 505 from Ambleside or Hawkshead Village, will drop you off 1½ miles from Brantwood at Monk Coniston. From here you can walk or take a taxi to Brantwood. The steam yacht Gondola, another option, leaves from Coniston for Brantwood after cruising the lake five times daily between March and October. For information, call 015394/41288.

About 2½ miles along the eastern lake shore from Coniston is
★ **Brantwood,** the home of Victorian artist, critic, and social reformer John Ruskin (1819–1900). It's a rambling white 18th-century house (with Victorian alterations) set in a 250-acre estate. Here you'll find a collection of Ruskin's own paintings, drawings, and books, as well as much of the art he collected in his long life, including a superb group of drawings by Turner. Ruskin's coach and private boat are

still here, too. The extensive grounds, complete with woodland walks, were laid out by Ruskin himself, and visitors can take morning coffee, lunch, or afternoon tea in **Jumping Jenny's** (tel. 015394/41715), Brantwood's brasserie and tearoom, which is appropriately decorated in Pre-Raphaelite style. *Brantwood, tel. 015394/41396. Admission: £3 adults, £1.50 students, children under 16 free. Open mid-Mar.–mid-Nov., daily 11–5:30; mid-Nov.–mid-Mar., Wed.–Sun. 11–4.*

Barrow-in-Furness

The regular bus route from Windermere to Barrow is the No. 518 from Windermere rail station. The journey takes about 2 hours, 10 minutes. For more information, call Cumberland Motor Services at Barrow (tel. 01229/821325).

Barrow-in-Furness is a rather gloomy iron- and steel-producing town, but you can visit the ruins of **Furness Abbey,** once one of the wealthiest monasteries in Britain, in the darkly named Vale of Deadly Nightshade, 1½ miles north of town. Founded in 1124, this Cistercian abbey once owned large tracts of land all over the Lake District. The red sandstone ruins are extensive; what's left intact is a series of graceful arches overlooking the cloisters, and some magnificent canopied seats in the presbytery (the part of the church reserved for the officiating priest). A small visitor center and museum provide information about the abbey's history. *Tel. 01229/823420. Admission: £2 adults, £1.50 senior citizens, £1 children. Open Apr.–Sept., daily 10–6; Oct.–Mar., Tues.–Sun. 10–1, 2–4.*

Dining **Bay Horse Inn.** This restaurant, 1¼ miles east of Ulverston, is a pub
Splurge and bistro combined, with the bistro situated on a veranda over the water. The cooking here is thoroughly imaginative and unexpected, with the set lunch (about £15, excluding drinks), particularly good value. There may be cheese and fennel soup, pork cutlet with sage and apple purée, venison in mustard-and-red-wine sauce, or sweetbreads with tongue and mushrooms in marsala listed on one of the ever-changing menus. There's a great view over the Morecambe estuary. *Canal Foot, Ulverston, tel. 01229/583972. Reservations necessary. MC, V. Closed Sun., Mon. lunch, Jan.–Feb.*

Levens Hall

Levens Hall is on most of the guided tours available in the region and can be reached by local bus from Barrow. It is also easily reached from either Windermere rail station or Kendal bus station on hourly runs on Bus 555/556, weekdays 7:15 AM–7:40 PM, Saturday 7:58 AM–7:40 PM.

★ Sixteenth-century **Levens Hall** is famous for its rare topiary **garden** laid out in 1692, with yew and box hedges cut into curious and elaborate shapes. The hall is also notable for its ornate plasterwork, oak paneling, and leather-covered walls. It has a spacious deer park, a fascinating steam engine collection, a store, and a cafeteria. *Levens Park, Levens, tel. 015395/60321. Admission: house and gardens, £4.20 adults, £3.20 senior citizens, £1 children; gardens only, £2.50 adults, £2.30 senior citizens, £1.40 children. Open Easter–Sept., Sun.–Thurs. 11–5.*

Kendal

Kendal is accessible on Bus 555/556. The most regular services (hourly throughout the day) are from Grasmere, Ambleside, and Windermere; slightly less regular services run from Keswick. Kendal tourist office: Town Hall, Highgate., tel. 01539/725758.

Kendal, 5 miles to the north, was one of the most important textile centers in northern England before the Industrial Revolution. Once you're away from the busy main road, you'll discover quiet, narrow, winding streets and charming courtyards, many dating from medieval times. Take a pleasant stroll along the River Kent where you can visit **Abbott Hall.** Here the **Museum of Lakeland Life and Industry,** housed in the former stable block, offers interesting exhibits on blacksmithing, wheelwrighting, farming, weaving, printing, local architecture and interiors, and regional customs. In the main building is the **Art Gallery,** featuring works by Ruskin and 18th-century portrait painter George Romney, who worked (and died) in Kendal. *Abbott Hall, Kirkland, tel. 01539/722464. Combined admission to museum and gallery: £4 adults, £2 senior citizens, students, and children, £10 family ticket. Admission to one building: £3 adults, £1.50 senior citizens, students, and children, £6 family ticket. Open Apr.–Oct., Mon.–Sat. 10:30–5, Sun. 2–5; Nov.–Mar., weekdays 10;30–4, weekends 2–5.*

At the northern end of town, close to the train station, the **Kendal Museum** details the flora and fauna of the Lake District and contains displays related to Alfred Wainwright, the region's most avid chronicler of countryside matters, who died in 1991. Wainwright's multivolume walking guides to the Lake District are famous the world over; you'll see them in every local book and gift shop. *Station Rd., tel. 01539/721374. Admission: £2 adults, £1.25 senior citizens, £3.75 family ticket. Open Mon.–Sat. 10.30–5, Sun. 2–5.*

Lodging **Martindales.** This well-appointed guest house is just three minutes'
£ walk from the town center. All the bedrooms have baths en suite, TV, and tea/coffeemakers. An evening meal is available for £9, though you must book this in advance. *9–11 Sandes Ave., LA9 4LL, tel. 01539/724028. 8 rooms with bath. MC, V.*

¢ **Holmfield.** Set in its own grounds in Kendal, 10 minutes' walk from
★ the center, this fine nonsmoking establishment treats its guests well; the public rooms have open fireplaces, there's a pool, and advice is freely offered on local walks. *41 Kendal Green, LA9 5PP, tel. and fax 01539/720790. 3 rooms with separate bath. No credit cards.*

Dining **The Moon.** A bistro ambience prevails in this small, centrally located
££ restaurant, whose good reputation has been won with quality home-
★ made foods. There's always a strong selection of vegetarian dishes, and the cooking can be adventurous, using Mediterranean and Asian flourishes at times. Good house wines are available, too. *129 Highgate, tel. 01539/729254. Reservations advised. MC, V. Closed lunch, and mid-Jan.–mid-Feb.*

The Arts and The **Brewery Arts Centre** in Kendal is a converted brewery that now
Nightlife holds an **art gallery, a theater, a theater workshop,** and a **cinema.** One of the most active centers of creative performance in the southern part of the Lake District, it offers special events, festivals, and art exhibitions throughout the year. One of the main annual events is the Jazz and Blues Festival, held every November; the Arts Centre can provide program details. It also has an excellent coffee bar, a real-ale bar, and a health food café open for lunch. *Highgate, tel. 01539/725133. Open Mon.–Sat. 9 AM–11 PM. Free parking.*

Tour 2: Keswick and the Northern Lakes

Keswick (pronounced "Kezzick") is our alternative choice to Windermere as a touring center for the Lake District, though both towns are equally crowded in the summer. If you want to explore on foot, however, Keswick is your better bet. There are regular bus routes to Keswick across the central Pennines from York on the east coast, so you could make a visit to the Lakes from there.

Keswick

Keswick tourist office: Moot Hall, Market Sq., tel. 017687/72645.

Keswick is the next stop north after Windermere on the bus and train routes from London (*see* Traveling within the Lake District *in* Tour 1, *above*, for details); it's also one of the terminal points of Bus 555/556, with regular services to and from Kendal, Windermere, Ambleside, and Grasmere.

The great Lakeland mountains of Skiddaw and Blencathra brood over the gray slate houses of Keswick on the scenic shores of Derwentwater. An old market and mining center, Keswick was transformed by the arrival of the railroad. Many of the best hiking routes radiate from here, so it is more of a touring base than a tourist destination. People stroll the congested, narrow streets in boots and corduroy hiking trousers, and there are plenty of mountaineering shops, as well as hotels, guest houses, pubs, and restaurants.

With a population of only 6,000, Keswick is a compact town, and all the interesting sights lie within easy walking distance of the central streets: Market Place, Main Street, and Lake Road. The town received its market charter in the 13th century, and its Saturday market is still going strong. Later centuries brought a wealth of industries, especially textile manufacturing, which was dependent on power from the area's fast-flowing streams. The introduction of lead and copper mining in the 16th century brought scores of skilled German laborers here.

The handsome 19th-century **Moot Hall** (assembly hall) on Market Place has served as both the Keswick town hall and the local prison. Now it houses the main **tourist information center** for the region.

Keswick offers a number of outdoor attractions, among them **Hope Park,** just beside the lake, with a putting green and an aviary. **Fitz Park,** a garden area bordering the River Greta (just behind the town center), is pleasant for picnics and leisurely strolls. Here you will also find the **Keswick Museum and Art Gallery.** Exhibits include manuscripts by Wordsworth and other Lakeland writers, a diorama of the Lake District, a local geological and natural history collection, some unusual "musical" stones, and an assortment of watercolor paintings. *Station Rd., tel. 017687/73263. Admission: £1 adults, 50p children. Open Easter–Oct., Sun.–Fri. 10–noon and 1–4.*

Castlerigg Stone Circle stands on the eastern edge of town. A clearly marked route leads to a 200-foot-long path running through a pasture; beyond this, set in a great natural hollow called St. John's Vale, stands an intriguing circle of Neolithic or Bronze Age stones, none of them tall, but nonetheless impressive in this awesome setting ringed with mountains. The circle can be visited during daylight hours, and there is no admission charge.

Another aspect of Keswick's history comes into sharp focus at the **Cumberland Pencil Museum.** Keswick was the first place in the world to manufacture pencils, as graphite (the material from which pencil lead is made) was discovered in neighboring Borrowdale in the 16th century. Pencils are still produced here. The museum, housed in the factory just off Main Street, outlines the history of pencils from early times to the present. *Southey Works, Greta Bridge, tel. 017687/73626. Admission: £2 adults, £1 senior citizens and children, £4.50 family ticket. Open daily 9:30–4.*

Hill walks originating in Keswick include routes across the **Latrigg** and **Skiddaw** mountains, and the great ridge of **Blencathra.** You can reach Latrigg (1,203 feet), the nearest of the three, from Station Road: Pass the Keswick Hotel, then follow the road under the old railroad bridge, keeping left, toward Briar Rigg. After about 100 yards, a sign on the right indicates the trail to Latrigg—a 2-hour round-trip from Keswick.

★ To understand why **Derwentwater** is considered one of England's finest lakes, take a short walk from Keswick's town center to the lake shore, and follow the **Friar's Crag** path—about 15 minutes' level walk from the center. This pine-tree-fringed peninsula is a favorite vantage point, with its view over the lake, the surrounding ring of mountains, and many tiny wooded islands. Ahead you will see the crags that line the **Jaws of** Borrowdale and overhang a dramatic mountain ravine—the perfect setting for a Romantic painting or poem.

Another essential excursion is a wooden-launch cruise around Derwentwater. Between late March and November, cruises set off every hour in each direction from a wooden dock at the lake shore. You can also rent a rowboat here. Landing stages around the lake provide access to some spectacular hiking trails in the nearby hills. (*See* Tour 1 By Boat section, *above.*)

Walking is perhaps the best way to discover the delights of this area. Don't worry if you don't have all the equipment; you can buy all the relevant maps and provisions in Keswick and even rent a pair of hiking boots. You may want to leave your car behind, as parking is difficult in the higher valleys, and both the Derwentwater launches and the Borrowdale bus service between Keswick and Seatoller run frequently. A number of pleasant country hotels, guest houses, and B&Bs, both on the lake and in the interior valley, can provide a base for your walking excursions. For more information, contact Keswick's Lake District National Park information center (Lake Rd., tel. 017687/72803).

Lodging **Acorn House.** This large B&B is sited in its own attractive garden,
££ but close to the town center. The rooms are spacious, with tea/
★ coffeemakers. The best room here has a four-poster bed. *Ambleside Rd., CA12 4DL, tel. 017687/72553. 10 rooms, 4 with bath. MC, V.*

£ **Greystones.** Aptly named, this guest house is built from the local gray slate; it has fine views over the fells and is situated near the center of town. Rooms are comfortably furnished and have TVs and tea/coffeemakers, while a small garden has outdoor seating in the summer. The owner is knowledgeable about walks in the surrounding area and will help you plan routes. Note that prices rarely stray above £45 per double room, and that longer stays attract discounts. *Ambleside Rd., CA12 4DP, tel. 017687/73108. 9 rooms with bath or shower. Facilities: garden. V.*

£ **Ravensworth.** A century-old imposing guest house built of Lakeland slate, this comfortable haven is located close to Fitz Park and the town center. All the bedrooms have tea/coffeemakers and evening meals are available. *29 Station St., CA12 5HH, tel. 017687/72476. 8 rooms with bath. AE, MC, V.*

Dining **La Primavera.** The River Greta runs below this stylish restaurant at
££ the north end of town. Here you have a choice of English or Italian dishes—the grilled steaks are particularly tasty—and a good wine

list. *Greta Bridge, High Hill, tel. 017687/74621. Reservations advised. MC, V. Closed Mon. and Jan.*

£ **Four in Hand.** This is a typical Cumbrian pub, with a 19th-century paneled bar decorated with horse brasses and bank notes. The imaginative touches in its lunch and dinner menu include hot asparagus rolled in ham, and pâté with red currant jelly; the traditional dishes are steaks, meat pies, and Cumberland sausage. *Lake Rd., tel. 017687/72069. No credit cards.*

¢ **Abraham's Café Tea Room.** Located inside George Fisher's outdoor equipment shop, this casual eatery is open daily for nourishing snacks and meals. Vegetarian dishes are available, as are beers, wines, and mulled wine—just the thing after a long winter's walk. *2 Borrowdale Rd., tel. 017687/72178. No credit cards.*

Penrith

Penrith is 40 minutes from Keswick by Cumberland Bus X5. There are five buses a day Monday–Saturday, two on Sunday. Penrith tourist office: Robinson's School, Middlegate, tel. 01768/67466.

The town of **Penrith** was the capital of the semi-independent kingdom of Cumbria in the 9th and 10th centuries. Later, Cumbria became part of the Scottish kingdom of Strathclyde; in the year 1070, it was incorporated into England. Even at this time, Penrith was a thriving market town and an important staging post on the road to Scotland. The warning beacon on the hill above the town (**Beacon Pike,** where a stone tower still stands) was lit to alert townsfolk of approaching enemies, usually Scots. The last invasion from Scotland was that of the Jacobites in 1745, who followed Bonnie Prince Charlie in his romantic but ill-fated attempt to restore the Stuart dynasty to the British throne. Charlie and his aides stayed in part of the present **George Hotel** (*see below*) before their retreat.

To find out more about Penrith's history, stop in at the **Penrith Museum** on Middlegate. Built in the 16th century, the building served as a school from 1670 to the 1970s; it now contains a fascinating exhibit of local historical artifacts. Ask at the museum about the historic "town trail" route. It takes you through narrow byways to the **plague stone** on King Street, where food was left for the plague-stricken; to a churchyard with 1,000-year-old "hog-back" tombstones (i.e., stones carved as stylized "houses of the dead"); and finally to the ruins of the 15th-century red sandstone **castle.** *Robinson's School, Middlegate, tel. 01768/64671, ext. 228. Admission free. Open Easter–June and Oct., Mon.–Sat. 10–5, Sun. 1–5; June–Sept., Mon.–Sat. 10–7, Sun. 1–6; Nov.–Easter, Mon.–Sat. 10–5.*

Three miles southwest of town is **Dalemain,** a country house with a 12th-century peel (tower) built to protect the occupants from raiding Scots. A medieval hall was added, as well as a number of extensions from the 16th to the 18th centuries, culminating in an imposing Georgian facade of local pink sandstone. The result is a delightful hodgepodge of architectural styles. Inside you can see a magnificent oak staircase, furniture dating from the mid-17th century (including Cumbrian "courting" chairs), a Chinese drawing room adorned with hand-painted wallpaper, a 16th-century "fretwork room" with intricate plasterwork, a nursery complete with an elaborate 18th-century dollhouse, and many fine paintings, including masterpieces by Van Dyck. The tower houses a small military museum with mementos from local army regiments. There's also a coffee shop, a picnic area, and sweeping gardens, which include an intriguing Tudor grotto. *Penrith, tel. 01768/486450. Admission to house, garden, and museum: £4 adults, £3 children, £11 family ticket. Open Easter–mid-Oct., Sun.–Thurs. 11:15–5.*

Dining and   **George Hotel.** This centrally located, 300-year-old, dignified estab-
Lodging   lishment—once a coaching inn—features paneling, antique furni-
  ££   ture, and big bay windows. Food is served in both the bar and the
restaurant, but stay at the bar for the less expensive fare, which
should cost you well under £20; there are particularly good-value set
lunches and dinners. *Devonshire St., Penrith, CA11 7SU, tel. 01768/
62696, fax 01768/68223. 31 rooms, 30 with bath. Facilities: restaurant, bar. MC, V.*

*Bus 108 runs from Penrith to Patterdale via Ullswater (Pooley
Bridge) eight times a day in the summer months, five in winter;
journey time is normally just less than an hour.*

Visitable from Penrith (only 6 miles away) is **Ullswater,** the region's
second-largest lake. Hemmed in by towering hills, it is spectacular.
Follow the main road around to **Glenridding** and **Patterdale** at the
★ southern end of the lake and you'll reach the foot of **Helvellyn** (3,118
feet). It is an arduous climb to the top and shouldn't be attempted in
poor weather or by inexperienced hikers. If you do try, paths run
from the road between Glenridding and Patterdale, on the way passing Red Tarn, which, at 2,356 feet, is the highest Lake District tarn.
For those who'd rather see Ullswater from a less exalted level,
steamers leave Glenridding's pier for Pooley Bridge, offering a
pleasant tour along the lake.

Lodore, Grange, and Seatoller

*Bus 79 travels from Keswick to Lodore, Grange, and Seatoller four
times a day, Monday–Saturday, at 10:25 AM, 1:20 PM, 4 PM, and 5:40
PM. Total trip time to Lodore is 11 minutes, 16 minutes to Grange, and
28 minutes to Seatoller; for information, call Keswick tourist office
(see above).*

Lodore's spectacular waterfall, behind the Lodore Swiss Hotel, is
well worth a slight detour from the main road. Go about a mile south
★ to the village of **Grange,** at the head of the **Borrowdale Valley.** This is
a popular center for walkers, particularly in the summer. An assortment of cafés allows you to fuel up before beginning your vigorous
walk across the fells.

From Grange, the bus travels south about 2 miles to **Rosthwaite,** a
tranquil farming village with an ample supply of local B&Bs and
guest houses. Here you're in the Borrowdale valley, whose varied
landscape of green valley floor and surrounding crags has long been
considered one of the region's most magnificent spots. Not all walks
in Borrowdale have to be full-fledged hikes or climbs; you can con-
fine yourself to relatively easy valley and woodland routes, or take a
stroll along Stonethwaite Beck, the lovely little river that runs
through Rosthwaite.

Seatoller, also reached by Bus 79, is the southernmost village in the
Borrowdale valley, lying at 1,176 feet; it's the starting and terminus
point for buses to and from Keswick. It is also the location of a Lake
District National Park information center (Dalehead Base,
Seatoller Barn, tel. 017687/77294). Behind Seatoller, the steep
Borrowdale Fells rise dramatically. Get out and walk wherever inspiration strikes, and in the spring, keep an eye open and your camera ready for newborn lambs roaming the hillsides. From here, to
the south, you can also see England's highest mountain, **Scafell Pike**
(3,210 feet). The usual route up the mountain, for experienced walkers, is from the hamlet of Seathwaite, just a mile or so south of
Seatoller.

Lodging   **The Grange.** This slate-built B&B, with its own garden, is located in
  ¢   the village of Grange-in-Borrowdale. The atmospheric accommoda-
★ tion makes a great base for walking and boating. Most of the cozy
bedrooms have excellent views, and the owners are very welcoming.

Grange-in-Borrowdale, CA12 5UQ, tel. 017687/77251. 7 rooms, 1 with bath. No credit cards. Closed Nov.–mid-Mar.

Dining **Yew Tree Restaurant.** The atmosphere here is intimate and gracious,
££ and the inventive menu is based largely on local produce. Specialties include pan-fried trout and, as an appetizer, marinated and smoked fish. Other English country dishes, including venison, hare, eel, and salmon, are seasonally available. The low-beamed ceiling, long open fireplace, and excellent bar add to the pleasure of eating here. *Borrowdale, tel. 017687/77634. Reservations advised. MC, V. Closed Mon., Fri. lunch, and Jan.–mid-Feb.*

Cockermouth

Cumberland Bus 35/36/X5 runs a daily service from Keswick to Cockermouth, leaving eight times a day Monday–Saturday, three times a day Sunday. Check with the Keswick tourist office for the latest schedule (see above).

Cockermouth, 13 miles north, along the **Crummock Water,** was the birthplace of William Wordsworth. His childhood home, **Wordsworth House,** is a typical 18th-century north-country gentleman's home, now owned by the National Trust. Some of the poet's furniture and personal items are on display here, and you can explore the garden he played in as a child. *Main St., tel. 01900/824805. Admission: £2.40 adults, £1.20 children. Open Apr.–Oct. weekdays 11–5, Sat. in July and Aug., 11–5.*

Wordsworth's father is buried in the churchyard nearby, and in the church itself is a stained-glass window in memory of the poet. Outside is the site of the old grammar school Wordsworth attended, now covered with other buildings. Another pupil here was Fletcher Christian, ringleader of the notorious mutiny on HMS *Bounty;* he was born in 1764 at **Moorland Close,** a farmhouse in the village of Eaglesfield, about 2 miles outside of town. It is not open to the public. If you wander around Cockermouth, you will find a maze of narrow streets, a ruined Norman castle (public access is not permitted), and a traditional outdoor market, held each Monday. An old bell is still rung at the start of trading.

Dining **Trout Hotel.** The Trout Hotel is quite large (23 bedrooms), but it's
££ above an affordable range for lodging. However, the food that's
★ served in the red plush bar is very reasonably priced; there's also a decent restaurant with a set menu of locally inspired dishes costing under £20 per person. The garden leads down to the River Cocker for pleasant summer eating. *Crown St., tel. 01900/823591. MC, V.*

11 East Anglia

Cambridge, Bury St. Edmunds, Norwich, Colchester, Lincoln

Occupying an area of southeastern England that juts out, knoblike, into the North Sea, East Anglia comprises the counties of Essex, Norfolk, Suffolk, and Cambridgeshire. If you take the Network Southeast rail lines from London, the region is only 1 to 2 hours away: Its beautiful towns make convenient and fairly inexpensive excursions from the capital. A number of bus lines also offer leisurely and scenic tours through some of the most picturesque countryside in England.

For the budget traveler, East Anglia is a good region to explore, by land or by water, and it doesn't cost very much in transportation. Also, this part of England abounds with stimulating cultural and scenic attractions that are inexpensive, if not free. Historically the region has played a vital role in Britain's past, and visitors can amble through the land and see evidence of the Celts, Romans, Vikings, and scholars who have left their impressions through the ages.

North Essex's Saffron Walden—named for the prized saffron that grows in its fields—is one of the most resplendent towns in southern England. A walk through the streets will reveal the many well-preserved wood-frame houses, several with pargeting, the ancient decorative art of plasterwork that typically has vine and leaf patterns.

In flat Cambridgeshire, the bleakness of the Fens is tempered by the broad sweep of the sky and provides a startling landscape against which Ely Cathedral, or the "Ship of the Fens," stands in dramatic relief. Cambridge boasts some of the greatest institutional architecture in the world, befitting its stature as one of the most famous university towns. It retains its small, market-town atmosphere, however, and bookworms will find an unrivaled collection of secondhand books here.

The Fens give way to the gently rolling and still largely rural inland of Suffolk, its coast a refuge for birds and other wildlife. The wetland reasserts itself in Norfolk, but then surrenders to the most spectacular broadland in the British Isles: famous for its natural waterways and lakes, its reed beds, and bird life.

Our tour also takes in neighboring Lincolnshire, across that arm of the North Sea known as The Wash. Here too, in Lincoln itself, a great cathedral towers over the plains, built on the site of a Roman settlement. And here too, the tourist will seldom be troubled by crowds.

Essential Information

Lodging   For the most part, the hotels in East Anglia's towns are small and intimate, and even the larger accommodations have fewer than 100 rooms. As a result of their modest sizes, the lodgings in this region tend to have friendly atmospheres and can offer more personal service. The relatively few hotels in downtown Cambridge are rather overpriced: There simply isn't room for hotels among the historic buildings crowded together, but there are many guest houses in the suburbs. The town fills up in the summer months, and you may have to look farther afield for accommodations. Prices tend to be below London levels, but because East Anglia has long been one of the most prosperous sections of England, you must search carefully for hotel bargains. Highly recommended establishments are indicated by a star ★.

Dining   East Anglia is a rich agricultural region with excellent produce. Traditional favorites such as Norfolk Black turkeys and a variety of game are frequently available. The long coastline provides a number of delicacies such as Cromer crabs and Yarmouth bloaters (a kind of smoked herring), and you'll find a wide selection of fish year-round. Around the Essex coast near Colchester you can get your fill of oysters.

Among the touring bases, Norfolk is particularly well served with downtown restaurants. Cambridge, which was once a gastronomic desert, has seen a renaissance, probably as a result of its economic upturn. As for pub food, the quality often varies, but generally you'll be able to get a hearty, cheap lunch or dinner for under £5.

Unless otherwise noted, reservations are not needed and dress is casual. Highly recommended restaurants are indicated by a star ★.

Shopping   Cambridge is a main shopping area for a wide region, and it has all the usual chain stores, many situated in the **Grafton Centre Shopping Precinct.** More interesting—and expensive—are the small specialty stores found among the colleges in the center of town, especially in and around Trinity Street, King's Parade, Rose Crescent, and Market Hill.

Biking   The flat landscape of the Fens in Norfolk and Cambridgeshire provides ideal country for bicycling. Keep in mind, however, that the country surrounding Cambridge can get very congested with auto traffic. Suffolk, with its gently rolling hills, will provide more of a challenge, and its beauty is equally rewarding. If you want to rent a bicycle, these shops are all near the train stations or centrally located: in Cambridge, **Geoff's Bike Hire** (65 Devonshire Rd., tel. 01223/65629); in Great Yarmouth, **Lawford's** (224 Northgay St., tel. 01493/842741); in Norwich, **ABC Cycles** (72A Gloucester St., tel. 01603/632467); and in Ipswich, **Bicycle Doctor** (18 Bartholomew St., tel. 01473/259853).

Hiking   **Peddar's Way,** the most walkable Roman road in England, runs for 50 miles from Knettishall on the Norfolk/Suffolk border due northwest to Holme-next-the-Sea, close to Hunstanton. Although you can do the whole distance, perhaps the best part is from Castle Acre, just north of Swaffham, to Holme, about 20 miles.

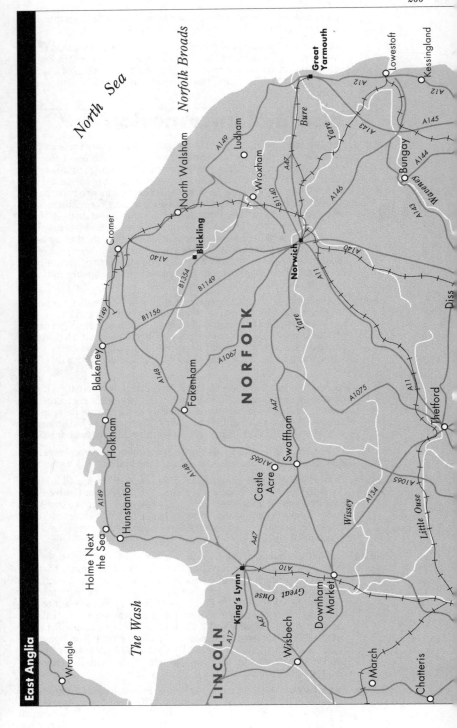

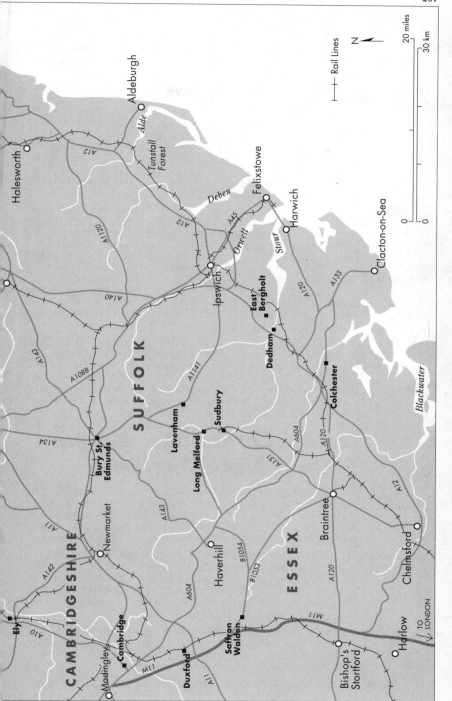

N

—+— Rail Lines

0   20 miles
0   30 km

Halesworth

Aldeburgh

Alde

Tunstall
Forest

Deben

A12

A12

A1120

Felixstowe

A45

Harwich

Orwell

Stow

Ipswich

East
Bergholt

A140

Clacton-on-Sea

A133

A143

A1088

Dedham

A120

SUFFOLK

A1141

Colchester

Blackwater

Lavenham

Sudbury

A134

Long Melford

A604

Bury St.
Edmunds

A131

A120

A12

Newmarket

A143

Haverhill

A11

Braintree

A120

A142

B1054

ESSEX

Chelmsford

CAMBRIDGESHIRE

Ely

A10

Madingley

B1053

Saffron
Walden

Cambridge

M11

Duxford

A11

Bishop's
Stortford

Harlow

M11

TO
LONDON

Beaches Beautiful and substantial beaches can be found on the north Norfolk coast. On the more exposed segments of the East Coast, beaches tend to shelve steeply, while those in Suffolk are always more appealing at low tide, when there is normally a strip of clean sand. Public toilets and changing facilities are usually located on the beach.

The Arts and Nightlife The **Cambridge Arts Theatre** puts on major touring productions and a Christmas pantomime every year, and one of the classical Greek dramas is presented every three years. For the past 30-some years the annual Cambridge Footlights Review, training ground for much comic talent, has been hosted here. The **Arts Cinema** (8 Market Passage, tel. 01223/352001) is an important venue for art films and the annual Cambridge Animated Film Festival. The **ADC Theatre** is the headquarters of the University Amateur Dramatics Club. Anything but amateur, the club stages productions comparable with those of the best professional theater.

Festivals For the entire month of July, several festivals in succession take over the city of **Cambridge**. Three separate festivals are devoted to classical music—the **Cambridge Summer Recitals** feature organ music performed in the college chapels. The **Cambridge Film Festival** focuses on some aspect of cinema from around the world. The **Cambridge Folk Festival**, on the last weekend of the month at Cherry Hinton Hill, is Britain's premier showcase for acoustic music of all types. Like all self-respecting British festivals, there's also a **Fringe Festival**, while **Summer in the City** is a program of events such as fireworks displays for families. Full schedules and information can be obtained by calling 01223/463363.

The wide-ranging **King's Lynn Festival** (King's Lynn Festival Office, 27 King St., King's Lynn, PE30 1HA, tel. 01553/773578), based at the King's Lynn Arts Centre, encompasses concerts, exhibitions, theater, dance, films, literary events, and children's programs. Smaller festivals are held in Lincoln, Bury St. Edmunds, and Ely during the summer. Check with tourist information centers for details.

Tour 1: Cambridge and the Suffolk Wool Churches

The hub of this tour is the university town of Cambridge, 54 miles north of London. Frequent train and bus service connects Cambridge to Ely, Audley End, and Saffron Walden. Included here is a popular walking tour from Cambridge to Grantchester, the village made famous by Rupert Brooke, the World War I poet.

From London *By Train* The quickest service to Cambridge takes less than an hour from Liverpool Street (tel. 0171/928–5100) or King's Cross (tel. 0171/278–2477) stations in London. The longest service takes about 1 hour, 20 minutes. Four trains per hour generally depart Monday–Saturday 6:40 AM–11:20 PM; Sunday service begins at 8:11 AM and runs hourly (two trains per hour) until 11:11 PM.

By Bus **National Express** (tel. 0171/730–0202) buses depart from London's Victoria Coach Station daily at least once every hour between 9 AM and 9 PM, taking 2 hours for the trip. Call in Cambridge (tel. 01223/460711) for information on local connecting service.

By Car From London, Cambridge is just off M11. At Exit 9, M11 connects with A11 to Norwich (114 miles); A45, off A11, goes to Bury St. Edmunds. London to Cambridge takes about 75 minutes; Cambridge to Bury St. Edmunds, about 45 minutes; Cambridge to Norwich, about 90 minutes. The drive from London to Bury St.

This guidebook teaches you how to budget your money.

This page is for slow learners.

We all make mistakes. So if you happen to find yourself making a costly one, call Western Union. With them, you can receive money from the States within minutes at any of our European locations. Plus, it's already been converted into the appropriate currency.

Just call our numbers in Austria 0222 892 0380, Belgium 02 753 2150, Denmark 800 107 11, Finland 9 800 20440, France 161 43 54 46 12, Germany 069 2648201, 0681 933 3328, Greece 01 687 3850, Ireland 1 800 395 395,* Italy 039 6 167016840, Netherlands 06 0566,* Poland 22 37 1826, Spain 93 301 1212, Sweden 020 741 742, United Kingdom 0 800 833 833,* or if you're in the United States 1 800 325 6000.*

And since nobody's perfect, you might want to keep these numbers in your wallet, for those times when nothing else is in there.

WESTERN UNION | MONEY TRANSFER®

*The fastest way to send money worldwide.*ᴼᴹ

Edmunds is about 1 hour, 45 minutes; London to Norwich is about 2 hours.

Cambridge

Guide Friday operates city tours of Cambridge on open-top buses throughout the year, taking in the Backs, the colleges, and the American war cemetery (daily, every 15 minutes, June–Sept; at least once per hour Oct.–May; tel. 01223/62444 for current schedule). Tickets (£6.50 adults, £4.50 students and senior citizens, and £2 children under 12), can be bought from the office at Cambridge train station or on the bus itself, and you can join the tours either at the station or at any of the specially marked bus stops in the city. From Cambridge train station, Cambuses go into the center of town until 6 PM. **Premier Travel** *(tel. 01223/237262) and* **Cambus** *(tel. 01223/423554) also provide connecting service within East Anglia. Cambridge tourist office: Wheeler St. (just behind the Corn Exchange), tel. 01223/322640.*

With the spires of the university buildings framed by towering trees and expansive meadows, and the medieval streets and passages enhanced by gardens and the riverbanks, the city of **Cambridge** is among the loveliest in England. The city—situated on a bend of the River Cam, on the edge of the once uninhabited and inhospitable Great Fen—has been settled since prehistoric times. It was once a Roman town, and later the Cam helped to protect it from Danish raiders. During the Middle Ages, Cambridge gained its real importance with the founding of the university, which is still the heart of the city. Several college buildings survive from the medieval period, and most generations since have added more. These were often designed by the best architects of the day and financed by kings and princes, with the result that Cambridge is an illustrated history of the best of English architecture.

For centuries the university has ranked among the world's greatest seats of learning, and since the time of its most famous scientific alumnus, Sir Isaac Newton, it has outshone Oxford in the natural sciences. During the past 10 years, the university has focused its research facilities on computer technology and other high-tech fields. Cambridge is now one of Britain's "Silicon Valleys," and a new prosperity has enlivened the city center.

The colleges are built around a series of courts, or quadrangles, whose velvety lawns are the envy of many an amateur gardener. As students and fellows (faculty) live and work in these courts, access for tourists is restricted, especially at term time (when the university is in session), and during the examination period, from April to mid-June. Tourists are not normally allowed into college buildings other than chapels and dining halls. The peace of the college courts is quite remarkable, and just to stroll through them gives an immediate sense of the more than 700 years of scholastic calm.

Numbers in the margin correspond to points of interest on the Cambridge map.

1 The oldest college is **Peterhouse,** on Trumpington Street, which was founded in 1281 by the bishop of Ely. Parts of the dining hall date from 1290; the chapel, in late Gothic style, dates from 1632. On the river side of the buildings is a large and tranquil deer park—without any deer, but with some good apple trees!

2 Across the road stands **Pembroke College,** whose first court has some of the oldest buildings in Cambridge and dates from the 14th century. On the south side, Christopher Wren's chapel (completed in 1665) looks like a distinctly modern intrusion. You can walk through the college, around a delightful garden, and past the fellows' bowling green.

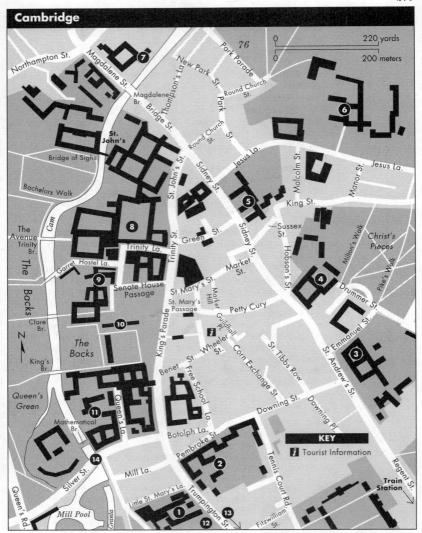

Cambridge

Christ's College, **4**

Emmanuel College, **3**

Fitzwilliam
Museum, **12**

Jesus College, **6**

King's College
Chapel, **10**

Magdalene College, **7**

Pembroke College, **2**

Peterhouse, **1**

Queens' College, **11**

Sidney Sussex
College, **5**

Silver Street Bridge
and Mill Lane, **14**

Trinity College, **8**

Trinity Hall, **9**

University Botanic
Garden, **13**

Down Pembroke and Downing streets, on St. Andrew's Street, is **Emmanuel College,** whose chapel and colonnade are also by Christopher Wren. Among the portraits of famous members of the college hanging in Emmanuel Hall is one of John Harvard, founder of Harvard University. Indeed, a number of the Pilgrim Fathers were Emmanuel alumni, and they remembered their alma mater in naming Cambridge, Massachusetts. The gateway of **Christ's College,** also on St. Andrew's Street, bears the enormous coat of arms of its patroness, Lady Margaret Beaufort, mother of Henry VII. **Sidney Sussex College,** located where St. Andrew's Street becomes Sidney Street, is a smaller foundation with many 17th- and 18th-century buildings. Oliver Cromwell was a student here in 1616: The hall contains his portrait, and his head has been buried here since 1960.

In contrast to the compact Sidney Sussex College is its spacious neighbor, **Jesus College.** Parts of its chapel were built in the Middle Ages for the nunnery of St. Radegund, which existed on the site before the college. Victorian restoration of the building includes some Pre-Raphaelite stained-glass windows. Uniquely in Cambridge, this college incorporates cloisters, also a remnant of the nunnery.

Across Magdalene (pronounced "maudlin") Bridge, a cast-iron 1820 structure, is **Magdalene College,** originally a 15th-century hostel for Benedictine monks, distinguished by pretty redbrick courts. The college's Pepys Library contains the books and desk of the 17th-century diarist, Samuel Pepys. *Admission free. Open Apr.–Sept., daily 11:30–12:30 and 2:30–3:30, Oct.–Mar., daily 2:30–3:30.*

Trinity, the largest of the colleges, with nearly 700 undergraduates, can sometimes be approached by a bridge that joins it with neighboring St. John's College (which straddles the river by means of the Bridge of Sighs). This approach gives a fine view of Christopher Wren's magnificent library, colonnaded and seemingly constructed as much of light as of stone. Many of Trinity's features match its size, not least its 17th-century "great court," and the massive and detailed gatehouse where you'll find Great Tom, a giant clock that strikes each hour with high and low notes. At the end of the 1960s Prince Charles was an undergraduate here.

Cambridge's celebrated **Backs** are gardens and meadows running down to the River Cam's banks; some colleges back onto them. A good vantage point from which to appreciate the Backs is Trinity's neighbor, **Trinity Hall,** where you can sit on a wall by the river and watch students in punts (flat-bottomed boats with square ends that are guided with a pole) manipulate their poles under the ancient bridges. Between the bridges is one of the few strictly university buildings (i.e., not part of a particular college), the **Senate House,** a classical structure of the 1720s, which is used for graduation ceremonies.

★ **King's College Chapel,** one of the most beautiful buildings in England, is for most people the high point of their visit to Cambridge. Begun in the mid-15th century by Henry VI, it was not completed for 100 years, mainly because of lack of funds. Built in the late-Gothic English style known as Perpendicular, its great fan-vaulted roof is supported only by a tracery of soaring side columns, and it seems to float over a huge space, lit by ever-changing light from the vast and ancient stained-glass windows. Rubens's *Adoration of the Magi* hangs behind the altar. Every Christmas Eve, a festival of carols performed by the college choir is broadcast from the chapel to the world.

★ Tucked away on Queens Lane, next to the wide lawns that lead down from King's to the Backs, is **Queens' College,** named after the consorts of Henry VI and Edward IV. The secluded "cloister court" looks untouched since its completion in the 1540s. Queens' boasts a very different kind of masterpiece from King's College Chapel in the

Mathematical Bridge (best seen from the Silver Street road bridge), an arched wooden structure across the river that was originally held together without fastenings. The present bridge, dating from 1902, is securely bolted.

⑫ Trumpington Street, where a stream runs beside the road, has elegant 18th-century houses and the **Fitzwilliam Museum,** a classical building with an outstanding collection of art (including paintings by John Constable) and antiquities, with a particularly good display from ancient Egypt. The museum has a coffee bar and restaurant. *Tel. 01223/332900. Admission free but £2 donation preferred. Open Tues.–Sat. 12:30–5:30, Sun. 2:15–5. Guided tours every Sun. at 2:30.*

⑬ Just beyond central Cambridge, in Bateman Street off Trumpington Road, is the **University Botanic Garden,** which was laid out in 1846 and contains, among its rare specimens, a limestone rock garden. *Cory Lodge, Bateman St., tel. 01223/336265. Admission free except on weekends, Mar.–Oct. £1.50 adults, £1 children. Open May–Sept., daily 10–6, Sun. 10–6; Feb.–Apr., Oct., daily 10–5; Nov.–Jan., daily 10–4.*

⑭ The **Silver Street Bridge** and **Mill Lane** are good places to rent punts on the river. You can either punt along the Backs to Magdalene Bridge and beyond, or punt upstream to **Grantchester,** a village celebrated by Rupert Brooke, one of a generation of poets lost in World War I. Grantchester is a long way for the inexperienced punter, so you may prefer to make the scenic 2-mile trip on foot. The path roughly follows the river, going through college playing fields and the Grantchester Meadows.

Lodging **Arundel House Hotel.** This elegantly proportioned Victorian row ho-
££ tel overlooks the River Cam, with Jesus Green in the background. Bedrooms have been redecorated and are furnished very comfortably with locally made mahogany furniture. The restaurant serves French and English cuisine, children's and vegetarian menus, and bar meals, and it has a reputation for offering some of the best and most reasonably priced food in the area. *53 Chesterton Rd., CB4 3AN, tel. 01223/67701, fax 01223/67721. 105 rooms with bath or shower. Facilities: restaurant, bar, TV with video of guided tour of Cambridge. AE, DC, MC, V. Closed Dec. 25–26.*

£ **Suffolk House.** Set to the north of the city in a secluded garden, this large, renovated 1930s detached house with a gabled front maintains a high standard of privacy, comfort, and cleanliness, and its staff warmly welcomes all guests. You can walk to the city center from the hotel in less than 20 minutes. *69 Milton Rd., CB4 1XA, tel. 01223/352016. 11 rooms, all with shower or bath. MC, V.*

¢ **Benson House.** Situated opposite Newhall College in North Cam-
★ bridge, and within a 10-minute walk from the city center and university, this well-established guest house offers comfortable and convenient accommodations for as low as £30 a night. Be sure to try one of the traditional English breakfasts, and meet with other guests in the residents' lounge. Benson House especially welcomes children, and pets are allowed. *24 Huntingdon Rd., CB3 0HH, tel. 01223/311594. 9 rooms, 4 with shower or bath. MC, V.*

¢ **Christina's Guest House.** This modern building in a quiet location is a 15-minute walk from the colleges and city center. All bedrooms include color TV, and guests are invited to enjoy the comfortable lounge area. Each room has a tea/coffeemaker. *47 St. Andrews Rd., CB4 1DL, tel. 01223/65855. 6 rooms, 5 with bath. No credit cards.*

Dining **Three Horseshoes.** This early 19th-century thatched cottage in-
££ cludes a recently added conservatory. A pub restaurant serves beautifully prepared grilled fish, and the conservatory menu offers traditional English fare and seafood, also beautifully presented. There are homemade sorbets and ice cream for dessert. *Madingley*

(3 mi outside Cambridge, 10-min taxi ride), tel. 01954/210221. AE, DC, MC, V.

£ **Browns.** This handy eatery is part of a small chain; there's another in Brighton. Opposite the Fitzwilliam Museum, this property is constantly busy and has good salads, hamburgers, and daily specials such as venison or lamb steak. The desserts are always inviting. *23 Trumpington St., tel. 01223/461655. AE, MC, V.*

£ **Peking Restaurant.** Cambridge's best-value restaurant, located in a pedestrianized shopping area, features friendly service, large portions, and a tasty Peking duck. Also try the crispy seaweed. Come either a bit early or a bit late to avoid student crowds. *21 Burleigh St., tel. 01223/354755. No credit cards.*

¢ **Hobbs Pavilion Restaurant.** The building housing this crêperie is a former cricket pavilion, and its terrace still commands enjoyable views of the playing fields of Parker's Piece, a large open green in the middle of Cambridge (near the city center and the colleges). The food, predominantly a wide assortment of savory and sweet pancakes, is served in generous portions, and the informal atmosphere and low prices appeal to the college community. Expect informal service to match. *Parker's Piece, Park Terrace, tel. 01223/67480. No credit cards. Closed Sun., Mon, and mid-Aug.–mid-Sept.*

Shopping **Heffer's** is one of the world's biggest bookstores, with an enormous stock of rare and imported books as well as best-sellers. The main bookstore (20 Trinity St., tel. 01223/358351) is spacious, with a galleried upper floor, and there is a charming children's branch (30 Trinity St.). Cambridge is also known for its secondhand bookshops. Antiquarian books can be found at **G. David** (3 & 16 St. Edward's Passage, tel. 01223/354619), which is tucked away near the Arts Theatre. Three doors away, **The Haunted Bookshop** (9 St. Edward's Passage, tel. 01223/312913) offers a great selection of old, illustrated books. Across the bridge at 24 Magdalene Street, **The Bookshop** (tel. 01223/62457), with a wide variety, is the best secondhand shop.

Handcrafted jewelry and leather goods, much of it made on the premises, can be found at **Workshop Designs** (31 Magdalene St., tel. 01223/354326). **Primavera** (10 King's Parade, tel. 01223/357708) is an excellent gallery where top-class craftspeople exhibit in a small but lively ground floor and basement. All the works are for sale, at prices that can be as low as £50; some of the exquisite jewelry pieces can cost up to £1,000, but there are also some genuine bargains. Also on King's Parade is the **Benet Gallery** (No. 19, tel. 01223/353784), which specializes in antique prints and lithographs.

The Arts **The Cambridge Arts Theatre** productions honor discounts for students, the elderly, and the disabled. Concession prices (discount rates) range from £5 to £6; regular prices range from £7.50 to £10.50. Music recitals sponsored by individual colleges cost about £4. The ADC (University Amateur Dramatics Club) productions usually cost about £4–£5. Buy tickets for all these events through the Cambridge Arts Theatre (Peas Hill, tel. 01223/352000).

Pick up one of the United Counties (tel. 01234/262151) buses that depart at 35 minutes past the hour from the Roman Catholic church in Cambridge to Madingley, 4 mi away. Tickets: £1.25 adults, 75p children.

About 4 miles west of Cambridge, you can visit the **American Military Cemetery** at Madingley, now more or less a suburb of Cambridge. It contains the graves of 3,811 U.S. servicemen who lost their lives during World War II. There is also a memorial wall for more than 5,000 American servicemen who have no known graves.

Ely

*Trains leave about every half hour from Cambridge train station for
the 20-minute ride to Ely.*

From Cambridge, make a single foray north to **Ely,** the Fenland's
"capital," and the center of what used to be a separate county called,
appropriately, the Isle of Ely. It is a small, dense town dominated by
its cathedral. The shopping area and little market square lie to the
north and lead down to the attractive riverside, while the well-preserved medieval buildings of the cathedral grounds and the King's
School (which trains cathedral choristers) spread out to the south
and west.

★ **Ely Cathedral,** on one of the few ridges in the whole of the Fens, can
be seen for miles. Known affectionately as "the Ship of the Fens,"
the cathedral was begun by the Normans in 1083, on the site of a
Benedictine monastery founded by the Anglo-Saxon Queen
Etheldreda in the year 673. In the center can be seen a true marvel of
medieval architecture, the octagonal lantern—a sort of stained-
glass skylight of vast proportions. Much of the decorative carving of
the Lady Chapel was defaced during the Reformation (mostly by
knocking off the heads of the statuary), but enough of the delicate
tracery work remains to show its original beauty. The fan-vaulted,
carved ceiling remains intact, as it was too high for the iconoclasts to
reach.

A major program of restoration is being undertaken on the cathedral's main fabric. The diocese of Ely was one of the first to charge
admission to a cathedral, not only to help with the restoration, but
to cover the enormous maintenance costs of a building this size. The
cathedral also includes a stained-glass museum, reached up a flight
of 41 steps. *Chapter Office, The College, tel. 01353/667735. Cathedral admission: £2.80 adults, £2 senior citizens and children under
16 (up to 2 accompanied children free); free on Sun. Open Mon.–
Sat. 7:30–6, Sun. 7:30–5. Stained-glass museum, tel. 01353/778645.
Admission: £1.80 adults, £1 senior citizens and children. Open
Mar.–Oct., weekdays 10:30–4, Sat. 10:30–4:30, Sun. noon–3.30;
Nov.–Feb., Sat. 10:30–4:30, Sun. noon–3:30.*

Lodging **Black Hostelry.** A different sort of bed-and-breakfast establish-
£ ment, the Black Hostelry has enormous rooms situated right in the
★ cathedral grounds, in one of the finest medieval domestic buildings
still in use. It's adjacent to the Chapter House, at the end of Firmary
Lane. Extremely comfortable, with antiques and old-fashioned English furnishings, this medieval hostel offers a lot of privacy. It's so
popular that you will need to reserve a room well in advance. *Cathedral Close, The College, CB7 4DL, tel. 01353/662612. 2 rooms with
bath or shower. Facilities: full English breakfast in the Undercroft.
No credit cards. Closed Dec. 24–26.*

£ **Old Egremont House.** This wonderful 17th-century house, just five
★ minutes' walk from the center, has beautiful views of the cathedral
from its two largest rooms. Inside the oak-beamed house, everything is immaculate—a family still lives here—and there are books
and antiques all around. The lovely private garden is a delight to sit
in during the summer. The price includes an excellent English
breakfast. *31 Egremont St., tel. 01353/663118. 3 rooms, 1 with bath.
No credit cards. Closed Christmas week.*

Dining **Dominique's.** This delightful little restaurant not far from the cathe-
£ dral serves brunch, lunch, and dinner in a totally nonsmoking environment. During the day it sees itself as more of a brasserie, while in
the evening the specialty is French cuisine with a focus on local
game. There are good-value set meals, or you can choose from the
blackboard daily specials, including a good range of hearty desserts.
There's an outdoor patio in summer and stripped pine floors

throughout. *8 St. Mary's St., tel. 01353/665011. Reservations advised for dinner. No credit cards. Dinner served Wed.–Sat. only; closed Mon. and Tues.*

Shopping   Handmade wooden crafts items are for sale at the **Steeplegate Tearoom and Gallery** (16 High St., tel. 01353/664731) and affordable paintings and prints by local Fenland artists at **The Old Fire Engine House** restaurant (25 St. Mary's St., tel. 01353/662582). The real treasure trove, however, is the **Waterside Antiques Warehouse,** where a wealth of antiques at very competitive prices are sold in an authentic river warehouse (The Wharf, tel. 01353/667066).

Duxford

Cambus 103 leaves the Drummer Street Bus Station in the center of Cambridge every hour 8:35–5:35 for the Duxford Airfield Museum.

Eleven miles south of Cambridge is the **Duxford Airfield,** a former Royal Air Force base used in the Battle of Britain and assigned to the U.S. Air Force in the latter years of World War II. It is now the Imperial War Museum's aviation branch, set up in the 1970s to house an extensive collection of fighters, bombers, and ancillary equipment. The original hangars, control tower, and other structures help the whole place to evoke a World War II air base in action. In addition, there are historic examples of civil aircraft, including a prototype Concorde, and occasional demonstration flights. *Duxford, tel. 01223/835000. Admission: £6 adults, £4 senior citizens, £3 children ages 5–15, £17 family ticket. Open Apr.–mid-Oct., daily 10–6; mid-Oct.–Mar., daily 10–4. Closed Dec. 24–26, Jan. 1.*

Saffron Walden

The Cambus (tel. 01223/423554) from Cambridge runs an hourly service daily, from 7 AM to 6 PM, for the 16-mile journey to Saffron Walden that takes 57 minutes. The train from Cambridge to London, which also stops at Audley End (tel. 01223/311999), takes about 20 minutes.

A few miles south of Duxford is the town of **Saffron Walden,** which owes its name to its saffron fields. It has many typical East Anglian, timber-frame buildings, some with elaborate pargeting (decorative plasterwork), which is especially notable on the walls of the former Sun Inn. The old **Grammar School** here was the World War II headquarters of the U.S. Air Force's 65th Fighter Wing.

★   A mile or so west of Saffron Walden is palatial **Audley End House,** a famous example of Jacobean (early 17th-century) architecture. Remodeled in the 18th and 19th centuries, it shows the architectural skill of Sir John Vanbrugh, Robert Adam, and Biagio Rebecca, as well as original Jacobean work in the magnificent Great Hall. You can also enjoy a leisurely walk around the park, which was landscaped by Capability Brown in the 18th century. *Tel. 01799/522842. Admission: house and park, £5.40 adults, £3.90 senior citizens, £2.60 children under 16; park only, £2.85 adults, £2.15 senior citizens, £1.40 children. Open Apr.–Sept., Wed.–Sun. and national holidays; park noon–6, house 1–5.*

Lodging   **Saffron Hotel.** This conversion of three houses into one has resulted
££   in a comfortable, modern hotel inside a 16th-century building. The conservatory restaurant has straightforward food, with plenty of local specialties, such as a delicious lamb dish. *10–18 High St., CB10 1AY, tel. 01799/522676, fax 01799/513979. 24 rooms with bath. AE, DC, MC, V.*

Dining   **Old English Gentleman.** This traditional, homey pub, built in 1912,
¢   has excellent food made on the premises. The menu includes a wide selection of classic English pub dishes, and there's real ale or a

choice of wines to accompany your meal. *Gold St., tel. 01799/523595. No credit cards.*

Sudbury

*Buses departing hourly from Cambridge run daily 7 AM–6 PM, with a change at Saffron Walden before continuing on to Sudbury. The trip to Saffron Walden takes 57 minutes, and an additional 45 minutes on to Sudbury. Call **Cambus** (tel. 01223/423554) or **Hedingham and District** (tel. 01787/60621) for more information.*

Sudbury, 15 miles east of Saffron Walden, is the fictionally famed "Eatanswill" of Dickens's *Pickwick Papers*. In real life, Thomas Gainsborough, one of the greatest English portrait and landscape painters, was born here in 1727; a statue of the artist holding his palette stands on Market Hill. His family's home is now a museum, containing paintings by the artist and his contemporaries, as well as an arts center. Although **Gainsborough's House** presents an elegant Georgian facade, with touches of the 18th-century neo-Gothic style, the building is essentially Tudor. In the walled garden behind the house, a mulberry tree planted in 1620 is still growing. *46 Gainsborough St., tel. 01787/72958. Admission: £2.50 adults, £2 senior citizens, £1.25 children, free in Dec. Open mid-Apr.–Oct., Tues.–Sat. 10–5, Sun. and national holidays 2–5; Nov.–mid-Apr., Tues.–Sat. 10–4, Sun. 2–5.*

Long Melford

*Buses departing hourly from Cambridge run daily 7 AM–6 PM, with a change at Saffron Walden before continuing on to Long Melford; the total trip takes 97 minutes. Call **Cambus** (tel. 0223/423554) or **Hedingham and District** (tel. 01787/60621) for information.*

Long Melford, one of the great wool towns of the area, lies just 2 miles north of Sudbury. The 2-mile-long main street broadens to include green squares and trees, and finally opens out into the large triangular green on the hill. The buildings of the town are an attractive mixture—mostly 15th-century half-timbered or Georgian—and many house antiques shops. Telegraph poles are banned from both Long Melford and nearby Lavenham, to preserve the towns' ancient look. On the hill, the **Church** is unfortunately obscured by **Trinity Hospital,** thoughtlessly built there in 1573. But close up, the delicate, flint flushwork (elaborate geometric decoration) and huge, 16th-century Perpendicular windows that take up most of the church's walls have great impact, especially as the nave is 150 feet long. Much of the original stained glass remains, notably the Lily Crucifix window. The indoor Lady Chapel has an unusual interior cloister with a wooden ceiling.

Melford Hall, now a National Trust property, distinguished from the outside by its turrets and topiaries, is a mid-16th-century house with a fair number of 18th-century additions. Much of the porcelain and other fine pieces in the house come from the *Santissima Trinidad*, a ship captured by one of the house's owners in the 18th century, when she was sailing back to Spain full of gifts from the emperor of China. The hall is set in parkland leading down to a walk by Chad Brook. *Tel. 01787/880286. Admission: £2.70 adults, £1.35 children; tours £2 adults, £1 children. Open Apr., weekends 2–5:30; May–Sept., Wed., Thurs., Sat., Sun. 2–5:30; Oct., weekends 2–5:30; tours May–Sept., Wed., Thurs.*

A 5- to 10-minute walk to the north of Long Melford Green will take you to **Kentwell Hall,** a redbrick Tudor manor house, surrounded by a wide moat. It was built at much the same time as Melford Hall, and has a similar interior design, though it was heavily restored inside after a fire in the early 19th century. Today, a restoration program is again under way, and the original gardens are being re-created. Throughout the summer—on Sunday from April until October, and increasing in frequency in peak season until it becomes daily from late July until late September—a reenactment of Tudor life is performed here by costumed "servants" and "farmworkers," with great panache and detail. Other theatrical and crafts events also take place here. *Tel. 01787/310207.* Admission: house and gardens £4.50 adults, £3.75 senior citizens, £2.75 children; increased fees for special events. Open Apr.–June, Sun. noon–5; late July–Sept., daily noon–5.

Lavenham

*Buses leave Cambridge Monday–Saturday every 2 hours 9:45–3:50. Change at Bury St. Edmunds for an **Eastern Counties** (tel. in Bury St. Edmunds, 01284/766171) bus meeting the **Cambus** (tel. 01223/423554) for Lavenham.*

Lavenham remains virtually unchanged from the way it appeared in the 15th and 16th centuries, when it was at the peak of its commercial success. The weavers' and wool merchants' houses occupy not just one show street, but most of the town. These are timber-framed in black oak, the main posts looking as if they could last for another 400 years. The grandest building of them all, the **Guildhall** of Corpus Christi (1529), is owned by the National Trust and is open to visitors. *Market Place, tel. 01787/247646. Admission: £2.50 adults, children free. Open Apr.–Oct., daily 11–5.*

The **Wool Hall** was torn down in 1913, but it was reassembled immediately at the request of Princess Louise, sister of the then-reigning king, George V. In 1962, it was joined to the neighboring Swan Hotel, a splendid Elizabethan building in its own right. The Swan Inn had a long history as a coaching inn, and in World War II served as the special pub for the U.S. Air Force's 48th Bomber Group.

You might enjoy having afternoon tea in one of the Swan's many cozy alcoves, by a roaring fire in winter, or in the charming garden in spring and summer. The freshly baked scones served with jam and clotted cream are particularly good and filling enough for lunch.

Lodging **The Angel.** This timbered inn, in the center of Lavenham opposite
£ the historic Guildhall, offers comfortable rooms and well-cooked meals in the English tradition. House specials, such as beef in Guinness and orange, cost up to £15 per person and are delicious. Room rates rise by about £10 on Fri. and Sat. nights. *Market Pl., CO10 9QZ, tel. 01787/247388, fax 01787/247057. 8 rooms with bath or shower. MC, V.*

Dining **Great House Restaurant.** An important family of weavers built this
Splurge 15th-century house that is one of the most beautiful and historically important homes in town. The building has undergone a careful restoration. Although the excellent French meals here may cost up to £30 per person, they are well worth the splurge, and the excellent fixed-price lunches and dinners only run to about half that price. *Market Pl., tel. 01787/247431. Reservations advised. AE, MC, V.*

Bury St. Edmunds

Trains leave Cambridge every 2 hours for the 40-minute trip, Monday–Saturday from 6:43 AM to 9:16 PM. On Sunday there are only four departures.

*Regular trains leave from London's Liverpool Street station Monday–Saturday, every 2 hours from 6:30 AM to 8:30 PM. The trip includes a change at Ipswich. For train information in Ipswich, call 01473/693396. **Cambus** (tel. 01223/423554) and **Eastern Counties** (tel. 01603/788890) buses connect all towns in the Bury St.*

Edmunds area. Also, buses leave Cambridge Monday–Saturday, every 2 hours from 9 to 5, for the 40-minute trip. Bury St. Edmunds tourist office: 6 Angel Hill, tel. 01284/764667.

Bury St. Edmunds rises from the pleasant valley of the Rivers Lark and Linnet. The town owes its unusual name and its initial prosperity to the martyrdom of Edmund, last king of Anglo-Saxon East Anglia, who was hacked to death by the pagan Danes in 869. He was subsequently canonized and his shrine attracted pilgrims, settlement, and commerce. In the 11th century the building of a great Norman abbey confirmed the town's importance as a religious center. Today only the Norman Gate Tower, the fortified Abbot's Bridge over the Lark, and a few picturesque ruins remain, for the abbey was yet another that fell during Henry VIII's dissolution of the monasteries. You can get some idea of the abbey's enormous scale, however, from the surviving gate tower. The ruins are now the site of the **Abbey Botanical Gardens,** with rare trees, including a Chinese tree of heaven originally planted in the 1830s. The abbey walls enclose separate, specialized gardens. One of these, the yew-hedged **Appleby Rose Garden,** was founded with the royalties from *Suffolk Summer,* a memoir by a U.S. serviceman, John Appleby, who had been stationed at nearby Rougham during World War II. *Tel. 01284/757490. Admission free. Open weekdays 7:30 AM–½ hour before dusk, weekends 9 AM–dusk.*

Originally there were three churches within the abbey walls, which shows the extent of the grounds, but only two have survived. **St. Mary's,** built in the 15th century, is the finer, with a blue-and-gold embossed "wagon" (i.e., barrel-shaped) roof over the choir. Mary Tudor, Henry VIII's sister and queen of France, is buried here. **St. James's** also dates from the 15th century; the brilliant paintwork of its ceiling and the stained-glass windows gleaming like jewels are the result of restoration in the 19th century by the architect Sir Gilbert Scott. Don't miss the memorial (by the altar) to an event in 1214, when the barons of England gathered here to take a solemn oath to force King John to grant the Magna Carta. The cathedral's original **Abbey Gate** was destroyed in a riot, and it was rebuilt in the 14th century on clearly defensive lines—you can see the arrow slits.

A walk along **Angel Hill** is a journey through the history of Bury St. Edmunds. Along one side, the Abbey Gate, cathedral, Norman Gate Tower, and St. Mary's Church make up a continuous display of medieval architecture. On the other side, the elegant Georgian houses include the **Athenaeum,** an 18th-century social and cultural meeting place and still the site of concerts and recitals, and the splendid **Angel** hotel, the scene of Sam Weller's meeting with Job Trotter in Dickens's *Pickwick Papers.* Dickens stayed here while he was giving readings at the Athenaeum. Farther along Angel Hill, the road becomes Crown Street, and off to the left, down Honey Hill, the **Manor House Museum** faces the abbey's grounds. The Georgian mansion contains excellent art and horological collections—paintings, clocks, watches. Furniture, costumes, and ceramics from the 17th to the 20th centuries are also on display. The clocks and watches in particular are extraordinarily beautiful. *Honey Hill, tel. 01284/757072. Admission: £2.50 adults, £1.50 senior citizens and children. Open Mon.–Sat. 10–5, Sun. 2–5.*

Continuing on to the end of Crown Street, turn right into Westgate Street to one of the National Trust's most unusual properties, the **Theatre Royal.** The theater (a working venue) was built in the 1800s and restored in 1982; it now presents pre- and post-London performances. (*See* The Arts and Nightlife, *below.*)

The shopping streets of Bury St. Edmunds follow an ancient grid pattern from Abbey Gate to Cornhill, with Abbeygate Street in the center. The public buildings within this area have a varied grandeur; there is, first, the medieval **Guildhall;** next, 18th-century classicism as interpreted by Robert Adam in the **Art Gallery;** and then Victorian classicism in the **Corn Exchange.** The Art Gallery has no permanent collections; instead there are changing exhibits of paintings, sculpture, and crafts, as well as frequent concerts. *Market Cross, Cornhill, tel. 01284/762081. Admission: 50p adults, 30p senior citizens and children. Open Tues.–Sat. 10:30–4:30, Sun. by appointment.*

Walk down to the end of Cornhill and turn right for the 12th-century **Moyse's Hall,** probably the oldest building in East Anglia, which houses in the original tiny rooms the local archaeological collections. The contemporary blood-and-thunder theatrical melodrama, *Maria Marten, or the Murder in the Red Barn,* is based on the macabre early 19th-century case, the Red Barn murder, about which there is a display here. *Buttermarket, tel. 01284/757072. Admission free. Open Mon.–Sat. 10–5, Sun. 2–5.*

Lodging **Chantry Hotel.** The older part of this pretty, 18th-century town
£ house is traditionally furnished, but the new extension has the best rooms and is completely modern. Single rooms are available for less than £45. *8 Sparhawk St., IP33 1RY, tel. 01284/767427. 17 rooms with bath. Facilities: restaurant, bar. MC, V.*

¢ **Dunstan Guest House and Hotel.** This reasonably priced Victorian guest house is five minutes' walk west from the center of town, near the A14 from Cambridge to Ipswich. Its comfortable rooms (all with TVs and tea/coffeemakers) are an excellent value. *8 Springfield Rd., IP33 3AN, tel. 01284/767981. 17 rooms, 10 with bath or shower. Facilities: garden, sun lounge. No credit cards.*

Dining **Mortimer's Seafood Restaurant.** Mortimer's gets its name from the
££ watercolors by Victorian artist Thomas Mortimer, which are dis-
★ played on the walls of the dining room. The seafood menu varies with the season's catch, but there are generally grilled fillets of local trout and Scottish salmon, and often mussels and oysters. You can have a cheaper counter lunch or a cheery, full-service meal in the two main dining rooms. *30 Churchgate St., tel. 01284/760623. Reservations required for weekends (at least a week in advance). AE, DC, MC, V. Closed Sat. lunch, Sun., national holiday Mon., and Tues.*

£ **Butterfly Hotel.** English/Continental cuisine, from a prix-fixe menu (starting at £10.50), is served in this cozy restaurant, whose kitchen maintains a high standard. You can enjoy your meal in a relaxed atmosphere, for an affordable price, in a large and airy conservatory. *45A Bury East exit, Symonds Rd., Moreton Hall, tel. 01284/760884. AE, DC, MC, V.*

¢ **Masons' Arms.** The setting of this lovely 17th-century timbered building presents a friendly and informal dining atmosphere. For less-expensive meals grab something from the bar, or choose to dine in the courtyard, weather permitting. All dishes are home cooked; specials include Dover sole and Japanese prawns. There's jazz on Sunday night. *Whiting St., tel. 01284/753955. No credit cards.*

Shopping The area around Abbeygate Street contains the best stores in town. The **Parsley Pot** (17 Abbeygate St., tel. 01284/760289) has a good selection of local crafts, and **Thurlow Champness** (14 Abbeygate St., tel. 01284/754747) has above-average silver, jewelry, and Copenhagen porcelain. The **Silk House** (14 Hatter St., tel. 01284/767138) concentrates on Macclesfield silk goods and men's neckties (Macclesfield has been the center of England's silk production for centuries).

The Arts and Bury St. Edmunds's splendid **Theatre Royal,** built in 1819, is run by
Nightlife the National Trust. A working theater offering a wide variety of touring shows, it is a perfect example of Regency theater design and a delightfully intimate place to watch a performance. It may be closed altogether during parts of the summer, so telephone first to

avoid disappointment. *Westgate St., tel. 01284/755127. Open Mon.–Sat. 10–8, and for performances. Closed Good Friday and national holiday Mon.*

Tour 2: Norwich and the Broads

The hub of this tour is Norwich, a city reminiscent of an illustration out of a medieval Book of Hours. The ancient capital of East Anglia, Norwich is an ideal base from which to explore the region's beautiful medieval churches, the many market towns and villages, the unique Broads, and the unparalleled coastline with its nature reserves, fishing villages, and peaceful harbors. Buses run from village to village, though service is sometimes irregular. It is recommended that you plan in advance and check schedules before you leave.

From London
By Train Trains depart from London's Liverpool Street Station (tel. 0171/928–5100) to Norwich, every hour on the half hour from 8:30 to 8:30. The trip is about 2 hours.

By Bus **National Express** (in London tel. 0171/730–0202) runs buses from Cambridge and London to Norwich.

By Car If you leave from northeast London, take the M11 to the A11, which you can take all the way into Norwich. Allow about 3 hours. From the northwest of London, take the M25 to the M11, and pick up the A11 into Norwich. This approach, too, will take about 3 hours. From Cambridge, take the A45 to the A11, and take it all the way into Norwich. Allow 1½ to 2 hours.

Norwich

Eastern Counties buses serve the local Norwich area (tel. 01603/788890). When planning to tour Norfolk by bus, check with Norfolk Bus Information (4 Guildhall Hill, Norwich, NR2 1JH, tel. 01603/613613) for schedules and village-to-village connections. Norwich tourist office: The Guildhall, Gaol Hill, tel. 01603/666071.

Established by the Saxons because of its fine trading position on the Rivers Yare and Wensum, **Norwich,** now a modern county town, still has its heart in the triangle between the two waterways, dominated by the castle and cathedral. The inner beltway follows the line of the old city wall, much of which is still visible, and it is worth driving around after dark to see the older buildings uncluttered by their much newer neighbors, thanks to skillful floodlighting.

Numbers in the margin correspond to points of interest on the Norwich map.

★ ❶ The spire of **Norwich Cathedral,** at 315 feet, is visible everywhere, but you cannot see the building itself until you go through St. Ethelbert's Gate. The cathedral was begun in 1096 by Herbert de Losinga, who had come from Normandy in 1091 to be its first bishop. His splendid tomb is by the high altar. The plain west front and dramatic crossing tower, with its austere, geometric decoration, are distinctively Norman. The remarkable length of the nave is immediately impressive; unfortunately, the similarly striking height of the vaulted ceiling makes it a strain to study the delightful colored bosses (ornamental knobs at junction points), where Bible stories are illustrated with great vigor and detail—look for Pharaoh and his cohorts drowning in a vivid Red Sea. Bring binoculars. Note also the woodcarving on the choir-stall misericords (semi-seats), a wonderful revelation of medieval skill and religious beliefs. The stalls were originally intended for the Benedictine monks who ran the cathedral, and the beautifully preserved cloister is part of what remains

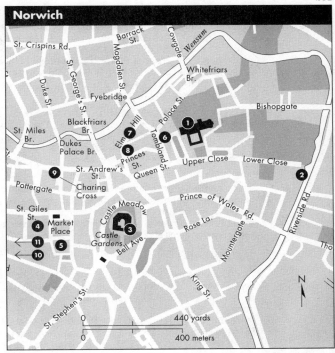

of their great priory. *62 The Close, tel. 01603/764385. Admission free; donation requested. Open mid-May–mid-Sept., daily 7:30–7; mid-Sept.–mid-May, daily 7:30–6; free guided tours June–Sept., weekdays 11 AM and 2:15 PM, Sat. 11 AM.*

Past the buildings of various periods on the cathedral grounds, a path leads down to the ancient water gate, **Pulls Ferry.** The grave of Norfolk-born nurse Edith Cavell, the British World War I heroine shot by the Germans for helping prisoners to escape from occupied Belgium, is outside the cathedral.

From Pulls Ferry retrace your steps to St. Ethelbert's Gate and proceed to the traffic lights where you will turn left and see the **castle** on the hill to your right. The castle is also Norman, but the wooden bailey (wall) on the castle mound was later replaced with a stone keep (tower). The thick walls and other defense works attest to the castle's military function, but the unique, decorated stone facing of the walls makes it seem like a child's illustration. For most of its history the castle has been a prison, and executions took place here well into the 19th century. There are daily guided tours of both the battlements and dungeons; call ahead for the current hours. An excellent museum here features displays of different facets of Norfolk's history, including a gallery devoted to the Norwich School of painters who, like the Suffolk artist John Constable, devoted their work to the everyday Norfolk landscape and seascape as revealed in the East Anglian light. *Norwich Castle, tel. 01603/223624. Admission: £2.20 adults, £1.50 senior citizens, £1 children. Open Mon.–Sat. 10–5, Sun. 2–5.*

At the castle, turn right at the traffic lights on the right, cross over, and go down the steps to the market. Behind the market, **City Hall** has one of the best views in Norwich from its steps, between the bronze Norwich lions. On the right rises the elaborate church tower of **St. Peter Mancroft,** below are the brightly colored awnings of the market stalls, and opposite looms the castle. Narrow lanes that used to be the main streets of medieval Norwich lead away from the mar-

6 ket, and end at **Tombland** by the cathedral. Neither a graveyard nor a plague pit, Tombland was the site of the Anglo-Saxon trading place, now a busy thoroughfare. In Tombland turn left and take the

7 second turn on the left which is **Elm Hill,** a cobbled street with a pleasing mixture of Tudor and Georgian houses, now mostly given over to gift shops and tearooms.

8 At the southern end of Elm Hill, on Princes Street, stands **St. Peter Hungate,** a 15th-century former church, which displays church art and furnishings; here you can try your hand at brass-rubbing. *Princes St., tel. 01603/667231. Admission: 50p adults, 40p senior citizens, 30p children; brass-rubbing charge £1–£5. Open Mon.– Sat. 10–5.*

From Princes Street, follow St. Andrew's Street to Charing Cross

9 where you'll find **Strangers Hall,** a good example of a medieval merchant's house. Built originally in 1320, it went on growing until the mid-18th century and is now a museum of domestic life, and each room is appropriately furnished. *Charing Cross, tel. 01603/667229. Admission: £1.40 adults, £1.20 senior citizens, 70p children. Open Mon.–Sat. 10–5.*

Norwich once owed much of its prosperity to the River Yare, which was a busy commercial waterway connecting the city with the North Sea at Great Yarmouth. Now the river is much quieter, but during the summer months you can have a different view of the city by taking a boat trip starting either from Roaches Court or from a berth near the railway station. The same company, Southern River Steamers (tel. 01603/501220), runs river trips of varied lengths to the nearer Broads on both the Yare and the River Wensum. There is also a marked riverside walk that follows the Wensum from St. George's Bridge to the city wall at Carrow Bridge.

In complete contrast to Norwich's historical composition, the

10 **University of East Anglia** (UEA)—1½ miles west of the center—is a modern construction, built during the great expansion of higher education in the 1960s. Its site on the slopes of the River Yare was used by the architect to give a dramatic, stepped-pyramid effect. The campus is linked by walkways that open out at different levels and center on a fountain courtyard.

11 Close by, the award-winning **Sainsbury Centre for the Visual Arts,** which was opened in 1972, holds the remarkable private art collection of the Sainsbury family, owners of a huge supermarket chain. The collection includes a large quantity of tribal art and 20th-century works, especially Art Nouveau, and includes pieces by Picasso and Giacometti. Both a coffee bar and a restaurant are located on the premises. Buses 12, 14, 23, 26, 27, 33, and 34 run from Norwich Castle Meadow to UEA, providing access to both the university and the Sainsbury Centre. *Earlham Rd., tel. 01603/456060. Admission: £1 adults, 50p senior citizens and children. Open Tues.–Sun. noon–5.*

Norfolk Broads To the east of Norwich, the **Norfolk Broads** stretch all the way to the coast. This is the popular image of Norfolk: a maze of small lakes, reed beds, and rivers that provides a haven for wildlife and boat lovers. Among its highlights is the 450-yard nature trail at **Ranworth Broad** that leads through oak woods, swamp, and reed beds to the moored floating Broadland Conservation Centre, which has an exhibition on the ecology of the Broads, and makes an ideal venue for bird-watching. *Ranworth, tel. 01605/49479. Admission: £1 adults, 75p students, senior citizens, and children. Open Apr.–Oct., Sun.– Fri. 10.30–5.30, Sat. 2–5.*

Lodging **The Beeches.** This hotel combining two Victorian houses is situated
££ on the west side of Norwich, a 10-minute walk to the city center. All

rooms have tea/coffeemakers and direct-dial phones, and breakfast is included in the basic price. Italian-style meals are served in the licensed restaurant every night except Sunday, with set menus starting at £9.50. *4–6 Earlham Rd., NR2 3DB, tel. 01603/621167, fax 01603/620151. 27 rooms with bath. AE, DC, MC, V.*

££ **Georgian House Hotel.** This central hotel offers comfortable, traditional accommodations in two tastefully converted and inter-connected Victorian houses. *32–34 Unthank Rd., NR2 2RB, tel. 01603/ 615655, fax 01603/765689. 27 rooms with bath or shower. Facilities: restaurant, bar. AE, DC, MC, V. Closed Christmas.*

¢ **Aspland Hotel.** This Victorian building, just 10 minutes' walk from the center of Norwich, offers very economical rooms, with modern furnishings and facilities to complement the surviving original features. The price includes breakfast. *6 Aspland Rd., NR1 1SH, tel. 01603/628999. 7 rooms, 6 with bath. MC, V. Closed Christmas.*

Dining **Green's Seafood Restaurant.** Seafood is served here, and fresh linen
££ and live piano music contribute to the pleasant ambience. Specialties include turbot with prawns and herb butter as well as poached salmon, or ask about the daily specials. There are some meat dishes, too, and an oyster bar serves seafood in a less formal atmosphere. *82 Upper St. Giles St., tel. 01603/623733. Reservations required. MC, V. Closed Sat. lunch, Sun., Mon. lunch.*

££ **Marco's.** The Georgian architecture of this building is comple-
★ mented inside by paneled walls, open fires, and pictures, all of which contribute to a warm, friendly, private atmosphere. Specialties of the Italian cuisine include *salmone al cartoccio* (salmon baked in parchment) and *gnocchi alla Marco* (potato dumplings). *17 Pottergate, tel. 01603/624044. Reservations advised. AE, DC, MC, V. Closed Sun., Mon., and mid-Sept.–mid-Oct.*

£ **Pinocchio's.** This spacious but intimate Italian restaurant in the fashionable St. Benedict's area is attractively furnished with scatter rugs and colorful murals. There's a wide choice of inventive pasta specials, such as chicken served with saffron noodles in a red pesto sauce, and regional Italian dishes—try the eggplant stuffed with walnut and spinach. Meals are accompanied by live jazz on Monday and Friday evenings. *11 St. Benedict's St., tel. 01603/613318. Reservations advised. AE, DC, MC, V. Closed Sun. eve.*

¢ **Boswell's Carvery.** An ideal place to lunch, this restaurant is in the historic heart of the city, along the cathedral wall in Tombland. The good selection of hot roast meats with fresh vegetables and a variety of salads should be topped off with one of the irresistible desserts. The average price for a meal is a little more than £8. *24 Tombland, tel. 01603/626099. AE, DC, MC, V.*

£ **Trafalgar Restaurant.** The pleasant and comfortable atmosphere here capitalizes on the striking views across the river, while the kitchen makes good use of the local produce. You can choose a classic English roast in the **Trafalgar Room,** or the less expensive light meals and snacks in the **Quarter-Deck Buttery,** to which the price rating for this review refers. *Hotel Nelson, Prince of Wales Rd., tel. 01603/760260. AE, DC, MC, V.*

Shopping The medieval lanes of Norwich, around Elm Hill and Tombland, contain the best stores. Antiquarian books can be found at **Peter Crowe** (75 Upper St. Giles St., tel. 01603/624800). The **Crome Gallery** (34 Elm Hill, tel. 01603/622827) features art by contemporary painters and old masters. Antiques shops abound in this area: **As Time Goes By** (5 Wrights Court, Elm Hill, tel. 01603/666508) specializes in clocks, and **St. Michael-at-Plea** (Bank Plain, tel. 01603/619129) is a church converted into an antiques market.

The **Elm Hill Craft Shop** (12 Elm Hill, tel. 01603/621076) has interesting stationery and dollhouses, while **Hovell's** (Bedford St., tel. 01603/626676) is a basketware specialist, among other things. Although some of the items sold here can be pricey, both shops house a wide range of mostly affordable stock.

The Arts In Norwich, the **Maddermarket Theatre** (Maddermarket, tel. 01603/620917), built on an Elizabethan theater design and founded in 1911 by an amateur repertory company, now stages all sorts of plays, including Shakespeare, to a high standard. Tickets cost from £2.50 to £7.50, with discounts offered to senior citizens and students. The theater is closed for performances in August, but there are guided tours all year. Norwich has a small **Puppet Theatre** (White Friars, tel. 01603/629921), housed in a former church. Not just for children, this theater has a national reputation in its field. Tickets run from £3.50 to £5, depending on the season and your age.

Great Yarmouth

*Trains from Norwich (tel. 01603/632055) make the half-hour journey to Great Yarmouth hourly Monday–Saturday 9:30 AM–10:20 PM (Sunday trains are less frequent). **Eastern Counties** (tel. 01603/788890) buses run about hourly 9–5 Monday–Saturday; less frequently on Sunday. Great Yarmouth Tourist Office: Town Hall, Hall Quay, tel. 01493/846345.*

Until recently, rivers were the main routes of trade for the Broads and much more important than roads, with traditional Norfolk sailing barges, known as wherries, plying their trade all over the area from their main port at **Great Yarmouth** (now mainly a seaside resort with a long, seafront promenade and a clean beach). In the late 19th and early 20th century, the leisure potential of these fine boats was first realized, and some were built as wherry yachts for luxurious vacations afloat. The *Albion*, based at Ludham, is the only working wherry left, maintained by the Norfolk Trust, while the *Norada* and the *Olive* are historic wherry yachts based at Wroxham. If you're in for a splurge, all may be chartered for cruises of up to 12 people. For information, call the *Albion* (Norfolk Wherry Trust, tel. 01603/413720) and the *Olive* and the *Norada* (tel. 01603/782470).

Blickling

Eastern Counties (tel. 01603/788890) buses run from Norwich to Aylesham; from Aylesham take a taxi or walk (ask bus driver for best route) the ½ mile.

★ Fourteen miles north of Norwich is **Blickling Hall,** now a National Trust property. It has belonged to a succession of historical figures, including Sir John Fastolf, the model for Shakespeare's Falstaff; Anne Boleyn's family, who owned it until Anne was executed by her husband, Henry VIII; and finally Lord Lothian, an ambassador to the United States. This redbrick Jacobean house is framed by a mighty yew hedge, and the grounds include a formal flower garden and parkland whose woods conceal a temple, an orangery, a pyramid, and a secret garden! Blickling Hall houses a National Trust textile conservation workshop, fine tapestries, and a long gallery with an intricate plasterwork ceiling decorated with Jacobean emblems. *Blickling, tel. 01263/733084. Admission: house and garden, £4.90 adults, £2.40 children; garden only £2.50 adults, £1.25 children. House and gardens open Apr.–Oct., Tues., Wed., Fri.–Sun., and national holidays; house 1–5, gardens 11–5.*

King's Lynn

Hourly trains make the 50-minute trip from Norwich Monday–Saturday (less frequently on Sunday) from 7:26 AM to 10:07 PM; change at Ely. Trains also run to King's Lynn (information, tel. 01553/772021) from London's King's Cross Station (tel. 0171/278–2477) and

London's Liverpool Street Station (tel. 0171/928–5100), traveling via Cambridge. Call for schedules. **Eastern Counties** buses (tel. 01603/ 788890) travel the half-hour trip direct from Norwich from 8:30 AM to 8:15 PM, with five departures daily. King's Lynn tourist office: The Old Gaol House, Saturday Market Place, tel. 01553/763044.

This tour from Norwich can finish in **King's Lynn,** situated close to the mouth of the Great Ouse (pronounced "ooze") on the Wash. Now an important container and fishing port, King's Lynn gained importance in the 15th century, especially for trade with northern Europe. **Trinity Guildhall,** with its striking checkered stone front, is now the Civic Hall of the Borough Council and is not generally open to the public, although you can visit it during the King's Lynn Festival. It is possible, however, to explore the **Regalia Rooms,** housed in the Guildhall Undercroft, with the aid of a recorded audio tour played on a personal cassette player. The rooms, entered through the **Old Gaol** (jail) **House** (now the tourist information center), exhibit charters dating from the time of King John (reigned 1199–1216), as well as the 14th-century chalice known as King John's Cup. *Market Pl., tel. 01553/763044. Admission: £2 adults, 1.50p senior citizens and children. Open Apr.–Oct., daily 10–5; Nov.–Mar., Fri–Sun 10–5.*

Another early 15th-century guildhall, St. George's, forms part of the **King's Lynn Arts Centre,** now a thriving arts and theater complex administered by the National Trust, and the focal point for the annual King's Lynn Festival. There is also an art gallery, and a crafts fair every September. The center's coffee bar serves snacks all day. **St. George's Guildhall** is the largest surviving English medieval guildhall, and it adjoins a Tudor house and a warehouse used during the Middle Ages. *27 King St., tel. 01553/774725. Admission free. Open Apr.–Sept., weekdays 10–5, Sat. 10–1 and 2–5; Oct.–Mar., weekdays 11–5, Sat. 11–1 and 2–4. Gallery closed Mon.*

Lodging **Russet House Hotel.** One of the rooms at this charming Victorian
£ house has a four-poster bed, and the other rooms are equally pleasant. There's a garden and a lounge bar, and a wide-ranging à la carte dinner menu is served for less than £13 per person, every night except Sunday. *53 Goodwin's Rd., PE30 5PE, tel. 01553/773098. 12 rooms with bath or shower. AE, DC, MC, V. Closed Christmas and New Year's.*

¢ **Guanock Hotel.** Close to the historic Southgates, next to the Jubilee Gardens, and just a few minutes from the town center, this hotel is conveniently placed in a pleasant part of the neighborhood. Offering a variety of room sizes (all rooms with TV), it suits the needs of just about everyone. Guests may use the residents' lounge and roof garden. *Southgates, PE30 5JG, tel. 01553/772959. 17 rooms, 2 with bath, 3 with shower. AE, DC, MC, V.*

Dining **Riverside Rooms.** Part of the Arts Centre, the building housing this
£ restaurant reflects the style of the original 15th-century warehouse. There are some tables outside. The English cuisine emphasizes locally caught fish and Cromer crabs. An inexpensive coffee shop in the historic undercroft serves homemade snacks and pastries. *27 King St., tel. 01553/773134. MC, V. Closed Sun.*

Shopping The **King's Lynn market** is in the great English tradition of open markets: stalls set up in a large outdoor space, selling everything from mussels and cockles to used Turkish rugs and period bric-a-brac. The atmosphere is bustling and friendly, and the savvy tourist can find good deals on just about everything. Looking for a piece of Irish lace to make into a collar, a pound of tart satsuma oranges, or a slightly tarnished set of brass candlesticks? This is the place to come.

The Arts Much of the wide-ranging **King's Lynn Festival,** held in July, is based at the King's Lynn Arts Centre and encompasses concerts, exhibitions, theater, dance, films, literary events, and children's programs. *King's Lynn Festival Office, 27 King St., PE30 1HA, tel. 01553/773578.*

Tour 3: Colchester and Environs

The town of Colchester is a wonderful mix of old and new; ancient streets blend with one of the country's most modern shopping centers to offer travelers remarkably diverse browsing. There is affordable shopping in Colchester; anyone willing to spend time looking can find good bargains, both in smaller town shops and in the modern shopping center. Apart from the shops, Colchester's history is ever present. From this town, exploring Constable Country is simple.

From London
By Train

Trains make the 45-minute trip to Colchester from London's Liverpool Street Station (tel. 0171/928–5100) weekdays 6:25 AM–11:30 PM. There are about three trains per hour. On Saturday and Sunday, two trains per hour run 7:30 AM–11:30 PM.

By Bus

National Express (tel. 0171/730–0202) runs buses from London's Victoria Coach Station to Colchester. Five buses daily make the 2 hour, 15-minute trip, 8–7.

Colchester

For specific bus schedules in Colchester, contact the tourist office. Colchester tourist office: 1 Queen St., CO1 2PJ, tel. 01206/712920.

Less than an hour's journey from London is **Colchester**, England's oldest recorded town. Recent archaeological research indicates a settlement at the head of the Colne estuary in Colchester at least as early as 1100 BC. At the turn of the millennium it was the center of the domain of Cunobelin (Shakespeare's Cymbeline), who was king of the Catuvellauni. On Cunobelin's death, the Romans invaded in AD 43 and the Emperor Claudius—who, according to legend, entered Colchester on an elephant—built his first stronghold here and made it the first Roman colony in Britain, appropriately renaming the town *Colonia Victricensis* ("Colony of Victory"). Colchester had to wait another millenium, however, before it received its royal charter in 1189, from King Richard the Lionheart.

Evidence of Colchester's four centuries of Roman history is visible everywhere. Although the Romans prudently relocated their administrative center to London after the Celtic Queen Boudicca burned the place in AD 60, Colchester was important enough for them to build massive fortifications around the town. The **Roman Walls**—dating largely from the reign of Emperor Vespasian (AD 69–79)—can still be seen, especially along Balkerne Hill (to the west of the town center), with its splendid Balkerne Gate, and along Priory and Vineyard streets, where there is now a Roman drain exposed halfway along. In Maidenburgh Street, near the castle, the remains of a Roman amphitheater have been discovered—the curve of the foundations is outlined in the paving stones of the roadway, and part of the walls and floor have been exposed and preserved in a modern building, where they can be viewed through the window.

Colchester has always had a strategic importance, and is still home to a military garrison; a tattoo (military spectacle) is held in even-numbered years. The **castle** was built by William the Conqueror in about 1076, one of the earliest to be built of stone (largely taken from the Roman ruins) and although all that survives is the keep (main tower), it is the largest in Europe. The castle was actually built over the foundations of the huge Roman Temple of Claudius, and in the vaults you can descend through 1,000 years of history. A museum inside contains an ever-growing collection of Roman and prehistoric remains, mostly from Colchester itself. Spread across two floors of the castle vaults, highly engaging displays chart the original Celtic inhabitation of the region before recording in detail the Roman invasion and subsequent occupation, while recent additions bring the story through to the Norman Conquest. To really make your visit come alive, take a guided tour of the Roman vaults and castle dungeons (daily July and Aug., weekends Apr.–June and Sept.). *Tel. 01206/712931 or 712932 (information about all Colchester's museums is available at these numbers). Admission £2.50 adults, £1.50 senior citizens and children. Open Mar.–Nov., Mon.–Sat. 10–5, Sun. 2–5; Dec.–Feb., Mon.–Sat. 10–5; closed Christmas week.*

Next door to the castle is **Hollytrees,** a pleasing early 18th-century brick house with a collection of costumes, dolls, and toys that spans three centuries of English design. *High St., tel. 01206/712931. Admission free. Open Tues.–Sat. 10–noon and 1–5.*

Opposite Hollytrees is a group of graceful 18th-century town houses, two of which have been turned into an art gallery known as **The Minories.** The gallery has 19th-century works by John Constable and Auguste Rodin. The collection of 20th-century works by modern East Anglian artists John and Paul Nash can be viewed by appointment. There are also temporary exhibitions. The restaurant provides light meals and drinks during the gallery's opening hours. *74 High St., tel. 01206/577067. Admission free. Open Tues.–Sat. 10–5, Sun. 2–4; closed Christmas week.*

Opposite the castle, in High Street, **All Saints Church** has been turned into a county museum of natural history, while **Holy Trinity Church** on Trinity Street, which was begun around the year 1000 and which incorporates visible Roman materials, has been converted into the **Trinity Museum** of town and country life in Colchester over the past two centuries. Opening times are the same as for the Hollytrees (*see above*), and admission to both is free. The church of **St. Mary-at-the-Wall** is now an arts center, offering a varied program throughout the year.

Not far from St. Mary's and near Balkerne Gate is Colchester's **Mercury Theatre.** At the theater, turn right and walk down Balkerne Passage, which leads to the top of North Hill; there, turn right again into High Street, which follows the line of the main Roman road. Along High Street you will pass the Victorian **Town Hall,** standing on the site of the original Moot (assembly) Hall. The narrow, medieval streets behind the town hall are called the **Dutch Quarter** because weavers from the Low Countries settled here in the 16th century. Across the High Street and beyond the modern Culver Square pedestrian mall lie the medieval streets of Long Wyre Street, Short Wyre Street, and Sir Isaac's Walk, where there are many small antiques stores, and crafts and gift shops.

Off Culver Street West, on Trinity Street, **Tymperley's Clock Museum** displays a unique collection of Colchester-made clocks in the surviving wing of an Elizabethan house. *Tel. 01206/712943. Admission free. Open Apr.–Oct., Tues.–Sat. and national holidays, 10–1 and 2–5.*

Lodging **Four Sevens.** This guest house, within easy walking distance from
¢ the town center, makes a relaxed and friendly base. All rooms have TV, and videos are available, too. The breakfast served is excellent, and you can order a very reasonably priced dinner for just £8. In the past, the owners have also made bicycles available to their guests. *28 Inglis Rd., CO3 3HU, tel. 01206/46093. 6 rooms, 2 with bath. No credit cards.*

¢ **The Maltings.** This very friendly B&B establishment is about 4 miles
★ south from the center of Colchester. The house dates back to the

15th century, which means a preponderance of oak beams. Cottage-style rooms (which can run as low as £30 a night) are homey and guests have their own dining room and lounge with an open fire. Light snacks, such as beans and toast, are available for very low prices: £1.50–£3.50. *Mersea Rd., Abberton, CO5 7NR, tel. 01206/735780. 3 rooms, 1 family room with bath. Facilities: open-air swimming pool in garden. No credit cards. Closed Christmas week.*

Dining **Pasquale.** This cheerful and friendly Italian restaurant serves well-
£ prepared pastas and other classic dishes in a light, simple, Italian-style dining room near the Roman Balkerne Gate and the Mercury Theatre. *2–4 Balkerne Passage, tel. 01206/549080. Reservations advised on weekends. MC, V. Closed Sun.*

¢ **Jacklins Restaurant.** This first-floor restaurant in the town center is
★ located above the remains of the pottery shops of Roman Colchester. In the lovely oak-paneled rooms, inexpensive breakfasts, lunches, and afternoon teas are served. *147 High St., tel. 01206/572157. AE, MC, V. Closed Sun.*

The Arts Colchester's **Mercury Theatre** (Balkerne Gate, tel. 01206/573948) stages a wide variety of plays, including tour productions, pre–West End runs, and local productions. It's in a modern building not far from the **Colchester Arts Centre** (St. Mary-at-the-Walls, Church St., tel. 01206/577301), which hosts theater, exhibitions, and workshop events. Jazz is featured every other Thursday, with top names from Britain, the Continent, and America.

East Bergholt and Dedham

*For bus service from Colchester to Dedham, call the **Eastern National Bus Co.** (01206/571321); for service from Colchester to East Bergholt, call the **Eastern Cities Bus Company** in Ipswich (01473/253734). Call in advance for specific schedules.*

Colchester is the traditional base for exploring **Constable Country,** that quintessentially English rural landscape on the borders of Suffolk and Essex that was made famous by the early 19th-century painter, John Constable. This area runs north and west of Colchester along the valley of the River Stour, and includes his birthplace at **East Bergholt** (7 miles northeast of Colchester) and nearby **Dedham,** where he went to school and whose church and other town features served as inspiration for his works.

Tour 4: Lincoln and Environs

This tour begins with Lincoln in the northeast, an old settlement dating from Roman times and earlier. Using Lincoln as a base, you can explore the countryside and the town of Boston, from which the Pilgrims originally tried to set sail.

From London Trains to Lincoln from London's **King's Cross Station** (tel. 0171/278–
By Train 2477) travel the 2-hour trip weekdays from 6 AM to 10 PM every hour; Saturday, hourly 6 AM–7:30 PM; Sunday, hourly 8:25 AM–8:10 PM. A change is made in Newark.

By Bus For bus information to Lincoln and the surrounding area, call **Eastern National Thameslink/Link** (tel. 01245/256151) or **National Express** (tel. 0171/730–0202).

Lincoln

Lincoln tourist office: 9 Castle Hill, tel. 01522/529828.

Northeast of the area already covered in this section lies **Lincoln,** with its crowning glory, the great **Cathedral of St. Mary** (which you should try to see at night, when it is floodlit). Commanding views

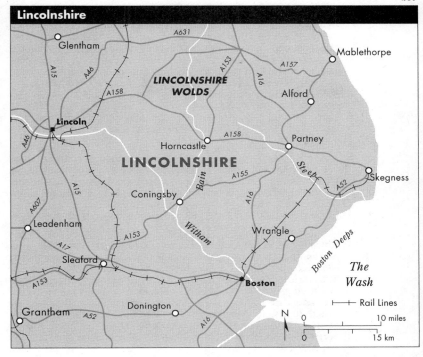

from the top of the steep limestone escarpment above the River Witham reveal the strategic advantages of the city's site from earliest times. Weapons from the pre-Roman, tribal era have been found in the river; later, the Romans (always quick to see the potential of a site) left their usual permanent underpinning; and a wealth of medieval buildings—quite apart from the cathedral and castle—seem to tumble together down the steep hillside lanes leading to the river.

★ The **cathedral** is the most obvious starting point for any visitor to Lincoln. For hundreds of years, it was the tallest building in Europe, but this magnificent medieval building is now among the least known of the European cathedrals. It was begun in 1072 by the Norman bishop Remigius; the Romanesque church he built was irremediably damaged, first by fire, then by earthquake (in 1185), but you can still see parts of the ancient structure at the west front. The next great phase of building, initiated by Bishop Hugh of Avalon, is mainly 13th century in character. The west front, topped by the two west towers, is a unique structure, giving tremendous breadth to the entrance. It is best seen from the 14th-century Exchequer Gate arch in front of the cathedral or from the castle battlements beyond.

Inside, a breathtaking impression of space and unity belie the many centuries of building and rebuilding. The stained-glass window at the north end of the transept, known as the Dean's Eye, is one of the earliest (13th-century) traceried windows, while its opposite number at the south end shows a 14th-century sophistication in its tracery, such as interlaced designs. St. Hugh's Choir in front of the altar and the Angel Choir at the east end behind it have remarkable vaulted ceilings and intricate carvings. Look for the famous Lincoln Imp up on the pillar nearest to St. Hugh's shrine, and even farther up (binoculars or a telephoto lens will help!), look for the 30 angels who are playing musical instruments, and for whom this part of the cathedral is named.

Among the many chapels is one commemorating Lincolnshire's connections with North America and Australia. Through a side door on the north side lies the chapter house, a 10-sided building that sometimes housed the medieval Parliament of England. The chapter house, notable for its grotesquely amusing ceiling bosses, is connected to the 13th-century cloisters. The cathedral library, a restrained building by Christopher Wren, was built onto the north side of the cloisters after the original library collapsed. *Lincoln Cathedral, tel. 01522/544544. Requested donation: £2.50 adults, £1 senior citizens and children. Open late May–Aug., Mon.–Sat. 7:15 AM–8 PM, Sun. 7:15–6; Sept.–late May, Mon.–Sat. 7:15–6, Sun. 7:15–5.*

In the **Minster Yard,** which surrounds the cathedral on three sides, are buildings of various periods, including graceful examples of Georgian architecture. A statue of Alfred, Lord Tennyson, who was born in Lincolnshire, stands on the green near the chapter house exterior, and the medieval **Bishop's Palace,** on the south side, is open to the public. *Tel. 01522/527468. Admission: 80p adults, 60p senior citizens, 45p children. Open Apr.–Sept., daily 10–6.*

Lincoln Castle, facing the cathedral across Exchequer Gate, was originally built on two great mounds by William the Conqueror in 1068, incorporating part of the remains of the Roman garrison walls. The castle was a military base until the 17th century, after which it was used primarily as a prison. In the extraordinary prison chapel you can see the cagelike stalls in which Victorian convicts were compelled to listen to sermons. *Tel. 01522/511068. Admission: £2 adults, £1.20 senior citizens and children. Open Apr.–Oct., Mon.–Sat. 9:30–5:30, Sun. 11:30–5:30; Nov.–Mar., Mon.–Sat. 9:30–4, Sun. 11:30–4.*

The Roman presence in Lincoln is particularly evident near the cathedral. At the end of Bailgate, traffic still passes under the **Newport Arch,** once the north gate of the Roman city, *Lindum Colonia.* Ermine Street, stretching north from the arch to the River Humber, replaced an important Roman road lying 8 feet below the surface. The foundations of the east gate have been excavated and permanently exposed in the forecourt of the Eastgate Post House Hotel, and the columns of a 175-foot Roman colonnade are marked along the roadway in Bailgate.

South of the cathedral the ground slopes away sharply down to the river. Here narrow medieval streets cling to the hillside, with the aptly named **Steep Hill** at their center. Well-preserved domestic buildings, such as the early 12th-century Jew's House, and 14th- and 15th-century timbered buildings, such as Harding House and the Harlequin and Dernstall House (at the end of High St.), now contain bookstores, antiques shops, boutiques, and restaurants. These hillside streets lead into Lincoln's shopping district (mainly pedestrianized).

Through the busy shopping district, where you can walk under the 15th-century **Stonebow Arch** with the **Guildhall** above it, the River Witham flows unobtrusively, crossed by the incongruously named **High Bridge**—a low, vaulted Norman bridge topped by 16th-century, timber-framed houses. West of High Bridge the river opens out into **Brayford Pool,** still busy with river traffic (and, unfortunately, road traffic, as a large, unsightly, multistory parking lot has been built on one side). Here you can rent various kinds of boats.

Lodging   **Hillcrest Hotel.** A small, unpretentious Victorian hotel, formerly a
£   rectory, Hillcrest is in a very quiet area about five minutes' walk
★   north of the cathedral. The interior features simple but pleasing modern furnishings. Rooms at the back overlook the garden and arboretum. An English breakfast is included in the room rate. *15 Lindum Terrace, LN2 5RT, tel. and fax 01522/510182. 17 rooms*

with bath. Facilities: restaurant, bar, garden, arboretum. AE, MC, V. Closed 2 weeks at Christmas.

¢ **Carline Guest House.** Situated in a quiet spot, just five minutes from one of the most beautiful and historic cathedrals in Britain, this lodging is well placed. Family rooms, doubles, and singles are available, and the whole establishment is nonsmoking. The full English breakfast includes free-range eggs from the owners' hens. *1 & 3 Carline Rd., LN1 1HL, tel. 01522/530422. 12 rooms, 11 with bath or shower. No credit cards.*

££ **Duke William Hotel.** This 18th-century stone house stands 100 yards
★ from Newport Arch on the old coaching road. Attractive rooms have good views, and the food is very good value: Large portions of classic English cuisine are on offer, and room rates include a filling English breakfast, which most certainly could carry you through the day. *44 Bailgate, LN1 3AP, tel. 01522/533351. 11 bedrooms with shower. Facilities: restaurant, bar, garden. AE, DC, MC, V.*

Dining **Jew's House.** Situated in the 12th-century Jew's House, one of
££ Lincoln's oldest buildings, this restaurant has an intimate atmos-
★ phere that is enhanced by antique tables and oil paintings on the walls. The cosmopolitan menu, featuring Continental specialties, changes daily, and the restaurant is renowned for its rich desserts, all homemade. *15 The Straight, Steep Hill, tel. 01522/524851. Reservations advised. AE, DC, MC, V. Closed Sun. and Mon. lunch. Closed 2–4 weeks in Feb. each year for redecoration.*

££ **Wig and Mitre.** This interesting downtown pub-café-restaurant stays open all day until 11 PM, serving an extremely varied range of food, from breakfast to full evening meals. Produce comes from the local markets and dishes may include fresh fish or warming seasonal soups, European specialties or classic English pies and roasts. *29 Steep Hill, tel. 01522/535190. Reservations advised for dinner. AE, DC, MC, V. Closed Christmas.*

Shopping Lincoln's main shopping area, mostly pedestrianized, is at the bottom of the hill below the cathedral, around the Stonebow gateway and Guildhall, and along High Street. However, the best stores are on Bailgate, Steep Hill, and the medieval streets leading directly down from the cathedral and the castle. Steep Hill has several good bookstores, antiques shops, and crafts and art galleries, such as **Harding House, Steep Hill Galleries,** and **The Long Gallery** (the top of High St.). **David Hansord** (32 Steep Hill, tel. 01522/530044) specializes in antiques, especially antique scientific instruments.

Lincolnshire Wolds

*Trains (tel. 01522/539502) depart from Lincoln every 2 hours (sometimes hourly) and stop in many towns throughout the area. Trains make the 1-hour trip Monday–Saturday 8 AM–9 PM, and less frequently on Sunday. Buses depart from Lincoln to Louth (located in the Wolds) every 2 hours Monday–Saturday 8:55–5:15. For bus information call **Eastern National Thamesline/Link** (tel. 01245/256151). For information about the area, call Lincolnshire County Travel Hotline (tel. 01522/553135).*

The countryside around Lincoln, especially the **Lincolnshire Wolds** (chalk hills) to the northeast, consists of rolling hills and copses, with dry-stone (unmortared) walls dividing well-tended fields. The unspoiled rural area of the Wolds, strikingly evoked in Tennyson's poetry, is particularly worth a visit, while the long coastline, with its miles of sandy beaches and its North Sea air, offers all the usual, if occasionally tacky, seaside facilities for the family.

Boston

*Trains run to Boston direct from Lincoln, hourly Monday–Saturday 8 AM–9 PM (Sunday service is less frequent). Buses from Lincoln to Skegness connect in Boston. These run Monday–Saturday 9–2, but they are extremely irregular. For information call **Eastern National Thamesline/Link** (tel. 01245/256151). Boston tourist office: Spain La., tel. 01205/356656.*

The River Witham flows right through the Lincolnshire Fens, from Lincoln to the port of **Boston**, whose 14th-century **Church of St. Botolph** has a lantern tower (288 feet high) known affectionately as "Boston Stump." It can be seen for 20 miles from both land and sea and serves as a directional beacon for aircraft as well. The Pilgrims, who were finally to reach Massachusetts in 1620, originally tried to sail from Boston to Holland in their search for religious freedom, but were captured and imprisoned here in 1607. The 15th-century guildhall, now the **Boston Borough Museum,** contains the courtroom where they were tried, and the cells where they were held. *St. Mary's Guildhall, South St., tel. 01205/365954. Admission: 90p adults, 65p senior citizens, accompanied children free; free to all on Thurs. Admission includes a 45-min personal audio guided tour. Open Mon.–Sat. 10–5, Sun. (Apr.–Sept. only) 1:30–5.*

Among several other reminders of Boston's transatlantic links is the 18th-century **Fydell House,** next to the guildhall, which is now a school where a room is set aside for welcoming visitors from Boston, Massachusetts. *South St., tel. 01205/351520. Admission free. Open weekdays 9:30–12:30 and 1:30–4:30.*

12 York and the Northeast

Harrogate, Haworth, Scarborough, Bridlington, Durham, Hexham, Berwick

England's northeast corner is relatively unexplored by tourists. Consequently, visitors who do make their way here are often impressed by the wide-open spaces and empty country roads; they also like the value for their money in shopping and accommodations, the unspoiled villages and uncrowded beaches, and the warmth and friendliness of the people.

Mainly composed of the two large counties of Durham and Northumberland (also known as Northumbria), the Northeast includes among its attractions the English side of the Scottish Border area, renowned in ballads and romantic literature for feuds, raids, and battles. Hadrian's Wall, which served to mark the northern limit of the Roman Empire, runs through this region; much of it, remarkably, is still intact. Farther north, on the coast near the border, is the market town of Berwick-upon-Tweed, which has changed hands between England and Scotland several times over.

To the east, the bleak areas of moorland that characterize Yorkshire are linked by lush, green valleys. Here, the high rainfall produces luxuriant vegetation, swift rivers, sparkling streams, and waterfalls that contrast with the dark, heather-covered Moors. In the center of the fertile plain that separates the Pennines (the range of hills that stretches from the Peak District almost to the border with Scotland) from the Moors lies York, dominated by the towers of its great minster. This medieval walled city is one of the best preserved in Europe. North of York is Durham, with its great cathedral, which for 1,000 years was the seat of bishops who had their own armies and ruled as prince bishops with quasi-royal authority.

In more recent times, steel, coal, railroads, shipbuilding, and chemicals backed the prosperity of towns and cities such as Darlington and Middlesbrough. Reflecting the area's industrial history are such attractions as the Railway Museum at Darlington.

Yorkshire and the Dales

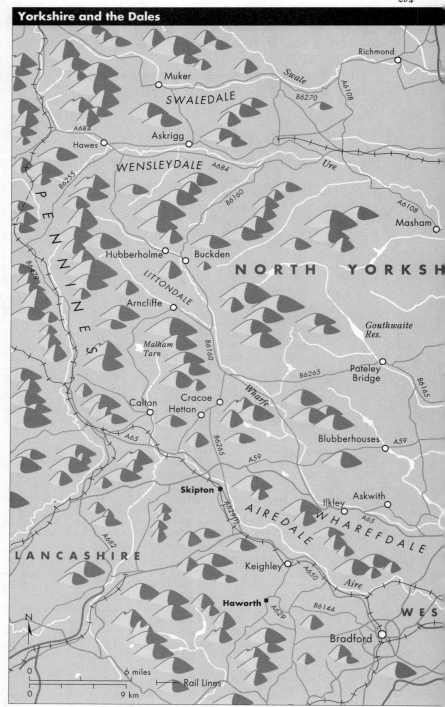

Richmond

Muker

Swale

SWALEDALE

B6270

A6108

A684

Askrigg

Hawes

WENSLEYDALE

A684

Ure

B6255

P

E

N

N

I

N

E

S

B6160

A6108

Masham

Hubberholme

Buckden

LITTONDALE

N O R T H   Y O R K S H

Arncliffe

Gouthwaite Res.

Malham Tarn

B6160

B6265

Pateley Bridge

B6165

Calton

Cracoe

Hetton

Wharfe

Skipton

B6265

A65

A59

Blubberhouses

A59

Skipton ■

A59(?)

AIREDALE

WHAREFDALE

Ilkley

Askwith

A65

LANCASHIRE

A682

Keighley

A650

Aire

Haworth ■

A629

B6144

W E S

Bradford

N

0   6 miles

0   9 km

Rail Lines

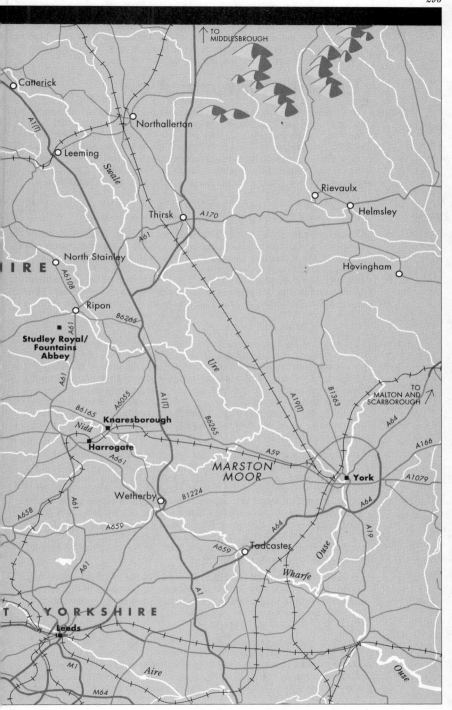

TO
MIDDLESBROUGH

Catterick

A1(M)

Northallerton

Leeming

Swale

Rievaulx

Helmsley

Thirsk

A170

A61

North Stainley

Hovingham

A6108

IRE

Ripon

B6265

A61

Studley Royal/
Fountains
Abbey

Ure

A1(M)

A61

A6055

B1363

TO
MALTON AND
SCARBOROUGH

A64

B6165

A1(M)

Knaresborough

B6265

Nidd

A166

Harrogate

A59

A1079

A661

MARSTON
MOOR

York

A64

Wetherby

B1224

A658

A61

A659

A64

A19

Tadcaster

A659

Ouse

Wharfe

A1

T YORKSHIRE

Leeds

M1

Aire

Ouse

M64

This is a good region for visitors who want to alternate tours of historic sites with countryside walks that cost no money. Almost all attractions can be reached by local buses and trains, but if you want to explore some of the more remote areas or Hadrian's Wall thoroughly, it may be worth splurging on a rental car for a day or so.

Essential Information

Lodging Bed-and-breakfast accommodations are usually an excellent value, with simple but comfortable rooms starting from around £20 per person. When touring the countryside by car, look for farmhouse B&Bs. In town, guest houses and small hotels are comparatively inexpensive and also include breakfast. Many guest houses offer traditional home-cooked dinners. Even if you travel by public transportation, you're not necessarily limited to accommodations in town centers: Many proprietors of places on the outskirts of town will pick you up at the train station or bus depot; it's worth giving them a call if you prefer a peaceful, out-of-the-way spot.

Prices are slightly higher in York and Durham than in the rest of the region, but the towns (particularly York) offer the widest range of restaurants, shopping, and nightlife. Skipton and Scarborough are provincial towns, yet each provides a peaceful place from which to explore the deeper countryside. The popularity of the Yorkshire Dales means that budget travelers should book ahead or arrange accommodations early in the day, because the inexpensive guest houses and B&Bs fill up quickly. Highly recommended establishments are indicated by a star ★.

Dining This part of the country, with its fresh air and exhilarating hilltop walks, positively encourages hearty appetites. Locally produced meat and vegetables are excellent. One not-to-be-missed specialty is Yorkshire pudding, a popover-like pastry cooked in meat juices and served with gravy. In the days when meat was a real luxury, it was offered as a first course in hopes of filling you up so you wouldn't want much to eat for the main course. Now it usually comes with succulent roast beef and vegetables, although some places still serve it in the traditional way.

In the Northeast, keep an eye out for restaurants that serve game from the Kielder Forest, local lamb from the hillsides, and fish both from streams threading through the wild valleys and from the fishing fleets plying their trade from the small harbors along the coast. Also, fresh fish from Whitby or Scarborough is a real treat with fried chips (thick french fries); don't bother asking for a fish-and-chips shop—just follow your nose! Cheese from Wensleydale has a subtle, honeyish flavour, while the famous Bakewell tart is a good, sticky sweet snack. Wherever you are, go for the freshly baked bread and homemade cakes.

Pubs are often the best (and in small villages, the only) places to find good, hearty meals for under £10. Here you can usually find home cooking and traditional fare. Unless otherwise noted, reservations are not needed and dress is casual. Highly recommended restaurants are indicated by a star ★.

Biking Several operators organize guided or self-guided bicycle tours and rent gear (some even have mountain bikes). In summer, it's best to write ahead and reserve your bike. Be sure to enclose International Reply Coupons (available from the post office) to cover the postage cost of the reply. In Yorkshire, Phil Webster at **Bike of Beyond,** at the Grinton Lodge youth hostel (Grinton, Richmond, N. York, tel. 01748/884206), rents mountain bikes and leads guided cycling tours of the region. **Cycle Scene** (Burton Stone Lane, York YO3 6EN (tel. 01904/653286) also rents bikes.

Hiking The **Ebor Way** ('Ebor' is short for the Roman name for York, Eboracum) runs 70 miles from Helmsley in the north to Ilkley in the west, just north of Haworth. The route goes through the city of York and across the Pennines. For other specific trails, check with the national parks offices; they all have guidebooks, guide services, and maps.

Beaches South of Scarborough, the long-established seaside resorts of **Filey** and **Bridlington** have long, sweeping, sandy beaches and good areas for walking, fishing, and bird-watching; Scarborough's beaches are a mixture of sand and rock. **Cayton Bay** and **Sandsend** are smaller, quieter, sandy beaches. In towns such as **Whitby** and **Staithes,** the atmosphere of an old fishing port and seafarers' town has been retained, but swimming isn't really an option.

Shopping Throughout the region, colorful local markets are popular, especially in York. Yorkshire and the surrounding region have a large number of "mill shops" where high-quality knitting wool, sweaters, and woven wool for skirts or suits can be bought at factory prices; the TIC will supply a full list of mill shops in the area.

The Arts and The northern cities have excellent facilities for theater, opera, and
Nightlife arts. Most of these cultural activities take place in the fall and winter months. For information on inexpensive theatrical and musical events, contact **Northern Arts,** the official body that promotes the arts in the Northeast. *9–10 Osborne Ter., Jesmond, Newcastle-upon-Tyne, NE2 1NZ, tel. 0191/281–6334.*

Festivals While the arts flourish during the winter, summer means country exhibitions and festivals for this region. The **Alnick Fair,** held from the last week in June through the first week in July, features a costumed reenactment of a medieval fair, processions, a market, and concerts. *Alnick Fair, Box 2, Alnick NE66 1AA, tel. 01665/605004 or 01665/602234.*

Billingham International Folklore Festival is held each year in the third week of August. Tickets range in price from £1 to £10, depending on the event. *Festival Office, Municipal Buildings, Town Center, Billingham (north of Middlesbrough), Cleveland, TS23 2LW, tel. 01642/558212.*

Each February York hosts the **Viking Festival,** a month-long celebration that includes free events, such as fireworks, torchlight processions, and theatrical presentations. The finale is the Jorvik Viking Combat, a re-enactment of ravaging Northmen confronting their Anglo-Saxon enemies. *Jorvik Viking Festival Office, Clifford Chamber, 4 Clifford St., YO1 1RD, tel. 01904/611944.*

An **Early Music Festival** is held in and around York each summer, except in Mystery Play years. *For details call 01904/613161.*

Tour 1: York

York, just under 2 hours by express train from London, is also convenient to many of the towns in this chapter, and is the hub for most of the tours that follow. Medieval walls encircle the city and its rich blend of architectural styles. From the Roman to the Victorian, each era has added its own flavor to the city landscape which takes on a special charm in February, during the month-long Viking festival.

York Minster, the 500-year-old Gothic cathedral, dominates all city views. But York has a long list of other attractions, not to mention many cozy pubs offering world-famous beers, such as Bass, Sam Smiths, and the wonderfully named Old Peculier (sic). The city's cycle of medieval mystery plays is performed every four years, either in the gardens of the Yorkshire Museum, formerly St. Mary's Abbey, or in the Theatre Royal; the next local performance is scheduled for 1996.

From London Several trains run the 168-mile trip to York from London's King's
By Train Cross Station (tel. 0171/278–2477): nine a day weekdays 7:30–7; eight Saturday 6:30–6:15; and six Sunday 9:15–6.

By Bus **National Express** buses leave three times daily (10:30 AM, 2:30 PM, and 6:30 PM) from London's Victoria Coach Station (tel. 0171/730–0202) for the 4½-hour journey.

By Car By car, York is 193 miles from London: take M1 to Leeds and then A64.

York

Regional Tourist Information: The Yorkshire and Humberside Tourist Board, 312 Tadcaster Rd., York, YO2 2HF, tel. 01904/707961. York tourist office: De Grey Rooms, Lendel Bridge, Exhibition Sq., tel. 01904/621756. **Guide Friday** *(8 Tower St., tel. 01904/640896) operates a city tour of York, including visits to the Minster, the Castle Museum, the Shambles, and the Jorvik Viking Centre. The circuit lasts about an hour, but you can leave and rejoin the bus at will. The cost is £6 adults, £1.50 children under 12, £4.50 senior citizens.* **Yorspeed Tours** *(tel. 01904/762622) has two tours of the city on cassette tape, "The Streets" and "The Walls," which cost £5 per tour or £6 for both (children half price). They can be rented from the Tourist Information Centre, the Jorvik Viking Centre, and Thomas Cook's Bureau de Change at the railway station.*

★ Spend as much time as you can in **York**; the layers of history within its walls cannot be explored quickly. Named "Eboracum" in Latin, York was the military capital of Roman Britain, and traces of Roman garrison buildings still survive in the Yorkshire Museum gardens, among other places. The base of the medieval **Multangular Tower** was also part of the garrison, and the foundations of York Minster (cathedral) itself rise from remains of the *principia*, or garrison headquarters. Following the fall of the Roman Empire in the 5th century, a Saxon town grew up over the ruins of the Roman fort. On Christmas Eve, AD 627, the Northumbrian King Edwin introduced Christianity to the area by being baptized in a little wooden church in York. The city grew in importance in the 9th century, after the Viking conquerors of northern and eastern England made York— which they called "Jorvik"—their English capital.

One memorable way to see the city is from atop the city walls. Originally earth ramparts erected by York's Viking kings to repel raiders, the present stone structure (probably replacing a stockade) dates from the 14th century and has been extensively restored. A narrow paved walk runs along the top of the walls (originally 3 miles in circumference), passing over fortified gates or "bars."

Because of its strategic position on the River Ouse, York developed throughout Norman and Plantagenet times (11th–14th centuries) into a trade center and inland port, particularly for the export of wool to the Continent. Wealthy guilds of craftsmen and merchants flourished, and kings and queens frequently visited the city: Henry II and Edward II held parliaments here, and Richard II gave the city its first Sword of State. The great York Minster, officially the Cathedral of St. Peter, was founded in Norman times, and its size and beauty reflect medieval York's wealth and importance. The archbishop of York is second only to the archbishop of Canterbury in the hierarchy of the Church of England.

The old city center of York is a compact, dense web of narrow streets and tiny alleys—"snickleways." Congestion has gotten so bad that traffic has been banned around the minster. Bus tours of the city leave from outside the train station, but you'll probably get a better sense of York by walking through it. Avoid July and August when crowds choke the narrow streets and cause long lines at the popular museums. April, May, and October are far better; April is also the time to see the embankments beneath the city walls filled with the pale gold ripple of daffodils.

Numbers in the margin correspond to points of interest on the York map.

❶ Start your tour in the north of the city, at the largest Gothic church in England, **York Minster:** It is 534 feet long, 249 feet across its transepts, and 90 feet from floor to roof; the central towers are 184 feet high. Mere statistics, however, cannot convey the scale and beauty of the building. Its soaring columns; the ornamentation of its 14th-century nave; the great east window; the enormous choir screen portraying somewhat whimsical images of every king of England from William the Conqueror to Henry VI; the Rose Window (just one of 128 in the Minster) commemorating the marriage of Henry VII and Elizabeth of York in 1486 (the event that ended the Wars of the Roses and began the Tudor dynasty)—all contribute to its magnificence. The minster also contains a rich array of chapels, monuments, and tombs, and don't miss the exquisite 13th-century **Chapter House** or the **Undercroft Museum and Treasury,** with Saxon and Roman remains. The crypt features some of the Minster's oldest treasures. After exploring the interior, climb the 275 steps up the great **central tower,** not only for the close-up view of the cathedral's detailed carving but also for a magnificent panorama of York and the surrounding Pennines and Yorkshire moors. *York Minster Undercroft Museum and Treasury, Chapter House, Crypt, and Central Tower, tel. 01904/624426. Admission: Minster free, although £1.50 donation appreciated; Foundations (including Treasury) £1.80 adults, £1.50 senior citizens, 70p children; Chapter House 70p adults, 30p senior citizens and children; Crypt 60p adults, 30p senior citizens and children; Central Tower £2 adults, £1 senior citizens and children. Minster open summer, daily 7 AM–8:30 PM, winter, daily; Undercroft, Chapter House, Crypt, and Central Tower open Mon.–Sat. 10–6:30, Sun. 1–6:30; gift shop open daily 9:30–4:30.*

❷ After leaving the Minster, walk down Low Petergate to Colliergate. **The Shambles** (right off Colliergate), is a perfectly preserved medieval street with half-timbered stores and houses whose overhangs are so massive you could almost reach across the street from one second-floor window to another.

❸ Walk the length of the Shambles, taking time to browse in the crafts and souvenir shops along the way, and into The Pavement. From here turn right into Fossgate where you'll find the **Merchant Adventurers' Hall** on the right. This former guildhall, dating from the mid-14th century, is the largest half-timbered hall in York, with a pretty garden in the back. *Tel. 01904/654818. Admission: £1.80 adults, £1.50 senior citizens, 50p children. Open Mar.–Nov., daily 8:30–5; Nov.–Mar., Mon.–Sat. 8:30–5.*

❹ From the Merchant Adventurers' Hall you can walk along the river a little way before turning right into an area containing two interesting museums: the Jorvik Viking Centre and the Heritage Centre in St. Mary's church. In the **Jorvik Viking Centre,** on an authentic Viking site, archaeologists have re-created a Viking street with astonishing attention to detail. Its "time-cars" take visitors through the streets to experience the sights, sounds, and smells of Viking England. *Coppergate, tel. 01904/643211. Admission: £3.95 adults, £3 senior citizens (seniors concession Nov.–Mar. only), £2 children. Open Apr.–Oct., daily 9–7; Nov.–Mar., daily 9–5:30.*

York's 20 or so surviving medieval churches—almost all of which can stand alone as architectural showpieces—tend to be largely ignored

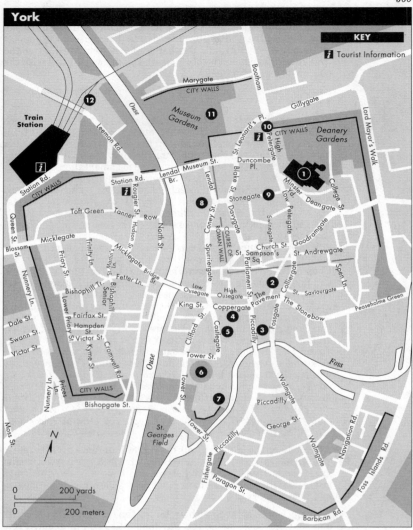

York

KEY

ℹ️ Tourist Information

Bootham Bar, **10**

Castle Museum, **7**

Clifford's Tower, **6**

Jorvik Viking Centre, **4**

Mansion House and
Guildhall, **8**

Merchant Adventurers'
Hall, **3**

National Railway
Museum, **12**

St. Mary's and the
York Story, **5**

The Shambles, **2**

Stonegate, **9**

York Minster, **1**

Yorkshire Museum, **11**

⑤ by tourists, and are therefore good places to explore without having to deal with crowds. An exception, however, is **St. Mary's,** which now houses **The York Story,** an exhibit devoted to the history of the city, with medieval-style embroidered panels, original artifacts, and a video. It's very crowded but a worthwhile attraction. *Castlegate, tel. 01904/628632. Admission: £1.60 adults, £1.10 senior citizens and children; joint ticket with the Castle Museum, £5.30 adults, £2.90 children, £12 family ticket. Open Mon.–Sat. 10–5, Sun. 1–5.*

Continue down Castlegate and turn right into Tower Street. On your ⑥ left you'll see **Clifford's Tower,** which dates from the early 14th century. It stands on the mound originally erected for the keep of York Castle, long since gone (the site now occupied by the Assize Courts and the Castle Museum. In 1190 this was the scene of one of the worst outbreaks of anti-Semitism in medieval Europe, when 150 Jews who had sought sanctuary in the castle were massacred. Information panels tell the story of the castle, including the massacre and the Civil War. *Tower St., tel. 01904/646940. Admission: £1.50 adults, £1.10 senior citizens, 75p children. Open Apr.–Oct., daily 10–6; Nov.–Mar., daily 10–4. Closed Christmas and Jan. 1.*

⑦ The **Castle Museum,** a former 18th-century debtors' prison, offers a number of detailed exhibitions and re-creations, including a cobblestoned Victorian street complete with crafts shops; a working water mill; domestic and military displays; and, most important, the Coppergate Helmet, a 1,200-year-old Anglo-Saxon helmet (one of only three ever found) discovered during recent excavations of the city. You can also visit the cell where Dick Turpin, the 18th-century highwayman and folk hero, spent the night before his execution. The museum also has a welcome tearoom serving simple snacks. *Clifford St., 01904/653612. Admission: £3.95 adults, £2.85 senior citizens and children. Joint ticket with York Story, £5.30 adults, £2.90 children, £12 family ticket. Open Apr.–Oct., Mon.–Sat. 9:30–5:30, Sun. 10–5:30; Nov.–Mar., Mon.–Sat. 9:30–4, Sun. 10–4. Closed Christmas and Jan. 1.*

A walk up Castlegate to Spurriergate into Coney Street brings you ⑧ to the **Mansion House** and the **Guildhall.** The mid-15th-century Guildhall has been restored after being damaged in World War II. *St. Helen's Sq., tel. 01904/613161. Admission free. Open May–Oct., Mon.–Thurs. 9–5, Fri. 9–4, Sat. 10–5, Sun. 2–5; Nov.–Apr., Mon.–Thurs. 9–5, Fri. 9–4.*

⑨ From the Guildhall, make your way across into **Stonegate,** a narrow street of Tudor and 18th-century storefronts and courtyards with considerable charm. A passage just off Stonegate, at 52A, leads to a 12th-century Norman stone house, one of the very few to have survived in England. Continue to the Minster and turn left onto High ⑩ Petergate. Walk out of the walled city through **Bootham Bar,** one of its old gates. To your left are the gardens and ruins of St. Mary's ⑪ Abbey, founded in 1089, which now houses the **Yorkshire Museum.** The museum itself covers the natural and archaeological history of the whole county, including a great deal of material on the Roman, Anglo-Saxon, and Viking aspects of York. *Museum Gardens, tel. 01904/629745. Admission: £3 adults, £1.75 senior citizens and children, £6 family ticket. Open Nov.–Mar., Mon.–Sat. 10–5, Sun. 1–5; Apr.–Oct., daily 10–5.*

Enjoy a stroll through the gardens and then make your way to Lendal Bridge and cross the river onto Station Road. Take a right ⑫ onto Leeman Road and follow the signs to the **National Railway Museum,** which houses Britain's national collection of locomotives and is the world's largest train museum. Among the exhibits are gleaming giants of the steam era, including *Mallard,* holder of the world speed record for a steam engine (126 mph). You can board some of the trains. Passenger cars used by Queen Victoria are also on display, along with hands-on exhibits that take train travel into the future. *Tel. 01904/621261. Admission: £4.20 adults, £2.80 senior citizens, £2.10 children, £11.50 family ticket. Open Mon.–Sat. 10–6, Sun. 11–6.*

Lodging

££

★

Curzon Lodge and Stable Cottages. This attractive, white-painted, 17th-century part-beamed building, near the racecourse (a mile or so from the train station), has been converted to a high standard of comfort. It is furnished with antiques, such as four-poster beds with brass bedsteads, and all rooms have TVs and tea/coffeemakers. Breakfast is served in the cozy, rustic dining room. (In July and August, prices are slightly higher, but the rooms are still a good value.) *23 Tadcaster Rd., Dringhouses, YO2 2QG, tel. 01904/703157. 10 rooms with bath and/or shower. Facilities: lounge, car park, walled garden. MC, V.*

££

Grasmead House. The comfortable bedrooms in this small family-run hotel all boast antique four-poster beds. Just beyond the city walls, the lodging is an easy walk from the city center, and the friendly owners are more than willing to share their local knowledge with guests. *1 Scarcroft Hill, YO2 1DF, tel. and fax 01904/629996. 6 rooms with bath or shower (3 are nonsmoking rooms). Facilities: bar, lounge, parking. MC, V.*

£

Acer House. This attractive little hotel is in a Victorian building on the edge of York, near the racecourse, 1½ miles from the center of town. The rooms—one of which, more expensive, is a suite with four-poster beds—are comfortable, all en suite, and all have TVs and tea/coffeemakers. Dinner, from £10, is available nightly, and lunch by arrangement. *52 Scarcroft Hill, The Mount, YO2 1DE, tel. 01904/653839. 6 rooms. AE, MC, V.*

£

Byron House Hotel. Ten minutes' walk from the train station and city walls, this friendly hotel retains much of its Victorian character, with comfortable furnishings throughout. Rooms are smart and modern, and rates include a full English breakfast. Dinner is also available, from £17.50. *The Mount, YO2 2DD, tel. 01904/632525, fax 01904/638904. 10 rooms, 7 with shower. AE, DC, MC, V.*

£

Hedley House. The accent at Hedley House is on friendly informality and attentive service. All the rooms have baths en suite and TVs and tea/coffeemakers. It is within easy walking distance (10 minutes) of the city center. The evening meals, at £10, are home-cooked, and special diets can be accommodated. *3–4 Bootham Terr., YO3 7DH, tel. 01904/637404. 15 rooms with bath. MC, V.*

¢

Abbey Guest House. This quaint, pretty guest house is a 10-minute walk from the train station and town center. Though small, it is very clean, friendly, and enjoys a lovely riverside location, with a peaceful garden right on the river. *14 Earlsborough Terr., Marygate, YO3 7BQ, tel. 01904/627782. 7 rooms with basins. Facilities: parking, picnic lunches and evening meal on request. AE, MC, V.*

¢

Arnot House. This late-Victorian bed-and-breakfast overlooks Bootham Park and the Minster. The rooms are large and comfortable, with such period features as fireplaces and attractively molded ceilings. There are tea/coffeemakers and TVs in all rooms. Evening meals, at £10, are available on request. The owner/manager is a professional musician with a helpful knowledge of artistic events in York. *17 Grosvenor Terr., YO3 7AG, tel. 01904/641966. 6 rooms, none with bath. No credit cards. Closed Dec. and Jan.*

Dining

££

Judge's Lodging. In one of York's finest 18th-century buildings, this small hotel's restaurant is a place to enjoy bar lunches, as well as dinners of local fish, meat, and vegetables in superb surroundings. The menu reflects the broad price range, so you can have a fine meal without dropping a bundle of cash. The wine cellar is well stocked. *9 Lendel, tel. 01904/638733. Reservations required. AE, DC, MC, V.*

££

Kites Restaurant. Climb a steep narrow staircase to find an innovative restaurant serving offbeat, health-conscious food. Recommended dishes include the chicken garda filled with raisins,

Parmesan, oregano, and a tamarind sauce. For dessert, the creamy bonoffi pie is a perennial favorite. *13 Grape La., tel. 01904/641750. Reservations advised. AE, D, MC, V. Closed Sun.*

£ **Hudson's Below Stairs.** Eat traditional English food, including fish
★ dishes as well as roast beef and Yorkshire pudding, in this atmospheric Victorian hotel restaurant a five-minute walk from the Minster. *60 Bootham, tel. 01904/621267. Reservations advised. AE, DC, MC, V.*

£ **Little Italy.** This bustling Italian restaurant serves steak, veal, piz-
★ zas (the "Little Italy," with mozzarella, mushroom, prawn, garlic, and tomato is a favorite), pasta, fish, and seafood. Desserts are irresistible, especially the amaretto cheesecake. It's close to the Minster. *Goodramgate, tel. 01904/623539. Reservations advised Sat. and Sun. AE, D, MC, V. Closed Mon. and Tues. mornings.*

¢ **Betty's.** This elegant restaurant and tea house, at the opposite end of Stonegate from the Minster, has been a York institution since 1912. Though it is best known for its teas and mouth-watering cakes (especially the "fat rascal," a plump bun bursting with cherries and nuts), it also has a wide selection of light meals (an inventive menu, from venison sausage with rosti to gourmet toasted sandwiches), all served with old-fashioned style and refinement. Get a table on the upper floor if you can, next to the ceiling-to-floor picture windows, etched with Art Nouveau stained glass. Come early for dinner, as it closes at 9 PM. *6–8 St. Helen's Sq., tel. 01904/659142. MC, V.*

¢ **Plunkets Restaurant, Ltd.** This cheerful restaurant, set in a 17th-century building, is located on one of York's main streets, near the Minster. Live low-key jazz and a menu including spicy Burmese curry, sizzling fajitas, and hamburgers make this a good informal place to have an inexpensive meal. *9 High Petergate, tel. 01904/637722. No credit cards.*

Shopping One mill shop worth visiting is the **Bridge of York** (3 Main St., tel. 01904/634508), where you'll find reasonably priced women's skirts and blouses in a selection of fabrics, and men's shirts and ties, made on the premises.

Although you are not likely to find any bargains in bookstores in York, the new and secondhand ones around Petergate, Stonegate, and the Shambles are excellent. **Blackwell's** (32 Stonegate, 01904/624531) holds new titles, some secondhand books, and a convenient mail order service. For a wide range of secondhand books, head for the **Minster Gate Bookshop** (8 Minster Gate, tel. 01904/621812), in the shadow of the Minster.

The Arts York's **Theatre Royal** (St. Leonard's Place, tel. 01904/623568) is a lively professional theater in a lovely old building, with many other events besides plays: string quartets, choral music, poetry readings, and art exhibitions.

Tour 2: Yorkshire Towns

Using York (*see* Tour 1) as its hub, this tour takes you to the inland towns of Knaresborough and Harrogate, both rich in heritage and natural beauty. In addition to its historic castle, which was partially destroyed under Cromwell's orders in 1648, Knaresborough also offers spectacular views of the river and gorge. Harrogate, on the other hand, is famous for its beautiful and extensive gardens and its springs. What originated as a spa town presently functions as a shopping and conference center.

Knaresborough

Trains make the 16-mile (24-minute) trip from York Railway Station (tel. 01904/642155) to Knaresborough hourly. Monday–Satur-

day 6:52 AM–9:50 PM; Sunday every other hour 12:14–9:21 PM. Knaresborough tourist office: 35 Market Pl., tel. 01423/866886.

A photogenic old town, **Knaresborough** is built in a steep, rocky gorge along the River Nidd. Its attractions include a medieval castle, a boat-filled river, a little marketplace, a house carved out of the cliff face, and a "petrifying well" that will cover anything placed in it with a thin layer of limestone in a matter of weeks.

Harrogate

Take the train to Knaresborough and transfer to the local bus that will take you on the 2-mile jaunt into Harrogate. The direct train from York to Harrogate takes 28 minutes. Harrogate tourist office: Crescent Rd., tel. 01423/525666.

The elegant town of **Harrogate** flourished during the Regency and early Victorian periods, when its mineral springs began to attract the noble and wealthy. You can still drink the evil-smelling (and tasting) spa waters at the newly restored **Royal Pump Room Museum,** which charts the story of Harrogate from its modest 17th-century beginnings. *Opposite Valley Gardens, tel. 01423/503340. Admission: £1.50 adults, 75p senior citizens and children, £3.50 family ticket. Open Mon.–Sat. 10–5, Sun. 2–5.*

Numerous coffee shops and wine bars line the town's gracious esplanades, and tea and toasted teacakes are served in the pump room in the **Royal Baths.** Here you can also still take a Turkish bath or a sauna in its exotic, tiled rooms.

When the spas no longer drew crowds, Harrogate shed its old image to become a modern business center and built a huge complex that attracts international conventions. The complex has been tactfully located so as not to spoil the town's landscape of Regency row houses, pleasant walkways, and sweeping green spaces (the one in the town center is known as "The Stray").

Dining **Gladstones.** This attractive Victorian-style pub near the town center
¢ is noted for its traditional ales and range of inexpensive homemade meat and vegetable pies with roast potatoes. *Prospect Pl., tel. 01423/564976. No credit cards. Lunch only (noon–2); closed Sun.*
Tap & Spile. This old English ale house is just 5 minutes from the bus and train stations and as good a place as any to stop for lunch. You can sample a range of traditional ales, complemented by fresh, home-cooked food. *31 Tower St., tel. 01423/526785. No credit cards.*

Shopping **Walton's Mill Shop** (41 Tower St., tel. 01423/520980), close to the town center, sells a wide range of textiles for the home, including linens, braids, and towels, at factory clearance prices.

Fountains Abbey

It is possible to reach Fountains Abbey on the York Tour Heritage Bus from the York British Rail station; for details, call 01904/ 640896.

The 18th-century water garden and deer park, **Studley Royal,** together with the ruins of **Fountains Abbey,** blends the glories of English Gothic architecture with a neoclassical vision of an ordered universe. The gardens include lakes, ponds, and even a diverted river, while waterfalls splash around classical temples, statues, and a grotto; the surrounding woods offer long vistas toward the great tower of Ripon Cathedral, some 3 miles north. Next to the Studley Royal grounds the majestic ruins of Fountains Abbey, with its own high tower and soaring 13th-century arches, make a striking picture on the banks of the River Skell. Founded in 1132, but not completed until the early 1500s, the abbey still possesses many of its original buildings, and it's one of the best places in England to learn how medieval monastic life was organized. The whole of this complex is now owned by the National Trust, which manages a small restaurant (lunch only) at the eastern entrance, as well as stores at both the east and west entrances, and an exhibition and video display in the 17th-century **Fountains Hall,** one of the earliest neoclassical buildings in northern England. *Tel. 01765/608888. Admission: £4 adults, £2 children, £10 family ticket. Abbey, Hall, and gardens open Jan.–Mar. 10–5 or dusk; Apr.–Sept. 10–7; Oct.–Dec. 10–5 or dusk. Closed Fri. Nov.–Jan.*

Tour 3: The Moors

Because Leeds is midway between London and Edinburgh and between Liverpool and Hull, the city serves as a strategic hub for travelers to the Moors.

From London Several trains depart from London's King Cross Station for the 2 ½-
By Train to 3-hour trip to Leeds. Trains leave hourly weekdays 7:30 AM–6:50 PM; 10 trains depart on Saturday 6:30 AM–7 PM, and 11 trains depart on Sunday 9:15 AM–7:15 PM. For train information in Leeds call 01132/448133.

By Bus **National Express Coaches** (tel. 0171/730–0202) depart from London's Victoria Coach Station for Leeds Central Bus Station (tel. 01132/457676) daily, every 90 minutes.

By Car Take the M1 from London to Leeds, 189 miles away.

Leeds

Leeds tourist office: 19 Wellington St., tel. 01132/478301.

The congested traffic and tangle of main routes that pass through the very industrialized city of **Leeds** may make it difficult for visitors to believe that the area surrounding the core makes up one the greenest cities in Europe. In addition to the parks, long green routes radiate from the **City Centre.** You can walk from Golden Acre Park along the Meanwood Valley Trail—the green route to the city—or follow the canal along the Aire Valley. The superb **Victorian Arcades** in the city are well known, but the Georgian squares and streets of Leeds's West End are just as notable. Among the streets you'll find old pubs tucked away and yards that were laid out in the 14th century. The **Art Gallery,** with its fine collection of 20th-century work, and **Henry Moore Study Centre, City Museum,** and **Craft Design Centre** are all adjacent to the **Town Hall.** Crafts of different kinds from all over the world can be found at **Granary Wharf** in the Canal Basin, which is reached via the **Dark Arches,** where the River Aire flows under the City Station. This is one of the many projects that are reviving the Leeds riverside.

Haworth

A trip to Haworth will require taking the train from London to Leeds, another train from Leeds to Keighley, and a bus on to Haworth. Trains run from Leeds to Keighley every half hour, Monday–Saturday 8 AM–9:30 PM; hourly Sunday 8–8. Local buses depart from Keighley on their way to Haworth every 30 minutes, Monday–Saturday 6:25 AM–10:45 PM; Sunday every 45 minutes 9:45 AM–10:45 PM.

*For bus information in Haworth, call 01535/645214. The other option for travel from Keighley to Haworth (a 15- to 20-minute trip) is a privately run steam train—kids love it—called the **Worth Valley Railway** (tel. 01535/645214). Although this is a daily service, schedules tend to be irregular, especially in the winter, so a call in ad-*

vance is advised. Round-trip tickets cost £4.20, £2.10 senior citizens and children; Day Rover tickets £6, £14 family tickets. Haworth tourist office: 2/4 West La., BD22 8EF, tel. 01535/642329.

Many are drawn to **Haworth,** a straggling stone village on the edge of the Yorkshire Moors, to pay homage to the Brontë sisters. It was here that they lived with their father and dissolute brother Bramwell at the Vicarage—a grim house set on the edge of a graveyard that faced the moors—and where Charlotte wrote *Jane Eyre* and Emily wrote *Wuthering Heights,* two of the most enduring 19th-century novels.

Haworth's steep, cobbled Main Street has changed little since the days of the famous sisters, and it is now largely free of traffic. At the end is the **Black Bull** pub, where Branwell drank himself into an early grave. Here also are the post office from which Charlotte, Emily, and Anne sent their manuscripts to their London publishers; an information center with guides and maps; the church, with its gloomy graveyard (Charlotte and Emily are buried inside the church); and

★ their house, the **Brontë Parsonage Museum,** which has some enchanting mementos, including their spidery, youthful graffiti on the nursery wall. *Tel. 01535/642323. Admission: £3.60 adults, £2.60 senior citizens, £1.10 children 16 and under, £8.30 family ticket. Open Apr.–Sept., daily 10–5; Oct.–Mar., daily 11–4:30. Closed mid-Jan.–early Feb. and Christmas.*

If you know and love the Brontës' works, you'll also probably want to walk (an hour or so) to the **Brontë Waterfall,** described in Emily's and Charlotte's poems and letters. Farther into the austere moor is **Top Withins,** the remains of a bleak hilltop farm, which was probably the main inspiration for Heathcliff's gloomy mansion, Wuthering Heights. Wear sturdy shoes and protective clothing: If you've read *Wuthering Heights,* you'll have a fairly good idea of what weather can be like on the Yorkshire moors!

Lodging **Old White Lion Hotel.** Nearly 300 years old, this lovely hotel in the
£ village center and near the Brontë Museum features comfortable rooms, all with TVs, en suite facilities, and tea/coffeemakers. The candlelit restaurant is recommended for traditional favorites like roast beef and Yorkshire pudding; full meals start at £9. The two Old World cocktail bars also dish up excellent bar meals, such as Brontë stew and dumplings. Weekend bargain breaks are often available. *Main St., W. Yorkshire BD22 8DU, tel. 01535/642313, fax 01535/ 646222. 14 rooms with bath. Facilities: restaurant, bars, lounge. AE, DC, MC, V.*

Dining **Weavers Restaurant & Bar.** This restaurant consists of converted
££ weavers' cottages, with a large collection of antiques on show. The stylish cooking with a Northern flare may include stews made from local produce and fresh fish. Weavers is situated near the Brontë Museum and the Worth Steam Railway, and the atmosphere is relaxed and informal. There's a low-price set dinner for early arrivals, so get there before 7 PM. *15 West La., tel. 01535/643822. Reservations suggested. AE, DC, MC, V. Open Tues.–Sat. dinner only and Sun. lunch (Oct.–Apr. only).*

Shopping In Haworth, at the **Brontë Weaving Shed and Edinburgh Woollen Mill** (Townend Mill, tel. 01535/646217) you can see handloom weavers making tweed the traditional way (weekends only); an attached store sells the finished product and is happy to accept U.S. currency or traveler's checks.

Skipton

Trains run about hourly from Leeds to Skipton Monday–Saturday 5:48 AM–10:33 PM, and Sunday 9:05 AM–7:10. For rail information in

Leeds call 01132/448133. Skipton tourist office: 8 Victoria Sq., BD23 1JF, tel. 01756/792809.

Skipton, a typical Dales market town (markets every day except Tuesday and Sunday), has as many farmers as tourists milling in the streets. At the top of busy High Street is **Skipton Castle,** built by the Normans and unaltered since the Civil War (17th century). In the central courtyard, a yew tree, planted 300 years ago by feminist and philanthropist Lady Anne Clifford, still flourishes. Lady Anne was the last of the Cliffords, one of England's most famous baronial families; you can see the striking heraldry on the tombs of her ancestors, the earls of Cumberland, inside Skipton Church. *Skipton Castle, tel. 07156/792442. Admission: £3.20 adults, £2.70 senior citizens, £1.60 children under 18. Open Mar.–Sept., Mon.–Sat. 10–6, Sun. 2–6; Oct.–Feb., Mon.–Sat. 10–4, Sun. 2–4.*

Lodging **Highfield Hotel.** Noted for its home cooking and its breakfast menus
¢ (included in room rate), this small, friendly hotel is also convenient to the bus and rail stations and town center. In the evening between 6 and 8, inexpensive bar meals are served. All rooms have TVs and tea/coffeemakers. *58 Keighley Rd., N. Yorkshire BD23 2NB, tel. 01756/793182. 10 rooms, 9 with bath. Facilities: bar, dining room, lounge. MC, V. Closed Christmas.*

¢ **Linden Guest House.** This friendly guest house on the Pennine Way,
★ 10 miles northwest of Skipton and just 3 miles from Malham Cove and Goredale Scar, is an ideal base from which to walk and tour. It boasts beautiful views of Malhamdale limestone country and superb cooking. Breakfasts are included in the room rate, but dinner costs an additional £10.95 per person. *Airton, N. Yorkshire BD23 4BE, tel. 01729/830418. 6 rooms, 5 with shower, 1 with bath. Facilities: dining room, lounge, bar. No credit cards. Closed Christmas.*

Tour 4: Scarborough and the North York Moors

This tour directs you from York through Malton and Castle Howard to Scarborough; south along the coast to Filey; and finally, to Bridlington. Scarborough, Yorkshire's principal coastal town, is just an hour from York and slightly more than 3 hours from London by fast train. The helpful TIC at Scarborough provides leaflets listing numerous walks.

Malton and Castle Howard

Trains from York (tel. 01904/642155) to Malton run the 25-minute trip hourly Monday–Saturday 7:42 AM–10:06 PM, and every 2 hours on Sunday 9:48 AM–10:32 PM.

*There is no public transport from Malton to Castle Howard; a taxi costs at least £10 each way. Although there are no public buses from York to Malton or Castle Howard, a tour bus from York leaves from the Royal Hotel next to the train station at 1 PM, 4 or less days a week (depending on the season). The bus costs £5.50 round-trip, with a 50p reduction if you book in advance, and goes straight to the castle. There is a £1 reduction in the admission ticket to Castle Howard if you take this bus. For more information call **York Tours** (tel. 01904/641737). Malton tourist office: Old Town Hall, tel. 01653/600048.*

Malton, a pleasant market town and once an important Roman post,
★ is the center for one of Yorkshire's most famous houses—**Castle Howard**—which lies to the west in the Howardian Hills. Perhaps best known these days as the setting for the TV series "Brideshead Revisited," it was designed by Sir John Vanbrugh, who also designed Blenheim, Winston Churchill's birthplace. Castle Howard

Scarborough and the North York Moors

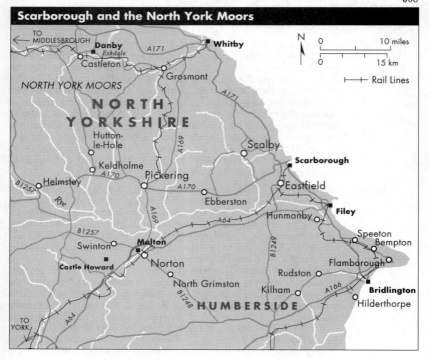

took 60 years to build (1699–1759), and its Baroque grandeur, both inside and out, is without equal in northern England. A magnificent central hallway spanned by a handpainted ceiling leads to a series of staterooms and galleries packed with furniture and works of fine art; there is also a costume gallery in the stables. A neoclassical landscape was created for the house: Carefully arranged woods, lakes, bridges, obelisks, temples, pyramids, and a mausoleum compose a scene far more like a painting than a natural English landscape. *Coneysthorpe, tel. 01653/648333. Admission: House and gardens £5.50 adults, 5 senior citizens, £3 children; gardens only £3 adults, £1.50 senior citizens and children. House open mid-Mar.– late Oct., daily 11–4:30. Grounds open all year 10–4:30.*

Scarborough

Trains from Malton to Scarborough make the 20-minute run hourly Monday–Saturday 6:25 AM–8:46 PM, Sunday hourly 9:20 AM–8:27 PM.

*Trains from London to Scarborough run hourly weekdays 7 AM–8 PM; Saturday trains travel irregularly 6 AM–7 PM; Sunday trains run irregularly 10 AM–8 PM. All involve a change in York for the three- or four-hour trip. For more rail information call **British Rail** in Scarborough at tel. 01723/373486. Scarborough tourist office: St. Nicholas Cliff, tel. 01723/373333.*

A great sweep of cliffs above its sandy bay, a rocky promontory capped by a ruined castle, and a harbor with a lighthouse make **Scarborough** the classic picture of an English seaside resort, though its beaches are a mixture of sand and rock. In fact, the city claims to be the earliest seaside resort in Britain, dating from the chance discovery in the early 17th century of a mineral spring on the foreshore. Not unexpectedly, this led to the establishment of a spa, whose users were encouraged not merely to soak themselves in seawater but also to drink it. By the late 18th century, when sea bathing was firmly in vogue, no beaches were busier than Scarborough's with "bathing machines," cumbersome wheeled cabins drawn by donkeys or horses into the surf and anchored there. These contraptions afforded swimmers, especially modest ladies, relative privacy, as the cabin door faced seaward.

Scarborough's initial prosperity dates from this period, as evidenced in the handsome Regency and early Victorian residences and hotels in the city. The advent of train travel further popularized seaside vacations in Britain, and the extension of the railroad from York to Scarborough in the mid-19th century made it accessible for larger numbers of people. Smaller hotels and boardinghouses sprang up, and an atmosphere of cheerful vulgarity soon became as characteristic of Scarborough as of the other British seaside resorts.

Yet Scarborough has kept its two distinct faces. Its older, more genteel side in the southern half of town consists of carefully laid-out crescents and squares, and clifftop walks and gardens with spectacular views across Cayton Bay. The northern side is a riot of ice-cream stands, cafés, stores selling "rock" (no British seaside vacation is complete without this hard candy), crab hawkers, bingo halls, and "candy floss" (cotton candy). The contrast between the two sides makes Scarborough all the more appealing. Enough also survives of the tight huddle of streets, alleyways, and red-roofed cottages around the harbor to give one an idea of what the city was like before the resort days. One revealing relic is a tall, 15th-century stone house, now a restaurant, which is said to have been owned by Richard III.

Scarborough harbor is busy with coastal fishing and shipping, as well as pleasure cruises. Stop in at the old harbor lighthouse, which doubles as a deep-sea fishing museum. Paths link the harbor with the ruins of **Scarborough Castle** on the promontory; dating from Norman times, it is built on the site of a Roman signal station and near a former Viking settlement. From the castle you can see across the North Bay to the beaches and the shore gardens. *Tel. 01723/ 372451. Admission: £1.50 adults, £1.10 students and senior citizens, 75p children. Open Apr.–Sept., daily 10–6; Oct.–Mar., Tues.–Sun. 10–4.*

At the little medieval church of **St. Mary**, near the castle on the way into town, you'll find the grave of Anne, the youngest of the Brontë sisters; she was taken to Scarborough from Haworth in a final desperate effort to save her life in the supposedly beneficial sea air. Happier literary associations are found at **Wood End** on the Crescent, vacation home of 20th-century writers Edith, Osbert, and Sacheverell Sitwell, a sister and two brothers. The early Victorian house with delightful grounds is now the **Woodend Museum of Natural History;** an adjoining house is the **Art Gallery.** *Tel. 01723/367326. Admission free. Open May–Sept., Tues.–Sun. 10–5; Oct.–Apr., Fri.–Sun. 11–4.*

A short walk below Wood End leads to the **Rotunda Museum,** an extraordinary circular building with archaeological and local history collections. Constructed in 1829 for the Scarborough Philosophical Society, it was one of the first museums in the country. *Vernon Rd., tel. 01723/374839. Admission and opening times same as Woodend Museum (see above).*

Scarborough's beaches are a mixture of sand and rock, but its proximity to outstanding countryside makes it an excellent touring base. The 55-mile stretch of coast from **Saltburn-by-the-Sea** north of Scarborough down to Bridlington has some of the sheerest seacliffs in the British Isles, and inland, the unspoiled country towns and villages provide a pleasant contrast to the sometimes garish esplanades of resorts and the overcrowded trailer parks.

Lodging
£

Old Mill Hotel. Located in the center of town, this atmospheric hotel features traditional-style rooms, with TVs, in a cobbled courtyard surrounding a lovely old windmill. The mill has been carefully renovated and houses a lounge and dining room, where you can order delicious meals on request. *Mill St., YO11 1SZ, tel. 01723/372735. 14 rooms with bath. Facilities: dining room, lounge. No credit cards.*

¢
★

Attenborough Hotel. This is a welcoming hotel set in a Victorian crescent, overlooking attractive gardens. It's in the center of town, close to the train and bus station. Breakfast and dinner are served here. *28/29 Albemarle Crescent, YO11 1XX, tel. 01723/360857. 25 rooms, 5 with bath. Showers available. No credit cards.*

¢

Manor Heath Hotel. This attractive hotel overlooks Peasholm Park and North Bay. Conveniently situated, it is near all the attractions of this seaside resort: the beach, swimming pools, miniature railway, golf links, and cricket ground. Breakfast and dinner are available, and all rooms have TV and tea/coffeemakers. *67 Northstead Manor Dr., YO12 6AF, tel. 01723/365720. 16 rooms, 13 with bath. Facilities: lounge, bar. No credit cards.*

¢

St. Margaret's Guest House. A well-kept guest house, St. Margaret's is small and popular, so you should call well in advance to reserve a room. There's a lounge and dining room, and you're only 10 minutes' walk from the town center and beach. *8 Trafalgar Sq., YO12 7PY, tel. 01723/379983. 7 rooms with washbasins. No credit cards.*

Dining
££
★

Lanterna Restaurant. An intimate atmosphere and a high standard of cuisine make this Italian restaurant a good choice. The classic dishes are all represented, among them tender veal cooked with ham and cheese, but more unusual seasonal specials are worth investigating, too, using fresh vegetables and fish unavailable at other times of the year. The establishment is also noted for the quality of its service and its wine cellar. *33 Queen St., tel. 01723/363616. Reservations advised. MC, V. Closed Sun., Mon., and lunch.*

£

Central Hotel. This building forms part of an attractive Georgian crescent overlooking the Crescent Gardens. It's close to the bus and train stations, the town center, theaters, and South Bay Beach. The hotel is too expensive for the budget traveler, but the restaurant, with charcoal-grilled steaks and seafood, is reasonable. *1–3 The Crescent, YO11 2PW, tel. 01723/365766. V.*

The Arts

Alan Ayckbourne, a widely popular contemporary playwright in Great Britain, is from Scarborough. The **Stephen Joseph Theatre in the Round** at Valley Bridge near the train station (tel. 01723/370541) stages many of his plays before they head for London or Broadway. You might be lucky enough to catch an Ayckbourne premiere, directed by the master himself, at this small theater.

Filey and Bridlington

Trains to Filey from Scarborough run Monday–Saturday 7:10 AM– 7:35 PM, every 90 minutes; on summer Sundays irregular service begins at 11 AM. To reach Bridlington stay on the Scarborough–Filey train for another 13½ miles.

*The **East Yorkshire Bus Co.** (tel. 01759/302126) runs hourly buses from Scarborough, weekdays 7:35–7:25, and Sunday 10:25–7:25. The trip to Filey takes 30 minutes; to Bridlington it's a bit longer.*

Except for the hottest summers, England's northeastern seaboard isn't the warmest place for a beach vacation. Yet there are some good, sandy beaches at **Filey** and **Bridlington**.

Tour 5: Durham and Environs

From York you can connect with the industrial town of Darlington (about 50 mi) and travel on to the cathedral city of Durham, which has long dominated the Northeast. Durham is a good base for exploring Durham County, which is peppered with coal mines that are now closed and landscaped. From Durham or Darlington you can easily reach the medieval town of Bishop Auckland.

Another option is to take a train directly from London's King's Cross Station (tel. 0171/278–2477) to Durham, about 3 hours northeast. For unlimited train travel to Durham and surrounding towns, you may want to pick up a seven-day **Northeast Regional Rover** ticket (£57 adults), which includes the scenic Carlisle–Settle Line, or for short excursions, the one-day **Tees Ranger** ticket (£9.50 adults), which covers unlimited travel in the Teesside area, including the Heritage Line from the town of Bishop Auckland to the handsome Esk Valley.

National Express (tel. 0171/730–0202) provides service to the Northeast; buses from London make the trip to Durham in under 5 hours.

Darlington

*Two trains per hour make the 44-mile trip from York to Darlington in about 30 minutes and travel Monday–Saturday from 6:44 AM to midnight. Sunday's trains depart a bit irregularly but steadily from 9 AM to midnight. For more train information call **British Rail** in Darlington at tel. 01325/355111. Darlington tourist office: 4 West Row, tel. 01325/382698.*

To enter **Darlington** is to step into the 19th-century world of industrialization, when the town quickly expanded with the success of the railroads in the 1830s. That expansion brought not only prosperity but fame, for here, on the Stockton–Darlington route, the world's first steam passenger railroad was established by George Stephen-
★ son in 1825. The **Darlington Railway Centre and Museum** is housed in one of his original railroad stations, built in 1842. You can inspect historic engines, including Stephenson's *Locomotion I*, as well as photographs, documents, and models. *North Road Station, tel. 01325/460532. Admission: £1.80 adults, £1.30 senior citizens, 90p children. Open daily 10–5; closed Christmas and New Year's.*

Durham

Trains from Darlington to Durham depart twice hourly, weekdays 7:12 AM–12:55 AM; Saturday 7:15 AM–12:52 AM; Sunday 8:47 AM–1:45 AM. From London's King's Cross Station to Durham trains run weekdays, 6 AM–10 PM; Saturday 6 AM–12:45 AM; Sunday 9 AM–10 PM about once per hour. For more information call 0191/232–6262. Durham tourist office: Market Place, DH1 3NJ, tel. 0191/384–3720.

The cathedral and castle of the city of **Durham**, seat of Durham County, stand high on a wooded peninsula almost entirely encircled by the River Wear (rhymes with "beer"). For centuries these two ancient buildings have dominated the city—now a thriving university town—and the surrounding countryside. Durham was once the capital of the Anglo-Saxon kingdom of Northumbria (i.e., the land north of the River Humber, which flows into the North Sea at Grimsby). For 1,000 years, the city was also the seat of powerful "prince bishops" who exercised near-monarchical power within the diocese. The city's glorious past is proudly preserved and protected. Ingenious street plans keep pedestrians and traffic separate, and older buildings have been carefully restored. Recently the castle

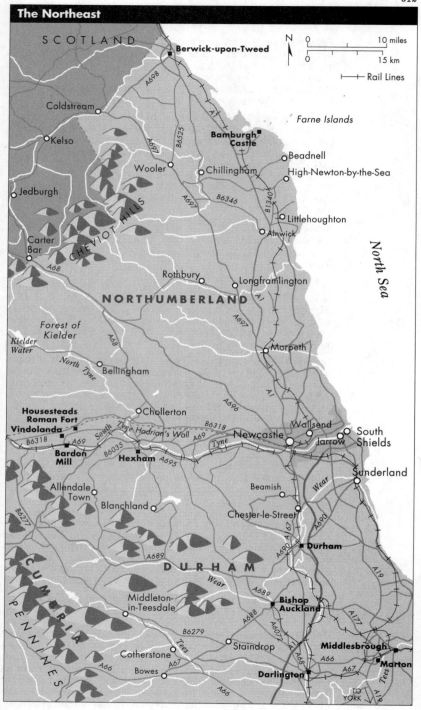

The Northeast

and cathedral were jointly designated a World Heritage Site in official recognition of their international importance.

Numbers in the margin correspond to points of interest on the Durham map.

★ ❶   The centrally located **cathedral** on Palace Green is an ideal starting point for a walking tour of Durham. Architectural historians come from all over the world to admire and study the great church's Norman features, such as the relief work on its massive pillars and the rib vaulting in the roof. But no special expertise is needed to appreciate its exceptional position, impressive size, and wealth of detail.

The origins of the cathedral go back to the 10th century. Monks fleeing a devastating Viking raid in the year 875 on Lindisfarne Abbey (on Holy Island off the northeast coast, 78 miles from Durham) had carried the body of St. Cuthbert from the shrine at Lindisfarne to this site. By 995, the wealth attracted by Cuthbert's shrine paid for the construction of a cathedral. The prestige of the area grew until the bishop of Durham acquired his title of "prince bishop," a title held until the 19th century. This gave the bishop power to rule Durham County in both a political and a religious sense, and even to raise armies, mint coins, and appoint judges. The **prince-bishop's throne** in the cathedral is still the loftiest in all Christendom; his miter is the only one to be encircled by a coronet, and his coat of arms is the only one to be crossed with a sword as well as a crosier.

Many visitors take a snapshot of the 12th-century **bronze knocker,** shaped like the head of a ferocious mythological beast, on the massive north entrance door. By grasping the ring clenched in the animal's mouth, medieval felons could claim sanctuary; cathedral records show that 331 criminals (especially murderers) sought this protection between 1464 and 1524. But the knocker now in place is, in fact, a replica; the original is kept for security in the cathedral **treasury.**

The power and the glory of the prince bishop, as manifested in the richly decorated **tomb of Bishop Hatfield** and the lofty episcopal throne described above, are a marked contrast to the simple **tomb and shrine of St. Cuthbert** (behind the high altar) and the tomb (in the Galilee Chapel) of the Venerable Bede, the scholar and saint whose body was brought here in 1020. Many more ornate features would have survived had not the cathedral been used to imprison 4,000 Scottish soldiers after the Battle of Dunbar in 1650. These fierce Protestants went on a rampage, smashing effigies and burning woodwork, although they spared the cathedral's elaborate **clock** because the thistle emblem of Scotland figures in its design.

The **Chapel of the Nine Altars** has soaring, polished pillars made from a local limestone known as Frosterley marble. Only the visible surfaces were polished (probe behind the pillars and you can feel the rough, unfinished parts). A restaurant in the Undercroft is open seven days a week. *Tel. 0191/386–2367. Admission: cathedral free but donation welcome; treasury £1 adults, 40p children. Cathedral open May–Sept., daily 7:15 AM–8 PM; Oct.–Apr. daily 7:15–5:30; treasury open Mon.–Sat. 10–4:30, Sun. 2–4:30; choral evensong service weekdays 5:15, Sun. 3:30.*

❷   On the opposite side of Palace Green is **Durham Castle,** which commands a strategic position overlooking the River Wear. For over 750 years the castle was the home of successive warlike prince bishops, and today it houses University College, of the University of Durham (the oldest in England after Oxford and Cambridge). You can tour the castle at certain times, and during college vacations tourist accommodations are available. The great hall, dating from 1284, is still in use, as are the original kitchens and buttery; the castle crypt serves as a student lounge, while the old servants' hall is now the

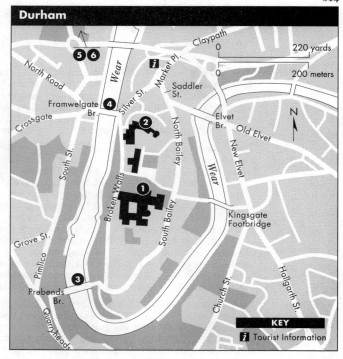

Durham

0 ─── 220 yards
0 ─── 200 meters

N

KEY
ℹ️ Tourist Information

college library. *Palace Green, tel. 0191/374–3800. Admission: £1.60 adults, £1 children. Open July–Sept., daily 10–noon, 2–4:30; Oct.–June (tours only), Mon., Wed., Sat. 2–4:30.*

③ *From the southern end of Palace Green, a path to* **Prebends Footbridge** (which bears an inscription of several lines by Sir Walter Scott) *leads across the river and along South Street. Recross the* **④** *River Wear at* **Framwelgate Bridge,** *and go into Silver Street, which leads to Market Place. From here, Saddler Street and North Bailey lead back to the cathedral. Many of the elegant town houses on these streets are now departments of the university. At every turn there are glimpses of river, castle, cathedral, and town. Durham Regatta, held on the river every year in mid-June, is the oldest rowing event in Britain, and attracts teams in all classes from the entire country.*

⑤ The **Durham Light Infantry Museum** at Aykley Heads (½ mile northwest of the city center on A691) is devoted to the history of the county regiment, exhibiting uniforms, weapons, and regalia alongside mementos of campaigns in India, Iran, the Crimea, and Africa. On the second floor is an arts center offering a changing program of events throughout the year. Outdoor events, such as brass-band concerts and military vehicle rallies, take place on the landscaped grounds. *Tel. 0191/384–2214. Admission: £1 adults, 50p senior citizens and children. Open Tues.–Sat. 10–4:30, Sun. 2–4:30.*

⑥ *The* **Durham University Oriental Museum** collections cover all parts of the East, showing everything from tiny, meticulously carved jade and ivory ornaments to full-size representations of Buddha, a Chinese portable bedroom, and an Egyptian mummy. *Elvet Hill, off South Rd. (A1050), near Van Mildert and Trevelyan colleges, tel. 0191/374–2911. Admission: £1 adults, 50p senior citizens and children. Open weekdays 9:30–1 and 2–5, weekends 2–5; closed 10 days at Christmas.*

Lodging **Castle View Guest House.** This 250-year-old building, in the heart of
£   the old city near St. Margaret's Church, is in close proximity to
woodland and riverside walks and has a magnificent view of the cathedral and castle. *4 Crossgate, DH1 4PS, tel. 0191/386–8852. 6
rooms, 3 with bath. Facilities: lounge. No credit cards. Closed
Christmas week.*

¢   **Castledene.** This Edwardian house is a half mile west of the market-
★   place and within walking distance of the riverside, cathedral, and
castle. Budget travelers can make the most of Castledene's prime
location. *37 Nevilledale Terr., DH1 4QG, tel. 0191/384–8336.++any
fax?++ 3 rooms without bath. Facilities: lounge. No credit cards.*

¢   **Neville's Cross Hotel.** This small family-run hotel, in a former 19th-
★   century coaching inn on the western outskirts of Durham, has open
fires and a warm hospitable atmosphere. It's a mile from Durham
city center: a 2-minute taxi ride along the city bus route or an easy
walk. It stands at what used to be a major crossroads on the north–
south road; Neville's Cross itself, now ruined, commemorated an
English victory over the Scots on this site in 1346. The food, which
will cost less than £10 per person, is very good: Specialties include
homemade steak and kidney pie, steaks grilled in red wine, and
duck braised in orange. Bar meals are also served. *Darlington Rd.,
Neville's Cross, DH1 4JX, tel. 0191/384–3872. 5rooms without bath.
AE, DC, MC, V.*

Dining **County Restaurant.** Located in the Royal County Hotel, a Georgian
Splurge   building that retains many of its historic details, this luxurious
downtown restaurant has romanesque decor and some extravagant
dishes on its menu. Specialties include wild boar steaks and traditional Northumbrian and Northern dishes such as roast beef with
Yorkshire pudding. If you select carefully from the menu, you don't
necessarily have to spend a lot of money here, although an average
meal could easily run you more than £25 per person. *Old Elvet, tel.
0191/386–6821. Reservations advised. Jacket and tie. AE, DC, MC,
V.*

Shopping The **University Bookshop** (55 Saddler St., tel. 0191/384–2095) offers
both general and academic books, with more than 25,000 volumes in
stock, including secondhand and antiquarian books. Here you'll find
the largest selection in this university city.

Bishop Auckland

*Trains run about hourly from Darlington to Bishop Auckland,
weekdays from 6:30 AM to 8:31 PM, Saturday from 7:04 AM to 8:45 PM,
Sunday from 8:24 AM to 7:58 PM.*

*Buses from Darlington to Bishop Auckland run twice hourly, Mon-
day–Saturday 7:30 AM–10:40 PM, and hourly on Sunday 11:10 AM–
9:10 PM. Local buses (5 per hour) make the 35-minute trip from Durham to Bishop Auckland, Monday–Saturday 7:11 AM–10:56 PM. On
Sunday, one bus per hour travels from 10:56 AM to 10:56 PM.*

The town of **Bishop Auckland** is where the prince bishops of Durham
had their official residence in **Auckland Castle** for 700 years. This
grand episcopal palace dates mainly from the 16th century, though
the chapel was built in 1665 from the ruins of a 12th-century banqueting hall. The unusual 18th-century "deerhouse," or hunting
lodge, of adjoining Bishops Park testifies to at least one of the bishops' extracurricular interests. The castle itself offers architectural
styles ranging from the medieval to the neo-Gothic. *Off Market
Place, tel. 01388/601627. Admission: £1.30 adults, 65p senior citizens and children. Open mid-May–Sept., Sun. and Wed. 2–5; chapel only on Thurs. 10–noon.*

Lodging **The Postchaise.** This authentic 17th-century coaching inn, with a
£   large public bar and à la carte restaurant, still retains most of its

original woodwork. The food is excellent, whether you choose the homemade pies in the bar or the succulent fish and steaks in the restaurant proper. All the rooms are equipped with TVs. *36 Market Pl., DL14 7NX, tel. 01388/661296. 12 rooms with bath. Facilities: restaurant, bar. AE, DC, MC, V.*

Dining   **Bishops Bistro.** This central eatery (close to the rail station) is
£   housed in a connected row of converted cottages. You can have a pre-
★   prandial drink in the cozy bar, then select one of the daily specials from the blackboard. Try the roast leg of lamb with rosemary if it's available. *17 Cockton Hill Rd., tel. 01388/602462. Reservations advised. MC, V. Closed Sun. and Mon.*

Tour 6: Middlesbrough to Whitby

From Darlington, head east to the industrial town of Middlesbrough. With a stop in Danby continue southeast toward the coast to the port-turned-resort-town of Whitby, once the home of explorer Captain James Cook.

Middlesbrough

Trains depart about every 30 minutes from Darlington to Middlesbrough Monday–Saturday 7:10 AM–10:29 PM; Sunday 9:39 AM–9:54 PM. The trip is about 27 minutes. For more rail information for Middlesbrough and Darlington, call 01325/355111.

For bus information in Middlesbrough, call 0642/210131. Middlesbrough tourist office: 51 Corporation Rd., tel. 01642/243425.

About 12 miles east of Darlington lies the industrial town of **Middlesbrough.** In 1802, a mere dozen people lived here, but the local discovery of iron ore spawned a boom based on the manufacture of steel; later, development focused on chemical industries. The town's unusual claim to fame is its iron transporter bridge, built in 1911 to replace a ferry crossing. The largest of its kind in the world, this vast structure looms up like a giant's erector-set model. A gantry system still takes 12 cable cars, holding 200 passengers each, across the river every 20 minutes. A special viewing platform stands on the south bank. Upstream you'll find **Newport Bridge,** the world's largest lift-span bridge. For travelers willing to forsake the usual tourist routes, these structures present a remarkable sight. *Tel. 01642/247563. Crossing time, 2 minutes. Fare: 25p pedestrians, 70p cars. Open Mon.–Sat. 5 AM–11 PM, Sun. 2–11.*

Marton

Buses from Middlesbrough to Marton depart Monday–Saturday, every half hour 4:43 AM–6:10 PM, then hourly to 10:55. On Sunday buses run hourly 10:55 AM–10:55 PM.

Middlesbrough's more conventional attraction is the **Captain Cook Birthplace Museum** in the leafy suburb of **Marton.** The great explorer, the son of a Scottish laborer and an English domestic servant, was born here in 1728. His life and times are vividly depicted, with a special focus on his remarkable voyages to Australia, New Zealand, Canada, Antarctica, and Hawaii, where he met his death in 1779. A conservatory near the museum houses specimens of the exotic plants Cook discovered during his travels. *Stewart Park, Marton, off A174, south of city center, tel. 01642/311211. Admission: £1.40 adults, 70p senior citizens and children. Open Oct.–Apr., Tues.–Sun. 9–3:30; May–Sept., Tues.–Sun. 10–4:45. Conservatory tel.*

01642/300202. Admission free. Open Easter–Sept., weekends 11 until dusk.

Danby

You can reach Danby from Middlesbrough via the train to Whitby (see Scarborough and the North York Moors map in Tour 4, above). Four trains depart daily from Middlesbrough to Danby, Monday–Saturday 7:12–5:40, Sunday 9:55–3:30. The trip takes about 50 minutes. In the fall and winter service becomes less frequent, with no Sunday trains. Danby tourist office: Lodge La., tel. 01287/660654.

Take time if you can to visit the National Park's **The Moors Centre** at **Danby Lodge,** Eskdale (not far from Danby Station). Here, in a converted country house, exhibitions, displays, and a wide range of pamphlets and books about the area are available, as well as a varied program of lectures, guided walks, and national park events. *Tel. 01287/660654. Admission free. Open Mar.–Oct., daily 10–5.*

Whitby

The train from Middlesbrough continues after Danby for 15 more miles to Whitby (see Scarborough and the North York Moors map in Tour 4, above).

Now a small resort, **Whitby** was once a great whaling port, and it was here that Captain James Cook (1728–79), explorer, circumnavigator, and discoverer of Australia, served his apprenticeship. Visit the **Captain Cook Memorial Museum** in the 18th-century house where Cook lived between voyages, and see mementos of his epic expeditions, including maps, diaries, and fascinating Polynesian prints. *Grape La., tel. 01947/601900. Admission: £1.80 adults, £1.20 senior citizens, £1 children, family tickets £4.50. Open Apr.–Oct., daily 9:45–5; Mar. weekends 11–3.*

Climb the 199 steps from Whitby harbor, and you are at the romantic ruins of **Whitby Abbey,** set high on the cliffs. St. Hilda founded the abbey in AD 657, and Caedmon (died c. 670), the first identifiable poet in the English language, was a monk here. The nearby Mariners' Church of **St. Mary** is designed in the style of an 18th-century ship's deck. It was in this churchyard that Bram Stoker's Dracula claimed Lucy as his victim. *Tel. 01947/603568. Admission: £1.50 adults, £1.10 senior citizens, 80p children. Open Apr.–Sept., daily 10–6; Oct.–Mar., daily 10–4. Closed between Christmas and New Year.*

Dining
£
★
Magpie Café. This restaurant, situated in a onetime whaling port, is a real bargain! With the fishing quay within a stone's throw, everything is ultra fresh. Go for the set lunch, with Whitby crab if you're lucky, and sole, haddock, plaice, or even lobster to follow. The Mackenzie family has been running the Magpie for upward of 40 years, and what they don't know about fish isn't worth knowing. *14 Pier Rd., tel. 01947/602058. MC, V. Last orders at 6:30 Sun.–Thurs., 9 Fri.–Sat. Closed late Nov.–mid-Feb.*

Tour 7: Hexham and Hadrian's Wall

From Durham, you can connect with Newcastle (about 15 miles north), and change to the scenic **Carlisle line,** which travels through the Tyne Valley on to Hexham, the historic market town known as the gateway to Hadrian's Wall country. Nearby is Bardon Mill, where you can see an archaeological excavation of parts of the wall.

Also from Newcastle you can take the train north to the coastal market town of Berwick-upon-Tweed, about an hour away.

When you travel around Hexham, consider using the **North East Rail Rover** pass. During school summer holidays (end of July to beginning of September) a round-trip coach service runs from Hexham station to Haltwhistle, taking in Hadrian's Wall attractions, Vindolanda near Bardon Mill, and a number of other neighboring sites.

Hexham

Trains leave Newcastle for Hexham every half hour for the 40-minute trip. Hexham tourist office: Manor Office, Hallgate, Northumberland NE46 1XD, tel. 01434/605225.

The best day to visit **Hexham** is Tuesday, when the weekly market is held in Market Place. In 1761, the marketplace was the site of a massacre of protesting lead miners by the North Yorkshire Militia, henceforth known as "The Hexham Butchers." Tuesday is also the day for the town's livestock market, the third largest in the country, and the air is thick with the sounds of animals being traded between local farmers.

From Market Place, you can enter ancient **Hexham Abbey,** which forms one side of the square. Inside, climb the 35 worn stone "night stairs," which once led from the main part of the abbey to the canon's dormitory, to overlook this tranquil, peaceful place where Christ has been worshiped for more than 1,300 years. Most of the present building dates from the 12th century, with much of the stone being taken from the Roman fort at Corstopitum a few miles northeast. Near the foot of the stairs, a Roman tombstone set into the wall records the death of one Flavinus, a 25-year-old standard-bearer, shown on horseback above a crouched Briton armed with a dagger. Death is also starkly depicted on the unusual altar screen, which is ornamented with skeletons. Fugitives could claim sanctuary by sitting on the stone throne called both the Frith Stool and St. Wilfred's Chair, after the abbey's founder. *Beaumont St., tel. 01434/602031. Admission free; suggested donation £2. Open May–Sept., daily 9–7; Oct.–Apr., daily 9–5. No tours during services.*

Upon leaving the abbey, you can either stroll through the gardens and parkland opposite or explore the shops around Market Place. From the bowling green there is a particularly fine view of the abbey. Paths lead to the cheerful-looking bandstand and on to **Queen's Hall,** built in the style of a French chateau and now incorporating a library, a 400-seat theater, an arts center, and exhibition galleries. On display is the Tynedale Tapestry (8 × 14 feet), made in the early 1980s by more than 300 people working from a loom on a scaffold. The tapestry illustrates the theme of "theater," with the bright, traditional figures of Harlequin, Columbine, and Pantaloon. *Beaumont St., tel. 01434/607272. Admission free. Galleries open Mon.–Sat. 9:30–5:30.*

Continuing away from the abbey and past Queen's Hall, turn left down Battle Hill to Priestpopple, and go down Fore Street, a thronged, traffic-free shopping area that leads back into Market Place. On the side of Market Place opposite the abbey an exhibition gallery now occupies the ground floor of the Moot Hall in which the archbishop's court was held. A little way beyond, toward the main parking lot, the Manor Office, built as a jail in 1330, now houses the TIC.

Manor Office also hosts the **Border History Museum.** Photographs, models, drawings, a reconstructed blacksmith's shop, a Border house interior, armor, and weapons help tell the story of the "Middle March"—the medieval administrative area governed by a warden and centered in Hexham. *The Old Gaol, Hallgate, tel. 01434/652200, ext. 235. Admission: £1.50 adults, 75p senior citizens and children, £4 families. Open Feb.–Easter and Nov., Sat.–Tues. 10–4; Easter–Oct., daily 10–4.*

Hexham is the best base from which to explore **Hadrian's Wall,** recently designated a World Heritage Site. Begun after the Roman emperor Hadrian's visit in AD 121 following repeated barbarian invasions from Scotland, the wall spanned 73 miles from Wallsend ("Wall's End") just north of Newcastle, in the east, to Bowness-on-Solway beyond Carlisle, in the west. Each mile was reinforced by a "milecastle," or small fort, and each third of a mile by a turret. In addition, at strategic points, large garrison forts were built behind the wall. This formidable line of fortifications marked the northern border of the Roman Empire, which ran east for 2,500 miles to what is now Iraq.

Although a path can be followed along the entire wall, this is rugged country, unsuited to the inexperienced hiker. Most trekkers here organize their routes around the various excellent visitor centers, which are near the best-preserved sections of the wall or in the area of milecastles, turrets, or excavations.

Lodging **Amber House.** This comfortable B&B, close to the railway station
¢ and within easy walking distance of central Hexham, offers single rooms only at £15, equipped with basic amenities such as TVs, teakettles, and hair dryers. *2 Woodlands, NE46 1HT, tel. 01434/602148. 2 rooms without bath. No credit cards.*

Dining and **County Hotel.** An old-fashioned, homey establishment, known to the
Lodging local people who frequent the hotel bar simply as "the County," this
££ hotel is usually crowded with farmers on auction days. Food is served all day in the paneled dining room and in the more informal lounge. High teas (late-afternoon meals) are a specialty (5:30–6:30), and homemade meat pies, pastries, and Northumbrian lamb are often featured on the menu, along with international dishes. A good lunch can be had here for £6–£10, depending on your selection, and you can stay the night for under £60. *Priestpopple, NE46 1PS, tel. 01434/602030. 9 rooms, 6 with bath. Facilities: restaurant, bar, lounge. Restaurant reservations advised. AE, MC, V.*

Dining **Harlequin's Restaurant.** Occupying the ground floor of the Queen's
¢ Hall Arts Centre, this light and airy place overlooks the park and abbey. The dining room is decorated with original modern paintings, and the cheerful staff is busy at lunchtime serving neighborhood workers and shoppers. Local game and fish are the specialties, but there are also vegetarian and pasta dishes. *Beaumont St., tel. 01434/607230. Dinner reservations advised. AE, DC, MC, V. Closed Sun. and national holidays.*

Splurge **Black House.** This restaurant is housed in converted farm buildings, fitted with lots of old furniture and attractive china. The menu is changed monthly and is always imaginative and wisely limited. This splurge will cost about £25 a head. *Dipton Mill Rd., tel. 01434/604744. Reservations advised. MC, V. Closed Sun. and Mon. Open for dinner only.*

Shopping Run by church authorities, the **Abbey Gift Shop** (Beaumont St., tel. 01434/603057) next to the abbey provides a good selection of moderately priced gifts, some unique to the abbey, such as commemorative plates, tapes of on-site choir and music recitals, and various hallmarked items.

Abbey Prints (22 Hallgate, tel. 01434/602244) features a collection of paintings and prints by local artists. It's a good place to look for images of Hadrian's Wall and the surrounding countryside.

Vindolanda

Trains (about one every 90 minutes) from Hexham to Bardon Mill (on the Carlisle line) run Monday–Saturday 7:06 AM–9:44 PM; on Sunday there are four trains from 10:45 AM to 8:17 PM.

At Bardon Mill a one-lane road leads north about 2 miles to the great garrison fort of **Vindolanda.** If you choose to walk the 1-mile route, maps are available at the Hexham tourist office. Excavations are always going on here, and a section of the wall has been reconstructed. Recorded information interprets the site. *Near Bardon Mill, tel. 01434/344277. Admission: grounds only, £1.75 adults, £1.25 senior citizens, £1 children; grounds and museum, £3.25 adults, £2.50 senior citizens, £2 children. Museum open July–Aug., daily 10–6:30; May–June, daily 10–6; Apr., Sept., daily 10–5:30; Mar., Oct., daily 10–5; second half of Feb., first half of Nov., daily 10–4. (last admission ½ hr before closing). Grounds also open Nov.–Feb, daily 10–4.*

Housesteads Roman Fort

From Bardon Mill take a taxi 4 miles to Housesteads Roman Fort.

If you have time to visit only one Hadrian's Wall site, **Housesteads Roman Fort** is your best bet. It offers an interpretive center, views of long sections of the wall, the excavated 5-acre fort itself, and a museum. It's a steep, 10-minute walk up from the parking lot to the site, but it's worth the effort, especially for the view of the wall disappearing over hills and crags into the distance. The excavations reveal granaries, gateways, barracks, and the commandant's house. There are also altars, inscribed stones, and models. *3 mi northeast of Bardon Mill, tel. 01434/344363. Admission: £2.20 adults, £1.75 senior citizens, £1.10 children. Open Apr.–Sept., daily 10–6; Oct–Mar., daily 10–4. Closed Christmas and New Year's Day.*

Berwick

Local trains make the 67-mile journey from Newcastle to Berwick in about 50 minutes. Thirteen trains run per day, weekdays 6:30 AM–10:10 PM. On Saturday trains run 7:50 AM–9:22 PM, and Sunday 10:37 AM–9:28 PM. Weekend service is less frequent. For information, call Berwick (tel. 01289/306771). Berwick tourist office: Castlegate Car Park, tel. 01289/330733.

Historians estimate that **Berwick-upon-Tweed,** located on the coast just within England's border, has changed hands between the Scots and the English 14 times. The market on Wednesday and Saturday draws plenty of customers from both sides of the border. The town's 16th-century walls are among the best-preserved in Europe (a path follows the ramparts). The parish church, Holy Trinity, was built during Cromwell's Puritan Commonwealth with stone from the castle.

In Berwick's **Military Barracks,** built between 1717 and 1721, three accommodation wings surround a square, with the decorated gatehouse forming the fourth side. An exhibition called "By Beat of Drum" depicts the life of the common soldier from the 1660s to the 1880s. *The Parade, off Church St. in town center, tel. 01289/304493. Admission: £2.20 adults, £1.60 senior citizens, £1.10 children. Open Apr.–Sept., daily 10–6; Oct.–Mar., Wed.–Sun. 10–4. Closed Christmas, New Year's.*

Lodding **Old Vicarage.** This guest house is in a roomy Victorian building that
¢ has been refurbished recently. The rooms all have tea/coffeemakers and TVs, and there are ground-floor bedrooms if mobility is a concern. The Old Vicarage is a 10-minute walk from the town center. *24*

Church Rd., Tweedmouth, TD15 2AN, tel. 01289/306909. 7 rooms, 4 with shower. No credit cards.

Dining and Lodging

£

Funnywayt'Mekalivin. This has become famous as an idiosyncratic eatery, and with a name like that who could resist? Set in a 17th-century building in the heart of town, crammed with eccentric oddities and a mere 20 yards from the Elizabethan walls, it's very much a one-woman show. In the seven-table dining room, chef/owner Elizabeth Middlemiss produces her own much-acclaimed variations on local specialties such as venison casserole, seafood crumble, or carrot and apple soup. Lunch buffets provide a chance to sample her cooking at bargain prices. Three basic guest rooms are available upstairs for visitors who can't bear to leave. *41 Bridge St., TD15 1ES, tel. 01289/308827. 3 rooms, without bath. Facilities: restaurant (dinner reservations required). MC, V. Open Tues.–Sat. lunch and Thurs.–Sat. evenings.*

13 Scotland: Edinburgh and Environs

St. Andrews, Melrose, and Kelso

Travelers who want a taste of Scotland but have limited money and time may want to visit only Edinburgh (pronounced Edinbro'), one of Europe's most distinctive and dramatic urban environments. Among its many attributes, the city has an outstanding geographic position: Like Rome, Edinburgh is built on seven hills, and it has an Old Town district that retains striking evidence of a colorful history. Its many outstanding buildings were conceived during the upsurge of Scottish intellectual, scientific, and artistic activity in the second half of the 18th century.

The result for today's visitor is a skyline of sheer drama and an aura of grandeur. Edinburgh Castle watches over the city, frowning down on Princes Street, the main downtown shopping area, as if disapproving of its modern commercial razzmatazz. Its ramparts still echo with gunfire each day when the traditional one o'clock gun booms out over the city, startling unwary shoppers. To the east, the top of Calton Hill is cluttered with sturdy, neoclassical structures, like the abandoned set for a Greek tragedy.

Also conspicuous from Princes Street, springing up just behind the spires of the Old Town, is Arthur's Seat. This child-size mountain, which juts 800 feet above its surroundings, offers steep slopes and little crags, like a miniature highlands right in the middle of the busy city.

From George Street, parallel to Princes Street, you will see, not an endless cityscape, but blue sea and a patchwork of fields. This is the county of Fife, beyond the inlet of the North Sea called the Firth of Forth—a reminder, like the highlands to the northwest visible from Edinburgh's highest points, that the rest of Scotland lies within easy reach.

The Borders area comprises the great rolling hills, moors, wooded river valleys, and farmland that stretch south from Lothian, the region crowned by Edinburgh, to England. All the distinctive features of Scotland—paper currency, architecture, opening hours of pubs and stores, food and drink, and accent—begin at this border; you won't find the Borders a dilute form of England.

Getting around Edinburgh is quite easy because many buses pass along Princes Street on their routes across town. Also, since the city is so compact, it is basically walkable. In the Borders, there are no train services apart from the east coast main line, which only skirts the region. The good bus network, however, will enable you to make

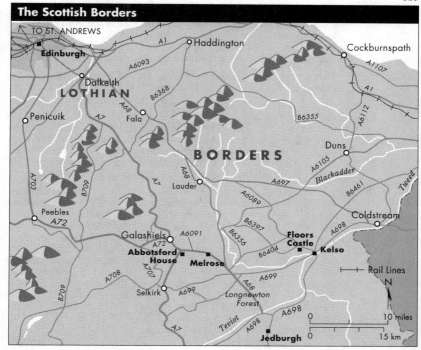

The Scottish Borders

a variety of day trips, although if you intend to spend more than a day in the Borders, hiring a car is your best option.

Essential Information

Lodging In Scotland, a budget accommodation is generally defined as a bed-and-breakfast. Such establishments usually advertise by hanging signs outside the house, but the local tourist information center can also provide you with listings. If you stay in a small B&B, you may share public rooms with the family—what better way of getting to know the Scots? Check in advance whether or not an evening meal is served. Traditional Scottish breakfasts are substantial. Because Edinburgh is a long-established tourist center, budget accommodations are easy to find, although the city becomes very crowded around the time of the Edinburgh Festival in August.

When choosing a hotel or inn anywhere in Scotland, follow the Scottish Tourist Board's grading and classification system: Look for the low-price places that are "Highly Commended," or at least "Commended." A local accommodation can be booked at the tourist information center in the particular town. Except for the cost of the telephone call, this service is usually free. The tourist information centers also offer "Book a Bed Ahead" for travel outside the locality up to 24 hours in advance (£2.50 for booking, plus a room deposit). Highly recommended establishments are indicated by a star ★.

Dining Edinburgh is a sophisticated city, with an interesting, diverse mix of traditional and exotic cuisine, from Scottish dishes to varied ethnic fare. However, one word of warning: The fact that a menu is written in creaking, mock-antique Scots does not guarantee that it is adventurous. For instance, "tassie o' bean bree"—"tassie" being an uncommon word for "cup," and "bree" usually meaning "soup" or "brine"—translates as a plain cup of coffee.

If you want good local fare, look for the "Taste of Scotland" sign in the windows. Most restaurants offer set menus that will usually allow you to eat a 2- to 3-course meal for about £10. An even less expensive option is a "take-out" sandwich or filled roll (from £1). Princes Gardens provides pleasant surroundings in which to eat.

Unless otherwise noted, reservations are not necessary and dress is casual. Highly recommended restaurants are indicated by a star ★.

Shopping   As befits Scotland's capital, shopping in Edinburgh is varied, although it does not compare with Glasgow when it comes to high-fashion clothing. Along Princes Street and the Royal Mile a number of shops sell quality tartans and tweeds. The best buys in the woolen goods for which the region is famous are at the mills in the Borders towns. Though the prices for shetlands and tweeds may be a bit higher in Edinburgh, the selection in the city is usually better.

Biking   It's reasonably easy to get around Edinburgh on a bicycle, although it's hilly. For the most part, destinations north of Princes Street are downhill; to the south, the town rises to its outskirts and into the Pentland Hills. Within the city are few designated bike paths, but even on the main roads motorists are fairly considerate of cyclists. Borders routes—sometimes called the Southern Uplands—are quiet but particularly hilly; fit and experienced cyclists will probably enjoy this challenging terrain. Bicycles can be rented from **Sandy Gilchrist Cycles** (1 Cadzow Pl., tel. 0131/652–1760), **Secondhand Bike Shop** (31–33 Iona St., Leith, tel. 0131/553–1130), and **Central Cycle Hire** (13 Lochrin Pl., tel. 0131/228–6333). Weekly rates in summer start from about £30 for a 3-speed, £40 for a 10-speed, and £40–£50 for a mountain bike.

Hiking   Edinburgh's **Water of Leith** walkway leads upstream from the city to the outskirts by way of leafy riverbanks and paved footpaths. **Arthur's Seat,** Edinburgh's own mountain in miniature, is also a pleasant walk and has rewarding city views. In the Borders, there is the **Southern Upland Way** (the only east–west trail marked with signs), which runs 212 miles from Portpatrick in Galloway to Cockburnspath on the Borders coastline to the east. In addition, this region offers a wide choice of forest, country park, and hill walks. Local tourist offices can give you information on selected routes.

Beaches   Few people visit Edinburgh for its beaches, but there is an acceptable one at **Portobello,** just east of the city. Also to the east is the **East Lothian coastline,** with some beautiful sandy beaches, such as **Gullane,** about 15 miles away. With the exception of the pleasant **St. Abbs,** the Borders lacks sandy beaches. For the most part, the coastline is rocky, with some of the most spectacular cliffs in southern Scotland. To the north across the Firth of Forth, in Fife, is the especially peaceful and striking St. Andrews's beach, which is just steps from the university town.

The Arts and   Good traditional theater productions and concerts by the Royal
Nightlife   Scottish Orchestra and the Scottish Opera can be seen in Edinburgh. Owing to the high standards set by the Edinburgh Festival, summer performances tend to be consistently good.

Edinburgh's nightlife is quite diverse, including both discos and Scottish musical evenings or "ceilidhs" (pronounced "kay-lees") for the older set. The Edinburgh and Scotland Tourist Information Centre above Waverley Market (3 Princes St., tel. 0131/557–1700) can supply up-to-date information on nightlife, especially where there's dinner-dancing.

Festivals   Among many others are the Edinburgh International Festival, the Edinburgh Festival Fringe, the Edinburgh Film Festival, the Edinburgh Military Tattoo, and the Edinburgh Folk Festival.

Edinburgh, the Borders, and St. Andrews

The hub of this tour is Scotland's capital city, Edinburgh, which offers easy access to St. Andrews in Fife, over the Firth of Forth—a town famous for its Royal and Ancient Golf Club. Also within easy reach of the capital is the Borders in the south, recognized as the heart of Scotland's woolen industry and known for its four great ruined abbeys. Edinburgh is easily reached by train or coach from Glasgow or from London's airports. Transatlantic travelers to Scotland should fly direct into Glasgow airport, 50 miles from Edinburgh, thereby avoiding the crunch at Heathrow.

From Glasgow Airport
By Train Trains leave for Glasgow's Queen Street from Paisley Gilmour Street Station, 2 miles from the airport; bus shuttle service between the airport and station operates every 10 minutes. The train from Queen Street Station to Edinburgh takes about 50 minutes and runs at least every half hour. There is also a service from Glasgow Central Station to Edinburgh, but this takes 1½ hours, with frequent stops at intermediate stations, and is not recommended.

By Bus Regular bus services run the 8-mile route from the airport to Glasgow's city center in about 20 minutes. The Buchanan Street bus station is adjacent to Queen Street rail station, from which trains depart for Edinburgh. Alternatively, **Scottish Citylink** (tel. 0141/332–9191) operates a regular bus service to Edinburgh that takes about an hour. For information on local connecting services from Edinburgh, contact St. Andrews Square bus station (tel. 0131/556–8464).

By Car Glasgow Airport is about an hour's drive (just over 50 miles) from Edinburgh via M8.

From London
By Plane Three airlines offer regular flights to Edinburgh: **British Airways** and **British Midland** fly from London's Heathrow (which is on the London Underground rail system). **Air UK** flies from the generally less crowded London Stansted and London Gatwick airports. There are main-line rail connections to London from both airports. Planes leave about every hour and the flight takes 1 hour, 15 minutes. Competition between the airlines can produce bargain prices that compare well with the cost of train travel, so check any special fares when planning your trip. From Edinburgh Airport, buses run at 15-minute intervals to Waverley Bridge downtown; they are less frequent after rush hours and on weekends. The 25-minute journey costs about £3.

By Train **ScotRail** Intercity trains from London's King's Cross (tel. 0171/278–2477) can take from 4 to 5 hours to reach Edinburgh's Waverley Station. Trains run at about hourly intervals, and an overnight sleeper service, which costs from £30 more, is available on this route.

By Bus **Scottish Citylink** (tel. 0131/556–8464) and **National Express** (tel. 01738/33481) run regular services to Edinburgh from London. From London's Victoria Coach Station, the journey takes about 8 hours.

By Car Edinburgh is about 400 miles from London, and the trip takes 7 to 8 hours. The quickest route is via M1, which becomes M6, to the west and then A7 from Carlisle; an alternative route is A1(M) and A1 to the east.

Edinburgh

Lothian Region Transport (tel. 0131/554–4494) and S.M.T. (tel. 0131/556–8464) offer bus tours in and around the city. The Cadies–Witchery Tours (tel. 0131/225–6745) organizes a variety of walking tours of Edinburgh. The cost is about £5 per person for about a 1¼-hour tour. Edinburgh tourist office: 3 Princes St., adjacent to Waverley Rail Station, tel. 0131/557–1700.

The dark, brooding presence of the castle dominates **Edinburgh,** the very essence of Scotland's martial past. The castle is built on a crag of hard, black volcanic rock formed during the Ice Age when an eastward-moving glacier scoured around this resistant core, forming steep cliffs on three sides. On the fourth side, a "tail" of rock was left—a ramp from the top that gradually runs away eastward—which became the street known as the Royal Mile, the backbone of the Old Town.

Time and redevelopment have swept away some of the narrow "closes" (alleyways) and tall tenements of the Old Town, but enough survives for you to be able to imagine the original shape of Scotland's capital, straggling between the guardian fortress on its crag at one end of the Royal Mile and the royal residence, the Palace of Holyroodhouse, at the other. It was not until the Scottish Enlightenment, a civilizing time of expansion in the 1700s, that the city fathers decided to break away from the Royal Mile's rocky slope and build another Edinburgh, a little to the north, below the castle. This is the New Town, with elegant squares, classical facades, wide streets, and harmonious proportions. The main street, Princes Street, was conceived as an exclusive residential address with an open vista to the south. It has since been completely altered by the demands of business, especially of shopping.

Victorian expansion and urban sprawl have hugely increased the city's size, and the Old and New Towns are now separated by Princes Street Gardens (and the railroad), yet their contrasting identities are still the key to understanding Edinburgh.

Numbers in the margin correspond to points of interest on the Edinburgh map.

From Waverley Station, turn southwest to walk up **The Mound** past the **Royal Scottish Academy** and the **National Gallery of Scotland.** At the High Street traffic lights, turn right up to the castle. Probably every visitor to the city tours **Edinburgh Castle**—which is more than can be said for many residents! Its popularity as an attraction is due not only to the castle's symbolic value as the center of Scotland but to the outstanding views offered from its battlements.

Recent archaeological discoveries have established that the rock was inhabited as far back as 1000 BC, in the later part of the Bronze Age. There have been fortifications here since the mysterious people called Picts first used it as a stronghold in the 3rd and 4th centuries AD. The Picts were dislodged by Saxon invaders from northern England in AD 452, and for the next 1,300 years the site saw countless battles and skirmishes.

The castle has been held by Scots and Englishmen, Catholics and Protestants, soldiers and royalty; during the Napoleonic Wars, it even contained French prisoners of war, whose carvings can still be seen on the vaults under the great hall. In the 16th century Mary, Queen of Scots, chose to give birth here to the future James VI of Scotland, who was also to rule England as James I. In 1573, it was the last fortress to hold out for Mary as rightful Catholic queen of Britain, only to be virtually destroyed by English artillery.

The oldest surviving building in the complex is the tiny 11th-century **St. Margaret's Chapel,** the only building spared when the castle was razed in 1313 by the Scots, who had won it back from their English foes and were determined never to surrender it again. Also worth seeing are the **crown room,** which contains the **regalia of Scotland**—the crown, scepter, and sword—that once graced the Scottish monarch; the **old parliament hall;** and **Queen Mary's apartments,** where

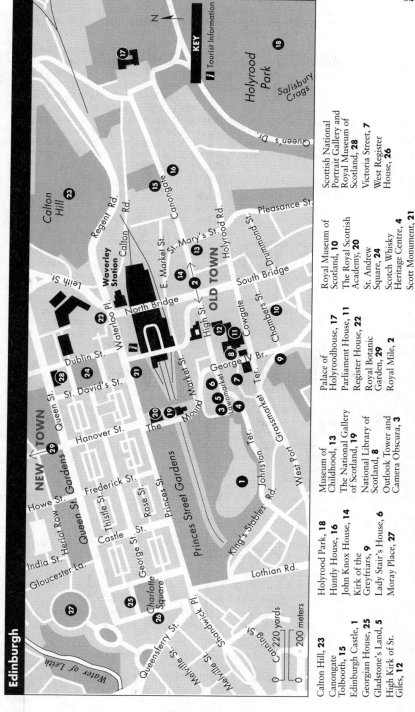

Edinburgh

N

KEY

i Tourist Information

Holyrood Park

Salisbury Crags

Calton Hill

Calton Hill, **23**
Canongate Tolbooth, **15**
Edinburgh Castle, **1**
Georgian House, **25**
Gladstone's Land, **5**
High Kirk of St. Giles, **12**

Holyrood Park, **18**
Huntly House, **16**
John Knox House, **14**
Kirk of the Greyfriars, **9**
Lady Stair's House, **6**
Moray Place, **27**

Museum of Childhood, **13**
The National Gallery of Scotland, **19**
National Library of Scotland, **8**
Outlook Tower and Camera Obscura, **3**

Palace of Holyroodhouse, **17**
Parliament House, **11**
Register House, **22**
Royal Botanic Garden, **29**
Royal Mile, **2**

Royal Museum of Scotland, **10**
The Royal Scottish Academy, **20**
St. Andrew Square, **24**
Scotch Whisky Heritage Centre, **4**
Scott Monument, **21**

Scottish National Portrait Gallery and Royal Museum of Scotland, **28**
Victoria Street, **7**
West Register House, **26**

NEW TOWN

OLD TOWN

Waverley Station

Holyrood Park

Calton Hill

Water of Leith

Princes Street Gardens

0   220 yards
0   200 meters

she gave birth to James. The **great hall** features an extensive collection of arms and armor, and has an impressive vaulted, beamed ceiling.

There are several military features of interest, including the **Scottish National War Memorial,** the **Scottish United Services Museum,** and the famous 15th-century cannon Mons Meg, which is so huge that 100 men, five carpenters, and a large number of oxen were needed to heave it into position. The **Esplanade,** the huge forecourt of the castle, was built in the 18th century as a parade ground, using earth from the foundation of the Royal Exchange to widen and level the area. Although it now serves as the castle parking lot, it comes alive with color each year when it is used during the Festival for the Tattoo, a magnificent military display and pageant. *Tel. 0131/244–3101. Admission: £5 adults, £3 senior citizens, £1 children under 16. Open Apr.–Sept., daily 9:30–5; Oct.–Mar., daily 9:30–4:15.*

2 The **Royal Mile** starts immediately below the Esplanade. It runs roughly west to east, from the castle to the Palace of Holyroodhouse (*see below*), and progressively changes its name from Castlehill to Lawnmarket, High Street, and Canongate. As you stroll downhill from the castle you'll need to look closely to spot the numerous details, such as historic plaques or ornamentation, that make the excursion more than simply a parade of buildings. Note on Castlehill, for example, the bronze plaque that recalls the people who were burned here in the late 16th century because they were thought to be witches. Notice also the cannonball imbedded in the wall of Cannonball House. Although legend says it was fired from the castle during the Jacobite rebellion in 1745 led by Bonnie Prince Charlie, the most romantic of the Stuart pretenders to the British throne, it's probably an early height marker related to Edinburgh's water supply.

3 On the north side of Castlehill, the **Outlook Tower and Camera Obscura** offer armchair views of the city. The building that houses this optical instrument was originally constructed in the 17th century, but was significantly altered in the 1840s and 1850s with the installation of the camera obscura, which, on a clear day, projects an image of the city onto a white, concave table. *Tel. 0131/226–3709. Admission: £3.20 adults, £2.50 students, £2 senior citizens, £1.60 children, £8.90 family ticket. Open Apr.–Oct., weekdays 9:30–6, weekends 10–6; Nov.–Mar., weekdays 10–5, weekends 10–3:30 (shop 10–5).*

4 Opposite, the **Scotch Whisky Heritage Centre** reveals the mysterious process that turns malted barley and spring water into one of Scotland's most important exports. *358 Castlehill, tel. 0131/220–0441. Admission: £3.80 adults, £3.20 students, £2.30 senior citizens, £2 children, £10.60 family ticket. Open daily 10–5 (extended hours in the summer season; closed Christmas and New Year's).*

Farther down on the left, the **Tolbooth Kirk** ("kirk" means "church"), built in 1842–44 for the General Assembly of the Church of Scotland, boasts the tallest spire in the city—240 feet.

From Lawnmarket you can start your discovery of the **Old Town closes,** the alleyways that are like ribs leading off the Royal Mile backbone.

5 The six-story tenement known as **Gladstone's Land,** just beside the Assembly Hall, is a survivor from the 17th century, demonstrating typical architectural features, including an arcaded ground floor and an entrance at second-floor level. It is furnished in the style of a 17th-century merchant's house. *Tel. 0131/226–5856. Admission: £2.60 adults; £1.30 students, senior citizens, and children. Open Apr.–Oct., Mon.–Sat. 10–5, Sun. 2–5 (last admission 4:30).*

⑥ Close by Gladstone's Land, down yet another close, is **Lady Stair's House,** a good example of 17th-century urban architecture. Built in 1622, it evokes Scotland's literary past with exhibits on Sir Walter Scott, Robert Louis Stevenson, and Robert Burns. *Off Lawnmarket, tel. 0101/225–2424, ext. 6593. Admission free. Open June–Sept., Mon.–Sat. 10–5:30, Sun. during Edinburgh Festival 2–5; Oct.–May, Mon.–Sat. 10–5.*

⑦ For a worthwhile shopping diversion, turn right down George IV Bridge, then down **Victoria Street** to the right, to a 19th-century extension of the Old Town. Its shops offer antiques, clothing, and quality giftware. The shopping continues down in the **Grassmarket,** which for centuries was, as its name suggests, an agricultural market.

⑧ To visit another of Edinburgh's historic churches, walk from the Grassmarket back up Victoria Street to George IV Bridge, where straight ahead is the **National Library of Scotland** (free exhibitions; open weekdays 9:30–8:30, Saturday 9:30–1). Farther down, to the
⑨ south, the **Kirk of the Greyfriars** stands on the site of a medieval monastery. Here, in 1638, the National Covenant was signed, declaring the independence of the Presbyterian Church in Scotland from government control. The covenant plunged Scotland into decades of civil war. *Greyfriars Pl., tel. 0131/225–1900. Admission free. Open Easter–Sept., weekdays 10–4, Sat. 10–2; Oct.–Easter, Thurs. 1:30–3:30.*

★ ⑩ You might also detour down Chambers Street, which leads off from George IV Bridge. Here, in a lavish Victorian building, currently undergoing a major extension, the **Royal Museum of Scotland** displays a wide-ranging collection drawn from natural history, archaeology, scientific and industrial history, and the history of mankind and civilization. The great Main Hall's architecture, with its soaring roof, is interesting in its own right. *Chambers St., tel. 0131/225–7534. Admission free. Open Mon.–Sat. 10–5, Sun. noon–5.*

⑪ Return to High Street and, near Parliament Square, look on the right for a heart set in the cobbles. This marks the site of the vanished Tolbooth, around which was the center of city life from the 15th century until 1817, when it was demolished. This ancient civic building, formerly housing the Scottish parliament, then used as a prison from 1640 onward, inspired Scott's novel *The Heart of Midlothian.* Nearly every city and town in Scotland at one time had a tolbooth—originally a customs house where tolls were gathered. The name came to mean the town hall and later a prison, since the detention cells were located in the basement of the town hall. **Parliament House**—the seat of Scottish government until 1707, when the crowns of Scotland and England were united—is partially hidden by the bulk of St. Giles's Cathedral. *Parliament Sq., 0131/225–2595. Admission free. Open weekdays 9:30–4:30.*

⑫ The **High Kirk of St. Giles,** originally the town's parish church, became a cathedral in 1633, and is now usually called St. Giles's Cathedral. There has been a church on the site since AD 854, although most of the present structure dates from 1829. The spire, however, was completed in 1495, the choir is mostly 15th-century, and four of the interior columns date from the early 12th century. The **Chapel of the Order of the Thistle,** bearing the belligerent national motto "Nemo Me Impune Lacessit" ("No one assails me with impunity"), was added in 1911. *High St., tel. 0131/225–4363. Admission free; Thistle Chapel, 50p. Open Mon.–Sat. 9–5 (7 in summer), Sun. 2–5 (services 8 AM, 10 AM, 11:30 AM, and 8 PM.*

Another landmark in Old Town life can be seen just below St. Giles's: The **Mercat Cross** ("mercat" means "market"), a focus of public attention for centuries, is still the site of royal proclamations.

On the right, two blocks below the North Bridge–South Bridge
13 junction, is the **Museum of Childhood,** a celebration of toys that even
adults may well enjoy. *42 High St., tel. 0131/225–2424. Admission
free. Open June–Sept., Mon.–Sat. 10–5:30, Sun. during Edinburgh
Festival 2–5; Oct.–May, Mon.–Sat. 10–5.*

14 Opposite is **John Knox House,** a 16th-century dwelling. It is not abso-
lutely certain that Knox, Scotland's severe religious reformer
(1514–72), lived here, but mementos of his life are on view inside. *45
High St., tel. 0131/556–9579 or 0131/556–2647. Admission: £1.25
adults, £1 senior citizens, 75p children. Open Mon.–Sat. 10–4:30.*

Beyond this point, you would once have passed out of the safety of
the town walls. A plaque outside the **Netherbow Theatre** depicts the
Netherbow Port (gate), which once stood here. Below is the
Canongate, named for the canons who once ran the abbey at
Holyrood Palace. Canongate was original-
ly an independent "burgh," a Scottish term meaning, essentially, a
community with trading rights granted by the monarch. This ex-
15 plains the presence of the handsome **Canongate Tolbooth,** on the
left, where the town council once met but which is now the setting
for "The People's Story" exhibition, which tells the history of the
people of Edinburgh.

Almost next door, in the graveyard of **Canongate Kirk,** are buried
some notable Scots, including Adam Smith, author of *The Wealth of
16 Nations* (1776). Opposite the tolbooth is the gable-fronted **Huntly
House,** a museum of local history. *142 Canongate, tel. 0131/225–
2424. Admission free. Open June–Sept., 10–5:30, Sun. during
Edinburgh Festival 2–5; Oct.–May, Mon.–Sat. 10–5.*

Facing you at the end of Canongate are the elaborate wrought-iron
★ **17** gates of the **Palace of Holyroodhouse,** official residence of the queen
when she is in Scotland. Holyrood Palace came into existence originally as a guest house for the medieval abbey founded in 1128 by
Scottish king David I, after a vision of the cross ("rood" means
"cross") saved his life on a hunting trip. Since then the palace has
been the setting for high drama, including at least one notorious
murder, a spectacular funeral, several major fires, and centuries of
the colorful lifestyles of larger-than-life, power-hungry personalities. The murder occurred in 1566 when Mary, Queen of Scots, was
dining with her trusted counselor, David Rizzio, who was hated at
court for his social climbing. Mary's second husband, Lord Darnley,
burst into the chamber with his henchmen, dragged Rizzio into an
antechamber, and stabbed him more than 50 times. When Charles II
ascended the British throne in 1660, he ordered Holyrood rebuilt in
the architectural style of the French "Sun King," Louis XIV, and
that is the palace that visitors see today. When the royal family is
not in residence, you can go inside for a conducted tour. *Tel. 0131/
556–7371; recorded information, tel. 0131/556–1096. Admission:
£3.50 adults, £3 senior citizens, £1.80 children, £9 family ticket.
Open Apr.–Oct., Mon.–Sat. 9:30–5:15, Sun. 10:30–4:30; Nov.–
Mar., Mon.–Sat. 9:30–3:45, Sun. 10–3.45; closed during royal and
state visits.*

18 Behind the palace lie the open grounds of **Holyrood Park,** which enclose Edinburgh's own minimountain, Arthur's Seat. The park was
the hunting ground of early Scottish kings.

In 1767, a civic competition to design a new district for Edinburgh
was won by an unknown young architect, James Craig. His plan was
for a grid of three main east–west streets, balanced at either end by
two grand squares. These streets survive today, though some of the
buildings that line them were altered by later development. Princes
Street is the southernmost, with Queen Street to the north and
George Street as the axis, punctuated by St. Andrew and Charlotte
squares. A look at the map will show you its geometric symmetry,

unusual in Britain. Even Princes Street Gardens are balanced by Queen Street Gardens to the north.

Start your walk on **The Mound,** the sloping street that joins Old and New Towns. Two galleries tucked immediately east of this great linking ramp are both the work of W. H. Playfair (1789–1857), an architect whose neoclassical buildings contributed greatly to Edinburgh's earning the title, the "Athens of the North." **The National Gallery of Scotland,** immediately east of the Mound, has a wide-ranging selection of paintings, from the Renaissance to Postimpressionism, with works by Velásquez, El Greco, Rembrandt, Turner, Degas, Monet, and Van Gogh, among many others, as well as a fine collection of Scottish art. The rooms of the gallery are attractively decorated, making it a pleasure to browse. *Tel. 0131/556–8921. Admission free. Open Mon.–Sat. 10–5 (extended during Edinburgh Festival), Sun. 2–5.*

The other gallery, **The Royal Scottish Academy,** with its imposing columned facade overlooking Princes Street, holds an annual exhibition of students' work. *Princes St., tel. 0131/225–6671. Admission charges vary depending on exhibition. Open late Apr.–July, Mon.–Sat. 10–5, Sun. 2–5, and during the Edinburgh Festival.*

The north side of **Princes Street** is now one long sequence of chain stores whose unappealing modern storefronts can be seen in almost any large British town. Luckily, the other side of the street is occupied by well-kept gardens, which act as a wide green moat to the castle on its rock. Walk east until you reach the unmistakable soaring Gothic spire of the 200-foot-high **Scott Monument,** built in 1844 in honor of Scotland's most famous author, Sir Walter Scott (1771–1832), author of *Ivanhoe, Waverley,* and many other novels and poems. Note the recently renovated marble statue of Scott and his favorite dog. *Princes St. Admission: £1.50. Open Mon.–Sat. 9–6 (last admission 5:45).*

Register House, on the north side opposite the main post office, marks the end of Princes Street. This was Scotland's first custombuilt archives depository and was partly funded by the sale of estates forfeited by Jacobite landowners following their last rebellion in Britain (1745–46). Robert Adam, Scotland's most famous neoclassical architect, started work on the building in 1774. The statue in front is of the duke of Wellington. *Tel. 0131/556–6585. Admission free. Open weekdays, legal collection 9:30–4:30, historical collection 9–4:30.*

★ The monuments on **Calton Hill,** growing ever more noticeable ahead as you walk east along Princes Street, can be reached by continuing along Waterloo Place, and either climbing steps to the hilltop or taking the road farther on that loops at a more leisurely pace up the hill. Beyond the photogenic collection of columns and temples, the views from Calton Hill range over the Lomond Hills of Fife in the north, to the Pentland Hills southwest, behind the spire of St. Giles's. The incomplete Parthenon look-alike, known as Edinburgh's Disgrace, was intended as a National War Memorial in 1822 but contributions did not come in. On the opposite side of the road, in the Calton Old Burying Ground, is a monument to Abraham Lincoln and the Scottish-American dead of the Civil War. (An impressive American monument to the Scottish soldiers of World War I stands in West Princes Street Gardens, among various memorials of Scottish and foreign alliances.) The tallest monument on Calton Hill is the 100-foot-high **Nelson Monument,** completed in 1816 in honor of Britain's naval hero. *Tel. 0131/225–2424. Admission: £1. Open Mon.–Sat. 10–3 (extended hours in summer).*

Make your way to **St. Andrew Square** by cutting through the recently refurbished **St. James Centre** shopping mall and the bus station to the headquarters of the **Royal Bank of Scotland;** take a look inside at the lavish decor of the central banking hall. In the distance, at the other end of George Street, on Charlotte Square, you can see the copper dome of the former St. George's Church. In Craig's symmetrical plan for the New Town, a matching church was intended for the bank's site, but Sir Lawrence Dundas, a wealthy and influential baronet, somehow managed to acquire the space for his town house: Pulling strings at city hall is nothing new! The grand mansion was later converted into the bank, and St. Andrew's Church, originally intended for the site, is a little way down George Street.

Walk west along George Street, with its variety of shops, to Charlotte Square. Note the palatial facade of the square's north side, designed by Robert Adam and considered one of Europe's finest pieces of civic architecture. Here you will find the **Georgian House,** which the National Trust for Scotland has furnished in period style to show the elegant domestic arrangements of an affluent family of the late 18th century. Note, for instance, how the hallway was designed to take sedan chairs, in which 18th-century grandees were carried through the streets. *7 Charlotte Sq., tel. 0131/225–2160. Admission: £3.50 adults, £1.50 senior citizens and children. Open Apr.–Oct., Mon.–Sat. 10–4:30, Sun. 2–4:30.*

Also in the square, the former St. George's Church, mentioned above as part of the New Town plan, now fulfills a different role as **26** **West Register House,** an extension of the original Register House. *Tel. 0131/556–6585. Admission free. Open weekdays, exhibitions 10–4, research room 9–4:30.*

27 To explore further in the New Town, choose your own route northward, down to the wide and elegant streets centering on **Moray Place,** a fine example of an 1820s development, with imposing porticoes and a central, secluded garden. The area remains primarily residential, in contrast to the area around Princes Street. The gardens in the center of the square are still for residents only.

28 An unusual red-sandstone neo-Gothic building on Queen Street houses the **Scottish National Portrait Gallery** and the Queen Street premises of **the Royal Museum of Scotland.** The gallery contains a magnificent Gainsborough, and portraits by the Scottish artists Ramsay and Raeburn. In the museum, don't miss the 16th-century Celtic harps and the Lewis chessmen—mysterious, grim-faced chess pieces carved from walrus ivory in the Middle Ages. *Tel. 0131/225–7534. Admission free to both. Both open Mon.–Sat. 10–5, Sun. 2–5.*

29 Another attraction within reach of the New Town is the **Royal Botanic Garden.** Walk down Dundas Street, the continuation of Hanover Street, and turn left across the bridge over the Water of Leith, Edinburgh's small-scale river. These 70-acre gardens offer the largest rhododendron and azalea collection in Britain; peat, rock, and woodland gardens; a magnificent herbaceous border; an arboretum; and capacious greenhouses. There is also a convenient cafeteria and small art gallery. *Inverleith Row, tel. 0131/552–7171. Admission free; donations accepted for greenhouses. Open Mar.–Oct., daily 10–one hour before sunset; Nov.–Feb., daily, 10–sunset. Greenhouses close at 5 PM Mar.–Oct. (3:45 PM Nov.–Feb.).*

The **Scottish National Gallery of Modern Art,** also close to the New Town, occupies a former school building on Belford Road, and features paintings and sculpture, including works by Picasso, Braque, Matisse, and Derain. *Belford Rd., tel. 0131/556–8921. Admission free. Open Mon.–Sat. 10–5, Sun. 2–5 (extended during the Edinburgh Festival).*

Lodging **Dorstan Private Hotel.** This villa, dating from the Victorian era, is
££ located in a quiet neighborhood a fair way from the city center, but for that reason is a relaxing place to lodge. The moderately expen-

sive bedrooms have been modernized to offer both the charm of the old and the ease of the new. Peaceful pastel colors predominate in the decor, adding to this hotel's restfulness. *7 Priestfield Rd., EH16 5HJ, tel. 0131/667–6721, fax 0131/668–4644. 14 rooms, 9 with bath or shower. MC, V. Closed Dec. 24–Jan. 2.*

££ **Stuart House.** Located just a few minutes from the city center (although it's an uphill walk), this thoughtfully decorated, restored Georgian-style town house is a good-value accommodation. *12 E. Claremont St., EH7 4JP, tel. 0131/557–9030, fax 0131/557–0563. 6 rooms with bath/shower. No smoking. MC, V.*

£ **Ashdene House.** Set in a residential neighborhood along the bus route, this Victorian town house with many original features is fairly well situated, just 15 minutes from the city center. *23 Fountainhall Rd., EH9 2LN, tel. 0131/667–6026. 5 rooms with shower. No credit cards.*

£ **Ashlyn Guest House.** This handsome 19th-century stone building, in a residential area of the city, is on a main bus route to the city center. (Traffic noise is occasionally a little intrusive.) *42 Inverleith Row, EH3 5PY, tel. 0131/552–2954. 8 rooms, 4 with bath/shower. No credit cards.*

£ **Ellesmere House.** A typical Edinburgh terraced home, this one is not far from the city center, within walking distance of a good selection of shops and restaurants. *11 Glengyle Terr., EH3 9LN, tel. 0131/229–4823. 6 rooms, 2 with shower, 1 with bath. No credit cards.*

£ **Galloway Guest House.** Within walking distance of the city center and the Royal Botanic Garden, this New Town terraced guest house has a friendly and knowledgeable local owner. There is free street parking outside; rooms are about £45. *22 Dean Park Crescent, EH4 1PH, tel. 0131/332–3672. 10 rooms, 6 with bath/shower. No credit cards. Closed Christmas and New Year's Day.*

£ **Teviotdale House.** Situated along the bus route to town (2 miles away), in an upscale Edinburgh neighborhood, this elegant Victorian town house is convenient to shopping and entertainment. It has many original features that have been restored, and touches such as home-baked bread in the mornings that give this inn an at-home feel. *53 Grange Loan, EH9 2ER, tel. and fax 0131/667–4376. 7 rooms with bath/shower. MC, V.*

¢ **Balquidder Guest House.** This former church manse is a detached Victorian house that stands on its own grounds and overlooks a public park. There's easy access to the bus into the city. *94 Pilrig St., EH6 5AY, tel. 0131/554–3377. 6 rooms, 5 with bath/shower. No credit cards.*

¢ **Bruntsfield Youth Hostel.** This International Youth Hostel (IYH) affiliate, in a quiet residential district only 10 minutes from downtown, offers dormitory-style accommodations for less than £20. Features of this year-round facility include a large sitting room, a TV room, and a dining room with two kitchens. Doors are open until 2 AM, but you must register before 11:30 PM. *7 Bruntsfield Crescent, tel. 0131/447–2994. 172 beds. No credit cards.*

¢ **Crannoch But & Ben.** Convenient for the airport and 3 miles from the city center on a good bus route, this is a top-of-the-range bed-and-breakfast with a residents' lounge and excellent breakfasts. *467 Queensferry Rd, EH4 7M, tel. 0131/336–5688. 2 rooms with bath/shower. No credit cards. Closed Oct.–Apr.*

★ ¢ **Eglinton Youth Hostel.** Located on a tree-lined court in Edinburgh's west end, this IYH affiliate is only a 10-minute walk from downtown. Rather than dormitory accommodations, Eglinton offers 4–6 small bedrooms (a very good deal), in addition to the recently renovated dining rooms, kitchens, and well-stocked shops. There is also a cafeteria for meals. Doors stay open until 2 AM and the hostel is open year-round. *18 Eglinton Crescent, tel. 0131/337–1120. 200 beds. No credit cards.*

¢ **Mrs. Valerie Livingstone.** This is a modern terraced villa near Arthur's Seat, with views over the Firth of Forth. The house is no-smoking, and Mrs. Livingstone maintains a high standard of accommodation and meals. *50 Paisley Crescent, EH8 7JQ, tel. 0131/661–6337. 2 rooms (no private bathrooms). No credit cards. Closed Oct.–Apr.*

¢ **St. Valery.** This spacious New Town house is within easy access of Princes Street—one of Edinburgh's main shopping and sightseeing thoroughfares—and provides a full Scottish breakfast in the morning. Rooms rent for about £35 a night. *36 Coates Gardens, Haymarket, Edinburgh EH12 5LE, tel. 0131/337–1893. 11 rooms (2 shared baths). MC, V.*

¢ **Salisbury Guest House.** This guest house in a Georgian building is
★ located in a peaceful architectural conservation area. It is also convenient for city touring, and offers excellent value. *45 Salisbury Rd., EH16 5AA, tel. 0131/667–1264. 12 rooms, 9 with bath or shower. MC, V. Closed Christmas and Jan. 1.*

¢ **University of Edinburgh.** During the summer months, if you want to stay in the heart of Edinburgh yet look out onto grass, trees, and Arthur's Seat, stay at Pollock Halls beside Holyrood Park. The rooms are mainly singles in typical, modern student style—fitted furniture, painted walls, basic floor coverings and no frills—but you have a washbasin, use of kitchen, restaurant, lounge, and that wonderful view. *Pollock Halls, 18 Holyrood Park Rd., tel. 0131/667–1971, fax 0131/668–3217. 1,500 rooms (mainly singles, a few twins). MC, V. Closed late Sept.–late June.*

Splurge **King James Thistle Hotel.** Although this hotel is not much to look at from the outside, rooms are comfortable and dependable, and worth the £125 a night for a double. If you come here for any one thing, however, it should be for the competent and devoted staff who will go out of their way to make your stay easy and enjoyable. They're also very knowledgeable about Edinburgh. Rooms have remote-control TV, hair dryer, tea/coffeemaker, and a trouser press. *St. James Centre, EH1 3SW, tel. 0131/556–0111. 147 rooms, all with showers. Facilities: restaurant, bar. AE, MC, V.*

Splurge **Thrums Private Hotel.** There is a pleasing mix of the modern and traditional in this detached Victorian house, where rooms go for around £70 per night for two. It is small, cozy, and quiet, yet surprisingly close to downtown Edinburgh. *14 Minto St., EH9 1RQ, tel. 0131/667–5545. 14 rooms, 12 with bath. Facilities: restaurant, bar. No credit cards. Closed Christmas and Jan. 1.*

Dining **Indian Cavalry Club.** This restaurant is cool and sophisticated; its
££ menu reflects a confident, up-to-date approach—almost an Indian *nouvelle cuisine.* It features steamed specialties. The **Club Tent** in the basement serves light meals. *3 Atholl Pl., tel. 0131/228–3282. Reservations advised. AE, DC, MC, V.*

££ **Martins.** Don't be put off by the look of this restaurant on the outside. It's tucked away in a little back street, and has a typically forbidding northern facade. All's well inside, though, and the food is excellent, if sometimes pricey. (Watch how you order to stay under £25). Specialties are all light and extremely tasty, with fish in the lead—langoustine and gurnard (said to grunt when caught!) in phyllo pastry and a ginger sauce, halibut in a nettle and black-pepper sauce, plus gorgeous homemade sorbets. For just £11.95 you can choose from the satisfying two-course set-price lunch menu. *70 Rose St. North Lane, tel. 0131/225–3106. Reservations required. AE, DC, MC, V. Closed Sat. lunch, Sun. and Mon.*

££ **Ristorante Tinelli.** A little removed from downtown, this restaurant offers authentic Italian cuisine in a relaxed atmosphere. *139 Easter Rd., tel. 0131/652–1932. Reservations advised. AE, MC, V. Closed Sun.–Mon.*

£ **Doric Tavern.** Don't be put off by the rather tatty entrance plastered with posters and playbills; once inside, you will enjoy this café/bistro bar. With stripped wood floor, rustic tables and chairs, peach walls and navy velvet curtains, the decor plays along with the relaxed mood. Daily specials might be roast pigeon salad with raspberry vinegar dressing or fresh fish poached with basil and cream. The fixed-price dinner menu is very good value at about £12. Lunch can be anything from a large salad, perhaps with strips of venison, to chicken with tarragon or wild mushroom stir-fry. The fixed-price lunch for £9 is also good value. *15/16 Market St., tel. 0131/225–1084. Reservations advised Fri. and Sat. AE, MC, V. Closed Sun. Restaurant closes 11 PM, wine bar open till 1 AM.*

£ **Henderson's Salad Table.** This was Edinburgh's original vegetarian restaurant, long before that cuisine became fashionable. Try the vegetarian haggis! *94 Hanover St., tel. 0131/225–2131. AE, MC, V. Closed Sun. except during Edinburgh Festival.*

£ ★ **Kalpna.** This eatery has a reputation for outstanding value including a great buffet lunch. Indian art adorns the walls, enhancing your enjoyment of the exotic specialties like *shahi sabzi* (spinach and nuts in cream sauce), and mushroom curry. All dishes are vegetarian and are skillfully and deliciously prepared. *2–3 St. Patrick's Sq., tel. 0131/667–9890. Reservations advised. MC, V. Closed Sun.*

£ **La Lanterna.** The closely packed tables (and very comfortable chairs) are usually crowded with content locals, but the staff will always try to squeeze you in. The excellent Italian home cooking and daily chef's specials represent good value for money, and preparation is done in full view. *83 Hanover St., tel. 0131/226–3090. Reservations advised. MC, V. Closed Sun.*

£ **Mr. V's.** This friendly downtown restaurant, with a slightly rustic decor—expensive in the evening—is affordable if you choose the fixed menu at lunchtime. Bustling and popular, with a predominantly business clientele, Vito's specialties include *filleto d'agnello al caffe*, lamb fillet seasoned with crushed coffee beans in a coffee sauce, and tournedos Rossini. *7 Charlotte Lane, tel. 0131/220–0176. Reservations required. AE, DC, MC, V. Closed Sun., Mon.*

£ **Pierre Victoire.** Idiosyncratic service and improvised dining furniture are forgivable because of the consistently high quality of the food: good but simple French cooking. The reasonable fixed-price set lunches (around £6) are especially worthwhile. *10 Victoria St., tel. 0131/225–1721. Reservations advised. MC. Closed Sun.*

Splurge ★ **Vintner's Room.** Located in the Leith section of Edinburgh, this is a pleasant escape from the bustle of downtown, only a few minutes' walk away. Tasteful decor, including fine plasterwork, and a relaxed atmosphere combine with dishes such as sautéed scallops and smoked salmon, and grilled oysters with bacon and hollandaise sauce, to make any meal here a treat. Main courses range from £15 to £18 and appetizers start at £5. *The Vaults, 87 Giles St., Leith, tel. 0131/554–6767. Reservations advised. AE, MC, V.*

Splurge ★ **The Witchery.** A somewhat eerie ambience, complete with flickering candlelight, reigns here. There are, in fact, supposed to be three ghosts in the place, one of whom haunts the refrigerator! There's nothing spooky about the food, however, with fine venison Marie Stuart, and Auld Reekie fillet steak among the specialties. *Castlehill, Royal Mile, tel. 0131/225–5613. Reservations advised. AE, DC, MC, V.*

Shopping Edinburgh has many upscale shopping areas, among them Princes Street, George Street, Victoria Street, West Bow, Grassmarket, William Street, and Stafford Street. There are few bargains here, but you will find some stores of interest.

If you want to learn the background of your tartan accessories, try **Scotland's Clan Tartan Centre** (70–74 Bangor Rd., Leith, tel. 0131/553–5100), where extensive displays on various aspects of tartanry will keep you informed.

For some idea on exactly what Scotland has to offer in the way of crafts, use as your yardstick and price guide the **Royal Mile Living Craft Centre** (12 High St. tel. 0131/557–9350), where you can watch craftspeople as they work, then buy the results.

A popular gift selection comes from **Edinburgh Crystal** (Edinburgh Crystal Visitor Centre, Eastfield, Penicuik, tel. 01968/675128). Many department and gift stores in town stock this fine glassware, but you can also visit the firm's premises, which include a visitor center and a restaurant, as well as the largest crystal glassware store in Britain. It's just a few miles from the city and often you will be able to find good deals on special offers and factory seconds.

Jenners (4 Princes St. opposite the Scott Monument, tel. 0131/225–2442) is not only Edinburgh's last surviving independent department store, but is also (so it claims) the oldest of its type in the world. The **Scotch House** (39–41 Princes St., tel. 0131/556–1252) is another store popular with overseas visitors; it also offers top quality. Items at **Gleneagles of Scotland** (tel. 0131/557–1770) nearby, at the east end of Princes Street in Waverley Market, are fairly reasonably priced. You can combine visits to all three stores in one short trip.

A good selection of Scottish books can be found in the **James Thin Bookshop** (57 George St. tel. 0131/225–4495).

Quite close to the castle end of the Royal Mile, Victoria Street concentrates a number of specialty stores in a small area. The interior design shop **Ampersand** (18 Victoria St., tel. 0131/226–2734) stocks a large selection of sundry collectibles, mostly jugs, lamps, and vases, as well as unusual fabric. **Kinnels** (36 Victoria St., tel 0131/220–1150) combines a specialty coffee and tea shop with a relaxed Old World coffeehouse. **Robert Cresser's** brush store (40 Victoria St., tel. 0131/225–2181) features, not surprisingly, handmade brushes of all kinds.

In the Grassmarket, **Bill Baber** (No. 66, tel. 0131/225–3249) has wonderful knitwear (but prepare to splurge).

Flea Markets   Edinburgh is far too self-conscious to do this sort of thing really well. **Byzantium** (9A Victoria St., tel. 0131/225–1768), with its antiques, crafts, paintings, books, and jewelry, is the nearest, though perhaps too tasteful, clean, and restrained. **Jacksonville Furniture Bazaar** (108A Causewayside, tel. 0131/667–0616) is more authentically downscale, if a wardrobe circa 1950 is your idea of a souvenir of Edinburgh.

The Arts and   Edinburgh's main theaters are the **Royal Lyceum** (Grindlay St., tel.
Nightlife   0131/229–9697), which offers contemporary and traditional drama;
The Arts   the **King's** (Leven St., tel. 0131/229–1201), offering both "highbrow" material, such as ballet, and light entertainment, including Christmas pantomime; the **Traverse** (Cambridge St., tel. 0131/228–1404), which has toned down its previously avant-garde approach in an attempt to secure sponsorship and has just moved into new premises; and **Edinburgh Festival Theatre** (Nicolson St., tel. 0131/529–6000), which is the newest and hosts a variety of performances from the Scottish National Opera to Christmas pantomime.

Usher Hall (Lothian Rd., tel. 0131/228–1155) is Edinburgh's grandest, and the venue for the Royal Scottish Orchestra in season (Oct.–Mar.); the **Queen's Hall** (Clerk St., tel. 0131/668–3456) is more intimate in scale and hosts smaller recitals. The **Playhouse** (Greenside Pl., tel. 0131/557–2692) leans toward popular artists.

Festivals   The **Edinburgh International Festival** is probably Scotland's biggest cultural event. It takes place annually, for three weeks in late August and early September, bringing together music and theater of the highest caliber. *Edinburgh Festival Office, 21 Market St., Edinburgh, EH1 1BW, tel. 0131/226-4001.*

The less formal (and less expensive) **Edinburgh Festival Fringe,** which runs concurrently with the Festival, offers a variety of shows at venues all over the city, from serious drama to humor. *Edinburgh Festival Fringe, 180 High St., Edinburgh, EH1 1QS, tel. 0131/226-5257 or 0131/226-5259.*

The Edinburgh Military Tattoo, also held for most of August, might not be art, but it is certainly entertainment. It is sometimes confused with the Festival itself, partly because the dates overlap. This great celebration of martial music and skills is set on the castle esplanade and the dramatic backdrop augments the spectacle. Dress warmly for the late-evening performances. Even if it rains, the show most definitely goes on. *Tickets and information available from Edinburgh Military Tattoo, 22 Market St., Edinburgh, EH1 1QB, tel. 0131/225-1188.*

Away from the August–September festival overkill, the **Edinburgh Folk Festival** usually takes place around Easter each year. This 10-day event blends performances by Scottish and international folk artists of the very highest caliber. *Box 528, Edinburgh, EH10 4DU, tel. 0131/556-3181.*

Film The **Filmhouse** (88 Lothian Rd., Edinburgh, EH3 9BZ, tel. 0131/228-4051) is Edinburgh's year-round best venue for modern, highbrow, offbeat, or simply less commercial films. The **Edinburgh Film Festival,** held in August at the Filmhouse, is yet another aspect of this busy summer festival time.

Nightlife **Berkeley Casino Club** (2 Rutland Pl., tel. 0131/228-4446), **Casino Martell** (7 Newington Rd., tel. 0131/667-7763), and **Stakis Regency Casino** (14 Picardy Pl., tel. 0131/557-3585)—all private clubs—make membership available after a 48-hour waiting period.

Discos Discos and clubs in Edinburgh are very volatile and fashion-oriented. What is popular one week is often closed the next, so check with the tourist information center for the latest status.

Buster Browns (25–27 Market St., tel. 0131/226-4224) offers mainstream chart sounds Friday–Sunday 10:30 PM–3 AM (4 AM Saturday).

Century 2000 (31 Lothian Rd., tel. 0131/229-7670) is one of Edinburgh's busiest and biggest discos. Dance night is Friday and party night Saturday, but Century is open both nights 10 PM–4 AM.

Madison's (Greenside Pl., tel. 0131/557-3807) specializes in rock music and is open Friday and Saturday 10 PM–4 AM.

Red Hot Pepper Club (3 Semple St., tel. 0131/229-7733) is open Thursday–Saturday 10 PM–4 AM (3 AM Thur.).

The Venue (Calton Rd, tel. 0131/557-3073) hosts a variety of rock concerts and dance nights. Concerts 9 PM–12 midnight, Clubs 9 PM–3 AM.

Folk Clubs There are always folk performers in various pubs throughout the city. **Edinburgh Folk Club** (Cafe Royal, 17 Register St., tel. 0131/339-4083) features folk music every Wed. at 8:15 PM.

Scottish Evenings and Ceilidhs Several hotels have traditional Scottish music evenings, including the **Carlton Highland Hotel** (North Bridge, tel. 0131/556-7277) and the **George Hotel** (George St., tel. 0131/225-1251).

Another well-established Scottish entertainment is **Jamie's Scottish Evening** (King James Hotel, Leith St., tel. 0131/556-0111). The Scottish evenings at the **Scottish Experience and Living Craft Centre** (12 High St., tel. 0131/557-9350), with food, song, and dance for about £20 per person, are a good value.

St. Andrews

Trains leave hourly from Edinburgh's Waverley Station for the hour-long journey to Leuchars; from there it is a short bus (Nos. 95, 96) ride to St. Andrews. Buses also go to St. Andrews from Edinburgh's St. Andrews Square bus station; service operates every two hours, and the trip takes about 2 hours. St. Andrews tourist office: 78 South St., tel. 01334/72021.

St. Andrews is world-famous as the birthplace of the game of golf, originally played with a piece of driftwood, a shore pebble, and a convenient rabbit hole on the sandy, coastal turf. However, the town also offers a wide range of attractions for nongolfers. The cathedral, its ancient university (founded in 1411), and castle are poignant reminders that the town was once the ecclesiastical capital of Scotland. The now largely ruined cathedral was one of the largest churches ever built in Scotland. The castle, named St. Rule's Tower, is now approached via a visitor center with an audiovisual presentation. *Cathedral museum and St. Rule's Tower, tel. 01334/244–3101. Admission to museum and St. Rule's Tower: £1.50 adults, £1 senior citizens, 75p children, £4 family ticket. Admission to castle: £2 adults, £1.25 senior citizens, 75p children. Joint entry to all: £3 adults, £1.75 senior citizens, £1 children. Grounds, museum, and tower open Apr.–Sept., Mon.–Sat. 9:30–6, Sun. 2–6; Oct.–Mar., Mon.–Sat. 9:30–4, Sun. 2–4.*

Lodging
£ **Aslar Guest House.** This small and friendly Victorian terrace house is family-run and close to the town center and golf courses. *120 North St., KY16 9AF, tel. and fax 01334/73460. 5 rooms with bath/ shower. No credit cards.*

£ **University of St. Andrews.** For budget-wise accommodations within walking distance of all the town's attractions, it's hard to beat the university. Room sizes vary from adequate to spacious (in the older building); they have attractive pastel decor with light wood furnishings and the newer rooms have private baths. Rates for two vary from a bargain of about £40 for a room with washbasin to an inexpensive £50 for one with private facilities. *79 North St., tel. 01334/ 77641, fax 01334/77922. 350 rooms, 150 with shower (mostly singles). Facilities: restaurant, bar, lounge, TV room, laundry facilities. MC, V. Closed late Sept.–late June.*

Dining
££ **Grange Inn.** This old farmhouse-type building houses a simple, traditional restaurant where excellent bar lunches are individually prepared. Dinner is a candlelit affair, with fine food—try the gravlax with sweet dill mustard—and a good selection of single malt whiskeys. *Grange Rd., tel. 01334/72670. Reservations advised. AE, DC, MC, V.*
★

£ **Ziggy's.** With its rock-and-roll theme displayed vividly around the walls, this is a cheerfully brisk and busy student-frequented restaurant offering a no-frills cuisine with items such as burgers, steaks, salads. *Murray Pl., tel. 01334/73686. MC, V.*

Galashiels and Melrose

Lowland Scottish Bus 95 leaves approximately hourly for the 1½-hour trip to Galashiels from Edinburgh's St. Andrews Square bus station; from Galashiels, connecting service takes another 20 minutes to Melrose. Melrose tourist office: Priorwood Gardens, near Abbey, tel. 0189/682–2555 (open Apr.–Oct.).

One of the best ways to approach the Borders region is through the life and works of the man who focused world attention on this part of Scotland and is largely responsible for its romantic image—Sir Walter Scott. The route will take you through the Moorfoot Hills to Galashiels, then a mile farther on A6091 to **Abbotsford House,** the small, castellated mansion Scott built for himself between 1818 and

1823. He took a rather damp farmhouse on the banks of the River Tweed, and transformed it into a pseudo-monastic, pseudo-baronial hall. Ruskin called the result "the most incongruous pile that gentlemanly modernism ever devised." Here Scott entertained such visitors as Wordsworth and Washington Irving. Abbotsford is still owned by Scott's descendants; and Scott's library as well as a large collection of weapons, armor, and Scottish artifacts are on display. *Tel. 01896/2043. Admission: £2.60 adults, £1.30 children. Open late Mar.–Oct., Mon.–Sat. 10–5, Sun. 2–5.*

In the peaceful little town of **Melrose,** 3 miles east, you'll find the ruins of a Cistercian abbey that was the most famous of the great Borders abbeys. All the abbeys were burned in the 1540s in a calculated act of barbarism by English invaders acting on the orders of Henry VIII; Sir Walter Scott himself supervised the partial reconstruction of **Melrose Abbey,** one of the most beautiful ruins in Britain. *Tel. 0131/244–3101. Admission: £2.50 adults, £1.50 senior citizens, £1 children. Open Apr.–Sept., Mon.–Sat. 9:30–6, Sun. 2–6; Oct.–Mar., Mon.–Sat. 9:30–4, Sun. 2–4.*

★

Also worth a visit is the **Trimontium Exhibition** (Ormiston Institute, in the Market Square), which displays items excavated from Scotland's largest Roman fort at nearby Newstead. Tools and weapons, a blacksmith's shop, a pottery, and scale models of the fort are displayed. *Tel. 0189/682–2463. Admission: £1.50 adults, 75p children. Open Easter–Oct. daily, 10–12:30 and 2–4:30.*

Lodging **Woodlands House Hotel.** This wonderful hotel has stunning views
££ over Tweeddale. The main restaurant, too, is first class and specializes in fresh seafood and hearty Scottish cuisine. *Windyknowe Rd., Galashiels TD1 1RG, tel. and fax 01896/754722. 9 rooms with bath. Facilities: 2 restaurants, garden, golfing, horseback riding. Open all year. MC, V.*

¢ **Drummore.** This hillside bed and breakfast, set in an acre of wild garden full of birdlife, is well positioned both for touring the Borders and for visiting Edinburgh. The proprietors are particularly helpful in planning itineraries for day trips. *Venlaw High Rd., Peebles EH45 8RL, tel. 01721/720336, fax 01721/723004. 2 rooms (no private baths). No credit cards. Closed Nov.–Mar.*

¢ **Silverburn Steading.** Just outside Edinburgh in a rural setting at the foot of the Pentland Hills, Mr. and Mrs. Taylor's farmhouse B&B offers a relaxing base for sightseeing in the city or in the Borders. Good food and well-equipped rooms are other plus points. *Silverburn, Penicuik, Midlothian EH26 9LJ, tel. 01968/78420. 3 rooms, 2 with bath/shower. No credit cards.*

Splurge **Burts Hotel.** This distinctive black-and-white traditional town hostelry dates from the early 18th century, yet offers every modern comfort. The elegant dining room features dishes such as pheasant terrine, and venison with a whisky-and-cranberry sauce. *Market Sq., Melrose TD6 9PN, tel. 0189/682–2285, fax 0189/682–2870. 21 rooms with bath or shower. Facilities: restaurant; fishing and game shooting arranged. Restaurant reservations advised. AE, DC, MC, V.*

Dining **Marmion's Brasserie.** This cozy restaurant features outstanding
££ country-style cuisine. It is a great place to stop for lunch after a visit
★ to nearby Abbotsford. *Buccleuch St., tel. 0189/682–2245. Reservations advised. MC, V. Closed Sun.*

Kelso

Lowland Scottish Bus 30 operates from Edinburgh's St. Andrews Square bus station to Kelso at approximately 2-hour intervals throughout the day. The trip takes about 2 hours. Kelso tourist office: Turret House, tel. 01573/223464 (open Apr.–Oct.).

Kelso, where Scott attended the grammar school, has an unusual Continental air, with stout buildings surrounding a spacious, cobbled marketplace. Its abbey is a magnificent ruin, and the baker next door sells fresh Selkirk "bannocks" (the Scots are very good at baking cakes). Try the 18th-century coaching inn, the **Queen's Head** (Bridge St.), for ample helpings of home-cooked food and a selection of cool, authentic draft ales.

Rennie's Bridge on the edge of town provides good views of **Floors Castle.** Designed by Robert Adam in 1721 and later altered by John Playfair, this is the largest inhabited house in Scotland, an architectural extravagance of pepper-mill turrets and towers. *Tel. 01573/ 223333. Admission: £3.40 adults, £2.60 senior citizens, £1.70 children over 8, £8.50 family ticket, grounds £1.50. Open Easter and May–Sept., Sun.–Thurs. 10:30–5:30 (also Fri.–Sat., July–Aug.); Oct., Sun. and Wed. 10:30–4. Check locally for variations.*

Lodging **Queen's Head Hotel.** This historic coaching inn in one of Kelso's old-
¢ est streets has been refurbished to a very high standard. A decent night's sleep for less than £40 per person, including dinner and breakfast, is the draw. *24 Bridge St., TD5 7JD, tel. 01573/224636. 10 rooms, 8 with bath or shower. MC, V.*

Splurge **Ednam House Hotel.** This large, attractive hotel is right on the
★ banks of the River Tweed, close to Kelso's grand abbey and the many fine Georgian and early Victorian buildings in the old Market Square. Ninety percent of the guests are return visitors, and the open fire in the hall, sporting paintings, and cozy armchairs give the place a homey feel. *Bridge St., TD5 7HT, tel. 01573/224168, fax 01573/226319. 32 rooms with bath or shower. Facilities: restaurant, garden, fishing, golf, horseback riding. Closed Christmas–early Jan. MC, V.*

Jedburgh

*You can make a half hour journey to Jedburgh from Kelso on **Lowland Scottish** Bus 20, which departs about every 2 hours. (From Jedburgh, Bus 29 will return you to Edinburgh.) Jedburgh tourist office: Murray's Green, tel. 01835/63435.*

Jedburgh, a little town just 13 miles north of the border, lay in the path of marauding armies for centuries. **Jedburgh Abbey** is the most intact of the Borders abbeys and has an informative visitor center that explains the role of the abbeys in the life of the Borders until their destruction around 1545. *High St., tel. 01835/63925. Admission and opening hours same as Melrose Abbey (see Melrose, above).*

Lodging **Spinney Guest House.** Made up of unpretentiously converted and
£ modernized farm cottages, this is a B&B offering the very highest
★ standards for the price. *Langlee, TD8 6PB, tel. and fax 01835/ 63525. 3 rooms, 1 with bath, 2 with shower. No credit cards. Closed Nov.–Feb.*

14 Scotland: Glasgow and Environs

Stirling, Perth, Inverness, Fort William

Glasgow, Scotland's largest city, underwent a major transformation in the 1980s that took it from an industrial backwater town to what is arguably the most exciting place in Scotland, leaving staid, old Edinburgh behind. Glasgow is a very convenient touring center, too, in easy reach of coastal towns to the southwest, and excellent transportation links the city to the rest of the country.

The only Scottish city with an underground rail system, Glasgow has an efficient circuit to the inner city, in addition to having an aboveground suburban rail network. Adequate bus services not only accommodate the city, but link Glasgow to nearby towns as well. As for the Highlands, public transportation by bus and train covers the main towns, but because the population is sparse, services can be limited, especially off-peak. A better bet for more remote areas are postbuses, run by the Royal Mail (Britain's letter delivery service). Instead of small vans, postmen drive minibuses that also pick up and drop off passengers on regular schedules.

The Dumfries and Galloway region to the southwest is a hilly and sparsely populated area, divided from England by the Solway Firth. Dumfries is associated with Robert Burns (1759–96), whose poems and songs, such as "Auld Lang Syne" and "A Red, Red Rose," are among the best-loved lyrics the world over. The "Burns Trail" runs from his birthplace near Ayr on the Clyde coast to his mausoleum in St. Michael's Church, Dumfries. During 1996, the 200th anniversary of his death, a major celebration of Burns's life and work, the Burns 96 International Festival, takes place all over Ayrshire and Dumfriesshire throughout the year.

Stirling was one of the most important cities in Scotland's history, with the proud title of "Scenic Gateway to the Highlands." Commanding the strategic route linking north and south Scotland, its castle is second only to Edinburgh's in grandeur. In a ring around Stirling are other ancient towns that have contributed much to Scotland's colorful past, including Perth, former seat of Scottish kings. Northwest of Stirling lie the Trossachs with their woodlands and lochs, the Highlands in miniature.

West and north are the Highlands—the romance of "Caledonia stern and wild," the clans, the shaggy cattle, the red deer, the golden eagles, the Celtic mists and legends, and a mixture of scenic splendor and profound tranquillity found hardly anywhere else in the world. The great surprises to unprepared visitors are the changing scenery

Southwest Scotland and the Western Highlands

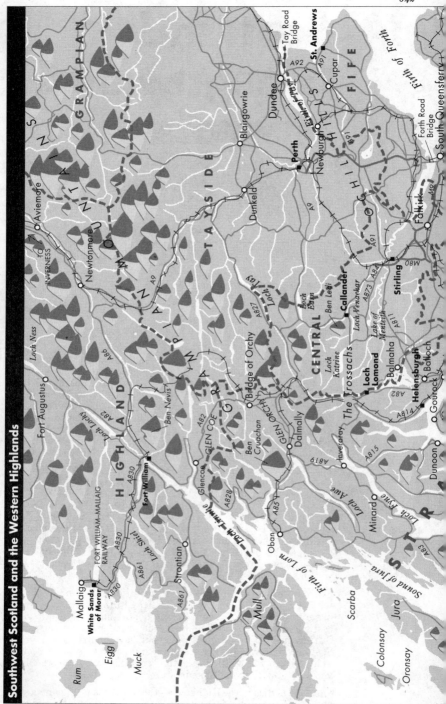

Culzean Castle
and Country Park

NORTHERN
IRELAND
++++ Rail Lines

N

20 miles
30 km

and the stunning effects of light and shade, cloud, sunshine, and rainbows. Sea inlets cut deep into the coastline, and roads often have to detour far inland to get around them. The misty shapes of the isles beckon temptingly across the water. Westward, the next stop is North America.

Essential Information

Lodging For general information about accommodations, *see* Lodging in Chapter 13, Scotland: Edinburgh and Environs. In the Highlands region, the more populous areas, such as Fort William, can get quite busy during peak season (July–August); book accommodations in advance. Tourist information centers can help. Highly recommended establishments are indicated by a star ★.

Dining You'll find a good selection of restaurants and small cafés in Glasgow. In the Highlands, there are some outstanding country house restaurants, but nothing like the choices available in cities. Unless otherwise noted, reservations are not needed and dress is casual. Highly recommended restaurants are indicated by a star ★.

Shopping Glasgow is rapidly challenging Edinburgh as a shopping center, and it's a lot more fun than its staid rival. Elsewhere in the region you will find excellent woolens and tweeds. Keep an eye out for unusual designs in Scottish jewelry, especially when they employ local stones. Scotland has always been a very bookish country, priding itself on the high rate of literacy, and you will often find a surprisingly well-stocked secondhand bookshop in a fairly remote town. You'll probably find that the boutiques and small shops here are more expensive than those in Edinburgh. Chain store prices, however, will be fairly consistent.

Biking Glasgow is not quite as compact as Edinburgh, but it is flatter. Traffic is very heavy here, as well as between cities, so the best route to the Highlands for cyclists is the **Glasgow to Killin Cycleway,** which uses Forestry Commission tracks, out-of-use railway lines, and other private or little-used roads to take the cyclist past some of Scotland's best scenery. The tourist information centers in Glasgow (tel. 0141/204–4400) and Stirling (tel. 01786/475019) have details. Bikes can be rented from **Lee's Cycle Hire** (Fort William, tel. 01397/704204); **Off Beat Bikes** (Fort William, tel. 01397/704008); **Highland Wheelers** (Spean Bridge, tel. 01397/712408); **Mountain Madness** (Ballachulish, tel. 01855/811728); **Wheels** (Manse La., Callander, tel. 01877/331100); **Trossachs Cycle Hire** (Trossachs Holiday Park, Aberfoyle, tel. 01877/382614); and **Pedlars Mountain Bike Hire** (Main St., Killin, tel. 01567/820652).

Hiking The best-known long-distance footpath is the **West Highland Way,** which runs 98 miles from the outskirts of Glasgow to Fort William via the banks of Loch Lomond and the wilderness of Rannoch Moor and Glencoe. However, the Highlands offer a vast choice of routes leading to the summits of the Munros, the collective name for a number of Scotland's hills that reach more than 3,000 feet.

Beaches The **White Sands of Morar,** near the Fort William–Mallaig road and railway, is probably the most famous beach in the west, but there are few sandy beaches along this rocky coast. In the southwest, the coastline around Ayr has sandy beaches. To the east of Inverness, there are some spectacular empty beaches (just you and the sea birds) at Nairn and eastward to Culbin Sands and Lossiemouth.

The Arts and Nightlife Glasgow is the headquarters of the **Royal Scottish Orchestra** and national opera and ballet companies, sure signs that this artistic center is thriving. In the Highlands, arts and culture are in part dependent on touring groups, though concerts and *ceilidhs* are fairly widespread, especially in summer. The ceilidhs tend to be inexpensive, and other arts events in Glasgow have a wide range of ticket prices to suit all pockets, while in the Highlands, touring companies can be enjoyed at very reasonable rates.

Festivals   Glasgow's Mayfest (held throughout May), the second-largest Scottish festival after Edinburgh's, features theater, dance, music, and street events.

Tour 1: Glasgow, Clyde Valley, and the Southwestern Coast

The hub of this tour is Scotland's largest city, Glasgow, which lies 42 miles west of Edinburgh. Glasgow and the surrounding towns have a good train service; the city is also a departure point for the rail routes north (*see* Tour 2, *below*), and thus a good base for budget travelers. You can easily take day trips to Loch Lomond; to Helensburgh (famous for Hill House, designed by Glasgow native Charles Rennie Mackintosh); to Ayrshire and the towns associated with Robert Burns; and to Culzean Castle, jewel in the crown of the National Trust for Scotland and closely associated with General Eisenhower.

From Glasgow   Paisley Gilmour Street Station is 2 miles from the airport, with fre-
Airport   quent trains to Glasgow's Central Station, a 10-minute trip away.
By Train   Take a taxi or use the bus that leaves from the airport entrance every 10 minutes.

By Bus   There is frequent bus service from the airport to Buchanan Street Bus Station downtown. The journey takes about 20 minutes, a bit longer during rush hour.

By Car   The M8 links the airport with downtown Glasgow.

From London   **Intercity** trains make hourly departures to western Scotland from
By Train   London's Euston Station (tel. 0171/387–7070). The average travel time to Glasgow is 5½ hours; an overnight sleeper service, for an additional £25–£30, is available on this route.

By Bus   **National Express** (tel. 0141/332–9191) is one of the operators offering service four times per day from London's Victoria Coach Station to Glasgow. The average travel time is 7 hours.

By Car   The quickest route from London to Glasgow is M6, which becomes A74 (397 miles).

Traveling   The **Freedom of Scotland Travelpass** offers unlimited travel on
Around the   Scotland's rail network (with a few exceptions, such as day tours). It
Highlands   is also valid for free travel on most Caledonian MacBrayne west coast ferry links (except Raasay and Scalpay), and will also give a one-third discount on many Scottish bus routes. It is available for trips lasting 8 days, 15 days, or 8 out of any consecutive 15 days, and though you can buy it at any main station, it is cheaper if bought from a stateside Britrail office.

Postbuses   There are more than 140 postbuses in Scotland, providing an important transport link for many rural communities, especially in the Highlands and Islands. Regular timetable services are operated by postmen driving minibuses, who pick up and drop off passengers in addition to delivering the mail. Further information and timetables are available from tourist information centers, and from the Postbus Controller (tel. 01463/234111, ext. 273).

Glasgow

Glasgow tourist office: 35–39 St. Vincent Place, just across George Square from Queen Street Station, tel. 0141/204–4400.

★ Until fairly recently a depressed city, infamous for its slums, **Glasgow** today is one of the liveliest cities in Britain. The renewal shows in its trendy downtown stores, a booming and diverse cultural life, stylish restaurants, and above all, a general air of confidence.

Glasgow's development over the years has been unashamedly commercial, tied up with the wealth of its manufacturers and merchants, who constructed a vast number of civic buildings throughout the 19th century. Many of these have been preserved, and Glasgow claims, with some justification, to be Britain's greatest Victorian city.

Numbers in the margin correspond to points of interest on the Glasgow map.

❶ From Queen Street Station or Buchanan Street Bus Station, turn east up West George Street to **George Square,** the focal point of Glasgow's business district. This is the natural starting point for any walking tour. The magnificent Italian Renaissance-style **City Chambers** on the east side of the square was opened by Queen Victoria in 1888. *Tel. 0141/227–4017. Free guided tours weekdays at 10:30 and 2:30 (may be closed for occasional civic functions).*

❷ Leave the square by Queen Street to the south, and note the fine neoclassical facade of the Royal Exchange of 1827, now the **Glasgow Gallery of Modern Art.** Contact the Glasgow tourist office (*see above*) for further details.

❸ Pass through Royal Exchange Square and under the arch to the pedestrian section of Buchanan Street. (The elegant **Princes Square** shopping mall is here.) Next, turn east into Argyle Street, another important shopping district where you can wander without the threat of traffic. Discover the new face of Glasgow shopping at the **St. Enoch Centre,** then head toward the River Clyde, via Stockwell Street.

❹ In the nearby park, Glasgow Green, is the **People's Palace.** Opened in 1898 and recently refurbished, it has extensive exhibits on Glasgow's social history. The rear half of the premises is a Victorian greenhouse called the Winter Gardens. *Tel. 0141/554–0223. Admission free. Open Mon.–Sat. 10–5, Sun. 11–5.*

❺ Taking place every weekend just north of Glasgow Green is Glasgow's market, **the Barras,** whose stalls are covered, despite the name ("barrows," or pushcarts). You can find just about anything here, in any condition, from very old model railroads to almost new cheese rolls. You may strike pay dirt—or leave empty-handed. *Tel. 0141/552–7258. Admission free. Open weekends 9–5.*

❻ Make your way next up High Street, which was the center of the downtown area before Glasgow expanded westward in the 18th century. These days, High Street seems unimpressive, but keep a lookout for **Provand's Lordship,** the oldest building in Glasgow. This 15th-century town house, built as a residence for churchmen, has period room displays and a curious ambience of ancient dustiness— very atmospheric. It is said to be haunted as well. *Castle St., tel. 0141/552–8819. Admission free. Open Mon.–Sat. 10–5, Sun. 11–5.*

❼ **Glasgow Cathedral,** on a site sacred since St. Mungo founded a church there in the late 6th century, is an unusual double church, one above the other. Its 13th-century crypt was built to hold the relics of St. Mungo, also called St. Kentigern. *Cathedral St., tel. 0131/ 244–3101. Admission free. Open Apr.–Sept., Mon.–Sat. 9:30–6, Sun. 2–5; Oct.–Mar., Mon.–Sat. 9:30–4, Sun. 2–4 and for services.*

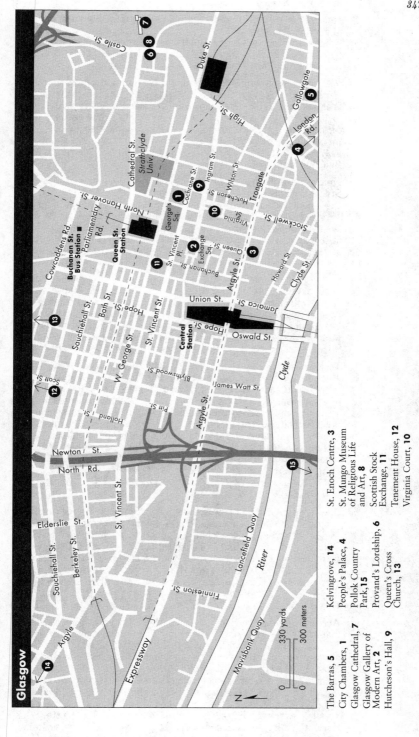

Glasgow

The Barras, **5**
City Chambers, **1**
Glasgow Cathedral, **7**
Glasgow Gallery of
Modern Art, **2**
Hutcheson's Hall, **9**

Kelvingrove, **14**
People's Palace, **4**
Pollok Country
Park,**15**
Provand's Lordship, **6**
Queen's Cross
Church, **13**

St. Enoch Centre, **3**
St. Mungo Museum
of Religious Life
and Art, **8**
Scottish Stock
Exchange, **11**
Tenement House, **12**
Virginia Court, **10**

⑧ Nearby is the **St. Mungo Museum of Religious Life and Art,** a gallery of world religions and the art inspired by them, with exhibits on the religious history of Glasgow. Among the works on display is Dali's *Christ of St. John of the Cross. 2 Castle St., tel. 0141/553–2557. Admission free. Open Mon.–Sat. 10–5, Sun. 11–5.*

Walk south on High Street, west on Trongate, and north on Hutcheson Street on your return to George Square, and enjoy the architecture of this area known as "the Merchant City." Just ahead
⑨ look for **Hutcheson's Hall,** a visitor center, shop, and regional office for the National Trust for Scotland. The elegant, neoclassical building was designed by David Hamilton in 1802. *158 Ingram St., tel. 0141/552–8391. Admission free. Open weekdays 9:30–5, Sat. 10–4. Shop open Mon.–Sat. 10–5.*

Nearby, the buildings on Virginia Street just south of Ingram Street recall the days of the rich "tobacco barons" who traded with the Americas. At No. 33, a former tobacco exchange survives.
⑩ **Virginia Court,** somewhat faded now, also echoes those far-off days. (Peer through the bars of the gates and note the wagon-wheel ruts still visible in the roadway.) Today's commercial trading takes place
⑪ at the **Scottish Stock Exchange,** on Nelson Mandela Place, worthwhile for the exterior alone: It was built in 1877 in an ornate "French Venetian" style.

⑫ Just beyond the downtown area, the **Tenement House** in the Garnethill area north of Charing Cross Station, is a fascinating time capsule, painstakingly preserved with the everyday furniture and belongings of half a century of occupation by the same owner. The building dates from 1892. *145 Buccleuch St., tel. 0141/333–0183. Admission: £2 adults, £1 children. Open Mar.–late Oct., daily 1:30–5.*

To learn more about the Glasgow-born designer Charles Rennie
⑬ Mackintosh, head for **Queen's Cross Church,** now the Mackintosh Society Headquarters. Although one of the leading lights in the turn-of-the-century Art Nouveau movement, Mackintosh died in 1928 with his name scarcely known, least of all in his native city. Now he is confirmed as a leading innovator. This center provides further insight into Glasgow's other Mackintosh-designed buildings, which include the Scotland Street School, the Glasgow School of Art, and reconstructed interiors of his house, which can be seen in the Hunterian Art Gallery (*see below*). *870 Garscube Rd., tel. 0141/946–6600. Admission free. Open Mon., Wed. 10–4; Tues., Thurs., Fri. noon–5; Sun. 2:30–5.*

⑭ The city's main art gallery and museum, **Kelvingrove**—looking like a combination of cathedral and castle—in Kelvingrove Park, west of the M8 beltway, houses what is claimed to be Britain's finest civic collection of British and Continental paintings, with 17th-century Dutch art, a selection from the French Barbizon school, French Impressionists, Scottish art from the 17th century to the present, silver, ceramics, European armor, and even Egyptian archaeological finds. *Tel. 0141/357–3929. Admission free. Open Mon.–Sat. 10–5, Sun. 11–5.*

Across Kelvingrove Park are two other important galleries, both maintained by Glasgow University. They house the collections of William Hunter, an 18th-century Glasgow doctor who assembled a staggering quantity of extremely valuable material. The **Hunterian Museum,** the city's oldest (1807), displays Hunter's hoards of coins, manuscripts, and archaeological artifacts in a striking Gothic building. Even more interesting is the **Hunterian Art Gallery,** which has the doctor's pictures plus other collections bequeathed to the university—works by Reynolds, Rodin, Rembrandt, Tintoretto, Whistler, and a large section devoted to the work of Charles Rennie Mackintosh, including reconstructed interiors of his house. *Museum: tel. 0141/330–4221. Admission free. Open Mon.–Sat. 9:30–5.*

*Gallery: tel. 0141/330–5431. Admission free. Open Mon.–Sat.
9:30–5 (Mackintosh House closed 12:30–1:30).*

⑮ Pollok Country Park provides a peaceful green oasis off Paisley
Road, just 3 miles southwest of the city center. To reach it, take
Strathclyde Transport Bus 45, 48, or 57 from the Glasgow city center, or a train to Pollockshaws West Station from Central Station.
The key attraction here is the **Burrell Collection,** Scotland's finest
art collection. An airy and elegant modern building houses treasures of all descriptions, from Chinese ceramics, bronzes, and jade to
medieval tapestries, stained glass, and 19th-century French paintings, the magpie collection of an eccentric millionaire. *Tel. 0141/
649–7151. Admission free. Open Mon.–Sat. 10–5, Sun. 11–5.*

Also located in Pollok Country Park is **Pollok House,** which dates
from the mid-1700s and contains the Stirling Maxwell Collection of
paintings, including works by El Greco, Murillo, Goya, Signorelli,
and William Blake. Fine 18th- and early 19th-century furniture, silver, glass, and porcelain are also on display. *Tel. 0141/632–0274. Admission free. Open Mon.–Sat. 10–5, Sun. 11–5.*

Lodging   **Kirklee Hotel.** Located in a quiet district of Glasgow near the univer-
££   sity, this bed-and-breakfast is small and cozy. Its owners take pride
in being friendly and helpful and in keeping the hotel spotless and
comfortable. *11 Kensington Gate, G12 9LG, tel. 0141/334–5555, fax
0141/339–3828. 9 rooms with bath. MC, V.*

££   **Town House.** A handsome old terraced house in a quiet cul-de-sac
bordering playing fields, the Town House thrives on repeat business
from very happy guests. The owners are particularly welcoming.
Evening meals can be served on request, and there is a comfortable
sitting room with books and information leaflets to browse through.
*4 Hughenden Terrace, G12 9XR, tel. 0141/357–0862, fax 0141/339–
9605. 10 rooms with shower. MC,V.*

£   **St. Enoch Hotel.** A location right in the city center makes this hotel a
good sightseeing base. Recently completely refurbished, the hotel
is decorated throughout in an unimaginative modern style with few
pretensions, but the low room rates compensate for the lack of atmosphere. There is a Continental café bar serving inexpensive,
quick meals. *St Enoch Sq., 44 Howard St., G1 4EE, tel. and fax
0141/221–2400. 45 rooms with shower. AE, MC, V.*

¢   **Glasgow International Youth Hostel.** This IYH-affiliated youth hostel is in a quiet residential area, within a 10-minute walk of downtown. Facilities include sitting and dining rooms, a well-stocked
shop with everything from maps to emergency rations for campers,
and a meal service. Doors stay open until 2 AM, and you can actually
stay for under £20. *7–8 Park Terrace, G3 6BY, tel. 0141/332–3004.
120 beds. No credit cards.*

¢   **University of Strathclyde.** If you want to be right in the city center,
★   but at a budget price, forget all your preconceptions about student
accommodations and book one of the university's excellent single,
double, or twin rooms, or apartments with kitchen facilities in the
Campus Village, a five-minute walk from George Square. Decor is
light wood, with pastel walls and upholstery—not at all what you
may remember from your own student days. Unfortunately, most
are available only in summer. *Residence & Catering Services, 50
Richmond St., tel. 0141/553–4148, fax 0141/553–4149. 1,200 rooms,
400 with bath or shower. No credit cards. Most available late June–
late Sept., with limited availability during the academic year.*

¢   **Victorian House.** Centrally located, but on a quiet residential street,
this overgrown bed-and-breakfast is a block from the Charles
Rennie Mackintosh–designed Glasgow School of Art. The plain and
uninteresting bedrooms are rather disappointing after the dramatic, dark red decor of the entrance hall, reception area, and stairs,
but the staff is welcoming. No meals are served other than breakfast, but there are plenty of restaurants on nearby Sauchiehall

Street. *212 Renfrew St., G3 6TX, tel. 0141/332–0129, fax 0141/353–3155. 37 rooms with shower. MC, V.*

Splurge **Babbity Bowster.** This wonderful old pub-restaurant-lodging house
★ in the heart of the Merchant City is an atmospheric hangout for musicians and artists. Both the public bar and the restaurant serve a mixture of traditional Scottish and French food, the bedrooms are pine-furnished with few frills. This is the place to experience Glasgow as it really is, but do not try to get to bed early—the bar stays open late and is noisy. *16–18 Blackfriars St., tel. 0141/552–5055. 6 rooms with shower. AE, MC, V. About £60 for 2 people.*

Splurge **Cathedral House.** This small, friendly, freshly decorated hotel is in the heart of old Glasgow, near the cathedral, and is convenient for sightseeing. The lunch in the café-bar is a good value and worth trying. *28–32 Cathedral Sq., tel. 0141/552–3519, fax 0141/552–2444. 7 rooms with bath. MC, V. About £65 for 2 people.*

Dining **Café Gandolfi.** This restaurant in the heart of the Merchant City, is
££ cozy and atmospheric with its carved wooden tables and chairs by Scottish artist Tim Stead. Food is interesting, innovative, and reasonably priced. The cold smoked venison and finnan haddie are particularly good. *64 Albion St., tel. 0141/552–6813. Reservations advised. MC, V.*

££ **Ubiquitous Chip.** Much loved locally, this restaurant has a glass-cov-
★ ered courtyard with lush greenery and a dining room with exposed ceiling beams. The upstairs restaurant is far more affordable than the fancier one downstairs. Specialties depend on what is available fresh at top quality but will usually include fish and seafood, venison, haggis, and lamb. The wine list is outstanding. *12 Ashton La., tel. 0141/334–5007. Reservations advised. AE, DC, MC, V.*

£ **Colonial.** In a traditional dining room you will find a wide range of Indian cuisine, especially dishes from the south (that is, hotter and spicier). Goanese fish and prawns, *sali boti* (a selection of dishes using sun-dried fruits, spices, and cream), and dishes using wine and cognacs are specialties. *25 High St., tel. 0141/552–1923. Reservations advised. AE, DC, MC, V.*

£ **Fazzi Café Bar.** This inexpensive Italian café bar (with delicatessen food at one side), with its red-and-white checked cloths and bentwood chairs set on a quarry-tiled floor, is a cheerful place for a quick plateful of gnocchi a la pomarda, or ravioli with ricotta and spinach. *65–67 Cambridge St., tel. 0141/332–0941. Reservations not required. AE, MC, V.*

¢ **Ali Baba's Balti Bar.** Balti—a kind of Indian stir-fry served in the pan in which it is cooked—has become very popular in Scotland in recent years; this establishment was the first Balti restaurant in Glasgow. A sofa to sprawl in for pre-dinner drinks and spacious dining areas decorated à la Arabian Nights, combined with fast, efficient service, create a relaxing ambience to experience this special cuisine. Try the pakora, lamb kofta, or delicious aloo sag (potato and spinach) balti. *54 West Regent St., tel. 0141/332–6289. Reservations not required. AE, MC, V.*

¢ **CCA Café/Bar.** Attached to the Centre for the Contemporary Arts, this is a bright, white-painted warehouse-style café serving a particularly good selection of vegetarian dishes along with offerings for carnivores, and backed up by a good wine and beer list. *350 Sauchiehall St., tel. 0141/332–7864. Reservations not required. AE, DC, MC, V (minimum charge £7).*

¢ **Drum and Monkey.** This Victorian restaurant-bar, an upscale meet-
★ ing place for business men and women, offers delicious snacks and bar meals that are surprisingly good value. The bistro is much more expensive, but worth it if you are in the mood to splurge. *93–95 St. Vincent St., tel. 0141/221–6636. AE, MC, V.*

¢ **Harry Ramsden's.** This world-famous fish-and-chip restaurant is not quite as cheap as your average "chippie," but the food is much better than average (and you are still eating for less than £6 per person). *251 Paisley Rd., tel. 0141/429–3700. Reservations not required. MC, V.*

¢ **Koh-I-Noor.** This excellent Indian restaurant has a special gourmet buffet dinner every Monday evening from 7 to 9. At £9.95 per person, this all-you-can-eat offer has to be one of the best deals in the city. *235 North St., Charing Cross, tel. 0141/221–1555 or 0141/204–1444. Reservations advised. No credit cards. No Sun. dinner.*

¢ **Willow Tea Room.** The restored Art Nouveau archetype is styled after the original Charles Rennie Mackintosh design. Here you can have coffee, a light lunch, fresh-baked cakes, and a pot of tea for a minimal charge. *217 Sauchiehall St., tel. 0141/332–0521. No credit cards. Closed dinner.*

Shopping Glasgow's main shopping districts occupy the southeastern part of town, in a square grid that runs south to Clyde Street on the banks of the river, north to St. Vincent Street, and east–west from City Hall to the Central Station. **Princes Square,** off Buchanan Street, is a chic and modern mall, with specialty shops on three levels and a café complex above, all under a glittering dome. It's mostly a case of "window shop and dream," as the shops here are pricey, but try the **Scottish Craft Centre** (the Courtyard, tel. 0141/248–2885) for unusual, high-quality items—no tartan dolls. **Stockwell China Bazaar** (67–77 Glassford St., tel. 0141/552–5781) specializes in fine china and giftware.

William Porteous & Co. Ltd. (9 Royal Exchange Pl., tel. 0141/221–8623) features maps, souvenir books and prints, and Scottish-made crafts and gifts. **John Smith & Son (Glasgow) Ltd.** (57 Vincent St., tel. 0141/221–7472) prides itself on being a thoroughly Scottish bookshop, founded in the mid-18th century, and has a particularly good selection of Scottish guidebooks.

Glasgow's weekend market, the **Barras,** just north of Glasgow Green, may be the best place for travellers on a budget to pick up a bargain—or then again, you may not be lucky. It offers a dizzying array of items, from antique toys to fresh vegetables, but there is a lot of dross to sift through before striking paydirt.

The Arts Glasgow is better endowed with functioning theaters than Edinburgh. One of the most exciting in Britain is the **Citizen's Theatre** (119 Gorbals St., tel. 0141/429–0022), where productions of often hair-raising originality are the order of the day. Contemporary works are also staged at the **Cottier Theatre** (93 Hyndland St., tel. 0141/339–5868) in a converted church, while the **Centre for the Contemporary Arts** (350 Sauchiehall St., tel. 0141/332–7521) stages not only modern plays but also exhibitions, films, and musical performances. The **King's Theatre** (Bath St., tel. 0141/227–5511) stages light entertainment and musicals. The enchanting **Theatre Royal** (Hope St., tel. 0141/332–9000) is the home of Scottish Opera.

Loch Lomond

Regular coach trips to Loch Lomond, about 20 miles and about 30 minutes from downtown Glasgow, are operated by local bus and coach companies. For up-to-date information, contact the tourist information office in Glasgow.

★ **Loch Lomond,** at 23 miles long, is the largest and most famous of Scotland's lochs. The town of **Balloch** is the southern gateway to the loch, but it is not especially attractive. The very best view of Loch Lomond is from **Duncryne Hill,** farther east. The loch, dotted with tiny islands, spreads out beyond the fields and lush lowland hedgerows, then narrows and extends northward into the Highlands. Scenic cruises leave from a number of loch-side communities, including

Balloch on the south side, Balmaha on the east, and Tarbet and Luss on the west.

Helensburgh

Strathclyde Transport (0141/204–2844) trains leave from Glasgow's Queen Street Station (lower level) every half hour for the 30-minute trip to Helensburgh. Helensburgh tourist office: The Clock Tower, tel. 01436/672642 (open Apr.–Oct.).

Just 5 miles west of the loch is the port town of **Helensburgh,** where you can embark on a Clyde Estuary cruise. The Clyde coast was once the playground for Glasgow's prosperous merchants, who built their splendid Victorian country homes here. These mansions line the shores of the Gare Loch and fill the resort of Helensburgh. The Mackintosh-designed **Hill House,** complete with his custom-designed furniture, is here in a calm, leafy suburb on the hill just behind the promenade. It was originally built for Glasgow publisher William Blackie in 1902–1904. *Upper Colquhoun St., tel. 01436/ 673900. Admission: £3 adults, £1.50 children and senior citizens. Open Apr.–Dec. 23, daily 1:30–5:30 (last admission 5).*

Ayr

ScotRail trains travel to Ayr from Glasgow's Central Station (every half hour) on an hour-long trip. From Ayr Railway Station, take a bus to Alloway, about 10 minutes away. Ayr tourist office: Burns House, 16 Burns Statue Sq., tel. 01292/288688.

Among the many attractions of **Ayr** is **Alloway,** a suburb closely associated with poet Robert Burns. Here, among the many middle-class residences, you'll find the one-room thatched **Burns Cottage,** where the poet was born in 1759. A museum beside the cottage contains various items that belonged to Burns, such as a family bible, and manuscripts. *Tel. 01292/441215. Admission: £2.20 adults, £1.25 senior citizens and children, £6 family ticket. Open Jun.–Aug., Mon.–Sat. 9–6, Sun. 10–6; Apr., May, Sept., Oct., Mon.–Sat. 10–5, Sun. 1–5; Nov.–Mar., Mon.–Sat. 10–4.*

Down the road from Burns Cottage and around the corner from Alloway's ruined church, is the new **Tam o' Shanter Experience.** *Tam o' Shanter,* one of Burns's most famous poems, is brought to life in a three-screen theatrical set, while the audience is transported to 18th-century Ayr. There are also a restaurant and gift shop. *Tel. 01292/443700 or contact local tourist information center for details of opening times and charges.*

Auld (old) **Alloway Kirk** (church) is where Tam o' Shanter, hero of Burns's poem, unluckily passed a witches' revel—with Old Nick himself playing the bagpipes—on his way home from a night of drinking. Close by is the **Brig o' Doon** ("brig" is Scots for "bridge") which Tam, in flight from the witches, managed to cross just in time. His gray mare, Meg, lost her tail to the closest witch. (Any resident of Ayr will tell you that witches cannot cross running water.) The **Burns Monument** (entrance fee included in charge for Burns Cottage) overlooks the Brig o' Doon.

Culzean Castle and Country Park

From Ayr take a local bus 12 miles (30 minutes) to Culzean (a stop en route to Girvan). Bus service is sometimes infrequent, so call for transportation details in advance (Ayr tourist office tel. 01292/ 288688).

★ For a different perspective on Ayrshire's history, visit **Culzean** (pronounced "Ku*lain*") **Castle and Country Park,** the National Trust for

Scotland's most popular property. The castle, complete with walled garden, is a superb neoclassical mansion designed by Robert Adam in 1777. The country park welcomes 300,000 visitors a year, yet remains unspoiled. In addition to marvelous interiors, the castle contains the National Guest Flat, given by the people of Scotland in appreciation of General Eisenhower's services during World War II. As president he stayed once or twice at Culzean and his relations still do occasionally. Between visits it is used by the N.T.S. for official hospitality. Rooms evoke World War II: mementos of Glenn Miller, Winston Churchill, Vera Lynn, and other personalities of the epoch all help create a suitably 1940s mood. The self-service restaurant at Culzean Castle offers light meals and afternoon teas of the scones-and-cakes variety. You can also pick up an ale or a glass of wine. *Tel. 01655/760269. Castle admission: £5.50 adults, £3 senior citizens and children. Country park admission: £3 adults, £1.50 senior citizens and children. Castle open Apr.–Oct., daily 10:30–5:30. Country park open all year, daily 9:30–sunset (grounds only).*

Tour 2: Stirling, Perth, Inverness, and Fort William

This circular tour takes you north by train to Stirling and its great castle, a royal residence of the Stuart monarchs; on to the Fair City of Perth; then to Inverness, capital of the Highlands; and finally, west by bus to Fort William. Highlights of this journey include traveling along Loch Ness and down the Great Glen, and from Fort William you have the option of a train trip to Mallaig on the famous West Highland Line or circling back to Glasgow. Although you can travel this entire route by bus (in addition to the Inverness–Fort William leg), the train is recommended because it is faster and service is more frequent.

From Glasgow
By Train   Trains leave Glasgow's Queen Street Station approximately hourly for the 30-minute journey to Stirling.

By Bus   **Scottish Citylink** (tel. 0141/332–9191) buses run from Buchanan Street Bus Station to Stirling hourly. Journey time is about 1 hour. For information on local connecting bus services, phone Midland Bluebird at Stirling bus station (tel. 01786/473763).

By Car   The A80/M80 takes you direct to Stirling.

From Edinburgh
By Train and Bus   Trains leave Edinburgh Waverley Station about every 30 minutes for Stirling; the journey time is about 45 minutes. Local bus services run hourly from St. Andrew Square bus station to Stirling, and the drive takes about 1½ hours.

By Car   Take M9, a direct route to Stirling.

Stirling

Stirling tourist office: 41 Dumbarton Rd., almost opposite Rob Roy statue, tel. 01786/475019.

Stirling, about 23 miles northeast of Glasgow, is another of Britain's great historic towns. The Royal Burgh of Stirling Visitor Centre on
★ the battlements of **Stirling Castle** is a good starting point for an appreciation of Stirling's historic role as a strategic center controlling Scotland. Even when the castle is not open—it has, incidentally, its own visitor center—the Esplanade commands sweeping views towards the Highlands and across the central belt of Scotland. The castle, built in the 15th and 16th centuries, was a royal residence of the Stuart kings, who were—in every sense of the word—monarchs of all they surveyed. Take time to inspect this lovely Renaissance cit-

adel of crow-stepped gables, stone carvings, and twisted chimneys. The hammer-beamed Parliament Hall still whispers of dark 16th-century deeds, and across the courtyard, the fine regimental museum of the Argyll & Sutherland Highlanders houses more recent battle memories. Mary, Queen of Scots, lived here in her infancy before she was sent to France. An embrasure on the battlements with the inscription "MR 1561" is still called Queen Mary's Lookout. *Tel. 0131/244–3101. Admission: £3.50 adults, £2 senior citizens, £1 children. Open Apr.–Sept., daily 9:30–5:15; Oct.–Mar., daily 9:30–4:15.*

On the right as you go down into the town is **Mar's Wark,** the roofless ruin of a mansion that the earl of Mar, premier earl of Scotland, put up in 1570. The building of slightly later date on the left, the **Argyll Ludging** ("ludging" was "lodging," a nobleman's town house), was for many years a military hospital.

Before you descend to modern Stirling's shopping streets, you pass the old **Town House** (City Hall); the **Mercat Cross,** where proclamations were made; and the parish church of the **Holy Rude** (rood, cross), a fine medieval building dating from 1456. Here King James VI was crowned at the age of one year; the presiding clergyman was John Knox, the Scottish religious reformer and leader of the Scottish Reformation.

Close by, in Back Walk, stands the quaint 17th-century **Cowane's Hospital,** built as a refuge for the old. It is now known as the Guildhall and is a popular venue for traditional ceilidhs in the summer months. You can walk from here along the south side of the castle hill to the **Smith Art Gallery and Museum.** *Dumbarton Rd., tel. 01786/471917. Admission free. Open Apr.–Sept., Tues.–Sat. 10:30–5, Sun. 2–5; Oct.–Mar., Tues.–Fri. noon–5, Sat. 10:30–5, Sun. 2–5.*

Stirling Castle at one time commanded the only overland route between the Highlands and Lowlands, at the River Forth's lowest bridging point. Many decisive battles were fought near here. The story of the great battle of **Bannockburn** in 1314, which regained Scotland's independence for 400 years, is told at the National Trust for Scotland's **Bannockburn Heritage Centre,** 2 miles from Stirling's town center on A91, and accessible by bus or taxi. *Glasgow Rd., tel. 01786/812664. Admission: £2 adults, £1 children. Open Mar. and Nov.–Dec. 23, daily 11–3; Apr.–Oct., daily 10–5:30. Site open daily all year.*

Just north of the town, high on the Abbey Craig, is the 200-foot-high **National Wallace Monument,** commemorating Scotland's 13th-century freedom-fighter, William Wallace, with an exhibition and audiovisual presentation. Afterward, you can climb to the top. *Tel. 01786/472140. Admission: £2.50 adults, £1.50 senior citizens and children. Open Feb. and Nov., weekends 10–4; Mar.–May and Oct., daily 10–5; June and Sept., daily 10–6; July and Aug., daily 9:30–6:30. Closed Dec. and Jan.*

Lodging **Castlecroft.** This modern house, set atop a hill just beneath Stirling ¢ Castle, offers extensive views to the Trossachs hills. Owner Bill ★ Salmond is particularly friendly and knowledgeable about the surrounding area. *Ballengeich Rd., FK8 1TN, tel. 01786/474933. 6 rooms with bath or shower. No credit cards.*

¢ **Firgrove Guest House.** Only a five-minute walk from the town center, this spacious guest house has large comfortable rooms and private parking for guests. *13 Clifford Rd., FK8 2AQ, tel. 01786/475805. 3 rooms with bath/shower. No credit cards. Closed Nov.–Mar.*

¢ **Lochend Farm.** Extensive views, wholesome farm cooking and peace are the hallmarks of this working farm. About 5 miles south of Stirling by the M9/M80, it makes a good touring base. The traditionally furnished, comfortable bedrooms have wash basins and share a private bathroom. *Carronbridge, Denny, Stirlingshire FK6 5JJ, tel. 01324/822778. 2 rooms. No credit cards.*

¢ **West Plean.** This handsome house is part of a working farm. It also has a walled garden and woodland walks. Well-cooked food and spacious rooms make certain that your stay is enjoyable. *Denny Rd., FK7 8HA, tel. 01786/812208. 3 rooms with bath or shower. No credit cards.*

¢ **Youth Hostel.** Built within the shell of a former church, the hostel offers high-grade 4- and 6-bedded rooms with en suite baths. Use of the television room, dining room, and fully equipped kitchen is included in the bargain tab of only £10.15 per person for bed and breakfast. *Erskine Marykirk, St. John's St., Stirling FK8 IDU, tel. 01786/473442. 128 beds. MC, V.*

Splurge **Terraces Hotel.** This centrally located Georgian town house has been comfortably converted into a good reliable lodging where rooms run about £80 a night for two. The comparatively small size of the hotel means, in this case, attentive service. *4 Melville Terr., FK8 2ND, tel. 01786/472268. 18 rooms with bath or shower. AE, DC, MC, V.*

Dining **Heritage.** This elegant 18th-century establishment is run by a
££ French family. The decor is all fanlights and candles; the menu features French and Scottish classics. *16 Allan Park, tel. 01786/473660. Reservations advised. MC, V. Closed Jan. 1.*

£ **Cross Keys Hotel.** A quaint, stone-walled dining room makes an atmospheric setting for this restaurant's varied, traditionally Scottish menu. *Main St., Kippen (just west of Stirling), tel. 01786/ 870293. Reservations advised. MC, V.*

£ **No. 39.** Only 200 yards from the castle, this highly recommended res-
★ taurant has a menu for varied tastes and budgets, featuring Scottish meats, fish, and game cooked in traditional style. *39 Broad St., tel. 01786/473929. Reservations advised. MC, V.*

¢ **Darnley Coffee House.** The building where Lord Darnley (the second husband of Mary, Queen of Scots) stayed when Mary was in residence at Stirling Castle now serves excellent coffee and homemade cakes and light lunches. *16–18 Bow St., tel. 01786/474468. No credit cards. Open Easter–mid-Dec. 10–5.*

The Arts Stirling has the dynamic **MacRobert Arts Centre** (Stirling University Campus, tel. 01786/461081), which offers a wide range of theatrical performances, as well as films. Tickets for films cost £3 (£2 for discounted tickets); tickets for theater and concerts cost £5–£10, depending on the production.

Callander and the Trossachs

*There is a local bus service to Callander, departing hourly from Stirling town center. From Callander, you can travel to the Trossachs by postbus (tel. 01463/234111, ext. 273), which is a cheap means of travel, and is feasible if you plan your itinerary carefully. Alternatively, it may be worth hiring a car for a day from **Europcar Ltd.** (Drip Rd., tel. 01786/472164) to discover the delightful Trossachs, coined "the Highlands in miniature." Rob Roy and Trossachs Visitor Centre: Ancaster Sq., tel. 01877/330342.*

At **Callander,** the peak of **Ben Ledi** (2,882 feet) looms impressively at the end of the main street. The town itself is unashamedly tourist-oriented—an accommodation and refreshment stop on the route west—but worth exploring nonetheless. If you tire of shopping, explore the **Callander Crags** or the less steep **Bracklinn Falls** (both behind the town) for a sample of Highland scenery.

For a little break, stop by **Pip's Coffee House** (Ancaster Sq., right in the center, tel. 01877/330470), a bright and cheerful eating place that offers soups, salads, and Scottish baking in the daytime and more substantial fare at night from May through September. There is also a picture gallery where you can browse. Pip's is closed Wednesdays.

The **Trossachs** have been a tourist mecca since the late 18th century, and **Loch Venachar** marks the beginning of the region's lochs. The area initially attracted tourists not just for its harmonious scenery of hill, loch, and wooded slopes but also because it was the first "wild" part of Scotland encountered by visitors straying from the central belt of Scotland. Its appeal, therefore, owes something at least to its geographic location. The Trossachs represent the very essence of what the Highlands are supposed to be like: birchwood and pine; vistas down lochs where the woods creep right to the water's edge; and in the background, mountain peaks that rise not as high as their neighbors farther north and west—but quite high enough to give the first tourist adventurers a thrill. The Trossachs are almost a Scottish visual cliché, but they're very popular right through the year, especially with regular Sunday afternoon tourists from Glasgow and Edinburgh.

Though there is a range of forest tracks and trails, for many people the easiest way to enjoy the Trossachs' splendor is to walk from the main car park along the north bank of **Loch Katrine** (pronounced "*Kǎ*-trin"). This is on a well-surfaced road owned by Strathclyde Water Board and open only to pedestrians and cyclists.

The steamer *Sir Walter Scott* leaves from a nearby pier on its Loch Katrine cruise. Take the cruise if time permits, as the shores of Katrine remain undeveloped and impressive. This loch is the setting of Scott's narrative poem, *The Lady of the Lake,* and Ellen's Isle is named after his heroine. It was Scott's influence that made the Trossachs a major tourist attraction. *Trossachs Pier, tel. 0141/955–0128. Cruise cost: £3.40 adults, £2 children and senior citizens, £9 family ticket. Apr.–Sept., Sun.–Fri., cruises at 11, noon, 1:45, 3:15; Sat. at 2, 3:30.*

Lodging **Arran Lodge.** This delightful bungalow, situated by the river on the
£ outskirts of Callander, offers luxurious accommodations at a bar-
★ gain price. If you've gone fishing, the staff will even cook your catch for your dinner. *Leny Rd., FK17 8AT, tel. 01877/330976. 4 rooms, 3 with bath, 1 with hall bathroom. No credit cards. Closed Jan.*

¢ **Arden House Guest House.** Set in extensive grounds above the town, with wonderful views of the Trossachs, this entirely nonsmoking guest house is comfortably furnished and offers evening meals if required. *Bracklinn Rd., FK17 8EQ, tel. 01877/330235. 6 rooms with bath or shower. No credit cards. Closed Dec.–Feb.*

Perth

Trains leave hourly for the 40-minute journey from Stirling to Perth. Perth tourist office: Lower City Mills, West Mill St., tel. 01738/627958, fax 01738/630416.

Perth does not give the impression of being an ancient historical site, yet this old town was the Scottish capital from the 12th century until James I, the king of Scotland, was assassinated here in 1437. His successor, James II, moved the court to the better fortified castle at Stirling. Today Perth is a bustling place, where the country folk from the prosperous hinterland of Lowland farms and Highland estates mix with strolling tourists on the busy shopping streets.

★ Perth's main historic interest lies in nearby **Scone Palace** (2 miles northeast and easily reached by local bus). This grandly embellished, castellated mansion stands on the site of earlier royal palaces. While still the home of the earl of Mansfield, it is well equipped to deal with visitors who flock to view its vast collections of 16th-century needlework, china, furniture, vases, and other objets d'art. Within its grounds is **Moot Hill,** the ancient coronation place of the

Scottish kings. To be crowned, they sat upon the Stone of Scone, which was seized in 1296 by Edward I of England, Scotland's greatest enemy, and placed in the coronation chair at Westminster Abbey in London, where it is still on view. Some Scots hint darkly that Edward was fooled by a substitution, and that the real stone is hidden north of the border, waiting for Scotland to regain her independence. *Tel. 01738/552308. Admission: £4.50 adults, £3.70 senior citizens, £2.50 children, £13 family ticket. Open Easter–Oct., daily 9:30–5.*

Lodging **Sunbank House Hotel.** This early Victorian graystone mansion is in
££ a fine residential area near Perth's Branklyn Gardens. Recently re-
★ decorated in traditional style, it offers solid, unpretentious comforts along with great views over the River Tay and the city. *50 Dundee Rd., PH2 7BA, tel. 01738/624882, fax 01738/442515. 10 rooms, 5 with bath, 5 with shower. MC, V.*

£ **Beechgrove Guest House.** Once a manse (house for the minister of the local church), this peaceful guest house stands in its own grounds but is only minutes away on foot from the town center. It retains its former gracious character, offering the highest standards of bed-and-breakfast accommodation. *Dundee Rd., PH2 7AD, tel. 01738/636147. 6 rooms with bath or shower. MC, V.*

¢ **Park Lane Guest House.** This Georgian house is especially well situated, close to the river, and to the South Inch park and the golf course, and a short walk from the city center. *17 Marshall Pl., PH2 8AG, tel. 01738/637218, fax 01738/643519. 6 rooms with bath or shower. MC, V.*

Dining **Number Thirty Three Seafood Restaurant.** Right in the center of
££ town, with restful pink and gray decor, this establishment offers the
★ choice of eating in the main restaurant, or at the Oyster Bar or informal "front of house" area. The emphasis, as one might expect, is on fish—perhaps salmon or king scallops might tempt you—but top-quality meat entrées are also served. *33 George St., tel. 01738/633771. Reservations advised. AE, MC, V. Closed Sun. and Mon.*

£ **Lang Bar and Restaurant.** Within the Perth Repertory Theatre's premises in High Street are, firstly, a coffee bar, offering light meals and home-baked goods both at lunchtime and in the evening and a chance to enjoy exhibitions of work by local artists. A short flight of stairs leads to the restaurant, which has a more elaborate menu featuring favorites such as stuffed roast loin of lamb or salmon in filo pastry. *185 High St., tel. 01738/639136. Reservations advised for restaurant. AE, MC, V. Closed Sun.*

Shopping Perth, with its upscale shopping aspirations, is not the town for budget shoppers. However, if you're in the market for fine jewelry or china and have put some money aside, you'll find quality selections here. **Cairncross Ltd., Goldsmiths** (18 St. John's St., tel. 01738/624367) use native freshwater pearls in their superb gold designs. **Timothy Hardie** (25 St. John's St., tel. 01738/633127) sells fine jewelry and antique silver. **William Watson & Sons** (163–167 High St., tel. 01738/639861) specializes in quality china and glassware.

The Arts Perth has a repertory company that performs at **Perth Repertory Theatre** (High St., tel. 01738/621031). Tickets average £8.

Inverness

There are regular trains from Perth to Inverness, running approximately every 2 hours (with some more frequent services), and taking about 2½ hours. Scottish Citylink (tel. 01463/711000) runs bus services between Perth and Inverness, approximately two buses hourly. Inverness tourist office: Castle Wynd, tel. 01463/234353.

Known for centuries as "the Capital of the Highlands," **Inverness** is not exclusively Highland in flavor. Part of its hinterland includes the

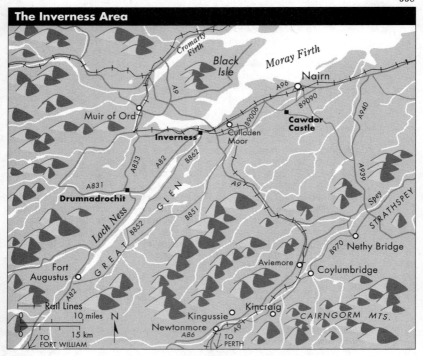

The Inverness Area

farmlands of the Moray Firth coastal strip, as well as of the Black Isle. It is open to the sea winds off the Moray Firth, while the high hills, although close at hand, are mainly hidden. Few of Inverness's buildings are of great antiquity—thanks to the Highland clans' careless habit of burning the town to the ground. Even its castle is a Victorian replacement on the site of a fort blown up by Bonnie Prince Charlie. Now bypassed by A9, in summer the town does not simply bustle, it positively roars. Be careful in its one-way traffic system, whether walking or driving.

From Inverness post office, in the town center, buses depart five times daily for the 5-mile trip to **Culloden Moor,** the site of the last battle fought on British soil. Here, on a cold April day in 1746, the outnumbered Jacobite forces of rebel Bonnie Prince Charlie, ill-fed and badly led, exhausted by a night march, were decimated by the superior firepower of George II's army, which included the Campbells, among other Highlanders, as well as Lowland Scottish regiments. The victorious commander, the duke of Cumberland (George II's son), earned the name of "Butcher" Cumberland for the bloody reprisals carried out by his men on Highland families, Jacobite or not, who were caught in the vicinity.

The National Trust for Scotland has re-created the battlefield as it looked in 1746. The eerie silence of the open moor almost drowns out the merry clatter from the visitor center's coffee shop and the tinkle of the cash registers. *Tel. 01463/790607. Admission (visitor center and audiovisual display): £1.80 adults, 90p children, senior citizens, and students. Open Feb., Mar., Nov., and Dec. daily (except Dec. 25, 26) 10–4; Apr.–Oct. daily, 9–6.*

Lodging **Ballifeary House Hotel.** A redecorated and well-maintained Victori-
££ an property, this offers especially high standards of comfort and
★ service and is within easy reach of downtown Inverness. *10*

Ballifeary Rd., IV3 5PJ, tel. 01463/235572. 8 rooms with bath. MC, V. No smoking in hotel. Closed Nov.–Feb.

£ **Atholdene House.** This family-run late-19th-century stone villa offers a friendly welcome and modernized accommodations. The bus and railway stations are a short walk away. *20 Southside Rd., IV2 3BG, tel. 01463/233565. 9 rooms, 7 with shower. No credit cards.*

¢ **Clach Mhuilinn.** This modern family home in a residential area is set in a pretty garden and has good parking. It offers bed and breakfast of very high standard in a no-smoking environment. *7 Harris Rd., IV2 3LS, tel. 01463/237059. 3 rooms, 1 with shower, 1 with private bath (not en suite). MC, V. Closed Dec.–Feb.*

Dining **Nico's.** This bistro bar with its oak panelling and Victorian decor
£ is found inside the Glen Mhor Hotel. While the hotel's Riverview Seafood Restaurant has a much more elaborate (and expensive) menu, Nico's offers a price-conscious choice of tasty pasta, grilled dishes, and some vegetarian options. Some lunch dishes cost well under £10. *Glen Mhor Hotel, Ness Bank, tel. 01463/234308. AE, DC, MC, V.*

Shopping As you would expect, Inverness features a number of shops with a distinct Highland flavor. **James Pringle Weavers** (Holm Woollen Mill, Dores Rd., tel. 01463/223311) offers self-guided tours of the mill; a fine shop on the premises sells lovely tweeds, tartans, and, of course, wool clothing. **Duncan Chisholm & Sons** (49 Castle St., tel. 01463/234599) is another fine shop specializing in Highland tartans, woolens, and crafts.

In addition to these traditional stores, more unusual crafts shops are nearby. **Highland Aromatics Ltd.** (Drumchardine, 7 miles west on A862, tel. 01463/831625) sells perfumed toilet soap made with Scottish ingredients, and all manner of perfumes, colognes, bath salts, and toiletries. **Highland Wineries Ltd.** (2 miles farther on B9164, at Moniack Castle, Kirkhill, tel. 01463/831283) makes wine from local products, including sap from silver birch trees.

The Arts Inverness's theater, the **Eden Court** (tel. 01463/221718), is a reminder that just because a town is in northern Scotland, it need not be an artistic wasteland. This multipurpose 800-seat theater and its art gallery offer varied programs throughout the year.

Loch Ness at Drumnadrochit

*The **Highland Bus and Coach Company** (tel. 01463/233371) Bus 19 travels from Inverness down the Great Glen beside Loch Ness and on to Fort William, 4 times a day (limited service on Sunday; more frequent service in summer). Break your trip at Drumnadrochit.*

Inverness is one of the northern gateways to the Great Glen—Glen Mor, the 60-mile-long valley (and geological fault) that's the result of an ancient earth movement that dislocated the entire top half of Scotland. The main road south from Inverness runs along the west
★ bank of **Loch Ness.** Monster-watchers should visit the "official" **Loch Ness Monster Exhibition** at **Drumnadrochit,** midway on the west bank. Loch Ness's huge volume of water has a locally warming effect on the weather, making the lake conducive to mirages in still, warm conditions. These are often the circumstances in which the "monster" appears, but you may draw your own conclusions. *Tel. 01456/450573 or 01456/450218. Admission: £4 adults, £2.50 children, £3 students and senior citizens, £10.50 family ticket. Open daily, Easter–May 9:30–5:30; June and Sept. 9:30–6:30; July and Aug. 9–8:30; Oct.–Mar. 10–4 (last admission 1 hr before closing).*

Lodging **Borlum Farmhouse.** Close to Drumnadrochit and with beautiful
¢ views over Loch Ness, this traditional farmhouse is set on a working hill farm. Freshly decorated rooms boast many period features, and

the good home cooking is a bonus. *Drumnadrochit, IV3 6XN, tel. 01456/450358. 5 rooms, 2 with bath/shower. MC, V. No smoking.*

Fort William

Travel by bus direct from Inverness (see above), or on from Drumnadrochit. The Inverness–Fort William trip takes about 2 hours. Fort William tourist office: Cameron Centre, Cameron Sq., in the center of town, tel. 01397/703781.

Fort William originated as a military outpost, first established by Cromwell's General Monk in 1655 and refortified in 1715 to help combat an outbreak by the turbulent Jacobite clans. It remains the southern gateway to the Great Glen and to the far west. Scotland's (and Britain's) highest mountain, the 4,406-foot **Ben Nevis,** looms over Fort William less than 4 miles from the sea. Only fit and well-equipped walkers should attempt to hike to its summit.

A day trip from Fort William to Mallaig, along the scenic **West Highland Line,** is recommended. For details, phone Fort William Railway Station (tel. 01397/703791). From the train you can take in views of birch- and bracken-covered wild slopes, with misty glimpses of the Hebridean islands of Rhum, Eigg, and Muck.

Once you arrive at Mallaig, take a look at the **Heritage Centre,** with exhibits and films on all aspects of local history. *Station Rd., tel. 01687/462085. Admission: £1.50 adults, 75p senior citizens and children, £4 family ticket. Open mid-May–Sept., Mon.–Sat. 10–5 (also Sun. noon–5 in July and Aug.); telephone for spring and autumn opening times. Closed Jan.–mid-Mar.*

Facing the harbor at **Mallaig Marine World** are fish and shellfish in aquariums that replicate their natural habitat, a display on the local fishing tradition, a video, and gift shop. *The Harbour, tel. 01687/462292. Admission £2.50 adults, £2 senior citizens and students, £1.50 children, £7 family ticket. Open daily 10–5 (closed Christmas, New Year's Day, and late Jan.–early Feb.)*

Lodging
££ **Innseagan House Hotel.** Right beside Loch Linnhe, with beautiful loch and mountain views, this comfortable hotel is a brisk 20-minute walk from the town center and much quieter than many of the town's hotels. The proprietors pride themselves on maintaining very high standards, supported by friendly staff. *Achintore Rd., PH33 6RW, tel. 01397/702452, fax 01397/702606. 24 rooms, 21 with bath or shower. AE, MC, V.*

£ **Crolinnhie.** A detached late Victorian house in a large garden bright
★ with flowers all summer, this bed-and-breakfast is top-of-the-range in every respect except price. The owners are particularly welcoming and many guests return again. *Grange Rd., PH33 6JF, tel. 01397/702709. 5 rooms, 3 with shower, 1 with private bath not en suite. No credit cards. Closed Dec.–Feb.*

¢ **Lochview Guest House.** This modern, well-decorated guest house
★ has attractive gardens and panoramic views of Loch Linnhe and the Ardgour hills. All bedrooms have color TV and tea/coffeemaker. *Heathercroft Rd., PH33 6RE, tel. 01397/703149. 8 rooms with bath or shower. No credit cards.*

Dining
££ **Crannog Seafood Restaurant.** Set right on the pier, here the seafood
★ really does seem to "leap from the sea into the pan," as the fishing boat unloads its catch directly to the kitchen door. Nothing in the understated decor detracts from the flavors on your plate, whether you have chosen bouillabaisse, skate with capers, or langoustine. Don't miss the cranachan (whipped cream, raspberries, and toasted oats enlivened with whiskey) for dessert. *Town Pier, tel. 01397/705589, fax 01397/705026. Reservations advised. MC, V. Closed Christmas Day and New Year's Day.*

Index

NOTES

NOTES

NOTES

NOTES

NOTES

NOTES

NOTES

Fodor's Travel Publications

Available at bookstores everywhere, or call 1–800–533–6478, 24 hours a day.

Gold Guides

U.S.

Alaska

Arizona

Boston

California

Cape Cod, Martha's Vineyard, Nantucket

The Carolinas & the Georgia Coast

Chicago

Colorado

Florida

Hawaii

Las Vegas, Reno, Tahoe

Los Angeles

Maine, Vermont, New Hampshire

Maui

Miami & the Keys

New England

New Orleans

New York City

Pacific North Coast

Philadelphia & the Pennsylvania Dutch Country

The Rockies

San Diego

San Francisco

Santa Fe, Taos, Albuquerque

Seattle & Vancouver

The South

U.S. & British Virgin Islands

USA

Virginia & Maryland

Waikiki

Washington, D.C.

Foreign

Australia & New Zealand

Austria

The Bahamas

Barbados

Bermuda

Brazil

Budapest

Canada

Cancún, Cozumel, Yucatán Peninsula

Caribbean

China

Costa Rica, Belize, Guatemala

The Czech Republic & Slovakia

Eastern Europe

Egypt

Europe

Florence, Tuscany & Umbria

France

Germany

Great Britain

Greece

Hong Kong

India

Ireland

Israel

Italy

Japan

Kenya & Tanzania

Korea

London

Madrid & Barcelona

Mexico

Montréal & Québec City

Morocco

Moscow, St. Petersburg, Kiev

The Netherlands, Belgium & Luxembourg

New Zealand

Norway

Nova Scotia, New Brunswick, Prince Edward Island

Paris

Portugal

Provence & the Riviera

Scandinavia

Scotland

Singapore

South America

South Pacific

Southeast Asia

Spain

Sweden

Switzerland

Thailand

Tokyo

Toronto

Turkey

Vienna & the Danube

Fodor's Special-Interest Guides

Branson

Caribbean Ports of Call

The Complete Guide to America's National Parks

Condé Nast Traveler Caribbean Resort and Cruise Ship Finder

Cruises and Ports of Call

Fodor's London Companion

France by Train

Halliday's New England Food Explorer

Healthy Escapes

Italy by Train

Kodak Guide to Shooting Great Travel Pictures

Shadow Traffic's New York Shortcuts and Traffic Tips

Sunday in New York

Sunday in San Francisco

Walt Disney World, Universal Studios and Orlando

Walt Disney World for Adults

Where Should We Take the Kids? California

Where Should We Take the Kids? Northeast

Special Series

Affordables

Caribbean

Europe

Florida

France

Germany

Great Britain

Italy

London

Paris

Fodor's Bed & Breakfasts and Country Inns

America's Best B&Bs

California's Best B&Bs

Canada's Great Country Inns

Cottages, B&Bs and Country Inns of England and Wales

The Mid-Atlantic's Best B&Bs

New England's Best B&Bs

The Pacific Northwest's Best B&Bs

The South's Best B&Bs

The Southwest's Best B&Bs

The Upper Great Lakes' Best B&Bs

The Berkeley Guides

California

Central America

Eastern Europe

Europe

France

Germany & Austria

Great Britain & Ireland

Italy

London

Mexico

Pacific Northwest & Alaska

Paris

San Francisco

Compass American Guides

Arizona

Canada

Chicago

Colorado

Hawaii

Hollywood

Las Vegas

Maine

Manhattan

Montana

New Mexico

New Orleans

Oregon

San Francisco

South Carolina

South Dakota

Texas

Utah

Virginia

Washington

Wine Country

Wisconsin

Wyoming

Fodor's Español

California

Caribe Occidental

Caribe Oriental

Gran Bretaña

Londres

Mexico

Nueva York

Paris

Fodor's Exploring Guides

Australia

Boston & New England

Britain

California

Caribbean

China

Florence & Tuscany

Florida

France

Germany

Ireland

Italy

London

Mexico

Moscow & St. Petersburg

New York City

Paris

Prague

Provence

Rome

San Francisco

Scotland

Singapore & Malaysia

Spain

Thailand

Turkey

Venice

Fodor's Flashmaps

Boston

New York

San Francisco

Washington, D.C.

Fodor's Pocket Guides

Acapulco

Atlanta

Barbados

Jamaica

London

New York City

Paris

Prague

Puerto Rico

Rome

San Francisco

Washington, D.C.

Rivages Guides

Bed and Breakfasts of Character and Charm in France

Hotels and Country Inns of Character and Charm in France

Hotels and Country Inns of Character and Charm in Italy

Short Escapes

Country Getaways in Britain

Country Getaways in France

Country Getaways Near New York City

Fodor's Sports

Golf Digest's Best Places to Play

Skiing USA

USA Today The Complete Four Sport Stadium Guide

Fodor's Vacation Planners

Great American Learning Vacations

Great American Sports & Adventure Vacations

Great American Vacations

National Parks and Seashores of the East

National Parks of the West